PAGE 54 | **ON THE ROAD**

YOUR COMPLETE DESTINATION GUIDE
In-depth reviews, detailed listings
and insider tips

Nor...

Central Coast & Elba (p164)

Siena & Central Tuscany (p190)

Southern Tuscany (p236)

Elba

PAGE 325 | **SURVIVAL GUIDE**

VITAL PRACTICAL INFORMATION TO
HELP YOU HAVE A SMOOTH TRIP

Language

welcome to Florence & Tuscany

Living History

Home to some of the world's most recognisable tourist icons, Tuscany has been enticing visitors ever since the Etruscans arrived here to party and decided to stay. The Romans came to pave roads and stock their grain silos, Christians came to walk the stages of a medieval pilgrimage route, and British aristocrats came to admire art, drink way too much of the local wine and complete their Grand Tour. Once here, these visitors swiftly fell into the local swing of things, partaking of the food and wine with gusto and soaking up the region's rich historical and cultural heritage. You're sure to do the same.

An Artistic Powerhouse

Then there's the art. And oh, what art! The Etruscans indulged their fondness for a classy send-off with exquisite funerary objects that are still being excavated to this day, and the Romans, always partial to puffing up their own importance, left their usual legacy of monumental sculptures. But it was during the medieval and Renaissance periods that Tuscany really hit its artistic stride, with painters, sculptors and architects creating the masterpieces that now entice visitors into churches, museums and galleries across the region. Giotto, Brunelleschi, Leonardo, Michelangelo, Botticelli – these and dozens of equally famous names hailed from Tuscany and left seminal works for us to enjoy.

Travel writers and tour operators tend to deploy the word 'idyllic' far too often, devaluing it in the process. But here in Tuscany, it really does apply.

Taking It Slowly...and Enjoying Every Minute

It's not all about art and history, though. The local obsession with food and wine trumps every other regional characteristic, and then some. Three of Italy's greatest wines – Brunello di Montalcino, Vino Nobile di Montepulciano and Vernaccia di San Gimignano – are produced here, and gastronomic gems such as *bistecca alla fiorentina* (chargrilled T-bone steak), *cacciucco* (Livornese fish stew) and *pici con ragù di cinghiale* (hand-rolled pasta with wild-boar sauce) are just some of the region's signature dishes. Tour here and you'll develop a true understanding of what Slow Food is, and how truly delectable it can be.

Postcard-Perfect Landscapes

Yes, the scenery really *is* that gorgeous. Central Tuscany is dotted with medieval hilltop fortresses and sculptural stands of cypress trees; the northwest and east harbour boast dramatic mountain ranges and fecund forests; and the central and southern coasts feature a garland of islands floating tantalisingly close to a shoreline teeming with wildlife. The range of outdoor activities on offer is equally diverse, contributing to the region's reputation as a repository of grand-slam sights and experiences unmatched anywhere in the world. Enjoy!

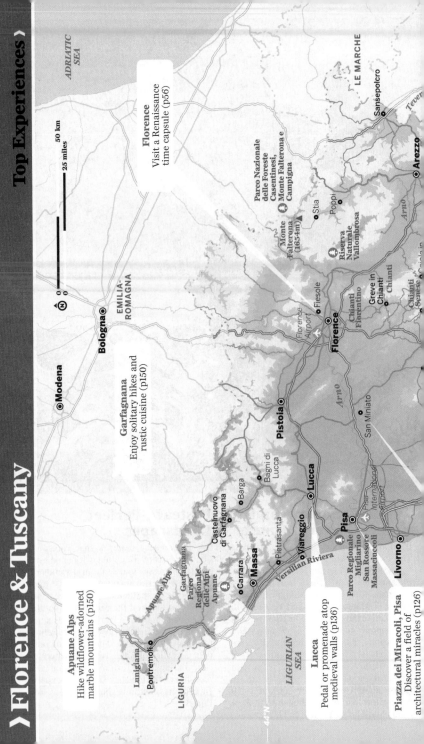

❯ Florence & Tuscany

Top Experiences ❯

Apuane Alps
Hike wildflower-adorned marble mountains (p150)

Garfagnana
Enjoy solitary hikes and rustic cuisine (p150)

Florence
Visit a Renaissance time capsule (p56)

Lucca
Pedal or promenade atop medieval walls (p136)

Piazza dei Miracoli, Pisa
Discover a field of architectural miracles (p126)

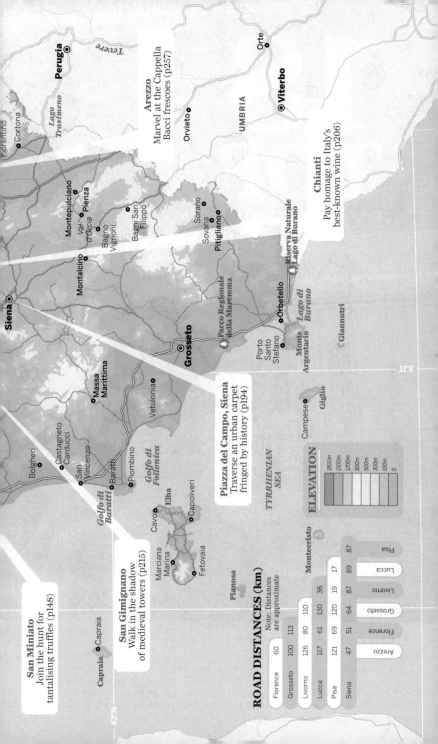

San Miniato
Join the hunt for tantalising truffles (p148)

San Gimignano
Walk in the shadow of medieval towers (p215)

Piazza del Campo, Siena
Traverse an urban carpet fringed by history (p194)

Arezzo
Marvel at the Cappella Bacci frescoes (p257)

Chianti
Pay homage to Italy's best-known wine (p206)

TYRRHENIAN SEA

UMBRIA

Riserva Naturale Lago di Burano

Parco Regionale della Maremma

Tevere

Perugia

Lago Trasimeno

Cortona

Fiorentino

Arezzo

Orvieto

Orte

Viterbo

Montepulciano

Pienza

Val d'Orcia

Bagno Vignoni

Bagni San Filippo

Sorano

Sovana

Pitigliano

Montalcino

Siena

Grosseto

Massa Marittima

Vetulonia

Bolgheri

Castagneto Carducci

San Vincenzo

Baratti

Piombino

Golfo di Baratti

Golfo di Follonica

Capraia

Capraia

Cavo

Elba

Marciana Marina

Capoliveri

Fetovaia

Pianosa

Montecristo

Campese

Giglio

Porto Santo Stefano

Monte Argentario

Lago di Burano

Orbetello

Giannutri

43°N

11°E

ELEVATION

	1800m
	1500m
	1200m
	800m
	500m
	300m
	100m
	0

ROAD DISTANCES (km)

Note: Distances are approximate

	Arezzo	Florence	Grosseto	Livorno	Lucca	Pisa
Florence	60					
Grosseto	100	113				
Livorno	126	80	110			
Lucca	117	61	130	36		
Pisa	121	69	120	19	17	
Siena	47	51	64	87	89	87

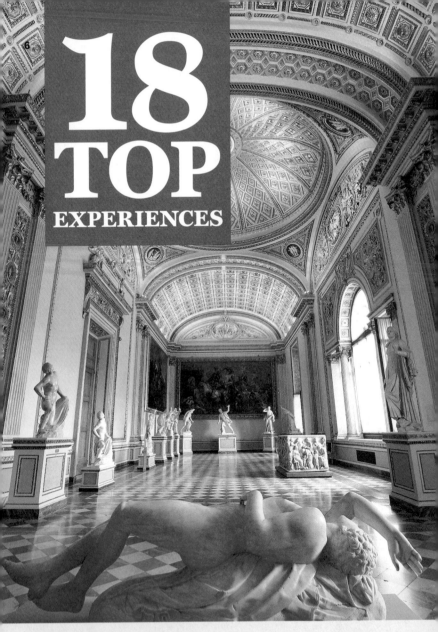

18 TOP EXPERIENCES

Uffizi Gallery, Florence

1 Visiting this magnificent art gallery twice or even three times during your stay in Florence is highly recommended. In fact, we'll go on record to say that limiting yourself to a mere morning – as many visitors do – could almost be described as criminally negligent. Chock-full of Renaissance masterpieces, this Medici-built palace (p61) is home to major works by Giotto, Botticelli, Michelangelo, da Vinci, Raphael, Titian and Caravaggio, and is one of only a few cultural institutions in the world that deserves a life-long program of revisits.

Piazza del Campo, Siena

2 Horses race around it twice a year, local teenagers treat it as an impromptu picnic spot and tourists inevitably gasp on seeing it for the first time – Siena's strangely sloping and perfectly paved central piazza (p194) is where the city's geographical and historical heart lies. Presided over by the graceful Palazzo Comunale and fringed with bustling cafe terraces, it's where you should come to promenade, take photographs and experience this magically intact Gothic city in all its glory.

Chianti

3 'A jug of wine, a loaf of bread and thou': the Persian poet Omar Khayyam could well have been extolling the joys of Chianti when he wrote the *Rubáiyát's* oft-quoted stanza. Come to Tuscany most romantic destination (p206) and you'll end up waxing lyrical, too – luxurious accommodation, stunning scenery and the very best of modern Tuscan cuisine provide the ingredients for an idyllic short escape, particularly when accompanied by generous pourings of Italy's best-known wine, the ruby-red, violet-scented Chianti Classico.

DAMIEN SIMONIS/LONELY PLANET IMAGES ©

The Flavours of Tuscany

4 'To cook like your mother is good, but to cook like your grandmother is better', says the Tuscan proverb. Here, age-old recipes passed between generations form the backbone of the cuisine and make any visit a gastronomic delight (p294). Forget fusion food, molecular madness and other culinary claptrap beloved of celebrity chefs from Paris, London and New York – in Tuscany, cooking is dictated by the season, is packed full of flavour and is locovore to the letter. *Buon appetito!*

Relaxing in an Agriturismo

5 Do something for both the local economy and your soul – stay in an *agriturismo* (farm stay; p32). Established to supplement a farm's income, *agriturismi* offer an authentic peek into traditional Tuscan country life and the opportunity to relax in oft-idyllic rural surrounds. Particularly popular with families, they offer opportunities to do everything from helping to bring in the grape or olive harvest to taking a cooking course or feeding the farm animals. Usually offering amenities such as swimming pools and home-cooked dinners, they're havens of Tuscan tranquillity. Villa Vignamaggio, south of Greve in Chianti

CUBOIMAGES SRL/ALAMY ©

The Truffle Hunt

6 The most precious product in the Italian pantry is sourced east of Pisa, in the woods surrounding the hilltop town of San Miniato. Here, in the loamy soil, grow white truffles – lots and lots of them. Come here between mid-October and mid-December to join the excitement of a truffle hunt (p149), or follow your nose to San Miniato on the last three weekends of November, when the Mostra Mercato Nazionale del Tartufo Bianco (National White Truffle Market) takes over the town.

The Duomo, Florence

7 A building that graces a million postcards (and then some), the duomo (p68) isn't just the most spectacular structure in Florence – it's also one of Italy's most recognisable built icons. The polychrome marble facade is wonderful, but what makes the building so extraordinary is Filippo Brunelleschi's massive red-brick dome, one of the greatest architectural achievements of all time.

The Garfagnana

8 Head to the hills north of Lucca (p150) to feast on fruits of the forest (chestnuts, honey and mushrooms), hike through wildflower-festooned fields and make a leisurely progress from one laid-back medieval mountain village to another. Base yourself in an *agriturismo* and spend your days hiking, mountain biking and eating wonderfully well. From here, the beaches and artistic enclaves of the Versilian coast aren't too far away, but most visitors find that once they've discovered this tourist-free corner of Tuscany, they never want to leave. Bridge over the Serchio at Castelnuovo di Garfagnana

Vacationing in a Villa

9 If only life could always be this good! Book a room in a country villa, or go for broke and rent the whole joint – it's the quintessential Tuscan holiday experience (p31). Villas come in every shape and size: former medieval monasteries, ornate Renaissance country houses, simple but charming *fattorie* (farmhouses) and designer retreats sporting every mod-con you can imagine. For the perfect holiday formula, day-trip in the morning, laze by the pool in the afternoon and dine in rustic local eateries at night. A villa near Pienza

Medieval Festivals

10 Tuscans have more than a few peculiarities. They won't eat foreign food (and that includes dishes from the neighbouring regions of Lazio and Emilia-Romagna), they don't put seats on their toilets (go figure) and they adore dressing up in medieval costumes and playing with giant crossbows or lances (p24). Almost every town hosts an annual festival in which locals don fancy dress and join neighbourhood teams battling for trophies such as golden arrows and silk banners. Between May and September you'll be able to join in the fun. Standard bearers at Siena's Palio

Art Scene, Arezzo

11 Though way off the well-trod tourist trail, eastern Tuscany's major city has loads to offer the visitor. Chief among its attractions is Piero della Francesca's fresco cycle of the *Legend of the True Cross* in the Chiesa di San Francesco (p257), but there are also three other churches and four museums housing significant works of art. Come here on the first weekend of the month and you may even be able to purchase a masterpiece of your own – the city's antiques fair is one of the most famous in Italy. Museo di Casa di Vasari

Piazza dei Miracoli, Pisa

12 History will resonate when you stand in the middle of this piazza (p126). Showcasing structures built to glorify God and flaunt civic riches (not necessarily in that order), this cluster of Romanesque church buildings possesses an architectural harmony that is remarkably refined and very rare. Hear the acoustics in the baptistry, marvel at Giovanni Pisano's marble pulpit in the *duomo* and confirm that, yes, the famous tower really does lean. It truly is a field full of miracles.

Touring by Vespa

13 What could be more Italian than hopping on a Vespa and cruising the countryside, stopping to visit wine estates, medieval *pieve* (rural churches) and hilltop towns along the way? The famous scooter – nicknamed a *vespa* (wasp) by its original manufacturer Enrico Piaggio – is ubiquitous throughout the region and ideally suited to slow travel. If you hire one, the only accessories you'll need for a perfect day or two of touring are a driving map and gourmet picnic provisions.

Pedalling Through Lucca

14 The Lucchesi version of the Giro d'Italia is shorter and considerably less strenuous. Hire a bike, provision yourself with picnic supplies and freewheel along the city's cobbled streets (p136), zooming through a progression of piazzas and stopping to pay your respects at the city's clutch of architecturally important churches. Next, hit the popular bicycle path atop the monumental city walls (such fun!) or head into the surrounding countryside to visit opulent villas surrounded by formal gardens and scenic parkland. Piazza Anfiteatro, Lucca

Medieval Towers, San Gimignano

15 They form one of the most enchanting skylines in the world, house everything from local families to contemporary art, and bring history alive for every visitor – San Gimignano's medieval towers are one of Tuscany's signature sights. You can't climb many these days (the exception is the Torre Grossa in the Palazzo Comunale; p216), but you can explore in their shadow and reflect on the civic pride and neighbourhood rivalry that prompted their construction and have given this diminutive hilltop town its unique appearance.

Exploring the Apuane Alps

16 This rugged mountain range (p150), protected within the Parco Regionale delle Alpi Apuane, beckons hikers, bikers and drivers with a trail of isolated farmhouses, medieval hermitages and hilltop villages. Its most spectacular sights are the slopes providing a backdrop to the town of Carrara, which are scarred with marble quarries that have been worked since Roman times. Come here to visit a quarry and – if you dare – sample *lardo di colonnata* (thinner-than-wafer-thin slices of local pig fat), one of Tuscany's greatest gastronomic treats, in the tiny village of Colonnata.

Aperitivo

17 Tuscans love a tipple or two, and who's to blame them? While you're here, be sure to join them in the age-old ritual of *aperitivo* (pre-dinner drinks accompanied by cocktail snacks) or in the recent phenomenon of *apericena* (drinks with a snack buffet so generous that it can double as dinner). Best enjoyed after a leisurely *passeggiata* (early evening stroll), *aperitivo* is most seductive in the larger cities and towns, when people-watching is an important component. *Salute!*

JOHN ELK III/LONELY PLANET IMAGES ©

Franciscan Pilgrimage Sites

18 Offering a heady mix of scenery, art, history and religion, the Santuario della Verna in eastern Tuscany (p269) and the hilltop town of Assisi (p273) in neighbouring Umbria are two of the most important Christian pilgrimage sites in the world. Visit the windswept monastery in the Casentino where St Francis is said to have received the stigmata, and then move on to his birthplace, where Giotto's famous fresco series in the upper church stuns every beholder with its beauty and narrative power. Basilica di San Francesco, Assisi

need to know

Currency
» euro (€)

Language
» Italian

When to Go

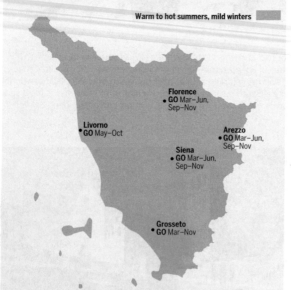

Warm to hot summers, mild winters

Florence
● GO Mar–Jun, Sep–Nov

Livorno
● GO May–Oct

Arezzo
● GO Mar–Jun, Sep–Nov

Siena
● GO Mar–Jun, Sep–Nov

Grosseto
● GO Mar–Nov

High Season
(May, Jun, Sep, Oct)

» Accommodation prices rise by up to 50%

» Perfect weather for travelling, but it can be crowded

» Major festivals are held from June to September

Shoulder
(Apr, Jul & Aug)

» In April the weather is pleasant and prices are reasonable

» High summer can be hot away from the coast and crowded on the coast

» Most attractions stay open to sundown during summer

Low Season
(Nov–Mar)

» Accommodation bargains abound, but many country hotels close for the season

» Some tourist information offices close

» Many restaurants close for annual holidays

Your Daily Budget

Budget less than
€70

» Dorm bed: €25–30

» Sandwich: €4

» Many sights have free entry

» Trattoria dinner: €20

» Coffee drunk at the bar: €0.90

Midrange
€70– 200

» Midrange-hotel double room: €100–200

» Restaurant meal: €35

» *Aperitivo*: €8

» Average museum entry: €5

» Walking tours: €10–50

Top End over
€200

» Top-end-hotel double room: €200 and over

» Dinner of modern Tuscan cuisine: €50

» Coffee sitting on a cafe terrace: €4

» Tour guide for two hours: €120

Money

» ATMs widely available. Credit cards accepted in most hotels and many restaurants; exceptions are noted in reviews.

Visas

» Not needed for residents of Schengen countries or for many visitors staying for less than 90 days. See p332.

Mobile (Cell) Phones

» Local SIM cards can be used in European and Australian phones. Other phones must be set to roaming.

Accommodation

» A wide range of accommodation styles is available. See p31.

Websites

» **Turismo in Toscana** (www.turismo.intoscana. it) Official Tuscan tourism authority site.

» **Toscana & Chianti News** (www. toscanaechiantinews. com) News and listings.

» **Firenze Made in Tuscany** (www. firenzemadeintuscany. it) Design-driven guide.

» **Informacittà Toscana 24hr** (www. informacitta.net, in Italian) Events listings.

» **Lonely Planet** (www. lonelyplanet.com/ italy/tuscany) Loads of practical information.

» **Angloinfo Tuscany** (http://tuscany.angloinfo. com) Expat website.

Exchange Rates

Australia	A$1	€0.73
Canada	C$1	€0.70
Japan	¥100	€0.90
New Zealand	NZ$1	€0.58
UK	UK£1	€1.13
USA	US$1	€0.70

For current exchange rates see www.xe.com.

Important Numbers

Italy country code	☎39
International access code	☎00
Ambulance (free call from a landline)	☎118
Local police (free call from a landline)	☎113
Pan-European emergency number & all emergency services from a mobile phone	☎112

Arriving in Tuscany

» **Pisa International Airport**
Bus – €1.10 to central Pisa; €10 to central Florence
Train – €1.10 to Stazione Pisa Centrale; €5.80 to Florence's Stazione di Santa Maria Novella
Taxi – €10 to central Pisa

» **Florence airport**
Bus – €5 to central Florence
Taxi – €20 flat rate into central Florence, plus €1 per bag and surcharges at night and on Sunday and holidays
For more information, see p135 for Pisa and p119 for Florence.

Driving in Tuscany

Cars drive on the right side of the road and overtake on the left. Unless otherwise indicated, you must always give way to cars entering an intersection from a road on your right.

Tuscany has an excellent road network, including autostradas and major highways. Most of these are untolled, with the main exceptions being the A11 and A12 (FI-PI-LI) autostrada connecting Florence, Pisa and Livorno and the A1 autostrada linking Milan and Rome via Florence and Arezzo.

Many Tuscan towns and cities have a *Zona a Traffico Limitato* (ZTL; Limited Traffic Zone) in their historic centre. This means that only local vehicles with parking permits can enter – all other vehicles must stay outside the ZTL or be hit with a hefty fine.

For more information, see p335.

first time

Everyone needs a helping hand when they visit a country for the first time. There are phrases to learn, customs to get used to and etiquette to understand. The following section will help demystify Tuscany so that your first trip goes as smoothly as your fifth.

Language

Tourism is an extremely important part of the Tuscan economy, so most locals speak at least one language other than Italian. English is the most common, but many locals also speak French. That said, your travels will be easier if you master a few basic phrases in Italian. See the Language chapter (p339) for useful words and phrases.

Booking Ahead

Reserving your accommodation in advance is highly recommended. Most hotel reservation staff speak and write English, but in situations where this isn't the case, the following phrases should help when making a booking by email or telephone:

Hello.	Buongiorno.
I would like to book...	Vorrei prenotare...
a single room	una camera singola
a double room	una camera doppia con letto matrimoniale
in the name of...	in nome di...
from... to... (date)	dal... al...
How much is it...?	Quanto costa...?
per night/per person	per la notte/per persona
Thank you (very much).	Grazie (mille).

What to Wear

A sense of style is vital to Tuscans, who take great pride in their dress and appearance. Here, maintaining *la bella figura* (ie making a good impression) is extremely important. In general, steer clear of shorts and flip-flops unless you're at the beach and always dress up, not down, at restaurants, clubs and bars. Smart-casual outfits will cover you in most situations, though trainers and jeans are frowned upon for evening wear.

Cover yourself when entering a church (no shorts, short skirts or sleeveless or off-the-shoulder tops) and also, to a degree, when on the beach – topless and nude bathing are unacceptable in most instances. It pays to bring a sweater (jumper) and rain jacket in all periods except high summer. Take sensible shoes in every season, as streets are cobbled and often totally unsuited to high heels or thin soles.

What to Pack

» Passport
» Credit cards
» This guidebook
» International Driver's Licence
» Phrasebook
» Driving map
» Travel plug (adaptor)
» Mobile phone (cell phone) and charger
» Earplugs
» Sunscreen
» Sunhat
» Sunglasses
» Swimming towel
» Umbrella
» Rainproof jacket
» Torch (flashlight)
» Pocketknife with corkscrew
» Camera
» Medical kit

Checklist

» Check the validity of your passport

» Check if you need a visa (p332)

» Organise an International Driver's Licence

» Organise a youth, student or teacher card if applicable (p327)

» Organise travel insurance (p328)

» Book ahead for accommodation and major sights

» Check the airline baggage restrictions

» Organise international roaming on your phone if needed (p331)

Etiquette

» **Greetings**
Shake hands, make eye contact and say *buongiorno* (good morning/afternoon), *buonasera* (good evening) or *piacere* (pleased to meet you). If you know someone well, air-kissing on both cheeks (starting on the left) is standard.

» **Polite Language**
Say *mi scusi* to attract attention or say 'I'm sorry', *grazie (mille)* to say 'thank you (very much)', *per favore* to say 'please', *prego* to say 'you're welcome' or 'please, after you' and *permesso* if you need to push past someone in a crowd.

» **Cafes**
Don't hang around at an espresso bar; drink your coffee and go. It's called espresso for a reason.

» **Body Language**
Avoid making a circle with two hands ('I'll kick your ass'), an OK signal ('You might be gay'), or the devil horns with your hand ('Your wife is cheating on you').

» For advice on table etiquette, see p40.

Tipping

» **Taxis**
Round the fare up to the nearest euro.

» **Restaurants**
Many locals don't tip waiters, but most visitors leave 10% if there's no service charge.

» **Cafes**
Leave a coin (as little as €0.10 is acceptable) if you drank your coffee at the counter or 10% if you sat at a table.

» **Hotels**
Bellhops usually expect €1 to €2 per bag; it's not necessary to tip the concierge, cleaners or front-desk staff.

Money

Credit and debit cards are widely accepted, though there may be a minimum purchase of €10. Visa and MasterCard are the most popular options; American Express is only accepted by international chain hotels, luxury boutiques and major department stores, and few places take Diners Club and JCB. Always check if restaurants take cards before you order; most bars and cafes do not. Chip-and-pin is the norm for card transactions – few places accept signatures as an alternative.

Bancomats (ATMs) are everywhere; most offer withdrawal from overseas savings accounts and cash advances on credit cards. Both transactions will incur international transaction fees. If you don't want to rely on plastic, you can usually change cash and travellers cheques at a bank, post office or *cambio* (exchange office).

what's new

For this new edition of Florence & Tuscany, our authors have hunted down the fresh, the transformed, the hot and the happening. These are some of our favourites. For up-to-the-minute recommendations, see www.lonelyplanet.com/italy/tuscany.

Firenze Card, Florence
1 Florence finally has its own museum pass, shaving euros off admission fees for culture-keen visitors (p61).

Le Murate, Florence
2 Knitting lounges, sound installations, screenings, tastings and exhibitions – this former jail and nunnery is being transformed into one of the city's most exciting cultural spaces (p112).

Museo Galileo, Florence
3 Though fabulous, most of Florence's museums have been around for centuries. This museum, with its cutting-edge interactive exhibits, bucks the trend (p77).

Palazzo Accommodation, Florence
4 They don't carry any stars, but Florence's new breed of luxury accommodation – palatial suite rooms in historical *palazzi* such as Residenza del Moro (p100) and Palazzo Vecchietti (p99) – really do raise the bar.

2Italia, Lucca
5 These contemporary self-catering apartments are aimed squarely at families with kids and – most unusually – are available on a nightly basis (p139).

Podere del Grillo, San Miniato
6 Artists, gourmets and music lovers flock to this hybrid dining-drinking address for outstanding farm-sourced cuisine and an urban vibe – all in backwater Tuscany (p150).

Waterfront, Livorno
7 The waterfront in downtown Livorno has never looked so good: there's a brand-new aquarium – very dashing – and the *belle epoque* Grand Hotel Palazzo has reopened for business (p168 and p170).

Museo del Vino, Greve in Chianti
8 Where better to locate a museum of Italian wine than in the centre of the Chianti region? Its eclectic collection and slick audiovisual presentation will pique your interest and your palate (p207).

Castello di Ama
9 The artworks adorning the sculpture park at this highly regarded winery southwest of Gaiole in Chianti are resolutely cutting-edge and only recently opened to public view (p213).

Colline Metallifere
10 Industrial history may be an acquired taste, but everyone is sure to be fascinated by the weird and wonderful sites within this newly gazetted member of the European Geopark Network (p241).

Archaeological Finds, Vetulonia
11 Recent excavation works have uncovered the most intact villa from the Etruscan-Roman era in existence, and hint at many more exciting finds in the future (p243).

Walking Tours, Arezzo & Cortona
12 Maximise your time and budget by signing up for one of Colori Toscani's cheap-as-chips guided English-language walking tours (p262 and p273).

if you like...

Food

Tuscan cooks serve up meals that satisfy every sense, inspired by produce that bursts with flavour, smells divine and looks even better. Forget the terms 'pre-prepared', 'out-of-season' and 'fusion' – food here is simple, seasonal and straight from the heart.

Bistecca alla fiorentina Chargrilled T-bone steak comes rare, unadorned and packed full of flavour. Sample it in the Val di Chiana (p231), where it's a local art form.

Chianti The home of Italy's signature wine and the incubator of modern Tuscan cuisine should top every foodie's must-do list (p206).

Antipasto Toscano Follow the local lead and start your meal with a plate of cured meats, *pecorino* (sheep's-milk cheese) and toasts topped with chicken liver pâté.

Fruits of the forest Fossicking here really pays off, particularly in autumn when truffles, *porcini* mushrooms and chestnuts are harvested. Join the fun of a truffle hunt (p149).

Wine

Dante, Petrarch and Boccaccio all waxed lyrical about Tuscan wine, and we're not surprised. In fact, we hazard a guess that you'll be spouting poetry of your own after sampling the joys of Brunello di Montalcino, Vino Nobile di Montepulciano and Vernaccia.

Aperitivo Florence's *aperitivi* (pre-dinner drinks) scene has taken the city by storm. See what the fuss is about in the city's fabulous wine bars (p107).

Strade del Vino For a road trip with a difference, follow a regional wine itinerary, visiting vineyards, *cantine* (cellars) and local artisan food producers (p210).

Super Tuscans To taste what the international wine press is raving about, head to Bolgheri on the Etruscan Coast, home of the groundbreaking Sassicaia (p173).

Montalcino Be there for the release of the new vintage of Brunello in February (p224). Bliss.

Architecture

Tuscan architects have been innovating, inspiring and transforming flights of imagination into brick-and-mortar reality for centuries. City-hop here and you'll see some of the most beautiful and influential buildings ever constructed.

Siena The city's historical centre is a showcase of the Gothic style, with the *duomo* (cathedral) being the jewel in its crown (p197).

Florence Climb to the top of Brunelleschi's dome to survey the city's skyline in all its Renaissance splendour (p68).

Insider Florence Every visitor sees the *duomo,* but true architecture buffs head straight to Brunelleschi's more modest commissions: the Ospedale degli Innocenti (p84) and Cappella de' Pazzi (p85).

Pisa The Piazza dei Miracoli lives up to its name, delivering a monumental arrangement of Romanesque buildings that has battled the threat of subsidence and stood the test of time (p126).

» Autumn hues in a Chianti landscape (p206)

Renaissance Art

The term 'embarrassment of riches' seems appropriate here. Tuscany is packed to the gunwales with Renaissance masterpieces, many of which have been expertly and lovingly restored and most of which are on public display.

Uffizi Gallery It doesn't get any better than this. The repository of the Medici art collection is so wonderful that even superlatives seem inadequate when trying to describe it (p61).

Museo Civico Secular art takes centre stage in Siena's town hall, courtesy of Ambrogio Lorenzetti's *Allegories of Good and Bad Government* fresco cycle (p195).

Piero della Francesca Follow a trail of the great painter's works in eastern Tuscany, marvelling at the tenderness of the *Madonna del Parto* and the masterful storytelling of the *Legend of the True Cross* (p265).

Collegiata Decipher a medieval cartoon strip and be enchanted by Domenico Ghirlandaio's tribute to Santa Fina at San Gimignano's *duomo* (p215).

Contemporary Art

There's more to the Tuscan art scene than 15th-century frescoes. Come here to embrace the cutting edge, wandering through formal gardens full of site-specific sculptures and visiting sleek commercial galleries unexpectedly housed in centuries-old buildings.

Castello di Ama Works by some of the art world's biggest names are showcased in the formal gardens of this wine estate in Chianti (p213).

Fattoria di Celle Industrialist Giuliano Gori has commissioned an extraordinary collection of site-specific artworks at his vast family estate outside Pistoia (p148).

Galleria Continua One of Europe's most impressive contemporary art galleries is located in the medieval time capsule of San Gimignano (p218). Go figure.

Giardino dei Tarocchi A whimsical labour of love by Franco-American artist Niki de Saint Phalle, this sculpture garden south of Grosseto brings the tarot card pack to life (p254).

Natural Landscapes

From the marble mountains of the Apuane Alps to the marshy flatlands of the southern coast, there's a huge variety of Tuscan landscapes to keep nature lovers satisfied.

Parco Nazionale dell'Arcipelago Toscano Europe's largest marine protected area covers the whole of the Tuscan archipelago and has at its centre the magical island of Elba (p176).

Parco Regionale Migliarino, San Rossore, Massaciuccoli Climb Pisa's Leaning Tower and you'll be able to see this haven of bird life west of the city. Explore it on foot, by bicycle, on horseback or in a horse-drawn carriage (p133).

Apuane Alps The snowy-white mountain peaks forming the backdrop to the town of Carrara aren't capped with snow – they're topped with vast quarries where marble has been gouged out of the landscape since Roman times (p150).

The Casentino Dense forests, crystal-clear river streams and hidden medieval monasteries await in the northeastern corner of the region (p266).

If you like... opera, visit Lajatico for the once-a-year performance staged by locally born operatic superstar Andrea Bocelli. It's held in the purpose-built, evocatively named Teatro del Silenzio in July (p151).

Scenic Drives

Hit the road to see the real Tuscany – the provincial variety rather than the autostrada. Most of these can be explored by 2WD and offer opportunities galore for cultural stops, nature walks and great meals.

The Passo del Vestito Ascend this spectacular mountain pass from Castelnuovo di Garfagnana to Massa on the Versilian coast (p155).

Elba off season Wait until the crowds have gone home, then wind your way along the stunning road on the island's southwest coast, stopping for a seafood lunch at the enchanting hilltop town of Capoliveri (p176).

The Crete Senese Explore the gently rolling, cypress-topped hills of this postcard-perfect pocket of Tuscany (p230).

Chianti Every road seems to lead to immaculately maintained vineyards and olive groves, honey-coloured stone farmhouses, graceful Romanesque *pieve* (rural churches) and imposing castles (p206).

Picnics

Provisioning alfresco lunches couldn't be easier – the shelves at local shops groan under the weight of artisan-made cheeses and meat, freshly baked bread and plump olives. Wine is cheap and plentiful, and fruit or biscuits make a great finale.

Parco Archeologico di Baratti e Populonia Lay down your picnic blanket between ancient Etruscan tombs at this vast green archaeological park (p175).

Piazza del Campo Fill your picnic basket at Morbidi and join the locals lounging on Siena's famous urban carpet (p194).

Bagni San Filippo Take a dip in these tumbling thermal cascades in Tuscany's deep south before noshing in the slightly sulphurous surrounds (p227).

Afloat in Elba Commandeer a sea kayak and enjoy an offshore snack. Even better, make a night of it and catch your own fish to BBQ on the beach before pitching a tent beneath the stars (p176).

Pilgrimage Sights

Christian history and beliefs resonate here, with every village, town and city having its own religious traditions and structures. Churches and religious art are ubiquitous, but there are also many important sites that draw pilgrims from surrounding areas and beyond.

Via Francigena Drive or walk parts of this medieval pilgrimage route, stopping at evocative destinations including the Abbazia di Sant'Antimo along the way (p162 and p225).

Santuario della Madonna del Monte Take the half-day walk from the pretty town of Marciana on Elba through scented parasol pine and chestnut woods to this hilltop chapel (p184).

Santuario della Verna Visit the windswept monastery in the Casentino where St Francis of Assisi is said to have received the stigmata (p269).

Cattedrale di San Martino Pay your respects to the *Volto Santo*, a simply fashioned image of a dark-skinned, life-sized Christ that is Lucca's most revered religious icon (p137).

month by month

Top Events

1 **The Palio**, July and August

2 **Carnevale**, February to March

3 **Puccini Festival**, July to August

4 **Maggio Musicale Fiorentino**, April to June

5 **Giostra del Saracino**, June and September

February

It's only towards the end of this month that locals are coaxed out of their winter hibernation. Weather conditions can be bone-chillingly cold in mountainous areas and windswept hill towns can appear all but deserted.

 Carnevale
Kicking off 40 days before Ash Wednesday and the restrictions of Lent, Viareggio's famous month-long street party involves fireworks, floats, parades and revelry galore. It's usually held in February to early March (p161).

March

Locals start to get into the springtime swing of things in the weeks leading up to Easter. Many regular visitors time their trips for this period to take advantage of low-season prices and uncrowded conditions.

Settimana Santa
Easter Week is celebrated in neighbouring Umbria with processions and performances in Assisi. Other Easter celebrations in the region include Florence's Scoppio del Carro (Explosion of the Cart) on Easter Sunday (p98).

April

Wildflowers carpet the countryside, market stalls burst with new-season produce and classical music is staged in wonderfully atmospheric surrounds. Easter sees the tourist season kicking off in earnest.

Maggio Musicale Fiorentino
This arts festival – Italy's oldest – is held in Florence's Teatro del Maggio Musicale Fiorentino and stages world-class performances of theatre, classical music, jazz and dance from April to June (www.maggiofioren tino.com).

May

Medieval pageants take over the streets of towns and cities across the region from late spring to early autumn, highlighting ancient neighbourhood rivalries and the modern-day love of street parties.

Balestro del Girifalco
In Massa Marittima, crossbow teams from the town's three *terzieri* (districts) dress in medieval costumes and compete for trophies, including a painted banner. Held on the first Sunday after 20 May and again in July or August.

Giostra dell'Archidado
More crossbows, this time in Cortona, when a full week of medieval merriment in late May or June culminates in an exciting competition between representatives from the town's five residential quarters.

June

It's summertime and, yes, the living is easy. The start of the month is the perfect time to tour the paradisaical isle of Elba, and any time is right to gorge on seafood and strawberries.

Luminaria

On the night of 16 June, Pisans honour their city's patron saint with thousands of candles and blazing torches along the banks of the Arno, as well as a spectacular fireworks display.

Giostra del Saracino

A grand, noisy affair involving extravagant fancy dress and neighbourhood rivalry, this medieval jousting tournament (www.giostradel saracino.arezzo.it, in Italian; p262) is held in Arezzo on the third Saturday in June and first Sunday in September.

July

Cyclists and walkers take to the mountains but everyone else heads to the beach, meaning that accommodation prices in inland cities and towns drop as a result. Summer music festivals abound.

Festivals in Cortona

The hill town of Cortona is alive with the sound of music at its annual Festival of Sacred Music (www.cortona cristiana.it), held early in the month, and Tuscan Sun Festival (www.tuscansun festival.com), held late July to early August.

Music in Montalcino

Sip a glass or two of Brunello while mingling with Montalcino's winemakers at the town's refined International Chamber Music Festival (www.musica-reale.com) and laid-back Jazz & Wine

(above) The colourful street pageant that takes place as part of Siena's Palio
(below) A spectacular float in Viareggio's month-long Carnevale celebrations

Festival (www.montalcino jazzandwine.com).

⭐ Puccini Festival
Opera buffs from around the world make a pilgrimage to the small town of Torre del Lago for this annual event in July and August (www. puccinifestival.it; p142). Performances are staged in an open-air lakeside theatre next to the great man's house.

✨ The Palio
The most spectacular event on the Tuscan calendar is held on 2 July and 16 August in Siena (see the boxed text, p203). Featuring colourful street pageants, a wild horse race and generous doses of civic pride, it exemplifies the living history that makes this region so compelling.

⭐ Lucca Summer Festival
This month-long music festival (www.summer -festival.com) lures big-name international pop, rock and blues acts to lovely Lucca, where they serenade crowds under the stars in some of the city's most atmospheric piazzas.

August
Locals take their annual holidays and the daily tempo of life in the cities slows to a snail's pace. Be warned: the weather can be oppressively hot and beaches are inevitably crowded.

✨ Volterra AD 1398
On the third and fourth Sundays of August, the citizens of Volterra roll back the calendar some 600 years, take to the streets in period costume and participate in this medieval festival (www.volterra1398. it, in Italian).

September
Autumn/fall is when La Vendemmia (the grape harvest) is celebrated and when the forests proffer their highly anticipated harvests of intensely scented porcini mushrooms and creamy chestnuts.

 Grapes in Greve
The major town in the Chianti wine district holds its annual wine fair in the first or second week of September.

✨ Palio della Ballestra
Sansepolcro's party-loving locals don medieval costumes and peacock around town on the second Sunday of September while hosting a crossbow tournament between local archers and rivals from the nearby Umbrian town of Gubbio.

November
This is when restaurateurs and truffle tragics come from every corner of the globe to sample and purchase Tuscany's bounty of strong-smelling and utterly delicious white truffles.

🍴 Mostra Mercato Nazionale del Tartufo Bianco
The streets of San Miniato are filled with one of the world's most distinctive aromas at the National White Truffle Market (p149), held on the last three weekends in November.

itineraries

Whether you've got six days or 60, these itineraries provide a starting point for the trip of a lifetime. Want more inspiration? Head online to lonelyplanet. com/thorntree to chat to other travellers.

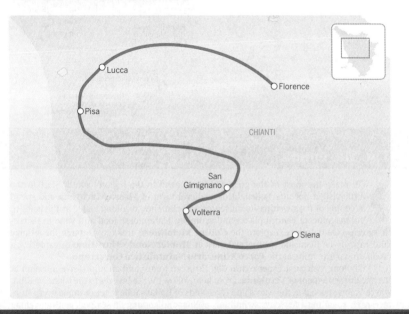

10 Days
Only the Best

Florence anchors any 'best of' tour. You'll need at least three days to do this magnificent city justice – any less and you'll be selling both it and yourself short. Spend one day visiting the Uffizi, another wandering through the San Marco and San Lorenzo neighbourhoods, and the third crossing the Arno to explore the artisan's neighbourhood of Oltrarno. After having eaten, drunk, shopped and seen more Renaissance masterpieces than you would previously have thought possible, it's time to slow down the pace and move on to the enchanting walled city of **Lucca** for two days. Hire a bike and use pedal power for a leisurely exploration of its cobbled city streets and villa-studded surrounding countryside. On day six, pop into **Pisa** to scale its Leaning Tower, leaving after lunch to arrive at a Tuscan farmhouse in **Chianti** before dusk. Check-in for three nights, visiting wineries, taking a day trip to **San Gimignano** or **Volterra**, exploring sculpture gardens and feasting on modern Tuscan food during your stay. On day nine, head to gloriously Gothic **Siena**, home to museums, cafes and churches that will supply a truly fabulous two-day finale to your trip.

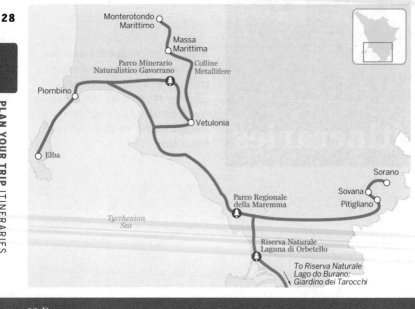

12 Days
The Maremma

> To make the most of the great outdoors, head to the region's south. Start in the little-visited but utterly delightful medieval town of **Massa Marittima** and spend a couple of days visiting its museums and churches, drinking coffee at the cafes in its magnificent central piazza and sampling Maremmese food and wine in its rustic eateries. On day three, explore the **Colline Metallifere**, trekking through the strange landscape of 'Le Biancane' geothermal park at **Monterotondo Marittimo** or exploring a fascinating pyrite mine at the **Parco Minerario Naturalistico Gavorrano**.

On day four, visit an archaeological dig, Etruscan tombs and an impressive museum at the ancient settlement of **Vetulonia**. From here, follow the sea breezes to the island of **Elba**, where Venus sported in the waves and thousands of Italians follow her example every summer. After spending a few days swimming, cycling and gorging on seafood, continue along the coast to the wild and wonderful **Parco Regionale della Maremma** to walk, canoe, cycle or horse-ride alongside the famous cowboys known as the *butteri*.

On day nine, those interested in bird-watching should visit the **Riserva Naturale Lago do Burano** or the **Riserva Naturale Laguna di Orbetello**, both operated by the Italian branch of the WWF (World Wide Fund for Nature), whereas art-lovers should head to the whimsical **Giardino dei Tarocchi**, a sculpture garden that takes its inspiration from the cards in a tarot pack. End your journey inland amid the stunning surrounds of the *Paese del Tufa* (Land of the Tufa), where you can visit Etruscan necropolises, and walk along the enigmatic sunken roads known as *vie cave*.

Also here are three enchanting and historically intact towns: **Pitigliano**, where you can visit an historic ghetto that was once home to the largest Jewish community in Italy; **Sovana**, an atmosphere-rich hamlet with two beautiful Romanesque churches; and **Sorano**, known for its majestic 11th-century fortress. To make the most of your time here, consider taking the 8km walk from Pitigliano to Sovana, which incorporates stretches of *vie cave* – a truly unique experience.

To Orvieto & Assisi

12 Days
Into the East

Mix it up a bit by balancing well-known destinations with some intriguing off-the-beaten-track alternatives. Spend three days admiring the Renaissance splendour of **Florence** before branching out east into the little-visited Casentino region, home to the idyllically isolated Parco Nazionale delle Foreste Casentinesi, Monte Falterona e Campigna. Base yourself around the fortified hill town of **Poppi** for three days, sampling the area's rustic and delicious cuisine, visiting the medieval monasteries of **Camaldoli** and **La Verna**, following the stretch of our driving tour between the **Castello di Romena** and **Pratovecchio**, and walking a few trails in the national park. Next, meander southeast to **Sansepolcro**, proud possessor of charming medieval churches, great restaurants and a museum showcasing the paintings of Piero della Francesca.

Tear yourself away after two nights and continue to your final destination, the Val di Chiana. Book into a rural retreat and spend a few days eating and drinking your way around the valley. While here, pop into the provincial capital, **Arezzo**, where locals outnumber tourists by a healthy margin and where churches are the highlight – don't miss the Cappella Bacci, Pieve di Santa Maria and Cattedrale di San Donato.

A number of nearby medieval hilltop towns are also well worth visiting – **Castiglion Fiorentino** and **Lucignano** are extremely pretty, but both pale in comparison with **Cortona**, which deserves a full-day visit at the very least. Be sure to walk up the steep cobbled streets to its Fortezza Medicea, and also check out the collections at the Museo dell'Accademia Etrusca and the Museo Diocesano.

When your time runs out, head south towards Rome on the A1 autostrada, stopping to visit the stunning cathedral at **Orvieto** en route to admire Luca Signorelli's famous fresco cycle of *The Last Judgement*. Alternatively, head into the neighbouring region of Umbria to visit one of Italy's most famous pilgrimage centres, **Assisi**, home to the Basilica di San Francesco where Giotto's extraordinary frescoes portraying the life of St Francis stun all beholders.

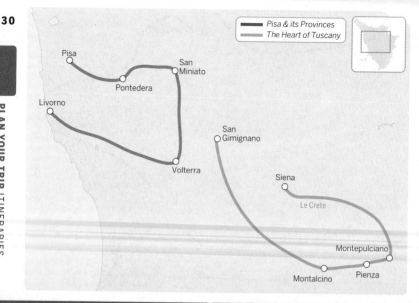

Pisa & its Provinces
The Heart of Tuscany

One Week
Pisa & its Provinces

> Start your peregrination in **Pisa**, spending two days admiring the marble pulpits in the Baptistry and *duomo*, the paintings and sculpture in the Museo Nazionale di San Matteo and the exquisite exterior decoration of the Chiesa di Santa Maria della Spina. Conclude your visit at the Piazza dei Miracoli, home to that famous engineering project gone horribly wrong, the Leaning Tower. On day three, spend the morning paying homage to Italy's famous Vespa scooter at the Museo Piaggio in **Pontedera** before driving through gently rolling hills covered in olive groves and vineyards to hunt truffles and sleep in style at the gourmet destination of **San Miniato**. From here, head to spectacularly sited **Volterra** in the Val di Cecina, where visits to alabaster ateliers and an extraordinary museum of Etruscan art await. Spend two nights here and then finish your tour in the neighbouring province and city of **Livorno**, home to an atmospheric central market, the delectable seafood stew known as *cacciucco* and the world-famous Sassicaia super Tuscan wine.

One Week
The Heart of Tuscany

> Head to the sun-kissed centre of Tuscany to indulge in some of Italy's best wine, architecture and scenery. Kick off in **Siena**, where you should gravitate towards Gothic glories such as the Museo Civico and Opera della Metropolitana. During your two days here be sure to nibble on the city's famous sweet biscuits – preferably accompanied by a glass of local Vin Santo – and explore the atmospheric streets and piazzas of the incredibly intact *centro storico* (historic centre). From Siena, head south through the stunning scenery of **Le Crete** and base yourself at a rural retreat somewhere in the area for four nights. From here, you'll be able to explore the Val d'Orcia and Val di Chiana, visiting the charming hill towns of **Montepulciano**, **Pienza** and **Montalcino** and sampling the gastronomic products that this part of Tuscany is known for – Chianina beef, *cinta senese* (indigenous Tuscan pig), and Brunello and Vino Nobile wine. In between meals, visit medieval abbeys, take a scenic driving tour and soak in ancient hot springs. End your Sienese sojourn with one night in romantic **San Gimignano**, home to medieval tower houses and golden-hued Vernaccia wine.

Staying in Tuscany

Best Agriturismi

Best Boutique Hotels

Best on a Budget

Best Country Hotels

Choosing Your Accommodation

Travellers are spoiled for choice when it comes to finding places to stay in this part of Italy, so it pays to research thoroughly. Choose somewhere with the atmosphere, services and amenities that you want, and always check hotel websites for special deals.

Accommodation Types

» **Affittacamere** A room in a private house. Tourist offices can often provide lists of these budget accommodation options.

» **Agriturismo** A working farm or vineyard offering rooms to visitors on holiday; many have on-site restaurants.

» **Albergo** A hotel; these come in all shapes and forms, including business hotels, luxury hotels and characterful midrange choices.

» **B&B** A small guesthouse offering bed and breakfast at a reasonable price. Most offer double rooms with a private bathroom.

» **Boutique hotel** A growing trend in Tuscan cities, where they often occupy magnificent *palazzi* (palaces). The Ferragamo fashion empire is a major player in this sector, operating six hip hotels in Florence under its Lungarno Collection brand.

» **Country hotel** Tuscan rural retreats come in many varieties. As well as *agriturismi* and villas, you'll find self-catering apartments in a *borgo* (farm hamlet), spa hotels and resort-style hotels with lots of sporting amenities.

» **Foresteria** These offer rooms and dorm beds in religious communities such as monasteries and convents. Though catering predominantly for pilgrims or people on religious retreats, they are also popular with families and budget travellers.

» **Locanda** A country inn offering B&B in rustic surrounds; most will provide dinner if you request this in advance.

» **Ostello** A hostel offering dorm beds and rooms to budget travellers.

» **Pensione** A small, family-run guesthouse offering B&B. The owners usually live on site.

» **Rifugio** A mountain hut kitted out with bunk rooms sleeping anything from two to a dozen or more people. Many offer half-board (dinner, bed and breakfast) and most are open from mid-June to mid-September.

» **Villa** The stuff of which dreams are made. Historic villas and *fattorie* (farmhouses) can be rented in their entirety or sometimes by the room. Most have swimming pools and are set in idyllic landscapes.

Booking Your Accommodation

It is wise to book well ahead for all accommodation, particularly in Florence and Siena and along the coast in summer. Note that in busy periods, some hotels may impose a multinight stay (this usually applies at beach hotels over July and August, and always applies in Siena during the Palio).

WHEN TO GO

Most urban accommodation is open year-round; country hotels, *locande*, villas and *agriturismi* often close in winter. For info about seasons, see p16.

Most hotels will give you the choice of a *camera doppia* (room with twin beds) or a *camera matrimoniale* (room with double bed). Many hotels do not have *camera singola* (single rooms); instead, lone travellers will pay a slightly reduced price for a double room.

Credit cards are accepted at many – but not all – places to stay. MasterCard and Visa are more widely accepted than American Express or Diners Club International. When booking directly with the hotel, a deposit of up to 30% may be requested; you can organise this by faxing or emailing your credit-card details.

See p326 for a guide to the accommodation price ranges we have used in this book.

Useful Resources

Associazione Italiana Alberghi per la Gioventù (Association of Italian Youth Hostels, AIG; www.aighostels.com) Affiliated with Hostelling International (HI).

BB Italia (www.bbitalia.it) B&B website.

Beds & Blessings in Italy: A Guide to Religious Hospitality (St Pauls Publications) English-language version of the Centro Italiano Sociale Turismo's annual guide to accommodation

---

AGRITURISMI

Agriturismi (farm stays) have long been popular in Tuscany. By definition, an *agriturismo* is required to grow at least one of its own products, but beyond this common thread they can run the gamut from a rustic country house with a handful of olive trees to a luxurious country estate with an attached vineyard to a fully functioning farm where guests can help with the harvest. They are vital to small communities, as they inject money into local economies, provide employment and often cross-subsidise the production of artisanal farm produce. In many ways, they embody the concept of Slow Travel – we love them to bits, and have recommended many in this book.

To research *agriturismi,* check out the following sites:
Agritour (www.agritour.net)
Agriturismo.com (www.agriturismo.com)
Agriturismo.it (www.agriturismo.it)
Agriturismo-Italia.net (www.agriturismo-italia.net)
Agriturismo.net (www.agriturismo.net)
Agriturismo Vero (www.agriturismovero.com)
Agriturismoitalia.com (www.agriturismoitalia.com)
Agriturist (www.agriturist.com, in Italian)

in religious institutions. Available on Amazon and the Book Depository.

Campeggi e Villaggi Turistici (Camping & Holiday Villages in Italy; TCI) An annually published list (in Italian) of all Italian camping grounds published by Touring Club Italiano (TCI). Available from bookshops throughout the region.

Camping.it (www.camping.it) Useful website listing camp sites across the region.

Club Alpino Italiano (CAI; www.cai.it) Has a database of CAI-operated *rifugi*.

Guest in Italy (www.guestinitaly.com) Online agency for apartment rental.

Invitation to Tuscany (www.invitationtotus cany.com) Wide range of villa rentals.

Locande d'Italia (Slow Food Editore) Compendium of Slow Food–recommended accommodation. Published in Italian only; available from bookshops throughout the region.

MonasteryStays.com (www.monastery stays.com) A well-organised online booking service for monastery and convent stays.

Slow Travel (www.slowtrav.com/italy) Excellent commercial booking website that carries a huge amount of information about the region.

Summer's Leases (www.summerleases.com) More villa rentals.

Turismo in Toscana (www.turismo.into scana.it) The regional tourism authority's handy accommodation-booking website.

Veronica Tomasso Cotgrove (www.vtcitaly. com) London-based company offering a small, hand-picked list of country properties.

What to Expect

You can expect a warm welcome, particularly when staying in rural areas. Whether they be cosy *pensioni,* grand villas or sleek boutique hotels, Tuscan sleeping choices inevitably have personable and professional staff and offer clean and comfortable rooms.

Hotels are non-smoking by national law and many offer accommodation for mobility-impaired guests. Most offer free wi-fi and/or an internet kiosk (indicated by wi-fi and internet symbols in reviews).

Leisure Facilities

Country hotels will usually offer one or two leisure activities. Swimming pools are commonplace, and many hotels have mountain bikes for guest use. Tennis courts, horse

---

WWOOF ITALIA

For an accommodation option with a difference, investigate **World Wide Opportunities on Organic Farms Italia** (www.wwoof.it), an organisation that facilitates the trade of your labour for accommodation on an organic farm. There are plenty of options in Tuscany to choose from, including the fabulous Il Benefizio (p154) in Barga.

---

stables and wellness centres are less common, but can be found reasonably regularly. Of these, horse-riding usually incurs an extra charge, as do certain treatments in wellness centres (massage etc). For a list of *agriturismi* offering horse-riding opportunities, see p47. Options with the best leisure facilities:

» Montebelli Agriturismo & Country Hotel, Molinetto Caldana (p244)

» Tenuta del Fontino, Massa Marittima (p241)

» La Cerreta, Castagneto Carducci (p174)

» Il Borro, San Giustino Valdarno (p262)

» Borgo Corsignano, Poppi (p268)

» Rosselba Le Palme, Portoferraio (p182)

» Hermitage, Marciana (p184)

» Villa Scacciapensieri, Siena (p204)

» Villa I Barronci, San Casciano in Val di Pesa (p209)

» Villa Vignamaggio, Greve in Chianti (p209)

» Hotel Posta Marcucci, Bagno Vignoni (p228)

» Villa Fontelunga, Foiano della Chiana (p262)

» Hotel Saturno Fontepura, Saturnia (p249)

Dining

The vast majority of hotels include breakfast in their room rate; this can take the form of anything from a simple coffee and *cornetto*

ON-THE-GROUND ASSISTANCE

Tourist offices throughout the region can help you to source accommodation. Check their websites (which are listed under Resources at the start of each regional chapter) or visit offices on the ground for advice and recommendations.

UNIQUE SLEEPS

Tuscany has more than its fair share of atmospheric hotel settings, but for a truly unique experience consider sleeping in one of the following:

Castles
» Castello delle Serre, Serre di Rapolano (p214)
» Hotel della Fortezza, Sorano (p250)

Convents
» Hotel Alma Domus, Siena (p203)
» Foresteria Monastero di San Girolamo, San Gimignano (p219)
» Chiosco delle Monache, Volterra (p223)
» Hotel Morandi alla Crocetta, Florence (p100)
» Ostello Santa Monaca, Florence (p101)

Medieval Tower Houses
» Hotel Relais dell'Orologio, Pisa p133)

Palazzi
» Palazzo Vecchietti, Florence (p99)
» Residenza del Moro, Florence (p100)
» Palazzo Guadagni Hotel, Florence (p101)
» Palazzo Magnani Feroni, Florence (p101)
» Albergo Pietrasanta, Pietrasanta (p159)
» Hotel Scoti, Florence (p98)

Olive Oil Mills
» Hotel Vecchia Oliviera, Montalcino (p226)

(croissant) to a full Western-style buffet. Many *agriturismi,* country hotels and boutique hotels also offer in-house dining, usually in the form of a set dinner menu that changes daily. Options with the best in-house dining:

» Pradaccio di Sopra, Castelnuovo di Garfagnana (p151)
» Podere San Lorenzo, Volterra (p222)
» Montebelli Agriturismo & Country Hotel, Molinetto Caldana (p244)
» Tenuta del Fontino, Massa Marittima (p241)
» Il Borro, San Giustino Valdarno (p262)
» Locanda del Giglio, Sansepolcro (p264)
» Fattoria Collebrunacchi, San Miniato (p149)
» Grand Hotel Palazzo, Livorno (p170)
» La Cerreta, Castagneto Carducci (p174)
» Canessa, Golfo di Baratti (p175)
» Podere Riparbella, Massa Marittima (p241)

Handy Hints

» Prior to your arrival, print out location information from your hotel's website; many places in cities are secreted in hard-to-find laneways and courtyards, and country retreats are often in obscure locations that don't appear on standard road maps. Don't rely on GPS, either – our experiences would indicate that it can be unreliable here.

» If driving, check with the hotel as to the most convenient and cost-effective place to park. And beware the infamous *Zona a Traffico Limitato* (ZTL; Limited Traffic Zones; p336).

» Ask hotel staff for restaurant recommendations – they often know about great local eateries and will usually be happy to make reservations for you.

» Check when the hotel swimming pool will open for the season – Italians don't usually swim until high summer and pools often remain closed until this time.

» If you're allergic to animals, mention this when booking. Many country hotels have cats and dogs.

» It's often possible to negotiate a discount if you stay five nights or more.

Eat & Drink Like a Local

When to Go

Feasting is year-round; for more details of food and wine festivals, see p24.

Spring

Markets burst with baby artichokes, asparagus, fresh garlic and – towards the season's end – cherries, figs and courgette flowers desperate to be stuffed.

Summer

Strawberries, peppers and the start of San Gimignano's long saffron harvest (July to November) as the first purple crocus flowers bloom. Beat the heat by the sea with seafood, and elsewhere with a gelato – go local with chestnut, fig and honey, or saffron and pine-nut flavours.

Autumn

Food festivals galore, the olive and grape harvests, and forest gems such as chestnuts, *porcini* mushrooms (late August to October) and game. Oenophiles head to Greve in Chianti in September for Chianti's biggest wine fair. Mid-October opens the white-truffle-hunting season near Pisa.

Winter

The truffle season, which continues until mid-December, peaks with San Miniato's truffle market. Montalcino wine producers crack open the new vintage at February's Benvenuto Brunello.

Culinary Art

For Tuscans, eating and drinking is as much a fine art as their masterpiece surrounds. And exceedingly well around a shared table is how they eat, thanks to an ancient cuisine sourced in the family farmstead from seasonal fruits of the land and sea. Titillate taste buds with these food-trip essentials and further your Tuscan Table appreciation on p294.

Food Experiences
Meals of a Lifetime

» **Enoteca Pinchiorri, Florence** (p104) Tuscany's only Michelin three-star address, stratospheric and smug in a 16th-century Florentine *palazzo*.

» **Peperino, San Miniato** (see the boxed text, p150) Dinner for two at the world's smallest, and possibly most romantic, restaurant.

» **Barbialla Nuova, Montaione** (see the boxed text, p149) Hunt down your own white truffle in damp, musky woods then head to a trattoria in a nearby village to eat it simply shaved over pasta or a *bistecca alla fiorentina* (chargrilled T-bone steak).

» **Osteria di Passignano, Badia di Passignano** (p212) Exceedingly fine abbey dining on the estate of one of Chianti's oldest, best-known winemaking families, the Antinori.

» **Il Pellicano, Monte Argentario** (p253) For sensational seafood dishes and glorious sea views.

WHAT TO BOOK

Generally, all high-end and popular restaurants should be booked in advance, especially on Friday and Saturday evenings and Sunday lunch. In Florence, Siena and other tourist-busy towns and resorts (such as Forte dei Marmi or Porto Ercole), the 'book ahead' rule applies every day in summer high season and during the Easter and Christmas periods.

Tuscany's only Michelin three-star address, Florence's Enoteca Pinchiorri (p104) requires booking a couple of weeks or more in advance depending on the day of the week you desire to dine. Ditto for Tuscany's other high-profile places to eat, such as Pepenero (p150) and Peperino in San Miniato (see the boxed text, p150); and butcher Dario's celebrity meat meccas in Panzano in Chianti, Officina della Bistecca and Solociccia (see the boxed text, p212).

» **Ristorante Albergaccio, Castellina in Chianti** (p214) Creative, five-course feasts of local, seasonal and organic produce in an old farmhouse restaurant.

» **Enoteca I Terzi, Siena** (p205) Siena's golden ticket recasts the traditional *enoteca* (wine bar) in modernity.

In the Making

» **Martelli, Lari** (see the boxed text, p134) Workshop visits at an artisanal pasta maker, in the biz since 1926.

» **Il Benefizio, Barga** (p154) Say ciao to the bees and watch honey being made.

» **Oliveto Fonte di Foiano, Castagneto Carducci** (p175) Olive farm tours, oil tastings and accommodation.

» **Tenuta La Chiusa, Portoferraio** (see the boxed text, p183) Wine tasting and dreamy sleeps between seashore, olive grove and vineyard on Elba's oldest wine-producing estate.

» **Podere San Lorenzo, near Volterra** (p222) Join the workforce; harvest olives.

» **Poggio Antico, near Montalcino** (p226) Cellar tours, wine tasting and sublime dining in Tuscany's most famous wine region.

» **Agienza Regionale Agricola di Alberese, Parco Regionale della Maremma** (p252) The only Tuscan farm to breed free-range Maremma cows, using *butteri* (traditional cowboys) to boot – tours, workshops and tastings in a cowboys' saddle room.

Cheap Treats

» **Pecorino** A nutty, crumbly ewe's-milk cheese perfect in fresh, crunchy *pane* (bread).

» **Porchetta rolls** Warm sliced pork (roasted whole with fennel, garlic and pepper) in a crispy roll.

» **Torta di ceci** Savoury chickpea pancake.

» **Castagnaccio** Hybrid cake-crepe, sweet and made from chestnut flour.

» **Pizza al taglio** 'Pizza by the slice'.

» **Gelato** The best Tuscan gelato uses seasonal, natural ingredients: figs, chestnuts, pine nuts, honey, saffron, wild strawberries...

Dare to Try

» **Bistecca alla fiorentina** Brilliantly blue and beautifully bloody is the only way Florence's iconic T-bone steak is served.

» **Tripe panino** Cow's stomach chopped up, boiled, sliced, seasoned and bunged between bread – Florence's favourite fast food (see the boxed text, p102).

» **Lampredotto** Cow's fourth stomach, chopped and simmered for hours like a stew.

» **Trippa alla fiorentina** Tripe cooked in a rich tomato sauce.

» **Lardo di colonnata** Carrara's luscious pig lard, aged in marble vats, keeps cardiologists in the black.

» **Biroldo** Local version of haggis, best sampled in Castelnuovo di Garfagnana.

» **Mallegato** San Miniato's Slow Food–accredited blood sausage.

Local Specialities

Spicy green olives, extra-virgin olive oils, full-bodied red wines, smoky *porcini* mushrooms and bags of beans are culinary trademarks across the Tuscan board, but delve deeper to discover geographic differences every gourmet will revel in. Rejoice.

Florence

Endowed with more quality eating addresses than you can possibly consume in a weekend or week, Tuscany's leading lady

» (above) A mouth-watering display at Olio & Convivium (p106), Florence
» (left) *Porcini* mushrooms offer a taste of autumn

» (above) Ingredients for *ribollita*,
Tuscan style (p295)
» (left) Cheese for sale, including the
ewe's-milk *pecorino* (p296)

is a born-and-bred gourmet. Be it slow food or fine dining, *panino* in a piazza or tripe at a street cart, Florence meets every gastronomic taste with style and panache.

» **Aperitivo & Apericena** (p107) The early-evening drink scene is big and buzzing – younger Florentines forgo dinner and feast for free instead on copious buffets fashioned by trendy *aperitivo* bars from 7pm onwards.

» **Bistecca alla fiorentina** The icon of Tuscan cuisine, legendary because of its gluttonous size and rebel reputation as former outlaw; Trattoria Mario (p103) is the best place to watch the feisty steak sizzle on the grill before sinking your teeth in.

Northwestern Tuscany

An unexpected culinary nest-egg wedged between wind-whipped sea and mountain, known for its fresh *pecorino* cheese, *zuppe di cavolo* (cabbage soup) and other humble farm fare.

» **Lucca** As sweet as the walled town where it has been baked since 1881, sugared bread loaf *buccellato* is studded with sultanas and aniseed.

» **San Miniato** Known for its exceptional white truffles, hunted and consumed with passion from mid-October to mid-December.

» **Castelnuovo di Garfagnana** Fresh autumnal *porcini,* chestnuts, sweet *castagnaccio* (chestnut cake) and farm-grown *farro* (spelt).

» **Colonnata** Pig fat is aged in Carrara marble vats and eaten 12 or 24 months later, as wafer-thin slices.

Central Coast & Elba

Two words: sensational seafood.

» **Livorno** A grimy port known for its superb affordable dining and *cacciucco,* a zesty fish stew swimming with octopus, rock fish and a shoal of other species.

» **Bolgheri** The Super Tuscan Sassicaia and other legendary full-bodied reds are a perfect match for *cinghiale* (wild boar); spunky olive oils, too.

» **Elba** Along with the raft of sun-drenched wines grown on this island, sweet red Aleatico Passito DOCG is the one to look for.

Siena & Central Tuscany

Something of a gastronomic giant, Siena is the GPS coordinate where Tuscan cuisine originates, say locals in Siena. True or otherwise, its kitchen and cellar (stashed with Tuscany's finest reds and Terre di Siena DOP olive oils) are superb.

» **Coffee and cake** Meeting at historic Pasticceria Nannini (p205) in Siena for a *caffè* (coffee) and slice of *panforte* (a rich cake of almonds, honey and candied fruit, originally eaten only at Christmas) is one of the city's sweet, timeless trends.

» **Chianti** The number-one stop for serious foodies: cheery, dry, full red wines; butcher legend Dario Cecchini (p212); tip-top Chianti Classico DOP olive oils; *finocchiona briciolona* (pork salami made with fennel seeds and Chianti) from Antica Macelleria Falorni (p207); and some of Tuscany's most exciting, modern 'New Tuscan' cuisine.

» **Montalcino** Famed internationally for red Brunello wine, the consistently good Rosso di Montalcino, prized extra-virgin olive oils, *pecorino* cheese, *porcini* mushrooms, truffles and *cinta senese* (indigenous Tuscan pig).

» **Montepulciano** Home of Vino Nobile red and its equally quaffable second-string Rosso di Montepulciano. Savour local *cinta senese* and Terre di Siena extra-virgin olive oil.

» **Val di Chiana** This rolling green valley is where the world-famous Chianina beef comes from, making it the perfect place to sample *bistecca alla fiorentina*. *Pici* (a type of hand-rolled pasta) and *ravaggiolo* (sheep cheese wrapped in fern fronds) are other local treats.

» **San Gimignano** Fiery red San Gimignano saffron was the first in Europe to get its own DOP (protected origin) stamp of quality. Its aromatic Vernaccia is Tuscany's pale golden white wine of note.

» **Pienza** Cheese aficionados note: the *pecorino* crafted here is among Italy's greatest.

Southern Tuscany

When it comes to quality-guaranteed beef, chicken and game, Maremma is the byword.

» **Grosseto** Mecca for sweet tooths thanks to handmade biscuits (including traditional Jewish honey-and-walnut pastry, *lo sfratto*) from Dolci Tradizioni dalla Maremma Toscana (p251).

How to Eat & Drink Like a Local

It pays to know what and how much to eat, and when – adopting the local pace is key to savouring every last exquisite gastronomic moment of the Tuscan day.

When to Eat

» **Colazione (breakfast)** Breakfast for most Tuscans is a quick dash into a bar or cafe for a short sharp espresso and *cornetto* (Italian croissant) or *brioche* (breakfast pastry) balanced on the saucer standing at the bar.

» **Pranzo (lunch)** Traditionally, the main meal of the day, though many Tuscans now tend to share the main family meal in the evening. Many businesses close for *la pausa* (afternoon break). Standard restaurant times are noon or 12.30pm to 2.30pm, though most locals don't lunch before 1pm.

» **Aperitivo (aperitif)** Fabulously popular in Florence, that all-essential post-work, early-evening drink can take place any time between 5pm and 10pm when the price of your cocktail (€8 to €10 in Florence) includes an eat-yourself-silly buffet of nibbles, finger foods, even salads, pasta and so on.

» **Apericena** This growing trend among 20- and 30-something Florentines sees that copious *aperitivo* buffet double as *cena* (dinner).

» **Cena (dinner)** Traditionally, dinner is lighter than lunch though still a main meal. The traditional Tuscan belt-busting, five-course whammy only happens on Sunday and feast days. Standard restaurant times are 7.30pm to around 10pm (often later in Florence and across the board in summer).

Choosing Your Restaurant

» **Ristorante (restaurant)** Crisp linen, classic furnishings, a more formal service and refined dishes make restaurants the obvious choice for special occasions.

» **Trattoria** A family-owned version of a restaurant, with cheaper prices, more relaxed service and classic regional specialities. Avoid places offering tourist menus.

» **Osteria** Intimate and relaxed, this has its origins in a traditional inn serving wine with a little food on the side; these days it is often hard to differentiate between an *osteria* and trattoria.

» **Enoteca (wine bar)** A real trend in Tuscany, wine bars are increasingly casual, atmospheric places to dine as well as taste dozens of different Tuscan wines by the glass.

» **Agriturismo (farm stay)** Dining on a farm is oftentimes the very best of Tuscany – a copious, never-ending feast of homemade cooking with local farm produce against a quintessential Tuscan backdrop of old stone farmhouse, cypress alley and pea-green rolling hills.

» **Pizzeria** A top place for a cheap feed, cold beer and a buzzing, convivial vibe, the best pizzerias are often crowded. Be patient.

» **Gelateria (ice-cream shop)** Come rain, hail or shine, a queue outside the door marks the very best of Tuscany's many ice-cream shops. The astonishing choice of flavours – fruits, creamy, unexpected – will have you longing for an Italian ice cream long after you've left Tuscany. Chestnut, pine kernel and fig and honey are distinctive local flavours not to miss.

Menu Advice

» **Menù a la carte** Choose whatever you like from the menu.

» **Menù di degustazione** Degustation or tasting menu, usually consisting of six to eight 'tasting size' courses.

» **Menù turistico** Good value as it might appear, the dreaded 'tourist menu' is a pale reflection of authentic fare consumed by locals. Steer clear!

» **Coperto** Cover charge, usually €1 to €3 per person, charged to cover complimentary bread.

» **Piatto del giorno** Dish of the day.

» **Antipasto** A hot or cold appetiser; for a mix of appetisers go for the *antipasto misto* (mixed antipasto).

» **Primo** First course, usually a substantial pasta, rice or *zuppa* (soup) dish.

» **Secondo** Second course, comprising *carne* (meat) or *pesce* (fish).

» **Contorno** Side dish, usually *verdura* (vegetables).

» **Dolce** Dessert, often *torta* (cake).

» **Nostra produzione** Made in-house; used to describe anything from bread and pasta to *liquori* (liqueurs).

» **Acqua minerale (mineral water)** Jugs of tap water aren't really in, but ordering a bottle of *frizzante* (sparkling) or *naturale* (still) with a meal is a Tuscan standard – and it's cheap; pay €1 or €2 max for a 1L bottle.

» **Vino della casa (house wine)** Wine in restaurants is reasonably priced and generally very good; the cheapest is house wine or *vino da tavola* (table wine), which can be ordered in carafes of 25cl, 50cl, 75cl or a litre.

Etiquette

» **Multiple courses** Don't feel obliged to order the Full Monty when dining out; it's quite acceptable to go for antipasto and *primo*, antipasto and *secondo* or *primo* and *dolce* – whatever you fancy!

» **Bread** Is plentiful (and unsalted, and butterless) but don't expect a side plate; put it on the table. Sauce mopping is not allowed.

» **Dress** Decent is best, particularly in Florence, where working Florentines go home to freshen up between *aperitivo* and dinner.

» **Spaghetti** Twirling it around your fork as if you were born twirling is the only way – no spoons please.

» **Fussy kids** If there really isn't anything on the menu to appease fussy kids (hard to believe), it is acceptable to ask for a simple plate of pasta with butter and Parmesan.

» **Cantucci and Vin Santo** If you don't feel like a fully fledged, rich dessert this is a great alternative – and yes, you dunk the dry almond-studded biscuits into the sweet wine.

» **Coffee** Easily Europe's best. Never order a cappuccino after 11am, and certainly not after a meal, when an espresso is the only respectable way to end a meal (with, perhaps, a digestive of grappa or other fiery liqueur).

» **Il conto (the bill)** Whoever invites usually pays.

» **Splitting the bill** Common enough, though itemising it is *molto vulgare* (very vulgar).

» **Tipping** If there is no *servizio* (service charge), leave a 10% to 15% tip.

Outdoor Experiences

Best Short Walks
Vie Cave, along Etruscan sunken roads below **Pitigliano**

Guided nature walks in hills around **San Gimignano**

Montalcino to Abbazia di Sant'Antimo, **Val d'Orcia**

Best Easy Bike Rides
With elegance atop the city walls of **Lucca**

Around **Chianti** vineyards and olive groves

Elba island touring

Best at Sea
Sea kayaking and diving offshore from **Elba**

Slicing silent waterways with a canoe in the **Parco Regionale della Maremma**

Best Spa Towns
Old English literati fave **Bagni di Lucca**

Ancient Roman soak **Bagno Vignoni**

Montecatini Terme of Puccini fame

Best Magnificent Drives
Marble mountain to Med blue sea: **Castelnuovo di Garfagnana to Massa**

Elba's giddying southwest coast

Pienza to Serre di Rapolano, **Le Crete**

When Renaissance man's brilliance overwhelms, flee into the open arms of Mother Nature. Be it tramping through Tuscan woods in autumn, hiking around marble or plunging head first into sea-blue waters where the goddess Venus once rose from the waves, this green part of Italy has bags of natural beauty to get lost in. And the only prerequisite is go slow: to skip the myriad of outdoor activities underscoring Tuscany's natural splendour is to zap the very essence of this unique region.

On Your Marks
Efficient pretrip planning of your outdoor action ensures you can revel in the Tuscan thrill without any unexpected spill once in situ.

When to Go?
Lapping up all that fresh mountain and sea air, heady with the scent of wild sage and maritime pine, is an integral part of the Tuscan activity experience. Spring and autumn with their abundance of wild flowers and forest fruits are the prettiest times to be outdoors. Autumn, when the harvests start in the vineyards and olive groves, has a particularly mellow appeal and with summer's warmth lingering well into October, there is plenty of daylight for outdoor activities.

BEST WALKS IF YOU LIKE ...

» **Etruscan ruins** – Golfo di Baratti (p175), Pitigliano (see the boxed text, p245)

» **Birdwatching** – Lago di Burano (p254); Laguna di Orbetello (p253); Parco Regionale Migliarino, San Rossore, Massaciuccoli (see the boxed text, p133)

» **Cowboys** – Parco Regionale della Maremma (p252)

» **Geology** – Monterotondo Marittimo (see the boxed text, p241)

» **Wine** – Chianti (p206), San Gimignano to Volterra hike (see the boxed text, p223), Montalcino (p224), Montepulciano (p231)

» **Pilgrim paths** – Marciana (p184), Abbazia di Sant'Antimo (see the boxed text, p225)

» **Coastal panoramas** – Monte Capanne (p184), Marciana (p184)

Best Times

» **April–June** Pleasantly warm dry days and valleys drenched in poppies and wildflowers – all created solely with cyclists in mind.

» **July** Water-sports enthusiasts flock to the Med, hot and a tad less crowded than August. Hiking in the Apuane Alps is best this month.

» **September–October** Cooler days means mellow hikes through dewy mornings, crunchy leaves and mushroom-rich forests.

Avoid

» **Easter** The first key holiday period of the year for Italians, this two-week slot in late March or April sees too many people jostle for too little picnic-table and trail space.

» **August** Italians take their summer holidays, crowding trails, cycling routes and roads. On lower terrain, the intense heat of August can be oppressive.

» **Autumn** Often means slippery wet roads and poor visibility for cyclists.

Where to Go

Whatever outdoor activity rocks your boat, there is a part of Tuscany with your name on it. For token outdoor activists, essentially urban at heart, plump for Florence as a base – the city has bags of bike-tour operators running two-wheel day trips to Chianti (see the boxed text, p47).

» **Chianti** (p206) Tuscany's key wine-growing area means easy walking and cycling between achingly pretty vine and olive groves; lots of tour groups.

» **Apuane Alps & Garfagnana** (p150) Ruggedly scenic and off the mainstream tourist radar, with the region's most dramatic mountains, marble quarries and forested valleys: serious hiking, caving, mountain biking, horse-riding and five magnificent road trips (see the boxed text, p155).

» **Etruscan Coast** (p172) Hit the beach, July and August, for sand, sea, sailing and water-sport action galore. Inland, cycling is dirt track to silky smooth, and seriously big among Italians.

» **Elba** (p176) A summer island idyll with stunning sea kayaking, sailing, diving and snorkelling; beautiful family walks from cove to cove, and through scented *macchia* (herbal scrub) and parasol pines.

» **Val d'Orcia** (p224) Family walking and cycling near Siena.

» **Maremma** (p250) Hiking, biking and backwater canoeing on Tuscany's southern coast.

» **Casentino** (p266) Easy walking to strenuous hikes in eastern Tuscany's forested national park.

Get Set

Before diving into Tuscany's ethereal landscape, get set with the necessary nuts-and-bolts info and gear to ensure a silky-smooth ride up mountains, down soft rolling hills, through vineyards and around olive groves.

Information

The **Region of Tuscany** (www.turismo.into scana.it) is a useful one-stop resource for background information, interactive maps and inspiring routes on foot, by bike or horseback. Caving, spas and water sports are other activities it covers.

Throughout Tuscany, tourist offices and national-park offices have mountains of information on outdoor activities, including lists of guides to contact and accommodation

NATIONAL & REGIONAL PARKS

For serious outdoor enthusiasts the cream of the action is found in Tuscany's national parks and nature parks. Created to protect a diverse booty of land, river, lake and marine ecosystems, they are naturally rich in outdoor experiences.

PARK	WEBSITE	FEATURES
Parco Nazionale dell'Arcipelago Toscano	www.islepark.it	Europe's largest marine park covering 18,000 hectares of land and 60,000 sq metres of sea; typical Mediterranean island flora and fauna
Parco Nazionale delle Foreste Casentinesi, Monte Falterona e Campigna	www.parcoforeste casentinesi.it	source of the river Arno and Italy's most extensive, best-preserved forest: ancient pines, beech, five maple types and the rare yew; deer, wild boar, mouflon, wolves and 97 nesting bird species
Parco Alpi Apuane	www.parcapuane. toscana.it	mountainous regional park cascading to the sea from the Garfagnana; golden eagles, peregrine falcons, buzzards and the rare chough (the park's symbol)
Parco Regionale Migliarino, San Rossore, Massaciuccoli	www.parcosanros sore.org	coastal reserve stretching from Viareggio to Livorno; extraordinary birdlife (over 200 species) in its marshes, dunes and wetland
Parco Regionale della Maremma	www.parco-marem ma.it	regional park comprising the Uccelllina mountains, pine forest, agricultural farmland, marshland and 20km of unspoiled coastline; oak and cork oak, herbal maquis (scrubland); Maremma cows, horses and chickens

options en route. Be aware that printed brochures detailing actual trails etc are increasingly scarce – if you can, buy maps and guides online before leaving home.

Maps

Florentine cartographer **Edizioni Multigraphic** (www.edizionimultigraphic.it; Via Arcangelo Corelli 55, Florence) produces maps for walkers and mountain-bike riders with *sentieri* (walking trails), *mulattiere* (mule tracks, especially good for mountain bikes), mountains huts and so on superimposed on the map. Its *Carte dei Sentieri* (1:25,000) and *Carte Turistica e dei Sentieri* (1:25,000 or 1:50,000) map series are both available online at **Omnimap** (www.omnimap.com).

Books & Guides

» *50 Hikes In & Around Tuscany* (Jeff Taylor)

» *Italy's Sibillini National Park* (Gillian Price) Walking and hiking guide.

» *The Alps of Tuscany* (Francesco Greco) Selected hikes in the Apuane Alps.

» *Treading Grapes* (Rosemary George) Walking through the vineyards of Tuscany.

» *Walking & Eating in Tuscany & Umbria* (James Lasdun and Pia Davis) Forty varied itineraries with tips for restaurants and overnight stays.

» *Walking in Tuscany* (Gillian Price) Fifty walks and hikes of a none-too-strenuous nature.

» *Bicycle Touring in Tuscany* (David Cleveland) Eight multiday tours, each with detailed route map.

Activity Specialists

Stacks of companies can help you hit the Tuscan road. For organised activities in the Apuane Alps and Garfagnana, see the boxed text, p154; for the island of Elba, see p176. Or try:

75esimaaventura (www.75avventura.com) Outdoor adventure specialist based 3km from Montieri in southern Tuscany: hiking, biking, horse-riding, quad bikes, tree climbing, caving, kayaking.

What to Take

Tuscany is not Everest and generally you'll only need the minimum of items – for easy, undemanding walks or bike rides, a pair of comfortable trainers. A small daypack should contain an extra layer of clothing and wet-weather gear (the Apuane Alps get the greatest concentration of rainfall in all of Tuscany).

Sunblock, sunglasses and a hat (helmet for cyclists) are essential. Budget at least one bottle of water, calculating for at least 1.5L per walker or cyclist for a summertime day.

ACTIVITIES	BEST TIME TO VISIT	PAGE
sea kayaking, sailing, diving, snorkelling, water sports, walking, cycling, wine tasting	spring and summer	p176
walking, hiking, birdwatching	spring and autumn	p269
hiking, mountain biking, caving	summer and autumn	p150
easy walking, cycling, horse-riding, birdwatching, canoeing	spring, summer and autumn	see the boxed text, p133
walking, hiking, cycling, horse-riding, canoeing	spring and autumn (mid-Jun–mid-Sep visits by guided tour only)	p252

A fistful of light, high-nutrition, easily assimilated food, such as power bars, dried fruit or nuts, can stave off hunger and impart a quick kick of energy.

Obviously you need a map and a compass if you're planning to head off the beaten track. Wild camping is not permitted in the high mountains, meaning you'll need to plan your overnight stops around the availability of beds in *rifugi* (mountain huts); bring a sleeping bag.

Go

Pretrip planning done, go, do Tuscany. But don't expect machine-gun adrenalin rushes and life-changing palpitations of the heart. In typical Tuscan style, outdoor action is beaded with serenity – a lazed, go-slow experience designed wholly with appreciation of masterpiece landscape and cuisine in mind. Go, savour.

Walking

People have been criss-crossing Tuscany for millennia, creating paths and trails as they went. One of the most important pilgrim routes in Europe during the Dark Ages was the **Via Francigena** (see the driving tour, p162), in its time a veritable highway across Tuscany. Starting in the Magra river valley and winding through the wild Lunigiana territory of the northwest, the trail hugged the coast for a while before cutting inland to Siena via San Gimignano and then turning south to Rome, the capital of Christianity. Parts of the route can be walked today. *Via Francigena in Toscana* (1:50,000) is an excellent hiking map (for details, see the boxed text on p223).

The other extreme is the 24-stage **Grande Escursione Appenninica**, an arc for the truly ambitious that goes from the Due Santi pass above La Spezia southeast to Sansepolcro in eastern Tuscany.

Chianti is the big favourite among all walkers and is the essence of what Tuscan walking is about – rambling from vineyard, to wine cellar, to century-old farm where the day ends with a feast of homemade pasta, salami, meat and other tasty farm products enjoyed with gusto around a shared table. Several atmospheric overnights in *agriturismi* (farm-stay accommodation) punctuate the classic walk from Florence to Siena. **Il Mugello**, northeast of Florence, is another area within easy reach of Florence for half- and full-day walks.

On Elba (a prime hiking spot, more for its dramatic scenery than challenging peaks) the only real stiff hike is up **Monte Ca-panne** (p184); for more on hiking Elba, see the boxed text on p186.

Alpine Practicalities

Serious hikers seeking exciting medium-mountain walking head to the **Apuane Alps** and the **Garfagnana** on the spine of the Apennines in northwest Tuscany. Main town Castelnuovo di Garfagnana is the choice base camp with its invaluable information resources and sleeping/eating options – see p153.

Castelnuovo di Garfagnana is also the place to pick up information on *rifugi,* mountain huts with basic dorm-style accommodation (bring your own sleeping bag) found at higher altitudes on longer hiking trails in the Apuane Alps – the only real part of Tuscany with such off-the-beaten-track accommodation. Most *rifugi* can only be reached on foot; open June to September plus spring/autumn weekends; and have basic kitchen facilities and/or serve meals. Some are privately run; many are part of Italy's national alpine association **Club Alpino Italiano** (www.cai.it), which has local clubs in Florence, Lucca, Siena, Grosseto and Arezzo.

Trail Etiquette

» *Buongiorno* – greet your fellow walkers with a cheery 'hello'.

» Ascending walkers have right of way over those descending on narrow paths.

» Leave farm gates as you find them.

» Wildflowers look their blooming best in the wild; many are protected species.

» Marmots prefer holes to camera lenses. Keep a considerate distance from wild animals.

» As the old chestnut goes: take nothing but photos, leave nothing but footprints. Carry out what you have carried in.

Cycling

Whether you're out for a day's gentle pedal around Florence, a sybaritic weekend winery tour in Chianti with friends, or a serious workout with a week or more of pedal power, Tuscany cooks up bags of cycling scope with its varied landscapes and wide choice of roads and routes.

The most versatile bicycle for Tuscan roads is a comfortable all-terrain bike that is capable of travelling over paved and country roads and, more importantly, able to climb hills without forcing you to over-exert yourself. Ideally, it should give you a relaxed posture, have front suspension and be equipped with a wide range of gears.

The picturesque **Strada Chiantigiana** (SS222) waltzes through the heart of Chianti wine country on its way from Florence to Siena, while **Le Crete** and **Val d'Orcia** in central Tuscany wheels out a fanfare of golden wheat fields and cypress alleys for passing cyclists.

BEST KID-SHORT WALKS

Perfect with young kids in tow (no strollers) and accompanied by a long lazy picnic.

» **Parco Sculture del Chianti**, Chianti (see the boxed text, p213) Bring out the artist in them with a sculpture-studded stroll.

» **Parco Archeologico di Baratti e Populonia**, Golfi di Baratti (p175) Incredible trails around remains of Etruscan tombs and quarries on the Etruscan Coast.

» **Santuario della Madonna del Monte**, Marciana (p184) Follow in Napoleon's footsteps along an old mule track to this ancient pilgrimage site on Elba – mind-blowing coastal panorama!

» **Vie Cave**, Pitigliano (see the boxed text, p245) Excite young historians with this three-hour trail along sunken roads linking sacred Etruscan necropolis.

» **Elba** (see the boxed text, p186) The largest island in the Tuscan archipelago is especially well geared for short walks and, with its pretty capes and beaches, is appealing to families.

» **'Le Biancane' Monterotondo Marittimo**, Maremma (see the boxed text, p241) Easy two-hour walk.

» **Lago di Burano**, Maremma (p254) Short lake-bound trail in a World Wide Fund for Nature (WWF) nature reserve; spot birds and meet a tame kestrel.

Paved roads are particularly suited to high-tech racing bikes (watch out for the Sunday swarm of identically clad riders from the local club as the peloton sweeps by) or travelling long distances on touring bikes.

Back roads and trails are an interesting option for the fairly fit with a multigear mountain bike – rural Tuscany is mainly hilly. **Monte Amiata** is the perfect goal for aspiring hill climbers, while **Chianti** and **Le Crete** sport ample hilly itineraries with short but challenging climbs.

For those seeking a gentler ride, the **Etruscan Coast** and **south of Livorno** along the scenic wine and oil road are favourites. For itinerary suggestions, see the boxed text, p173.

If you are bringing your own bike from home, check in advance with your airline if there's a fee and how much, if any, disassembling and packing it requires. Bikes can be transported by train in Italy, either with you or to arrive within a couple of days.

Practicalities

For those not willing or able to haul their bikes from home there are plenty of places in Tuscany to rent a pair of wheels and buy the colour-coordinated lycra. Book through **EcoRent** (www.ecorent.net), or upon arrival at bike-rental outlets in Florence, Pisa, Lucca, Siena and other towns. Many hotels and *agriturismi* also organise bike rental.

While most historic town and city centres are closed to cars, cyclists are free to enter at will. But the real joy is once you head out into Tuscany's green belt of wild-flower meadows, sage-scented hedgerows and kilometre after kilometre of traffic-free road.

Horse-Riding

The rhythmic crunch of hooves as you saunter serenely on horseback through chestnut and cork oak wood, past fields of bright yellow sunflowers and wild red poppies, and between vines, is hypnotically calming, aromatic – and oh-so-Tuscan.

Riding is big region-wide, with plenty of *agriturismi* having horses for guests to ride. Several farms, especially in southern Tuscany's **Parco Regionale della Maremma**, specialise in equestrian holidays and offer treks of one or several days. Combining the intimacy of *agriturismi* and meals around a shared table with the formality of a riding school, these equestrian farms are the most atmospheric way of experiencing Tuscany on horseback.

On the Etruscan Coast a horseback itinerary takes riders from Livorno 170km southeast to Sassetta along a melody of sun-scorched coastal paths (best in spring and autumn), agricultural cart tracks, and summer-cool shady tracks through the forested hinterland (best in summer). It recommends accommodation en route for both horses and riders, and several half- and one-day loops feed off the main trail creating ample choice for riders of all abilities.

One of the easiest and greenest spots to saddle up is at riding centre **Equitiamo** (☑338 3662431; www.equitiamo.it; Località Cascine Vecchie 11a), within the Parco Regionale Migliarino, San Rossore, Massaciuccoli (see the boxed text, p133). Positioned between the sea and the city of Pisa, its treks are invariably invigorating, nature-driven romps on the sand.

Then there's the Maremma cowboy experience; see p252 for details.

Ballooning

Drifting noiselessly over pea-green vineyards and silvery olive groves is the essence of Tuscan travel – slow, serene and cinematic in scenery.

The ballooning season runs from late spring to early autumn and take-off is around 6am (before the wrong wind whips up from the coast). Flights last 1¼ hours and cost around €240 per person, often including a champagne breakfast.

Jump in a basket and take to the skies with the following outfits:

Tuscany Ballooning (www.tuscanyballooning.com) Near Florence.

Ballooning in Tuscany (www.ballooningintuscany.com) South of Siena.

Chianti Ballooning (www.chiantiballooning.com) Chianti-based.

Water Sports

Most can easily imagine Tuscany's signature cypress trees and medieval hilltop villages, but few slot in the shimmering blue wedge of water on the horizon speckled with a handful of wave-kissed islands. Add a sea kayak or surfboard to the ensemble, and a secret sandy cove perhaps – reached only from the sea – and you have the real picture: the Tuscan coast and its offshore islands are unexpected, inspired and the source of great outdoor action.

Diving & Snorkelling

The island of **Elba** is among Italy's top year-round diving spots (although you'll shiver without a semidry wetsuit between November and May): if you're into wrecks, you can plunge into blue waters at Pomonte, where the *Elvisco* cargo boat sits on the seabed 12m deep, or gawp through a mask at the

German WWII plane *Junker 52,* wrecked at a more challenging depth of 38m near Portoferraio.

Otherwise, aquatic flora and fauna is protected and dramatic. Diving facilities are generally of a high standard and several diving schools on the island rent all the gear and organise guides, courses and so on. Less intrepid water lovers can snorkel. For more details, see the boxed text, p185.

Back on the mainland, you can also dive along the **Etruscan Coast** and further south in Porto Ercole on **Monte Argentario**.

Kayaking & Canoeing

Hot sultry summer afternoons are best spent lapping up the slow, natural rhythm of Tuscan travel in a sea kayak or canoe – from beach to beach along **Elba's** magnificent cove-clad coast (bring provisions along given it will just be you, kayak, sand, sea and one or two monumental wind-sculpted rocks) or past sand dunes in the **Parco Regionale della Maremma** (where there's a fabulous guided canoe trail).

For practical details on how to, see p177 and p252 respectively.

Sailing & Surfing

The coves of the Tuscan archipelagos and around **Monte Argentario** are superb for sailing, as well as windsurfing, kite surfing and sea kayaking. Rent equipment and receive instruction at all the major resorts. **Viareggio** holds several annual sailing regattas.

Travel with Children

Best Regions for Kids

Florence
Interactive museums, fantastic *gelaterie* (ice-cream shops) and public gardens make Tuscany's major city a top choice for families.

Northwestern Tuscany
Head to the hills (in this case the Apuane Alps and Garfagnana) for the opportunity to swing through trees like Tarzan, see marble miners at work in a mountain quarry and run up and down wildflower-carpeted hillsides. Down on the plain, the city of Lucca has lots to offer the little ones.

Central Coast & Elba
Beaches and boats. Enough said.

Southern Tuscany
This pocket of the region is full of nature reserves, national parks and archaeological sites where kids can play hide and seek in the ruins. It's the perfect place for them to run off their frightening reserves of excess energy.

Tuscany for Kids

If you're looking for a family-friendly destination, Tuscany certainly fits the bill. Your children might whinge about the number of churches and museums on the daily itinerary, but they'll be quickly appeased by gelato (yay!) and accommodation that often features a swimming pool, farm animals and plenty of space to run around in (double yay!).

The only family members who might not be thrilled about your choice of holiday destination are teenagers – there are no malls or theme parks here and PlayStations and Xboxes aren't among the usual amenities in hotel rooms. This means that they'll have to join the rest of the family in enjoying the huge number of outdoor and cultural activities on offer. But guess what? In the process, they might even enjoy themselves.

Are We There Yet?

Most visitors tend to drive when they're in Tuscany. Fortunately, distances between destinations aren't particularly long and there are inevitably plenty of 'spot the sheep' and 'count the churches' opportunities.

When in cars, remember that children under 12 are not allowed to sit in the passenger seat, and that child restraints and seatbelts are mandatory.

If you're travelling on public transport, note that a seat on a bus costs the same whether you're an adult or child. You don't need to pay for toddlers and babies who sit on your lap, though. On trains, big discounts can apply if you're travelling in a family group – check the 'Offers and Deals' pages of the Trenitalia website (www.trenitalia.com) for details.

Discounts

If they are EU citizens, your kids will almost always be eligible for discounted or free entry to museums and other attractions. These discounts don't always apply to non-EU citizens, though. There's usually three tiers of discount: free entry for kids under four years of age, another tier for kids under 12 and a third for students up to the age of 26.

Beaches

Families from North America and Australasia may well find Tuscan beaches disappointing. There's little surf, not much sand and hardly any room in summer. Most disconcerting, though, is the fact that many tracts of beach have been privatised – you may have to pay for a chair and beach umbrella.

While sunblock is used by some locals, protective beachwear with an Ultraviolet Protection Factor (UPF) – recommended by skin cancer organisations in Australia and North America – are not readily available here. Bring your own and expect your kids to attract a few strange looks when they enter the water wearing them.

For the best beach experiences in the region, head to Elba (p176).

Museums & Churches

Hmm. What's the solution when the adults in the travelling party can't wait to visit churches and museums, but the kids can't imagine anything worse (and are quick to say so)? Bribery inevitably works, but there's also the possibility of visiting museums with interactive displays or child-oriented guided tours. We've identified these throughout the book. When all else fails in an art gallery or church, we've been known to play 'Spot a realistic-looking Baby Jesus painting'. It's never going to happen (one of the great mysteries of Renaissance art), but there's nothing like a challenge to keep kids engaged!

Children's Highlights

For experiences that keep your kids active and engaged and that you might enjoy too, consider the suggestions below. Also check p97 for the low-down on Florence for kids, and p46 for a list of great kid-friendly walks.

Stuff to Climb

» **Torre del Mangia, Siena** Steep steps (lots of them) and awesome views at the top.

» **Duomo and Campanile, Florence** Climb up Giotto's *campanile* (bell tower) or into Brunelleschi's dome.

» **Leaning Tower, Pisa** Yes, it really does lean. And yes again, it's loads of fun to take photographs simulating your kids holding it up.

Gardens to Explore

» **Parco Sculture del Chianti, central Tuscany** A 1km walking trail and lots of weird artworks to gawk at.

» **Giardino dei Tarocchi, southern Tuscany** If you thought the Parco Sculture del Chianti's artworks were weird, wait until you see the giant sculptures at this place!

BRIBERY: THE PARENT'S BEST FRIEND

Maybe you're trying to coax the junior members of the family to accompany you to a museum or church. Or perhaps you're keen to ensure a low whine factor on car trips. Whatever the situation, there's nothing wrong with a spot of parental bribery. Consider the following:

» **Agriturismi** Book into a farm stay and you'll usually be able to ensure a full morning's sightseeing by promising that the afternoon will be spent by the pool or patting the resident dogs, cats and farm animals.

» **Gelato** Anywhere, any time. It almost always works.

» **Pizza** Usually, pizzerias only open in the evening. This means that the prospect of a pizza dinner can sometimes ensure a full day's good behaviour.

» **Pinocchio** Tuscany is the birthplace of the cute wooden boy with the long nose, and souvenir stalls everywhere sell Pinocchio marionettes, wooden figures and other toys that little kids love.

Cool Stuff

» **Cava di Fantiscritti, Carrara** Take a Bond-style 4WD tour of the open-cast quarry or follow miners into the core of the mountain.

» **Selva del Buffardello, northwestern Tuscany** This park is awesome! Fly from tree to tree along rope ladders, elevated walkways and pulleys.

» **Museo Piaggio, northwestern Tuscany** Scooters. Way cool.

» **City walls, Lucca** Hire a bike and ride along the top of these, stopping for a picnic along the way.

Wildlife Encounters

» **Museo di Storia Naturale del Mediterraneo, Livorno** Come here to visit the skeleton of Annie the whale.

» **Parco Regionale Migliarino, San Rossore, Massaciuccoli, northwestern Tuscany** Take a horse-drawn carriage ride around this natural reserve just outside Pisa.

» **Parco Regionale della Maremma, southern Tuscany** Visit the aquarium and then spot loads of wildlife and birds while hiking, cycling or canoeing through this huge coastal park.

» **Riserva Naturale WWF Lago di Burano, southern Tuscany** See a tame kestrel and walk through a butterfly garden.

Knights & Castles

» **Fortezza Medicea, Cortona** Your kids won't have any trouble walking uphill to the town's highest point. The same, alas, cannot be said for all parents (it's really steep, so consider yourself warned).

» **Castello dei Conti Guidi, eastern Tuscany** A real castle, complete with dungeons and a suit of armour.

» **Palazzo Vecchio, Florence** Not really a castle (it's a palace), but there are secret staircases, hidden rooms and you can meet the original residents (well, sort of).

regions at a glance

Florence

Food ✓✓✓
Art ✓✓✓
Shopping ✓✓✓

Gourmet Paradise
The city's exceptional dining scene encompasses everything from inventive fast food (eg tripe *panini* from old-fashioned street carts) to noisy mad-busy trattorias, bustling food markets and the only restaurant in Tuscany to possess three Michelin stars.

Renaissance Beauty
The Uffizi is one of the world's most famous art galleries, but it's not the only repository of artistic masterpieces in the city. Churches, chapels and a bevy of lesser-known museums safeguard myriad riches, from extraordinary frescoes to Michelangelo-designed staircases.

Fashion & Old-Fashioned Crafts
From the designer boutiques on the chic shopping strip of Via de' Tornabuoni to tiny artisan workshops hidden down back lanes and alleys in the traditional craft district of Oltrarno, the city where Gucci was born really is the last word in quality shopping.

p56

North-western Tuscany

Food ✓✓✓
Mountains ✓✓
The Outdoors ✓✓

White Truffles
No single food product is lusted over/excites more than the white truffle – here, they're hunted in dew-kissed autumn forests around San Miniato and eaten with gusto.

Majestic Marble
Take a drive from the Garfagnana through rugged peaks and richly forested valleys laced with walking trails to witness the Apuane Alps' majestic marble mountains in their full glory.

On Your Bike!
No spot on earth so perfectly suits hiking, biking and eating as the trio of valleys forming the Garfagnana region. Trails criss-cross chestnut woods and forests rich in berries and *porcini* mushrooms – gorgeous!

p121

Central Coast & Elba

Food ✓✓✓
Beaches ✓✓✓
History ✓✓

Seafood in Livorno
The feisty locals in this gritty waterside city are staunchly proud of *cacciucco,* a remarkable seafood stew swimming with at least five types of fish.

Coastal Capers
Visit Elba, the palm tree–clad paradise where Napoleon was banished. This bijou island offers a sensational mix of sunbathing, sea-kayaking, snorkelling and swimming.

Etruscan Heritage
Exploring the remains of ancient Etruscan tombs and temples hidden beneath sky-high parasol pines on the Golfo di Baratti's sandy shoreline is an extraordinary experience. Pair it with gentle walking and a picnic lunch for the perfect day.

p164

Siena & Central Tuscany

Food ✓✓✓
Wine ✓✓✓
Hill Towns ✓✓✓

Sweet Temptations
Sample the biscuits and cakes that Siena is famous for, preferably accompanied by a glass of sweet Vin Santo.

In Vino Veritas
When it comes to wine, it doesn't get any better than this. Brunello, Vino Nobile, Chianti Classico and Vernaccia all hark from here, and estates throughout the region produce the stuff that makes wine buffs happy.

Take to the Hills
Sign up for a cardio workout with a difference, braving the steep but scenic streets of towns such as Montalcino, Montepulciano, Volterra and San Gimignano. Here, the intact medieval architecture is as impressive as the views – and that's saying something.

p190

Southern Tuscany

Food ✓✓✓
Archaeology ✓✓
Nature ✓✓✓

Slow Food
This is a no-fuss zone when it comes to cuisine. Local chefs buy local, stick to the season and subscribe to the concept of Slow Food. You've gotta love that.

Waves of Civilisation
The Etruscans certainly left their mark here, and the countryside of the extraordinary *Paese del Tufa* (Land of the Tufa) is littered with their tombs. The Romans didn't shirk in this respect either, as a visit to Roselle or Vetulonia will attest.

Land of the Big Sky
Europe's bird species stop here on their migration to North Africa for good reason – huge tracts of pristine landscape boast an impressive range of flora and fauna.

p236

Eastern Tuscany

Food ✓✓✓
Holy Sites ✓✓
Art ✓✓✓

The Real McCoy
Come here to eat Italy's best *bistecca alla fiorentina,* a succulent, lightly seared piece of locally raised Chianina beef.

Holy Places
St Francis left his stamp on this part of Tuscany. Born in nearby Assisi, he is said to have received the stigmata at the Santuario della Verna in the wonderfully wild Casentino forest.

Arty Itineraries
The old adage 'quality before quantity' applies here. Follow a trail highlighting the works of Piero della Francesca, but also look out for works by Cimabue, Fra' Angelico, Lorenzetti and della Robbia.

p255

See the Index for a full list of destinations covered in this book.

On the Road

Florence

Best Places to Eat

» Il Santo Bevitore (p105)
» L'Osteria di Giovanni (p102)
» Trattoria Cibrèo (p104)
» Targa (p107)
» Trattoria Mario (p103)

Best Places to Stay

» Hotel L'Orologio (p100)
» Palazzo Guadagni Hotel (see the boxed text, p101)
» Hotel Torre Guelfa (p99)
» Palazzo Vecchietti (p99)
» Academy Hostel (p100)

Why Go?

Return time and again and you still won't see it all. Stand on a bridge over the Arno river several times in a day and the light, the mood and the view changes every time. Surprisingly small as it is, this riverside city is like no other. Cradle of the Renaissance and of tourist masses that flock here to feast on world-class art, Florence (Firenze) is magnetic, romantic, unrivalled and too busy. Its urban fabric has hardly changed since the Renaissance, its narrow streets evoke a thousand tales, and its food and wine are so wonderful the tag 'Fiorentina' has become an international label of quality assurance.

Fashion designers strut their stuff on Via de' Tornabuoni. Gucci was born here, as was Roberto Cavalli who, like many a smart Florentine these days, hangs out in the wine-rich hills around Florence. After a while in this intensely absorbing city, you might want to do the same.

When to Go

Spring, before the high-season crowds arrive, is by far the best time to visit Florence – days are cooler, queues are substantially shorter and museums are less packed out. June brings with it Italy's oldest arts festival, Maggio Musical Fiorentino, that crescendos in a magnificent flurry of concerts in the city. Then there is autumn, the most foodie-fabulous time of the year to visit, with its abundance of freshly harvested *porcini* mushrooms and chestnuts from the forest and wealth of creative cooking it inspires.

Itineraries

David Tour Follow the world's most famous naked man: start with Michelangelo's original in the Galleria dell'Accademia, saunter past Piazza della Signoria's famous copy, then hit Museo del Bargello to see versions by Donatello and Andrea Verrocchio. Later, enjoy Michelangelo creations in the Biblioteca Medicea Laurenzia and watch the sun set on Piazzale Michelangelo. For a souvenir of your day, buy a replica in chocolate from Scudieri.

Fabulous Frescoes Begin with a coffee and breakfast at Caffè Gilli or one of its historic siblings. Then visit Domenico Ghirlandaio's vibrant frescoes in the Basilica di Santa Maria Novella. Grab a casual lunch at Trattoria Mario or La Mescita before admiring Fra' Angelico's religious reliefs at the Museo di San Marco and Benozzo Gozzoli's gorgeous Cappella dei Magi at the Palazzo Medici-Riccardi (reserve in advance).

Both Sides of the Arno Spend the morning at the Uffizi (buy a ticket in advance), followed by a wine-bar lunch at Cantinetta dei Verrazzano or La Canova di Gustavino, or a *panino* at 'Ino. Refreshed, get set to embark on (should you have been smart enough to organise in advance) a guided tour of the Vasarian Corridor; otherwise, consider our Walking Tour with a detour along Via de' Tornabuoni for some upmarket shopping and a truffle *panino* at Procacci. Come evening, cross the Arno for a wine-tasting aperitif at Le Volpe e L'uva and dinner at Il Santo Bevitore, Il Guscio or Trattoria Cammillo.

GETTING AROUND

Buses (p119) link both Florence and Pisa airports with Florence's central train station, Stazione di Santa Maria Novella, from where the city centre is a 10-minute walk – spot the dome of the *duomo* and you're there! Florence itself is small and best navigated on foot, with most major sights being within easy walking distance of one another. Otherwise, there are bicycles to rent (p119) and an efficient network of buses and trams. Unless you're mad, forget a car.

Where to Stay

Florence is unexpectedly small, rendering almost anywhere in the centre convenient. Budget hotels tend to be clustered around the main train station in the Santa Maria Novella area and around the Mercato Centrale in neighbouring San Lorenzo. Santa Croce and the Oltrarno are hipper and packed with great dining addresses.

DON'T MISS

Florence's faintly lesser-known gems: Palazzo Strozzi (blockbuster art exhibitions), Museo del Bargello (early Michelangelos), Museo di San Marco (superb frescoes), Chiesa di Orsanmichele (medieval statuary) and Biblioteca Medicea Laurenziana (Michelangelo staircase).

Blogs to Excite

» Emiko Davies: www.emikodavies.com

» Tuscan Traveler: http://tuscantraveler.com

Advance Planning

» Cut out the queue by booking tickets for the Uffizi and Galleria dell'Accademia.

» Work out which museum pass suits best and buy online (see p61).

» Reserve a tour of the Vasarian Corridor and Palazzo Vecchio; also reserve for Cappella Brancacci and Cappella dei Magi.

» Buy tickets for springtime's Maggio Musicale Fiorentino (p98).

Resources

» The Florentine: www.theflorentine.com

» Florence Museums: www.firenzemusei.it

» Florence Tourism: www.firenzeturismo.it

» Low Cost Florence: www.firenzelowcost.it

» Lonely Planet: www.lonelyplanet.com/italy/florence

Florence Highlights

1 Visit the world's most extraordinary collection of medieval and Renaissance paintings at the **Uffizi Gallery** (p61)

2 Admire sculptural tombs of Florentine luminaries and an exquisite Brunelleschi chapel at **Basilica di Santa Croce** (p85)

3 Scale new heights inside the **duomo** (cathedral; p68): climb its unforgettable dome and bell tower

4 Contemplate the monastic life, times and genius of Fra' Angelico at **Museo di San Marco** (p83)

5 Explore artisan workshops on the 'other side' of the Arno, where real Florentines live, work and meet for *aperitivi,* in **Oltrarno** (p88)

6 Revel in the most expensive hot chocolate of your life on a historic cafe terrace beneath *David's* (a copy) gaze on the **Piazza della Signoria** (p72)

7 Hike uphill to meet another copy of *David* and the most magnificent panorama of the city, best at sunset, at the **Piazzale Michelangelo** (p94)

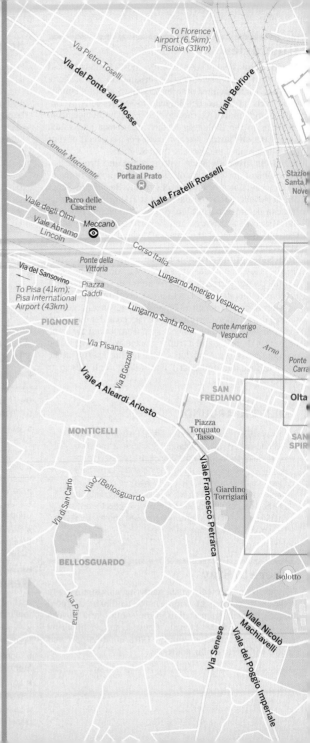

Piazza della Libertà

Piazza Savonarola

Viale Spartaco Lavagnini

Viale Giacomo Matteotti

ppo Strozzi

tezza Basso

0 ——— **400 m**
0 ——— **0.2 miles**

See San Lorenzo & San Marco Map (p82)

Piazza della Indipendenza

Giardino dei Semplici

Giardino della Gherardesca

4
Museo di San Marco

See The Duomo & Santa Maria Novella Map (p66)

See Santa Croce Map (p86)

SANTA CROCE

Piazza del Duomo **3**

Piazza C Beccaria

Piazza della Signoria
6

Ponte Santa Trinita

Uffizi Gallery **1**

Basilica di Santa Croce
2

Ponte alle Grazie

To Arezzo (57km)

Lungarno Serristori

Lungarno Benvenuto Cellini

Ponte S Niccolo

Piazza F Ferrucci

Giardino di Bardini (Bardini Gardens)

Piazzale Michelangelo
7

Viale Michelangelo

See Oltrarno & Boboli Map (p90)

Giardino di Boboli (Boboli Gardens)

Via di San Leonardo

SAN NICCOLÒ

MONTE ALLE CROCI

Basilica di San Miniato al Monte

Viale Galileo Galilei

Via della Torre del Gallo

Viale Nicolò Machiavelli

Viale Michelangelo

Florence's history stretches to the time of the Etruscans, who based themselves in Fiesole. Julius Caesar founded the Roman colony of Florentia around 59 BC, making it a strategic garrison on the narrowest crossing of the Arno in order to control the Via Flaminia linking Rome to northern Italy and Gaul.

After the collapse of the Roman Empire, Florence fell to invading Goths, followed by Lombards and Franks. The year AD 1000 marked a crucial turning point in the city's fortunes, when Margrave Ugo of Tuscany moved his capital from Lucca to Florence. In 1110 Florence became a free *comune* (city-state) and by 1138 it was ruled by 12 consuls, assisted by the Consiglio di Cento (Council of One Hundred), whose members were drawn mainly from the prosperous merchant class. Agitation among differing factions in the city led to the appointment in 1207 of a foreign head of state called the *podestà*, aloof in principle from the plotting and wheeler-dealing of local cliques and alliances.

Medieval Florence was a wealthy, dynamic *comune,* one of Europe's leading financial, banking and cultural centres, and a major player in the international wool, silk and leather trades. The sizeable population of moneyed merchants and artisans began forming guilds and patronising the growing number of artists who found lucrative commissions in this burgeoning city. But a political crisis was on the horizon.

Struggles between the pro-papal Guelphs (Guelfi) and the pro-Holy Roman Empire Ghibellines (Ghibellini) started in the mid-13th century, with power yo-yoing between the two for almost a century. Into this fractious atmosphere were born revolutionary artist Giotto and outspoken poet Dante Alighieri, whose family belonged to the Guelph camp. After the Guelphs split into two factions, the Neri (Blacks) and Bianchi (Whites), Dante went with the Bianchi – the wrong side – and was expelled from his beloved city in 1302, never to return.

In 1348 the Black Death spirited away almost half the population. This dark period was used as a backdrop by Boccaccio for his *Decameron.*

The history of Medici Florence begins in 1434, when Cosimo the Elder (also known simply as Cosimo de' Medici), a patron of the arts, assumed power. His eye for talent and tact in dealing with artists saw the likes of Alberti, Brunelleschi, Luca della Robbia, Fra' Angelico, Donatello and Fra' Filippo Lippi flourish under his patronage.

In 1439 the Church Council of Florence, aimed at reconciling the Catholic and Eastern churches, brought to the city Byzantine scholars and craftsmen, whom they hoped would impart the knowledge and culture of classical antiquity. The Council, attended by the pope, achieved nothing in the end, but it did influence what was later known as the Renaissance. Under the rule of Cosimo's popular and cultured grandson, Lorenzo il Magnifico (1469–92), Florence became the epicentre of this 'Rebirth', with artists such as Michelangelo, Botticelli and Domenico Ghirlandaio at work. Lorenzo's court, which was filled with Humanists (a school of thought begun in Florence in the late 14th century affirming the dignity and potential of mankind and embracing Latin and Greek literary texts), fostered a flowering of art, music and poetry, turning Florence into Italy's cultural capital.

Florence's golden age was not to last though, effectively dying (along with Lorenzo) in 1492. Just before his death, the Medici bank had failed and two years later the Medici were driven out of Florence. In a reaction against the splendour and excess of the Medici court, the city fell under the control of Girolamo Savonarola, a humourless Dominican monk who led a stern, puritanical republic. In 1497 the likes of Botticelli gladly consigned their 'immoral' works and finery to the flames of the infamous 'Bonfire of the Vanities'. The following year Savonarola fell from public favour and was burned as a heretic.

The pro-French leanings of the subsequent republican government brought it into conflict with the pope and his Spanish allies. In 1512 a Spanish force defeated Florence and the Medici were reinstated. Their tyrannical rule endeared them to few and when Rome, ruled by the Medici pope Clement VII, fell to the emperor Charles V in 1527, the Florentines took advantage of this low point in the Medici fortunes to kick the family out again. Two years later though, imperial and papal forces besieged Florence, forcing the city to accept Lorenzo's great-grandson, Alessandro de' Medici, a ruthless transvestite whom Charles made Duke of Florence. Medici rule continued for another 200 years, during which time they gained control of all of Tuscany, though after the

ⓘ MUSEUM PASSES

The all-new **Firenze Card** (www.firenzecard.it; €50) is valid for 72 hours and covers admission to 33 museums (it covers all the biggies), villas and gardens in Florence, as well as unlimited use of public transport. Buy it online (and collect upon arrival in Florence) or in Florence at tourist offices or ticketing desks of the Uffizi (Entrance 2), Palazzo Pitti, Palazzo Vecchio, Museo del Bargello, Cappella Brancacci, Museo di Santa Maria Novella and Giardini Bardini. If you're an EU citizen, your card also covers under 18 year olds travelling with you.

The big downside of the Firenze Card is it only allows one admission per museum. So, for example, if you want to split your Uffizi forays into a couple of visits and/or you're not from the EU and are travelling with kids, the annual **Friends of the Uffizi Card** (www.amicidegliuffizi.it; adult/under 26yr/family of 4 €60/40/100) is a better deal. Valid for a calendar year (expires 31 December), it covers admission to 22 Florence museums (including Galleria dell'Accademia, Museo del Bargello and Palazzo Pitti) and allows as many return visits as you fancy (have your passport on you as proof of ID to show at each museum with your card). Buy online or from the **Amici degli Uffizi Welcome Desk** (☑055 21 35 60; ⊙10am-5pm Tue-Sat) next to Entrance 2 at the Uffizi.

reign of Cosimo I (1537–74), Florence drifted into steep decline.

The last male Medici, Gian Gastone, died in 1737, after which his sister, Anna Maria, signed the grand duchy of Tuscany over to the House of Habsburg-Lorraine (at the time effectively under Austrian control). This situation remained unchanged, apart from a brief interruption under Napoleon from 1799 to 1814, until the duchy was incorporated into the Kingdom of Italy in 1860. Florence briefly became the national capital a year later, but Rome assumed the mantle permanently in 1871.

Florence was badly damaged during WWII by the retreating Germans, who blew up all of its bridges except the Ponte Vecchio. Devastating floods ravaged the city in 1966, causing inestimable damage to its buildings and artworks. However, the salvage operation led to the widespread use of modern restoration techniques that have saved artworks throughout the country. In 1993 the Mafia exploded a massive car bomb, killing five, injuring 37 and destroying a part of the Uffizi. Just over a decade later and amid a fair amount of controversy, this world-class gallery embarked on its biggest-ever expansion, end date yet to be confirmed.

⊙ Sights & Activities

Florence seriously overwhelms. Its wealth of museums and galleries house many of the world's most important and exquisite examples of Renaissance art, and its architecture is unrivalled. Yet the secret is not to feel pressured to see and do everything on offer here: combine your personal pick of the major sights with ample meandering through the city's warren of narrow streets.

Most churches enforce a strict dress code for visitors: no shorts, sleeveless shirts or plunging necklines. Note that museum ticket offices usually shut 30 minutes before closing time.

For one week of the year (usually some time in spring), admission to state museums is free of charge; dates change, making it impossible to plan a trip around this, so keep your eyes open. One date that doesn't shift is 18 February, the day Anna Maria Louisa de' Medici (1667–1743) died. In honour of the last of the Medici family, who bequeathed the city its vast cultural heritage, admission to all state museums is free on this day.

EU passport holders aged under 18 and over 65 get into Florence's state museums for free, EU citizens aged 18 to 25 pay half-price. Have your ID with you at all times.

DUOMO & PIAZZA DELLA SIGNORIA

Florence's big-hit sights lie in the geographic, historic and cultural heart of the city – the tight grid of streets between Piazza del Duomo and cafe-strung Piazza della Signoria.

Uffizi Gallery ART MUSEUM
(Galleria degli Uffizi; Map p66; www.uffizi.firenze.it; Piazzale degli Uffizi 6; adult/reduced €6.50/3.25, with temporary exhibition €11/5.50; ⊙8.15am-6.50pm Tue-Sun) There are some museums that tower over all others in terms of the quality of their collections – think MoMA, the Egyptian Museum, the Hermitage, the Louvre, the Prado and the Vatican. But this

The Uffizi

JOURNEY INTO THE RENAISSANCE

Navigating the Uffizi's main art collection, chronologically arranged in 45 rooms on one floor, is straightforward; knowing which of the 1500-odd masterpieces to view before gallery fatigue strikes is not. Swap coat and bag (travel light) for floor plan and audioguide on the ground floor, then meet 16th-century Tuscany head-on with a walk up the palazzo's magnificent bust-lined staircase (skip the lift – the Uffizi is as much about masterly architecture as art).

Allow four hours for this journey into the High Renaissance. At the top of the staircase, 2nd floor, show your ticket, turn left and pause to admire the full length of the first corridor sweeping south towards the river Arno. Then duck left into room 2 to witness first steps in Tuscan art – shimmering altarpieces by **Giotto 1** et al. Journey through medieval art to room 8 and **Piero della Francesca's 2** impossibly famous portrait, then break in the corridor with playful **ceiling art 3**. After Renaissance heavyweights **Botticelli 4** and **da Vinci 5**, meander past the Tribuna (potential detour) and enjoy the daylight streaming in through the vast windows and panorama of the **riverside second corridor 6**. Lap up soul-stirring views of the Arno, crossed by Ponte Vecchio and its echo of four bridges drifting towards the Apuane Alps on the horizon. Then saunter into the third corridor, pausing between rooms 25 and 34 to ponder the entrance to the enigmatic Vasari Corridor. End on a high with High Renaissance maestros **Michelangelo 7** and **Raphael 8**.

The Ognissanti Madonna
Room 2
Draw breath at the shy blush and curvaceous breast of Giotto's humanised Virgin (*Maestà*; 1310) – so feminine compared to those of Duccio and Cimabue painted just 25 years before.

Diptych of Duke & Duchess of Urbino
Room 8
Revel in realism's voyage with these uncompromising, warts-and-all portraits (1465–72) by Piero della Francesca. No larger than A3 size, they originally slotted into a portable, hinged frame that folded like a book.

Start of Vasari Corridor (linking the Palazzo Vecchio with the Uffizi and Palazzo Pitti)

Entrance to 2nd Floor Gallery

Palazzo Vecchio

Piazza della Signoria

Grotesque Ceiling Frescoes
First Corridor
Take time to study the make-believe monsters and most unexpected of burlesques (spot the arrow-shooting satyr outside room 15) waltzing across this eastern corridor's fabulous frescoed ceiling (1581).

The Genius of Botticelli
Room 10–14
The miniature form of *The Discovery of the Body of Holofernes* (c 1470) makes Botticelli's early Renaissance masterpiece all the more impressive. Don't miss the artist watching you in *Adoration of the Magi* (1475), left of the exit.

View of the Arno
Indulge in intoxicating city views from this short glassed-in corridor – an architectural masterpiece. Near the top of the hill, spot one of 73 outer towers built to defend Florence and its 15 city gates below.

Second Corridor

Tribuna

First Corridor

Arno River

Portrait of Pope Leo X
Room 26
Stare into the eyes of the trio in this Raphael masterpiece (1518) and work out what the devil they're thinking – a perfect portrayal of High Renaissance intrigue.

Entrance to Vasari Corridor

Third Corridor

Matter of Fact
The Uffizi collection spans the 13th to 18th centuries, but its 15th- and 16th-century Renaissance works are second to none.

Doni Tondo
Room 25
David's creator, Michelangelo, was essentially a sculptor and no painting expresses this better than *Doni Tondo* (1506–08). Mary's muscular arms against a backdrop of curvaceous nudes are practically 3D in their shapeliness.

Annunciation
Room 15
Admire the exquisite portrayal of the Tuscan landscape in this painting (c 1475–80), one of few by Leonardo da Vinci to remain in Florence.

Value Lunchbox
Try the Uffizi rooftop cafe or – better value – gourmet *panini* at 'Ino (www.ino-firenze.com; Via dei Georgofili 3-7r).

list wouldn't be complete without adding Florence's jewel in the crown, the Uffizi. Filling the vast, oversized U-shaped Palazzo degli Uffizi, the collection spans the whole gamut of art history from ancient Greek sculpture to 18th-century Venetian paintings, but its core is the masterpiece-rich Renaissance collection.

Cosimo I commissioned Vasari to design and build the gargantuan U-shaped palace in 1560 – a government office building (*uffizi* means offices) for the city's administrators, judiciary and guilds. Following Vasari's death in 1564, architects Alfonso Parigi and Bernando Buontalenti took over the Uffizi project, Buontalenti modifying the upper floor of the palace to house the works of art keenly collected by Francesco I, a passion inherited from his father. In 1580 the building was finally complete. By the time the last of the Medici family died in 1743, the family's private art collection was enormous. Fortunately, it was bequeathed to the City of Florence on the strict proviso that it never leave the city.

Over the years, sections of the collection have been moved to the Museo del Bargello and Museo Archeologico, and other collections in turn have been moved here. Several artworks were destroyed or badly damaged in 1993 when a car bomb planted by the Mafia exploded outside the gallery's west wing, killing five people. Documents cataloguing the collection were also destroyed.

Visits are best kept to three or four hours max. When it all gets too much, head to the rooftop cafe (aka the terraced hanging garden where the Medici clan listened to music performances on the square below) for fresh air and fabulous views.

Tuscan Masters: 13th Century to 14th Century

Works in the Uffizi are displayed on the 2nd floor in a series of numbered rooms off two dramatically long corridors. Arriving in the Primo Corridoio (First Corridor), the first room to the left of the staircase (Room 2) highlights 13th-century Sienese art and is designed like a medieval chapel (look up to admire those great wooden ceiling trusses) to reflect its fabulous contents: three large altarpieces from Florentine churches by Tuscan masters Duccio di Buoninsegna, Cimabue and Giotto. These clearly reflect the transition from the Gothic to the nascent Renaissance style. Note the overtly naturalistic realism overtones in Giotto's portrayal of the *Madonna and Child* among angels and saints, painted some 25 years after that of Duccio and Cimabue (c 1306–10).

The next room stays in Siena but moves into the 14th century. The highlight is Simone Martini's shimmering *Annunciation* (1333), painted with Lippo Memmi and setting the Madonna in a sea of gold. Also of note is the *Madonna with Child and Saints* triptych (1340) by Pietro Lorenzetti, which demonstrates a realism similar to Giotto's; unfortunately both Pietro and his artistic brother Ambrogio died from the plague in Siena in 1348.

THE NEW UFFIZI

The lighting in places is atrocious; the vital statistics of some works are not even marked; and world-class masterpieces jostle for limited wall space. Hundreds if not thousands more art works are kept under wraps in storage, simply because of lack of display space. Historic, vast, world famous and rammed to the rafters with the very best of the Renaissance it might be, but Italy's iconic art gallery sucks in terms of museum design and efficiency.

The so-called Nuovi Uffizi (New Uffizi; www.nuoviuffizi.it) project is meant to sort all this out. The ongoing and vastly overdue €65 million refurbishment and redevelopment project, announced way back in 1997 but not actually started until 2007, will double exhibition space and add a lovely new exit (possibly designed by Japanese architect Arato Isozaki if everyone agrees to the radical contemporary design that was accepted, then disputed, discussed and discussed still more).

Five years on, in true Italian fashion no one, including Uffizi architect Antonio Godoli in charge of the works, will commit to a final completion date, originally set at 2010, shifted to 2013 and now clearly some time beyond that. The eventual Nuovi Uffizi once finished (don't hold your breath) will hopefully be fabulous, but in the meantime expect to find some rooms temporarily closed and the contents of others dramatically changed.

HAVE YOUR SAY

Found a fantastic restaurant that you're longing to share with the world? Disagree with our recommendations? Or just want to talk about your most recent trip?

Whatever your reason, head to lonelyplanet.com, where you can post a review, ask or answer a question on the Thorntree forum, comment on a blog, or share your photos and tips on Groups. Or you can simply spend time chatting with like-minded travellers. So go on, have your say.

Masters in 14th-century Florence paid as much attention to detail as their Sienese counterparts, as works in the next room demonstrate: savour the depth of realism and extraordinary gold-leaf work of *San Reminio Pietà* (1360–65) by gifted Giotto pupil, Giottino (otherwise known as Giotto di Stefano).

International Gothic

Rooms 5 and 6 (actually one large room) are dedicated to works of the International Gothic style, with the knockout piece being Gentile da Fabriano's *Adoration of the Magi* (1423), originally commissioned by Palla Strozzi for Santa Trìnita.

Renaissance Pioneers

A concern for perspective was a hallmark of the early-15th-century Florentine school (Room 7) that pioneered the Renaissance. One panel (the other two are in the Louvre and London's National Gallery) from Paolo Uccello's striking *Battle of San Romano*, which celebrates Florence's victory over Siena, shows the artist's efforts to create perspective with amusing effect as he directs the lances, horses and soldiers to a central disappearing point.

In Room 8, Piero della Francesca's famous profile portraits (1465) of the crooked-nosed, red-robed Duke and Duchess of Urbino are wholly humanist in spirit: the former painted from the left side as he'd lost his right eye in a jousting accident, and the latter painted a deathly white, reflecting the fact that the portrait was painted posthumously.

Carmelite monk Fra' Filippo Lippi had an unfortunate soft spot for earthly pleasures, eloping with a nun from Prato and causing a huge scandal. Search out the artist's self-portrait as a podgy friar in *Coronation of the Virgin* (1439–47) and don't miss his later *Madonna and Child with Two Angels* (1460–65), an exquisite work that clearly influenced his pupil, Sandro Botticelli.

Another related pair, brothers Antonio and Piero del Pollaiolo, fill Room 9, where their seven cardinal and theological values of 15th-century Florence – commissioned for the merchant's tribunal in Piazza della Signoria – burst forth with fantastic energy. More restrained are Piero's *Portrait of Galeazzo Maria Sforza* and Antonio's *Portrait of a Lady in Profile*.

The only canvas in the theological and cardinal virtues series not to be painted by the Pollaiolos was *Strength* (1470), the first documented work by Botticelli.

Botticelli Room

The spectacular Sala del Botticelli, numbered 10 to 14 but in fact one large hall, is one of the Uffizi's most popular rooms and is always packed. Of the 15 works by the Renaissance master known for his ethereal figures, *Birth of Venus* (c 1484), *Primavera* (Spring; c 1478), the deeply spiritual *Cestello Annunciation* (1489–90), the *Adoration of the Magi* (1475; featuring the artist's self-portrait on the extreme right) and *The Madonna of the Magnificat* (1483) are the best known, but true aficionados rate his twin set of miniatures depicting a sword-bearing Judith returning from the camp of Holofernes and the discovery of the decapitated Holofernes in his tent (1495–1500) as being among his finest works.

Leonardo Room

Room 15 displays two early Florentine works by Leonardo da Vinci: the incomplete *Adoration of the Magi* (1481–82), drawn in red earth pigment, and his *Annunciation* (c 1472).

La Tribuna

The Medici clan stashed away their most precious masterpieces in this exquisite octagonal-shaped treasure trove (Room 18) created by Francesco I. Today their family portraits hang on the red upholstered walls and a walkway leads visitors around the edge. The popular favourites here are the Bronzino portraits of the family of Cosimo I, including his wife Eleonora di Toledo (painted with their son Giovanni), the duke himself, young Giovanni holding a bird, daughter Bia and son Francesco.

FLORENCE

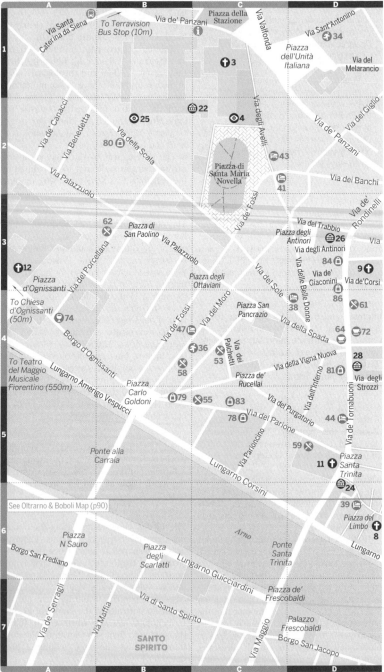

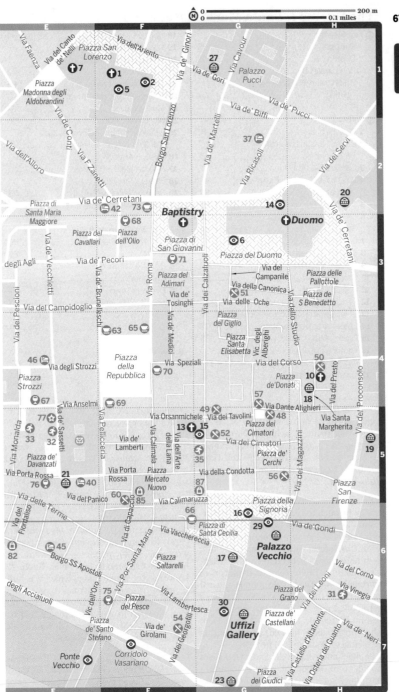

The Duomo & Santa Maria Novella

Flemish & German Masters

Rooms 20 to 23 house works by Northern Renaissance painters including Dürer (*Adoration of the Magi;* 1504), Lucas Cranach the Elder (*Adam and Eve;* 1528) and Hans Memling (*Madonna and Child Enthroned With Two Angels;* 1480).

High Renaissance to Mannerism

Passing through the loggia or **Secondo Corridoio** (Second Corridor) visitors enjoy wonderful views of Florence before entering the **Terzo Corridoio** (Third Corridor). The first room here (Room 25) is home to Michelangelo's dazzling *Tondo Doni,* a depiction of the Holy Family. The composition is unusual and the colours as vibrant as when they were first applied in 1504–06. It was painted for wealthy Florentine merchant Agnolo Doni (who hung it above his bed) and bought by the Medici for Palazzo Pitti in 1594.

Raphael and Andrea del Sarto works rub shoulders in Room 26, where Raphael's charming *Madonna of the Goldfinch* (1505–

06) holds centre stage, though his striking portrait of *Pope Leo X with Giulio de' Medici and Luigi de' Rossi* is just as impressive.

The work of Venetian masters graces Room 28, where 11 Titians are displayed. Masterpieces include the sensual nude *Venus of Urbino* (1538), the seductive *Flora* (1515) and the striking portrait of *Eleonora Gonzaga, Duchess of Urbino* (1536–37).

Room 29 is notable for Parmigianino's oddly elongated *Madonna of the Long Neck* (1534–40), and subsequent rooms feature works by Paolo Veronese, Tintoretto, Rubens and Rembrandt. Don't miss Room 42, known as the Niobe Room, which was built to house a group of statues representing Niobe and her children. Discovered in a Roman vineyard in 1583 and brought to Florence in 1775, the works are 4th century BC Roman copies of Greek originals.

Duomo CATHEDRAL
(Map p66; Cattedrale di Santa Maria del Fiore or St Mary of the Flower; www.duomofirenze.it; ⊙10am-

5pm Mon-Wed & Fri, to 3.30pm Thu, to 4.45pm Sat, to 3.30pm 1st Sat of month, 1.30-4.45pm Sun, Mass in English 5pm Sat) Not only is Florence's *duomo* the city's most iconic landmark, it's also one of Italy's 'Big Three' (with Pisa's Leaning Tower and Rome's Colosseum). Its famous red-tiled dome, graceful *campanile* (bell tower) and breathtaking pink, white and green marble facade have the wow factor in spades.

Begun in 1296 by Sienese architect Arnolfo di Cambio, the cathedral took almost 150 years to complete. Its neo-Gothic facade was designed in the 19th century by architect Emilio de Fabris to replace the uncompleted original, torn down in the 16th century. The oldest and most clearly Gothic part of the cathedral is its south flank, pierced by Porta dei Canonici (Canons' Door), a mid-14th-century High Gothic creation (you enter here to climb up inside the dome).

When Michelangelo went to work on St Peter's in Rome, he reportedly said: 'I go to build a greater dome, but not a fairer one.'

One of the finest masterpieces of the Renaissance, Florence's famous cathedral dome (admission €8; ⊙8.30am-7pm Mon-Fri, to 5.40pm Sat) is indeed a feat of engineering and one that cannot be fully appreciated without climbing its 463 interior stone steps.

The dome was built between 1420 and 1436 to a design by Filippo Brunelleschi. Taking his inspiration from Rome's Pantheon, Brunelleschi arrived at an innovative engineering solution of a distinctive octagonal shape of inner and outer concentric domes resting on the drum of the cathedral rather than the roof itself, allowing artisans to build from the ground up without needing a wooden support frame. Over four million bricks were used in the construction, all of them laid in consecutive rings in horizontal courses using a vertical herringbone pattern. The final product is 91m high and 45.5m wide.

The climb up the spiral staircase is relatively steep, and should not be attempted if you are claustrophobic. Make sure to pause

ℹ CUT THE QUEUE: PREBOOKED TICKETS

In July, August and other busy periods such as Easter, unbelievably long queues are a fact of life at Florence's key museums – if you haven't prebooked your ticket in advance, you could well end up standing in line queuing for four hours or so.

For a fee of €3 per ticket (€4 for the Uffizi and Galleria dell'Accademia), tickets to all 13 *musei statali* (state museums) can be reserved, including the Uffizi, Galleria dell'Accademia (where *David* lives), Palazzo Pitti, Museo del Bargello and the Medicean chapels (Cappelle Medicee). In reality, the only museums where prebooking is vital are the Uffizi and Accademia – to organise your ticket, go to www.firenzemusei.it or call **Firenze Musei** (Florence Museums; ☏ 055 29 48 83; ☺ booking line 8.30am-6.30pm Mon-Fri, to 12.30pm Sat), with ticketing desks (open 8.30am to 7pm Tuesday to Sunday) at the Uffizi (p61) and Palazzo Pitti (p89).

At the Uffizi, signs point prebooked ticket holders to the building opposite the gallery where prebooked tickets can be collected; once you've got the ticket you go to Door 1 of the museum (for prebooked tickets only) and queue again to enter the gallery. It's annoying, but you'll still save hours of queuing time overall.

Many hotels in Florence also prebook museum tickets for guests.

when you reach the balustrade at the base of the dome, which gives an aerial view of the octagonal *coro* (choir) of the cathedral below and the seven round stained-glass windows (by Donatello, Andrea del Castagno, Paolo Uccello and Lorenzo Ghiberti) that pierce the octagonal drum.

Look up and you'll see flamboyant late-16th-century frescoes by Giorgio Vasari and Federico Zuccari, depicting the *Giudizio Universale* (Last Judgement).

As you climb, snapshots of Florence can be spied through small windows. The final leg – a straight flight up the curve of the inner dome – rewards with an unforgettable 360-degree panorama of one of Europe's most beautiful cities.

After the visual wham-bam of the facade and dome, the sparse decoration of the cathedral's vast interior, 155m long and 90m wide, comes as a surprise – most of its artistic treasures have been removed over centuries according to the vagaries of ecclesiastical fashion, and many are now on show in the Museo dell'Opera di Santa Maria del Fiore. The interior is also unexpectedly secular in places (a reflection of the sizeable chunk of the cathedral not paid for by the church): down the left aisle two immense frescoes of equestrian statues portray two *condottieri* (mercenaries) – on the left Niccolò da Tolentino by Andrea del Castagno (1456) and on the right Sir John Hawkwood by Uccello (1436) – who fought in the service of Florence in the 14th century.

Between the left (north) arm of the transept and the apse is the Sagrestia delle Messe (Mass Sacristy), its panelling a marvel of inlaid wood carved by Benedetto and Giuliano da Maiano. The fine bronze doors were executed by Luca della Robbia – his only known work in the material. Above the doorway is his glazed terracotta *Resurrezione* (Resurrection).

A stairway near the main entrance of the cathedral leads down to the crypt (admission €3; ☺ 10am-5pm Mon-Wed & Fri, to 4.45pm Sat), where excavations between 1965 and 1974 unearthed parts of the 5th-century Chiesa di Santa Reparata that originally stood on the site.

The steep 414-step climb up the 85m-high campanile (adult/child €6/free; ☺ 8.30am-7.30pm), designed by Giotto, offers the reward of a view nearly as impressive as that from the dome. The queues here are usually much shorter, too.

The first tier of bas-reliefs around the base of the *campanile* are copies of those carved by Pisano, but possibly designed by Giotto, depicting the Creation of Man and the *attività umane* (arts and industries). Those on the second tier depict the planets, the cardinal virtues, the arts and the seven sacraments. The sculptures of the Prophets and Sibyls in the niches of the upper storeys are copies of works by Donatello and others; see the originals in the Museo dell'Opera di Santa Maria del Fiore.

Museo dell'Opera di
Santa Maria del Fiore   MUSEUM
(Cathedral Museum; Museo dell'Opera di Duomo; Map p66; www.operaduomo.firenze.it; Piazza del

Duomo 9; adult/child €6/free; ⊙9am-6.50pm Mon-Sat, to 1pm Sun) Surprisingly overlooked by the crowds, this museum on the northern (street) side of the cathedral safeguards treasures that once adorned the *duomo*, Baptistry and *campanile*. It is one of the city's most impressive museums.

Make a beeline for the glass-topped courtyard with its awe-inspiring display of seven of the original 10 panels from Ghiberti's glorious masterpiece the *Porta del Paradiso* (Door of Paradise), designed for the Baptistry.

The nearby large room is devoted to statuary from Arnolfo di Cambio's original never-to-be-completed Gothic facade. Pieces include several by Arnolfo – *Pope Boniface VIII, The Virgin and Child* (with its somewhat strange glass eyes) and *Santa Reparata* – as well as Donatello's 1408 statue of *St John,* which was the sculptor's first large-scale work. Next door, the smaller space is home to exquisite marble panels from the *duomo's coro* (choir), carved by Baccio Bandinelli and Giovanni Bandini in 1547.

On the stair landing is the museum's best-known piece, Michelangelo's *Pietà,* a work he intended for his own tomb. Vasari recorded in his *Lives of the Artists* that, dissatisfied with both the quality of the marble and of his own work, Michelangelo broke up the unfinished sculpture, destroying the arm and left leg of the figure of Christ. A student of Michelangelo's later restored the arm and completed the figure.

Continue upstairs, where a pair of exquisitely carved *cantorie* (singing galleries) or organ lofts – one by Donatello, the other by Luca della Robbia – face each other. Originally in the cathedral's sacristy, their scenes of musicians and children at play add a refreshingly frivolous touch amid so much sombre piety. There are also several carvings by Donatello here, including his *Prophet Habakkuk,* originally in the *campanile,* which has always been known as *'lo zuccone'* (big head). Vasari wrote that he visited Donatello in his studio one day to find him looking intensely at this extremely life-like statue and commanding it to talk (he'd obviously been working far too hard!). Don't miss the same sculptor's wooden representation of a gaunt, desperately desolate *Mary Magdalene* in the same room, a work completed late in his career.

Baptistry   CHURCH
(Map p66; Piazza di San Giovanni; admission €4; ⊙12.15-7pm Mon-Sat, 8.30am-2pm 1st Sat of the month & Sun) The gilded bronze bas-reliefs adorning the doors at the eastern entrance of this wonderful, 11th-century Romanesque Baptistry were designed by Lorenzo Ghiberti, who jointly won a 1401 competition involving the greatest artists of the day for the honour of undertaking this task. His co-winner was Filippo Brunelleschi, who was so annoyed at not winning outright that he withdrew from the project. Looking at their entries, both of which are now in the collection of the Museo del Bargello (p87), Brunelleschi's tantrum seems providential: Ghiberti's graceful panel, which was cast in a single piece and is clearly more unified in conception and execution, is much more impressive.

Ghiberti's finished product – which depicts assorted scriptural subjects, comprises 10 panels and took over two decades to complete – was so extraordinary that, many years later, Michelangelo stood before the doors in awe and declared them fit to be the *Porta del Paradiso* (Gate of Paradise), hence their name. What we see today are copies; most of the originals are on display in the Museo dell'Opera di Santa Maria del Fiore.

The Gate of Paradise is one of the Baptistry's three sets of doors, conceived as a series of panels in which the story of humanity and the Redemption would be told. The earliest (now south) door is by Andrea Pisano (1336) and illustrates the life of St John the Baptist in 28 panels. Ghiberti sculpted the panels for both the east (1425–52) and north (1403–24) doors. The top 20 panels of the north door recount episodes from the New Testament, and the eight lower ones show the four Evangelists and four fathers of the Church.

The building itself is an octagonal striped structure of white and green marble that was built on the site of a Roman temple. The

WHAT'S IN A NAME

Medieval dyers changed the colour of wool in *caldaie* (vats) on Via delle Caldaie; Renaissance *calzaiuoli* (hosiers) handcrafted fine shoes in workshops on Via dei Calzaiuoli; tanners made a stink in *conce* (tanneries) on Via delle Conce. (And yes, those Medici did keep caged lions, although nothing caused quite a stir as the giraffe given to Lorenzo Il Magnifico by an Egyptian sultan in 1486.)

earliest documentation in existence dates from 897, although the building is thought to be much older than that and incorporates Roman columns with Corinthian capitals. The interior is encrusted in magnificent mosaics, the oldest of which (c 1250) covers the apse. The glittering (and wonderfully lit) dome mosaics date from the end of the 13th century and took many decades to complete. Look for the *Christ in Majesty* and *Last Judgement.*

To the right of the apse lies the magnificent tomb of Baldassare Cossa (1370–1419) sculpted by Donatello. Better known as the antipope John XXIII, Cossa was hardly a saint, but as antipope he had helped Giovanni di Bicci de' Medici (1360–1429) – the Medici credited with making the Medici rich – break into papal banking. So when Cossa asked in his will to be buried in the Baptistry, it was the least Giovanni could do. The tomb is remarkable for its elegant carving and for the fact that it is squeezed into the narrow space between two Roman columns but still seems perfectly proportioned.

Piazza della Signoria   PIAZZA

(Map p66) Edged by historic cafes, crammed with Renaissance sculptures and presided over by the magnificent bulk of Palazzo Vecchio, this photogenic piazza is the hub of Florentine life, and has been so for centuries.

ⓘ TOP 5: LOSE THE CROWD

» Florence can be overwhelming: flee to **Fiesole** (see the boxed text, p118) in the Florentine hills for peace, quiet and lunch with a spectacular view.

» Take tea with a panoramic city view in the manicured gardens of **Giardino Bardini** (p93).

» Join the privileged few in an exclusive, cross-river stroll along the enigmatic **Vasarian Corridor** (see opposite).

» Motor out of the city through vineyards and olive groves in a vintage Fiat 500 with the **500 Touring Club** (see the boxed text, p96).

» Follow Florentines out of town for a gastronomic breath of fresh air (p106) – on the banks of the Arno or in a flowery garden.

Whenever the city entered one of its innumerable political crises, the people would be called here as a *parlamento* (people's plebiscite) to rubber-stamp decisions that frequently meant ruin for some ruling families and victory for others. Scenes of great pomp and circumstance alternated with those of terrible suffering: it was here that vehemently pious preacher-leader Savonarola set fire to the city's art – books, paintings, musical instruments, mirrors, fine clothes and so on – during his famous 'Bonfire of the Vanities' in 1497, and where he was hung in chains and burnt as a heretic, along with two other supporters a year later.

The same spot where both fires burned is marked by a bronze plaque embedded in the ground in front of Ammannati's **Fontana di Nettuno** (Neptune Fountain). With its pin-headed bronze satyrs and divinities frolicking at its edges, this huge fountain is hardly pretty and is much mocked as *il biancone* (the big white thing), not to mention a waste of good marble, by many a Florentine. Far more impressive are the equestrian statue of Cosimo I by Giambologna in the centre of the piazza, the much-photographed copy of Michelangelo's *David* that has guarded the western entrance to the Palazzo Vecchio since 1910 (the original stood here until 1873 but is now in the Galleria dell'Accademia) and two copies of important Donatello works – *Marzocco,* the heraldic Florentine lion (for the original visit the Museo del Bargello) and Giuditta e Oloferne (Judith and Holofernes, c 1455; original inside Palazzo Vecchio).

Facing this line-up is the 14th-century **Loggia dei Lanzi** (Map p66; admission free), an open-air museum where works such as Giambologna's *Rape of the Sabine Women* (c 1583), Benvenuto Cellini's bronze *Perseus* (1554) and Agnolo Gaddi's *Seven Virtues* (1384–89) are displayed. The loggia owes its name to the *Lanzichenecchi* (Swiss bodyguards) of Cosimo I, who were stationed here, and the present day guards live up to this heritage, sternly monitoring crowd behaviour and promptly banishing anyone carrying food or drink.

The piazza is a favourite *passeggiata* (evening stroll) choice for Florentines, who saunter around it and surrounding streets in the early evening and all day on the weekend, dodging herds of camera-toting tourists before stopping for a coffee, hot chocolate or *aperitivo* at the city's most famous cafe, Caffè Rivoire (see the boxed text, p111).

Bathed in mystery, this must be the world's most infamous and enigmatic corridor. Look above the jewellery shops on the eastern side of Ponte Vecchio to see – most dramatically at sunset – Florence's Corridoio Vasariano, an extraordinary elevated covered passageway joining the Palazzo Vecchio on Piazza della Signoria with the Uffizi and Palazzo Pitti on the other side of the river. Around 1km long, it was designed by Vasari for Cosimo I in 1565 to allow the Medicis and court's high dignitaries to wander between the two palaces in privacy and comfort. From the 17th century, the Medicis strung it with self-portraits – a collection of 700-odd art works today that includes self-portraits of Andrea del Sarto (the oldest), Rubens, Rembrandt, Canova and others.

The original promenade incorporated tiny windows (facing the river) and circular apertures with iron gratings (facing the street) to protect those who used the corridor from outside attacks. But when Hitler visited Florence in 1941, his chum and fellow dictator Benito Mussolini had big new windows punched into the corridor walls on Ponte Vecchio so that his guest could enjoy an expansive view down the Arno from the famous Florentine bridge.

On the Oltrarno, the corridor passes by Chiesa di Santa Felicità (Map p90; Piazza di Santa Felicità; admission free; ☉9.30am-noon & 1.30-5.30pm Mon-Sat), thereby providing the Medici with a private balcony in the church where they could likewise attend Mass without mingling with the minions. Stand in front of the small Romanesque church on Piazza di Santa Felicità and admire the trio of arches of the Vasarian Corridor that runs right above the portico outside the otherwise unnotable church facade. Inside, walk towards the altar and look backwards to see the Medici balcony up high (and imagine the corridor snaking behind it). Oh, and before leaving the church, don't miss Ghirlandaio's *Meeting of St Anne and St Joachim* hung at the end of its right transept.

The Vasarian Corridor is open to just a privileged few – look for spots in the Uffizi and elsewhere where you can get sneak peeks of the corridor. To actually visit it – a memorable experience – either join a guided tour of just five people (in Italian only) sporadically organised by Firenze Musei (€15 including Uffizi admission and booking fee) – tours are advertised in advance on the Uffizi website (www.uffizi.firenze.it). Or pay the price for an English-language tour in a group of 15 organised by Florence Town (Map p66; ☎055 012 39 94; www.florencetown.com; Via de' Lamberti 1; adult/6-12yr €89/45 incl Uffizi admission; ☉2 to 3 times weekly). Whichever option you plump for, reserve well in advance.

Palazzo Vecchio   MUSEUM, TOWN HALL
(Old Palace; Map p66; www.palazzovecchio-family museum.it; Piazza della Signoria; adult/reduced €6/4.50; ☉9am-7pm Mon-Wed & Fri-Sun, to 2pm Thu) The traditional seat of government, Florence's imposing fortress palace with its striking crenellations and 94m-high tower Torre d'Arnolfo was designed by Arnolfo di Cambio between 1298 and 1314 for the *sig-noria* (city government) that ruled medieval and Renaissance Florence, hence its original name, Palazzo della Signoria. During their short time in office the nine *priori* (consuls) – guild members picked at random – of the *signoria* lived in the palace. Every two months nine new names were pulled out of the hat, ensuring ample comings and goings.

In 1540 Cosimo I made the palace his ducal residence and centre of government, commissioning Vasari to renovate and deco-rate the interior. Not too long after the renovation, he and his wife Eleonora di Toledo (famously immortalised in Bronzino's portrait in the Uffizi collection) decided that the newly renovated apartments were too uncomfortable for their large family to live in year-round and he purchased Palazzo Pitti as a summer residence. After the death of Eleonora and their sons Giovanni and Garzia from malaria in 1562, Cosimo moved the rest of his family to Palazzo Pitti permanently. At this time, the building became known as Palazzo Vecchio. It remains the seat of the city's power, home to the mayor's office and the municipal council.

The best way to discover this den of political drama and intrigue is by thematic guided tour. Interior highlights include the magnificent 53m-long, 22m-wide Salone dei Cinquecento (aka La Sala Grande), created within the original building in the

1. Palazzo Vecchio (p73)

Florence's imposing Old Palace has long been a den of political drama and intrigue.

2. Piazza di Santa Croce (p85)

This square is dominated by the Basilica di Santa Croce, burial place of many famous Florentines.

3. Palazzo Pitti (p89)

From the Medici to the Savoy, Palazzo Pitti has a remarkable pedigree of powerful residents.

4. Piazza del Duomo (p68)

The steep climb up Giotto's campanile affords a spectacular view in Florence's most famous spot.

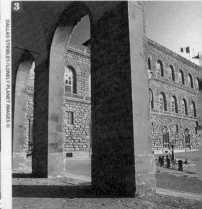

DALLAS STRIBLEY/LONELY PLANET IMAGES ©

1490s to accommodate the Consiglio dei Cinquecento (Council of 500) that ruled Florence at the end of the 15th century. Star of the show at floor level is Michelangelo's sculpture *Genio della Vittoria* (Genius of Victory), destined for Rome and Pope Julius II's tomb, but left unfinished in the artist's studio when he died.

Sheer size aside, what impresses most about this room are the swirling battle scenes, painted floor to ceiling by Vasari and his apprentices. These glorify Florentine victories by Cosimo I over arch-rivals Pisa and Siena: unlike the Sienese, the Pisans are depicted bare of armour (play 'Spot the Leaning Tower'). To top off this unabashed celebration of his own power, Cosimo had himself portrayed as a god in the centre of the exquisite panelled ceiling – but not before commissioning Vasari to raise the original ceiling 7m in height. It took Vasari and his school, in consultation with Michelangelo, just two years (1563–65) to construct the ceiling and paint the 34 gold-leafed panels,

which rest simply on a wooden frame. The effect is mesmerising.

Off this huge space is the Chapel of SS Cosmas and Damian, home to Vasari's 1557–58 triptych panels of the two saints depicting Cosimo the Elder as Cosmas (on the right) and Cosimo I as Damian (on the left). Next to the chapel is the Sala di Leo X, the private suite of apartments of Cardinal Giovanni de' Medici, the son of Lorenzo Il Magnifico, who became pope in 1513.

Up the stairs and across the balcony (from where you can enjoy wonderful views of the Salone dei Cinquecento), are the Quartiere di Eleonora di Toledo, the private apartments for both Eleonora and her ladies-in-waiting. These bear the same heavy-handed decor blaring the glory of the Medici as the rest of the palace. Of note is the ceiling in the Camera Verde (Green Room) by Ridolfo del Ghirlandaio, inspired by designs from Nero's Domus Aurea in Rome, and the vibrant frescoes by Bronzino in the chapel.

Also on the 2nd floor, the Sala dei Gigli, named after its frieze of fleur-de-lis, repre-

PALAZZO VECCHIO TOURS

Palazzo Vecchio cleverly markets itself as a 'slow museum for visitors who want to be more than spectators'. And indeed, the only way to get the most out of this dynamic, well-thought-out museum is to join one of its excellent guided tours (☑055 276 82 24; info.museoragazzi@comune.fi.it; ◷9.30am, 12.30pm, 3.30pm & 6.30pm Mon-Wed & Fri, 9.30am & 12.30pm Thu, 10am, 1.30pm, 3pm & 6.30pm Sat & Sun). Best reserved in advance to avoid disappointment, tours last 1¼ hours and take you into parts of the building otherwise inaccessible; many are in English.

The best of the adult bunch is probably the 'Secret Passages' tour, in which groups of 12 are led along the secret staircase built between the palace's super-thick walls in 1342 as an escape route for French Duke of Athens Walter de Brienne, who seized the palace and nominated himself Lord of Florence only to be sent packing back to France by the Florentines a year later. It follows this staircase to the Tesoretto (Treasury) of Cosimo I – a tiny room no larger than a cupboard for his private collection, entered by one carefully concealed door and exited by another – and the equally intimate but substantially more sumptuous Studiolo (Study) of his introverted, alchemy-mad son Francesco I. Cosimo commissioned Vasari and a team of top Florentine Mannerist artists to decorate the study, Francesco appearing in one of the 34 emblematic paintings covering the walls not as a prince, but as an inconsequential scientist experimenting with gunpowder. The lower paintings concealed 20 cabinets in which the young prince hid his shells, stones, crystals and other curious treasures. The tour ends in the palace roof above the Salone dei Cinquecento, where you can see the huge wooden trusses that hold up Vasari's ornate ceiling.

The wonderful children's tours see actors dressed in Renaissance costume who rope young participants into the performance. A sumptuously attired Eleonora of Toledo, clearly shocked by the casual attire of today's children, has been known to give advice about proper grooming for young ladies, and Cosimo I is happy to lay down the law about the proper age for a Medici to take on duties as a cardinal (the answer is 14, the age of his son Ferdinando when he became a cardinal).

Two Days

Start with a coffee on historic Piazza della Repubblica before hitting the **Uffizi**. After lunch head to **Piazza del Duomo** to visit the **cathedral**, **baptistry** and **Museo dell'Opera di Santa Maria di Fiore**. Dedicated art buffs can finish the day with an *aperitivo* at **Caffè Giacosa** and an evening visit (if it's Thursday) to **Palazzo Strozzi** (then a late dinner at **Obikà**). Next morning, follow our walking tour (p95), then head to San Marco to visit the **Galleria dell'Accademia** and **Museo di San Marco**. For *aperitivo* and dinner, venture across the Arno to the Oltrarno, stopping en route to admire the sunset from the **Ponte Vecchio**, and later **Piazzale Michelangelo**.

Four Days

On day three, explore **Palazzo Pitti**, the **Giardino di Boboli** and the **Giardino Bardini**. Alternatively, visit the city's major basilicas – **San Lorenzo**, **Santa Croce** and **Santa Maria Novella**. For dinner, enjoy good food and entertainment at **Teatro del Sale**. On day four, take a guided tour of **Palazzo Vecchio** in the morning and explore the city's artisanal **shops** in the afternoon.

One week

With three extra days, you'll be able to fit in gems such as **Cappella Brancacci** (reserve in advance), **Cappella dei Magi** at Palazzo Medici-Riccardi and the **Museo del Bargello**. Or take a day trip to **Fiesole**.

---

senting the Florentine Republic, is home to Donatello's original *Judith and Holofernes*. Domenico Ghirlandaio's fresco on the far wall in this room, depicting figures from Roman history, was meant to be one of a series by other artists, including Botticelli.

A small study off the hall is the chancery, once Niccolò Machiavelli's office. Another room, the Sala delle Carte Geografiche (Map Room), houses Cosimo I's fascinating collection of 16th-century maps charting everywhere in the known world at the time, from the polar regions to the Caribbean.

For details about the special cumulative ticket for Palazzo Vecchio and the Cappella Brancacci, see the boxed text, p89.

Piazza della Repubblica   PIAZZA
(Map p66) Originally the site of a Roman forum and the heart of medieval Florence, this busy civic space was created in the late 1880s as part of a controversial plan of 'civic improvements' involving the demolition of the old market, Jewish ghetto and surrounding slums, and the relocation of nearly 6000 residents. Fortunately, Vasari's lovely *Loggia del Pesce* (Fish Market) was saved and re-erected on Via Pietrapiana. Today the piazza is known for its concentration of historic cafes, the bars of which are filled day and night with Florentines catching up with friends

and family, recovering after shopping exertions or grabbing a caffeine fix on the way to or from work (the terraces tend to be tourist-only territory).

TOP CHOICE **Museo Galileo**   MUSEUM
(Map p66; www.museogalileo.it; Piazza dei Giudici 1; adult/reduced €8/4; ⊗9.30am-6pm Wed-Mon, to 1pm Tue) Smart on the river next to the Uffizi in 12th-century Palazzo Castellani – look for the sundial telling the time on the pavement outside – is this state-of-the-art History of Science museum, named after the great Pisa-born scientist who was invited by the Medici court to Florence in 1610 (don't miss two of his fingers and a tooth displayed in the museum). A tour of the museum unravels a mesmerising curiosity box of astronomical and mathematical treasures (think telescopes, beautiful painted globes, barometers, watches, clocks and so on) collected by Cosimo I and other Medicis from 1562 and, later, the Lorraine dynasty. Temporary exhibitions hosted by the museum are equally compelling.

TOP CHOICE **Chiesa e Museo di Orsanmichele**   CHURCH, MUSEUM
(Map p66; Via dell'Arte della Lana; admission free; ⊗church 10am-5pm daily, museum 10am-5pm Mon) This thoroughly unusual and inspirational

church with a splendid Gothic tabernacle by Andrea Orcagna was created when the arcades of an old grain market (1290) were walled in and two storeys added during the 14th century. A real must-see, its exterior is exquisitely decorated with niches and tabernacles bearing statues. Representing the patron saints of Florence's many guilds, they were commissioned in the 15th and 16th centuries after the *signoria* ordered the city's guilds to finance the church's decoration.

These statues represent the work of some of the greatest Renaissance artists. Only copies adorn the building's exterior today but all the originals except one are beautifully displayed in the church's little-known, light and airy museum, open only on Monday in two floors above the church.

Via de' Tornabuoni
STREET

(Map p66) Renaissance palaces and the flagship stores of Italian fashion houses border Via de' Tornabuoni, the city's most expensive shopping strip. Named after a wealthy Florentine noble family (which died out in the 17th century), it is sometimes referred to as the 'Salotto di Firenze' (Florence's Drawing Room).

From the *duomo*, walk west along Via de' Pecori and its extension, Via degli Agli, crossing three streets before coming to Via de' Tornabuoni. Straight ahead, at the T-intersection, is Palazzo Antinori (1461–69), owned by the Antinori family since 1506. One of Florence's most aristocratic families, the Antinori are known for the wines they produce on their Tuscan estates in Chianti (p206). Opposite, huge stone steps lead up to 17th-century Chiesa di San Gaetano.

Palazzo Strozzi
PALACE, GALLERY

(Map p66; www.palazzostrozzi.org; cnr Via de' Tornabuoni & Via degli Strozzi; admission prices & opening hr vary according to exhibition, to 11pm Thu)

ⓘ MONDAY & THURSDAY IN FLORENCE

The Uffizi, Galleria dell'Accademia and most other state museums are shut on Monday. But it's the perfect day for visiting hidden-gem museum Museo di Orsanmichele (p77), above the church of the same name.

Thursday is the day to catch an evening of great art – for free – at Palazzo Strozzi.

This 15th-century palazzo, host to some of the city's most exciting art exhibitions, is one of Florence's most impressive Renaissance mansions. It was built for wealthy merchant Filippo Strozzi, one of the Medicis' major political and commercial rivals. Half palace/half fortress as befits its era and the Strozzi family history (Filippo's entire family was banished from Florence in 1434 and didn't return until 1466), it was built over three levels from large stone blocks. The design, in which Strozzi is thought to have been heavily involved, is incomplete, as he died two years after building commenced and his son soon ran out of money.

The blockbuster exhibitions held here today in its upstairs spaces and the contemporary work in both its basement gallery and imposing internal courtyard are well worth a trip to Florence. Pushchair (stroller) tours, art workshops for kids (see the boxed text, p97) and other activities aimed squarely at families make it a firm favourite with pretty much everyone: There's always a buzz around this place, with young Florentines congregating in the courtyard cafe – one of the best spots in the city for free and easy-to-access wi-fi!

Continuing south along Via de' Tornabuoni you hit Florence's main concentration of luxury designer boutiques, strung along both sides of the street like jewels on a particularly precious necklace. Prada, Gucci, Ferragamo, Gianfranco Ferre, Armani, Pucci and McQueen are all here. Two streets radiating west off Tornabuoni, Via della Spada and Via Della Vigna Nuova, are where more edgy boutiques are found.

Chiesa di Santa Trìnita
CHURCH

(Map p66; Piazza Santa Trinita; admission free; ⓧ8am-noon & 4-6pm Mon-Sat, 4-6pm Sun) Heading towards the Ponte Santa Trìnita, built over the Arno in 1567 and painstakingly restored after being blown up by the Nazis in 1944, you pass this 14th-century church. Built in Gothic style and later given a Mannerist facade of indifferent taste, it shelters some of the best frescoes in the city. The church interior has little natural light, so you'll need to spring for a few coins to illuminate the chapels.

Don't miss Lorenzo Monaco's *Annunciation* (1422) in the Cappella Salimbenes/Bartholini, badly damaged by the 1966 flood but subsequently restored. During the restoration process, another fresco was found underneath, and this was removed

Italy's most divine poet was born in 1265 in a wee house down a narrow lane in the back-streets of Florence. Tragic romance was what made him tick and there's no better place to unravel the medieval life and times of Dante than the Museo Casa di Dante (Map p66; Via Santa Margherita 1; adult/reduced €4/2; ⊗10am-5pm Tue-Sun).

When Dante was just 12 he was promised in marriage to Gemma Donati. But it was another Florentine gal, Beatrice Portinari (1266–90), that was his muse, his inspiration, the love of his life (despite only ever meeting her twice in his life): in *Divina Commedia* (Divine Comedy) Dante broke with tradition by using the familiar Italian, not the formal Latin, to describe travelling through the circles of hell in search of his beloved Beatrice.

Beatrice, who wed a banker and died a couple of years later aged just 24, is buried in 11th-century Chiesa di Santa Margherita (Map p66; Via Santa Margherita 4), tucked down an alley near Dante's house. This was also where the poet married Gemma in 1295. Dimly lit with just a few candles, the tiny chapel remains much as it was in medieval Florence. Top off the old-world experience at neighbouring hole-in-the-wall Da Vinattieri (Via Santa Margherita 4) with a tripe *panino* (sandwich) eaten squatting on a simple wooden stool on this old-fashioned alley in backstreet Florence (see the boxed text, p102).

and placed in the chapel next door. Look out for the crest of the Salimbenes/Bartholini family on the floor of the chapel – it features poppies and the motto *'Per Non Dormire'* (For Those Who Don't Sleep), a reference to the fact that the family fortune resulted from the acquisition of an important cargo of wool from Northern Europe, a deal sealed unbeknown to their business rivals, who had been doped with opium-laced wine at a lavish party the night before the cargo was due to arrive in Florence.

Even more eye-catching are the wonderfully preserved frescoes in the Cappella Sassetti to the right of the altar, which were painted by Ghirlandaio from 1483 to 1485. These depict the life of St Francis of Assisi and include the portraits of many prominent Florentines of the time – Lorenzo Il Magnifico is portrayed with Francesco Sassetti, the merchant who commissioned the work, in *St Francis Receiving the Rule of the Order from Pope Honorius,* which is set in Piazza della Signoria; and Ghirlandaio portrayed himself in the *Miracle of the Boy Brought Back to Life,* which takes place on Piazza Santa Trìnita (he's on the far right, wearing a red cloak).

Museo Salvatore Ferragamo   MUSEUM
(Map p66; www.museoferragamo.it; Via de' Tornabuoni 2; ⊗10am-6pm Wed-Mon) Opposite Chiesa di Santa Trìnita, the splendid 13th-century Palazzo Spini-Feroni has been the home of the Ferragamo fashion empire since 1938. The ground floor is a showcase for its classy shoes, handbags, clothes and accessories

and anyone with even the faintest tendency towards shoe addiction or interested in the socio-historical context of fashion should not miss the esoteric but oddly compelling shoe museum it has in its basement museum.

Classic Ferragamo shoes, many worn by Hollywood stars such as Marilyn Monroe, Judy Garland, Greta Garbo and Sofia Loren, are showcased here and a free audioguide tells the tale of the Ferragamo empire.

Museo di Palazzo
Davanzati   HISTORICAL RESIDENCE
(Map p66; Via Porta Rossa 13; adult/reduced €2/1; ⊗8.15am-1.50pm, closed 1st, 3rd & 5th Mon, 2nd & 4th Sun of month) Tucked inside a 14th-century warehouse and residence aka Palazzo Davanzati, home to the wealthy Davanzati merchant family from 1578, this palazzo museum is a less-visited gem. Peep at the carved faces of the original owners on the pillars in the inner courtyard and don't miss the 1st-floor reception room with its painted wooden ceiling or the exquisitely decorated Sala dei Pappagalli (Parrot Room) and Camera dei Pavoni (Peacock Bedroom).

SANTA MARIA NOVELLA

Radiating west and south from the venerable basilica, the neighbourhood of Santa Maria Novella is blessed with chic boutiques, impressive palaces and art-adorned churches.

Basilica di Santa Maria Novella   CHURCH
(Map p66; Piazza di Santa Maria Novella; adult/child €3.50/free; ⊗9am-5.50pm Mon-Thu, 11am-5.30pm

Fri, 9am-5pm Sat, 1-5pm Sun) Just south of the central train station, Stazione di Santa Maria Novella, this church was begun in the mid-13th century as the Dominican order's Florentine base. Although it was mostly completed by 1360, work on the facade and embellishment of the interior continued well into the 15th century.

The lower section of the green-and-white marble facade is transitional from Romanesque to Gothic, while the upper section and the main doorway were designed by Leon Battista Alberti and completed between 1456 and 1470.

The interior is full of artistic masterpieces. As you enter, look straight ahead and you will see Masaccio's superb fresco *Trinity* (1424–25), one of the first artworks to use the then newly discovered techniques of perspective and proportion. Close by, hanging in the nave, is a luminous painted *Crucifix* by Giotto (c 1290).

The first chapel to the right of the altar, Cappella di Filippo Strozzi, features spirited late 15th-century frescoes by Filippino Lippi (son of Fra' Filippo Lippi) depicting the lives of St John the Evangelist and St Philip the Apostle. Behind the main altar itself are the highlights of the interior – Domenico Ghirlandaio's series of frescoes in the Sanctuary. Relating the lives of the Virgin Mary, St John the Baptist and others, these vibrant frescoes were painted in the late 15th century and are notable for their depiction of Florentine life during the Renaissance. They feature portraits of Ghirlandaio's contemporaries and members of the Tornabuoni family, who commissioned them. To the far left of the altar is the Cappella Strozzi, covered in wonderful frescoes by Narno di Cione; the fine altarpiece here was painted by his brother Andrea, better known as Andrea Orcagna.

Museo di Santa Maria Novella   MUSEUM
(Map p66; Piazza di Santa Maria Novella; adult/reduced €2.70/2; ⊙9am-5pm Mon-Thu & Sat) The indisputable highlight of this museum – arranged around the monastery's tranquil Chiostro Verde (Green Cloister; 1332–62), which takes its name from the green earth base used for the frescoes on three of the cloister's four walls – is the spectacular Cappellone degli Spagnoli (Spanish Chapel). On the north side of the cloister, the chapel is covered in extraordinary frescoes (c 1365–67) by Andrea di Bonaiuto. The vault features depictions of the *Resurrection, As-*cension and *Pentecost,* and on the altar wall are scenes of the *Via Dolorosa, Crucifixion* and *Descent into Limbo.* On the right wall is a huge fresco of *The Militant and Triumphant Church* – look in the foreground for a portrait of Cimabue, Giotto, Boccaccio, Petrarch and Dante. Other frescoes in the chapels depict the *Triumph of Christian Doctrine,* 14 figures symbolising the Arts and Sciences, and the *Life of St Peter.*

On the west side of the cloister, a passage leads to the 14th-century Cappella degli Ubriachi and a large refectory featuring ecclesiastical relics and a 1583 *Last Supper* by Alessandro Allori.

FREE Officina Profumo-Farmaceutica
di Santa Maria Novella   PHARMACY, MUSEUM
(Map p66; www.santamarianovella.com.br; Via della Scala 16; ⊙pharmacy 9.30am-7.30pm Mon-Sat, 10.30am-8.30pm Sun, museum 10am-5.30pm Mon-Fri) In business since 1612, this perfumery-pharmacy began its life when the Dominican friars of Santa Maria Novella began to concoct cures and sweet-smelling unguents using medicinal herbs cultivated in the monastery garden. The shop is an absolute treasure, having changed little over centuries, and its palatial salesrooms stock a wide range of fragrances, remedies, teas and skincare products. After a day battling crowds at the Uffizi or Accademia, you may want to come here for some Aqua di Santa Maria Novella, which is said to cure hysterics.

Chiesa d'Ognissanti   CHURCH
(Map p66; ⊙7am-12.30pm & 4-8pm Mon-Sat, 4-8pm Sun) Stroll the length of lengthy Borgo d'Ognissanti, from Piazza Carlo Goldoni towards ancient city gate Porta al Prato, past antiques shops and designer boutiques to reach this 13th-century church, built as part of a Benedictine monastery. Much altered in the 17th century and given a new facade in the 19th century, it possesses a number of significant paintings, including Domenico Ghirlandaio's fresco of the *Madonna della Misericordia* protecting members of the Vespucci family, the church's main patrons. Amerigo Vespucci, the Florentine navigator who gave his name to the American continent, is supposed to be the young boy whose head peeks between the Madonna and the old man. Also here are a *Crucifixion* by Taddeo Gaddi, Ghirlandaio's *St Jerome* (1480) and Botticelli's pensive *St Augustine* (also 1480). Botticelli, who grew up in a house on Borgo d'Ognissanti, is buried here (look for

the simple round tombstone marked 'Sandro Filipepe' in the south transept).

Museo Stibbert — MUSEUM
(off Map p66; www.museostibbert.it; Via Stibbert 26; adult/reduced €6/4; ⊙10am-2pm Mon-Wed, to 6pm Fri-Sun) Anglo-Italian, Florence-born Frederick Stibbert (1838–1906) was one of the grand 19th-century wheeler-dealers on the European antiquities market and amassed an intriguing personal collection, showcased in Villa di Montughi aka the Stibbert Museum. The Sala della Cavalcata (Parade Room), where life-sized figures of horses and their riders in all manner of suits of armour from Europe and the Middle East rub shoulders, is particularly great for kids. Other varied exhibits include clothes, furnishings, tapestries and 16th- to 19th-century paintings.

Take bus 4 from Stazione di Santa Maria Novella to the 'Gioia' stop on Via Fabroni, from where it is a short walk.

SAN LORENZO
This is Medici territory – come here to see their palace, church, library and mausoleum, all decorated with extraordinary works of art.

Basilica di San Lorenzo — CHURCH
(Map p66; Piazza San Lorenzo; admission €3.50; ⊙10am-5.30pm Mon-Sat year-round, 1.30-5.30pm Sun Mar-Oct) In 1425 Cosimo the Elder, who lived nearby, commissioned Brunelleschi to rebuild the basilica on this site, which dated to the 4th century. The new building would become the Medici parish church and mausoleum – many members of the family are buried here. Considered one of the most harmonious examples of Renaissance architecture, the basilica has never been finished – Michelangelo was commissioned to design the facade in 1518 but his design in white Carrara marble was never executed, hence the building's rough unfinished appearance.

In the austere interior, columns of *pietra serena* (soft grey stone) crowned with Corinthian capitals separate the nave from the two aisles. Donatello, who was still sculpting the two bronze pulpits (1460–67) adorned with panels of the Crucifixion when he died, is buried in the chapel featuring Fra' Filippo Lippi's *Annunciation* (c 1450). Left of the altar is the Sagrestia Vecchia (Old Sacristy), designed by Brunelleschi and decorated in the main by Donatello.

A combined ticket to the basilica and Biblioteca Medicea Laurenziana costs €6.

Biblioteca Medicea Laurenziana — LIBRARY
(Map p66; www.bml.firenze.sbn.it; Piazza San Lorenzo 9; admission €3, basilica & biblioteca €6; ⊙9.30am-1.30pm Mon-Fri) To the left of the basilica's entrance are peaceful cloisters, off which an extraordinary staircase designed by Michelangelo leads to the Biblioteca Medicea Laurenziana, commissioned by Guilio de' Medici (Pope Clement VII) in 1524 to house the extensive Medici library that had been started by Cosimo the Elder and greatly added to by Lorenzo Il Magnifico. The real attraction here is Michelangelo's magnificent vestibule and staircase, designed in walnut but subsequently executed in grey *pietra serena*. Its curvaceous steps are a sign of the master's move towards Mannerism from the stricter bounds of Renaissance architecture and design.

Cappelle Medicee — MAUSOLEUM
(Map p66; Piazza Madonna degli Aldobrandini; adult/reduced €6/3; ⊙8.15am-4.50pm Tue-Sat & 1st & 3rd Sun & 2nd & 4th Mon of month) Nowhere is Medici conceit expressed so explicitly as in their mausoleum, the Medician Chapels. Sumptuously adorned with granite, the most precious marble, semiprecious stones and some of Michelangelo's most beautiful sculptures, it is the burial place of 49 members of the dynasty. Francesco I lies in the grandiose Cappella dei Principi (Princes' Chapel) alongside Ferdinando I and II and Cosimo I, II and III. Lorenzo il Magnifico is buried in the stark but graceful Sagrestia Nuova (New Sacristy), Michelangelo's first architectural work and showcase for three of his most haunting sculptures: *Dawn and Dusk* on the sarcophagus of Lorenzo, Duke of Urbino; *Night and Day* on the sarcophagus of Lorenzo's son Giuliano; and *Madonna and Child*, which adorns Lorenzo's tomb.

Palazzo Medici-Riccardi — PALACE
(Map p66; www.palazzo-medici.it; Via Cavour 3; adult/reduced €7/4; ⊙9am-7pm Thu-Tue) Cosimo the Elder entrusted Michelozzo with the design of the family's townhouse in 1444. The result was this palace, a blueprint that influenced the construction of Florentine family residences such as Palazzo Pitti and Palazzo Strozzi for years to come.

Confident that his power base was solid, Cosimo determined that it wasn't necessary to build a fortress townhouse and allowed Michelozzo to create a self-assured, stout but not inelegant pile on three storeys. The rusticated facade of the ground floor gives a

San Lorenzo & San Marco

rather stern aspect to the building, though the upper two storeys are less aggressive, maintaining restrained classical lines – already a feature of the emerging Renaissance canon. The heavy timber roof has broad eaves protruding over the street below.

The Medici lived here until 1540, making way for the Riccardi family a century later, who gave the palace a comprehensive remodelling and built the sumptuously decorated Sala Lucca Giordano on the 2nd floor. Giordano adorned the ceiling with his complex *Allegory of Divine Wisdom* (1685), a rather overblown example of late baroque dripping with gold leaf and bursting with

colour. The *palazzo* now houses the offices of the Florence Provincial Authority and hosts temporary exhibitions in its public rooms.

The main reason to visit Palazzo Medici-Riccardi, however, is for its upstairs chapel, the Cappella dei Magi. It houses one of the supreme achievements of Renaissance painting and is an absolute must-see for art lovers. The tiny space is covered in a series of wonderfully detailed and recently restored frescoes (c 1459–63) by Benozzo Gozzoli, a pupil of Fra' Angelico. His ostensible theme of *Procession of the Magi to Bethlehem* is but a slender pretext for portraying members of the Medici clan in their best light; try to spy Lorenzo il Magnifico and Cosimo the Elder in the crowd. The chapel was reconfigured to accommodate a baroque staircase – hence the oddly split fresco of a Patriarch on a grey horse. The mid-15th-century altarpiece of the *Adoration of the Child* is a copy of the original (originally here) by Fra' Filippo Lippi. Only 10 visitors are allowed in at a time for a maximum of just five minutes; reserve your slot in advance at the palace ticket desk.

Mercato Centrale   MARKET
(Central Market; Map p82; Piazza del Mercato Centrale; ☺7am-2pm Mon-Fri, to 5pm Sat) Housed in a 19th-century iron-and-glass structure, Florence's oldest and largest food market is noisy, smelly and full of wonderful fresh produce to cook and eat. For a snack while you're here, follow the stream of stallholders making their way to Da Nerbone (p103).

SAN MARCO
This part of the city boasts far more than the city's most famous resident, one Signore *David*. The frescoes in the Museo di San Marco are nothing short of superb.

Galleria dell'Accademia   ART GALLERY
(Map p82; ☎055 29 48 83; Via Ricasoli 60; adult/reduced €6.50/3.25; ☺8.15am-6.50pm Tue-Sun) A lengthy queue marks the door to this gallery, built especially to house one of the greatest masterpieces of the Renaissance, Michelangelo's original *David*.

Fortunately, the most famous statue in the world is worth the long wait. The subtle detail (not quite as illuminated on copies) of the real thing – the veins in his sinewy arms, the muscles in his legs, the change in expression as you move around the statue – is impressive. Carved from a single block of marble already worked on by two sculptors before him (both of who gave up), Michelangelo's most famous work was also his most challenging – he didn't choose the marble himself, it was veined and its larger-than-life dimensions were already decided.

And when the statue of the nude boy-warrior, depicted for the first time as a man in the prime of life rather than a young boy, assumed its pedestal in front of Palazzo Vecchio on Piazza della Signoria in 1504, Florentines immediately adopted it as a powerful emblem of Florentine power, liberty and civic pride.

Michelangelo was also the master behind the unfinished *San Matteo* (St Matthew;

1504–08) and four *Prigioni* ('Prisoners' or 'Slaves'; 1521-30) on display here. The Prisoners seem to be writhing and struggling to free themselves from the marble; they were meant for the tomb of Pope Julius II, itself never completed. Adjacent rooms contain paintings by Andrea Orcagna, Taddeo Gaddi, Domenico Ghirlandaio, Filippino Lippi and Sandro Botticelli.

TOP / CHOICE **Museo di San Marco**   MUSEUM
(Map p82; Piazza San Marco 1; adult/reduced €4/2; ☺8.15am-1.50pm Mon-Fri, to 4.50pm Sat & Sun, closed 1st, 3rd & 5th Sun of month & 2nd & 4th Mon) At the heart of Florence's university area sits the **Chiesa di San Marco** and adjoining 15th-century Dominican monastery where both gifted painter Fra' Angelico (c 1395-1455) and the sharp-tongued Savonarola piously served God. Today the monastery showcases the work of Fra' Angelico. It is one of Florence's most spiritually uplifting museums.

Enter via Michelozzo's **Cloister of Saint Antoninus** (1440). Turn immediately right to enter the **Sala dell'Ospizio** (Pilgrims' Hospital), where Fra' Angelico's attention to perspective and the realistic portrayal of nature comes to life in a number of major paintings, including the *Deposition of Christ* (1432), originally commissioned for the church of Santa Trìnita.

Giovanni Antonio Sogliani's fresco *The Miraculous Supper of St Domenic* (1536) dominates the former monks' **refectory** in the cloister; and Fra' Angelico's huge *Crucifixion and Saints* fresco (1441-42) decorates the former **chapterhouse**. But it is the 44 **monastic cells** on the 1st floor that are the most haunting: at the top of the stairs, Fra' Angelico's most famous work, *Annunciation* (c 1440), commands all eyes. A stroll around each of the cells reveals snippets of many more fine religious reliefs by the Tuscan-born friar, who decorated the cells between 1440 and 1441 with deeply devotional frescoes to guide the meditation of his fellow friars. Most were executed by Fra' Angelico himself; others are by aides under his supervision, including Benozzo Gozzoli. Among several masterpieces is the magnificent *Adoration of the Magi* in the cell used by Cosimo the Elder as a meditation retreat (Nos 38 to 39). Quite a few of the frescoes are extremely gruesome – check out the cell of San Antonino Arcivescovo, which features a depiction of Jesus pushing open

WHO'S THAT BLOKE?

Name *David*

Occupation World's most famous sculpture.

Vital statistics Height: 516cm tall, weight: 19 tonnes of mediocre-quality pearly white marble from the Fantiscritti quarries in Carrara.

Spirit Young biblical hero in meditative pose who, with the help of God, defeats an enemy more powerful than himself. Scarcely visible sling emphasises victory of innocence and intellect over brute force.

Commissioned In 1501 by the Opera del Duomo for the cathedral, but subsequently placed in front of the Palazzo Vecchio on Piazza della Signoria where it stayed until 1873.

Famous journeys It took 40 men four days to transport the statue on rails from Michelangelo's workshop behind the cathedral to Piazza della Signoria in 1504. Its journey from here, through the streets of Florence, to its current purpose-built tribune in the Galleria dell'Accademia in 1873 took seven long days.

Outstanding features (a) His expression which, from the left profile, appears serene, Zen and boy-like, from the right, concentrated, manly and highly charged in anticipation of the gargantuan Goliath he is about to slay; (b) the sense of counterbalanced weight rippling through his body, from the tension in his right hip on which he leans to his taut left arm.

Why the small penis? In classical art a large or even normal-sized packet was not deemed elegant, hence the daintier size.

And the big head and hands? *David* was designed to stand up high on a cathedral buttress in the apse, from where his head and hand would have appeared in perfect proportion.

Beauty treatments Body scrub with hydrochloric acid (1843); clay and cellulose pulp 'mud pack', bath in distilled water (2004).

Occupational hazards Over the centuries he's been struck by lightning, attacked by rioters and had his toes bashed with a hammer. The two pale white lines visible on his lower left arm is where his arm got broken during the 1527 revolt when the Medici were kicked out of Florence. Giorgio Vasari, then a child, picked up the pieces and 16 years later had them sent to Cosimo I who restored the statue, so the story goes.

the door of his sepulchre, squashing a nasty-looking devil in the process. After centuries of being known as 'Il Beato Angelico' (literally 'The Blessed Angelic One') or simply 'Il Beato' (The Blessed), the Renaissance's most blessed religious painter was made a saint by Pope John Paul II in 1984.

Contrasting with the pure beauty of these frescoes are the plain rooms that Savonarola called home from 1489. Rising to the position of prior at the Dominican convent, it was from here that the fanatical monk railed against luxury, greed and corruption of the clergy. Kept as a kind of shrine to the turbulent priest, they house a portrait, a few personal items, the linen banner Savonarola carried in processions and a grand marble monument erected by admirers in 1873.

Piazza della Santissima Annunziata PIAZZA

(Map p82) Giambologna's equestrian statue of Grand Duke Ferdinando I de' Medici commands the scene from the centre of this square, which teems with more students than tourists. Across the street, Chiesa della Santissima Annunziata was established in 1250 by the founders of the Servite order, and rebuilt by Michelozzo and others in the mid-15th century. It is dedicated to the Virgin Mary and has frescoes by Perugino (in the fifth chapel) and Andrea del Sarto (in the atrium). Visitors often find it hard to squeeze in between the seven Masses held each morning.

The Ospedale degli Innocenti (Hospital of the Innocents) was founded on the southeastern side of the piazza in 1421 as Europe's first orphanage, hence the 'Innocents' in its name. Brunelleschi designed the classically influenced portico, which Andrea della Robbia (1435–1525) famously decorated with terracotta medallions of babies in swaddling clothes. At the north end of the portico, the false door surrounded by railings was once a revolving door where unwanted children were left. Inside, the **Museo degli Innocenti** (Map p82; www.istitutodeglinnocenti.it; Piazza della Santissima Annunziata 12; adult/reduced €5/4; ⊙10am-7pm daily) on the 2nd floor displays works by Florentine artists, including Domenico Ghirlandaio's striking *Adoration of the Magi* (1488), two wonderfully serene wooden sculptures of the *Madonna* and *St Joseph* by Marco della Robbia (c 1505), a *Madonna with Holy Child and Angel* (1465-66) by Botticelli and a charming *Madonna of the Innocents* (c 1440) by Domenico di Michelino. Less valuable, but even more moving, is the display case of 19th-century markers left on the clothing of abandoned babies to allow for eventual reunification with their mothers.

About 200m southeast of the piazza is the **Museo Archeologico** (Map p82; Via della Colonna 38; adult/reduced €4/2; ⊙8.30am-7pm Tue-Fri), whose rich collection of finds, including most of the Medici hoard of antiquities, plunges you deep into the past and offers an alternative to Renaissance splendour. On the 1st floor you can either head left into the ancient Egyptian collection or right for the smaller section on Etruscan and Graeco-Roman art.

SANTA CROCE

Presided over by the massive Franciscan basilica of the same name on the neighbourhood's main square, this area has a slightly rough veneer to it.

Piazza di Santa Croce   PIAZZA
(Map p86) This square was initially cleared in the Middle Ages, primarily to allow hordes of the faithful to gather when the church itself was full. In Savonarola's day, heretics were executed here.

Such an open space inevitably found other uses, and from the 14th century it was often the colourful scene of jousts, festivals and *calcio storico* matches. Still played in this square in the third week of June each year, *calcio storico* (www.calciostorico.it) is like a combination of football and rugby with few rules (headbutting, punching, elbowing and choking are allowed, but sucker-punching and kicks to the head are forbidden). Look

for the marble stone embedded in the wall below the gaily frescoed facade of **Palazzo dell'Antella**, on the south side of the piazza; it marks the halfway line on this, one of the oldest football pitches in the world.

Curiously enough, the Romans used to have fun in much the same area centuries before. The city's 2nd-century amphitheatre took up the area facing the western end of Piazza di Santa Croce. To this day, Piazza dei Peruzzi, Via de' Bentaccordi and Via Torta mark the oval outline of the north, west and south sides of its course.

Basilica di Santa Croce   CHURCH
(Map p86; Piazza di Santa Croce; adult/reduced incl Museo dell'Opera di Santa Croce €5/3, audioguide 1/2 people €5/7; ⊙9.30am-5.30pm Mon-Sat, 1-5.30pm Sun) When Lucy Honeychurch, the heroine of EM Forster's *A Room With a View*, is stranded in Santa Croce without a Baedeker, she first panics and then, looking around, wonders why it's thought to be such an important building. After all, doesn't it look just like a barn ('a black and white facade of surprising ugliness')?

On entering, many visitors share the same reaction. This massive Franciscan basilica has an austere interior can come as something of a shock after the magnificent neo-Gothic facade, which is enlivened by varying shades of coloured marble (both it and the *campanile* are 19th-century additions). The church itself was designed by Arnolfo di Cambio between 1294 and 1385 and owes its name to a splinter of the Holy Cross donated by King Louis of France in 1258.

Though most visitors come to see the tombs of famous Florentines buried inside this church – including Michelangelo, Galileo, Ghiberti and Machiavelli – it's the frescoes by Giotto and his school in the chapels to the right of the altar that are the real highlights. Some of these are substantially better preserved than others – Giotto's murals in the **Cappella Peruzzi** are in particularly poor condition. Fortunately, those in the **Cappella Bardi** (1315-20) depicting scenes from the life of St Francis have fared better. Giotto's assistant and most loyal pupil, Taddeo Gaddi, frescoed the neighbouring **Cappella Majeure** and nearby **Cappella Baroncelli** (1332-38); the latter takes as its subject the life of the Virgin.

Taddeo's son Agnolo painted the **Cappella Castellani** (1385) with delightful frescoes depicting the life of St Nicholas (later

FLORENCE

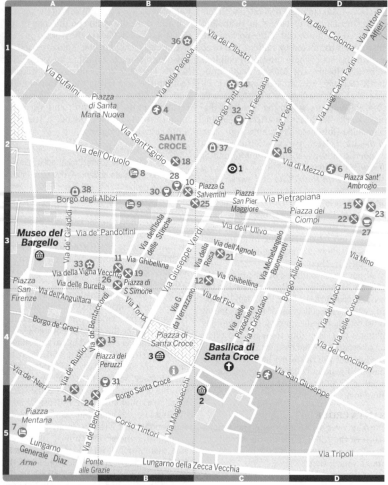

transformed into 'Santa Claus') and was also responsible for the frescoes above the altar.

From the transept chapels a doorway designed by Michelozzo leads into a corridor, off which is the Sagrestia, an enchanting 14th-century room dominated on the left by Taddeo Gaddi's fresco of the Crucifixion. There are also a few relics of St Francis on show, including his cowl and belt. Through the next room, the church bookshop, you can access the Scuola del Cuoio (p96), a leather school where you can see the goods being fashioned and buy the finished products. At the end of the corridor is a Medici chapel with a fine two-tone altarpiece in glazed terracotta by Andrea della Robbia.

Brunelleschi designed the second of Santa Croce's two serene cloisters just before his death in 1446. His unfinished Cappella de' Pazzi at the end of the first cloister is notable for its harmonious lines and restrained terracotta medallions of the Apostles by Luca della Robbia, and is a masterpiece of Renaissance architecture. It was built for, but never used by, the wealthy banking family destroyed in the 1468 Pazzi Conspiracy – when papal sympathisers sought to overthrow Lorenzo il Magnifico and the Medici dynasty.

Museo del Bargello ART MUSEUM

(Map p86; Via del Proconsolo 4; adult/reduced €7/3.50; ⊙8.15am-5pm Tue-Sun & 1st & 3rd Mon of month) It was behind the stark exterior of Palazzo del Bargello, Florence's earliest public building, that the *podestà* meted out justice from the late 13th century until 1502. Today the building safeguards Italy's most comprehensive collection of Tuscan Renaissance pieces and some of Michelangelo's best early works.

Michelangelo was just 21 when a cardinal commissioned him to create the drunken grape-adorned *Bacchus* (1496–97) displayed in Bargello's downstairs Sala di Michelangelo. Unfortunately the cardinal didn't like the result and sold it to a banker. Other Michelangelo works to look out for here include the marble bust of *Brutus* (c 1539–40), the *David/Apollo* from 1530–32 and the large, uncompleted roundel of the *Madonna and Child with the Infant St John* (1503–05, aka the *Tondo Pitti*).

After Michelangelo left Florence for the final time in 1534, sculpture was dominated by Baccio Bandinelli (his 1551 *Adam and Eve,* created for the *duomo,* is displayed in the Sala di Michelangelo) and Benvenuto Cellini (look for his playful 1548–50 marble *Ganimede* in the same room).

On the 1st floor, to the right of the staircase, is the Sala di Donatello. Here, in the majestic Salone del Consiglio Generale where the city's general council met, works by Donatello and other early-15th-century sculptors can be admired. Originally on the facade of Chiesa di Orsanmichele and now within a tabernacle at the hall's far end, Donatello's wonderful *St George* (1416–17) brought a new sense of perspective and movement to Italian sculpture. Also look for the bronze bas-reliefs created for the Baptistry doors competition by Brunelleschi and Ghiberti.

Yet it is Donatello's two versions of *David,* a favourite subject for sculptors, which really fascinate: Donatello fashioned his slender, youthful dressed image in marble in 1408 and his fabled bronze between 1440 and 1450. The latter is extraordinary – the more so when you consider it was the first free-standing naked statue to be sculpted since classical times.

Criminals received their last rites before execution in the palace's 1st-floor Cappella del Podestà, also known as the Mary Magdalene Chapel, where *Hell* and *Paradise* are

Located off the first cloister, the Museo dell'Opera di Santa Croce features a *Crucifixion* by Cimabue, restored to the best degree possible after flood damage in 1966, when more than 4m of water inundated the Santa Croce area.

Other highlights include Donatello's gilded bronze statue *St Louis of Toulouse* (1424), originally placed in a tabernacle on the Orsanmichele facade; a wonderful terracotta bust of St Francis receiving the stigmata by the della Robbia workshop; and frescoes by Taddeo Gaddi, including *The Last Supper* (1333).

Santa Croce

frescoed on the walls, as are stories from the lives of Mary of Egypt, Mary Magdalene and John the Baptist. These remnants of frescoes by Giotto were not discovered until 1840, when the chapel was turned into a storeroom and prison.

The 2nd floor moves into the 16th century with a superb collection of terracotta pieces by the prolific della Robbia family, including some of their best-known works, such as Andrea's *Ritratto idealizia di fanciullo* (Bust of a Boy; c 1475) and Giovanni's *Pietà* (1514). Instantly recognisable, Giovanni's works are more elaborate and flamboyant than either father Luca's or cousin Andrea's, using a larger palette of colours.

OLTRARNO

Literally 'other side of the Arno', atmospheric Oltrarno is the traditional home of the city's artisanal workshops. It embraces the area south of the river and west of Ponte Vecchio and its backbone is busy Borgo San Jacopo, clad with restaurants, shops and a twinset of 12th-century towers, Torre dei Marsili (Map p90) and Torre de' Belfredelli (Map p90).

When you reach the stage of museum overload and need to stretch your legs and see some sky, the tier of parks and gardens behind Palazzo Pitti – not to be missed at sunset when its entire vast facade is coloured a vibrant pink – are just the ticket.

Ponte Vecchio   LANDMARK
(Map p90) The first documentation of a stone bridge here, at the narrowest crossing point along the entire length of the Arno, dates from 972. The Arno looks placid enough, but when it gets mean, it gets very mean. Floods in 1177 and 1333 destroyed the bridge, and in 1966 it came close to being destroyed again. Many of the jewellers with shops on the bridge were convinced the floodwa-

ters would sweep away their livelihoods; however – fortunately – the bridge held.

They're still here. Indeed, the bridge has twinkled with the glittering wares of jewellers, their trade often passed down from generation to generation, ever since the 16th century, when Ferdinando I de' Medici ordered them here to replace the often malodorous presence of the town butchers, who used to toss unwanted leftovers into the river.

The bridge as it stands was built in 1345 and was the only one saved from destruction at the hands of the retreating Germans in 1944. What you see above the shops on the eastern side is the infamous Corridoio Vasariano built rather oddly around – rather than straight through – the medieval Torre dei Mannelli (Map p90) at the bridge's southern end. For details about the Corridoio Vasariano, see the boxed text, p73.

Basilica di Santo Spirito
CHURCH

(Map p90; Piazza Santo Spirito; admission free; ☺9.30am-12.30pm & 4-5.30pm Thu-Tue) The facade of this Brunelleschi church, smart on Florence's most shabby chic (some might say grungy) piazza, is most striking on summer nights when it forms an atmospheric backdrop to open-air concerts and a buzzing outdoor social scene.

Inside, the entire length of the basilica is lined by a series of semicircular chapels, and the colonnade of grey *pietra forte* Corinthian columns lends an air of monumental grandeur. Artworks to look out for include Domenico di Zanobi's *Madonna of the Relief* (1485) in the Cappella Velutti, in which the Madonna wards off a little red devil with a club, and Filippino Lippi's poorly lit *Madonna with Child and Saints* (1493–94) in the Cappella Nerli in the right transept. The main altar, beneath the central dome, is a voluptuous baroque flourish, rather out of place in Brunelleschi's characteristically spare interior. Ask an attendant to show you the sacristy, where you'll find a poignant

COMBINATION TICKETS

If you plan to visit the Cappella Brancacci and Palazzo Vecchio (p73) buy a combined ticket costing €8/6 (adult/reduced) and valid for three months.

wooden crucifix attributed by some experts to Michelangelo.

Next door to the church is the Cenacolo di Santo Spirito (Map p90; Piazza Santo Spirito 29; admission €2.50; ☺9am-5pm Sat Apr-Oct, 10.30am-1.30pm Sat Nov-Mar). Andrea Orcagna decorated this refectory with a grand fresco depicting the *Last Supper* and the *Crucifixion* (c 1370). Also on display is a collection of rare pre-Romanesque sculptures.

Cappella Brancacci
CHAPEL

(Map p90; ☎055 276 82 24, 055 76 85 58; Piazza del Carmine; admission €4; ☺10am-5pm Wed-Sat & Mon, 1-5pm Sun) On the southern flank of Piazza del Carmine, now a car park, 13th-century church Basilica di Santa Maria del Carmine was all but destroyed by fire in the late 18th century. Fortunately the fire spared the magnificent frescoes in its Cappella Brancacci, entered via the entrance to the cloisters, to the right of the church entrance. A maximum of 30 visitors are allowed into the chapel at a time, and you *must* book in advance. Visits are often marred by the belligerent attitude taken by the attendants, who strictly enforce the ridiculous 15-minute-visit rule that applies here. How the authorities think that this is enough time to appreciate the magnificent frescoes on show is an absolute mystery.

This chapel is a treasure of paintings by Masolino da Panicale, Masaccio and Filippino Lippi. Masaccio's fresco cycle illustrating the life of St Peter is considered among his greatest works, representing a definitive break with Gothic art and a plunge into new worlds of expression in the early stages of the Renaissance. *The Expulsion of Adam and Eve from Paradise* and *The Tribute Money,* both on the left side of the chapel, are his best-known works. Masaccio painted these frescoes in his early 20s, taking over from Masolino, and interrupted the task to go to Rome, where he died, aged only 27. The cycle was completed some 60 years later by Filippino Lippi. Masaccio himself features in his *St Peter Enthroned;* he's the one standing beside the Apostle, staring out at the viewer. The figures around him have been identified as Brunelleschi, Masolino and Alberti. Filippino Lippi also painted himself into the scene of *St Peter's Crucifixion,* along with his teacher, Botticelli.

Palazzo Pitti
MUSEUM

(Map p90; Piazza Pitti 1; adult with/without temporary exhibition & Museo degli Argenti, Museo

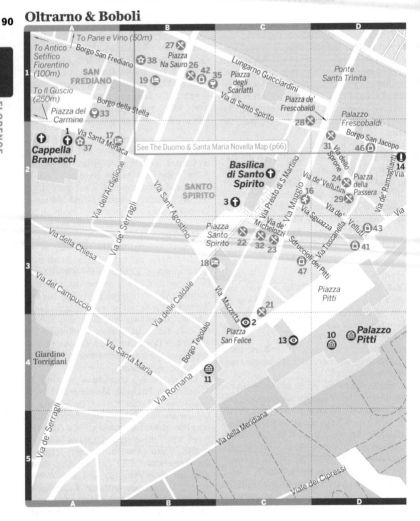

delle Porcellane & Galleria del Costume €10/7, adult with/without temporary exhibition & Galleria Palatina, Galleria d'Arte Moderna & Appartamenti Reali €12/8.50, adult 3-day ticket valid when no temporary exhibition €11.50) Wealthy banker Luca Pitti commissioned Brunelleschi to design this forbidding-looking palace in 1457, but by the time it was completed the family fortunes were on the wane, forcing them to sell it to arch-rivals, the Medici, in 1549. Following the demise of the Medici dynasty, the *palazzo* remained the residence of the city's rulers, the Habsburg-Lorraine grand dukes of Tuscany. When Florence was made capital

of the nascent Kingdom of Italy in 1865, it became a residence of the Savoy royal family, who presented it to the state in 1919.

Our recent stroll around the ground-floor Museo degli Argenti (Silver Museum; ☺8.15am-7.30pm Jun-Aug, shorter hr rest year, closed 1st & last Mon of month) was notable for the fact that no silver was on display. Go figure. Come instead to see the elaborately frescoed audience chambers, which host temporary exhibitions. These include the Sala di Giovanni da San Giovanni, which sports lavish head-to-toe frescoes (1635–42) celebrating the life of Lorenzo Il Magnifico –

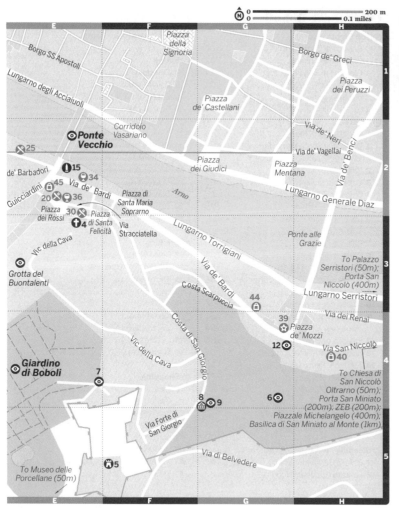

FLORENCE SIGHTS & ACTIVITIES

spot Michelangelo giving Lorenzo a statue. 'Talk little, be brief and witty' is the curt motto above the painted staircase in the next room, the public audience chamber, where the grand duke received visitors in the presence of his court.

Raphaels and Rubens vie for centre stage in the enviable collection of 16th- to 18th-century art amassed by the Medici and Lorraine dukes in the 1st-floor **Galleria Palatina** (⊘8.15am-6.50pm Tue-Sun), reached by a staircase from the palace's central courtyard. This gallery has retained the original display arrangement of paintings (squeezed

in, often on top of each other) so can be visually overwhelming – go slow and focus on the works one by one.

Highlights include Fra' Filippo Lippi's *Madonna and Child with Stories from the Life of St Anne* (aka the Tondo Bartolini; 1452–53) and Botticelli's *Madonna with Child and a Young Saint John the Baptist* (c 1490–95) in the Sala di Prometeo; Raphael's *Madonna of the Window* (1513–14) in the Sala di Ulisse; and Caravaggio's *Sleeping Cupid* (1608) in the Sala dell'Educazione di Giove. Don't miss the Sala di Saturno, which is full of magnificent works by Raphael,

Oltrarno & Boboli

including the *Madonna of the Chair* (1511) and portraits of Anolo Doni and Maddalena Strozzi (c 1506). Nearby, in the Sala di Giove, the same artist's *Lady with a Veil* (aka *La Velata;* c 1516) holds court alongside Giorgione's *Three Ages of Man* (c 1500). The sentimental favourite, Tiberio Titi's charming portrait of the young Prince Leopoldo de' Medici, hangs in the Sala di Apollo, and the Sala di Venere shines with Titian's *Portrait of a Lady* (c 1536).

Past the Sala di Venere are the Appartamenti Reali (Royal Apartments; ⊘8.15am-6.50pm Tue-Sun Feb-Dec), a series of rooms presented as they were circa 1880–91, when they were occupied by members of the House of Savoy. The style and division of tasks assigned to each room is reminiscent of Spanish royal palaces, all heavily bedecked with drapes, silk and chandeliers. Each room has a colour theme, ranging from aqua green to deep-wine red.

Forget about Marini, Mertz or Clemente. By 'modern' the curators of Palazzo Pitti's 2nd-floor Galleria d'Arte Moderna (Gallery of Modern Art; ⊘8.15am-6.50pm Tue-Sun) mean 18th and 19th century (again, go figure). Late-19th-century works by artists of the Florentine Macchiaioli school (the local equivalent of Impressionism), including Telemaco Signorini (1835–1901) and Giovanni Fattori (1825–1908), dominate the collection.

Few visitors get as far as the Galleria del Costume (Costume Gallery; ☺8.15am-7.30pm Jun-Aug, shorter hr rest year, closed 1st & last Mon of month), thus missing its absolutely fascinating, if somewhat macabre, display of the semidecomposed burial clothes of Cosimo I, his wife Eleonora di Toledo and their son Don Garzia. Considering their age and the fact that they were buried for centuries, Eleanora's gown and silk stockings are remarkably preserved, as are Cosimo's satin doublet and wool breeches and Garzia's doublet, beret and short cape. In contrast, the sculptural 1990s haute couture pieces by Maurizio Galante look as if they've just been created – they're guaranteed to impress.

FREE Giardino di Boboli   PALACE GARDEN
(Map p90; Piazza Pitti; ☺8.15am-sunset) Behind Palazzo Pitti, the Boboli Gardens laid out in the mid-16th century according to a design by architect Niccolò Pericoli are a prime example of a formal Tuscan garden and they are great fun to get lost in: skip along the Cypress Alley; let the imagination rip with a gallant frolic in the walled Giardino del Cavaliere (Knights' Garden); dance around 170-odd statues; meditate next to the Isoletto, a gorgeous ornamental pool; discover birdsong and species in the garden along the signposted nature trail; or watch Venere (Venus) by Giambologna rise from the waves in the Grotta del Buontalenti (☺guided visits hourly 11am-6pm Jun-Sep, to 5pm Mar, May & Oct, to 4pm Nov-Feb), a fanciful grotto designed by the eponymous artist. Other typical Renaissance garden features include a six-tier amphitheatre, originally embellished with 24 niches sheltering classical statues surrounded by animals; an orangery (limonaia; 1777), which stills keeps around 500 citrus trees snug in winter; and a botanical garden. The 17th-century maze, a Tuscan horticultural standard, was razed in the 1830s to make way for a driveway for carriages. Don't miss the monumental 'face' sculpture (1998) by Polish sculptor Igor Mitoraj (b 1944), who lives in Pietrasanta near Carrara today.

GARDEN STROLL

An easy footpath leads from Giardino di Boboli to Giardino Bardini; the gate between the two – a mere five-minute walk – shuts at 5pm.

At the upper, southern limit of the gardens, fantastic views over the Florentine countryside fan out beyond the box-hedged rose garden where the Museo delle Porcellane (Porcelain Museum) is located. This is home to Sèvres, Vincennes, Meissen, Wedgwood and other porcelain pieces collected by Palazzo Pitti's wealthy tenants.

TOP CHOICE Giardino Bardini   GARDEN
(Map p90; www.bardinipeyron.it; entrances at Via de' Bardi 1r & Costa di San Giorgio 2; adult/reduced incl Giardino di Boboli & Museo delle Porcellane €10/5; ☺8.15am-sunset) Florence's little-known Giardino Bardini was named after art collector Stefano Bardini (1836–1922), who bought the villa in 1913, restored much of its medieval garden and created new garden elements. Smaller and more manicured than the Boboli, it has all the features of a quintessential Tuscan garden – artificial grottos, orangery, marble statues, fountains, loggia, amphitheatre and a monumental baroque stone staircase staggering up the beautiful tiered gardens – but not the crowds. A springtime stroll is an extra-special joy when its azaleas, peonies, wisteria (all April and May) and irises (June) are in bloom. Its somewhat idyllic, summer cafe terrace, set in a stone loggia overlooking the Florentine skyline, is a wonderful spot for a *panino* lunch, ice cream or afternoon tea.

Inside the villa, the Museo Bardini (www. bardinipeyron.it, in Italian; adult/reduced €6/4; ☺10am-6pm Wed-Sun Apr-Sep, to 4pm Wed-Fri, to 6pm Sat & Sun Oct-Mar) hosts a collection of Roberto Capucci–designed haute couture and temporary exhibitions.

Casa Guidi   MUSEUM
(Map p90; ☎055 28 43 93; www.browningsociety. org; Piazza San Felice 8; admission free; ☺3-6pm Mon, Wed & Fri Apr-Nov) It was here, on the ground floor of 15th-century Palazzo Guidi, across from the south wing of Palazzo Pitti, that Robert and Elizabeth Browning rented an apartment in 1847, a year after their marriage. Robert wrote *Men and Women* in the apartment they called home for 14 years and poetess Elizabeth both gave birth to their only child here and died here. Britain's Eton College owns the literary-rich apartment today, which can be rented for short stays.

TOP CHOICE Museo di Storia Naturale – Zoologia La Specola   MUSEUM
(Map p90; Via Romana 17; adult/reduced €6/3, family ticket €12; ☺10.30am-5.30pm daily) One

of several sections of Florence's natural history museum (part of Florence University) dating back to 1775, La Specola showcases a vast collection of 5000-odd animals (out of an unbelievable depository of 3.5 million). But the big highlight, not recommended for the squeamish or young children, is the collection of wax models of bits of human anatomy in varying states of bad health. An offbeat change from all that art and history!

Via de' Bardi STREET
(Map p90) Walking east from Ponte Vecchio, the first stretch of Via de' Bardi shows clear signs of its recent history. This entire area was flattened by German mines in 1944, and hastily rebuilt in questionable taste after the war. The street spills into Piazza di Santa Maria Soprarno. Follow the narrow Via de' Bardi (the right fork) away from the square and you enter a pleasantly quieter corner of Florence. The powerful Bardi family once owned all the houses along this street, but by the time Cosimo the Elder wed Contessina de' Bardi in 1415, the latter's family was on the decline.

Via de' Bardi ends on Piazza de' Mozzi, surrounded by the sturdy facades of grand residences. Pope Gregory X stayed at Palazzo de' Mozzi (Map p90; Piazza de' Mozzi 2) when brokering peace between the Guelphs and Ghibellines.

Forte di Belvedere FORTRESS
(Map p90) From Piazza de' Mozzi turn east down Via dei Renai, past leafy Piazza Nicola Demidoff, dedicated to the 19th-century Russian philanthropist who lived nearby in Via San Niccolò. At the end of Via dei Renai, 16th-century Palazzo Serristori (off Map p90) was home to Joseph Bonaparte in the last years of his life until his death in 1844; a humble end to the man who, at the height of his career, had been appointed king of Spain by his brother Napoleon.

Turn right and you end up on Via San Niccolò; walk east along this street to emerge at the tower marking Porta San Niccolò (off Map p90), all that is left of the city walls. To get an idea of what the walls were once like, walk south from Chiesa di San Niccolò Oltrarno through Porta San Miniato (off Map p90). The wall extends a short way to the east and for a stretch further west, up a steep hill that leads you to Forte di Belvedere, a rambling fort designed by Bernardo Buontalenti for Grand Duke Ferdinando I at the end of the 16th century. From this massive bulwark soldiers kept watch on four fronts – as much for internal security to protect the Palazzo Pitti as against foreign attack. At the time of research the fort was closed for restoration.

Piazzale Michelangelo VIEWPOINT
(off Map p90) Turn your back on the bevy of ticky-tacky souvenir stalls flogging *David* statues and boxer shorts and take in the spectacular city panorama from this vast square, pierced by one of Florence's two *David* copies. Sunset here is particularly dramatic. It's a 10-minute uphill walk along the serpentine road, paths and steps that scale the hillside from the Arno and Piazza Giuseppe Poggi; from Piazza San Niccolò walk uphill and bear left up the long flight of steps signposted Viale Michelangelo. Or take bus 13 from Stazione di Santa Maria Novella.

Basilica di San Miniato al Monte CHURCH, VIEWPOINT
(Map p90; Via Monte alle Croce; ☉8am-7pm May-Oct, 8am-noon & 3-6pm Nov-Apr) The real point of your exertions up to Piazzale Michelangelo is five minutes' further uphill to this wonderful Romanesque basilica – the view of the city skyline from its terrace is superb. The church is dedicated to St Minias, an early Christian martyr in Florence who is said to have flown to this spot after his death down in the town (or, if you care to believe an alternative version, to have walked up the hill with his head tucked underneath his arm).

The church dates from the early 11th century. Its typically Tuscan multicoloured marble facade, which features a mosaic depicting Christ between the Virgin and St Minias, was added a couple of centuries later and is one of the most beautiful in all Italy. Inside, 13th- to 15th-century frescoes adorn the south wall and intricate inlaid marble designs line the length of the nave, leading to a fine Romanesque crypt. The raised choir and presbytery have an intricate marble pulpit and screen, rich in complex geometrical designs. The sacristy in the southeast corner features frescoes by Spinello Aretino depicting the life of St Benedict.

Slap bang in the middle of the nave is the bijou Cappella del Crocefisso, a 15th-century tabernacle designed by Michelozzo and decorated by artists including Agnolo Gaddi and Luca della Robbia. The 15th-century Cappella del Cardinale del Portogallo, beside the north aisle, features a tomb by Antonio Rossellino and a tabernacle ceiling in terracotta by Luca della Robbia.

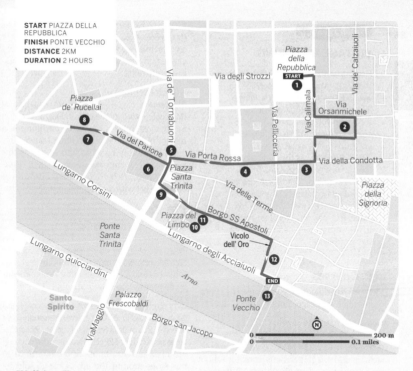

Walking Tour
Quintessential Florence

❯ Start with coffee on ❶ **Piazza della Repubblica**, then walk one block south along Via Calimala and turn left onto Via Orsanmichele to ❷ **Chiesa e Museo di Orsanmichele**, a unique church with ornate statuary adorning its facade and a fascinating museum inside. Backtrack to Via Calimala and continue walking south until you see the loggia of ❸ **Mercato Nuovo**. The 16th-century market building was called the 'New Market' to differentiate it from the Mercato Vecchio (Old Market) on the same site since the 11th century. Florentines know it as 'Il Porcellino' (The Piglet) after the bronze statue of a wild boar on its southern side. Rub its snout to ensure your return to Florence.

Walk past the market and along Via Porta Rossa to ❹ **Palazzo Davanzati** with its magnificent studded doors and fascinating museum inside. A few doors down, next to the Slowly bar, peep through the sturdy iron gate and look up to admire the ancient brick vaults of this dark hidden alley – this is hidden Florence of 1001 fabulous doors and lost alleys at its best!

Continue to ❺ **Via de' Tornabuoni** with its luxury designer boutiques. Swoon over frescoed chapels in ❻ **Chiesa di Santa Trinita**, then wander down Via del Parione to visit paper marbler ❼ **Alberto Cozzi** and puppet maker ❽ **Letizia Fiorini**.

Backtrack to Via de' Tornabuoni and turn right, past 13th-century ❾ **Palazzo Spini-Feroni**, home of Salvatore Ferragamo's flagship store and a rather stylish shoe museum, to Borgo Santissimi Apostoli. A short way ahead on Piazza del Limbo is the Romanesque ❿ **Chiesa dei Santissimi Apostoli**, in a sunken square once used as a cemetery for unbaptised babies.

After browsing for Tuscan olive oil in ⓫ **La Bottega dell' Olio**, continue east and turn right into Vicolo dell' Oro, home to the ⓬ **Hotel Continental**, whose sleek rooftop terrace, open to nonguests, is the perfect spot for a sundowner with a ⓭ **Ponte Vecchio** view.

DON'T MISS

VINTAGE MOTORING

Hook up with Florence's **500 Touring Club** (Map p66; ☏334 9965836; www.500touringclub.com; Via Vinegia 23r) for a guided tour in a vintage motor – with you behind the wheel! Every car has a name in this outfit's fleet of gorgeous vintage Fiat 500s from the 1960s (Giacomo is the playboy, Sergio the speed-fiend king, Anna the girl with style and so on). Motoring tours are guided – hop in your car and follow the leader – and themed; families love the picnic trip, couples wine tasting. March to November tours need to be booked well in advance.

🍴 Courses

Florence has zillions of schools running courses in Italian language, culture and cuisine.

Scuola di Arte Culnaria
Cordon Bleu   COOKING
(Map p86; ☏055 234 54 68; www.cordonbleu-it.com; Via di Mezzo 55r) Serious cooking school for amateurs and professionals with heaps of short-term, long-term and one-off courses; courses for kids too.

Scuola del Cuoio   LEATHER WORKING
(Map p86; ☏055 24 45 34; www.scuoladelcuoio.com; Via San Giuseppe 5r) Leather-working courses in a leather school created by Franciscan friars after WWII.

In Tavola   COOKING
(Map p90; ☏055 21 76 72; www.intavola.org; Via dei Velluti 18r) Take your pick from dozens of carefully crafted courses for beginners and professionals: pizza and gelato, pasta making, easy Tuscan dinners etc.

Food & Wine Academy   COOKING
(Map p66; ☏055 012 39 94; www.florencecookingclasses.com; Via de' Lamberti 1; 1-day class with lunch €79) Shop at the market with charismatic chef Giovanni, learn how to cook what you've bought, then eat it.

La Cucina del Garga   COOKING
(Map p66; ☏055 21 13 96; www.divinacucina.com; Via del Moro 48r; 1-day class with lunch €155) Delve into the secrets of Florentine trattoria cuisine at Trattoria Garga with American-born, Florence-based Sharon Oddson.

Florence for Fun   COOKING
(Map p86; ☏055 247 66 05; www.florenceforfun.org; Via della Pergola 10a) Mainstream cookery classes and pizza-, gelato- and sorbet-making workshops.

British Institute of
Florence   ART HISTORY, ITALIAN
(Map p66; www.britishinstitute.it; Piazza Strozzi 2) Study masterpieces in situ by enrolling in a history of art course (art in Renaissance Florence, Florentine Frescoes and so on) at this well-regarded cultural institute in a 15th-century *palazzo* behind Palazzo Strozzi – or combine art with an Italian language course.

🚩 Tours
Bus
CAF Tours   BUS
(Map p66; ☏055 21 06 12; www.caftours.com; Via Sant'Antonino 6r) Half- and full-day city bus tours (€45 to €190), including designer-outlet shopping tours (€35, six hours).

City Sightseeing Firenze   BUS
(Map p82; ☏055 29 04 51; www.firenze.city-sightseeing.it; Piazza della Stazione 1; tickets incl audioguide adult/5-15yr €22/11) Explore Florence by red open-top bus, hopping on and off at 15 bus stops around the city. Tickets, sold by the driver, are valid for 24 hours.

Cycling
I Bike Florence   BIKE
(Map p66; ☏055 012 39 94; www.ibikeflorence.com; Via de' Lamberti 1) Guided history tours of Florence by bike (€29, two hours) and guided day trips to Chianti (€80 including lunch and wine tasting).

Tuscany Bike Tours   BIKE
(Map p66; ☏055 386 04 95; www.tuscany-biketours.com; Via Ghibellina 34r) One-day, 23km-long bike tours in Chianti with lunch, castle tour, wine and oil tasting (€75); transfer to Chianti by minibus.

Walking
ArtViva   HISTORY, WINE
(Map p66; ☏055 264 50 33, 329 6132730; www.italy.artviva.com; Via de' Sassetti 1) Marketed as the 'Original & Best', these excellent one- to three-hour city walks (€25 to €39) are led by historians or art history graduates; tours include the Uffizi, the Original David tour and an Evening Walk/Murder Mystery Tour. ArtViva also runs trips further afield to Chianti (wine tasting) and a Renaissance villa outside Florence (villa lunch and swim).

FLORENCE FOR CHILDREN

Children are welcomed pretty much anywhere, anytime, in Florence, families frequently going out with young children in the evenings, strolling riverside with a *gelato* or dining al fresco on summertime restaurant terraces. That said, Florence is not the easiest city to visit with very young children; green spaces and playgrounds are scarce and, while some of the pricier hotels can provide baby-sitters, there's no organised service for tourists.

Books & Guides

Teems of locally published books help children discover Florence – the museum book-shops in Palazzo Vecchio and the Uffizi have particularly tip-top selections. Nancy Shroyer Howard's activity-driven book *Fun in Florence* kits out six to 10 year olds with pencils and do-and-find sections for major sites (*Mischief in Tuscany: Running Wild in a Famous Italian Painting* by the same author is an absolute kid must-read); while Ellen and Marvin Mouchawar's *Treasure Hunt Florence* sets the same age group chasing around the city looking for items or opportunities to carry out simple tasks. For older children consider Penelope Dyan's *Walk the Renaissance Walk: A Kids' Guide to Florence* and *Florence; Just Add Water* by Simone Frasca; and *Florence: Playing with Art* by Maria Salvia Baldini.

Tours & Workshops

Florence proffers plenty of guided activities designed with kids in mind, including the fabulous and engaging tours for children aged three to 11 years at Palazzio Vecchio (see the boxed text, p76) and the special pushchair (stroller) tours for toddler-laden families at Palazzo Strozzi (p78); watch out for the two-hour 'Art Weekend' workshops at the latter, held the first weekend of every month (☎055 277 64 61; from 3.30pm to 5.30pm Saturday, 10.30am to 12.30pm Sunday; reservations required). Or consider a pizza-, gelato- or pasta-cooking course for your child.

Next to the Ospedale degli Innocenti in San Marco, La Bottega dei Ragazzi (☎055 247 83 86; www.istitutodeglinnocenti.it; Via dei Fibbiai 2; 1/3 workshops €10/20; ☉9am-1pm & 3-7pm Mon-Sat) is an inspirational 'play and learn with art' space that runs workshops (in English and Italian) for children aged three to five years and six to 11 years; book in advance. Anytime, parents and kids can pop in to play with its many toys, books and games.

Museums & Monuments

While they're totally unsuitable for anyone with kids in pushchairs, for older kids there's nothing like scaling Florentine heights with an energy-burning hike up the *duomo campanile* or around the inside of its astonishing dome. Treat them afterwards to the tastiest and most expensive hot chocolate of their life at Caffè Rivoire (see the boxed text, p111) or the pick of more ice-cream flavours than they could ever imagine across the river at La Carraia (see the boxed text, p108).

Art museums aside, recommended museums for the over six year olds include the Museo di Storia Naturale – Zoologia La Specola (p93), with its unique menagerie of stuffed animals and waxworks; the Museo Stibbert (p81), with its knights – lots of them – in shining armour; and Florence's state-of-the-art History of Science Museum, Museo Galileo (p77) – rent a touch-screen TrackMan (interactive video guide) at the entrance, select the itinerary for kids and you're away!

Parks & Playgrounds

If you don't know where they are, you'll never find them: The best playgrounds for under six year olds are near the *duomo* on Piazza Massimo d'Azeglio and across the river on Lungarno Santa Rosa (Map p58) and Piazza Torquato Tasso (Map p58). The vintage carousel on Piazza della Repubblica never stops enchanting.

Children over six year olds never tire of playing hide-and-seek between statues in Giardino di Boboli (p93) or tearing round 118-hectare Parco delle Cascine, which in summer has an open-air swimming pool to splash around in.

Faith Willinger – Lessons & Tours CULINARY
(www.faithwillinger.com) Food lovers' walking tour, a market stroll, gelato crawl and much more by American-born, Florence-based food writer Faith Willinger, who runs cooking courses, hands-on 'market to table' sessions, tastings, demonstrations and culinary visits, including meaty field trips to Panzano in Chianti.

Accidental Tourist WINE, CULINARY
(☑055 69 93 76; www.accidentaltourist.com) Become an Accidental Tourist (membership €10), then sign up for a wine tour (€50), cooking class (€60), picnic (€70) and so on; tours happen in and around Florence.

Freya's Florence ART, HISTORY
(☑349 0748907; www.freyasflorence.com; per hr €60) Recommended Australian-born, Florence-based private tour guide; pay admission fees on top of guiding fee.

⭐ Festivals & Events

Festa di Anna Maria Medici HISTORICAL EVENT
Florence's Feast of Anna Maria Medici marks the death in 1743 of the last Medici, Anna Maria, with a costumed parade from Palazzo Vecchio to her tomb in the Cappelle Medicee; 18 February.

Scoppio del Carro EASTER
A cart of fireworks is exploded in front of the cathedral at 11am on Easter Sunday – get there at least two hours early to grab a good position.

Maggio Musicale Fiorentino ARTS
(www.maggiofiorentino.com) This arts festival – Italy's oldest – held in Florence's Teatro del Maggio Musicale Fiorentino stages world-class performances of theatre, classical music, jazz and dance; April to June.

Festa di San Giovanni MIDSUMMER
Florence celebrates its patron saint, John, with a *calcio storico* match on Piazza di Santa Croce and fireworks over Piazzale Michelangelo; 24 June.

Sant'Ambrogio Summer Festival ARTS
(www.firenzejazz.it) The streets between Borgo La Croce and Piazza Beccaria become an evening stage for art, dance, jazz and theatre; June to July.

Jazz & Co MUSIC
(www.santissima.it) On summer nights Piazza della Santissima Annunziata is filled with tables of people enjoying an *aperitivo* or dinner catered by Slow Food International while listening to jazz musicians from Italy and overseas perform; late June to September.

Festival Firenze Classica MUSIC
July sees Florence's highly regarded Orchestra da Camera Toscana (www.orcafi.it) performing classical music in the atmospheric settings of the Oratorio di San Michele a Castello and Palazzo Strozzi.

Festa delle Rificolone RELIGIOUS
During the Festival of the Paper Lanterns children carrying lanterns, accompanied by drummers, *sbandieratori* (flag throwers), musicians and others in medieval dress, process through the streets from Piazza di Santa Croce to Piazza della Santissima Annunziata to celebrate the Virgin Mary's birthday; 7 September.

🛏 Sleeping

Too many hotels and boutique B&Bs competing for too little business means some great deals for the traveller, especially in winter when there are bargains to be had in all price ranges – a midrange double in a gorgeous 16th-century *palazzo* can cost as little as €45.

Many top-end boutique options are secreted in hidden courtyards or behind the inconspicuous door of a *residenza d'epoca* (historical residence) – not listed as hotel or graced with any stars, making such addresses all the more exclusive, atmospheric and oh-so-fabulously Florentine.

DUOMO & PIAZZA DELLA SIGNORIA
Incredibly, for such a dead-central part of Florence, this area has some excellent budget addresses. And if your hotel lacks an internet connection, free wi-fi hotspot Palazzo Strozzi (p78), with its wonderfully airy and very hip courtyard, is just a minute's walk away.

TOP
CHOICE **Hotel Scoti** HISTORIC HOTEL €
(Map p66; ☑055 29 21 28; www.hotelscoti.com; Via de' Tornabuoni 7; s €29-75, d €45-125, tr €75-150, q €85-175; ☎🖳) Wedged between Prada and McQueen, this *pensione* is a splendid mix of old-fashioned charm and brilliant value for money. Run with smiling aplomb by Australian Doreen and Italian Carmello, the hotel is enthroned in a 16th-century *palazzo* on Florence's smartest shopping strip. The 16 rooms – ask for one of 11 facing courtyard rooftops and beautifully quiet, bar the peal

of church bells – are clean and comfortable, but the star of the show is the floor-to-ceiling frescoed living room dating to 1780. Breakfast, brought to your room, is €5.

TOP CHOICE Hotel Torre Guelfa HISTORIC HOTEL €€
(Map p66; ☎055 239 63 38; www.hoteltorreguelfa.com; Borgo SS Apostoli 8; d €70-170, tr €130-210; ❄@🤙) If you wanna kip in a Real McCoy Florentine *palazzo* without breaking the bank, this 31-room hotel with fortress-style facade is the address. Scale its 13th-century, 50m-tall tower – Florence's tallest privately owned *torre* – for a sundowner overlooking Florence and you'll be blown away. A couple of its spacious rooms, all with high ceilings and faded period furnishings, share the same staggering panorama.

Hotel Davanzati HOTEL €€
(Map p66; ☎055 28 66 66; www.hoteldavanzati.it; Via Porta Rossa 5; s €72-122, d €122-189, q €222-342; ❄@🤙❄) Don't be put off by the 26 steps leading up to this 1st-floor hotel snug against Palazzo Davanzati. A beguiling labyrinth of enchanting rooms, unexpected frescoes and up-to-the-minute comforts, it has bags of charisma – and that includes Florentine debonair Tommaso and father Fabrizio, who run the show. A twinset of mezzanines make Room 100 a top family choice; there's a laptop in every room and iPads in reception to gen up on the daily news.

Palazzo Vecchietti HISTORIC HOTEL €€€
(Map p66; ☎055 230 28 02; www.palazzovecchietti.com; Via degli Strozzi 4; d €284-734; ❄@🤙) Wow, and wow again! This *residenza d'epoca* with 14 hopelessly romantic rooms and loggia in a 15th-century *palazzo* is a buzzword for hotel chic. Tapestries, bookshelves and works of art adorn old stone walls and colour schemes mix traditional hues with bolder blues, reds and violets. Every room has a walk-in dresser, coffee machine and kitchenette, and three have a terrace to breakfast in style between rooftops. No surprise: all this is the handiwork of top Florentine interior designer Michele Bönan.

Hotel Cestelli BOUTIQUE HOTEL €
(Map p66; ☎055 21 42 13; www.hotelcestelli.com; Borgo SS Apostoli 25; s without bathroom €40-60, d €70-100, d without bathroom €50-80; ⊘closed 4 weeks Jan-Feb, 3 weeks Aug) Wonderfully set a stiletto hop and a skip from the Arno and fashionable Via de' Tornabuoni, this eight-room hotel in a 12th-century *palazzo* is a

---

FLEE THE CROWD **99**

Should you want to get away from it all and stay out of town, two remarkable 'prince and pauper' addresses leap out.

In a 17th-century villa framed by extensive grounds, HI-affiliated **Villa Camerata** (off Map p66; ☎055 60 14 51; www.ostellofirenze.it; Viale Augusto Righi 2-4; d/tr/q €65/75/88, dm without bathroom €20; 🅿@🤙) is among Italy's most beautiful hostels (and oh so typically Tuscan!). Bus 17 from Stazione di Santa Maria Novella stops 400m from the hostel; count on 30 minutes travel time.

Then there's five-star **Grand Hotel Villa Cora** (off Map p90; ☎055 22 87 90; www.villacora.it; Viale Machiavelli 18; d from €310; 🅿@🤙⊠), a glorious 19th-century mansion guaranteed to make your head spin with its sumptuous frescoes, fabrics, chandeliers and art works just steps from Giardino di Boboli.

---

real gem. Its large, quiet rooms ooze understated style – think washbasin with silk screen, vintage art and original wooden shutters. Before stepping out quiz Italian photographer Alessio and Japanese wife, Asumi, on the latest best addresses to drink, dine and shop.

Hotel Perseo HOTEL €
(Map p66; ☎055 21 25 04; www.hotelperseo.it; Via de' Cerretani 1; s €50-125, d €80-165, tr €80-185, q €90-220; ❄@🤙) Twenty-room Perseo is a great family choice with its large rooms and unpretentious, down-to-earth decor. Family rooms have bunk beds and those on the top floor smooch with the rooftops and gorgeous views of the *duomo*. Should you have trouble tracking down (black) No 1 on the street, look for red No 23.

Floroom 2 B&B €€
(Map p66; ☎055 230 28 02; www.floroom.com; Via del Sole 2; d €120-200; ❄@🤙) Small, chic and with every mod-con is what this bijou design address is all about. Tucked on the 2nd floor of an old building with whitewashed beams, it has four rooms crisply dressed in neutral hues of white, cream and oyster grey. Breakfast is around a shared table with coffee machine et al at hand around the clock. Floroom runs another four-room B&B across the river at Via del Pavone 7.

SANTA MARIA NOVELLA

TOP CHOICE **Hotel L'Orologio**   DESIGN HOTEL €€
(Map p66; ☑055 27 73 80; www.hotelorologio florence.com; Piazza di Santa Maria Novella 24; d from €160; P❄@🖘) The type of seductive, super-stylish address James Bond would feel right at home in, this elegant new hotel oozes panache. Designed to be something of a showcase for the (very wealthy) owner's (exceedingly expensive) luxury wristwatch collection, the hotel has four stars, rooms named after watches and clocks pretty much everywhere. Don't be late ...

Residenza del Moro   HISTORIC HOTEL €€€
(Map p66; ☑055 29 08 84; www.residenzadelmoro. com; Via del Moro 15; d from €265; P❄@🖘) Hidden a little off the tourist track in an inspiring, 16th-century *palazzo* with columned interior courtyard, this residence epitomises a new breed of Florentine accommodation – luxurious suites emblazoned with precious frescoes and art in a historical building. All 11 rooms are unique and palatial, and the icing on the cake is the tree-shaded roof garden. Bliss.

Hotel Rosso 23   BOUTIQUE HOTEL €€
(Map p66; ☑055 27 73 00; www.hotelrosso23. com; Piazza di Santa Maria Novella 23; s €79-100, d €85-195; ❄@🖘) Its entrance is so discrete you could well walk straight pass this stylish townhouse with a beautiful facade and smart, oyster-grey and red interior colour

---

WORTH A TRIP

HAPPENING HIDEAWAY

Named after the Salviati family who transformed the 14th-century villa into the ravishing, swoon-worthy 17th-century ode to luxury it is today, **Il Salviatino** (☑055 90 411; www.salviatino. com; Via del Salviatino 21; d from €345; P❄@🖘≋), hidden among cypress trees in the hills 3.5km east of Florence, is the stuff of Tuscan dreams. Italian literati gathered here in the 17th and 18th centuries, and today it is Europe's moneyed hipsters who check-in to spoil themselves rotten in the spa, lounge in the cascading infinity pool or perfectly manicured Italian gardens, and ogle smugly at the dome of Florence's cathedral from the terrace bar. No wonder this place was voted Italy's 'best boutique hotel' in 2010 ...

---

scheme. Rooms, all 42 of them, are thoroughly modern and breakfast is served in a bijou interior courtyard.

SAN LORENZO & SAN MARCO

TOP CHOICE **Academy Hostel**   HOSTEL €
(Map p82; ☑055 239 86 65; www.academyhostel. eu; Via Ricasoli 9; s & d per person €35-42, dm €34-40; ❄@🖘) Cheap accommodation shouldn't compromise on comfort is the much-appreciated philosophy of this small modern hostel, snug on the 1st floor of a 17th-century *palazzo*. Dorms with four or six beds are crisp white with brightly coloured lockers and chic flower-adorned screens. No credit cards for payments under €150.

Hotel Morandi alla Crocetta HISTORIC HOTEL €€
(Map p82; ☑055 234 47 47; www.hotelmorandi.it; Via Laura 50; s €70-140, d €110-220, tr €130-195; q €150-370; P❄🖘) This medieval convent-turned-hotel away from the madding crowd in San Marco is a real stunner. Rooms are refined, tasteful and full of authentic period furnishings and paintings. A couple of rooms have handkerchief-sized gardens to laze in, but the pièce de résistance is frescoed No 29, the former chapel.

Sette Angeli Rooms   B&B €
(Map p82; ☑393 939490810; www.setteangeli rooms.com; Via Nazionale 31; s €45-60; d €85-110, tr €95-135; ❄🖘) Tucked behind the Mercato Centrale on a mainstream shopping street, Seven Angels is a tantalising mix of great value and recent renovation. Its rooms are perfectly comfortable and guests can pay an extra €10 to use the self-catering kitchen corner.

Ostello Archi Rossi   HOSTEL €
(Map p82; ☑055 29 08 04; www.hostelarchirossi. com; Via Faenza 94r; dm €21-27, s €40-60, d €60-90, tr €75-105, all incl breakfast & sheets; ⊘closed 2 weeks Dec; @🖘) Guests' paintings and graffiti brighten up the walls at this private hostel near Stazione di Santa Maria Novella. Bright white dorms have three to 12 beds (those across the garden are quieter); there are washing machines, frozen meal dispensers and microwaves for guests to use. No curfew (knock to get in after 2am).

Johanna & Johlea   B&B €€
(Map p82; ☑055 463 32 92, 055 48 18 96; www. johanna.it; s €50-90, d €70-170; ❄🖘) One of the most established B&Bs in town, J&J has more than a dozen tasteful, impeccable, individually decorated rooms split between

five historic residences. Those desiring total luxury can ask about the suite apartments.

SANTA CROCE

Hotel Dalí
HOTEL €

(Map p86; ☑055 234 07 06; www.hoteldali.com; Via dell'Oriuolo 17; s €40, d €85, d without bathroom €70, apt 2/4/6 guests €90/140/200; P@♠⑭) This overwhelmingly friendly hotel with 10 spacious rooms like home simply goes from strength to strength. Run with unrelenting dynamism by world travellers-turned-parents Marco and Samanta ('running the hotel is like travelling without moving'), Dalí now has a kettle in every room, brand-new bathrooms, microwave for shared use and three gorgeous self-catering apartments – one with *duomo* view – sleeping two, four and six. No breakfast, but free parking in the leafy inner courtyard. Low season rates are 20% less.

Hotel Orchidea
HOTEL €

(Map p86; ☑055 248 03 46; www.hotelorchideaflorence.it; Borgo degli Albizi 11; s €30-55, d €50-75, tr €65-90, q €75-110, all without bathroom) This old-fashioned *pensione* in the mansion where the Donati family roosted in the 13th century (Dante's wife, Gemma, was allegedly born in the tower) is charm itself. Its seven rooms with sink and shared bathroom might be simple, but their outlook beats many a five-star pad hands down: Nos 5, 6 and 7 have huge windows overlooking a gorgeous garden while No 4 spills out onto an old stone terrace. Many guests return year after year, simply to enjoy the 100-year-old wisteria in bloom (May to June). No breakfast, but free tea- and coffee-making facilities around the clock.

Hotel Balestri
HOTEL €€

(Map p66; ☑055 21 47 43; www.hotel-balestri.it; Piazza Mentana 7; s/d/tr from €120/140/180; ✳@♠) Three-star Balestri is one of Florence's oldest and most traditional hotels, around since 1888 but adopted in the new millennium by the chic Whythebest Florence hotel group (they're the guys behind L'Orologio, Villa Cora and other chic pads). It sits bold on the banks of the Arno; superior rooms look out onto the water and the decor throughout is now comfortably contemporary.

OLTRARNO

Palazzo Magnani Feroni
HOTEL €€€

(Map p90; ☑055 239 95 44; www.florencepalace.com; Borgo San Frediano 5; d from €310-720;

DON'T MISS

ROOFTOP ROMANCE

Plump above Florence's most buzzing summertime square, **Palazzo Guadagni Hotel** (Map p90; ☑055 265 83 76; www.palazzoguadagni.com; Piazza Santo Spirito 9; d €100-150, f per person €35; ✳♠⑭), with impossibly romantic loggia is legendary – Zeffirelli shot several scenes of *Tea with Mussolini* here. Known for years as the shabby, overpriced but wholly irresistible Pensione Bandini (since shut), the Renaissance 16th-century palace has been brought back to life – in the most fabulous of manners – by local Florentines Laura and Ferdinando. Spacious rooms tastefully mix old and new, and that loggia terrace with wicker garden furniture is, well, dreamy ....

P✳@♠) This extraordinary old *palazzo* is the stuff of dreams. The 12 suites, which occupy four floors with the family's private residence wedged in-between, are vast and ooze elegance, featuring authentic period furnishings, rich fabrics and Bulgari toiletries. The 360-degree city view from the rooftop is magnificent and unforgettable.

Ostello Santa Monaca
HOSTEL €

(Map p90; ☑055 26 83 38; www.ostello.it; Via Santa Monaca 6; dm €17.50-19.50, d/q per person €24.50/20.50, breakfast/dinner €3.50/12; @♠) Once a convent, this large hostel run by a cooperative since the 1960s, comes warmly recommended. There is a bright kitchen with washing machine (€6.50 a wash) for guests' use, free safe deposits and two computers to surf. Single-sex dorms sleep four to 22 and are closed for cleaning between 10am and 2pm. Curfew 2am. Low season rates are €1 less.

Campeggio Michelangelo
CAMPGROUND €

(☑055 681 19 77; www.ecvacanze.it; Viale Michelangelo 80; adult €9.50-11.40, car & tent €11.40-13.80; P@) Just off Piazzale Michelangelo, this large and comparatively leafy campground has lovely city views. Take bus 13 from Stazione di Santa Maria Novella or walk – steeply uphill!

✕ Eating

Quality ingredients and simple execution are the hallmarks of Florentine cuisine, climaxing with the fabulous *bistecca alla fiorentina,* a huge slab of prime T-bone steak rubbed with olive oil, seared on the char grill, garnished with salt and pepper and served beautifully *al sangue* (bloody).

Other typical dishes include *crostini* (toasts topped with chicken-liver pâté or other topping), *ribollita* (a thick vegetable, bread and bean soup), *pappa al pomodoro* (bread and tomato soup) and *trippa alla fiorentina* (tripe cooked in a rich tomato sauce).

As equally an attractive option as the city's many restaurants is its wealth of *enoteca* – wine bars serving tasting platters of cheese, salami and cold meats as well as, quite often, full meals. See p108 for recommended *enoteca* addresses.

DUOMO & PIAZZA DELLA SIGNORIA

TOP CHOICE Obikà CHEESE BAR €€
(Map p66; ☎055 277 35 26; www.obika.it; Via de' Tornabuoni 16; 3/5 mozzarellas €19.50/30, pizza €9-14.50; ☺lunch & dinner) Given its exclusive location in Palazzo Tornabuoni this designer address is naturally ubertrendy. Taste different mozzarella cheeses with basil, organic veg or sundried tomatoes in the cathedral-like interior or snuggle beneath heaters in the star-topped courtyard. The mozzarella pizzas are particularly creative – as is the copious *aperitivi* salad buffet (€9 including one drink) and cheesy Sunday brunch.

Cantinetta dei Verrazzano BAKERY €
(Map p66; Via dei Tavolini 18-20; platters €4.50-12, focaccia €3-3.50, panini €2.50-4; ☺noon-9pm Mon-Sat) Together, a *forno* (baker's oven) and *cantinetta* (small cellar) equal a match made in heaven. Sit down at one of just five marble-topped tables, admire prized vintages displayed behind glass in wall-to-ceiling wooden cabinets and sip a glass of wine (€3.50 to €8) produced on the Verrazzano estate in Chianti. The focaccia, perhaps topped with caramelised radicchio or *porcini* mushrooms, is a must – as is a mixed cold-meat platter (try to ignore the bristly boar legs strung in the small open kitchen).

l'Parione TRATTORIA €€
(Map p66; ☎055 21 40 0 5; Via del Parione 74-76r; meals €40; ☺lunch & dinner Thu-Tue) Be it pea-green risotto with spinach and mozzarella, artichoke salad with parmesan shavings or wild boar *parppardelle,* cuisine is strictly seasonal at this upmarket address off Via de' Tornabuoni. Its wine cellar is particularly prized. The sole work of art strung on the walls depicts the church in Santa Croce.

Birreria Centrale TRATTORIA €€
(Map p66; www.birreriacentrale.com; Piazza dei Cimatori 1r; meals €35; ☺lunch & dinner) With a summer terrace spilling across one of the city's quaint little hidden squares, this traditional eating address is an attractive option. Its cosy interior snug beneath a centuries-old red-brick vaulted ceiling makes it a great winter hideaway, too, and the varied menu covers all gambits including vegetarian.

La Canova di Gustavino TUSCAN €
(Map p66; ☎055 239 98 06; Via della Condotta 29r; meals €25; ☺noon-midnight) The rear dining room of this atmospheric *enoteca* is lined with shelves of Tuscan wine – the perfect accompaniment to a soup, pasta or hearty main.

SANTA MARIA NOVELLA

TOP CHOICE L'Osteria di Giovanni TUSCAN €€
(Map p66; ☎055 28 48 97; www.osteriadigiovanni.it; Via del Moro 22; meals €45; ☺lunch & dinner Fri-

---

TRIPE: FAST-FOOD FAVOURITE

When Florentines fancy a fast munch-on-the-move, they flit by a *trippaio* – a cart on wheels or mobile stand – for a tripe *panini* (sandwich). Think cow's stomach chopped up, boiled, sliced, seasoned and bunged between bread.

Those great bastions of good old-fashioned Florentine tradition, *trippai* still going strong include the cart on the southwest corner of Mercato Nuovo (Map p66); L'Antico Trippaio (Map p66; Piazza dei Cimatori); Pollini (Map p86; Piazza Sant' Ambrogio) in Santa Croce; and hole-in-the-wall Da Vinattieri (Map p66; Via Santa Margherita 4), tucked down an alley next to Dante's Chiesa di Santa Margherita. Pay €3.50 for a *panini* with tripe doused in *salsa verde* (pea-green sauce of smashed parsley, garlic, capers and anchovies) or garnished with salt, pepper and ground chilli. Alternatively, opt for a bowl of *lampredotto* (cow's fourth stomach that is chopped and simmered for hours).

Count on paying between €5 and €8 for a lavishly filled *panino* (sandwich).

Mariano (Map p66; Via del Parione 19r; ⊙8am-3pm & 5-7.30pm Mon-Fri, 8am-3pm Sat) Our favourite for its simplicity, around since 1973. Sunrise to sunset this brick-vaulted, 13th-century cellar gently buzzes with Florentines propped at the counter sipping coffee or wine or eating salads and *panini*. Come here for a coffee-and-pastry breakfast, light lunch, *aperitivo* or a *panino* to eat on the move.

Gustapanino (Map p90; Piazza Santa Spirito; ⊙11am-8pm Mon-Sat, noon-5pm Sun) It's dead simple to spot what many Florentines rate as the city's best *enopaninoteca* (hip wine and sandwich stop) with no seating but bags of square space and church steps outside – just look for the long line at the front.

'Ino (Map p66; www.ino-firenze.com; Via dei Georgofili 3-7r; ⊙11am-8pm Mon-Sat, noon-5pm Sun) Artisan ingredients are sourced locally and creatively mixed at this stylish address near the Uffizi. Create your own combination or pick a house special and scoff on the spot with a glass of wine (included in the sandwich price).

I Due Fratellini (Map p66; www.iduefratellini.com; Via dei Cimatori 38r; ⊙9am-8pm Mon-Sat, closed Fri & Sat 2nd half of Jun & all Aug) This hole-in-the-wall has been in business since 1875. Wash *panini* down with a beaker of wine and leave the empty on the wooden shelf outside.

Oil Shoppe (Map p86; www.oleum.it; Via Sant'Egidio 22r) Queue at the back of the shop for hot subs, at the front for cold, at this busy student favourite. Choose your own or let chef Alberto Scorzon take the lead with his 10-filling wonder.

Mon, dinner Tue-Thu) It's not the decor or eclectic choice of wall art that stands out at this wonderfully friendly neighbourhood eatery. It's the cuisine, staunchly Tuscan and stunningly creative. Think chickpea soup with octopus or pear- and ricotta-stuffed *tortelli* (a type of ravioli) bathed in a leek and almond cream. Throw in the complimentary glass of sparkling *prosecco* as *aperitivo* and subsequent Vin Santo (with home-made *cantucci* – hard, sweet biscuits – to dunk in) at the end of the meal and you'll return time and again.

Osteria dei Centopoveri   TRATTORIA €€
(Map p66; ☎055 21 88 46; www.centopoveri.it; Via Palazzuolo 31r; meals €30; ⊙lunch & dinner) The 'hostel of the hundred poor people' is no soup kitchen, rather a modern dining option recommended in practically every guidebook. Creative Tuscan is its culinary spin.

Il Latini   TRATTORIA €€
(Map p66; ☎055 21 09 16; www.illatini.com; Via dei Palchetti 6r; meals €40; ⊙lunch & dinner Tue-Sun) A guidebook favourite built around melt-in-your-mouth *crostini,* Tuscan meats, fine pasta and roasted meats served at shared tables. There are two dinner seatings (7.30pm and 9pm); bookings mandatory.

SAN LORENZO & SAN MARCO

TOP CHOICE **Trattoria Mario**   TUSCAN €
(Map p82; www.trattoriamario.com; Via Rosina 2; meals €15-25; ⊙noon-3.30pm Mon-Sat, closed 3 weeks Aug) Get here on the dot at noon to ensure a stool around a shared table at this noisy, busy, fabulous trattoria – a legend in its own time that retains its soul and allure with locals despite being in every guidebook. The charming Fabio, whose grandfather Mario opened the place in 1953, is front of house while big brother Romeo and nephew Francesco cook up tasty, dirt-cheap dishes with speed and skill in the kitchen (watch them perform through glass while you eat). Monday and Thursday are tripe days, Friday is fish and Saturday sees local Florentines flock here for a brilliantly blue *bistecca alla fiorentina* (€35 per kilo). No advance reservations, no credit cards.

Da Nerbone   FOOD STALL €
(Map p82; Mercato Centrale, Piazza del Mercato Centrale; primi €4, secondi €5-9; ⊙7am-2pm Mon-Sat) Forge your way past cheese, meat and sausage stalls in Florence's Mercato Centrale to join the lunchtime queue at Nerbone, in the biz since 1872. Go local and order *trippa alla fiorentina* (tripe and tomato stew) or follow the crowd with a feisty *panini con*

FLORENCE

DON'T MISS

SHOW STEALER

Larger-than-life Florentine chef, Fabio Picchi, is one of the city's living treasures. Having colonised almost an entire block near Mercato di Sant'Ambrogio with his Cibrèo trio, he went on to steal the show with the fabulously eccentric and good-value **Teatro del Sale** (Map p86; ☎055 200 14 92; www.teatrodelsale.com; Via dei Macci 111r; breakfast/lunch/dinner €7/20/30; ⊙9-11am, 12.30-2.30pm & 7-11pm Tue-Sat Sep-Jul). Aptly set in an old Florentine theatre, it is a members-only club (everyone welcome, annual membership €5 valid yearly from September to July) open for breakfast, lunch and dinner, culminating at 9.30pm in a live performance of drama, music or comedy arranged by artistic director and famous comic actress (and Picchi's wife) Maria Cassi. Dinners are hectic affairs: grab a chair, serve yourself water, wine and antipasti, and wait for Picchi to yell out what's just about to be served before queuing at the glass hatch for your *primo* (first course) and *secondo* (second course). Dessert and coffee are laid out buffet style just prior to the performance.

bollito (a hefty boiled-beef bun, dunked in the meat's juices before serving). Eat standing up or fight for a table.

Il Vegetariano VEGETARIAN €
(off Map p82; ☎055 47 50 30; www.il-vegetariano.it; Via delle Ruote 30r; meals €15-20; ⊙lunch & dinner Tue-Fri, dinner Sat & Sun) This self-service veggie restaurant cooks up a great selection of Tuscan vegetable dishes, build-your-own salads and mains eaten around shared wooden tables. There's always a vegan option and the chalked-up menu changes daily.

La Mescita TUSCAN €
(Map p82; Via degli Alfani 70r; mains €5-10; ⊙10.30am-4pm Mon-Sat, closed Aug) Conveniently close to *David* and the Galleria dell'Accademia, this part *enoteca* part *fiaschetteria* (small tavern serving wine and snacks) is an unapologetically old-fashioned place from 1927. It serves Tuscan specialities such as *maccheroni* with sausage and *insalata di farro* (farro salad), and has a great marble-topped bar propped up by noontime tipplers.

SANTA CROCE

TOP
CHOICE **Trattoria Cibrèo** TRATTORIA €€
(Map p86; Via dei Macci 122r; meals €35; ⊙12.50-2.30pm & 6.50-11.15pm Tue-Sat Sep-Jul) Dine here and you'll instantly understand why a queue gathers outside before it opens. Once in, revel in top-notch Tuscan cuisine: perhaps ricotta and potato flan with a rich meat sauce, puddle of olive oil and grated parmesan (divine!) or a simple plate of polenta, followed by home-made sausages, beans in a spicy tomato sauce and braised celery. No

advance reservations, no credit cards, no coffee and arrive early to snag a table.

Pin Gusto ASIAN, FUSION €
(Map p86; www.pingusto.com; ☎055 23 44 397; Via della Mattonaia 2-18; lunch/dinner €10/20; ⊙lunch & dinner) A great cheap eat recommended by several savvy Florentines, this modern dining address behind Sant' Ambrogio market cooks up a bottomless lunch buffet (€10) built around hot and cold sushi, wok and fusion dishes. Dinner – a busy affair hence best to reserve one of two sittings (7.30pm and 9.30pm) – sees grilled meats added to the excellent-value, eat-as-much-as-you-can equation.

Ristorante Cibrèo MODERN TUSCAN €€€
(Map p86; ☎055 234 11 00; Via Andrea del Verrocchio 8r; meals €80; ⊙1-2.30pm & 7pm-midnight Tue-Sat Sep-Jul) The flagship of the Fabio Picchi empire, this elegant restaurant is an essential stop for anyone interested in modern Tuscan cuisine. Knock-out choices on our most recent visit were a *primo* (first course) of spicy fish soup and a *secondo* (second course) of roast pigeon with mustard fruits. The wine list is equally impressive.

Enoteca Pinchiorri GASTRONOMIC €€€
(Map p86; ☎055 24 27 77; www.enotecapinchiorri.com; Via Ghibellina 87r; meals €270, 7-/10-course tasting menus €225/275; ⊙lunch & dinner Thu-Sat, dinner Wed, closed Aug) Chef Annie Féolde applies French techniques to her versions of refined Tuscan cuisine and does it so well that this is the only restaurant in Tuscany to possess three Michelin stars. The setting is a 16th-century palace hotel, the wine list is mind-boggling in its extent and excellence,

and the prices reach the stratosphere. A once-in-a-lifetime experience.

Osteria del Caffè Italiano
TRADITIONAL TUSCAN €€

(Map p86; ☎055 28 90 20; www.caffeitaliano.it; Via dell'Isola delle Stinche 11-13r; meals €40; ☺lunch & dinner Tue-Sun) The menu at this cosy *osteria* (casual tavern or eatery presided over by a host) – something of a veteran in the Florence dining scene – is packed with simple classics such as *mozzarella di bufala* with Parma ham, ravioli stuffed with ricotta and *cavolo nero* (black cabbage), and the city's famous *bistecca alla fiorentina* (per kilo €50). Find it on the ground floor of 14th-century Palazzo Salviati.

Caffè Italiano Sud
ITALIAN €€

(Map p86; ☎055 28 93 68; Via della Vigna Vecchia; meals €25; ☺7.30-11pm Tue-Sun) Fronted by two potted olive trees, chef Umberto Montano's ode to southern Italy is a change from the Tuscan norm. Loads of home-made pasta, including unusual dishes from his native Puglia, stars on the menu.

Francesco Vini
TUSCAN €€

(Map p86; ☎055 21 87 37; www.francescovini.it; Piazza dei Peruzzi 8r; meals €40, pizza €6-10; ☺lunch & dinner) Built on top of Roman ruins, this surprise address with a striking glass facade sits on one of Florence's quintessentially quiet, stumble-upon-by-accident squares. Winter dining is between bottle-lined wall and red brick and in summer everything spills outside. But it is the wine list, packed with all the Tuscan greats, that is Francesco's real pride and joy.

La Pentola dell'Oro
FLORENTINE €€

(Map p86; ☎055 24 18 08; www.lapentoladelloro.it; Via di Mezzo 24-26r; meals €40; ☺lunch & dinner Mon-Sat) Long a jealously guarded secret among Florentine gourmands, Florence's old-style Golden Pot doesn't need to advertise. Word of mouth draws the culinary curious here to sample Renaissance dishes reinvented for modern tastes by culinary artist Giuseppe Alessi. Dine at substreet level or at the street-level offshoot with marble-topped tables, wooden benches and 25 place settings.

Antico Noè
OSTERIA €

(Map p86; Volta di San Piero 6r; meals €25; ☺noon-midnight Mon-Sat) Don't be put off by the dank alley in which this old butcher's shop with white marble-clad walls and wrought-iron meat hooks is found. The drunks loitering outside are generally harmless and the down-to-the-earth Tuscan fodder served is a real joy. For a quick bite, go for a *panini* from the adjoining *fiaschetteria* (small tavern). No credit cards.

Mercato di Sant'Ambrogio
MARKET €

(Map p86; Piazza Sant'Ambrogio; ☺7am-2pm Mon-Sat) Outdoor food market with an intimate, local flavour.

OLTRARNO

TOP CHOICE Il Santo Bevitore
MODERN TUSCAN €€

(Map p90; ☎055 21 12 64; www.ilsantobevitore.com; Via di Santo Spirito 64-66r; meals €35; ☺lunch & dinner Sep-Jul) Reserve in advance or arrive at 7.30pm to snag the last of the remaining tables at this raved-about address, an understated ode to stylish dining where

---

TIP-TOP PIZZERIE

Expect to pay around €8 for a pizza at these Florentine-recommended addresses:

Gustapizza (Map p90; Via Maggio 46r; ☺11.30am-3pm & 7-11pm Tue-Sun) Wow! This unpretentious pizzeria by Piazza Santa Spirito gives a new meaning to the word 'packed'. Arrive early to grab a bar stool at a wooden-barrel table and pick from eight pizza types.

Pizzeria del' Osteria del Caffè Italiano (Map p86; Via dell'Isola delle Stinche 11-13r; ☺7.30-11.30pm Tue-Sun) Simplicity is the buzz word at this pocket-sized pizzeria that makes just three pizza types – *margherita*, *napoli* and *marinara*. No credit cards.

PizzaMan (Map p86; Via dell' Agnolo 79; ☺noon-2.30pm & 6.30pm-midnight Mon-Fri, 6.30pm-midnight Sat & Sun) This cheap and cheerful pizzeria with booth-style seating gets rave reviews for its pizza baked in a wood-burning oven and bargain-basement prices. To lunch cheap, go for the PizzaMan's €6 pizza 'n fries deal or €8 menu.

Il Pizzaiuolo (Map p86; ☎055 24 11 71; Via dei Macci 113r; pizzas €5-10, pastas €6.50-12; ☺lunch & dinner Mon-Sat, closed Aug) Young Florentines flock to The Pizza Maker to nosh Neapolitan thick-crust pizzas hot from the wood-fired oven. Bookings essential for dinner.

gastronomes dine by candlelight in a cavernous whitewashed, wood and bottle-lined interior. The menu is a creative reinvention of seasonal classics, and different for lunch and dinner: hand-chopped beef tartare, chestnut *millefeuille* and lentils, pureed purple cabbage soup with mozzarella cream and anchovy syrup, acacia honey *bavarese* (type of firm, creamy mousse) with Vin Santo-marinated dried fruits ...

TOP CHOICE Il Ristoro TUSCAN €

(Map p90; ☎055 264 55 69; Borgo San Jacopo 48r; meals €20; ⊗noon-4pm Mon, noon-10pm Tue-Sun) A disarmingly simple address not to be missed, this two-room restaurant with deli counter is a great budget choice. Pick from classics like *pappa al pomodoro* or a plate of cold cuts and swoon at views of the Arno swirling beneath your feet.

Trattoria Camillo TRATTORIA €€€

(Map p90; ☎055 21 24 27; Borgo San Jacopo 57r; meals €50; ⊗lunch & dinner Thu-Mon) *Crostini* topped with aphrodisiacal white-truffle shavings, deep-fried battered green tomatoes or zucchini (courgette) flowers and home-made walnut liqueur are but a few of the seasonal highlights served beneath a centuries-old red-brick vaulted ceiling at this staunchly traditional trattoria. The quality of products used is exceptional and service is endearingly old-fashioned.

Pane e Vino TUSCAN €€

(☎055 247 69 56; Piazza di Cestello 3r; meals €40; ⊗dinner Mon-Sat) Sheer culinary reputation alone lures diners into this gourmet dining address, well away from the crowds in a quiet part of town. Imaginative and wholly sea-

---

DON'T MISS

PIAZZA DEL PASSERA

This bijou square with no passing traffic is a gourmet gem. Pick from cheap wholesome tripe in various guises at Il Magazzino (Map p90; ☎055 21 59 69; www.tripperailmagazzino.com; Piazza della Passera 2/3; meals €25; ⊗lunch & dinner) or pricier Tuscan classics at Trattoria 4 Leoni (Map p90; ☎055 21 85 62; www.4leoni.com; Piazza della Passera 2/3; meals from €35; ⊗lunch & dinner), known for its *bistecca alla fiorentina* (char-grilled T-bone steak) that it's cooked up since 1550; reservations essential.

---

sonal Tuscan cuisine is what the chef cooks up – think broad bean and chicory soup, pumpkin ravioli, *tagliatelle* (ribbon pasta) with black cabbage or a cardoon *timballi* (type of globe artichoke baked in a small pot) – and the wine list is extraordinary. Can't decide? Go for the €30 tasting menu.

Trattoria La Casalinga TRATTORIA €

(Map p90; ☎055 21 86 24; Via de' Michelozzi 9r; meals €25; ⊗lunch & dinner Mon-Sat) Family run and locally loved, this busy unpretentious place is one of Florence's cheapest trattorias. You'll be relegated behind locals in the queue – it's a fact of life and not worth protesting – with the eventual reward being hearty peasant dishes such as *bollito misto con salsa verde* (mixed boiled meats with green sauce).

Olio & Convivium TUSCAN €€

(Map p90; ☎055 265 81 98; Via di Santo Spirito 4; meals €40; ⊗lunch & dinner Tue-Sat, lunch Mon) A key address on any gastronomy agenda: your tastebuds will tingle at the sight of the legs of ham, conserved truffles, wheels of cheese, artisan-made bread and other delectable delicatessen products sold in its shop. Dine out the back.

Il Guscio TUSCAN €€

(☎055 22 44 21; www.ristoranteilgusciofirenze.com; Via dell'Orto 49; meals €40; ⊗lunch & dinner Tue-Sat) Exceptional dishes come out of the kitchen of this family-run gem in San Frediano. Meat and fish are given joint billing, with triumphs such as white bean soup with prawns and fish joining superbly executed mains, including guinea fowl breast in balsamic vinegar, on the sophisticated menu.

Trattoria Bordino TRATTORIA €

(Map p90; ☎055 21 30 48; www.trattoriabordino.it; Via Stracciatella 9r; meals €25; ⊗lunch & dinner Mon-Sat) If eat cheap is your mantra, Bordino is your address. Hidden behind Chiesa di Santa Felicità, not far from Ponte Vecchio, this pocket-sized trattoria cooks up all the classics and a great-value €7 lunch.

Dolcissima PASTRIES, CAKES €

(Map p90; www.dolcissimafirenze.it; Via Maggio 61r) This is a real favourite gourmet address for Florentines living this side of the river. Be it chocolates, cakes, pastries or pralines, it is *the* sweet stop extraordinaire.

OUT OF TOWN

When the summer city heat stifles, do what Florentines do – get out of town for an al

LOCAL KNOWLEDGE

GEORGIO TATTANELLI, FLORENTINE DEBONAIR

Before WWII his father made leather wallets in a tiny workshop on Piazza Pitti. By 1972 it had grown into an out-of-town factory where leather was cut into stylish shoes, bags and jackets for what had become a plush boutique on Piazza Pitti. A generation on, Georgio has retired and cuts a dashing figure as he passes by his family business **Casini Firenze** (Piazza Pitti 30-31r) each morning on his way to lunch – same place every day for 40 years – followed by a stroll and coffee with friends, every day, at Caffè Gilli or Caffè Rivoire (see the boxed text, p111). His insider tips on Florence:

Low-Key Lunch

Oltrarno shop owners, Ponte Vecchio jewellers, they all lunch at **Celestino** (Map p90; ☑055 239 65 74; Piazza di Santa Felicità; meals €30; ☺lunch & dinner, closed Sun Oct-Easter). I've been there every day since my mother died. Bruno knows his wine, is good at flambéed dishes and has an excellent daily special.

Sage Shopping

It is not only the design that is important, it is the fitting – and that is the difficult part. Good leather cannot be cheap – San Lorenzo's Mercato Centrale is full of cheap stuff, none from Florence. Look for shops that are clearly old family businesses.

Dinner Date

To eat well for little, try Trattoria La Casalinga. It is only Italian ladies – the youngest is about 50 – in the kitchen and the taste of the food is like my mother's. It's a family business, it's crowded, it's noisy, always lots of people ...

---

fresco lunch between flowers or riverside at these recommended addresses.

TOP CHOICE Targa MODERN TUSCAN €€

(☑055 677 377; www.targabistrot.net; Lungarno Colombo 7; meals around €35; ☺lunch & dinner Mon-Sat) 'Friendly food' is the strapline of this sleek, refreshingly modern address, a *bistrot Fiorentino* (Florentine bistro) bursting with green foliage on the banks of the Arno 1.1km east of Ponte San Niccolò. Dining is around Parisian-style wooden bistro tables – in or out on wooden decked verandah; the wine list is superb (lots of French as well as Italian etiquettes); and chef Gabriele Tarchiani takes real pride in his desserts, well worth saving a space for – his hot chocolate soufflé and lemon crepes are specialities raved about far and wide. Advance reservations essential.

Trattoria le Cave di Maiano TRATTORIA €€

(☑055 5 91 33; www.trattoriacavedimaiano.it; Via Cave di Maiano 16, Maiano; meals €35; ☺lunch & dinner, closed Mon winter) Every fine weekend Florentines flock to this restaurant in Maiano, a village 8km north of Florence near Fiesole, to indulge in long leisurely lunches on its outdoor terrace. The food is memorable: huge servings are the rule of thumb and everything is home-made, with pastas and vegetable dishes being particularly impressive. The rustic inclination of the chef is reflected in the number of dishes featuring rabbit, boar and suckling pig, all of which go wonderfully well with the quaffable house wine.

Trattoria Bibe TRATTORIA €€

(☑055 204 00 85; www.trattoriabibe.com; Via della Bagnese 1lr, Galuzzo; meals €35; ☺lunch & dinner Sat & Sun, dinner Mon, Tue, Thu & Fri Dec-Jan & Mar-Oct) Pigeon, frogs legs, hare and guineafowl are among the many meats roasted (count at least 40 minutes) at this wonderful old-fashioned inn – so legendary Italian poet Eugenio Montale wrote a poem about Grandfather 'Bibe' in 1927. Dine elegantly inside or amid flowers out. Find it 3km south of Florence; take bus No 46.

🍷 Drinking

Florence's drinking scene is split between *enoteche* (increasingly hip wine bars that invariably make great eating addresses too), trendy bars with lavish *aperitivo* buffets and straightforward cafes that quite often double as lovely lunch venues.

TOP 5 GELATERIE

Florentines take gelato seriously and there's healthy rivalry among local *gelaterie artigianale* (makers of handmade gelato) who strive to create the city's creamiest, most flavourful and freshest ice cream. Flavours are seasonal and a cone or tub costs €2/3/4/5 per small/medium/large/maxi.

Vivoli (Map p86; Via dell'Isola delle Stinche 7; ⊙7.30am-midnight Mon-Sat, 9am-midnight Sun Apr-Oct, to 9pm Nov-Mar) Inside seating tea-salon style alongside coffee, tea and cakes makes this ice-cream shop stand out. Pistachio and chocolate with orange are crowd favourites. Pay at the cash desk then trade your receipt for ice. No cones, only tubs.

Grom (Map p66; www.grom.it; Via del Campanile; ⊙10.30am-midnight Apr-Sep, to 11pm Oct-Mar) Rain, hail or shine, queues halfway down the street are a constant at this sweet address; flavours are all delectable and many ingredients organic. Rather tasty hot chocolate and milkshakes, too.

La Carraia (Map p90; www.lacarraiagroup.eu; Piazza N Sauro 25r; ⊙11am-11pm) Take one look at the constant queue out the door of this bright green-and-citrus shop with exciting flavours and know you're at a real Florentine favourite. Ricotta and pear anyone?

Gelateria dei Neri (Map p86; Via de' Neri 22r; ⊙9am-midnight) Semifreddo-style gelato that is cheaper than its competitors; known for its coconut, gorgonzola and ricotta and fig flavours.

Carabé (Map p82; www.gelatocarabe.com; Via Ricasoli 60r; ⊙10am-midnight, closed mid-Dec–mid-Jan) Traditional Sicilian gelato, granita (sorbet) and brioche (Sicilian ice-cream sandwich); handy address if you're waiting in line to see *David*.

Wine Bars

Nothing whets one's appetite for the Florentine way of living better than hanging out in an *enoteca* (wine bar), glass of Chianti in hand.

TOP CHOICE **Le Volpi e l'uva** WINE BAR
(Map p90; Piazza dei Rossi 1; cheese or meat platters €8-12; ⊙11am-9pm Mon-Sat) The city's best *enoteca con degustazione* (wine bar with tasting) bar none: this intimate address with marble-topped bar crowning two oak ageing wine barrels chalks up an extraordinarily impressive list of wines by the glass (€3.50 to €8) on its blackboard. To attain true bliss indulge in the most divine *crostini* (€6.50) topped with honeyed speck perhaps or *lardo*, a platter of boutique Tuscan cheeses (try the Rocco made by Fattoria Corzano e Paterno) or other delectable antipasti.

TOP CHOICE **Il Santino** WINE BAR
(Map p90; Via di Santo Spirito 34; ⊙daily) Just a few doors down from one of Florence's best gourmet addresses, Il Santo Bevitore, is this pocket-sized wine bar, run by the same gastronomic folk and packed every evening. Inside, squat modern stools contrast with old brick walls but the real action is outside, from around 9pm, when the buoyant wine-loving crowd spills onto the street.

Sei Divino WINE BAR
(Map p66; Borgo Ognissanti 42r; ⊙daily) This stylish 'wine gallery' hosts one of Florence's most happening *aperitivo* scenes, complete with music, the odd exhibition and plenty of pavement action.

Fiaschetteria Nuvoli WINE BAR
(Map p66; Piazza dell'Olio 15r; ⊙7am-9pm Mon-Sat) Pull up a stool on the street and chat with a regular over a glass of *vino della casa* (house wine) at this old-fashioned *fiaschetteria*, a street away from the *duomo*.

ZEB WINE BAR
(off Map p90; www.zebgastronomia.com; Via San Miniato 2r; ⊙9.30am-8pm Thu, Mon & Tue, to 10.30pm Fri & Sat) This modern, minimalist *enoteca* with a lovely choice of cold cuts at the deli-style counter sits at the foot of the hill leading up to Piazzale Michelangelo – enter the perfect pit stop post-panorama.

Bars

These are the addresses to head to for that all-essential *aperitivo* (pre-dinner drinks from around 7pm to 10pm) and/or late-night cocktails (around midnight before clubbing), two trends embraced with gusto by Florentines. Live music is the common denominator.

TOP CHOICE Sky Lounge Continentale SKY BAR

(Map p66; www.continentale.it; Vicolo dell'Oro 6r; ☺2.30-11.30pm Apr-Sep) This rooftop bar with wooden decking terrace accessible from the 5th floor of the Ferragamo-owned Hotel Continentale is as chic as one would expect of a fashion-house hotel. Its evening *aperitivo* buffet might be a modest affair, but who cares with that fabulous, drop-dead-gorgeous panorama of one of Europe's most beautiful cities. Dress the part or feel out of place.

Golden View Open Bar LOUNGE BAR

(Map p90; www.goldenviewopenbar.com; Via de' Bardi 58; ☺7.30am-1.30am) Of course it is touristy given its prime location near Ponte Vecchio, but its worth a pit stop nonetheless – preferably at *aperitivo* hour when chic Florentines sip cocktails (€10/12 at bar/table), slurp oysters (€15) and watch the Arno swirling below their feet. Art exhibitions and live jazz from 8.30pm.

Eby's Bar LATIN BAR

(Map p86; Via dell'Oriulolo 5r; ☺10am-3am Mon-Sat) A lively student crowd packs out this young, fun, colourful address with wooden-bench tucked outside in a covered alleyway. The kitchen is Mexican – think great-value lunch platters and all-day salads, crepes, burritos and so on – and the drinks menu, laden with fruity cocktails.

Slowly LOUNGE BAR

(Map p66; www.slowlycafe.com; Via Porta Rossa 63r; ☺9pm-3am Mon-Sat, closed Aug) Sleek and sometimes snooty, this lounge bar with a candle flickering on every table is known for

---

DON'T MISS

THE CLUBHOUSE

(Map p82; ☏055 21 14 27; www.theclub house.it; Via de' Ginori 6r; ☺noon-midnight) Rave reviews from Florentines as well as resident and visiting Anglophones is all this thoroughly modern American bar, pizzeria and restaurant in San Marco gets. Handily close to *David*, it is the perfect drinking-dining hybrid any time of day, and that includes Sunday brunch. Design buffs will love its faintly industrial, cavernous vibe.

APERICENA

Apericena, a brilliant cent-saving trick and trend among students and 20-somethings in Florence, translates as an *aperitivo* buffet so copious it doubles as *cena* (dinner). Firm Florentine favourites known for their exceptionally generous buffets include Kitsch, Slowly and Obikà (p102).

its glam interior, Florentine Lotharios and lavish fruit-garnished cocktails – €10 including buffet during the bewitching *aperitivo* hour, which rocks until 10.30pm. Ibiza-style lounge tracks dominate the turntable.

Kitsch RETRO BAR

(www.kitsch-bar.com; ☺6.30pm-2.30am; ☏) San Marco (Map p82; Via San Gallo 22r); Santa Croce (Map p86; Piazza Beccaria) Known among every cent-conscious Florentine for its lavish spread at *aperitivi* time (€8.50 including a drink, from 6.30pm to 10pm), the hipster American-styled bar in Santa Croce sports a dark-red theatrical interior and a bright 20s to early 30s crowd out for a good time. Chandelier-lit Kitsch, next to a 14th-century pilgrim hospice on Via San Gallo, has a lovely shabby-chic exterior, animal-print seats, pavement terrace and live bands every week.

Lochness Lounge MUSIC BAR

(Map p86; www.lochnessfirenze.com; Via de' Benci 19r; ☺7pm-2am) One sassy gal is Lochness, a vintage-cool music 'n' cocktail venue with a definite Andy Warhol twist to its bold red interior. Dane-turned-native Trine West is the creative force behind the place and DJs play alternative sounds most nights. Drinks cost €5 during the daily 7pm to 10pm happy hour; check Facebook for the week's line-up.

Dolce Vita BAR

(Map p90; www.dolcevitaflorence.com; Piazza del Carmine 6r; ☺5pm-2am Tue-Sun, closed 2 weeks Aug) For the city's hip set on the other side of the river, this '80s favourite remains *the* address. Live Brazilian beats and jazz set the mood both outside on the decking terrace and in the design-driven interior, host to small photography and art exhibitions.

Lion's Fountain IRISH PUB

(Map p86; www.thelionsfountain.com; Borgo degli Albizi 34r; ☺10am-2am) If you have the urge to hear more English than Italian – or local bands play for that matter – this is the place.

Plump on a pretty pedestrian square, Florence's busiest Irish pub buzzes in summer when the beer-loving crowd spills across most of the square. Live music.

Mojo
BAR

(Map p86; www.moyo.it; Via de' Benci 23r; ⊙8am-2am Mon-Sat, 9am-3am Sun; 🛜) Free wi-fi until 7.30pm pulls in a moneyed younger set at this trendy all-rounder, popular for breakfast (€7 to €10), lunch (€8), *aperitivi* or late-night drinks. Cocktails (€6 to €7) are big – cranberry martini with lemon juice and triple sec is the house speciality – and DJs spin tip-top tunes Thursday to Saturday. And the decor? Think chandelier and bamboo!

Colle Bereto
LOUNGE BAR

(Map p66; www.collebereto.com; Piazza Strozzi 5; ⊙8am-2am Tue-Sun; 🛜) The local fashion scene's bar of choice, uberstylish Colle Bereto is where the bold and the beautiful come to see or be seen for breakfast, lunch or at *aperitivo* hour.

Old Stove
IRISH PUB

(Map p66; Piazza di San Giovanni 3; ⊙11am-2am) A firm favourite among expats and foreign students, this small busy space has a tiny wooden decking terrace facing the Baptistery and a much sought-after terrace for two up top.

Rex Caffé
BAR

(Map p86; Via Fiesolana 25r; ⊙6pm-3am Sep-May) A firm long-term favourite, down-to-earth Rex sports great drinks and an artsy Gaudi-inspired interior.

Cafes

Cafes are a dime a dozen in Florence. Prime squares to sit and people-watch from a pavement terrace are Piazza della Repubblica, Piazza Santo Spirito and Piazza della Signoria.

Note that a coffee taken sitting down at a table is three to four times more expensive than one drunk standing up at a bar: a cappuccino costs around €1.40/5.50 standing up/sitting down and a hot chocolate €2.50/6.

La Terrazza
DEPARTMENT-STORE CAFE

(Map p66; La Rinascente, Piazza della Repubblica 1; ⊙9am-9pm Mon-Sat, 10.30am-8pm Sun) Three canvas parasols and a dozen tables make this hidden terrace on the roof of Florence's central department store a privileged spot. Gloat with the birds over coffee or a €7 *aperitivo* cocktail at achingly lovely views of the *duomo*, Piazza della Repubblica and Florentine hills beyond.

Procacci
CAFE

(Map p66; Via de' Tornabuoni 64r; ⊙10am-8pm Mon-Sat) The last remaining bastion of genteel old Florence on Via de' Tornabuoni, this tiny cafe was born in 1885 opposite the English pharmacy as a delicatessen serving truffles in its repertoire of tasty morsels. Bite-sized *panini tartufati* (truffle pâté rolls) remain the thing to order, best accompanied by a glass of *prosecco*.

Scudieri
HISTORIC CAFE

(Map p66; Piazza di San Giovanni 21r; ⊙7.30am-9pm) Around since 1939, Scudieri is known for its *schiaccata alla fiorentina* (traditional sugar-dusted flat cake) and chocolate replicas of Michelangelo's *David*.

Caffè Cibrèo
CAFE

(Map p86; Via Andrea del Verrocchio 5; ⊙8am-1am Tue-Sat Sep-Jul) Duck into this charming old-world cafe behind Mercato di Sant'Ambrogio for a coffee and *ciambella* (doughnut ring).

BEST FOR APERITIVI WITH...

» **Soul-Soaring View** Sky Lounge Continentale (p109), La Terrazza

» **The Jet Set** Colle Bereto, Golden View Open Bar (p109), Slowly (p109)

» **Stuff-Yourself-Silly Buffet** Kitsch (p109)

» **Great Choice of Wine by the Glass** Le Volpi e l'Uva (p108), Sei Divino (p108)

» **Free Wi-fi** La Cité (p112), Mojo

» **Courtyard Seating** Obikà (p102)

☆ Entertainment

Hanging out on warm summer nights on cafe and bar terraces aside, Florence enjoys a vibrant entertainment scene thanks in part to its substantial foreign-student population. The city has highly regarded theatres, a bounty of festivals (p98) and – from around midnight once *aperitivi* and dinner is done – a fairly low-key but varied dance scene.

Nightclubs

To savour the best of Florentine clubs, don't arrive before midnight – dance floors generally fill by 2am. June to September every-

DON'T MISS

TOP 5 HISTORIC CAFES

Few cafes have seen or heard as much as these fabulous old Florentine beauties. Remember a coffee taken sitting down at a table is three to four times more expensive than one standing up at the bar.

Caffè Giacosa (Map p66; www.caffegiacosa.com; Via della Spada 10r; ☺Mon-Sat) This small cafe, always packed, is famous for what it was – an 1815 child, inventor of the Negroni cocktail and hub of Anglo-Florentine sophistication during the interwar years – and what it is (hip cafe of local hotshot designer Roberto Cavalli, whose flagship boutique is next door). Giacosa is known for its reasonable prices and also runs the equally hip cafe across the street in the courtyard of Palazzo Strozzi.

Caffè Rivoire (Map p66; Piazza della Signoria 4; ☺Tue-Sun) The golden oldie to refuel inside or out after an Uffizi or Palazzo Vecchio visit, this pricey little number with unbeatable people-watching terrace has produced some of the city's most exquisite chocolate since 1872. Black-jacketed barmen with ties set the formal tone.

Caffè Gilli (Map p66; Piazza della Repubblica 3r) The most famous of historic cafes on the city's old Roman forum, Gilli has been serving utterly delectable cakes, chocolates, fruit tartlets and *millefoglie* (sheets of puff pastry filled with rich vanilla or chocolate Chantilly cream) to die for since 1733 (it moved to this square in 1910 and sports a beautifully preserved art nouveau interior).

Caffè Concerto Paszkowski (Map p66; www.paszkowski.com; Piazza della Repubblica 31-35r; ☺Tue-Sun) Born as a brewery overlooking the city's fish market in 1846, this Florentine institution with heated terrace and elegant, piano-clad interior lured a literary set a century on. Today it pulls the whole gambit of punters, mobile-touting Florentine youths, suit-clad businessmen and well-dressed old ladies sipping tea.

Giubbe Rosse (Map p66; Piazza della Repubblica 13-14r; mains around €15) This address has changed little since its heyday when die-hard members of the early-20th-century futurist artistic movement drank and debated here. Inside, long vaulted halls lined with old photos, sketches and artwork make a great place to linger for coffee.

---

thing grinds to a halt when most clubs – bar Central Park and Meccanò, which have outdoor dance floors – shut. Admission, variable depending on the night, is usually more expensive for males than females and is sometimes free if you arrive early (between 9.30pm and 11pm).

YAB NIGHTCLUB
(Map p66; www.yab.it; Via de' Sassetti 5r; ☺9pm-4am Oct-May) It's crucial to pick your night according to your age and tastes at Florence's busiest disco club, around since the 1970s behind Palazzo Strozzi. Thursdays is the evening the over 30s hit the dance floor – otherwise, the set is predominantly student.

Central Park NIGHTCLUB
(Via Fosso Macinante 1; ☺11pm-4am Wed-Sat) Flit between a handful of different dance floors at this mainstream club in city park Parco delle Cascine where everything from Latin to pop, house to drum and bass plays. From May the dance floor moves outside beneath the stars.

Cavalli Club NIGHTCLUB
(Map p90; ☎055 21 16 50; www.cavalliclub.com; Piazza del Carmine 8r; dinner €50; ☺7.30pm-2.30am Tue-Sun) Incongruously wedged beside 13th-century Basilica di Santa Maria del Carmine, designer Robert Cavalli's club – in a deconsecrated church, look for the shiny red door – is glitzy, glam, wildly theatrical and over-the-top. Love it or hate it. Dine upstairs or sip cocktails with seafood *antipastissimo* (€38) downstairs. Book your table in advance.

Montecarla Club NIGHTCLUB
(Map p90; Via de' Bardi 2; ☺10pm-6am) With its fearsome bouncers, boudoir furnishings and multilevel leopard-skin mosh pits, this small happening club exudes Late Empire decadence – as well as clubbing elitism. Dress to kill.

DON'T MISS

WATCH THIS SPACE! LE MURATE

Very much a work in progress, Le Murate (Map p86; www.lemurate.comune.fi.it; Piazza della Madonna della Neve; ⊘noon-midnight) is one of Florence's most exciting and interesting cultural spaces. Marketing itself as a 'home lab – free space for experimentation', it is housed in Florence's old city jail (1883–1985) and 15th-century nunnery behind Mercato di Sant'Ambrogio.

Arranged around an interior courtyard, the historic red-brick complex is, in itself, compelling: there's absolutely no mistaking the thick sturdy doors leading to the old prison cells, many of which now open onto a bookshop, wine bar, art gallery and so on. Le Carceri (Map p86; ☎055.247.93 27; www.ristorantelecarceri.it; Piazza della Madonna della Neve 3; meals €35; ⊘lunch & dinner) is a restaurant with a lovely terrace overlooking the ensemble, and other spaces within the arts centre host everything from wine tastings, exhibitions, performances and debates to knitting lounges (v trendy!), sound installations, screenings and a gaggle of other hot dates in Florence's increasingly happening arts diary.

Cargo Club NIGHTCLUB
(off Map p90; http://cargoclub.wordpress.com; Via dell'Erta Canina 12r; ⊘11pm-4am Wed-Sat) This club prides itself on being a tad underground; DJs spin all sounds.

Full Up NIGHTCLUB
(Map p86; Via della Vigna Vecchia 21r; ⊘11pm-4am Mon-Sat Sep-Jun) A variety of sounds energises the crowd at this popular Florentine nightclub where 20-somethings dance until dawn.

Meccanò NIGHTCLUB
(Viale degli Olmi 10; ⊘11pm-5am Tue-Sat) Big-crowd disco in the Parco della Cascine with three dance floors spinning house, funk and standard commercial music to a mainstream youthful set.

Live Music
Most venues are outside town and closed in July and/or August.

TOP
CHOICE / **La Cité** MUSIC CAFE
(Map p90; www.lacitelibreria.info; Borgo San Frediano 20r; ⊘10am-1am Mon-Sat, 4pm-1am Sun; ⊜) By day this cafe-bookshop is a hip cappuccino stop with an eclectic choice of vintage seating to flop down on and surf. By night, from 10pm, the intimate bookshelf-lined space morphs into a vibrant live music space: think swing, fusion, jam-session jazz ... The staircase next to the bar hooks up with mezzanine seating up top.

Jazz Club JAZZ CLUB
(Map p86; www.jazzclubfirenze.com; Via Nuovo de' Caccini 3; ⊘9pm-2am Tue-Sat, closed Jul & Aug) Catch salsa, blues, Dixieland and world music as well as jazz at Florence's top jazz venue.

Be Bop Music Club MUSIC CLUB
(Map p82; Via dei Servi 76r; admission free; ⊘8pm-2am) Inspired by the swinging sixties, this beloved retro venue features everything from Led Zeppelin and Beatles cover bands to swing jazz and 1970s funk.

Theatre, Classical Music & Ballet

Teatro del Maggio Musicale Fiorentino THEATRE
(☎055 28 72 22; www.maggiofiorentino.com; Corso Italia 16) The curtain rises on opera, classical concerts and ballet at this lovely theatre, host to the summertime Maggio Musicale Fiorentina (p98).

Teatro della Pergola THEATRE
(Map p86; ☎055 2 26 41; www.teatrodellapergola. com; Via della Pergola 18) Beautiful city theatre with stunning entrance; host to classical concerts October to April.

🛍 Shopping

Tacky mass-produced souvenirs (boxer shorts emblazoned with *David's* packet) are everywhere, not least at the city's two main markets, Mercato Centrale (Map p82; Piazza del Mercato Centrale; ⊘9am-7pm Mon-Sat) and Mercato Nuovo (Map p66; Loggia Mercato Nuovo; ⊘8.30am-7pm Mon-Sat), awash with cheap imported handbags and other leather goods.

But for serious shoppers keen to delve into a city synonymous with craftsmanship since medieval times, there are plenty of ateliers and studios to visit. In medieval Florence goldsmiths, silversmiths and shoemakers were as *alta moda* as sculptors and artists, and modern Florentines are just as enamoured of design and artisanship – keen to *fare la bella figura* (cut a fine figure), appearances are all-important in this city and high-end shops are patronised by people across the income scale. Some may purchase full wardrobes, others the occasional accessory, but all will be very conscious of the labels they and other people are wearing.

Those keen to take a distinctively Florentine treat home should consider leather goods, jewellery, hand-embroidered linens, designer fashion, perfume, marbled paper, wine, puppets or gourmet foods.

In addition to the following options, try Scuola del Cuoio (p96) behind Basilica di Santa Croce for leather and Officina Profumo-Farmaceutica di Santa Maria Novella (p80) for perfume.

Fashion & Accessories

TOP CHOICE **Mrs Macis**   FASHION
(Map p86; www.mrsmacis.it; Borgo Pinti 38r; ⏱10.30am-1pm & 4-7.30pm Mon-Sat) Workshop and showroom of the talented Carla Macis, this eye-catching boutique – dollhouse-like in design – specialises in very feminine 1950s, '60s and '70s clothes and jewellery made from new and recycled fabrics. Every piece is unique and fabulous.

TOP CHOICE **Pitti Vintage**   FASHION
(Map p86; Borgo degli Albizi 72r; ⏱10am-1.30pm & 3-7.30pm Tue-Sat, 4-7.30pm Mon & Sun) One of the city's most stylish vintage choices, this boutique is a Pandora's box of carefully selected couture pieces and one-off collectibles.

TOP CHOICE **Casini Firenze**   FASHION
(Map p90; www.casinifirenze.it; Piazza Pitti 30-31r) One of Florence's oldest and most reputable fashion houses, this lovely boutique across from Palazzo Pitti keeps its edge thanks to American-Florentine designer and stylist (she does personal wardrobe consultations) Jennifer Tattanelli.

Alessandro Gherardeschi   FASHION
(Map p66; www.alessandrogherardeschi.com; Via della Vigna Nuova 97r) Distinctive men's and women's shirts and blouses, short- and long-sleeved, in dozens of designs – floral, cupcakes, vintage cars, all sorts! – is what this colourful little designer boutique near the river sells. Count on paying €80 to €140.

Loretta Caponi   FASHION
(Map p66; www.lorettacaponi.com; Piazza degli Antinori 4r; ⏱Mon-Fri & Sat morning Mar-Oct, closed Mon afternoon Nov-Feb) An old family name dressing the aristocracy for ions, this utterly gorgeous shop sells hand-embroidered sleepwear, bed and table linen, as well as slippers, bathrobes and exquisitely smocked children's clothes.

Société Anonyme   FASHION
(Map p86; www.societeanonyme.it; Via Niccolini 3f) Near Mercato di Sant' Ambrogio, this urban concept store turns to London's Brick Lane, Berlin's Mitte and other hip neighbourhoods for inspiration. Look for its list of brands chalked on the board outside (and the Shared Platform design gallery next door).

Francesco da Firenze   SHOES
(Map p90; Via di Santo Spirito 62r; ⏱closed 2 weeks Aug) Hand-stitched leather is the cornerstone of this tiny family business specialising in ready-to-wear – and indeed made-to-measure – men's and women's shoes.

Alessandro Dari   JEWELLERY
(Map p90; www.alessandrodari.com; Via San Niccolò 115r) Flamboyant jeweller and classical guitarist Alessandro Dari creates unique and extremely beautiful pieces in his atmospheric 15th-century workshop-showroom in San Niccolò. He describes his pieces as 'sculpture that you can wear' and presents them in thematic collections.

Lorenzo Villoresi   PERFUME
(Map p90; ☎055 234 11 87; www.lorenzovilloresi.it; Via de' Bardi 14; ⏱10am-7pm Mon-Sat) Villoresi's perfumes and potpourris meld distinctively Tuscan elements such as laurel, olive, cypress and iris with essential oils and essences from around the world. His bespoke fragrances are highly sought after. Visiting

ⓘ DIGITAL RESOURCES

To find out what's on when ...

» **Firenze Spettacolo** (www.firenzespettacolo.it)

» **The Florentine** (www.theflorentine.net)

» **Notte Fiorentina** (www.nottefiorentina.it)

» **Viva Notte Firenze** (www.vivanotte.it)

» **ViviFirenze** (www.vivifirenze.it)

Shopping in Florence

Florence is naturally stylish – the city did spawn the Renaissance and Gucci after all – which translates as inspirational shopping. Be it the hottest big-name label to strut down the catwalk or something handmade and unique by a smaller designer, fashion is what many people come to Florence for.

At the Market

1 Open-air stalls at Mercato de San Lorenzo and Mercato Nuovo (p112) buzz with shoppers on the prowl for a handbag, belt or jacket. Florence's street markets only hawk cheap, imported leather (for quality Florentine leather head to an old family-run boutique).

Handmade

2 Watching artisans cut bags from calf skin, bookbinders marble paper with peacock patterns, puppeteers stitch and jewellers pore over gold is what shopping in Florence is really about: Scuola del Cuoio (p96), Letizia Fiorini (p116) and Giulio Giannini e Figlio (p116) are key artisan addresses to do just that.

Via de' Tornabuoni

3 The world's luxury brands sit smart on Florence's main shopping strip (p78), a line-up starring everyone from Prada to Cartier plus home-grown players Gucci, Cavalli and Ferragamo (with glittering shoe museum to boot).

Oltrarno

4 Cross the river and be transported into the Florence where real Florentines live and shop (p88): strut Borgo San Jacopo and Via Santo Spirito for avant-garde fashion, shoes, handcrafted wood and dazzling jewellery.

Vintage & Recycled

5 Move east into Santa Croce (p85) to mingle with some of Florence's most creative designers specialising in vintage and recycled fashion – Borgo degli Albizi, Borgo Pinti (Ciao Mrs Macis!) and Via di Mezzo are key streets.

Clockwise from top left
1. Mercato Nuovo **2.** Handcrafted paper **3.** High-end fashion on Via de' Tornabuoni

his showroom, which occupies his family's 15th-century *palazzo*, is quite an experience. Drop-ins welcome but better to call in advance to arrange your visit.

Madova
GLOVES

(Map p90; www.madova.com; Via Guicciardini 1r; ⊙Mon-Sat) Cashmere lined, silk lined, lambs wool lined, unlined – gloves in whatever size, shape, colour and type of leather you fancy by Florentine glovemakers in the biz since 1919.

Design

Slow
ECO-DESIGN STORE

(Map p90; www.slow-design.it; Sdruccioli dei Pitti 13r) Beautiful objects for the home in the main, all crafted from natural or recycled materials by local designers.

Food & Wine

TOP CHOICE Dolce Forte
CHOCOLATE

(Map p66; www.dolceforte.it; Via della Scala 21; ⊙3.30-7.45pm Tue, 10am-1pm & 3.30-7.45pm Wed-Sat & Mon) Elena is the passion and knowledge behind this astonishing chocolate shop that sells only the best. Think black-truffle flavoured chocolate, an entire cherry, stone et al, soaked in grappa and wrapped in white chocolate or – for the ultimate taste sensation – *formaggio di fossa* (a cheese from central Italy) soaked in sweet wine and enrobed in dark chocolate.

La Bottega dell'Olio
OLIVE OIL

(Map p66; Piazza del Limbo 2r; ⊙Mon-Sat) This bijou boutique next to 11th-century Chiesa dei Santissimi Apostoli takes great care with its

displays of olive oils, olive oil soaps, platters made from olive wood and skincare products made with olive oil (the Lepo range is particularly good).

Obsequium
WINE

(Map p90; www.obsequium.it; Borgo San Jacopo 17-39r) Occupying the ground floor of one of the city's best-preserved medieval towers, this shop offers a wide range of fine Tuscan wines, wine accessories and gourmet foods, including truffles.

Conti Stefano
OLIVE OIL

(Map p82; www.tuscanyflavours.com; Via Signa 300) This permanent market stall (inside Mercato Centrale) is the place in Florence to taste and buy bitter and spicy, typically Tuscan olive oil on white plastic teaspoons; don't hesitate to ask for help and advice.

Artisanal

TOP CHOICE Letizia Fiorini
PUPPETS

(Map p66; Via del Parione 60r; ⊙Tue-Sat) This charming shop is a one-woman affair – Letizia Fiorini sits at the counter and makes her distinctive puppets by hand in between assisting customers. You'll find Pulchinella (Punch), Arlecchino the clown, beautiful servant girl Colombina, Doctor Peste (complete with plague mask), cheeky Brighella, swashbuckling Il Capitano and many other characters from traditional Italian puppetry.

TOP CHOICE Giulio Giannini e Figlio
STATIONERY

(Map p90; www.giuliogiannini.it; Piazza Pitti) Easy to miss, this quaint old shopfront has

---

FLORENCE FASHION

If there is one Italian city that screams fashion it's Florence, birthplace of Gucci (Map p66; www.gucci.com; Via de' Tornabuoni 73), Emilio Pucci and Roberto Cavalli (Map p66; www.robertocavalli.com; Via de' Tornabuoni 83), alongside a bevy of lesser-known designers who beaver away to ensure Florence's continuing reputation as a city synonymous with beauty, creativity and skilled craftsmanship.

Which is precisely what Florence's Department of Tourism and Fashion strives to promote with its outstanding website (www.florenceartfashion.com), an authoritative guide to the city's fashion studios and workshops. Themed itineraries will walk you through small ateliers and boutiques that design and craft footwear, women's fashion, jewellery, accessories and so on; and you can also sign up for an on-the-ground guided fashion tour.

To DIY shop, legendary Via de' Tornabuoni (Map p66) – a fashionably quaint street with a pharmacy, bookshop, several cafes and small speciality stores until Florence Fashion dug in her manicured claws and turned it into the glittering catwalk of designer boutiques it is today – is the place to start. Via della Vigna Nuova (Map p66), the street where icon of Florence fashion Gucci started out as a tiny saddlery shop in 1921, is Florence's other fashion-hot street. Local designers to look for include Michele Negri, Enrico Coveri, Patrizia Pepe and Ermanno Daelli.

Keen to replenish your wardrobe with a few designer pieces but don't want to break the bank? Then head for Florence's out-of-town outlet malls where you can pick up previous-season designer clothing for 30% to 50% less. If you don't want to go it alone, CAF Tours (p96) organises day trips by bus to the following:

Barberino Designer Outlet (www.mcarthurglen.it; Via Meucci, Barberino di Mugello; ⏰10am-8pm Tue-Fri, to 9pm Sat & Sun, 2-8pm Mon Jan, Jun-Sep & Dec) Polo Ralph Lauren, D&G, Prada, Class Roberto Cavalli, Missoni, Furla, Benetton and Bruno Magli are just a few of the 100 labels with stores here. Outlet shuttle buses (return €12) depart from Piazza della Stazione in Florence at 10am and 2.30pm daily, departing for the return journey from the outlet, 40km north in Barberino di Mugello, at 1.30pm and 6pm.

The Mall (www.themall.it; Via Europa 8, Leccio; ⏰10am-7pm or 8pm daily) Gucci, Ferragamo, Burberry, Ermenegildo Zegna, Yves Saint Laurent, Tod's, Fendi, Giorgio Armani, Marni, Valentino et al are represented in this mall, 35km from Florence. Buses (€3.30, up to four daily) leave from the SITA bus station. By car, take the Incisa exit off the northbound A1 and follow signs for Leccio.

watched Palazzo Pitti turn pink with the evening sun since 1856. One of Florence's oldest artisan families, the Gianninis – bookbinders by trade – make and sell marbled paper, beautifully bound books, stationery and so on. Don't miss the workshop upstairs.

Antico Setifico Fiorentino   FABRIC
(www.anticosetificiofiorentino.com; Via Bartoini 4; ⏰9am-1pm & 2-5pm Mon-Fri) Precious silks, velvets and other luxurious fabrics are woven on 18th- and 19th-century looms at this world-famous fabric house where opulent damasks and brocades in Renaissance styles have been made since 1786.

Alberto Cozzi   STATIONERY
(Map p66; Via del Parione 35r) Florence is famous for its exquisite marbled paper and this well-known, fourth-generation bookbinder and restorer has been making sheets of the stuff by hand since 1908. Come here to buy paper, leather-bound journals and colourful cards.

Pineider   STATIONERY
(Map p66; www.pineider.com; Piazza della Signoria 13-14r) This exclusive stationer opened here in 1774 and once designed calling cards for Napoleon. You can order your own, or choose from a tempting range of paper products and elegant leather office accessories.

Officina de' Tornabuoni   PERFUME
(Map p66; www.officinadetornabuoni.com; Via de' Tornabuoni 19, ⏰Mon afternoon-Sun) This famous retailer of health and beauty products, tucked in a 16th-century *palazzo,* has been

selling sweet-smelling potions and lotions for every ailment or cosmetic need since 1843. It only uses natural products.

ⓘ Information

Emergency

Police station (Questura; ☎055 4 97 71; http://questure.poliziadistato.it; Via Zara 2; ⏰24hr)

Tourist Police (Polizia Assistenza Turistica; ☎055 20 39 11; Via Pietrapiana 50r; ⏰8.30am-6.30pm Mon-Fri, to 1pm Sat) English-speaking service for filing reports of thefts etc.

Medical Services

24-Hour Pharmacy (Stazione di Santa Maria Novella) In the main train station.

Dr Stephen Kerr: Medical Service (☎055 28 80 55, 335 8361682; www.dr-kerr.com; Piazza Mercato Nuovo 1; ⏰3-5pm Mon-Fri, or by appointment) Resident British doctor.

Hospital (Ospedale di Santa Maria Nuova; ☎055 2 75 81; Piazza di Santa Maria Nuova 1)

Tourist Information

Florence airport (☎055 31 58 74; ⏰8.30am-8.30pm)

Stazione di Santa Maria Novella (Map p58; ☎055 21 22 45; Piazza della Stazione 4; ⏰8.30am-7pm Mon-Sat, to 2pm Sun) Baby-changing facilities.

Santa Croce (Map p86; ☎055 234 04 44; www.comune.fi.it, in Italian; Borgo Santa Croce 29r; ⏰9am-7pm Mon-Sat, to 2pm Sun).

San Lorenzo (Map p82; ☎055 29 08 32; www.firenzeturismo.it; Via Cavour 1r; ⏰8.30am-6.30pm Mon-Sat)

FIESOLE DAY TRIPPER

One of the joys of Florence is leaving it behind and Fiesole provides the perfect excuse. Perched in hills 9km northeast of the city, this bijou hilltop village has seduced for centuries with its cooler air, olive groves, scattering of Renaissance-styled villas and spectacular views of the plain. Boccaccio, Marcel Proust, Gertrude Stein and Frank Lloyd Wright, among others, all raved about it.

10am

Hop aboard ATAF bus 7 (€1.20) from Florence's Piazza San Marco and alight 30 minutes later on Fiesole's central square, Piazza Mino di Fiesole. Founded in the 7th century BC by the Etruscans, Fiesole was the most important city in northern Etruria and its Area Archeologica (www.fiesolemusei.it; Via Portigiani 1; adult/reduced €12/8; ⊙10am-7pm Apr-Sep, to 6pm Mar & Oct, 10am-2pm Wed-Mon Nov-Feb), a couple of doors down from the tourist office (☑055 596 13 23; www.comune.fiesole.fi.it; Via Portigiani 3; ⊙10.30am-1pm & 1.30-4pm Mar-Oct, shorter hr rest of year), provides the perfect flashback to its fabulous past. Meander around the ruins of a small Etruscan temple, Roman baths and an archaeological museum with exhibits from the Bronze Age to the Roman period. Later, take a break al fresco on one of the stone steps of the 1st-century-BC Roman amphitheatre, where musicians, actors and artists take to the stage in summer during Italy's oldest open-air festival, Estate Fiesolana (www.estatefiesolana.it). July's Vivere Jazz Festival (www.viverejazz.it) is the other hot date at this atmospheric theatre.

Afterwards pop into the neighbouring Museo Bandini (Via Dupré; adult/reduced €5/3 or free with Area Archeologica ticket; ⊙9.30am-7pm Apr-Sep, to 6pm Oct & Mar, 10am-5pm Wed-Mon Nov-Dec, 11am-5pm Thu-Mon Jan & Feb) to view early Tuscan Renaissance art, including fine medallions (c 1505–20) by Giovanni della Robbia and Taddeo Gaddi's luminous *Annunciation* (1340–45).

Noon

From the museum, a 300m walk along Via Giovanni Dupré brings you to the villa of Museo Primo Conti (www.fondazioneprimoconti.org; Via Dupré 18; admission €3; ⊙9am-1pm Mon-Fri), where the eponymous avant-garde 20th-century artist lived and worked. Inside hang more than 60 of his paintings and the views from the garden are inspiring. Ring to enter.

1pm

Meander back to central square, Piazza Mino di Fiesole, host to an antiques market the first Sunday of each month, where cafe and restaurant terraces tempt on all sides. The pagoda-covered terrace of four-star hotel-restaurant Villa Aurora (☑055 5 93 63; www.villaurora.net; Piazza Mino da Fiesole 39), around since 1860, is the classic choice, not so much for its gourmet cuisine but rather for the spectacular panoramic view of Florence it cooks up. For a wholly rustic and typical Tuscan lunch built around locally produced salami and cheese, home-made pasta and Chianina T-bones eaten at a shared table, enoteca-cum-bistro Vinandro (☑055 5 91 21; www.vinandrofiesole.com; Piazza Mino da Fiesole 33; meals €25) is the hot spot on the square to grab a table.

3pm

Stagger around Cattedrale di San Romolo (Piazza Mino di Fiesole; ⊙7.30am-noon & 3-5pm), Piazza Mino di Fiesole's centrepiece, begun in the 11th century but heavily renovated in the 19th. A glazed terracotta statue of San Romolo by Giovanni della Robbia guards the entrance inside. Afterwards, from the far end of the square, slowly make your way up steep walled Via San Francesco and be blown away by the staggeringly beautiful panorama of Florence that unfolds from the terrace adjoining 15th-century Basilica di Sant'Alessandro (if you're lucky, the church might be open and even have a temporary exhibition inside). Grassy-green, afternoon-nap spots abound and the tourist office has brochures outlining several short trails (1km to 3.5km) fanning out from here should you prefer to carry on walking.

ℹ Getting There & Away

Air

Florence airport (FLR; ☎055 306 13 00; www.aeroporto.firenze.it) Also known as Amerigo Vespucci or Peretola airport, 5km northwest of the city centre; domestic and a handful of European flights.

Pisa International Airport (PSA; www.pisa-airport.com) Also known as Aeroporto Galileo Galilei, Tuscany's main international airport is closer to Pisa, but well linked with Florence by public transport.

Bus

Services from the **SITA bus station** (Map p66; www.sitabus.it; Via Santa Caterina da Siena 17r; ⊘information office 8.30am-12.30pm & 3-6pm Mon-Fri, 8.30am-12.30pm Sat), just west of Piazza della Stazione:

SAN GIMIGNANO (via Poggibonsi; €6.50, 1¼ hours, 14 daily)

SIENA (€7.10, 1¼ hours, at least hourly)

GREVE IN CHIANTI (€3.30, one hour, hourly)

Car & Motorcycle

Florence is connected by the A1 northwards to Bologna and Milan, and southwards to Rome and Naples. The Autostrada del Mare (A11) links Florence with Pistoia, Lucca, Pisa and the coast, but most locals use the FI-PI-LI – a *superstrada* (dual carriageway, hence no tolls; look for blue signs saying FI-PI-LI (as in Firenze-Pisa-Livorno). Another dual carriageway, the S2, links Florence with Siena. The much more picturesque SS67 connects the city with Pisa to the west, and Forli and Ravenna to the east.

Train

Florence's central train station is **Stazione di Santa Maria Novella** (Map p58; Piazza della Stazione). The **train information counter** (⊘7am-7pm) faces the tracks in the main foyer. The **left-luggage counter** (Deposito Bagagliamano; first 5hr €4, then per hr €0.60; ⊘6am-11.50pm) is located on platform 16 and the Assistenza Disabili (Disabled Assistance) office is on platform 5. International train tickets are sold in the **ticketing hall** (⊘6am-9pm). For domestic tickets, skip the queue and buy your tickets from the touch-screen automatic ticket-vending machines; machines have an English option and accept cash and credit cards.

Florence is on the Rome–Milan line. Services include the following:

BOLOGNA (€10.50 to €25, one hour to 1¾ hours)

LUCCA (€5.10, 1½ hours to 1¾ hours, half-hourly)

MILAN (€29.50 to €53, 2¼ hours to 3½ hours)

PISA (€5.80, 45 minutes to one hour, half-hourly)

ℹ SMS BUS TICKETS

If you prefer the speed and convenience of an SMS bus ticket, you'll need to first register your credit card (Visa or MasterCard) with **Bemoov** (www.bemoov.com). After that it's plain sailing: before hopping aboard send a text with the message 'ataf' to ☎339 9941264 and receive within seconds a reply containing an alphanumeric code that will keep any ticket controller happy. SMS tickets cost the same as paper tickets.

PISTOIA (€3.10, 45 minutes to one hour, half-hourly)

ROME (€17.25, 1¾ hours to 4¼ hours)

VENICE (€24 to €43, 2¾ hours to 4½ hours)

ℹ Getting Around

To/From the Airport

BUS ATAF operates a Volainbus shuttle (single/return €5/8, 25 minutes) between Florence airport and Florence's Stazione di Santa Maria Novella (Map p58) every 30 minutes between 6am and 11.30pm (5.30am to 11pm from city centre). **Terravision** (www.terravision.eu) runs daily services (single/return €10/16, 1¼ hours, hourly between 8.40am and 9.15pm) between the bus stop outside Florence's Stazione di Santa Maria Novella on Via Alamanni and Pisa's Galileo Galilei airport – buy tickets online, on board or from the **Terravision desk** (Via Alamanni 9r; ⊘6am-7pm) inside the Deanna Bar; at Galileo Galilei airport, the Terravision ticket desk dominates the arrival hall.

TAXI A taxi between Florence airport and town costs a flat rate of €20, plus surcharges of €2 on Sundays and holidays, €3 between 10pm and 6am and €1 per bag. Exit the terminal building, bear right and you'll come to the taxi rank.

TRAIN Regular trains link Florence's Stazione di Santa Maria Novella with Pisa's Galileo Galilei airport (€5.80, 1½ hours, at least hourly from 4.30am to 10.25pm).

Car & Motorcycle

Nonresident traffic is banned from the centre of Florence for most of the week and our advice if you can is to avoid the whole irksome bother of having a car in the city.

Bicycle & Scooter

Biciclette a Noleggio (Piazza della Stazione; per hr/day €1.50/8; ⊘7.30am-7pm Mon-Sat, 9am-7pm Sun, to 6pm Nov-Jan) Royal blue bikes to rent in front of Stazione di Santa Maria Novella.

ⓘ PARKING IN FLORENCE

There is a strict Limited Traffic Zone (Zona Traffico Limitato; ZTL) in Florence's *centro storico* (historic centre) between 7.30am and 7.30pm Monday to Friday and 7.30am to 6pm Saturday for all nonresidents, monitored by cyclopean cameras positioned at all entry points. The exclusion also applies on Wednesday, Friday and Saturday from 11pm to 4am mid-May to mid-September. Motorists staying in hotels within the ZTL are allowed to drive to their hotel to drop off luggage, but must tell reception their car registration number and the time they were in no-cars-land (there's a two-hour window) so that the hotel can inform the authority and organise a temporary access permit.

If you transgress, a fine of around €150 will be sent to you (or the car-hire company you have used). Many travellers have written to us to complain about credit-card charges from car-hire companies being levied months after their unknowing infraction of the ZTL occurred, often with administrative costs of up to €100 added to the fine. For more information (in English) and a map of the ZTL, go to www.comune.fi.it.

There is free street parking around Piazzale Michelangelo (park within blue lines; white lines are for residents only). Pricey (around €20 per day) underground parking can be found in the area around Fortezza da Basso and in the Oltrarno beneath Piazzale di Porta Romana. Otherwise, search for a car park on www.firenzeparcheggi.it or ask if your hotel can arrange parking for you.

Florence by Bike (www.florencebybike.com; Via San Zanobi 120r; ⊘9am-1pm & 3.30-7.30pm Mon-Sat) Top-notch bike shop, itinerary suggestions, bike tours and rental outlet (city bike/scooter per day €14.50/68).

Rental Point Ghiberti (Piazza Ghiberti; per hr/day €1.50/8; ⊘8.30am-7pm Mon-Sat May-Sep, shorter hr Oct-Apr) Open-air stand behind Mercato di Sant' Ambrogio.

Public Transport

Buses, electric *bussini* (minibuses) and, more recently, trams (all lines to be up and running by 2016) run by public transport company **ATAF** (☑800 424500, 199 104245; www.ataf.net/en) serve the city. Most buses – including bus 13 to Piazzale Michelangelo – start/terminate at the ATAF bus stops opposite the southeastern exit of Stazione di Santa Maria Novella. Tickets valid for 90 minutes (no return journeys) cost €1.20 (€2 on board – drivers don't give change!) and are sold at kiosks, tobacconists and the **ATAF ticket & information office** (Piazza della Stazione; ⊘7.30am-7.30pm), adjoining the train station. A carnet of 10 tickets costs €10, a handy *biglietto multiplo* (four-journey ticket) is €4.70 and a travel pass valid for 1/3/7 days is €5/12/18. Upon boarding time-stamp your ticket (punch on board) or risk a fine (€40 plus administrative costs on the spot or within five days; maximum fine €240).

Taxi

For a taxi, call ☑055 42 42 or ☑055 43 90.

Northwestern Tuscany

Best Places to Eat

» Villa Bongi (see the boxed text, p144)

» Podere del Grillo (p150)

» Osteria Vecchia Mulino (p151)

» Buca di Baldabò (see the boxed text, p156)

» Filippo (p160)

Best Places to Stay

» Barbialla Nuova (p149)

» Pradaccio di Sopra (p151)

» Il Benefizio (p154)

» Albergo Pietrasanta (p159)

» Fattoria di Stibbio (p149)

Why Go?

There is far more to this green corner of Tuscany than Italy's iconic Leaning Tower. Usually hurtled through at breakneck speed en route to Florence and Siena's grand-slam queue-for-hours sights, this is the place to take your foot off the brake and go slow – on foot, by bicycle or car. Allow for long lazy lunches of rustic regional specialities to set the pace for the day, meandering around a medieval hilltop village per-haps in the morning or along an ancient pilgrimage route.

Even the region's larger towns – university hub Pisa and 'love at first sight' Lucca with its 16th-century walls ensnar-ing a labyrinth of butter-coloured buildings, Romanesque palaces and gracious piazzas – have an air of tranquillity and tradition that begs the traveller to linger. This is snail-paced Italy, and you're sure to love it.

When to Go

Pisa makes an easy weekend break any time of year al-though July and August are best avoided if you don't like crowds: plan for June instead, when it's still warm and the city celebrates its patron saint with fireworks, a regatta and magical visits after dark of its iconic Leaning Tower. Else-where, spring and early summer is the best time to savour the Apuane Alps and Garfagnana's outdoor action, while October to December is the time to hunt and eat white truffles and catch San Miniato's famous white-truffle fair (November).

Culinary Experiences

» **Lardo di Colannata** (p158) Eat pig fat aged for 12 or 24 months in marble vats of herby olive oil.

» **Martelli Pasta** (see the boxed text, p134) Watch an artisan spaghetti maker at work.

» **Barbialla Nuova** (see the boxed text, p149) Hunt white truffles with a *tartufaio* (truffle hunter) and his dog.

Advance Planning

» Buy tickets online for Pisa's Leaning Tower (15 days in advance; p126).

» Books tickets/accommodation for Viareggio's famous carnival (p161).

» Buy a gold-dust ticket for Lucca's Puccini Festival (see the boxed text, p142).

» Put in your request to visit sculpture garden Fattoria di Celle (see the boxed text, p148).

Resources

» Pisa Tourism: www.pisaturismo.it

» Parco Regionale delle Alpi Apuane: www.parcapuane.it

» Toscana Mare: Tuscan Coast; www.tuscancoast.org

Itineraries

Biking Lucca Hire a bike, provision yourself with Forno Giusti's fresh-from-the-oven focaccia and pizza, and free-wheel along the city's medieval streets. Lunch atop the monumental city walls, or pedal east to picnic in Renaissance villa grounds. At day's end, listen to a Puccini recital in a medieval church.

Valdo Pisano Fall in love with backstreet Pisa – squirrel away the tower and Pisa's picture-perfect Piazza dei Miracoli until early evening. Next day watch how spaghetti is made in Lari, then continue to San Miniato for a mooch and lunch – in town or a nearby village. As the afternoon wanes, settle down for the night on a quintessential Tuscan farm or in a 15th-century villa built for members of the Medici family.

In the Name of Art: Mountain to Sea Shop for a picnic of local forest produce in Castelnuovo di Garfagnana, then motor up and over the Apuane Alps – allow plenty of time for pulling over to soak up vistas of monumental marble blocks being cut out of the mountainside. Picnic on the Passo del Vestito and visit its botanical garden, then drop down to the sea. In Massa, head north to Carrara (to see a marble quarry) or south to refined Pietrasanta (for contemporary art and creative dining).

GETTING AROUND

Major towns and cities are well connected by the A11 and A12, but it's more fun to veer off the motorways and onto scenic secondary roads and narrow rural routes, particularly in the Lunigiana and Garfagnana. Pisa and Lucca have strictly enforced Limited Traffic Zones (ZTL) in their *centro storico* (historic centres) – be careful where you park! Regular trains link Florence, Pisa, Lucca and Viareggio, but less obvious places such as Lari and Lajatico (with great off-beat things to see and do) require a car.

Where to Stay

Pisa is the obvious place to stay, but it's traffic busy and the choice of quality accommodation is limited. Opt instead for lovely Lucca (though parking is difficult), a farm stay around San Miniato, or stylish art gem Pietrasanta: all three are an easy drive to northwestern Tuscany's key sights, and will charm your socks off to boot.

PISA

POP 87,440

Once a maritime power to rival Genoa and Venice, Pisa now draws its fame from an architectural project gone terribly wrong. But the world-famous Leaning Tower is just one of many noteworthy sights in this compact and compelling city. Education has fuelled the local economy since the 1400s, and students from across Italy still compete for places in its elite university and research schools. This endows the centre of town with a vibrant and affordable cafe and bar scene, and balances what is an enviable portfolio of well-maintained Romanesque buildings, Gothic churches and Renaissance piazzas with a lively streetlife dominated by locals rather than tourists – a charm you will definitely not discover if you restrict your visit to Piazza dei Miracoli.

If you're looking for an easy half-day trip from Pisa, medieval Lari (see the boxed text, p134) with its artisanal spaghetti factory is just the ticket!

History

Pisa became an important naval base and commercial port under Rome and remained a significant port for centuries. The city's golden days began late in the 10th century, when it became an independent maritime republic and a formidable rival of Genoa and Venice. A century on, the Pisan fleet was sailing far beyond the Mediterranean, successfully trading with the Orient and bringing home new ideas in art, architecture and science. At the peak of its power (the 12th and 13th centuries), Pisa controlled Corsica, Sardinia and the Tuscan coast. Most of the city's finest buildings date from this period, when the distinctive Pisan-Romanesque architectural style with its use of coloured marbles and subtle references to Andalucian architectural styles flourished. Many of these buildings sported decoration by the great father-and-son sculptural team of Nicola and Giovanni Pisano.

Pisa's support for the imperial Ghibellines during the tussles between the Holy Roman Emperor and the pope brought the city into conflict with its mostly Guelph Tuscan neighbours, including Siena, Lucca and Florence. The real blow came when Genoa's fleet inflicted a devastating defeat on Pisa at the Battle of Meloria in 1284. After the city fell to Florence in 1406, the Medici court encouraged great artistic, literary and scientific endeavours and re-established Pisa's university, where the city's most famous son, Galileo Galilei, taught in the late 16th century. During WWII about 40% of old Pisa was destroyed.

◉ Sights & Activities

Many visitors to Pisa limit their sightseeing to the Piazza dei Miracoli monuments, but those in the know devote time to the *centro storico* (historic centre).

ALONG THE ARNO

Away from the crowded heavyweights of Piazza dei Miracoli, along the Arno river banks, Pisa comes into its own. Splendid *palazzo*, painted a multitude of hues, line the southern *lungarno* (riverside embankment), from where shopping boulevard Corso Italia legs it to the train station.

Pisa's medieval heart lies north of the water: from Piazza Cairoli, with its evening bevy of bars and *gelatarie*, meander along Via Cavour and get lost in the surrounding lanes and alleys. A daily fresh-produce market fills Piazza delle Vettovaglie, ringed with 15th-century porticoes and cafe terraces. Graffiti on the facade of Chiesa di San Michele in Borgo (Borgo Stretto) dates all the way back to a 15th-century election for the rector of a local school.

Chiesa di Santa Maria della Spina   CHURCH
(Lungarno Gambacorti; adult/reduced €2/1.50; ⊙11am-12.45pm & 3-5.45pm Tue-Fri, 11am-12.45pm & 3-6.45pm Sat & Sun) This breathtakingly exquisite church on the Arno's southern bank is a fine example of Pisan-Gothic. The now-deconsecrated church was built between 1230 and 1223 to house a reliquary of a *spina* (thorn) from Christ's crown. Its ornate, triple-spired exterior is encrusted with tabernacles and statues, but the interior is simple and perfectly suited to quiet reflection. The

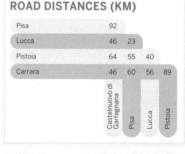

ROAD DISTANCES (KM)

	Pisa	Lucca	Pistoia	Castelnuovo di Garfagnana
Pisa	92			
Lucca	46	23		
Pistoia	64	55	40	
Carrara	46	60	56	89

North-western Tuscany Highlights

1 Pedal and picnic atop **Lucca**'s lovely Renaissance city walls (p137)

2 Fall in love with medieval **Pisa** – scale its iconic Leaning Tower at sunset (see the boxed text, p126)

3 Flee the Pisa and Lucca crowd: watch spaghetti being handmade, as it has been done by the same family, for almost a century in medieval **Lari** (see the boxed text, p134)

4 Hunt white truffles in autumnal woods at **Barbialla Nuova** (see the boxed text, p149)

5 Learn how to cook the Tuscan way with one of the region's tip-top celebrity TV chefs in **San Miniato** (p150)

6 Book a table for two in the world's smallest restaurant – it only has one table (see the boxed text, p150)

7 Revel in exciting contemporary art, cuisine and boutique shopping in gorgeous small-town **Pietrasanta** (p159)

8 Lose yourself in the best of rural Tuscany in the **Garfagnana** (p150)

9 See where Michelangelo sourced his marble and visit the quarries in **Carrara** (p157)

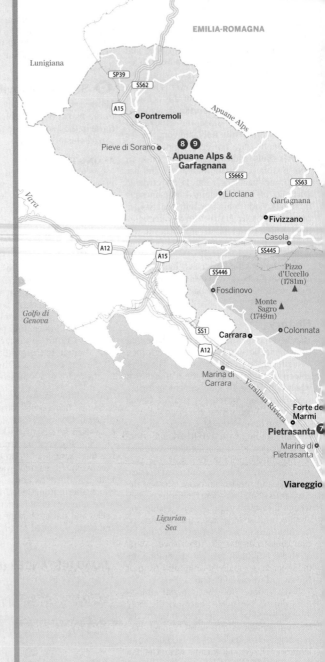

ℹ HOW TO FALL IN LOVE WITH PISA

Sure, the iconic Leaning Tower is Pisa's raison d'être and the reason everyone wants to go to Pisa. But once you've put yourself through the whole Piazza dei Miracoli madness (overzealous souvenir sellers, boisterous school groups, photo-posing pandemonium, you get the picture ...) most people simply want to get out of town.

To avoid leaving Pisa feeling oddly deflated by one of Europe's great landmarks, save the Leaning Tower & Co for the latter part of the day – or, better still, an enchanting visit after dark (mid-June to August) when the night casts a certain magic on the glistening white monuments and the tour buses have long gone.

Upon arrival, indulge instead in peaceful meanderings along the Arno river, over its bridges and through Pisa's medieval heart. Enjoy low-key architectural and art genius at the Chiesa di Santa Maria della Spina (p123) and Palazzo Blu (p126), and lunch with locals at Sottobosco (p133).

And only then, once you've fallen in love with the other Pisa, should you head for its tower.

focal point is Andrea and Nino Pisano's *Madonna and Child* (aka Madonna of the Rose; 1345–48), a masterpiece of Gothic sculpture that still bears traces of its original colours and gilding.

FREE Palazzo Blu   ART MUSEUM
(www.palazzoblu.it; Lungarno Gambacorti 9; ⊙10am-7pm Tue-Fri, 10am-8pm Sat & Sun) Facing the river is this magnificently restored, 14th-century building that has a striking dusty-blue facade. Inside, its over-the-top 19th-century interior decoration is the perfect backdrop for the Foundation CariPisa's art collection – predominantly Pisan works from the 14th to the 20th century, plus various temporary exhibitions.

Museo Nazionale di
San Matteo   ART MUSEUM
(Piazza San Matteo in Soarta, Lungarno Mediceo; adult/reduced €5/2; ⊙8.30am-7.30pm Tue-Sat, to 1.30pm Sun) This inspiring repository of medieval masterpieces sits in a 13th-century Benedictine convent on the Arno's northern waterfront boulevard, dwarfed either side by a gorgeous *palazzo*. The gallery's collection of 14th- and 15th-century Pisan sculptures, including pieces by Nicola and Giovanni Pisano, Andrea and Nino Pisano, Francesco di Valdambrino, Donatello, Michelozzo and Andrea della Robbia, is notable. But even better is its collection of paintings from the Tuscan school (c 12th to 14th centuries), with works by Berlinghiero, Lippo Memmi, Taddeo Gaddi, Gentile da Fabriano and Ghirlandaio on show. Don't miss Masaccio's *St Paul,* Fra Angelico's *Madonna of Humility* and Simone Martini's *Polyptych of Saint Catherine.*

PIAZZA DEI MIRACOLI

No Tuscan sight is more immortalised in kitsch souvenirs than the iconic tower teetering on the edge of this gargantuan piazza, also known as the Campo dei Miracoli (Field of Miracles) or Piazza del Duomo (Cathedral Sq). The piazza's expansive green lawns provide an urban carpet on which Europe's most extraordinary concentration of Romanesque buildings – in the form of cathedral, baptistry and tower – are arranged. With two million visitors every year, crowds are the norm, many arriving by tour bus from Florence for a whirlwind visit.

Each year from 16 June until the last Sunday in August or first in September, the Leaning Tower and Camposanta open their doors to visitors until 11pm – a magical experience not to be missed.

Leaning Tower   LANDMARK
(Torre Pendente; www.opapisa.it; admission ticket office/online €15/17; ⊙8.30am-8.30pm Apr–mid-Jun & Sep, 8.30am-11pm mid-Jun–Aug, 9am-7.30pm Oct, 9.30am-6pm Nov & Feb-Mar, 10am-5pm Dec-Jan) Yes, it's true: the Leaning Tower really *does* lean. Construction work started in 1173 but ground to a halt a decade later when the structure's first three tiers started tilting. In 1272 work started again, with artisans and masons attempting to bolster the foundations but failing miserably. Despite this, they kept going, compensating for the lean by gradually building straight up from the lower storeys and creating a subtle banana curve.

Over the centuries, the tower has tilted an extra 1mm each year. By 1993 it was 4.47m out of plumb, more than five degrees from the vertical. The most recent solution saw

Why Pisa Leans

When Bonnano Pisano set to work on the world's most famous *campanile* (bell tower) in 1173, he didn't realise what shaky ground he was on: beneath Campo dei Miracoli's lawns lay a treacherous mix of sand and clay, 40m deep. And when work stopped five years on, with just three storeys completed, Italy's stump of an icon already tilted.

When building resumed in 1272 workers compensated for the lean by building straight up from the lower storeys to create a subtle banana curve – not good. In 1990 the tower was closed to the public. Engineers placed 1000 tonnes of lead ingots on the north side to counteract the subsidence on the south side. Steel bands were wrapped around the 2nd storey to keep it together.

Then in 1995 the tower slipped a whole 2.5mm. Steel braces were slung around the 3rd storey of the tower and attached to heavy hydraulic A-frame anchors some way from the northern side. The frames were replaced by steel cables, attached to neighbouring buildings. The tower held in place, engineers gingerly removed 70 tonnes of earth from below the northern foundations, forcing the tower to sink to its 18th-century level – and correct the lean by 43.8cm. Success...

A good old scrub and polish followed and finally, in April 2011, work was complete. For the first time in 20 years Pisa's Leaning Tower could be viewed as intended – dazzling white, free of scaffolding (and still very firmly leaning).

LEANING CITY

» **Duomo & Baptistry** (Piazza Dei Miracoli) The tower's neighbours lean 25cm and 51cm respectively.

» **Chiesa di San Nicola** (Via Santa Maria) Nicola Pisano's octagonal *campanile* (bell tower) is another sacred edifice not dead straight.

» **Chiesa di San Michele degli Scalzi** (Via San Michele degli Scalzi) Note the wonky red-brick square tower.

Left

1. The Leaning Tower 2. Bell tower of Chiesa di San Nicola

The Humble Truffle

From Etruscan truffle hunts to hunting with a *tartufaio* (truffle hunter) and his dog near Florence, *tartufi* (truffles) are a mystery. They're not a plant, they don't spawn like mushrooms and cultivating them is impossible. Pig-ugly yet precious, these wild knobs of fungus excite and titillate.

Truffles grow in symbiosis with an oak tree and come in bianco (white – actually a mouldy old yellowish colour) or nero (black – a gorgeous velvety tone). They are sniffed out by highly trained dogs during the hunting season from mid-October to late December. Find them in San Giovanni d'Asso near Siena (p230) and San Miniato (p148), between Florence and Pisa.

Hunting truffles is like searching for gold or diamonds. It excites people, dogs – and wild boar, who ferret in dank autumnal woods to unearth the fungus. Truffles are said to have aphrodisiacal qualities and one whiff of their pungent aroma convinces: the smell of truffles, especially the more pungent white truffle, *is* seductive. Or rather, the smell *is* the taste (think fresh mint without its smell).

Truffles are typically served up with simple, mild-tasting dishes to give the palate full opportunity to revel in the subtle flavour. Buttered spaghetti topped with 10g of truffle shavings is a classic, as is a humble risotto laced with the extraordinary black specks.

BEST TASTING ADDRESSES

» **Barbialla Nuova**, Montaione (see the boxed text, p149) Tuscany's golden ticket for hunting white truffles.

» **Pepenero**, San Miniato (p150) Celebrity chef Gilberto Rossi gives truffles a creative spin.

» **La Tenda Rossa**, Cerbaia (p212) Send taste buds wild with a €90 truffle-tasting menu.

» **Ristorante Da Ventura**, Sansepolcro (p266) Nothing beats a simple omelette sprinkled with fresh truffle shavings.

Right

1. White truffles have a pungent aroma 2. Black truffle appetiser

steel braces slung around the third storey that were then joined to steel cables attached to neighbouring buildings. This held the tower in place as engineers began gingerly removing soil from below the northern foundations. After some 70 tonnes of earth had been extracted from the northern side, the tower sank to its 18th-century level and, in the process, rectified the lean by 43.8cm. Experts believe that this will guarantee the tower's future (and a fat tourist income) for the next three centuries.

Access to the Leaning Tower is limited to 40 people at one time – children under eight are not allowed in/up and those aged eight to 12 years must hold an adult's hand. To avoid disappointment, book in advance online or go straight to a ticket office when you arrive in Pisa to book a slot for later in the day. Visits last 30 minutes and involve a steep climb up 294 occasionally slippery steps. All bags, handbags included, must be deposited at the free left-luggage desk next to the central ticket office – cameras are about the only thing you can take up.

Duomo CATHEDRAL
(Piazza dei Miracoli; adult/reduced €2/1, free Nov-Mar & Sun year-round; ☉10am-8pm mid-Mar–Sep, 10am-7pm Oct, 10am-1pm & 2-5pm 1 Nov-Feb, 10am-6pm or 7pm early–mid Mar) Pisa's cathedral was paid for with spoils brought home after Pisans attacked an Arab fleet entering Palermo in 1063. Begun a year later, the cathedral, with its striking cladding of alternating bands of green and cream marble, became the blueprint floor for Romanesque churches throughout Tuscany. The elliptical dome, the first of its kind in Europe at the time, was added in 1380.

The cathedral was the largest in Europe when it was constructed; its breathtaking proportions were designed to demonstrate Pisa's domination of the Mediterranean. Its main facade – not completed until the 13th century – has four exquisite tiers of columns diminishing skywards, while the vast interior, 96m long and 28m high, is propped up by 68 hefty granite columns in classical style. The wooden ceiling decorated with 24-carat gold is a legacy from the period of Medici rule.

Inside, don't miss the extraordinary early-14th-century octagonal pulpit in the north aisle. Sculpted from Carrara marble by Giovanni Pisano and featuring nude and heroic figures, its depth of detail and heightening of feeling brought a new pictorial ex-

pressionism and life to Gothic sculpture. Pisano's work forms a striking contrast to the modern pulpit and altar by Italian sculptor Giuliano Vangi, which were controversially installed in 2001.

Visitors enter the cathedral through the Portale di San Ranieri – late 12th-century bronze doors of the south transept (facing the Leaning Tower) depicting the life of Christ in 20 panels and named after Pisa's patron saint, Raineri, whose preserved skeleton is in the Cappella Ranieri inside. A former wandering minstrel and party boy, Ranieri saw the error of his ways and became a poor and penitential monk. On the night of 16 June each year, 70,000 candles illuminate the streets running along the Arno to honour the saint. Palm trees, Moorish buildings and other Arab sculpted elements on the doors demonstrate just how influential the Islamic world was on Pisa at this time; the magnificent 11th-century bronze griffin that stood as a victory trophy atop the cathedral (see it in the Museo dell'Opera del Duomo today) until 1828 was booty, probably Egyptian in origin.

But it is the three pairs of firmly closed, 16th-century bronze doors of the main entrance (west), designed by the school of Giambologna to replace the wooden originals destroyed (along with most of the cathedral interior) by fire in 1596, that the crowds ogle over. Quite spellbinding, hours can be

---

ℹ️ **TOWER & COMBO TICKETS**

Reserve and buy tickets for the Leaning Tower from one of two well-signposted ticket offices (www.opapisa.it; Piazza dei Miracoli; ☉8am-7.30pm Apr-Sep, 8.30am-7pm Oct, 9am-5pm Nov & Feb, 9.30am-4.30pm Dec-Jan, 8.30am-6pm Mar): the main ticket office behind the tower or the smaller office inside Museo delle Sinópie. To guarantee your visit to the tower, we recommend you book tickets via the website at least 15 days in advance.

The ticket offices also sell combination tickets covering admission to the Baptistry, Camposanto, Museo dell'Opera del Duomo and Museo delle Sinópie: buy a ticket covering one/two/five admissions costing €5/6/10 (reduced €2/3/5, under 10 years free) and pick which sights to visit.

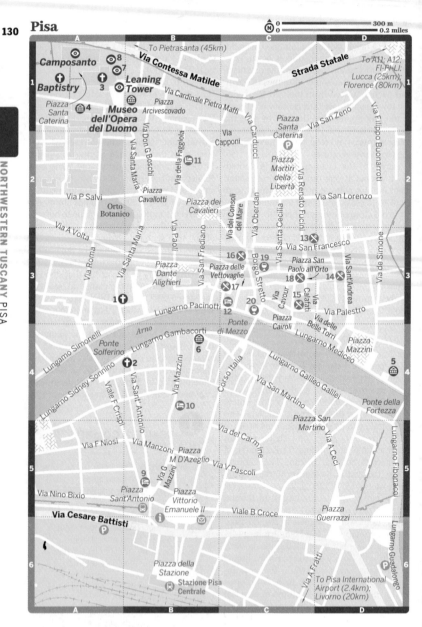

spent deciphering the biblical scenes illustrating the immaculate conception of the Virgin and birth of Christ (central doors), the road to Calvary and crucifixion of Christ etc (right), and the Ministry of Christ (left). Kids can play spot the rhino.

Baptistry BAPTISTRY
(Piazza dei Miracoli; adult/reduced €5/2; ⊗8am-8pm Apr-Sep, 9am-7pm Oct, 10am-5pm Nov-Feb, 9am-6pm Mar) The unusual round Baptistry has one dome piled on top of another, each roofed half in lead, half in tiles, and topped

by a gilt bronze John the Baptist (1395). Construction began in 1152, but it was notably remodelled and continued by Nicola and Giovanni Pisano more than a century later and was finally completed in the 14th century – hence its hybrid architectural style: the lower level of arcades is Pisan-Romanesque; the pinnacled upper section and dome are Gothic.

Inside, the beautiful hexagonal marble pulpit (compare it to Giovanni's notably more ornate one in the cathedral) carved by Nicola Pisano between 1259 and 1260 is the undisputed highlight. Inspired by the Roman sarcophagi in the Camposanto, Pisano used powerful classical models to enact scenes from biblical legend. His figure of Daniel, who supports one of the corners of the pulpit on his shoulders, was clearly modelled on an ancient statue of Hercules and is one of the earliest heroic nude figures in Italian art, often cited as the inauguration of a tradition that would reach perfection with Michelangelo's *David*.

Pisan scientist Galileo Galilei (who, so the story goes came up with the laws of the pendulum by watching a lamp in Pisa's cathedral swing), was baptised in the octagonal font (1246).

Don't leave the baptistry without (a) admiring the Islamic floor (b) climbing up to the gallery for a stunning overview (c) risking a whisper and listening to it resound; otherwise, the custodian demonstrates the double dome's remarkable acoustics and echo effects every half-hour.

Camposanto   CEMETERY
(Piazza dei Miracoli; adult/reduced €5/2; ☯8.30am–8pm Apr–mid-Jun & Sep, 8.30am–11pm mid-Jun–Aug, 9am–7pm Oct, 10am–5pm Nov-Feb, 9am-6pm Mar) Soil shipped from Calvary during the crusades – and reputed to reduce cadavers to skeletons within days – is said to lie within the white walls of this hauntingly beautiful, final resting place for many prominent Pisans, arranged around a garden in a cloistered quadrangle. Many of the more interesting sarcophagi are of Greco-Roman origin, recycled in the Middle Ages.

During WWII, Allied artillery destroyed many of the cloisters' precious frescoes. Those that are survived are the focus of the Museo delle Sinópie.

Museo delle Sinópie   FRESCO MUSEUM
(Piazza dei Miracoli; adult/reduced €5/2; ☯8am–8pm Apr-Sep, 9am-7pm Oct, 10am-5pm Nov-Feb, 9am-6pm Mar) Home to some wonderful pieces of wall art, this museum safeguards those precious few 14th- and 15th-century frescoes not destroyed by Allied artillery during WWII. Most notable is the *Triumph of Death,* a remarkable illustration of Hell attributed to 14th-century painter Buonamico Buffalmacco. Fortunately, the mirrors apparently once stuck next to the graphic, no-holds-barred images of the damned being roasted alive on spits have since been removed – meaning a marginally less uncomfortable visit for visitors who would have once seen their own faces peering out of the cruel wall painting.

DID YOU KNOW?

» In 1160 Pisa boasted 10,000-odd towers – but no *campanile* (bell tower) for its cathedral. Loyal Pisan Berta di Bernardo righted this in 1172 when she died, leaving a legacy of 60 pieces of silver in her will to the city to get cracking on a *campanile*.

» The Leaning Tower – a whimsical folly of its inventors – was built to lean: hotly debated in the early 19th-century, this theory was blown to shreds in 1838 when a clean-up job to remove muck oozing from its base revealed the true nature of its precarious foundations.

» Moscow will help restore the city of Pisa, shipping in construction workers by train from Odessa, Tashkent and Dushanbe to build skyscrapers around the cathedral and a vast car park beneath the Leaning Tower to resolve traffic congestion around one of Italy's most visited sights – the April Fools joke run by *The Moscow Times* on 1 April 2004.

» Seven bells, each sounding a different musical note and rung from the ground by 14 men, were added to the completed tower in 1370 but silenced in 1950s for fear of a catastrophic collapse.

Extensive restoration has also uncovered several *sinópie* (preliminary sketches), drawn by the artists in red earth pigment on the walls of the Camposanto before the frescoes were overpainted.

Museo dell'Opera del Duomo   ART MUSEUM
(Piazza dei Miracoli; adult/reduced €5/2; ⊘8am-8pm Apr-Sep, 9am-7pm Oct, 10am-5pm Nov-Feb, 9am-6pm Mar) No museum provides a better round-up of Piazza dei Miracoli's trio of architectural masterpieces than this museum inside the cathedral's former chapter house. A repository for works of art once displayed in the cathedral and baptistry, highlights include Giovanni Pisano's ivory carving of the *Madonna and Child* (1299), made for the cathedral's high altar, and his mid-13th-century *Madonna del colloquio*, originally from a gate of the *duomo*. Legendary booty includes various pieces of Islamic art, including the griffin that once topped the cathedral and a 10th-century Moorish hippogriff.

☞ Tours

Sightseeing Bus   BUS
(☑328 8090205; www.pisa.city-sightseeing.it; ticket valid 24hr adult/child €15/7; ⊘hourly 11am-4pm Mar-Oct) Passengers aboard these double-decker buses equipped with an English-language audio commentary and can hop on/off as they please during the route around town.

✯ Festivals & Events

Luminaria   FIREWORKS
The night before Pisa's patron saint's day is magical: thousands upon thousands of candles and blazing torches light up the river and riverbanks while fireworks bedazzle the night sky; 16 June.

Regata Storica di San Ranieri   SPORT
The Arno comes to life with a rowing regatta to commemorate the city's patron saint; 17 June.

Gioco del Ponte   MEDIEVAL BATTLE
During Gioco del Ponte (Game of the Bridge) two teams in medieval costume battle it out over the Ponte di Mezzo; last Sunday in June.

Palio delle Quattro Antiche Repubbliche Marinare   SPORT
In the Regatta of the Four Ancient Maritime Republics, the four historical maritime rivals – Pisa, Venice, Amalfi and Genoa – meet yearly in June for a procession of boats and a dramatic race; the next in Pisa will be held in 2014.

🛏 Sleeping

TOP CHOICE Royal Victoria Hotel   HOTEL €
(☑050 94 01 11; www.royalvictoria.it; Lungarno Pacinotti 12; s with shared bathroom €30-45, d with shared bathroom €40-55, d €65-80, tr €80-120, q €120-175; ✳🐕📶📧) This doyen of Pisan hotels, run with pride by the Piegaja family since 1837, offers old-world luxury accompanied by warm, attentive service. The word on the street says rooms vary, but those we saw were the perfect shabby-chic mix of Grand Tour antique – love the parquet floors and flashes of exposed stone – and modern-day comfort. The unquestionable highlight is an

aperitif flopped on a sofa on the flowery 4th-floor terrace, packed with potted plants. Garage parking/bike hire costs €20/15 per day, and wi-fi, only accessible in the lobby and 1st-floor rooms, is €2.50 per hour.

Hotel Bologna
HOTEL **€€**

(☑050 50 21 20; www.hotelbologna.pisa.it; Via Mazzini 57; s €59-99, d €79-179, tr €99-199, q €119-259; ❄@⑳❋) Nicely placed away from the Piazza dei Miracoli mayhem (a 1km walk or bike ride), this four-star choice on the south side of the Arno is a 68-room oasis of peace and tranquillity. Its rooms have wooden floors and high ceilings, and some are nicely frescoed. Those for four make it a practical, if pricey, family choice. Kudos to the small terrace garden out the back – a dream to breakfast on in summer. Courtyard parking/bike hire costs €10/12 per day.

Hotel Relais dell'Orologio
HOTEL **€€€**

(☑050 83 03 61; www.hotelrelaisorologio.com; Via della Faggiola 12-14; d €200-800; ❋⑳) Something of a honeymoon venue, Pisa's dreamy five-star hotel occupies a tastefully restored 14th-century fortified tower house in a quiet street. Some rooms have original frescoes and the flowery patio out the back makes a welcome retreat from the crowds. You'll need to pay for garage parking.

Dei Cavalieri
B&B **€**

(☑050 991 05 97, 2912 2880; www.deicavalieri.pisa.it; Piazza Sant' Antonio 4; s/d/tr/q €45/65/89/99; @⑳) Hidden in a 4th-floor apartment, views of the Pisan rooftops are lovely here. Count on €10 less a night for rooms with shared bathroom.

✖ Eating

Being a university town, Pisa has a good range of eating places, especially around Borgo Stretto, the university on cafe-ringed Piazza Dante Alighieri – always packed with students – and south of the river in the trendy San Martino quarter. Near Piazza dei Miracoli, a multitude of places tout €12 *menu turistici* (fixed lunch menus) along Via Santa Maria.

Local specialities include fresh *pecorino* (sheep's milk cheese) from San Rossore, *zuppe di cavolo* (cabbage soup), *pan ficato* (fig cake) and *castagnaccio* (chestnut-flour cake enriched by nuts). The local Denominazione d'Origine Controllata e Garantita (DOCG) is Chianti delle Colline Pisane, and though there's no Pisan Denominazione

d'Origine Controllata (DOC), Bianco Pisano di San Torpè, a Trebbiano-dominated wine with a delicate, dry flavour, is a popular substitute.

⌐TOP CHOICE⌐ Il Montino
PIZZERIA **€**

(Vicolo del Monte 1; pizza €4.20-7.50; ⊙10.30am-3pm & 5-10pm Mon-Sat) There is nothing flash or fancy about Il Montino, a brilliantly down-to-earth pizzeria with iconic status among Pisans, student or sophisticate. Order pizza to take away or grab one of a handful of tightly packed tables, inside or out, and munch on house specialities like *cecina* (chickpea pizza), *castagnacci* (chestnut cake) and *spuma* (sweet, nonalcoholic drink). Or go for a *foccacine* (flat roll) filled with salami, pancetta or *porchetta* (suckling pig). Hidden in a back alley, the quickest way to find Il Montino is to head west along Via Ulisse Dini from the northern end of Borgo Stretto (opposite the Lo Sfizio cafe at Borgo Stretto 54) to Piazza San Felice where it is easy to spot, on your left, a telling blue neon 'Pizzeria' sign.

⌐TOP CHOICE⌐ Sottobosco
CAFE, BOOKSHOP **€**

(www.sottoboscocafe.it; Piazza San Paolo all'Orto; lunch €15; ⊙10am-midnight Tue-Fri, noon-1am Sat, 7pm-midnight Sun) What a tourist-free breath of fresh air this creative cafe with a few books for sale is! Tuck into a sugary ring doughnut and cappuccino at a glass-topped table filled with artists' crayons perhaps, or a collection

---

GREEN PISA

Hop across the highway, towards the sea, and a sudden green landscape of sand dune, coastal wood and wetland ensnares Pisa's outskirts. Rich in bird life, the 23,000-hectare **Parco Regionale Migliarino, San Rossore, Massaciuccoli** laces the entire coastline west of Pisa, from just south of Viareggio to the northern tip of Livorno. Bare of surfaced roads, the regional nature park can only be explored on foot, by bicycle, on horseback or horse-drawn carriage. The visitors centre, **Centro Visite San Rossore** (☑050 53 01 01; www.centrovisitesanrossore.it; admission free; ⊙8am-7.30pm Apr-Sep, to 5.30pm Nov-Mar), 5.5km west of Pisa in Cascine Vecchie, has all the info as well as maps and trail guides.

of buttons. Lunch dishes (salads, pies and pasta) are simple and homemade, and come dusk, jazz bands play or DJs spin tunes.

Il Crudo SANDWICH SHOP €
(Piazza Cairoli 7; panini €4.50-6; ⊙11am-3.30pm & 6pm-1am Mon-Thu, to 2pm Fri, to 2am Sat, to 1am Sun) Grab a well-filled *panini* to munch on the move or enjoy one al fresco with a glass of wine at this pocket-sized *panineria* and *vineria* (wine bar) strung with ham legs. Find it by the river on one of Pisa's prettiest squares.

Il Colonnino OSTERIA €€
(☑050 313 84 30; Via Sant'Andrea 37-41; meals €30; ⊙lunch & dinner Tue-Sun) Hidden in the warren of medieval streets between Piazza San Francesco and the river, Il Colonnino is the sort of lunch, *aperitivo* or dinner spot that locals like. Modern-accented Italian is the cuisine. Go for spaghetti-like *tagliolini* sprinkled with San Miniato truffles, pork fillet in a balsamic and pink peppercorn sauce, or – for the springtime veggie in you – white asparagus with boiled egg sauce. The fixed €25 menu is excellent value.

biOsteria 050 ORGANIC, TUSCAN €
(☑050 54 31 06; www.zerocinquanta.com; Via San Francesco 36; meals €25; ⊙12.30-2.30pm & 7.45-10.30pm Mon & Wed-Sat, 7.45-10.30pm Sun) What a clever concept Zero Cinquante (Zero Fifty) is: 'Tradition and fantasy' is its strapline and the produce it uses to cook up its seasonal Tuscan dishes is strictly local and organic. There is ample choice for vegetarians and coeliacs, too. Try black cabbage, nut and gorgonzola risotto, rabbit with sweet mustard perhaps, or one of the excellent-value daily lunch specials chalked on the board outside.

Osteria del Porton Rosso OSTERIA €€
(☑050 58 05 66; Vicolo del Porton Rosso 11; meals €35; ⊙lunch & dinner Mon-Sat) Two menus – one from the land and one from the sea – tempt at this old-fashioned but excellent *osteria* (casual tavern or eatery presided over by a host) at the end of an alley – from riverside Lungarno Pacinotti look for the incongruous neon sign–lit doorway with red fly curtain. Pisan specialities such as fresh ravioli with salted cod and chickpeas happily coexist with Tuscan classics such as grilled fillet steak.

🍷 Drinking

Most of the student drinking action takes place on and around Piazza delle Vettovaglie and the university on cafe-ringed Piazza

---

WORTH A TRIP

MAKING SPAGHETTI

Snug in the heart of the medieval hilltop village of Lari (pop 8720), across from the thick red-brick walls of its huge 11th-century fortress, is an address no gastronome should miss: Martelli (☑0587 68 42 38; www.martelli.info; Via San Martino 3; ⊙10am-noon & 3-4pm Mon, Tue, Thu & Fri). Behind the canary-yellow facade of this *pastificio trazionale* (artisanal pasta maker), 35km southeast of Pisa, seven members of the Martelli family beaver away to make 1 tonne of pasta a year – an output any industrial factory would achieve in a matter of hours. Slowly kneaded dough is fed through a traditional bronze mould to create long strands of spaghetti and spaghettini, penne and macaroni. This is then air-dried for 50 hours (compared to three hours industrially), cut and packaged by hand in Martelli's trademark canary-yellow paper packets, deliberately designed to evoke the pre-1960s yellow paper that pasta in Tuscany was traditionally wrapped in at the market before industrial packaging changed it all.

Around since 1926, Martelli pasta – chewier and coarser in texture than many, meaning it marries particularly well with meat sauces and game – is shipped all over the world and sold in many a gourmet store, Harrods of London included. In Lari, buy it around the corner from the workshop at the village cafe and tobacconist, La Bottega delle Specialità (Via Diaz 14).

Workshop tours are completely informal. Stick your head around the shopfront, ask to visit (Luca, whose grandfather opened Martelli in 1926, speaks English), then nip down the neighbouring alley to reach the small room where the spaghetti action takes place. Spaghetti and spaghettini (the most fun to watch) are made every Tuesday and Friday, penne and macaroni (less fun) every Monday and Saturday.

Dante Alighieri, which is always packed with students.

Bazeel
BAR

(www.bazeel.it, in Italian; Lungarno Pacinotti 1; ☺5pm-2am) This bar draws a mixed clientele and is famous for its *aperitivo* spread. After 9pm there's usually live music or a DJ. Check its Twitter feed for what's on.

Bar Pasticceria Salza
CAFE

(Borgo Stretto 44; ☺8am-8.30pm Apr-Oct, shorter hr Tue-Sun Nov-Mar) This old-fashioned cake shop has been tempting Pisans off Borgo Stretto and into sugar-induced wickedness since the 1920s.

ℹ Information

Tourist office (www.pisaunicaterra.it); airport (☏050 50 25 18; ☺9.30am-11.30pm); town centre (☏050 91 03 50; tourist-point@comune. pisa.it; Piazza XX Settembre; ☺8.30-12.30pm); train station (☏050 4 22 91; Piazza Vittorio Emanuele II 13; ☺9am-7pm Mon-Sat, to 4pm Sun)

ℹ Getting There & Away

Air
Pisa International Airport (PSA, Aeroporto Galileo Galilei; www.pisa-airport.com) Tuscany's main international airport, 2.4km south of town; flights to most major European cities.

Bus
From its hub on Piazza Sant'Antonio, Pisan bus company **CPT** (www.cpt.pisa.it, in Italian) runs buses to/from Volterra (€6.10, two hours, up to 10 daily) and Livorno (€2.75, 55 minutes, half-hourly to hourly).

Car
Pisa is close to the A11 and A12. The SCG FI-PI-LI (SS67) is a toll-free alternative for Florence and Livorno, while the north–south SS1, the Via Aurelia, connects the city with La Spezia and Rome.

Train
Regional train services:
FLORENCE (€5.80, 1¼ hours, frequent)
LIVORNO (€1.90, 15 minutes, frequent)
LUCCA (€2.40, 30 minutes, every 30 minutes)
VIAREGGIO (€2.40, 15 minutes, every 20 minutes)

ℹ Getting Around

To/From the Airport
TRAIN Services run to/from Stazione Pisa Centrale (€1.10, five minutes, 33 per day); be

---

There is a strict Limited Traffic Zone (ZTL) in Pisa's *centro storico* (historic centre) that applies to all nonresidents, and this is rigorously enforced. If you drive into the zone, your car will be photographed and a fine will be sent to you (or to the car-hire company you are renting from). Many travellers have written to us to complain about credit card charges from car-hire companies being levied months after their unknowing infraction of the ZTL has occurred, often with administrative costs of up to €100 added to the fine. If you are staying at a hotel in the zone, you must supply the car's registration details to hotel staff as soon as you check-in so they can register you for a temporary permit. To obtain maps of the ZTL, go to https://secure.comune. pisa.it/tzi/info.jsp.

---

sure to purchase and validate your ticket before you get on the train.

BUS The LAM Rossa (red) bus line (€1.10, 10 minutes, every 10 to 20 minutes) passes through the city centre and the train station en route to/from the airport.

TAXI A taxi between the airport and city centre costs around €10. To book, call **Radio Taxi Pisa** (☏050 54 16 00; www.cotapi.it).

Bicycle
Most hotels rent bikes. Otherwise, stands at the northern end of Via Santa Maria and other streets off Piazza dei Miracoli rent four-wheel bikes (€5 per 40 minutes), quad bikes seating up to three/six people (€10/15 per hour) and regular bicycles (€2/3 per 30/60 minutes).

Car & Motorcycle
Parking costs up to €2 per hour, but you must be careful that the car park you choose is not in the city's Limited Traffic Zone (ZTL). There's a free car park outside the zone on Lungarno Guadalongo near the Fortezza di San Gallo on the south side of the Arno. Well-located pay parking:

» West of Piazza dei Miracoli, just outside Porta di Manin.

» At the bus station north of Piazza dei Miracoli.

» Piazza San Caterina, via Porta San Zeno.

» Via Cesare Battisti, near the train station.

VESPA TOUR

There's a certain romance to touring Tuscany on the back of a Vespa, Italy's iconic scooter that revolutionised travel when Piaggio launched it from its factory in Pontedera, 25km southeast of Pisa, in 1946. The 'wasp', as the two-wheeled utility vehicle was affectionately known, has been restyled 120 times since, culminating most recently in Piaggio's vintage-inspired GTV and LXV models. Yet the essential design remains timeless.

The complete Vespa story, from the Genovese company's arrival in Tuscany in 1921 to its manufacturing of four-engine aircraft and hydroplanes, WWII destruction and rebirth as Europe's exclusive Vespa producer, is grippingly told in Pontedera's Museo Piaggio (www.museopiaggio.it; Viale Rinaldo Piagio 7; admission free; ⊙10am-6pm Tue-Sat), in a former factory building.

Should Vespa's free-wheeling, carefree spirit take hold, hook up with Florence-based Tuscany by Vespa (☑055 012 39 94; Via de' Lamberti 1; www.tuscanybyvespa.com; per day €120 incl lunch & winery tour) or Entroterra Viaggi & Turismo (☑0571 41 71 75; www.entroterraturismo.com; Via Ser Ridolfo 10a; per day €85 incl lunch) in San Miniato (p148) for your very own Hepburn-style Vespa tour.

LUCCA

POP 84,640

Lovely Lucca is a precious pearl of a city that endears itself to everyone who visits. Hidden behind imposing Renaissance walls, its cobbled streets, handsome piazzas and shady promenades make it a perfect destination to explore on foot – as a day trip from Florence or in its own right. At the day's end, historic cafes and restaurants tempt visitors to relax over a glass or two of Lucchesi wine and a slow progression of rustic dishes prepared with fresh produce from the nearby Garfagnana.

If you have a car, the hills to the east of Lucca demand exploration. Home to historic villas and *belle epoque* Montecatini Terme where Puccini lazed in warm spa waters, they are easy and attractive day-trip destinations from Lucca.

History

Founded by the Etruscans, Lucca became a Roman colony in 180 BC and a free *comune* (self-governing city) during the 12th century, when it enjoyed a period of prosperity based on the silk trade. In 1314 it briefly fell to Pisa but regained its independence under the leadership of local adventurer Castruccio Castracani degli Anterminelli, and began to amass territories in western Tuscany, including marble-rich Carrara. Castruccio died in 1328 but Lucca remained an independent republic for almost 500 years.

Napoleon ended all this in 1805 when he created the principality of Lucca and placed one of the seemingly countless members of his family in need of an Italian fiefdom (this time his sister Elisa) in control of all of Tuscany. Ten years later the city became a Bourbon duchy before being incorporated into the Kingdom of Italy. It miraculously escaped being bombed during WWII, so the fabric of the *centro storico* has remained unchanged for centuries.

◉ Sights & Activities

Threading its way through the medieval heart of the old city, cobbled Via Fillungo is full of sleek, modern boutiques housed in buildings of great charm and antiquity – cast your eyes above the street-level bustle to appreciate ancient awnings and architectural details.

East of Via Fillungo is one of Tuscany's loveliest piazzas, oval cafe-studded Piazza Anfiteatro, so-called after the amphitheatre that was located here in Roman times. Look closely to spot remnants of the amphitheatre's brick arches and masonry on the exterior walls of the medieval houses ringing the piazza.

To track down a nature guide to take you on a three-hour bike ride along the river Serchio (€20) or your kids into the woods (€10), hook up with nature guides Eco Guide (see the boxed text, p154).

TOP CHOICE **Palazzo Pfanner** PALAZZO
(www.palazzopfanner.it; Via degli Asili 33; palace or garden adult/reduced €4/3.50, both €5.50/4.50; ⊙10am-6pm Apr-Oct) Fire the romantic in you with a stroll around this privately owned

17th-century palace where parts of *Portrait of a Lady* (1996) starring Nicole Kidman and John Malkovich were shot. Take the outdoor staircase to the frescoed and furnished *piano nobile* (main reception room), then visit the ornate, statue-studded 18th-century garden – the only one of substance within the city walls. (Felix Pfanner, may God rest his soul, was an Austrian émigré who first brought beer to Italy – and brewed it in the mansion's cellars.) From August to October watch out for the lovely chamber-music concerts that Palazzo Pfanner hosts.

City Walls   LANDMARK

Lucca's monumental mura (walls) were built around the old city in the 16th and 17th centuries and remain in almost perfect condition due to the long periods of peace the city has enjoyed over its history. Twelve metres high and 4km in length, the ramparts are crowned with a wide tree-lined footpath that looks down on the *centro storico* and out towards the Apuane Alps. This path is the favourite Lucchesi location for a *passeggiata* (traditional evening stroll), be it on foot, bicycle or inline skate. Children's playgrounds, swings and picnic tables beneath shady plane trees add a buzz of activity to Baluardo San Regolo, Baluardo San Salvatore and Baluardo Santa Croce – three of the 11 bastions studding the way – and older kids kick balls around on the vast green lawns of Baluardo San Donato. For bicycle hire, see p145.

Cattedrale di San Martino   CATHEDRAL

(Piazza San Martino; ◷9.30am-5.45pm Mon-Fri, 9.30am-6.45pm Sat, 9.30-10.45am & noon-6pm Sun) Lucca's predominantly Romanesque cathedral dates to the start of the 11th century. Its stunning facade was constructed in the prevailing Lucca-Pisan style and designed to accommodate the pre-existing *campanile*. The reliefs over the left doorway of the portico are believed to be by Nicola Pisano.

The cathedral interior was rebuilt in the 14th and 15th centuries with a Gothic flourish. The Volto Santo (literally, Holy Countenance) is not to be missed. Legend has it that this simply fashioned image of a dark-skinned, life-sized Christ on a wooden crucifix was carved by Nicodemus, who witnessed the crucifixion. In fact, the Volto Santo has recently been dated to the 13th century. A major object of pilgrimage, the sculpture is carried in procession through the streets on 13 September each year at dusk during the Luminaria di Santa Croce, a solemn torchlit procession marking its miraculous arrival in Lucca.

The cathedral's many other works of art include a magnificent *Last Supper* by Tintoretto above the third altar of the south aisle and Domenico Ghirlandaio's 1479 *Madonna Enthroned with Saints*. This impressive work by Michelangelo's master is currently located in the sacristy (adult/reduced €2/1.50). Opposite lies the exquisite, gleaming marble memorial to Ilaria del Carretto carved by Jacopo della Quercia in 1407. The young second wife of the 15th-century lord of Lucca, Paolo Guinigi, Ilaria died in childbirth aged only 24. At her feet lies her faithful dog.

Museo della Cattedrale   CATHEDRAL MUSEUM

(www.museocattedralelucca.it; Piazza San Martino; adult/reduced €4/2.50; ◷10am-6pm daily) Next door to the cathedral, this museum safeguards elaborate gold and silver decorations made for the Volto Santo, including a 17th-century crown and a 19th-century sceptre.

Chiesa dei SS Giovanni e Reparata   CHURCH

(Piazza San Giovanni; adult/reduced €2.50/1.50; ◷10am-6pm mid-Mar–Oct, 10am-5pm Sat & Sun Nov–mid-Mar) The 12th-century interior of this deconsecrated church is a hauntingly atmospheric setting for summertime opera recitals staged by Puccini e la sua Lucca (☑340 8106042; www.puccinielasualucca.com; adult/reduced €17/13; ◷7pm daily mid-Mar–Oct, 7pm Fri-Wed Nov–mid-Mar). Professional singers present a one-hour program of arias and duets dominated by the music of Puccini, but also featuring works by Verdi, Mozart, Mascagni and Cilea. Tickets are sold inside the church.

In the north transept of the church is a baptistry crowning an archaeological area comprising five building levels going back to the Roman period.

Chiesa di San Michele in Foro   CHURCH

(Piazza San Michele; ◷7.40am-noon & 3-6pm Apr-Oct, 9am-noon & 3-5pm Nov-Mar) One of Lucca's

---

❶ MONEY SAVER

If you're visiting the sacristy of the Cattedrale di San Martino, Museo della Cattedrale and baptistry of nearby Chiesa de SS Giovanni e Reparata, buy a cheaper combined ticket (adult/reduced €6/4) at any of the venues.

Lucca

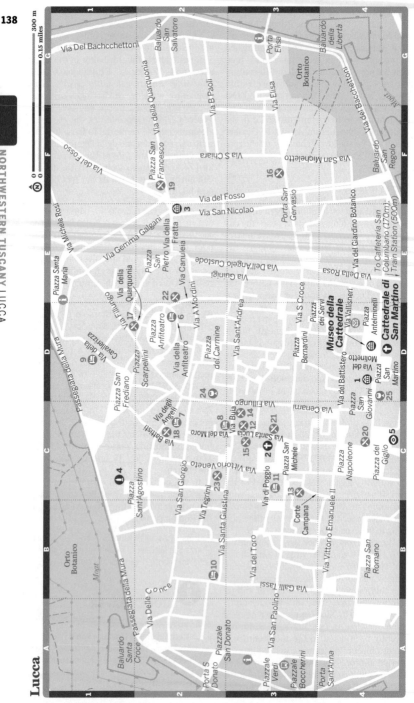

many architecturally significant churches, this lovely Romanesque edifice marks the spot where the city's Roman forum once was. The present building with exquisite wedding-cake facade was constructed on the site of its 8th-century precursor over a period of nearly 300 years, beginning in the 11th century. Crowning the structure is a figure of the archangel Michael slaying a dragon. Inside, don't miss Filippino Lippi's 1479 painting of Sts Helen, Jerome, Sebastian and Roch (complete with plague sore) in the south transept.

Lucca Center of Contemporary Art   ART GALLERY
(☎0583 57 17 12; www.luccamuseum.com; Via della Fratta 36; adult/reduced €7/5; ⊙10am-7pm Tue-Sun) A refreshing change from the historic Tuscan norm, Lucca's contemporary art museum hosts some riveting temporary exhibitions.

☆ Festivals & Events

Lucca Summer Festival   ARTS
(www.summer-festival.com) This month-long music festival lures international pop stars to Lucca; James Blunt and Elton John took to the stage on Piazza Napoleone in 2011; July.

🛏 Sleeping

Tourist offices have accommodation lists and, if you visit in person, can make reservations for you (free of charge); you pay a 10% on-the-spot deposit and the remainder at the hotel.

Alla Corte degli Angeli   BOUTIQUE HOTEL €€
(☎0583 46 92 04; www.allacortedegliangeli.com; Via degli Angeli 23; s €80-110, d €110-160; ❋@✿) Occupying three floors of a 15th-century townhouse, this four-star boutique hotel with just 10 rooms and an old-fashioned rocking horse (in the lovely beamed lounge) oozes charm. Beautifully frescoed rooms are named after flowers: lovers in the hugely romantic Rosa room can lie beneath a pergola and swallow-filled sky, while guests in Orchidea have their own private shower-sauna.

Piccolo Hotel Puccini   HOTEL €
(☎0583 5 54 21; www.hotelpuccini.com; Via di Poggio 9; d €75-95, tr €95-120, q €120-140; ❋✿) Snug around the corner from the great man himself (or at least a bronze copy of him) and the house where he was born, this elegant address is an ode to Puccini. Decor is an unobtrusive mix of period furnishings and historic collectables, and its 14 rooms wear dark rich fabrics and have crisp white bathrooms. April to October breakfast costs an extra €3.50.

2italia   SELF-CATERING €€
(☎3355 20 82 51; www.2italia.com; Via della Anfiteatro 74; apt for 2 adults & up to 4 kids €150-170; ✿👪) Not a hotel but a clutch of family-friendly self-catering apartments overlooking Piazza Anfiteatro. Available on a nightly basis (minimum two nights), the project is

1. Lucca (p136)

Lucca's centuries-old city walls provide an idyllic view.

2. Serchio River (p150)

Three stunning valleys have been formed by the Serchio and its tributaries.

3. Duomo, Carrara (p157)

The texture and purity of Carrara's Apuane white marble is unrivalled.

4. Lucca (p136)

Lovely Lucca is a precious pearl of a city that endears itself to everyone who visits.

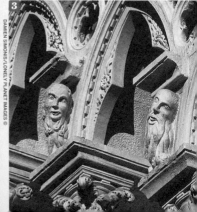

THE PUCCINI TRAIL

Lucca has a particular lure for opera buffs: it was here, in 1858, that the great Giacomo Puccini was born and baptised the following day in the Chiesa dei SS Giovanni e Reparata. The maestro, who came from a long line of Lucchesi musicians, grew up in an apartment at Corte San Lorenzo 9, which was turned into the house-museum Museo Casa Natale di Puccini (☎0583 584 028; Corte San Lorenzo 7; adult/child €7/free; ☉10am-6pm Wed-Mon Jun-Sep, 11am-5pm Wed-Mon Oct-Apr) – look for the imposing statue of the maestro at the front. During his teenage years, Puccini played the organ in the Cattedrale di San Martino and performed as a piano accompanist at the Teatro del Giglio (www.teatrodelgiglio.it; Piazza del Giglio 13-15), the 17th-century theatre where the curtain would later rise on some of his best-known operas: *La Bohème* (1896), *Tosca* (1900) and *Madame Butterfly* (1907).

In 1880 Puccini left Lucca to study at Milan's music conservatory, returning after his studies to Tuscany to rent a lakeside house in Torre del Lago, 15km west of Lucca on the shore of Lago Massaciuccoli. Nine years later, after the successes of *Manon Lescaut* (1893) and *La Bohème*, he had a villa built on the same lakeshore, undertaking the Liberty-style interior decoration himself. It was here that Puccini with his wife, Elvira, for 24 years, spent his time working, hunting on the lake and carousing with a diverse group of hunters, fishermen and bohemian artists. *Madame Butterfly, La fanciulla del West* (1910), *La Rondine* (1917) and *Il Trittico* (1918) were composed on the Forster piano in his front study, and he wrote his scores on the specially made walnut table in the same room.

The villa, now the Museo Villa Puccini (www.giacomopuccini.it; adult/reduced €7/3; ☉10am-12.40pm & 3-6.20pm Apr-Oct, 10am-12.40pm & 2.30-5.10pm Nov-Jan, 10am-12.40pm & 2.30-5.50pm Feb-Mar, closed Mon morning), has been preserved almost exactly as it was during Puccini's residence and is hence fascinating to visit (by guided tour every 40 minutes). In summer the villa grounds and lakeshore buzz with the world-famous Puccini Festival (www.puccinifestival.it), which sees three or four of the great man's operas in a huge purpose-built outdoor theatre. Tickets are like gold dust and need to be bought months in advance.

While living in Torre del Lago, Puccini was a frequent visitor to Montecatini Terme (www.termemontecatini.it), a charming spa resort 56km east, known for its mineral-rich waters – Verdi equally loved the place. May to October, spa lovers still flock to the place today to wallow in warm waters and indulge in various beauty treatments at its *terme* (thermal baths) in grand old buildings overlooking a beautifully maintained park; Leopoldine (1773) is the most impressive. The tourist office (☎0573 77 22 44; www.montecatiniturismo.it; Viale Verdi 66-68; ☉9am-12.30pm & 3-6pm Mon-Sat year-round, 9am-noon Sun Easter-Oct) on the main street has all the details.

In 1921 Puccini and Elvira moved to a villa in the nearby coastal town of Viareggio, where the composer became a regular fixture at Gran Caffè Margherita (p160). He worked on his last opera, the unfinished *Turandot* (1926), during this period. After Puccini's death in 1924, Elvira and son Antonio added a chapel to the Torre del Lago villa; Puccini's remains were interred there in 1926.

---

the brainchild of well-travelled parents-of-three, Kristin (English) and Kaare (Norwegian). Spacious apartments sleep up to six, have fully equipped kitchen and washing machine, and come with sheets and towels. Kristin and Kaare also organise cycling tours, cooking courses, wine tastings and olive pickings.

La Boheme B&B €€
(☎0583 46 24 04; www.boheme.it; Via del Moro 2; d €90-140; ✳@) A hefty dark-wood door locat-

ed on a peaceful backstreet heralds the entrance to this five-room bed and breakfast, which is run with charm and style by former architect Ranieri. Rooms are furnished in antique Tuscan style; some have breathtaking high ceilings and all have decent-sized bathrooms. Breakfast is generous.

Ostello San Frediano HOSTEL €
(☎0583 46 99 57; www.ostellolucca.it; Via della Cavallerizza 12; dm €21, without bathroom €19, d/tr/q €60/78/100; reception ☉7am-midnight; P@🛜)

Slap-bang in the centre of walled Lucca, inside a staggeringly historic and atmospheric building, hostellers won't get closer to the action than this. Top notch in comfort and service, this Hostelling International-affiliated hostel with 141 beds in voluminous rooms is serviced with a bar and grandiose dining room (breakfast €3, lunch or dinner €11). Non-HI members can buy a €3 one-night stamp.

Palazzo Alexander   BOUTIQUE HOTEL €€
(☑0583 58 35 71; www.hotelpalazzoalexander.com; Via Santa Guistana 48; s €80-120, d €90-150; ❄@�) An exuberant affair, this heavily frescoed palace hotel has plenty of over-sized mirrors, ornate gold-gilt bedheads and floor-to-ceiling drapes to woo history aficionados. Each of its 14 rooms are named after a Puccini or Verdi opera and the pièce de résistance is Bohème with frescoed ceiling and Tosca with rooftop balcony. Parking costs €14 per night.

✖ Eating

Lucca is known for its traditional cuisine and prized olive oil. Garfagnana is not far away and local chestnuts, *porcini* mushrooms, honey, *farro* (spelt), sheep's-milk cheese and *formenton* (ground corn) are abundant – and a perfect match with a delicate white Colline Lucchesi or a red Montecarlo di Lucca wine.

Pecora Nera   TRATTORIA €
(☑0583 46 97 38; www.lapecoraneralucca.it; Piazza San Francesco 4; pizza €5-9, meals €20; ☉Wed-Sat, lunch Sun) Plump on a big empty piazza, well away from the madding crowds, the Black Sheep – the only Lucca restaurant recommended by the Slow Food Movement – scores extra brownie points for social responsibility (its profits fund workshops for young people with Down Syndrome). Thirty-odd different pizza types and a handful of Tuscan classics is what's cooking in the kitchen.

TOP CHOICE **Da Felice**   PIZZERIA €
(www.pizzeriadafelice.com; Via Buia 12; focaccia €1-3.50, pizza slice €1.30; ☉10am-8.30pm Mon-Sat) This buzzing local favourite behind Piazza San Michele is easy to spot – come noon look for the crowd packed around two tiny tables inside, spilling out the door and squatting on one of two street-side benches. *Cecina*, a salted chickpea pizza served piping-hot from the oven, and *castagnacci* (chestnut cakes) are Felice's raison d'être.

Gli Orti di Via Elisa   FAMILY, TUSCAN €€
(☑0583 49 12 41; Via Elisa 17; meals €20; ☉lunch & dinner Mon, Tue & Thu-Sat, lunch Wed) Don't be surprised to see *'Siamo Completo'* (Fully Booked) chalked on the board outside this eating address, well away from the tourist action and busy! Gorge on gnocchi in zucchini (courgette) flower sauce, or bean soup with salt cod followed by grilled meat while the kids radiate happiness with pre-meal colouring, games and so on. Offers high chairs, bottle warmers and other kid stuff parents need.

Osteria del Manzo   TUSCAN €€
(☑0583 49 06 49; Via Battisti 28; meals €30; ☉lunch & dinner Mon-Sat) Quite often the local favourites are strictly inside, and this – simplicity in the making – is one of them. Enjoy typical local dishes beneath a beamed ceiling, watched on oddly enough by a collection of garden gnomes. Someone clearly collects miniature bottles too.

Trattoria Canuleia   TUSCAN €€
(☑0583 46 74 70; Via Canuleia 14; meals €40; ☉lunch & dinner Mon-Sat) What makes this dining address stand out from the crowd is its secret walled garden out the back – the perfect spot to escape the tourist hordes and listen to birds tweet over partridge risotto, artichoke and prawn spaghetti or a traditional *peposa* (beef and pepper stew).

Buca di Sant'Antonio   TUSCAN €€
(☑0583 5 58 81; www.bucadisantantonio.com; Via della Cervia 3; meals from €40; ☉Tue-Sat, lunch Sun) This atmosphere-laden restaurant, around since 1782, is an outstanding spot for tasting top-notch Italian wines. Its flattering lighting and banquette seating make it a favourite destination for romantic dinners, and its standards of service are unmatched in the city. The food doesn't quite live up to

---

TAKE HOME

The perfect accompaniment to a mid-morning or mid-afternoon espresso and a gift to take home, *buccellato* is a traditional sweet bread loaf with sultanas and aniseed seeds, baked in Lucca since 1881. **Taddeucci** (www.taddeucci.com; Piazza San Michele 34; ☉8.30am-7.45pm, closed Thu winter) is the *pasticceria* (pastry shop) to ogle at and shop for this traditional Lucchesi sweet treat. Pay €4/8/12 for a 300/600/900g loaf.

VILLA BONGI

Ask anyone from Lucca where to lunch on Sunday or flee the city to escape the stifling summer heat and the reply is invariably Villa Bongi (☑0583 51 04 79; www.villabongi. it; Via di Cocombola 640, Montuolo; meals €35; ☻dinner Tue-Sat, lunch & dinner Sun Mar-Dec, dinner Fri & Sat, lunch & dinner Sun Jan & Feb; ☝), 7km west of town. Born as a convent, the grand old villa overlooks olive groves and has a wonderful terrace on which diners feast al fresco on modern Tuscan cuisine and green views of soft rolling Lucchesi hills. Pasta is strictly homemade and traditional dishes enjoy a creative twist – the red-cabbage risotto with gorgonzola fondue is to die for, as is the saffron-scented *tagliatelle* (ribbon pasta) with prosciutto and prawns. Come winter, dining is all about snuggling up, glass of wine in hand, in front of a roaring fire. Advance reservations essential.

all of these attributes, alas, the rustic dishes on offer being similar to the fare served up in many other, less-expensive eateries around the region. Bookings essential.

Osteria Baralla
OSTERIA €€
(☑0583 44 02 40; www.osteriabaralla.it; Via Anfiteatro 5; meals €32; ☻lunch & dinner Mon-Sat) This busy *osteria,* rich in tradition (think 1860), is in every guidebook and for good reason. Feasting on local specialities beneath huge red-brick vaults is magnificent. Don't miss the soup with new-season olive oil, salt cod and chickpeas. On Thursday it's *bolito misto* (mixed boiled meat) day, Saturday roast pork.

Trattoria da Leo
TRATTORIA €
(☑0583 49 22 36; Via Tegrimi 1; meals €25; ☻lunch & dinner Mon-Sat) Another address everyone

knows and goes to, Leo is famed Lucca-wide for its friendly ambience and cheap food – which ranges from acceptable to delicious. Get here early to snag one of 10 tables lined up beneath racing-green parasols on the street outside and go for *vitello tonnato* (cold veal with a tuna and caper sauce) followed by fig and walnut tart. No credit cards.

Ristorante Giglio
TUSCAN €€€
(☑0583 49 40 58; www.ristorantegiglio.com; Piazza del Giglio 2; meals €45; ☻lunch & dinner Thu-Mon, dinner Wed) Set in the frescoed splendour of 18th-century Palazzo Arnolfini, this elegant restaurant serves refined versions of local specialities such as fresh *farro* pasta with rabbit sauce, polenta with *porcini* mushrooms, and *buccellato* (sweet fruit bread) filled with ice cream and berries.

🍷 Drinking

At almost every turn within the walls there is a pavement terrace to sit down at and savour a coffee or *aperitivo* – those on Piazza San Frediano are a particular favourite and not quite as tourist-packed as the cafe- and wine-bar terraces of Piazza Anfiteatro.

TOP CHOICE Enoteca Calasto
WINE BAR
(www.lucca-wine-treasures.com; Piazza San Giovanni 5; ☻11am-11pm) A Brit and a Dane are the creative duo behind this *enoteca* (wine bar) with terracotta-pot terrace overlooking the baptistry. Its wine list only features local Lucchesi production and Thursday evening ushers in wine tasting (€5) with a local producer.

Caffetiera San Colombano
CAFE
(Baluardo San Colombano; ☻Tue-Sun) This stylish cafe, to the right as you arise atop the city walls coming from the train station, is

ⓘ A WALLTOP PICNIC

When in Lucca, picnicking atop its city walls – on grass or at a wooden picnic table – is as lovely (and typical) a Lucchesi lunch as any.

Buy fresh-from-the-oven pizza and focaccia with a choice of fillings and toppings from fabulous 'n famed bakery Forno Amedeo Giusti (Via Santa Lucia 20; pizza & filled focaccia per kg €8-16; ☻7am-7.30pm Mon, Tue & Thu-Sat, 7am-1.30pm Wed, 4-7.30pm Sun), then nip across the street for a bottle of Lucchesi wine and Garfagnese *biscotti al farro* (spelt biscuits) at Antica Bodega di Prospero (Via Santa Lucia 13; ☻9am-1pm & 4-7.30pm); look for the old-fashioned shop window fabulously stuffed with sacks of beans, lentils and other local pulses.

a pleasant caffeine, ice-cream or light lunch stop during a wall-top city stroll or bike ride.

Caffè di Simo HISTORIC CAFE
(Via Fillungo 58; ⊙9am-8pm & 8.30pm-1am) For a respite from the sun's glare, immerse yourself in the chic Liberty (art nouveau) interior of Lucca's famous coffee shop. Its cakes are masterpieces.

❶ Information

Tourist offices (www.luccatourist.it) Piazza Santa Maria (✆0583 91 99 31; Piazza Santa Maria 35; ⊙9am-7pm); Piazzale Verdi (✆0583 58 31 50; Piazzale Verdi; ⊙9am-7pm daily Apr-Sep, to 5pm Oct-Mar); Via Eliza (Via Eliza 67; ⊙9am-1pm & 2-6pm Wed-Mon Apr-Sep)

❶ Getting There & Away

Bus

From the bus stops around Piazzale Verdi, **Vaibus** (www.vaibus.it) runs services throughout the region, including the following destinations:

BAGNI DI LUCCA (€3.40, one hour, eight daily)

CASTELNUOVO DI GARFAGNANA (€4.20, 1½ hours, eight daily)

PISA AIRPORT (€3.20, 45 minutes to one hour, 30 daily)

Car & Motorcycle

The A11 runs westwards to Pisa and Viareggio and eastwards to Florence. To access the Garfagnana, take the SS12 and continue on the SS445.

The easiest option is to park at Parcheggio Carducci, just outside Porta Sant'Anna. Within the city walls most car parks are strictly for residents only, and are indicated by yellow lines. Blue lines – few and far between – indicate where anyone, including tourists, can park (€1 to €1.50 per hour). If you are staying within the city walls, contact your hotel ahead of your arrival and enquire about the possibility of getting a temporary resident permit during your stay. The parks just outside the city walls have a time limit of one to two hours and are closely monitored.

Train

The train station is south of the city walls: take the path across the moat and through the tunnel under Baluardo San Colombano. Regional train services:

FLORENCE (€5.30, 1¼ to 1¾ hours, hourly)
PISA (€2.40, 30 minutes, every 30 minutes)
VIAREGGIO (€2.40, 25 minutes, hourly)

❶ Getting Around

Bicycle

Rent regular wheels (per hour/day €2.50/12; ID required) direct from the Piazzale Verdi tourist

---

WORTH A TRIP

A VILLA TOUR

Between the 15th and 19th centuries, successful Lucchesi merchants flouted their success to the world by building opulent summer residences in the hills around the city, and though a few have crumbled away or been abandoned, many are still inhabited.

Elisa Bonaparte, Napoleon's sister and short-lived ruler of Tuscany, once lived in handsome **Villa Reale** (www.parcovillareale.it; Via Fraga Alta, Marlia; garden tours €7; ⊙10am-1pm & 2-6pm Tue-Sun Mar-Nov), 7km north of Lucca in Marlia. The house isn't open to the public, but the statuary-filled gardens can be visited by hourly guided tour.

Neoclassical **Villa Grabau** (www.villagrabau.it; Via di Matraia 269; ⊙10am-1pm & 3-7pm Tue-Sun Jul-Aug, shorter hr rest of year, Sun only Nov-Mar), just north of Lucca in San Pancrazio, sits aplomb a vast parkland with sweeping traditional English- and Italian-styled gardens, splashing fountains, more than 100 terracotta pots with lemon trees and a postcard-pretty lemon house – host to fashion shows, concerts and the like – dating from the 17th century. It even has a clutch of self-catering properties to rent in its grounds should you happen to fall in love with the estate.

In the same village, the gardens of **Villa Oliva** (www.villaoliva.it; ⊙9.30am-12.30pm & 2-6pm mid-Mar–mid-Nov, by appointment rest of year), a 15th-century country residence designed by Lucchesi architect Matteo Civitali, demand a springtime stroll. Retaining its original design, the fountain-rich park staggers across three levels and includes a romantic cypress alley and stables reckoned to be even more beautiful that those at Versailles. Watch out for concerts held here.

To reach these villas, take the SS12 northeast from Lucca (direction Abetone) and exit onto the SP29 to Marlia. From Marlia, San Pancrazio is a mere 1.2km north.

office, or a city/mountain bike (per hour/day €3/4), racer (per hour €5) or tandem (per hour €6.50) from the following, either side of the Piazza Santa Maria tourist office:

Biciclette Poli (☑0583 49 37 87; www.bici clettepoli.com, in Italian; Piazza Santa Maria 42; ◷9am-7pm)

Cicli Bizzarri (☑0583 49 66 82; www.ciclibiz zarri.net, in Italian; Piazza Santa Maria 32; ◷9am-7pm)

Scooter & Vespa
Scooter Tuscany Rentals (☑0583 95 41 39; www.scootertuscany.com; Via della Caval-lerizza 23; ◷9am-7pm) Rent two motorised wheels from €55/210 per day/week; opposite Lucca's hostel.

PISTOIA

POP 90,200

Pretty Pistoia sits snugly at the foot of the Apennines. An easy day trip from Pisa, Luc-ca or Florence, it deserves more attention than it gets. A town that has grown well be-yond its medieval ramparts, its *centro stor-ico* is tranquil, well preserved and guardian to some striking contemporary art.

On Wednesday and Saturday a morn-ing market transforms Pistoia's vast main square, Piazza del Duomo, as well as its surrounding streets into a lively sea of blue awnings and jostling shoppers. Otherwise, on Monday to Saturday you'll find open-air stalls heaped with seasonal fruit and vege-tables on tiny Piazza della Sala, west of the cathedral.

◉ Sights

Pistoia's key sights are clustered around its beautiful cathedral square, Piazza del Duomo, edged by the distinctive green-and-white marble stripes of the 14th-century octagonal baptistry opposite the tourist office. Surrounding the square is a maze of narrow, shaded pedestrian streets made for hapless meandering.

Piazzetta degli Ortaggi   SQUARE
Don't miss pretty this beautiful bijou square with its laid-back cafe terraces and striking, life-size sculpture of three blindfolded men, Giro di Sole (Around the Sun; 1996) by contem-porary Pistoia artist Roberto Barni (b 1939). In the 18th century the market square, ad-joining Piazza della Sala and once home to a brothel, was the entrance to Pistoia's Jewish ghetto.

Cattedrale di San Zeno   CATHEDRAL
(Piazza del Duomo; ◷8.30am-12.30pm & 3.30-7pm) This cathedral with a beautiful Pisan-Romanesque facade safeguards a lunette of the Madonna and Child between two angels by Andrea della Robbia. Its other highlight, tucked in gloomy Cappella di San Jacopo off the north aisle, is the silver Dossale di San Giacomo (Altarpiece of St James) begun in 1287 and finished two centuries later by Brunelleschi. To visit, track down a church official.

Museo Rospigliosi e Museo
Diocesano   MUSEUM
(Piazza del Duomo; adult/reduced €4/2; ◷10am-1pm & 3-6pm Tue-Sat & 2nd Sun of month) The town museum is guardian of a wealth of ar-tefacts uncovered during restoration work of this former bishop's palace. Many treasures from the cathedral's collection are also here, including a 15th-century reliquary by Loren-zo Ghiberti supposedly housing a bone of St James and parts of his mother's and the Vir-gin's pelvic bones.

Museo Civico   ART MUSEUM
(Piazza del Duomo 1; adult/reduced €3.50/2; ◷10am-6pm Thu-Sun) Pistoia's Gothic Pal-azzo Communale is strung with works by Tuscan artists from the 13th to 20th cen-turies. Don't miss Bernardino di Antonio Detti's *Madonna della Pergola* (1498) with its modern treatment of St James, the Ma-donna and Baby Jesus; spot the mosquito on Jesus' arm.

Nearby, savour the rich portico of Os-pedale del Ceppo (Piazza Giovanni XXIII), with its detailed 16th-century polychrome terracotta frieze by Giovanni della Robbia. Dramatically contrasting with the ancient facade is La Luna nel Pozzo (The Moon in the Well; 1999), a striking iron sculpture smart on the spot in front of the old hospital where a well once stood.

Chiesa di San Andrea   CHURCH
(Via San Andrea; ◷8.30am-12.30pm & 3-6pm) This 12th-century church was built outside the original city walls, hence its windowless (fortified) state. The facade is enlivened by a relief of the *Journey and Adoration of the Magi* (1166) and inside is a marble pulpit carved by Giovanni Pisano (1298–1301).

Centro Documentazione e
Fondazione Marino Marini   ART MUSEUM
(www.fondazionemarinomarini.it; Corso Silvano Fedi; adult/reduced €4/2; ◷10am-5pm or 6pm Mon-Sat)

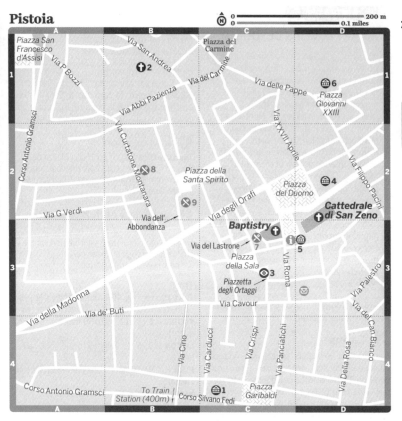

This museum-gallery is devoted to Pistoia's most famous modern son, the eponymous sculptor and painter (1901–80).

🎭 Festivals & Events

Giostra dell'Orso CULTURAL
Translated as Joust of the Bear, medieval jousting and other equestrian pranks fill Piazza del Duomo during Pistoia's celebration of its patron saint San Giacomo; 25 July.

🛏 Sleeping

Tenuta di Pieve a Celle COUNTRY MANOR **€€**
(📞0573 91 30 87; www.tenutadipieveacelle.it; Via di Pieve a Celle 158; d €140-160; 🅿❄☀) From the driveway lined with cypress trees to the olive grove and pool, this 1850s country estate 3km outside Pistoia, in the hills, is quintessential Tuscany at its best. Its five pretty rooms with canopy beds overlook expansive gardens and host Fiorenza cooks evening

Pistoia

◎ Top Sights
Baptistry	C3
Cattedrale di San Zeno	D2

◎ Sights
1	Centro Documentazione e Fondazione Marino Marini	C4
2	Chiesa di San Andrea	B1
3	Giro di Sole	C3
4	Museo Civico	D2
5	Museo Rospogliosi e Museo Diocesano	D3
6	Ospedale del Ceppo	D1
	Palazzo Comunale	(see 4)

✕ Eating
7	Osteria La BotteGaia	C3
8	Pasticceria Armando	B2
9	Trattoria dell'Abbondanza	B2

AN ART LOVER'S DETOUR

A tea house, aviary and other romantic 19th-century follies mingle with cutting-edge art installations created in situ by the world's top contemporary artists at Fattoria di Celle (www.goricoll.it, in Italian; Via Montalese 7, Santomato di Pistoia; ⊘visits by appointment only Mon-Fri May-Sep), 5km from Pistoia. The extraordinary private collection and passion of local businessman Giuliano Gori, this unique sculpture park showcases 70 site-specific installations sprinkled around his vast family estate. Visits – reserved for serious art lovers – require forward planning (apply by email at least five weeks in advance) and entail a guided three- to four-hour hike around the art-rich estate.

meals on request using seasonal produce fresh from her organic vegetable garden.

✕ Eating

Pistoia's eat street is pedestrian Via del Lastrone, packed with cafes, *gelatarie,* wine bars and traditional restaurants serving *carcerato* (a type of offal), *frittata con rigatino* (omelette with salt-cured bacon), *farinata con cavalo* (chickpea pancake with cabbage), *migliacci* (fritters made with pig's blood) and other local specialities. End your meal with *berlingozzo*, a sweet traditionally served with a glass of local Vin Santo.

TOP CHOICE Trattoria dell'Abbondanza   TRATTORIA €
(☑0573 36 80 37; Via dell'Abbondanza 10; meals €25; ⊘lunch & dinner Fri-Tue, dinner Thu) Dine beneath coloured parasols in an atmospheric alley outside or plump for a table inside where homey collections of door bells, pasta jars and so on catch the eye. The cuisine, once you've deciphered the handwriting on the menu, is simple Tuscan.

Osteria La BotteGaia   OSTERIA €€
(☑0573 36 56 02; www.labottegaia.it; Via del Lastrone 17; meals €30; ⊘lunch & dinner Tue-Sat, dinner Sun & Mon) Dishes range from staunchly traditional to experimental at this Slow Food–hailed *osteria*, known for its finely butchered cured meats and interesting wine

list. Reserve in advance or, if you fail to snag a table, opt for a salad (€7), *crostini* or *bruschetta* (€6 to €10) at La BotteGaia's *vineria* at No 4 on the same street.

Pasticceria Armando   PASTRIES, CAKES €
(Via Curtatone Montanara 38; ⊘6.30am-1pm & 3-8.30pm Tue-Fri, to 8pm Sat & Sun) Pistoia's best-known cafe has been plying locals with cakes, cocktails and coffees since 1947.

❶ Information

Tourist office (☑0573 2 16 22; Piazza del Duomo 4; http://turismo.provincia.pistoia.it; ⊘9am-1pm & 3-6pm Mon-Sat, 10am-1pm & 3-6pm Sun)

❶ Getting There & Around
Car
Find free parking in the Cellini car park on the city's eastern edge or cheap parking at Pertini car park near the train station.

Train
The train station is 400m south of the Old Town on Piazza Dante Alghieri. Regional train services:
FLORENCE (€3.10, 35 to 50 minutes, frequent)
LUCCA (€3.70, 45 minutes to one hour, half-hourly)
PISA (€4.70, 1¾ hours, one daily or change at Lucca)
VIAREGGIO (€4.70, one hour, hourly)

SAN MINIATO

POP 28,100

There is one delicious reason to visit this enchantingly sleepy, medieval hilltop town almost equidistant (50km) between Pisa and Florence: to eat, hunt and dream about the *tuber magnatum pico* (white truffle).

San Miniato town's ancient cobbled streets, burnt soft copper and ginger in the hot summer sun, are a delight to meander. Savour a harmonious melody of magnificent palace facades, 14th- to 18th-century churches and an impressive Romanesque cathedral, ending with the stiff hike up San Miniato's reconstructed medieval fortress tower, Rocca Fredericiana (admission €3.50; ⊘11am-5pm or 6pm Tue-Sun) to enjoy a great panorama. Before setting off buy a combined ticket to all the key sites (€5) at the tourist office (p150).

Then knuckle down to the serious business of lunch. Many local restaurants buy their meat from Sergio Falaschi (www.ser giofalaschi.it; Via Augusto Conti 18-20), the local *macellaria* (butcher) specialising in products made from *cinta senese* (indigenous Tuscan pig from the area around Siena), including the Slow Food favourite, *mallegato* (blood sausage). Other local products worth looking for on menus are *carciofo san miniatese* (locally grown artichokes) in April and May; chestnuts and wild mushrooms in autumn (fall); *formaggio di capra delle colline di san miniato* (the local goat's cheese); and locally raised Chianina beef.

🛏 Sleeping

📝 **Barbialla Nuova**   AGRITURISMO €€€
(☑0571 67 70 04; www.barbiallanuova.it; Via Casastada 49, Montaione; 2/4/6/8 person apt from €270/420/540/960, minimum 3/7 nights low/high season; P🖥🖥🛏) Creamy Chianina cows graze on the hillside and wild boars ferret for truffles between tree roots on this heavily wooded, 500-hectare biodynamic farm with just the right mix of adventure (unpaved roads) and panache (stylish decor). Apartments in old farmhouses dotted around the property offer self-catering accommodation, and there are plenty of opportunities to feed pigs, admire the livestock, walk (all guests are equipped with a map of marked trails

around the estate), stock up on fresh organic produce and truffles at the farm shop and, most memorably, hunt for white truffles (50% discount for guests on the farm's famous truffle hunts). Find Barbialla 20km south of San Miniato on the SP76; look for the white sign on your right 3km after the village of Carrazano.

Fattoria Collebrunacchi   AGRITURISMO €
(☑0571 40 95 93; Via Collebrunacchi 6a, San Miniato; d/tr/q from €50/60/80; P🖥) Hugely affordable prices aside, the big plus of this hilltop address with six simple but comfortable rooms and an apartment is the farm restaurant (closed Monday) it runs on the ground floor. It's a real local address, popular for its typical Tuscan dishes cooked just like grandma does. Look for the white sign on your right, 1km north of Collebrunacchi village, after which it is a breathtaking 1.8km drive uphill between fields and vines.

Fattoria di Stibbio   HISTORICAL RESIDENCE €€€
(☑0571 29 02 47; www.fattoriadistibbio.com; Via San Bartolomeo 72, Stibbio; d from €250; P🖥🖥🛏) Built by the Medicis in the 15th century, this super stylish and sophisticated villa set in extensive gardens 8km from San Miniato is the stuff of millionaire dreams.

149

SAN MINIATO SLEEPING

HUNTING WHITE TRUFFLES

An integral part of local culture since the Middle Ages, some 400 *tartufaio* (truffle hunters) in the trio of small valleys around San Miniato snout out the precious fungus, pale ochre in colour, from mid-October to mid-December. The paths and trails they follow are a family secret, passed between generations. The truffles their dogs sniff out are worth a small fortune after all, selling for €1500 per kilo in Tuscany and four times as much in London and other European capitals.

There is no better time to savour the mystique of this cloak-and-dagger truffle trade than during San Miniato's Mostra Mercato Nazionale del Tartufo Bianco (National White Truffle Market), the last three weekends in November, when restaurateurs and truffle tragics come from every corner of the globe to purchase supplies, sample truffle-based delicacies in the town's shops and restaurants, and breathe in one of the world's most distinctive aromas. San Miniato tourist office (p150) has a list of truffle dealers and can help you join a truffle hunt.

Best up are the early-morning truffle hunts at Barbialla Nuova (per person with 6-8 people €60, up to 6 people incl aperitif €300), a fabulous 500-hectare farm and estate, 20km south of San Miniato near Montaione, run by new-generation farmer Guido Manfredi. Two-hour hunts on the estate end with a glass of Chianti and local organic cheese and salami – or go with Guido to a local restaurant and savour your truffle shaved over pasta and after, a *bistecca alla fiorentina* (chargrilled T-bone steak). Famed far and wide for its enviable success rate when it comes to uncovering these nuggets of 'white' gold, Barbialla's *tartufaio* and his dog unearthed a staggering 20kg during the 2010 season (its seasonal record is 24kg).

✗ Eating

TOP **CHOICE** **Pepenero** MODERN TUSCAN €€€

(☑0571 41 95 23; www.pepenerocucina.it; Via IV Novembre 13, San Miniato; set menus €30-50; ⊙dinner Sat, lunch & dinner Sun & Wed-Fri) Chef and TV star Gilberto Rossi is one of the new breed of innovative Tuscan chefs using traditional products to create modern, seasonally driven dishes at this much-lauded restaurant. To share some of his secrets, sign up for one of his half-day cooking classes (€60 incl lunch & wine) followed by an informal lunch on the restaurant's terrace. Advance reservations are essential.

Podere del Grillo MODERN TUSCAN €

(☑0571 40 93 79; www.poderedelgrillo.eu; Via Serra 3, San Miniato; lunch/dinner tasting menu incl wine & coffee €10/20, tapas-style dishes €3-8; ⊙11am-3pm & 6-11pm Wed-Mon) Oh my goodness! The quality of ingredients here is just so extraordinary most dishes hardly need any cooking or other culinary intervention. Everything is sourced from local organic farms and it shows. Top off tasty salads, cold meats and cheeses with an artsy crowd, stylish location in a red-brick farmhouse and a positively urban bar vibe and you'll be back again and again. Occasional live music, art shows, cultural events.

Il Caminetto TRADITIONAL TUSCAN €

(☑0571 67 71 30; Via della Mura, Mura; meals €25; ⊙lunch & dinner Tue-Sun) Wholly traditional with no concessions to tourism bar an English-language menu, this simple village restaurant in Mura is all about feasting on hearty Tuscan fare. Think local *bruschetta* (rubbed with oil and garlic), tasty cheese

FOR THE ULTIMATE ROMANCE

Book the only table – a table for two – at Peperino (☑348 7804785; www.peperino. net; Via IV Novembre 1, San Miniato; meal incl wine €210; ⊙lunch & dinner daily), the world's smallest restaurant plump in the heart of Tuscany's most gourmet village, next to big brother, Pepenero. Decor is in-your-face romantic (think pink silk), furnishings are period and the waiter only comes when diners ring the bell. Reserve months in advance.

and pear gnocchi and – an absolute must in winter – a humble plate of pasta topped with shavings of fresh white truffle.

❶ Information

Tourist office (☑0571 4 27 45; www.cittadisan minato.it; Piazza del Popolo 1; ⊙9am-1pm Mon, 9am-1pm & 2-6pm Tue-Sun)

❶ Getting There & Away

Car

From Pisa or Florence, take the SCG FI-PI-LI (SS67); park on Piazza del Popolo in San Miniato.

Train

Train it to San Miniato then hop on a shuttle bus (€1, every 20 minutes) to the Old Town.

Regional train services:

FLORENCE (€3.70, 45 minutes, hourly)

PISA (€3.10, 30 minutes, hourly)

THE APUANE ALPS & GARFAGNANA

Rearing up inland from the Versilian Riviera (p158) are the Apuane Alps, a rugged mountain range protected by the Parco Regionale delle Alpi Apuane (www.parcapuane.it) and beckoning hikers with a trail of isolated farmhouses, medieval hermitages and hilltop villages.

Continue inland, across the Alps' eastern ridge and three stunning valleys formed by the Serchio and its tributaries – the low-lying Lima and Serchio Valleys and the higher Garfagnana Valley, collectively known as the Garfagnana – take centre stage. Thickly forested with chestnut woods and unknown to most, this is an unexplored land where fruits of the forest (chestnuts, *porcini* mushrooms and honey) create a very rustic and fabulous cuisine.

The main gateway to this staunchly rural part of Tuscany is Castelnuovo di Garfagnana, home to the regional park visitors centre (p153), some outstanding foodie addresses and a bevy of unique *agriturismi* (farm stays). Enthusiasts for military history come to the area around Borgo a Mozzano to see remnants of fortifications from the Linea Gotica (Gothic Line), the last major line of defence mounted by the retreating German army in the final stages of WWII. If faintly more 'cosmopolitan' rocks your boat as a base, consider Pietrasanta (p159) on the Apuane Alps' southern fringe.

AN OPERA BUFF'S DETOUR

Some 35km west of both Barbialla Nuova and San Gimignano (p215), ringed by a natural amphitheatre of soul-stirring hills, is Lajatico (pop 1390). This tiny village is the birth-place and family home of opera singer Andrea Bocelli (b 1958) who, each year in July, returns to his village to sing – for just one evening.

His stage is the astonishing Teatro del Silenzio (Theatre of Silence; www.teatrodelsi lenzio.it), a specially constructed, open-air theatre built in a green meadow on the fringe of the village where the natural silence is broken just once a year – by the Tuscan tenor and his friends (Placido Domingo, José Carreras, Sarah Brightman and Chinese pianist Lang Lang have all sung here). Each year different sculptures by contemporary artists are added to the ensemble, to striking effect. Gently rolling, fresh green hills as far as the eye can see is the astonishing 360 degree backdrop and listening to the tenor sing to an audience of 10,000 is an overwhelming experience. Tickets, usually released each year in March, cost €58 to €230 and are sold by TicketOne (www.ticketone.it).

True opera buffs can continue 5km to La Sterza to buy wine and olive oil produced on Bocelli's family estate at Cantina Bocelli (◷10am-12.30pm & 4-7pm Mon-Fri), a red-brick vaulted cellar at the southern end of the village on the SR439.

Castelnuovo di Garfagnana

POP 6110

The medieval eyrie of Castelnuovo crowns the confluence of the Serchio and its smaller tributary, the Turrite. Its heart is pierced by the burnt-red Rocca Ariostesca (Ariosto's Castle), built in the 12th century and named after Italian poet Ariosto who lived here between 1522 and 1525 as governor of the Garfagnana for the House of Este. The castle is now the town hall, with a tiny archaeo-logical museum (Piazza Ariosto; admission free; ◷10am-12.30pm & 4-7pm Thu, Sat & Sun) on the ground floor.

On the other side of the small piazza, old-world cake shop and chocolate-maker Fronte delle Rocca (Piazza Ariosto 1; ◷9am-1pm & 3-7.30pm Tue-Sun) has been the hub of local life since 1885. Should the hour be right indulge in a glass of *prosecco* (type of spar-kling wine) in the shade of the *rocca*, then follow Via Fulvio Testi to the nearby duomo (Piazza Duomo), with its lovely *Madonna and Two Saints* by Michele di Ridolfo del Ghirlandaio.

Footsteps away, across from the old city gate on Via Olinto Dini, sacks of beans, chickpeas, walnuts and *porcini* sit pretty as a picture outside local grocer's shop Ali-mentari Poli Roberto (Via Dini 1; ◷8.30am-1pm & 3.30-8.30pm daily) – his chestnut beer, beer made from locally grown *farro, farro*-encrusted *pecorino* and honey sold here are a prerequisite for any respectable Garf-

agnana picnic, as is *castagnaccio* (chestnut cake). This is also your chance to taste the local pride and joy, *biroldo* (a type of pork salami spiced with wild fennel).

Thursday morning is market day.

Sleeping & Eating

TOP CHOICE Pradaccio di Sopra AGRITURISMO €
(◷0583 66 69 66; www.agriturismopradaccio.it; Pieve Fosciana; d €60-75, q €100; ⓟ⊠⚶) Hugged by chestnut woods and fields of *farro,* this family farm (wheat, *farro* and corn) is an excellent-value *agriturismo* option. Rosy and Mariano have four rooms in their old farmhouse and a family room for four in the garden. Othello the donkey roams around the place and Rosa cooks up magnificent evening meals (€23) – lots of homemade *farro* pasta, chestnuts, salads fresh from the veggie patch and meats cooked to perfection in the wood-fuelled oven outside. Find the farm a five-minute drive from Castelnuovo in Pieve Fosciana. No credit cards.

TOP CHOICE Osteria Vecchia Mulino OSTERIA €
(◷0583 6 21 92, 347 3664566; www.vecchiomulino. info; Via Vittorio Emanuele 12; tasting menu incl wine €25; ◷lunch Tue-Sun, evening with advance reser-vation) If there is one place that stands out in this gastronomic valley for its staunchly local cuisine, top-quality products and unwaver-ing commitment to culinary tradition, it is this 160-year-old address. Run with passion and humour by the gregarious, charismatic Andrea Bertucci, the rustic *osteria* has no menu – rather a stunning symphony of cold

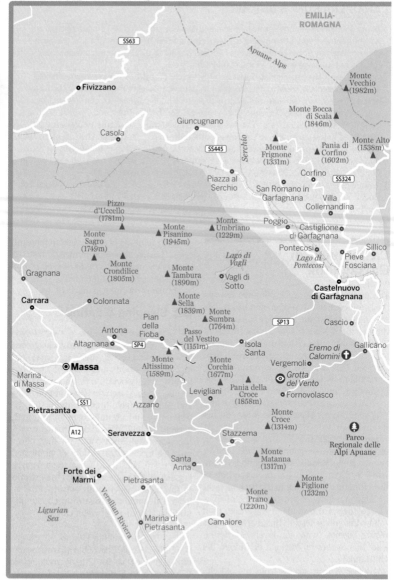

dishes crafted strictly from local products and brought out to shared tables one at a time. Advance reservations essential. Oh, and if you're renting a villa in the area, you can always arrange for Andrea to come to you to host a tasting evening.

TOP CHOICE Fuori Dal Centro GELATERIA €
(Piazza Olinto Dini 1f; 1/2/3/4/5 ice-cream balls €1/1.70/2.20/2.70/3.20) Dare we say it: having tried and tested dozens of Tuscan *gelaterie,* this bright modern ice-cream shop comes out on top. Fuori Dal Centro's regional-

Il Pozzo
PIZZERIA €

(📞0583 66 63 80; Via Europa 2a, Pieve Fosciana; pizza €5-10; ⊙lunch & dinner Thu-Tue) A great 'cheap meal' address with loads of outside seating, particularly handy on Sunday evening when everything else seems to be shut. Find it 3.5km north of Castelnuovo in Pieve Fosciano.

❶ Information

Centro Visite Parco Alpi Apuane (📞0583 6 51 69; www.turismo.garfagnana.eu; Piazza delle Erbe 1; ⊙9.30am-1pm & 3-7pm Jun-Sep, to 5.30pm Oct-May) The regional park visitors centre has information on walking, mountain biking, horse riding and other activities in the Apuane Alps; sells maps and has lists of local guides, *agriturismi* and *rifugi* (mountain huts).

Tourist office (📞0583 64 10 07; www.castelnuovagarfagnana.org; Piazza delle Erbe; ⊙9.30am-1pm & 3.30-6.30pm Mon-Sat) Opposite the regional park visitors centre.

❶ Getting There & Away

Car
Take the SS12 from Lucca (direction Abetone) and turn off onto the SS445. There's a car park at Piazza del Genio, off Via Roma on the opposite side of the river to the walled *centro storico*.

Train
Regional train services:
LUCCA (€3.70, one hour, nine daily)
PISA (€4.70, 1½ hours, four daily)

Barga
POP 10.300

This old hilltop village, 12km south of Castelnuovo di Garfagnana, is one of those irresistibly slow Tuscan hilltop towns with a disproportionately large and dynamic English-speaking community. Churches, artisan workshops, attractive stone houses and palaces built by rich merchants between the 15th and 17th centuries lace the steep streets leading up to Barga Vechia's crowning glory, the Romanesque **Duomo di San Cristoforo** (Piazza Beato Michele 1). Built in four stages between the 9th and 17th centuries, the church facade features local white Alberese stone that changes tone with the light, and the views of the Apuane and Apennine Alps from the terrace are quite breathtaking. Inside, Romanesque fittings and decorations include a baptismal font, a stoup for holy water, an arresting polychrome wooden statue of St Christopher dating from 1100

inspired flavours are simply magnificent – try chestnut, fig and honey, pine kernel and the to-die-for meringue. Keep an eye out for the amber-coloured canopied entrance, which is located just inside Castelnuovo's main city gate.

EMILIA-ROMAGNA

Passo di Radici (1529m)

Pievepelago

San Pellegrino in Alpe

Barga

Montefegatesi

Fornaci di Barga

Lucignano

San Cassiano

SS445

Calavorno

S12

Bagni di Lucca

Borgo a Mozzano

S12

Pieve di Brancoli

Villa Basilica

Vinchiana

0 — 6 km
0 — 3 miles

» **Tuscany Walking** (www.tuscanywalking.com) Family-run, English-speaking set-up in Barga offering guided and self-guided hikes.

» **Eco Guide** (www.eco-guide.it) Fabulous guided nature tours (on foot and by bicycle) by this creative Lucca-based set-up, including magical night walks in the Garfagnana, kids' walks and a 'Spectacular Apuane Alps' day hike.

» **Garfagnana Bikers** (www.garfagnanabikers.it) The Garfagnana is made for biking and these motorcyclists are the people to help you craft your route.

» **Sapori e Saperi Gastronomic Adventures** (www.sapori-e-saperi.com) Embark on a culinary tour of the Garfagnana with passionate foodie Heather Jarman: learn how bread is traditionally baked, sausages made, *pecorino* cheese produced as it's been done for generations; visit olive farms, harvest chestnuts, meet local cheesemakers and savour age-old recipes in local-endorsed restaurants.

and an exquisite marble pulpit. Later decorative additions include the baroque painting of *St Joseph, St Roche & St Anthony* (1500) in the chapel to the left of the main altar, which shows Barga and the cathedral in the background.

Across the grass from the church, inside the old prison, the **Museo Civico del Territorio di Barga** (Piazza dell'Arringo del Duomo; adult/reduced €3/2; ◎10.30am-12.30pm & 4.30-7pm Tue-Sun Jul & Aug, 10.30am-12.30pm Tue-Sat, 10.30am-12.30pm & 3-5pm Sun Sep-Jun) evokes local history and tradition from prehistory to the 17th century. An exhibition in the former cells explains how law and order was administered in the Florentine state.

✯ Festivals & Events

San Cristoforo   CULTURAL
Barga honours its patron saint, St Christopher, with a torchlight procession through the streets of Barga Vecchia and performances in its beautifully restored late 18th-century Teatro dei Differenti; 25 July.

🛏 Sleeping & Eating

Il Benefizio   AGRITURISMO €
(☑0583 72 22 01; www.albenefizio.it; Località Ronchi 4; apt from €70; P@🛜♨♿♨) Squeeze your car along the narrow road to this fabulous olive farm, framed by acacia and chestnut woods 2km from Barga. It has two well-equipped apartments (one sleeping two and the other four) in the old stables, both with spectacular views. Guests can swim to their heart's content, there are mountain bikes to use and a BBQ, too. But the real reason to visit is to get acquainted with owner Francesca, a walking guide and beekeeper who,

funnily enough, is a font of knowledge on local walking trails and beekeeping. With her you can visit the apiary, see how honey is extracted, and even sign up for an olive oil workshop. Husband Francesco, equally fascinating, is a sound engineer (hence the welcome presence of a state-of-the-art home theatre). No credit cards.

Casa Cordati   HOMESTAY €
(☑0583 72 34 50; www.casacordati.it; Via di Mezzo 17; s/d/tr €30/44/60; ◎Mar-Oct; @🛜) Run by genial Giordano Martinelli, who operates a small art gallery on the ground floor and often hosts musical evenings in his magnificent upstairs apartment, this atmospheric accommodation in Barga Vecchia offers excellent value. Rooms have lovely views, simple decor and good-sized bathrooms (some shared); the apartment is dark but well sized.

L'Osteria   TRADITIONAL TUSCAN €
(http://losteriabarga.com; Piazza Angelio; meals €25; ◎lunch & dinner daily) Tucked on the ground floor of a typical Old-Town house with rust-coloured facade and racing-green shutters, this casual *osteria* sits aplomb Barga's prettiest piazza. Cuisine is traditional – think *baccalà e ceci* (saltcod and chickpeas), grilled sausage with rosemary- and sage-scented beans, or a simple rack of lamb ribs – and its lovely wooden decking terrace buzzes on hot sultry summer nights.

ℹ Information

Tourist office (☑0583 72 47 45; www.comune.barga.lu.it; Via di Mezzo 47; ◎9am-1pm Mon-Fri, 9am-1pm & 3-5.30pm Sat, 10.30am-12.30pm & 3-5.50pm Sun, shorter hr Nov-Feb)

FIVE GREAT ROAD TRIPS

Nerves and stomach depending, dozens of narrow roads spaghetti from Castelnuovo into the rural depths of the Garfagnana and Apuane Alps.

Alpine Flora & Marble Mountain
Go west towards the Med and you'll be stunned. The first 17km along the SP13 is pretty straightforward, but once you fork right 2km south of Arni (following signs for Massa along the SP4), motoring turns into a relentless succession of hairpins, blindingly unlit tunnels hewn through rock and breathtaking aerial vistas of Carrara's marble quarries as you cross the Apuane Alps over the Passo del Vestito (1151m). November to April, the pass potentially requires snow chains and in summer it's busy with cyclists. Stop in Pian della Fioba to discover alpine flora in the Orto Botanico Pietro Pellegrini (Botanical Garden; ⊗9amnoon & 3-7pm daily May-Sep) and indulge in coffee or lunch at Rifugio Città di Massa (☎0585 81 90 43; www.rifugiodimassa.it; dm incl breakfast €25; ⊗May-Sep), a spick-and-span mountain hostel with an amazing panorama. From here the road drops steeply, passing through the postcard-pretty villages of Antona and Altagnana, each clinging for dear life to the hillside, to Massa on the Versilian coast. The entire drive is 42km.

Subterranean Rivers & Crystal-Brimmed Lakes
The SS445 follows the Serchio Valley to the east of the Apuane Alps and bores into the Lunigiana (p161). It's a twisting route that leads you through lush green hills pocked with an astounding 1300 caves. The most accessible and spectacular is Grotta del Vento (www.grottadelvento.com; adult/child 1hr guided visit €9/7, 2hr €14/11, 3hr €20/16; ⊗10amnoon & 2-6pm daily), 9km west of the SS445 along a horribly narrow road. Tourist-tacky from the outside, inside – a fresh 10°C – is an astonishing other world of underground abysses, lakes and caverns. April to October, choose between a one-, two- or three-hour guided tour – if you're up to the 800/1200 steps involved in the two- /three-hour tour (!) it's worth it. November to March, the one-hour tour (300 steps) is the only choice.

Medieval Rock Architecture
Returning to Castelnuovo from the Grotta del Vento you pass the Santuario Eremo di Calomini (☎0583 76 70 03; www.eremocalomini.it/agriturismo.php; admission free; ⊗9am-12.30pm & 3-6pm Jun-Sep, 9am-12.30 & 3-6pm Sat & Sun Oct-May), a medieval monastery spectacularly set at the bottom of a protruding rock face. Don't miss the sacristy, ancient kitchen and monks' quarters, all of which are hewn out of the rock. Sunday Mass is held at 11am and 5pm (11am and 4pm October to April), and in summer you can lunch at neighbouring farm Antica Trattoria dell' Eremita (☎0583 76 70 20; www.eremocalomini.it; meals €25; ⊗lunch & dinner daily, closed Mon lunch & Tue winter). Trout is the house speciality and it has rooms if you want to overnight.

Tree Climbing
Approaching Castelnuovo from the northwest along the wiggly S842 you drive through San Romano in Garfagnana, worth a stop for those with kids in tow: Selva del Buffardello (☎329 7715429; www.selvadelbuffardello.it; ⊗10am-7.30pm daily mid-Jun–mid-Sep, Sat & Sun only Easter–mid-Jun & mid-Sep–Oct) is an adventure park where aspiring Tarzans can fly from tree to tree along rope ladders, walkways, pulleys and so on. Set in 3 hectares of woods, the park has picnic tables, a barbecue area and children's playground. Last admission is 5pm.

Across a Mountain Pass
Spiralling north from Castelnuovo, a concertina of hairpin bends (the SS324) lifts you to Castiglione di Garfagnana and over the scenic Passo di Radici mountain pass, across the Apennines, into Emilia-Romagna. A minor parallel road to the south takes you to San Pellegrino in Alpe (1525m; www.sanpellegrinoinalpe.it), a hilltop village with a monastery and, in the old hospital, a Museo Etnografico (Ethnographic Museum; Via del Voltone 14; adult/reduced €2.50/1.50; ⊗10am-1pm & 2-6.30pm daily Jul & Aug, closed Mon & shorter hr rest of year) that brings traditional mountain life, scarcely changed for centuries, to life.

DON'T MISS

VICO PANCELLORUM

Precariously perched above chestnut and walnut forests on a hillock, angled so steeply it threatens to tumble down any second, is the tiny hamlet of Vico Pancellorum. Gazing in awe at its dramatic location aside, the main reason to come here is to experience Buca di Baldabò (☑0583 8 90 62; bucabaldabo@liberi.it; Via Prati 11; primi/secondi €8/9; ☻lunch & dinner daily Jun-Aug, dinner Wed-Sun, lunch with reservation mid-Sep–May). This is one of those iconic addresses every local foodie knows about.

Humbly placed at the back of the village bar where locals while away the day playing cards and *boccia* (boules) or watching TV, the much raved-about restaurant has no printed menu. Just listen to what's cooking that day and take your pick from a generous choice of homemade pastas and sauces cooked up daily by Giovanni (Enrico cooks the mains and Luisa the desserts). Game is generally big in the *secondi* choice (hence the boar's head trophy above the fireplace) and *contorni* (side dishes) are particularly creative (fennel with bitter greens, sweet cabbage with sausage and so on).

To get to Vico Pancellorum from Bagni di Lucca, head 9km north along the scenic S12 to Abetone and at the northern end of Ponte Coccia take the sharp turning on the left signposted 'Vico Pancellorum'; the restaurant is another 3km from here, at the foot of the hamlet, along a steep, narrow, curvaceous road. Advance reservations (and a double-check of opening hours that do vary depending if there's workmen in the village, a friend's birthday and so on) are essential.

❶ Getting There & Away

Bus

Vaibus (www.vaibus.it) runs services between Lucca and Barga (€4.10, 70 minutes, 10 daily). The buses stop at Piazzale del Fosso by Porta Mancianella.

Car

Take the SS12 from Lucca (direction: Abetone), veer left onto the SS445 and then turn right onto the SP7 at Fornacci di Barga. Barga is 5km further on. Park on Piazzale del Fosso or in the car park on nearby Via Hayange.

Train

Barga-Gallicano train station is a few kilometres below Barga Vecchia; walk or prebook a (pricey) taxi service through **Taxi Barga** (☑331 3378051) or **Biagiotti Taxi** (☑0583 7 51 13). Regional train service:

LUCCA (€3.50, 50 minutes, up to eight daily)

Bagni di Lucca

POP 6560

Small-town Bagni di Lucca, 28km south of Castelnuovo di Garfagnana on the banks of the Lima river, is small. Famed in the early 19th century for its thermal waters enjoyed by the gentry of Lucca and an international set (Byron, Shelley, Heinrich Heine and Giacomo Puccini were among the celebrity guests to take the waters), the spa town today is a pale shadow of its former splendid neoclassical self when it had its own casino, theatre and atypically ornate Anglican church (look for the stucco lion and unicorn motif above each window on the vivid burnt-red facade), now the municipal library. In the small British cemetery baroque tombs speak volumes.

There are two distinct areas: the smaller casino-clad Ponte a Serraglio, clustered around a bridge that crosses the Lima river; and the main town, 2km north, where most shops, restaurants and hotels are located.

❂ Sights & Activities

Bagni di Lucca Terme   THERMAL BATHS
(☑0583 8 72 21; www.termebagnidilucca.it; Piazza San Martino 11; ☻8am-12.30pm Mon-Fri & Sun, 8am-12.30pm & 2-4pm Sat) The thermal springs in this area have been popular spots for relaxation and revitalisation since Roman times. Its only spa today has two geothermal caves and a wellness centre offering various steam and thermal mud baths, massages (with salt, stone or olive oil) and beauty treatments.

Casino' delle Terme   CASINO
(www.casinodelleterme.com; Via del Casino) Strauss, Puccini and Liszt all played in the music room of this lovely riverside neoclassical building built in 1837. After their performances, they no doubt dallied at the handsome bar or squandered their performance

fee over the gaming tables. Lovers of trivia will be interested to know that this was the first licensed casino in Europe, and that one of its first managers, a Frenchman, went on to open the Monte Carlo Casino. Shut for many years, old-fashioned roulette tables were out, state-of-the-art slot machines were in, when the casino finally reopened in 2009.

🛏 Sleeping & Eating

TOP CHOICE Villa Stisted   B&B €

(✆348 4703201; www.villastisted.com; Via Roma 65; P@) Originally built for an Irish noblewoman, this elegant villa was the early 19th-century home to English poetess Elisabeth Stisted and is the perfect place to lap up the best of Bagni du Lucca. Period furnishings dress spacious rooms, its gardens are appropriately flowery, and guests can rent mountain bikes or canoes and kayaks to paddle down the Lima river. No credit cards.

Circolo dei Forestieri   TUSCAN €

(✆0583 8 60 38; Piazza Jean Varraud 10; à la carte €30; ⊙lunch & dinner Tue-Sun) Quell hunger pangs at the former home of the Foreigners' Club, an elegant *belle epoque* building on the river side of Viale Umberto I, southeast of the casino. Its grand dining room, chandeliers et al, provides a splendid setting in which to enjoy what could well be the cheapest tourist menu in Tuscany (€11 for three-course lunch).

ℹ Information

Tourist office (✆0583 80 57 45; www.bagni diluccaterme.info; Viale Umberto I 93; ⊙10am-1pm Mon & Wed-Sat)

ℹ Getting There & Away

Bus

Vaibus (www.vaibus.it) runs services between Lucca and Bagni di Lucca (€3.50, one hour, eight daily).

Train

Regional train services:

LUCCA (€2.40, 30 minutes, seven daily)
PISA (€3.70, 1¼ hours, five daily)

MOVING ON?

For tips, recommendations and reviews, head to shop.lonelyplanet.com to purchase a downloadable PDF of the Emilia-Romagna chapter from Lonely Planet's *Italy* guide.

Carrara

POP 65,600

Many first-time visitors assume the snowy-white mountain peaks forming Carrara's backdrop are capped with snow. In fact, the vista provides a breathtaking illusion – the white is 2000 hectares of marble gouged out of the foothills of the Apuane Alps in vast quarries that have been worked since Roman times.

The texture and purity of Carrara's white marble (derived from the Greek *marmaros,* meaning shining stone) is unrivalled and it was here that Michelangelo selected marble for masterpieces including *David* (actually sculpted from a dud veined block). Today it's a multi-billion-euro industry.

The quarries, 5km out of town, have long been the area's biggest employers. It's hard, dangerous work and on Carrara's central Piazza XXVII Aprile a monument remembers workers who lost their lives up on the hills. These tough men formed the backbone of a strong leftist and anarchist tradition in Carrara, something that won them no friends among the Fascists or, later, the occupying German forces.

Bar the thrill of seeing its mosaic marble pavements, marble street benches, decorative marble putti and marble everything else, the old centre of Carrara doesn't offer much for the visitor. The exception is July to October in even-numbered years, when Carrara stages a wonderful contemporary sculpture biennale (www.biennialfounda tion.org).

◉ Sights & Activities

Museo del Marmo   MUSEUM

(Viale XX Settembre; adult/child €4/free; ⊙9am-12.30pm & 2.30-5pm Mon-Sat) Opposite the tourist office, Carrara's Marble Museum tells the full story, from the old chisel-and-hammer days to the 21st-century's high-powered industrial quarrying. It also has a fascinating audiovisual oral history presentation documenting the lives of quarry workers in the 20th century.

Cava di Fantiscritti   MARBLE QUARRY

Next, make you way up the mountain to this *cava de marmo* (marble quarry), through a dramatic series of tunnels bored through rock and used by trains to transport marble until the 1960s (when trucks took over the weighty task). One of a handful of quarries, this is the easiest to visit – pick from

MARBLE MOUNTAIN

Zipping down a dank wet unlit tunnel in a dusty white minibus, grubby headlights blazing, driver incongruously dolled up in a shiny shocking-pink bomber jacket, it is all somewhat surreal. Five minutes into the pitch-black marble mountain, we are told to get out.

It is 16°C, foggy, damn dirty and slippery on foot (two Japanese had sensibly brought their wellies) and far from being a polished pearly white, it's grey – cold wet miserable grey. Rough-cut blocks, several metres long and almost as wide, are strewn about the place like toy bricks and marble columns prop up the 15m-high ceiling, above which a second gallery, another 17m, stands tall. The place is bigger than several football pitches, yet amazingly there is still plenty of marble mountain left for the five workers employed at Cava di Fantiscritti, 5km north of Carrara, to extract – with the aid of water and mechanical diamond-cutting chains that slice through the rock like butter – 10,000 tonnes of white marble a month (it takes one day to cut 7cm). The current market price is €200 to €1000 per tonne, with Carrara's very best commanding double that.

To learn how the Romans did it (with chisels and axes – oh my!), visit the open-air museum (admission free; ⊙9am-7pm), next to the souvenir shop across from the quarry entrance. Don't miss the B&W shots of marble blocks being precariously slid down the *lizza* (mountain pathway) to the bottom of the mountain where 18 pairs of oxen would pull the marble to Carrara port. In the 1850s tunnels (hence the tunnel tour groups use to drive into the mountain) were built for trains to do the job – which they did until the 1960s.

a 30-minute guided tour (www.marmotour.it; adult/child €8/4; ⊙11am-6pm daily Apr-Oct, 10.30am-5.30pm Jun-Aug, 9am-4pm Sep-May) by minibus/on foot of the marble quarry inside the mountain, or a Bond-style 4WD tour (www.carraramarbletour.it; adult/child €8/4; ⊙11am-6pm daily Apr-Oct, 10.30am-5.30pm Jun-Aug, 9am-4pm Sep-May) of the open-cast quarry above. Both are dramatic.

✕ Eating

The *only* place to lunch is in the hamlet of Colonnata, 2km from Fantiscritti, where one of Tuscany's greatest gastronomic treats, *lardo di colonnata* (thinner-than-wafer-thin slices of local pig fat) sits ageing in marble vats of herby olive oil. Once you're hooked, purchase a vacuum-packed slab (from €13.50 per kilo) to take home from one of the many *larderia* (shop selling *lardo*) in the village.

Ristorante Venanzio   TRADITIONAL TUSCAN   €€
(☎0585 75 80 62; Piazza Palestro 3, Colonnata; meals €35; ⊙lunch & dinner Mon-Wed, Fri & Sat, lunch Sun) Even those who initially find the idea of noshing on a hunk of fat off-putting are bound to be won over when sampling it melted over piping-hot *focaccette* (small, flat buns made of wheat flour and cornmeal) at this family-run restaurant with classical decor on Colonnata's central (marbled) square. Its €40 *menu degustazione* (tasting menu; minimum two people) is a real treat.

Locanda Apuana   TRADITIONAL TUSCAN   €€
(☎0585 76 80 17; www.locandaapuana.com; Via Communale 1, Colonnata; meals €35; ⊙lunch & dinner Tue-Sat, lunch Sun) The other key address in Colonnata, just off central Piazza Palestro, to feast on *crostini caldi con lardo* (warm toasts topped with lardo) et al.

ℹ Information

Tourist office (☎0585 84 41 36; Viale XX Settembre; ⊙9am-5pm Mon-Sat Apr & May, 9am-1pm & 4-8pm or 9pm Jun-Aug, 9am-1pm & 3-5pm Sep-Mar) Opposite the stadium; stop here to pick up a map of Carrara, its marble workshops and out-of-town quarries.

ℹ Getting There & Away

Train

The nearest station is Carrara-Avenza, between Carrara and Marina di Carrara. Regional train services:

PIETRASANTA (€1.90, 15 minutes, at least twice hourly)

VIAREGGIO (€2.40, 25 minutes, twice hourly)

THE VERSILIAN COAST

The beaches from Viareggio northwards to Liguria are popular with local holidaymakers and some tourists, but have been blighted by beachfront strip development and get unpleasantly packed with Italy's beach-loving hoi polloi during summer. We suggest steering clear of this coastal strip and instead heading inland to explore the hinterland town of Pietrasanta, known for its vibrant arts culture and *centro storico*.

Versilia is a major gateway to both the Apuane Alps, Garfagnana and Lunigiana with roads from the coastal towns snaking their way deep into the heart of the mountains and connecting with small villages and walking tracks.

Pietrasanta

POP 24,900

Often overlooked by Tuscan travellers, this refined art town is a real unexpected surprise. Its bijou historic heart, originally walled, is car-free and loaded with tiny art galleries, workshops and fashion boutiques – perfect for a day's amble broken only by lunch.

Founded by Guiscardo da Pietrasanta, *podestà* (governing magistrate) of Lucca in 1255, Pietrasanta was seen as a prize by Genoa, Lucca, Pisa and Florence, all of whom jostled for possession of its marble quarries and bronze foundries. As was so often the case, Florence won out and Leo X (Giovanni de' Medici) took control in 1513. Leo put the town's famous quarries at the disposal of Michelangelo, who came here in 1518 to source marble for the facade of San Lorenzo in Florence. The artistic inclination of Pietrasanta dates from this time, and today it is the home of many artists, including internationally lauded Colombian-born sculptor Fernando Botero whose work can be seen here.

Pietrasanta is a great base for exploring the Apuane Alps and a lovely day trip from Pisa or Viareggio.

◎ Sights & Activities

From Pietrasanta train station (Piazza della Stazione) head straight across Piazza Carducci, through the Old City gate and onto central square Piazza del Duomo, the main square that poses as an outdoor gallery for sculptures and other large works of art. It is impossible to miss the attractive Duomo di San Martino (1256) with its distinctive 36m-tall, red-brick bell tower – actually unfinished (the red brick was meant to have a marble cladding).

Next door, the deconsecrated 13th-century Chiesa di Sant'Agostino (Piazza del Duomo; ◎5-8pm Tue-Sun) is a wonderfully evocative venue for art exhibitions. Inside the convent adjoining the church dozens of moulds of famous sculptures cast or carved in Pietrasanta are showcased by the Museo dei Bozzetti (www.museodei bozzetti.it; Via S Agostino 1; admission free; ◎2-7pm Tue-Sat, 4-7pm Sun).

Cross to the other side of the square and meander along Via Giuseppe Mazzini, the town's main shopping strip bookended by contemporary street sculptures. Tucked between boutiques at No 103 is the superb Chiesa della Misericordia (Via Mazzini 103; ◎variable), frescoed with the *Gate of Paradise* and *Gate of Hell* by Botero (the artist portrays himself in hell).

🛏 Sleeping

TOP
CHOICE Albergo
Pietrasanta   BOUTIQUE HOTEL **€€€**
(☏0584 79 37 26; www.albergopietrasanta.com; Via Garibaldi 35; d €203-264; [P][✳][@][☎]) Should you find yourself totally smitten with Pietrasanta and unable to leave, this chic 17th-century *palazzo* – a perfect fusion of old and new – is among Tuscany's loveliest boutique town hotels. After a day spent sightseeing, its gorgeous courtyard, conservatory and beautifully appointed, classically elegant rooms are made for relaxing and pampering.

TOP
CHOICE Le Camere Filippo   B&B **€€**
(☏0584 7 00 10; www.lecameredifilippo.com; Via Stagio Stagi 22; d €100; [P][✳][@][☎]) A fabulous address loaded with two kitchens and four fantastic rooms, each with a different colour scheme and crisp design, run by the same team as Filippo (p160).

🍴 Eating & Drinking

The historic heart spoils for choice with its many artsy addresses spilling onto flower pot–adorned summer terraces. Pedestrian Via Stagio Stagi, parallel to main street Via Giuseppe Mazzini, has several appealing restaurants, while Piazza del Duomo is the al fresco favourite for a coffee or sundowner.

MOVING ON?

For tips, recommendations and reviews, head to shop.lonelyplanet.com to purchase a downloadable PDF of the Turin, Piedmont & the Italian Riviera chapter from Lonely Planet's *Italy* guide.

Filippo
MODERN TUSCAN €€

(☎0584 70 00 10; http://ristorantefilippo.com; Via Stagio Stagi 22; meals €30; ☉lunch & dinner daily, closed Mon winter) The foodie address locals rave about, Filippo is a stylish bistro with bottled-lined walls, tasteful art and an open kitchen. Cuisine is strictly seasonal and very creative – the pear, nut, rocket (arugula), *pecorino* and strawberry salad is divine, as is the unusual stuffed ravioli. To ensure you get a taste of the best, go for the €35 tasting menu. Chefs cook up stockfish every Thursday evening and *cervello e animelle fritte* (fried brains and sweetbreads) every Tuesday evening.

Pinocchio
SEAFOOD €€

(☎0584 7 05 10; Vicolo San Biagio 5; meals €50; ☉lunch & dinner Tue-Sun) This contemporary restaurant, a real favourite with the hip crowd, is not just about eye-catching design. The Virginia Woolf quote painted on the wall in Italian outside says it all: 'You cannot think well, love well or sleep well if you haven't eaten well' – fish and seafood in various creative guises in Pinocchio's case. Find its stark, grey-and-white facade a few doors down from Filippo on Via Stagio Stagi (entrance in the alley around the corner).

Quarantuno
CAFE €

(☎0584 77 25 07; www.quarantunopietrasanta. com; Via Stagio Stagi 41; ☉lunch & dinner daily) Savouring a light lunch or wine tasting in a Zen, relaxed, countryside style is what small sweet 41 is·all about. Look for the terracotta flower pots and baskets of fresh herbs on the pedestrian street.

TOP CHOICE Enoteca Marcucci
WINE BAR

(www.enotecamarcucci.it; Via Garibaldi 40; ☉10am-1pm & 5pm-1am Tue-Sun) Taste fine Tuscan wine on bar stools at high wooden tables or beneath big parasols on the street outside. Whichever you pick, the distinctly funky, artsy spirit of Pietrasanta's best-loved *enoteca* enthrals.

Caffè del Teatro
CAFE

(Piazza del Duomo; ☉7am-1am Wed-Mon) Straddling the corner of Via dei Piastroni, this busy cafe with pavement seating outside and tables beneath a red-brick vaulted ceiling inside is apparently Botero's favourite hang-out.

❶ Information

Tourist office (☎0584 28 32 84; www.pietra santamarina.it; Piazza Statuto; ☉9am-1pm & 4.30-7pm Mon-Wed, Fri & Sat, 4.30-7pm Thu, 9am-1pm & 4-7.30pm Sun)

❶ Getting There & Away

Bus
Vaibus (www.vaibus.it) runs buses to/from Lucca (€3.70, one hour, three daily) and Pisa airport (€3.50, 75 minutes, 15 daily) via Viareggio (€2.20, 30 minutes).

Train
Regional train services:
PISA (€3.10, 25 minutes, frequent)
VIAREGGIO (€1.90, 10 minutes, every 10 minutes)

Viareggio
POP 64,200

This hugely popular sun and sand resort is known as much for its flamboyant Mardi Gras Carnevale, second only to Venice for party spirit, as for its dishevelled line-up of old art nouveau facades, once grand, on its seafront that recall the town's 1920s and '30s heyday.

Literature lovers might like to pass by Piazza Shelley, the only tangible reference to the romantic poet who drowned in Viareggio; his body was washed up on the beach and his comrade-in-arms, Lord Byron, had him cremated on the spot.

◉ Sights & Activities

Beachfront
PROMENADE

Viareggio's vast golden sandy beachfront is laden with cafes, climbing frames and other kids' amusements and, bar the short public stretch opposite fountain-pierced **Piazza Mazzini**, is divided into *stabilimenti* (individual lots where you can hire cabins, umbrellas, loungers etc).

A handful of buildings on the waterfront retains something of the ornate stylishness they enjoyed in the 1920s and '30s, notably Puccini's favourite cafe, **Gran Caffè Margherita** (Viale Regina Margherita 30), around since 1929 and neighbouring wooden **Chalet Martini** (a clothes shop since 1860 with a fabulous interior).

Consorzio Marittimo Turistico
BOAT TRIP

(☎0187 73 29 87; www.navigazionegolfodeipo eti.it; adult/child 6-11 €30/15; ☉mid-Jun–mid-Sep) When the sea beckons in the height of summer, consider a day trip by boat to Porto Venere and Liguria's iconic cluster of medieval seaside villages known collectively as Cinque Terre. There is one boat daily, departing from Viareggio at 9am or 9.30am and returning at 6.45pm.

LA CITADELLA DI CARNEVALE

A couple of kilometres from the seafront you'll find La Citadella di Carnevale (Via Santa Maria Goretti; admission free; ⊘10am-noon Mon-Fri Jun-Aug, 10am-noon Mon, Wed & Fri Oct-May), where 16 gargantuan hangars serve as workshop and parking space for the fantastic floats crafted by Viareggio's prized *carrista* (floatbuilders) for its annual carnival. The largest floats featuring a papier-mâché merry-go-round of clowns, opera divas, skeletons, kings et al are 20m wide and 14m tall; take five months to build; and carry 200 people each during processions. Stroll around the complex and a *carrista* will inevitably invite you into his workshop. Otherwise, discover carnival history and the art of making *teste in capo* (the giant heads worn in processions) and *mascheroni a piedi* (big walking masks) in the small on-site Museo del Carnevale (Carnival Museum).

🎊 Festivals & Events

Carnevale di Viareggio CULTURAL
(www.viareggio.ilcarnevale.com) Viareggio's annual moment of glory lasts four weeks in February to early March when the city goes wild during carnival – a festival of floats, many featuring giant satirical effigies of political and other topical figures, which also includes fireworks and rampant dusk-to-dawn spirit. Tickets for the 3pm Sunday processions (adult/children under 10 years €15/free) can be bought on the same day from 30 ticket kiosks on the procession circuit or from Fondazione Carnevale (Piazza Mazzini 22).

ℹ️ Information

Tourist office (☑0584 96 22 33; www.apt versilia.it; Viale Margherita 20; ⊘9am-2pm & 3-7pm Mon-Sat) Across from the clock on the waterfront.

ℹ️ Getting There & Away

Train
Regional train services:
FLORENCE (€6.70, 1½ hours, at least hourly)
LIVORNO (€3.70, 35 minutes, 16 daily)
LUCCA (€2.40, 20 minutes, every 20 minutes)
PIETRASANTA (€1.90, 10 minutes, every 10 minutes)
PISA (€2.40, 15 minutes, every 20 minutes)

THE LUNIGIANA

This landlocked enclave of territory is bordered to the north and east by the Apennines, to the west by Liguria and to the south by the Apuane Alps and the Garfagnana. The few tourists who make their way here tend to be lunching in Pontremoli, a real off-the-beaten-track gastronomic gem, or following in the footsteps of medieval pilgrims along the Via Francigena.

Autumnal visits reward with fresh, intensely scented *porcini* mushrooms that sprout under chestnut trees in fecund woods and hills. Wild herbs cover fields, and 5000 scattered hives produce the region's famous chestnut and acacia honey. These fruits of the forest and other regional delicacies, including Zeri lamb, freshly baked *focaccette,* crisp and sweet *rotella* apples, boiled pork shoulder, *caciotta* (a delicate cow's-milk cheese), *bigliolo* beans, local olive oil and Colli di Luni wines, are reason alone to visit.

Pontremoli

POP 7820
It may be small, but this out-of-the-way town presided over by the impressive bulk of Castello del Piagnaro has a decidedly grand air – a legacy of its strategic location on the pilgrimage and trading route of Via Francigena. Its merchants made fortunes in medieval times, and adorned the Old Town with palaces, piazzas and graceful stone bridges.

The Old Town is a long sliver stretching north–south between the Magra and Verde rivers, which have historically served as defensive barriers. Meandering its streets takes you beneath colonnaded arches, through former strongholds of opposing Guelph and Ghibelline factions, and past a 17th-century cathedral and an 18th-century theatre.

👁 Sights

Castello del Piagnaro MUSEUM
(www.statuestele.org; adult/reduced €4/2, audioguide €1; ⊘9am-12.30pm & 3-6pm Tue-Sun May-Sep, 9am-12.30pm & 2-5.30pm Tue-Sun Oct-Apr) From central Piazza della Repubblica and adjacent Piazza del Duomo, walk along

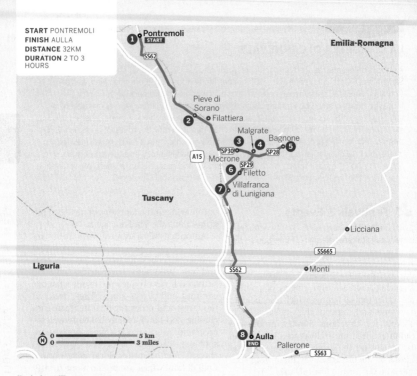

Emilia-Romagna

1 Pontremoli START

SS62

Pieve di Sorano

2 ● Filattiera

Malgrate

Bagnone

3 SP30 **4** SP28 **5**

A15 Mocrone

SP29

6 ● Filetto

7 ● Villafranca di Lunigiana

Tuscany

● Licciana

SS665

Liguria

SS62 ● Monti

0 _____ 5 km
0 _____ 3 miles
N

8 ● Aulla
END   Pallerone
●   SS63

Driving Tour
The Via Francigena

❯ This medieval pilgrimage route connected Canterbury with Rome. It was so popular with pilgrims making their way from Great Britain to the tomb of St Peter in Rome that in the 8th century the Lombard kings built churches, hospices and monasteries offering shelter and protection for pilgrims along its Lunigiana length. This tour explores some of them.

From **1** **Pontremoli** pick up the SS62 (direction Villafranca) and follow it 8km to Filattiera. Admire the hilltop village up high on your right (detour up should you fancy a meander) and, a little further, in a grassy roadside field, the Romanesque **2** **Pieve di Sorano** (1148), with traditional *piagnaro* roof and watchtower to signal its presence as a fortified stop on the pilgrimage route.

Continue for 2.5km along the SS62 then turn left onto the SP30 and drive 2.3km. In **3** **Mocrone** enjoy great views of fortified **4** **Malgrate** teetering on the hillside on your left. Soon after the road brings you into **5** **Bagnone**, an important trading stop on

the Via Francigena and now distinctive for its castle, church and eateries.

From Bagnone, continue towards Villafranca, veering slightly left onto the SP29 to reach the walled medieval hamlet of **6** **Filetto**. Park outside the monumental gate and have a wander through its tiny piazzas and narrow lanes.

Arrivng in **7** **Villafranca di Lunigiana** 1.5km south, you're on another key stop on the pilgrim route. Picturesquely set on the Magra river, it is an unassuming place to wander with its small ethnographical museum in an old 15th-century flour mill.

End the tour 12km south in **8** **Aulla**, known for its abbey founded in AD 884 and housing the remains of St Caprasio, the hermit monk who inspired the spread of monastic life in Provence from the 5th century.

Via Garibaldi then bear left along Vietata l'Affissione or Sdrucciolo del Castello, two pretty alleys and staircases that stagger uphill to this ramshackle castle. Former military barracks, it takes its name from the *piagnaro* (stone slabs) that were once widely used to roof Lunigianese buildings. Views across town from the castle are impressive and inside is a small museum showcasing primitive stelae statues found nearby. No one knows exactly what these stelae, which have been found throughout the Lunigiana, were for – most depict male and female idols and date from around 3000 BC.

🛏 Sleeping

Costa d'Orsola   HOTEL €€
(☎0187 83 33 32; www.costadorsola.it; d €98-120, tr €125-150, q €146-194; 🅿@🏊) For a true taste of this beautiful, untamed region, spend a few nights in the restored stone buildings of this 16th-century village hamlet in Orsola, 3.3km from the centre of Pontremoli and 1.6km from the motorway exit, at the end of a country lane. Wander through olive groves filled with grazing sheep, lounge by the swimming pool and admire the fabulous views, and savour regional cuisine in its tasty restaurant. Half-board rates also available.

🍴 Eating & Drinking

⌈TOP⌉ Antica Trattoria
⌊CHOICE⌋
Pelliccia   TRATTORIA €€
(☎0187 83 05 77; Via Garibaldi 137; meals €30; ⊗lunch & dinner Wed-Tue) Tucked down a rickety old stone road at the far end of the Old Town is this marvellous trattoria – a simple, unpretentious, paradise for gourmets keen to eat local. For *primo* (first course) go for *testaroli della Lunigiana al pesto* (type of savoury crepe cut into diamonds, cooked like pasta and served with pesto) or *lasagnette di faro* (sheets of spelt pasta) in a game and mushroom sauce, followed by simple oven-baked *agnello di Zeri* (lamb). But whatever you do, save space for dessert – sorbet (€4.50) is the house speciality and the flavours (lemon and sage, pistachio and pepper, strawberry and port, chestnut honey and Grand Marnier...) are unjustly good!

Da Bussè   TRATTORIA €
(☎0187 83 13 71; Piazza del Duomo 31; meals €25; ⊗dinner Mon-Thu, lunch & dinner Sat & Sun) This Slow Food favourite has been run by the same family since the 1930s, and brands itself as being 'predominantly for Pontremolese'. It

serves an almost exclusively regional menu, including *torta d'erbe della Lunigiana* (herb pie cooked over coals in a cast-iron pan lined with chestnut leaves to keep the mixture from sticking) and *lasagna bastarde* (broken lasagne sheets made with wheat and chestnut flour and served with olive oil and *pecorino*).

Osteria della Bietola   OSTERIA €
(☎0187 83 19 49; Via Bietola 4; meals €25; ⊗lunch & dinner Fri-Wed) Seating 25 and adhering to a somewhat capricious serving policy (if staff feel like closing early or leaving tables empty, that's what happens), this *osteria* is the place to come for *porcini* mushrooms in season and a very tasty rabbit cooked with herbs. In case you're wondering, *bietola* is a type of chard.

Caffè degli Svizzeri   PASTRIES, CAKES €
(Piazza della Repubblica 21-22; ⊗7am-8pm Tue-Sun, shorter hr rest of year) This historic cafe overlooking Pontremoli's central square opened in 1842 and was given an art nouveau makeover in 1910 that has been lovingly restored. Come here to eat cake – its *spongata degli svizzeri* (almond cake) and *biscotti della salute* (aniseed biscuits) are exceptionally fine, but pale into insignificance when contrasted with the utter delight of the *amor* (wafer filled with zabaglione-style cream).

Il Castagneto della
Manganella   MUSHROOMS €
(Via Garibaldi 3; ⊗daily) In the shade of the *duomo* is this tiny speciality shop, packed to the rafters with dried *porcini* mushrooms, sold by the handful (€15 per kilo) or packaged with herbs (€10 for a trio of 200g packets) in anticipation of that perfect risotto.

ℹ Information

Terre di Lunigiana (www.terredilunigiana.com) Excellent comprehensive website covering accommodation, nature, activities, dining and so on in the Lunigiana.

Tourist office (☎0187 83 20 00; Piazza della Repubblica; ⊗10am-1pm & 3-6.30pm Mon-Fri)

ℹ Getting There & Away

Bus

CAT (www.catspa.it) runs services to Carrara (€3.10, 1¾ hours, eight daily) via Aulla (€3.10, 40 minutes).

Train

Regional train services:

LA SPEZIA (€3.70 to €5.40, 40 to 55 minutes, frequent)

PISA (€6.30, 90 minutes, one daily)

Central Coast & Elba

Includes »

Best Places to Eat

» L'Ancora (p171)
» I'Ciocio (p174)
» Osteria Libertaria (p183)
» Ristorante Capo Nord (p184)
» Il Chiasso (p187)

Best Places to Stay

» Hotel al Teatro (p170)
» Pensione Bartoli (p172)
» La Cerreta (p174)
» Canessa (p175)
» Tenuta La Chiusa (p183)

Why Go?

Despite an enviable setting, this part of Tuscany is not burdened with well-known destinations. Anonymous working cities prevail, including primary-school girl-bully Livorno who dares you to like her – if she doesn't punch your lights out first. But saunter inland, along a trail of vineyards and olive groves, and pride is restored in the form of eye-catching medieval villages and astonishing Etruscan ruins woven together by tiny roads and blind switchbacks. Yes, car, bicycle or foot are the only ways to explore.

Meandering south, several sandy strands are worth a sun-drenched flop and seaside lunch, especially around the bijou Golfo di Baratti. But the best alfresco frolics are a ferry ride away on Elba, a classic Mediterranean island with orange trees, palms and not a single high-rise fronting its many hidden beach-laced coves. Tramp its rugged interior, mountain bike, and don't you dare leave without paddling a sea kayak.

When to Go

Late spring and early summer are perfect for touring the paradise-isle of Elba and its pinprick island counterparts. Come July and August, it is fast, hot and busy on the coast: bars open late, seafood restaurants are packed out, and beaches sizzle with water sports. Those preferring a slower pace might prefer the autumnal days of September and October, a mellow time of the year when the midday sun is less harsh, grapes are picked and villages along Livorno's coastal Strada del Vino celebrate the harvest with a bounty of food-and wine-driven festivals.

Itineraries

Stunning Seafood Livorno does seafood like nowhere else in Tuscany. Examine raw specimens bright and early at the Mercato Centrale, then walk across black-and-white checks on the Terrazza Mascagni followed by a seafood lunch at a Livorno eatery.

Along the Strada del Vino e dell'Olio Start inland from Livorno and wend your way scenically south through a rolling hinterland strung with medieval villages and laced with vineyards. Particularly fine tasting-stops – for wine and food – include San Guido and Bolgheri (linked by a beautiful, 5km-long Cypress Alley), from where it is a very wiggly 20km further south to Sassetta (a great place to overnight at La Cerreta). Next day focus on Val di Cornia DOC wines in Suvereto, then head 25km southwest to the Golfo di Baratti for a picnic between Etruscan ruins.

The Elba Experience The final leg of the Strada del Vino is across the water on this paradise island. Catch the ferry from Piombino to Portoferraio and spend the day exploring its waterfront, haggling with fishermen for the day's catch, lunching in the Old Town and visiting its forts. Elba's oldest wine estate, Tenuta La Chiusa is the place to stay – and taste/buy Elba's sweet red Aleatico dessert wine. Next day, explore western Elba, not missing a trip up Monte Capanne, an evening *passeggiata* in Marciana Marina and dinner at Ristorante Capo Nord.

GETTING AROUND

Livorno is a major port with ferries aplenty to Sardinia, Corsica and – closer to home – the tiny island of Capraia in the national park–protected Tuscan Archipelago; to sail to Elba drive 90km south along the A12 and subsequent SS1 and SP23 to Piombino. Livorno is on the Roma–La Spezia train line and is also connected to Florence and Pisa by train. Bus services throughout the region are limited and to explore properly you really need a car or bicycle.

Where to Stay

Livorno is the obvious place to stay but it is a busy port town. So if it's peace and tranquillity you're craving head south along the shore to the unpretentious Etruscan Coast, where pine-shaded beaches kiss vineyards and drop-dead gorgeous *agriturismi* (farm stays). For paradise island accommodation, Elba is the place.

Top Tastings

» **Cacciucco** Livorno's signature fish stew.

» **Wild boar & Sassicaia Super Tuscan** A marriage made in heaven.

» **Schiaccia & Aleatico Passita DOCG** Elban cake dunked in sweet wine.

Dramatic Drives

» **Colle d'Orano & Fetovaia** (p187) The road linking these two golden sands on Elba's western coast is the island's most dramatic.

» **Sassetta to Suvereto** (p174) Cyclists go wild over this hairpin-laced stretch of hinterland road.

Resources

» Costa degli Etruschi: www.costadeglietruschi.it

» Elba Link: www.elbalink.it

» Tuscan Archipelago Tourist Board: www.aptelba.it

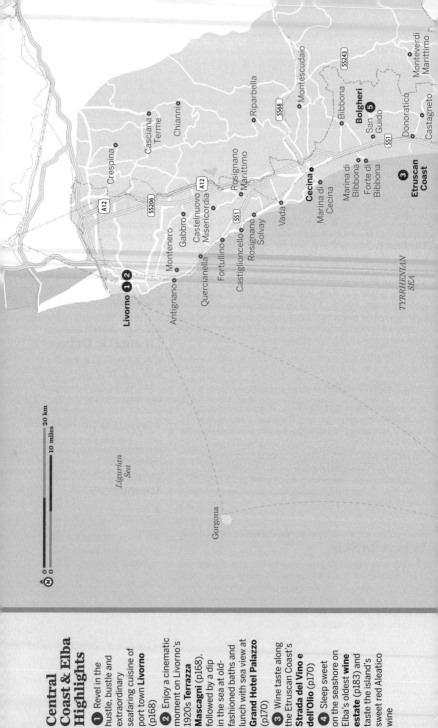

Central Coast & Elba Highlights

1 Revel in the hustle, bustle and extraordinary seafaring cuisine of port town **Livorno** (p168)

2 Enjoy a cinematic moment on Livorno's 1920s **Terrazza Mascagni** (p168), followed by a dip in the sea at old-fashioned baths and lunch with sea view at **Grand Hotel Palazzo** (p170)

3 Wine taste along the Etruscan Coast's **Strada del Vino e dell'Olio** (p170)

4 Sleep sweet on the seashore on Elba's oldest **wine estate** (p183) and taste the island's sweet red Aleatico wine

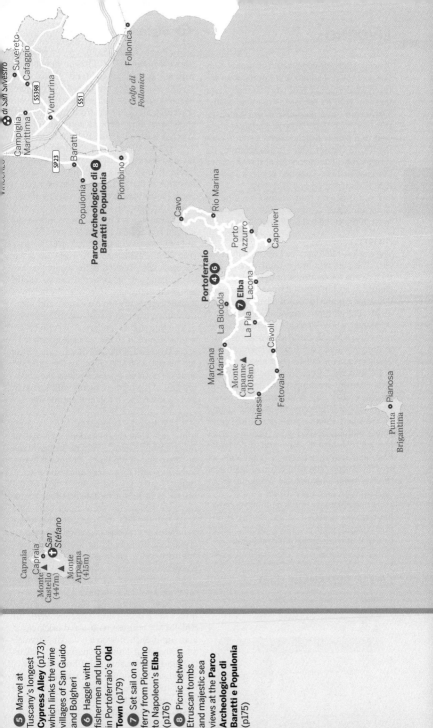

Golfo di
Follonica

Follonica

Suvereto
Cafaggio

di San Silvestro

SS398

Campiglia
Marittima

Venturina

SS1

SP23

Baratti

Populonia

Parco Archeologico di **8**
Baratti e Populonia

Piombino

Cavo

Rio Marina

Porto
Azzurro

Capoliveri

Portoferraio **4 6**

La Biodola

7 Elba

Lacona

Marciana
Marina

La Pila

Cavoli

Monte
Capanne ▲
(1018m)

Chiessi

Fetovaia

Punta
Brigantina

Pianosa

Capraia

Monte
Castello ▲
(447m)

San
Stéfano

Monte
Arpagna ▲
(415m)

5 Marvel at
Tuscany's longest
Cypress Alley (p173),
which links the wine
villages of San Guido
and Bolgheri

6 Haggle with
fishermen and lunch
in Portoferraio's **Old
Town** (p179)

7 Set sail on a
ferry from Piombino
to Napoleon's **Elba**
(p176)

8 Picnic between
Etruscan tombs
and majestic sea
views at the **Parco
Archeologico di
Baratti e Populonia**
(p175)

LIVORNO

POP 160,750

Tuscany's second-largest city is a quintessential port town. Though first impressions are rarely kind, this is a 'real' city that really does grow on you. Its seafood is the best on the Tyrrhenian coast, its shabby historic quarter threaded with Venetian-style canals is uber-cool, and pebbly beaches stretch south from the town's elegant *belle epoque* seafront. Be it short stay between ferries or day trip from Florence or Pisa, Livorno (Leghorn in English) is understated and agreeable.

From the main train station bus 1 heads along the coast road, stopping en route in front of the cathedral on Piazza Grande.

History

The earliest references to Livorno date from 1017. The port was in the hands of Pisa and then Genoa for centuries, until Florence took control in 1421. It was still tiny – by the 1550s it boasted a grand total of 480 permanent residents. But all that changed under Cosimo I de' Medici, who converted the scrawny settlement into a heavily fortified coastal bastion – to the point that even today it is known as a 'Medici town' by Italians elsewhere.

Livorno was declared a free port in the 17th century, sparking swift development. By the end of the 18th century it was a vital, cosmopolitan city, functioning as one of the main staging posts for British and Dutch merchants who were then operating between Western Europe and the Middle East, and had a permanent population of around 80,000. The 19th century again saw the city swell with notable development in the economy, arts and culture.

As one of Fascist Italy's main naval bases, the city was heavily bombed during WWII then rebuilt with a largely unimaginative face that only a sea captain could love.

ROAD DISTANCES (KM)

	Suvereto	Livorno	Piombino	Bolgheri
Livorno	79			
Piombino	24	86		
Bolgheri	39	50	38	
Baratti	16	70	8	31

◉ Sights & Activities

TOP CHOICE **Terrazza Mascagni**   PROMENADE

(Viale Italia) No trip to Livorno is complete without a stroll along (and photo shoot of) this dazzling 'work of art' – an elegant terrace with stone balustrades that sweeps gracefully along the seafront in a dramatic chessboard flurry of black and white checks. When it was built in the 1920s it was known as Terrazza Ciano after the leader of the Livorno *fascio* (fascist movement), Costanzo Ciano. But 40 years later the city changed its name to that of Livorno-born opera composer Pietro Mascagni (1863–1945) instead.

Wedged between the terrace and Livorno's naval academy a little further south is the elegant soft apricot facade of Bagni Pancaldi (www.pancaldiacquaviva.it; Viale Italia 56; adult/child €5/4; ☉8.30am-noon & 3-6pm Sat & Sun Apr-Sep), old-fashioned baths where you can swim, hang out in coloured canvas cabins and frolic in the sun. They were the height of sophistication, host to tea dances and musical soirées, when they first opened in 1846.

The thoroughly modern Acqvario Livorno (☎0586 26 91 11; www.acquariodilivorno.it; Piazzale Mascagni 1; adult/child €15/8; ☉11am-10pm Tue-Sun daily Jul & Aug, to 7pm Tue-Sun Jun & Sep, shorter hr rest of yr; ▣), overlooking the northern end of the terrace, swims with Etruscan and Mediterranean fish and marine life.

TOP CHOICE **Piazza dei Domenicani**   PIAZZA

End 'Little Venice' explorations on a high at this gorgeous piazza, across the bridge at the northern end of Via Borra. Chiesa di Santa Catarina, with its ancient, thick stone walls, stands sentry on the western side of the square as it did for the Medicis four centuries ago. Follow its walls along canal-side Scala del Refugio to Teatrofficina Refugio (http://teatrofficinarefugio.blogsome.com), a crumbling stone building if ever there was one with faded green shutters, gargantuan wooden doors and a thoroughly fabulous monthly calendar of happening theatre, music and cultural events.

Or stroll down the causeway by the bridge to La Bodeguita (Scala Rosciano 9), an equally hip address with a red-brick cellar and sun-drenched wooden-decking terrace afloat the canal. Lunch on pasta (€10), salads (€7) and generously topped bruschetta (€7) while members of the local rowing club ply the water with oars in front of you or, come dark, enjoy live music that gets practically the whole square jiving from 10pm.

Livorno

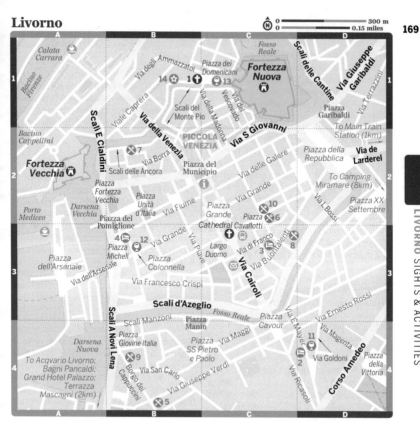

Livorno

◎ Top Sights

Piccola Venezia   HISTORIC QUARTER

The area known as Piccola Venezia or 'Little Venice' is crossed with small canals built during the 17th century using Venetian methods of reclaiming land from the sea. **Fortezza Nuova** (New Fort; admission free; ⊙24hr), built for the Medici court in the late 16th century, is the quarter's main attraction although little of it remains bar a park inside and its sturdy old walls out. Canals link it with the **Fortezza Vecchia** (Old Fort; admission free; ⊙24hr), constructed 60 years earlier on the site of an 11th-century building, on the waterfront. Deeply cracked and crumbling, it looks as though it might give up and slide into the sea at any moment.

Much more fun is to walk or jump on a tour boat and explore the waterways flanked by faded, peeling apartments and brightly decorated with strings of washing hanging out to dry. What this area lacks in gondolas and tourists, it makes up with a certain shabby-chic charm, tow paths intersected with hip waterside cafes and wine bars.

Museo Civico Giovanni Fattori   ART MUSEUM
(Via San Jacopo in Acquaviva 65; admission €4; ⊙10am-1pm & 4-7pm Tue-Sun) This museum in a pretty park features works by the 19th-century Italian Impressionist Macchiaioli school led by Livorno-born Giovanni Fattori. The group, inspired by the Parisian Barbizon school, flouted stringent academic art conventions and worked directly from nature, emphasising immediacy and freshness through patches, or 'stains' *(macchia)*, of colour.

Museo di Storia Naturale del Mediterraneo   MUSEUM
(Via Roma 234; adult/child €10/5; ⊙9am-1pm Wed & Fri, 9am-1pm & 3-7pm Tue, Thu & Sat, 3-7pm Sun; ⊛) Livorno's friendly and hands-on Natural History Museum is an exhaustive, first-rate museum experience for the natural sciences. Temporary exhibits rotate continually, while the highlight of the permanent collection is a 20m-long common whale skeleton called Annie.

DON'T MISS

THE WINE & OIL ROAD

If tasting wine on the seashore or pedalling between olive groves rocks your boat, then trip it – by car, bike or on foot in places – along the **Strada del Vino e dell'Olio** (www.lastradadelvino.com), a 150km tourist itinerary stretching south from Livorno to Piombino and across to Elba. It maps out cellars, wine estates and farms where you can taste and buy local wine and olive oil, and also recommends places to stay and eat. Its visitor centre is just outside Bolgheri.

🕝 Tours

For info on boat trips from Livorno to the wild Tuscan islets of Capraia and Gorgona, see p189.

Giro in Battello   BOAT
(☑348 738 20 94, 333 157 33 72; adult/child €10/5; ⊙11am, noon & 4pm daily Apr-Sep) Buy tickets for 45-minute guided tours by boat of Livorno's Medicean waterways from the tourist office.

🛏 Sleeping

TOP
CHOICE **Hotel al Teatro**   BOUTIQUE HOTEL €€
(☑0586 89 87 05; www.hotelalteatro.it; Via E Mayer 42; s €80, d €95-145; P❋@🤶) One of Tuscany's loveliest urban hotels, this bijou eight-room address with marble staircase, antique furniture, tapestries and individually designed rooms named after composers is irresistible. But the real stunner is the gravel garden out back where guests can lounge on green wicker furniture beneath a breathtakingly beautiful, 350-year-old magnolia tree.

Grand Hotel Palazzo   PALACE HOTEL €€
(☑0586 26 08 36; www.grandhotelpalazzo.com; Viale Italia 195; d €140-170; P❋@🤶🏊) A shimmering ship of a 19th-century palace on the seafront, this glamorous hotel deserves every one of its five stars. From its elegant oyster-grey and apricot facade to its perfectly thought out 123 rooms and glistening sea views, this is *belle epoque* Livorno relived. Dip into the small but perfectly placed infinity pool on the rooftop and, afterwards, gorge poolside on a sunset aperitif and the panoramic sea view. Dining in its rooftop garden restaurant (meals €60), face to face with the sea and the islet of Gorgona, is equally incredible.

Camping Miramare   CAMPGROUND €
(☑0586 58 04 02; www.campingmiramare.it; Via del Littorale 220; camping 2 people, car & tent €26-88; 🏊⊛) Be it tent pitch beneath trees or deluxe version with wooden terrace and sun-loungers on the sandy beach, this site – open year-round thanks to its village of mobile homes, maxi caravans and bungalows – has it all. Find it 8km south of town in Antignano.

Hotel Gran Duca   HOTEL €€
(☑0586 89 10 24; www.granduca.it; Piazza Micheli 16; s/d €90/110; ❋@🤶) Embedded in the little that survives of Livorno's 16th-century city walls, this hotel with dusty pink facade

across from the fishing docks is unique. Its 62 rooms are classic with regal-coloured fabrics and some have fortress views. For history buffs, those on the 2nd floor with private terrace in the red-brick ramparts of the Medici wall are straight out of a film. Wi-fi is €6 per day.

Hotel Città   HOTEL €

(📞0586 83 95 90; www.hotelcitta.it; Via di Franco 32; s €40-89, d €55-120, tr €75-135; ✴) In the heart of the market quarter of town, it is hard to spot the entrance for want of open-air stalls and general market to-ing and fro-ing at this very central joint. Once in, the collection of paintings by local artists is staggering, dazzling, mesmerising – as is the breakfast room wallpaper that recreates the beach. Room furnishings perfectly reflect the 35-odd years this place has been around.

✗ Eating

Sampling traditional *cacciucco,* a remarkable mixed seafood stew and the pride of many local eateries, is reason enough to visit Livorno, a town known for its abundance of affordable and exceptional restaurants.

TOP CHOICE L'Ancora   SEAFOOD €€

(📞0586 88 14 01; Scali delle Ancora 10; meals €25-35; ☺Wed-Mon) What a gorgeous address! Its canal-side terrace is naturally the white-hot ticket in good weather, though settling for a table in the elegantly simple 17th-century, Medici-built, barrel-ceilinged, brick boat house is hardly a hardship. You can get *cacciucco* here, but the *carbonara di mare* (seafood and pasta in white sauce) is the family's pride and joy. This is where locals send visitors looking for a 'nice' meal.

La Barrocciaia   OSTERIA €

(📞0586 88 26 37; Piazza Cavallotti 13; meals €20; ☺11am-2.30pm & 6-11pm Tue-Sat, 6-11pm Sun) Worst-kept dining secret in Livorno it may be, but locating Barrocciaia still takes a careful eye what with its inconspicuous facade being swamped by market stalls. With luck and timing, score a table to discover why every local speaks of La Barrocciaia with such reverence. The menu fluctuates continually, as does the art on the walls, with the exception of grandpa's picture, quietly supervising the third generation of management.

Cantina Senese   OSTERIA €

(📞0586 89 02 39; Borgo dei Cappuccini 95; meals €20; ☺Mon-Sat) Food- and value-conscious

DON'T MISS

THE CENTRAL MARKET

For self-catering nirvana, visit Livorno's late-19th-century **Mercato Centrale** (Via Buontalenti; ☺6am-2pm Mon-Sat), a magnificent, 95m-long neoclassical gem that miraculously survived Allied WWII bombing intact. Arresting both gastronomically and architecturally, the market is a gargantuan maze of tasty food stalls bursting with local produce, including the most astonishing fish and seafood.

Baby purple artichokes, golden courgette flowers, hot red peppers and other seasonal fruit and veg enliven nearby **Piazza Cavallotti** (☺6am-2pm Mon-Sat) in an orgy of colourful open-air stalls.

harbour workers are the first to fill the long wooden tables at this wonderfully unpretentious and friendly eatery, with neighbourhood families arriving later. Ordering is frequently done via faith in one's server, rather than by menu. The mussels are exceptional, as is the *cacciucco,* both served with piquant garlic bread.

Osteria del Mare   SEAFOOD €

(📞0586 88 10 27; Borgo dei Cappuccini 5; meals €25; ☺Fri-Wed) Despite its seafaring name, this smart old-world *osteria* (casual tavern presided over by a host) is not right by the sea. Yes, you can see the water from the doorway but it is for traditional fish dishes, cooked just the way grandma did, that lures in the punters. Go local with *riso nero* (black rice) and the catch of the day (€3.70 to €4 per 100g) or a simple plate of *fritto misto* (battered and deep-fried mix of tiny thumb-size fish).

🍷 Drinking

Il Vinaino   WINE BAR

(www.vinainolivorno.com; Piazza Colonnella 14; ☺6.30pm-10.30pm Tue-Sun) A wine bar couldn't be simpler: a faintly chaotic air adds atmosphere to its pocket-sized, bottle-busy interior, while live music (including lots of jazz) most evenings adds bags of buzz. Its pavement terrace, perfect for people-watching, faces the wonderful two-headed fountain at the water end of Livorno's main shopping street.

Enoteca DOC Parole e Cibi   WINE BAR
(Via Goldoni 40-44; ☺Tue-Sun) The wines are excellent at this self-styled *enoteca* (wine bar), *olioteca* (oil bar) and *whiskyteca* so you can be confident of getting top-quality lubricants, whatever your preference. Its menu (meals €30 to €35), built around fresh pasta dishes, superb seafood and a variety of carpaccio served with bread well worth the *coperto* (cover charge), changes weekly.

ⓘ Information
Tourist office (☏0586 20 46 11; www.costadeglietruschi.it; Piazza del Municipio; ☺7.30am-6.30pm daily Jun-Nov, shorter hr rest of yr)

ⓘ Getting There & Away
Boat
Livorno is a major port. Regular ferries for Sardinia and Corsica depart from Calata Carrara, beside the Stazione Marittima; and ferries to Capraia and Gorgona use the smaller Porto Mediceo near Piazza dell'Arsenale. Boats to Spain and Sicily, plus some Sardinia services, use Porto Nuovo, 3km north of the city along Via Salvatore Orlando.

Ferry companies:

Corsica Ferries/Sardinia Ferries (☏199 400500; www.corsicaferries.com, www.sardiniaferries.com) Two or three services per week (daily in summer) to Bastia, Corsica (deck-class €28 to €36, four hours), and four services per week (daily in summer) to Golfo Aranci, Sardinia (deck-class €32 to €40, six hours express, nine hours regular).

Grand Navi Veloci (☏010 209 45 91; www.gnv.it) Sailings three times weekly to/from Palermo, Sicily (€92, 19 hours).

Grimaldi Lines (☏0586 42 66 82; www.grimaldi-ferries.com) Sailings three times weekly to/from Barcelona (€235, 21 hours) and every four days to/from Valencia, Spain (32 hours).

Moby (☏199 303040; www.moby.it) Boats to/from Bastia, Corsica (€32 to €46, four hours) and Olbia, Sardinia (€44 to €67, six to 10½ hours).

Toremar (☏199 117733; www.toremar.it, in Italian) Daily services year-round to Elba and Capraia.

Car
The A12 runs past the city and the SS1 connects Livorno with Rome. There are several car parks near the waterfront.

Train
From the **main train station** (Piazza Dante) walk westwards along Viale Carducci, Via de Larderel, then Via Grande into central Piazza Grande, Livorno's main square. Trains are less frequent to Stazione Marittima, the station for the ports.

Florence (€6.70, 1½ hours, 16 daily)

Pisa (€1.90, 15 minutes, frequent)

Rome (€17.05 to €43, three to four hours, 12 daily)

ⓘ Getting Around
ATL (www.atl.livorno.it; Largo Duomo 2) has a service (bus 1) from the main train station to Porto Mediceo (€1.20, on board €1.70), via Piazza Grande. To reach Stazione Marittima, take bus 1 to Piazza Grande then bus 5 from Via Cogorano, just off Piazza Grande.

THE ETRUSCAN COAST

The coastline south from Livorno to just beyond Piombino and the ferry to the island of Elba lives up to its historically charged name, Costa degli Etruschi (Etruscan Coast), thanks to a smattering of Etruscan tombs unearthed on its shores. Its basic bucket-and-spade beaches are unstartling, but saunter inland into the hinterland to discover some of Tuscany's lesser-known, but often very good, wines against a backdrop of pretty hilltop villages and winemaking towns.

Castiglioncello

Agreeably unpretentious, this small seaside resort 30km south of Livorno is where Italian critic and patron of the arts, Digo Martelli, held court in the late 19th century. He would play host to the Florentine Impressionist artists of the period, giving birth to the artistic movement known as La Scuola di Castiglioncello (Castiglioncello School).

With its large, shaded terrace, redolent of the best of the 1950s, **Caffè Ginori** (Piazza della Vittoria), is where locals drop by to jaw at the bar. It was also the favourite hangout of Italian heart-throb Marcello Mastroianni when he had a summer villa in town.

Castiglioncello's best sandy beaches are on the north side of town. Get a map et al from the **tourist office** (☏0586 75 48 90; Via Aurelia 632; ☺9.30am-12.30pm & 4-6pm), within the train station. The town is linked by a regular train with Livorno (€2.40, 25 minutes).

ᵀᴼᴾCHOICE **Pensione Bartoli** (☏0586 75 20 51; www.albergobartoli.com; Via Martelli 9; s/d €55/76, half-board per person €58-72; ☺Easter-Oct; Ⓟ),

Those keen to explore by pedal-power can find a wonderfully conceived, detailed list of routes at www.costadeglietruschi.it. Here are some of the more appealing, easy-to-moderate routes.

Full Immersion in Nature

An entirely dirt-route affair, this 13.2km loop starts at La Cerreta near Sassetta and undulates through Casetta Fiorentina, past Podere I Colli and Podere La Pieve, where the landscape scenery peaks. Proceed downhill to the Lodano River valley and a small lake and back towards Podere I Colli. The signage gets pretty bad, but you'll eventually find a stony, tree-lined road heading down to Pian delle Vigne then left again towards La Cerreta.

Silent Livorno Hills

Requiring more fitness, this is a 20.5km lasso-loop route, starting at the Sanctuary of Montenero, about 10km south of Livorno, initially heading along Via del Poggio, then climbing past Castello. After transferring to a dirt road, proceed downhill, then ford a stream that you then follow along a flat road. After Palazzine, a rise leads to a wide firebreak, then a descent on a wide gravel road. The following climb ends with a view of Livorno and the coast. Going downhill, you reach an asphalt road heading back to Via del Poggio, then the Sanctuary of Montenero.

From the Coast to Val di Cornia

A moderately difficult, 63.5km loop that includes the sensational Sassetta–Suvereto run. Starting in Donoratico, an easy warm up through Il Bambolo, San Giusto and Castagneto Carducci leads to Sassetta. Soon after, the bending drop into the Val di Cornia begins. Passing scrubland and then into the valley itself, you sail past several olive grove–lined bends and into Suvereto. It's a gentle ride from here into San Lorenzo, then after passing the Petra wine cellar, a short climb and descent lead past Casalappi then Cafaggio. Next, an unrelenting 4km climb leads to Campiglia Marittima. An exhilarating downhill ride takes you the remaining distance to the coast and San Vincenzo.

aspiring to the very best of a 1950s boarding house, is a villa rich in character and offers unbeatable value. It's an old-fashioned 'let's stay with grandma' kind of place with 18 well-dusted, large rooms, lace curtains and venerable family furniture. Room 19, the largest, and room 21 have the best sea views. In June, July and August the only option is half-board.

Bolgheri & Around

This tiny walled village is dominated by its toy-like, red-brick castle taking in the city gate and Romanesque Chiesa di SS Giacomo e Cristoro, restructured towards the end of the 19th century. But the main reason people flock here, bar browsing its pricey tourist shops, is to taste wine – notably its locally produced, internationally famous 'Super Tuscan' Sassicaia.

From Bolgheri head 5.7km west along the SP16 to San Guido to pick up tasting notes and lists of wine estates where you can taste and buy at the Strada del Vino e dell'Olio visitor centre (☑0565 74 97 05; Castegneto Carducci 45; ☺9.30am-12.30pm Mon-Sat), within a pretty walled rose garden.

The short drive is stunning – along a dead-straight, impossibly romantic, century-old Cypress Alley made famous by Tuscan poet Giosuè Carducci in his 1874 poem *Davanti a San Guido*. Each year in July the 5km-long tree-lined avenue creates a green backdrop for Bolgheri Melody (www.bolgherimelody.com), a fabulous summer arts festival.

✖ Eating & Drinking

TOP CHOICE **Enoteca Tognoni**   WINE BAR €€
(☑0565 76 20 01; www.enotecatognoni.it; Via Lauretta 5; meals €25; ☺lunch & dinner Thu-Tue) This high-profile wine bar on Bolgheri's pretty central square is well worth a stop. Wines of the day to taste are chalked on the board outside, Sassicaia (€22 per 10cl) always featuring along with the 40-odd different wines

to taste by the glass (from €8 per 10cl). Order a €3 plate of mixed *crostini* (thick slices of Tuscan bread toasted and topped with pâté, oil, tomato and so on) to accompany your pick of wine and you'll be in foodie heaven.

Osteria San Guido WINE BAR €€
(✆0565 74 96 43; www.enotecasanguido.it; Località San Guido 50; meals €30; ⊙lunch & dinner) Just 100m from that inspirational Cypress Alley, within the Strada del Vino rose garden complex, this *enoteca* provides another fine wine-tasting op (€3 to €20 per glass). Dine alfresco while garden birds sing.

Castagneto Carducci

POP 8850

South from Bolgheri a densely wooded minor road rolls between vineyards and olive groves before climbing into the hills to this old fortified town. Behind its town walls lies a web of steep, narrow lanes crowded in by brooding houses and dominated by the castle of the Gherardesca clan that once controlled the surrounding area. (The stronghold was turned into a mansion in the 18th century.) The 19th-century poet Giosuè Carducci spent much of his childhood here.

From Castagneto, a winding forested hill road leads to the tiny hamlet of **Sassetta** (population 583), where houses hang on to their perches for dear life. A map at the entrance marks local walking trails.

🛏 Sleeping

🏠 **La Cerreta** AGRITURISMO, SPA €€
(✆0565 79 43 52; www.lacerreta.it; Località Pian delle Vigne, Sassetta; per person half-board €55-65; P🏊♿) Akin to the Tuscan dream, La Cerreta is a beautiful biodynamic estate with four stone cottages wedged between woods, vines, fig trees and sweeping views of rolling Tuscan hills. There are horses to ride, a double swing strung in one tree, and the charismatic Daniele happily takes guests around his 70-hectare farm and explains how he tends his *cinta senese* (indigenous Tuscan pigs), Maremma cows and rare Livornese chickens. Everything served for dinner comes from the estate with the exception of dinner on Friday – fish fresh from wife Vilma's fisherman friend in Piombino. The spirit of the place is 100% in harmony with nature, even down to the state-of-the-art thermal spa (admission €30), which has a series of pebble rock pools cascading down

---

DON'T MISS

SASSETTA TO SUVERETO

Deemed one of the best in Italy for cycling by many a serious cyclist, the undulating road from Sassetta south to Suvereto (population 3128) is well worth the relentless 13km-long wiggle. Once in Suvereto – seat of a bishopric, only incorporated into the Tuscan grand duchy in 1815 – it's a stiff hike up tortuous streets and steep cream-stone stairways, past well-tended flower balconies and windowsills, to the 12th- to 14th-century rocca (village 'castle'), abandoned as a defensive structure in the 1600s, subsequently turned into housing, and currently being restored to its original state.

Predictably, given the accolades of 'Slow Food town', 'wine town' and 'oil town' that it bears, Suvereto is a wonderful place to discover local Val di Cornia DOC wines and fine dine. The tourist office (✆0565 82 93 04; Via Matteotti 42; ⊙Apr-Sep) has information on where to taste and buy wine, as does the Consorzio per la Totela dei Vini DOC Val di Cornia (Via Matteotti 42) next door.

Or head up the hill to l'Ciocio (✆0565 82 99 47; www.osteriadisuvereto.it; Piazza dei Giudici; meals €32-38), a creative *osteria* with an appealing mix of old and new furnishings, and a menu squared firmly at foodies (the 12 different sugar types served after dinner with coffee says it all). At the other side of the village, Le Nuvole (✆0565 82 90 92; www. lenuvoleristobistro.it; Via Palestro 2; lunch/dinner €20/30; ⊙lunch & dinner Tue-Sun) is a modern 'risto bistro', particularly good value for lunch.

Enoteca dei Difficili (Via San Leonardo 2; ⊙6pm-2am Mon & Tue, to 3am Fri-Sun), just around the corner, is a spirited spot come dusk 'n' after dark, with brick-and-beam ceiling, stylish vintage chairs and a blockbuster selection of wines to discover. It has live music (check its Facebook page to see what bands are playing) and serves *crostini*, *panini*, bruschetta and various *taglieri* (wooden platters of wild boar, salami, Parmesan, honey etc).

the hillside. Grapes and olives are harvested in September, chestnuts in October.

Oliveto Fonte di Foiano
AGRITURISMO, OLIVE FARM €€

(☎0565 76 60 43, 347 4340047; www.fontedifoiano. it; Località Fonte di Foiano 48, Castagneto Carducci; apt per week €390-590; P☼) If you fancy staying on an olive farm where you can watch the sun sink out to sea behind the Tuscan isle of Capraia, then this is the address. Some 6000 olive trees cover the 18-hectare farm, tended by the same family since 1978, and there is a state-of-the-art mill where the olives are pressed to make extra virgin oil. Staying in one of its four, comfortable self-catering apartments during the olive harvest (end of October to mid-December) is particularly thrilling.

San Vincenzo

POP 7000

This moderately attractive seaside town is particularly popular in summer with Italian visitors, who flock here to flop on its sandy beaches. The beaches to the south are backed by herb-scented *macchia* (wild scrubland) and pine forest.

In town, yachties moor their vessels in the recently redeveloped Marina di San Vincenzo, which is smart, modern and endowed with a waterside line-up of chic, glass-box boutiques and bars. Bar del Porto (Piazza del Porto 2; ☼Wed-Sun), with lots of outside seating, is the designer address here. But if you like it shabby-chic, a little rough around the edges, it has to be beach shack Zanzibar (Piazzale Serini 2; ☼Tue-Sun), with vintage decor in old fishermen huts at the northern end of the marina.

A few kilometres inland, the Parco Archeominerario di San Silvestro (www.parchi valdicornia.it; 1/2/3 sites €9/13/15; ☼10.30am-7.30pm daily Jul & Aug, 10am-6pm Tue-Sun Jun & Sep, 10am-6pm Sat & Sun Mar-May & Oct) explores the valley's 3000-year mining history. Around 50m before the turn-off to the park entrance, a sunken lane on the right signposted *'forni fusori'* leads to the remains of some Etruscan smelting ovens, once used for copper production. The park itself comprises the ruins of the 14th-century mining town Rocca di San Silvestro, reached via an underground train that passes through the Temperino copper and lead mines (with a small mineral museum) en route. Guided tours taking in your pick of sites depart roughly hourly.

Golfo di Baratti

The drive from San Vincenzo to pretty waterside Baratti in the Baratti Gulf is a dead-straight 12km motor south along an avenue lined by sky-high parasol pines backing onto beautiful sandy beaches. Baratti itself is a gorgeous little fishing port with a couple of lovely restaurants.

◉ Sights & Activities

TOP CHOICE Parco Archeologico di Baratti e Populonia
ARCHAEOLOGICAL PARK

(www.parchivaldicornia.it; Populonia; Necropoli or Acropoli adult/child €9/6, entire park adult/child/family €15/11/39; ☼9.30am-7.30pm daily Jul & Aug, 10am-7pm Tue-Sun Jun & Sep, to 6pm Tue-Sun Mar-May & Oct, to 4pm or 5pm Sat & Sun Nov-Feb; ☼) Absolutely fascinating and a real highlight is this vast green archaeological park where five marked walking trails lead to various unearthed remains of several Etruscan tombs. Particularly impressive are the gigantic circular tumulus tombs in the Necropoli di San Cerbone immediately in front of the visitors centre – the Tomba dei Carri is an astonishing 28m in diameter.

Great for families (bring your own picnic to make a day of it), the easy Via delle Cave (two hours) trail leads through shady woodland to the quarries from which the soft ochre sandstone was extracted and into which tombs were later cut.

More demanding is the Via della Romanella (Metal Working Trail; 2½ hours) which leads to the Etruscan acropoli (acropolis) of Populonia. Digs here have revealed the foundations of an Etruscan temple dating to the 2nd century BC, along with its adjacent buildings. If you don't want to walk, you can drive here – follow signs for Populonia, a pretty three-street hamlet still owned by a single family and protected by a 15th-century castle with a tower that can be scaled for a fabulous panorama of park and coast.

Bring a sun hat, cream and sturdy shoes.

🍴 Sleeping & Eating

TOP CHOICE Canessa
HOTEL, SEAFOOD €€

(☎0565 2 95 30; www.canessacamere.it; Baratti; d €70-100, meals €30; ☼lunch & dinner, closed Mon Sep-Jun) What makes this contemporary seafood restaurant so unique is the ancient

15th-century watchtower by the sea that the modern building is wrapped around. Cuisine is fishy and fresh, and huge glass windows look right out onto the lapping waves. Should you fall in love with quaint Baratti (highly likely), Canessa has four lovely rooms up top with unbeatable sea views and romantic terraces on which to savour the outstanding location.

ELBA & THE TUSCAN ARCHIPELAGO

POP 31,000

A local legend says that when Venus rose from the waves, seven precious stones fell from her tiara, creating seven islands off the Tuscan coast. These little-known gems range from the tiny uninhabited island of Gorgona, just 2.23 sq km in size, to the biggest and busiest island, 224-sq-km Elba (Isola d'Elba), best known as the place where Napoleon (poor thing) was exiled to.

National Parks

The Parco Nazionale dell'Arcipelago Toscano (Tuscan Archipelago National Park; www.islepark.it) safeguards the delicate ecosystems of the seven islands as well as the 600 sq km of sea that washes around them, making it Europe's largest protected marine area.

Here, typical Mediterranean fish abound and rare species, such as the wonderfully named Neptune's shaving brush seaweed, unique to the archipelago, cling to life. Monk seals, driven from the other islands by human presence, still gambol in the deep underwater ravines off Montecristo. The islands serve as an essential rest stop for birds migrating between Europe and Africa. The shy red partridge survives on Elba and Pianosa and the archipelago supports over a third of the world's population of the equally uncommon Corsican seagull, adopted as the national park's symbol.

On Elba, the national park runs information offices in Portoferraio, Marciana and Enfola.

Elba

Napoleon would think twice about fleeing Elba today. Dramatically more congested than when the emperor was charitably dumped here in 1814 (he did manage to engineer an escape in less than a year), the island is an ever-glorious paradise setting of rocky beach-laced coves, vineyards, blue waters, thoroughly fabulous hairpin-bend motoring and mind-bending views crowned by the highest peak on the island, Monte Capanne (1018m). All this is supplemented by a very fine seafaring cuisine, some lovely island wines and a rugged terrain just made for hiking, biking and sea-kayaking.

With the exception of high season – actually only the month of August – when the island's beaches are sardine-packed and the few roads clogged to a standstill with too much traffic, Elba is something of a *Robinson Crusoe* paradise. In springtime, early summer and autumn, when grapes and olives are harvested, there are plenty of tranquil nooks on this stunningly picturesque, 28km-long, 19km-wide island. Why on earth did Napoleon ever want to leave?

History

Elba has been inhabited since the Iron Age and the extraction of iron ore and metallurgy were the island's principal sources of economic wellbeing until well into the second half of the 20th century. In 1917 some 840,000 tonnes of iron were produced, but in WWII the Allies bombed the industry to bits. By the beginning of the 1980s production was down to 100,000 tonnes. You can fossick around to your heart's content in museums dedicated to rocks.

Ligurian tribespeople were the island's first inhabitants, followed by Etruscans and Greeks from Magna Graecia. Centuries of peace under the Pax Romana gave way to more uncertain times during the barbarian invasions, when Elba became a refuge for those fleeing mainland marauders. By the 11th century, Pisa (and later Piombino) was in control and built fortresses to help ward off attacks by Muslim raiders and pirates operating out of North Africa.

In the 16th century, Cosimo I de' Medici grabbed territory in the north of the island, where he founded the port town of Cosmopolis, today's Portoferraio.

🏃 Activities

National park information offices are the obvious places to pick up information on the island's many walking trails, guided nature walks and outdoor activities; the visitors centre in Enfola (see the boxed text on p187) is particularly efficient and maps out a lovely circular walk around the cape starting from in front of the waterside office. From

May to October it organises guided botanical and bio-watching (as in observing biodiversity) walks.

Given its gorgeous crystal-clear waters, diving and snorkelling are predictably big on Elba – see the boxed text, p185, for the complete scoop. Otherwise, explore the island and its watery surrounds (not to mention a treasure trove of tiny hidden coves and beaches inaccessible on foot) by sailing boat, motor boat or kayak.

Sea Kayak Italy — TOP CHOICE — KAYAKING
(☑348 2290711; www.seakayakitaly.com) Organises sea-kayaking courses (€170 for 10 hours of tuition over two days), guided kayaking excursions (half/full day €53/70) and – the real experience not to be missed – a two-day kayaking trek departing from Marciana Marina with a spot of fishing, an overnight camp on the beach and a campfire dinner of just-caught fish (€130, minimum two people). True enthusiasts can encircle the entire island in seven magical days (€400).

Il Viottolo — TREKKING, BIKING
(☑348 3019709; www.ilviottolo.com) Vertical trekking, moonlight trekking, archaeological and mineralogy treks, mountain biking, snorkelling and sea kayaking are among the guided expeditions (ranging from two hours to all day) offered by this Marino di Campo–based adventure specialist.

Kikko Charter — BOATING
(☑348 3019709; www.kikkocharter.it) Charter a sailing boat with skipper in Portoferraio and sail out to sea – all day (€85), over an early-evening *aperitivo* (€40) or for dinner (6pm to midnight, €130).

EMPEROR NAPOLEON

At precisely 6pm on 3 May 1814, the English frigate *Undaunted* dropped anchor in the harbour of Portoferraio on Elba. It bore an unusual cargo. Under the Treaty of Fontainebleau, the emperor Napoleon was exiled to this seemingly safe open prison, some 15km from the Tuscan coast.

It could have been so much worse for the emperor, but the irony for someone who hailed from Corsica, just over the water, must have been bitter. Napoleon, the conqueror who had stridden across all of Europe and taken Egypt, was awarded this little island as his private fiefdom, to hold until the end of his days.

Elba would never quite be the same again. Napoleon, ever hyperactive, threw himself into frenetic activity in his new, humbler domain. He prescribed a mass of public works, which included improving the operations of the island's iron-ore mines – whose revenue, it is pertinent to note, now went his way. He also went about boosting agriculture, initiating a road-building program, draining marshes and overhauling the legal and education systems.

Some weeks after his arrival, his mother Letizia and sister Paolina rolled up. But he remained separated from his wife, Maria Luisa, and was visited for just two (no doubt hectic) days by his lover, Maria Walewska.

At the Congress of Vienna, the new regime in France called for Napoleon's removal to a more distant location. Austria, too, was nervous. Some participants favoured a shift to Malta, but Britain objected and suggested the remote South Atlantic islet of St Helena. The Congress broke up with no agreed decision.

Napoleon was well aware of the debate. Under no circumstances would he allow himself to be shipped off to some rocky speck in the furthest reaches of the Atlantic Ocean. A lifelong risk taker, he decided to have another roll of the dice. For months he had sent out on 'routine' trips around the Mediterranean a couple of vessels flying the flag of his little empire, Elba. When one, the *Incostante*, set sail early in the morning of 26 February 1815, no one suspected that the conqueror of Europe was stowed away on board. Sir Neil Campbell, his English jail warden, had returned to Livorno the previous day, confident that Napoleon was, as ever, fully immersed in the business of the island.

Napoleon made his way to France, reassumed power and embarked on the Hundred Days, the last of his expansionist campaigns that would culminate in defeat at Waterloo, after which he got his Atlantic exile after all, dying on St Helena in 1821, from arsenic poisoning – contracted, according to the most accepted contemporary theory, probably from the hair tonic he applied to keep that famous quiff glistening.

Elba

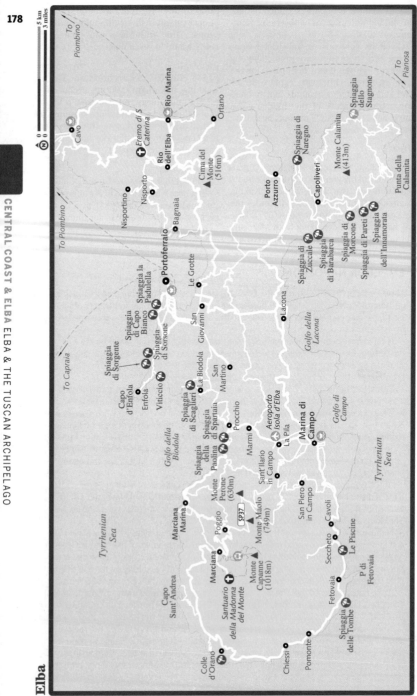

0 — 5 km
0 — 3 miles

To Piombino
To Pianosa
To Piombino
To Capraia

Cavo
Rio Marina
Eremo di S Caterina
Rio dell'Elba
Ortano
Nisporto
Nisportino
Bagnaia
Spiaggia di Narègno
Monte Calamita
Spiaggia dello Stagnone
Cima del Monte (516m)
Porto Azzurro
Capoliveri
Monte (413m)
Punta della Calamita
Portoferraio
Le Grotte
Spiaggia la Padulella
Spiaggia di Capo Bianco
Spiaggia di Sorsone
Spiaggia di Morcone
Spiaggia di Pareti
Spiaggia dell'Innamorata
Spiaggia di Zuccale
Spiaggia di Barabarca
Spiaggia di Sorgente
Capo d'Enfola
Enfola
Viticcio
San Giovanni
Lacona
Golfo della Lacona
Golfo della Biodola
La Biodola
San Martino
Spiaggia di Scaglieri
Spiaggia di Spartaia
Procchio
Aeroporto Isola d'Elba
La Pila
Marina di Campo
Golfo di Campo
Spiaggia della Paolina
Marmi
Sant'Ilario in Campo
Tyrrhenian Sea
Marciana Marina
Monte Perone (630m)
Poggio
SP37
Monte Maolo (749m)
San Piero in Campo
Cavoli
Capo Sant'Andrea
Marciana
Santuario della Madonna del Monte
Monte Capanne (1018m)
Secchéto
Le Piscine
P di Fetovaia
Colle d'Orano
Chiessi
Pomonte
Fetovaia
Spiaggia delle Tombe
Tyrrhenian Sea

Rent Boat Bagnaia BOATING
(347 6870275; www.rentboatbagnaia.it; Località Bagnaia) Motorised rubber dinghies and speed boats can be rented to explore the best of Elba's beaches; ask staff where to go before jetting off.

Getting There & Away
Elba is an easy one-hour ferry crossing from Piombino on the mainland to Portoferraio; ferries sail at least hourly year-round and in season a handful of extra boats sail from Piombino to the smaller Elban ports of Cavo and Rio Marina.

Elba's airstrip, **Aeroporto Isola d'Elba** (0565 97 60 11), just north of Marina di Campo, in La Pila, is served by seasonal domestic flights to/from Milan with **Elbafly** (www.elbafly.it).

Getting Around
Car is the easiest way to get around the island, except in traffic-clogged August when you really won't get very far at all. The island's southwest coast proffers the most dramatic and scenic motoring – with no traffic count one hour to motor the 35km from Procchio to Cavoli.

In Portoferraio, rent a mountain bike, scooter or bike from **Two Wheels Network** (0565 91 46 66; www.twn-rent.it; Viale Elba 32); or take an ATL bus from **Portoferraio bus station** (0565 91 43 92; Viale Elba 20), almost opposite the Toremar jetty.

PORTOFERRAIO & AROUND
POP 12,180
Known to the Romans as Fabricia and later Ferraia (since it was a port for iron exports), this small harbour was acquired by Cosimo I de' Medici in the mid-16th century, when its distinctive fortifications took shape.

Portoferraio can be a hectic place, especially in August when holidaymakers and day-trippers pour off the ferries from Piombino on the mainland every 20 minutes or so. But wandering the streets and steps of the historic centre, indulging in the exceptional eating options and haggling for sardines with fishermen at the old harbour more than makes up for the squeeze.

Sights & Activities
Old Town HISTORIC QUARTER
From the ferry terminal, it's a bit less than a kilometre along the foreshore to the Old Town, a spiderweb of narrow streets and alleys that stagger uphill from the old harbour and waterfront to Portoferraio's defining twinset of forts, **Forte Falcone** (closed) and the salmon-pink **Forte Stella** (Via della Stella; adult/child €2/1.50; 9am-7pm Easter-Sep) with deserted 16th-century ramparts to wander and scores of seagulls freewheeling overhead.

At the start of his fleeting exile on Elba in 1814, Napoleon was 'imprisoned' in the 15th-century **Torre del Martello** by the port entrance, which is the contemporary host to the modest **Museo Archeologica della Linguella** (Archaeological Museum; admission €3; 10am-1pm & 3.30-7.10pm Fri-Wed Apr-Oct).

Museo Villa Napoleonica
di San Martino HISTORICAL RESIDENCE
(San Martino; adult/child/parking €3/free/3; 9am-7pm Wed-Sat, 9am-1pm Sun) Set in hills about 5km southwest of town in San Martino, this villa – a remodelled farmhouse topped by a roof terrace with Napoleonic

DON'T MISS

HAGGLING FOR FISH

Hanging out with locals, waiting for the fishing boats to come in, is a quintessential Portoferraio pastime. The crowd starts to form on the quay around 9.30am and by the time the first boats dock at 10am there is quite a line-up of punters waiting to exchange hand-crumpled bank notes for the catch of the day.

The larger industrial fishing boats with crews of 10 or so dock midway between the ferry terminal and the old-town harbour on **Banchina d'Alto Fondale** (the quayside across the busy road from Piazza del Popolo). Occasionally they'll catch a huge tuna – which draws a real crowd, not to mention the fishing port authorities and all sorts – but in the main its wooden crates of sardines, mackerel and anchovies they sell from the side of their boat (€5 for a plastic-bag full).

Smaller boats with just one or two fishermen at most moor alongside **Calata Giacomo Matteotti** at the old harbour each morning any time from 8am onwards. And these are the guys who get the real catch – octopus, lobster, eel and swordfish on good days.

If haggling for fish is simply not your cup of tea, there's always harbourside fishmonger **Pescheria del Porto** (Calata Giacomo Matteotti 10; 8am-12.30pm Mon-Sat).

1. Populonia (p175)
A tiny hamlet offering a spectacular panorama of the Golfo di Baratti.

2. Portoferraio (p179)
A web of streets leads down to the waterfront in Elba's port town.

3. Parco Archeologico di Baratti e Populonia (p175)
Remains of Etruscan tombs offer a fascinating insight into the past.

4. Castagneto Carducci (p174)
A fortified town of steep, narrow lanes.

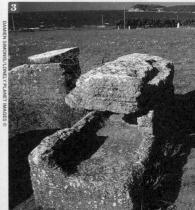

DAMIEN SIMONIS/LONELY PLANET IMAGES ©

stone eagles – was where Napoleon occasionally dropped in to escape the city heat. In the 1850s a Russian nobleman had the rather overbearing gallery built at its base, now host to temporary Napoleon-related exhibitions. Orange and palm trees colour its faintly shabby gardens and views from the rooftop terrace are lovely.

A combined ticket covering both this and Museo Nazionale della Residenza Napoleoniche costs €5 and is valid for three days.

Museo Nazionale della
Residenza Napoleoniche HISTORIC RESIDENCE
(Piazzale Napoleone; adult/child €3/1.50; 9am-7pm Mon & Wed-Sat, 9am-1pm Sun) Up on the bastions, between the two forts, is Villa dei Mulini (also known as Palazzo dei Mulini), home to Napoleon during his stint as emperor of this small isle. With its Empire-style furnishings, splendid library, fig tree–studded Italianate gardens and unbeatable sea view, the emperor certainly didn't want for creature comforts during his brief Elban exile – contrast his Elba lifestyle with the simplicity of his camp bed and travelling trunk when he was on the campaign trail.

Aquavision BOAT TRIP
(328 7095470; www.aquavision.it; Portoferraio harbour; adult/child €18/10; 10.30am daily mid-Apr–mid-Oct) It might seem a tad tourist-tacky but the sedentary two-hour voyages out to sea in a glass-bottom boat are a great way of seeing some of Elba's lovely coastline and aquatic fauna close up. Pillarbox-red *M/N Nautilus* sails west from Banchina d'Alto Fondale between the ferry port and the old harbour, past Portoferraio lighthouse, to Capo d'Enfola (Cape Enfola) and back again; crew throw bait into the water

DON'T MISS

SCALINATA MEDICI

From central square Piazza Cavour head uphill along Via Giuseppe Garibaldi to the foot of this monumental staircase, a fabulous mirage of 140 wonky stone steps cascading up through every sun-lit shade of amber to the dark, dimly lit church of 17th-century Chiesa della Misericordia (Via della Misericordia). Inside is Napoleon's death mask. Continue to the top of the staircase to reach the forts and Napoleonic villa.

to ensure a continuous shoal of fish for passengers to ogle at. Buy tickets on board.

🛌 Sleeping

Half-board is usually the only option in August and many hotels only open April to October. The best places to stay are a short drive from the town centre.

TOP CHOICE Lo Scoglio Bianco HOTEL €
(0565 93 90 36; www.scogliobianco.it; Viticcio; half-board per person €52-98; Apr-Oct; P) This thoroughly affordable address with bags of charm is perched above rocks and the sea in the hamlet of Viticcio, 5km west of town on Cape Enfola. The best rooms have small balconies with big blue views; others open onto a flowery interior courtyard. The closest beach, a pocket-sized shingle cove, is a steep climb down – as are the many smooth flat rocks begging to be basked on.

TOP CHOICE Hotel e Ristorante Mare HOTEL €€
(0565 93 30 69; www.hotelmare.org; Magazzini; half-board per person €43-122; Apr–mid-Oct;) One of the island's most modern choices, Hotel Mare has a distinct nautical feel to its architecture and decor – apt given that it sits on the waterfront of a picturesque little harbour just across the water from Portoferraio. And, yes, views of the town and peninsula from its rooftop terrace, pool and waterfront restaurant (meals €30, pizza €5 to €10) are all equally magnificent. Minimum three-night stay; parking €6.

Rosselba Le Palme CAMPGROUND €
(0565 93 31 01; www.rosselbalepalme.it; adult/child 3-8yr/tent/car €10.40/8.20/12.10/3.80; Apr–mid-Oct; P) Set around a botanical garden and considered one of Europe's best camp sites, this 'camping village' 9km east of Portoferraio town centre along the SP26 and SP28 is a green oasis of tropical palms. Among its many activities is diving, which is taught at its on-site diving school.

Villa Ombrosa HOTEL €
(0565 91 43 63; www.villaombrosa.it; Via Alcide de Gasperi 3; d from €95; P) One of the very few Portoferraio hotels open year-round, Ombrosa has a great location overlooking the sea (ask for a sea-facing room; those overlooking the back garden aren't half as nice) and Spiaggia delle Ghiaie (Ghiaie Beach).

Acquaviva CAMPGROUND €
(0565 91 91 03; www.campingacquaviva.it; adult/child 3-6yr/tent/car €11.20/7.50/15.60/3.70; mid-

TENUTA LA CHIUSA

Now this is what you call style: a walled estate on the seashore with a 17th-century farm-house, an 18th-century villa, almost 8 hectares of vineyards tumbling towards the sea, olive groves, palm trees and 10 self-catering apartments – some on the beach in former peasant-worker cottages. Upon landing on Elba in 1814 it was at Tenuta La Chiusa (☑0565 93 30 46; www.tenutalachiusa.it; Magazzini 93; d €65-120, up to 5 people €110-185, per week d €450-850, up to 5 people per week €750-1300; P⛵) that Napoleon stayed the night before heading next morning into Portoferraio to be received by the crowd.

Elba's oldest wine-making estate, La Chiusa, 8km east of Portoferraio along the SP26 and SP28, really is unique. It arranges wine-tasting (⊙8.30am-12.30pm & 4-8pm, shorter hr low season) and accommodation (minimum two nights from September to July, and five nights in August) has a simple charm. Guests can buy olive oil and wine direct from reception; and, should you fancy cooking (breakfast, lunch or dinner), harbour-side Hotel e Ristorante Mare is a wonderful two-minute stroll away along the pebbly seashore in the tiny harbour of Magazzini.

Apr–Oct) Portoferraio's nearest camping ground, located about 4km west of town near Enfola, is a more traditional camp-ground experience compared to many island schemes. Dirt paths encased in foliage connect pitches and modular Lego-like 'chalets' with common areas, including a tent restaurant. Modest apartments and 'mobile homes' are available as well. The beach, a humble but private 70m affair, is steps away, while other beaches are within reasonable walking distance.

✗ Eating

TOP CHOICE Osteria Libertaria   OSTERIA €€
(☑0565 91 49 78; Calata Giacomo Matteotti 12; meals €30; ⊙Apr-Oct) Smart on the water-front across from the fishing boats, this stylish dining address cooks up an outstanding fish-driven cuisine. Dishes are simple – think a mixed platter of marinated fish, fried calamari or *tonno in crosta di pistacchi* (pistachio-encrusted tuna fillet) – but fresher than fresh and cooked to perfection every time. Dine at one of two tile-topped tables on the traffic-noisy street outside or on the back-alley terrace. No coffee.

Il Castagnacciao   PIZZERIA €
(Via del Mercato Vecchio 5; pizza €4.50-8; ⊙9am-2.30pm & 4.30-11pm Thu-Tue) Hidden in an alley near central square Piazza Cavour, this iconic address with bench seating at wooden tables is tantamount to no-frills pizza bliss. Watch your thin-crust, rectangular-shaped pizza go in and out of the wood-fired oven and make sure you save space for dessert – *castagnaccio* (chestnut 'cake') baked in the

same oven. Big appetites can kick off the lip-smacking feast with *torta di ceci* (chickpea 'cake').

❶ Information

Info Park Are@ (☑0565 91 94 14; www.islepark.it; cnr Viale Elba & Calata Italia; ⊙9.30am-1.30pm & 3.30-7.30pm, closed Sun winter) Parco Nazionale dell'Arcipelago Toscano information centre.

Tourist office (☑0565 91 46 71; www.isoleditoscana.it; Calata Italia 43; ⊙9am-7pm Mon-Fri, to 1pm Sat & Sun, shorter hr winter) Near the ferry port.

❶ Getting There & Away

Year-round regular car and foot passenger ferries sail at least hourly from the Stazione Marittima (ferry port) in Piombino to Portoferraio. Unless it is a summer weekend or August, when queues can form, there is no need to buy a ticket in advance (online). Simply buy a ticket from one of the ticket booths at the port. Fares (from €15/45 one-way per person/car) vary according to the season. Sailing time is one hour. Companies include **Blunavy** (www.blunavytraghetti.com), **Moby** (www.mobylines.com) and **Toremar** (www.toremar.it, in Italian).

MARCIANA

POP 2240

From Portoferraio, cruise 18km west along the coast to Marciana Marina, an attractive resort which, unlike typical cookie-cutter marinas, has character and history to complement its pleasant pebble beaches. From here it's a twisting 9km inland to Marciana, the island's oldest and highest (375m) village crowned by a much-knocked-about fort (closed).

It's a joy to meander Marciana's stone streets, past arches, flower boxes and petite balconies to drop-offs revealing views of the coastline below. But the highlight is the short half-day walk from the village to the most important site of pilgrimage on the island.

◉ Sights & Activities

Santuario della Madonna del Monte
CHAPEL

(admission free) Park at the entrance to Marciana and head out of the village on foot along Via delle Fonti and its continuations, Via delle Coste and Via dei Monti, to this much-altered 11th-century church. Inside is a stone upon which a divine hand is said to have painted an image of the Virgin, believed to have miraculous powers. Outside the church a plaque commemorates Napoleon's visits here by horseback in 1814.

It is an invigorating 40-minute uphill walk through scented parasol pine and chestnut woods along an old mule track (lots of wild sage and thyme) and the coastal panorama that unfolds as you get higher is remarkable. Pace yourself with the aid of 14 Stations of the Cross and as you near the hilltop chapel (627m) play 'I Spy Corsica'. Once in situ, drink like Napoleon no doubt did from the old stone fountain (1695) across from the church entrance, then continue a further five minutes along the small footpath to ogle at Corsica in its full glory!

Museo Archeologico
ARCHAEOLOGY MUSEUM

(☑0565 90 12 15; Via del Pretorio 48; admission €2; ⊙4-7pm Wed-Mon) Down a cobbled lane, this modest museum harks back to medieval Marciana and beyond.

Cabinovia Monte Capanne
CABLE CAR

(Cableway; ☑0565 90 10 20; single/return €12/18; ⊙10am-12.50pm & 2.20-5pm Easter-Nov) If you only have time for one road trip from Portoferraio, it has to be this. Some 750m south of Marciana on the road to Poggio, the Cabinovia Monte Capanne whisks walkers up in open, barred cabins – imagine riding in a canary-yellow parrot cage – up the mountain to the summit of Elba's highest point, Monte Capanne (1018m). The trip takes 20 minutes and at the top you can hike around the peak to savour an astonishing 360-degree panorama of the entire island, surrounding Tuscan Archipelago, Etruscan Coast and Corsica 50km away.

🛏 Sleeping & Eating

Hermitage
HOTEL €€€

(☑0565 97 40; www.hotelhermitage.it; La Biodola; half-board per person €125-330; P❄@🛜⛱) If James Bond were to parachute onto Elba in a tuxedo, he'd land on the tennis courts of the Hermitage. One of the island's truly luxurious hotels, this is a simply gorgeous retreat complete with infinity pool overlooking the sea, golf course just over the fence, beauty centre

---

MARCIANA MARINA: A TRADITIONAL PASSEGGIATA

The loveliest moment of the day in laid-back Marciana Marina is late afternoon and early evening when what feels like the entire town slowly strolls the waterfront for that all-essential, oh-so-Tuscan *passeggiata* (early evening stroll).

Start on Piazza della Vittoria, at the eastern end of the seafront promenade, with its gigantic pineapple-shaped palm trees and restaurant terraces; the hip crowd gathers for *aperitivi* on the shabby-chic terrace of Enoteca Coltelli (Piazza della Vittoria 11), a wine bar and pub with a peeling-paint facade and strong party spirit.

Walk a couple of minutes west along waterside Viale Margherita and make a quick detour a block inland to Marciana Marina's old central square, Piazza Vittorio Emanuele. With its pretty peach-painted church and pristine carpet of perfect cobblestones, this is easily Elba's most beautiful piazza.

Backtrack to the water and continue meandering west past stylish boutiques selling all manner of wares – some great fashion. And, as the sun sinks, find yourself at the far end of the waterfront on Spiaggia di Capo Nord, a handsome beach of large smooth pebbles backed by a picture-postcard line-up of old-fashioned, green-and-white-striped bathing cabins (€23 per day). Marciana's 12th-century Torre Saracena (Saracen Tower) guards the enchanting ensemble.

End your *passeggiata* with dinner – octopus risotto, swordfish et al – looking out to sea from Ristorante Capo Nord (☑0565 99 69 83; Località Fenicia; meals €50; ⊙lunch & dinner Mar-Nov, closed Mon low season), an impossibly romantic seafood restaurant with splendid terrace on same said beach.

Coloured walls buzzing with eagle rays, sun fish and barracudas, and a couple of wrecks of Roman cargo boats off the coast of Capo Sant'Andrea makes Elba a top diving spot. From June to September, get set up with gear, tuition and guides at the following places.

Enfola Diving Center (☑339 6791367; www.enfoladivingcenter.it) Diving and snorkelling school on Enfola beach, 6km west of Portoferraio.

Rosselba Le Palme Diving Centre (☑0565 93 31 01; www.rosselbalepalme.it) Learn to dive without tanks with Jean-Jacques Mayol, son of legendary free diver Jacques Mayol of *Big Blue* fame, at his school 9km east of Portoferraio on the Rosselba Le Palme campground.

Diving in Elba (☑392 7816829; www.divinginelba.com) One of the island's largest centres, with schools in Portoferraio at Hotel Club Airone; in the beautiful wide-sand bay of La Biodola at the Hermitage hotel and in Procchio on **Sporting Life Beach** (Piazza del Mare 2). Exceptionally, it also runs snorkelling/diving courses specially designed for kids aged five to 14 years.

and pretty much every other spoil-yourself treat you could desire. Find it in the tiny hamlet of La Biodola, pretty much equidistant between Marciana Marina and Portoferraio.

Osteria del Noce   OSTERIA **€€**
(☑0565 90 12 85; Via della Madonna 27; meals €30; ☺lunch & dinner) This simple family-run place, a quintessential Slow Food address at the top of hilltop Marciana, cooks up a mean spaghetti laced with Granseolo Elbano (a large crab typical to Elba). Its *fritto del pescatore* (local deep-fried fish served in brown paper) is another fantastic dish to try – in the company of sweeping coastal views from its cosy covered terrace.

❶ Information

Casa del Parco di Marciana (☑0565 90 10 30, 348 7039374; below Fortezza Pisana; ☺10am-1pm & 5-6pm Thu-Sat) National park visitor centre with lots of walking and outdoor-activity info.

POGGIO

A twisting 4km ascent into the mountains from Marciana Marina brings you to the attractive inland village of Poggio on the SP25, famous for its spring water. It's an enchanting little place with steep, cobblestone alleys and stunning coastal views.

❂ Sights & Activities

Monte Perone   MOUNTAIN
If you follow the SP37 out of Poggio, park at the picnic site at the foot of Monte Perone (630m) – you can't miss it. To the left (east) you can wander up the mountain, with spectacular views across much of the island. To the right (west) you can scramble

fairly quickly to a height that affords broad vistas down to Poggio, Marciana and Marciana Marina.

Monte Maolo   MOUNTAIN
From Monte Perone, you could press on to Monte Maolo (749m), from where the road descends into the southern flank of the island passing en route the granite shell of the Romanesque **Chiesa di San Giovanni** and, shortly after, a ruined tower, the **Torre di San Giovanni**. Two small hamlets, Sant'Ilario in Campo and San Piero in Campo, make simple if uneventful stops to stretch your legs.

✘ Eating

Le Dolce Vita   CAFE **€**
(Piazza del Castagneto 3; snacks €4-8; ☺daily Easter-Oct) At the northern entrance to the village, this simple rooftop cafe is the place to lap up plunging views down to the coast over a simple *panino,* bruschetta or pizza. Cross the piazza for a couple more eating options.

Publius   SEAFOOD **€€**
(☑0565 9 92 08; meals €40; ☺lunch & dinner Tue-Sun Easter-Oct) Beneath Le Dolce Vita sits this formal restaurant with white tablecloths, large sea-facing windows and a refined, classically Tuscan cuisine.

MARINA DI CAMPO

This small fishing harbour on the south side of the island is Elba's second-largest town. Curling around a picturesque bay, the boats bobbing in the bay add personality to what is otherwise very much a holiday-oriented

BIKING & HIKING ON ELBA

A dizzying network of walking and mountain-biking trails blankets Elba. Many start in Portoferraio, but some of the best, far-flung trailheads kick off elsewhere on the island.

» **San Lucia to San Martino** A low-impact, 90-minute walking trail. It starts just outside Portoferraio at the church of San Lucia, traversing meadows and former farmland being repossessed by nature for about 2.2km and terminates at Napoleon's villa in San Martino.

» **Colle Reciso to San Martino and return** A 15km (round-trip), medium-difficulty mountain-bike trail that peaks at about 280m. The trail continues past San Martino, and descends into Marmi, but save some breath for the return trip, as circling back to Portoferraio from Marmi on the main road is neither pleasant nor particularly safe in high season.

» **Marciana to Chiessi** A 12km hike starting high up in Marciana, dribbling down-hill past ancient churches, sea vistas and granite boulders for about six hours to the seaside in Chiessi.

» **The Great Elba Crossing** A three- to four-day, 60km east–west island crossing, including Monte Capanne, Elba's highest point (1018m), overnighting down on the coast as camping is not allowed on the paths. The highlight is the final 19km leg from Poggio to Pomonte, passing the Santuario della Madonna del Monte and the Masso dell'Aquila rock formation.

town. Its beach of bright, white sand pulls in vacationers by the thousands; coves further west, though less spectacular, are more tranquil.

Northeast of town, signposted off the SP30 to Lacona, over 150 Mediterranean species swim, crawl and wave about in the Acquario dell'Elba (www.acquarioelba.com; adult/child €7/3; ☺9am-11.30pm Jun–mid-Sep, to 7.30pm mid-Mar–May & mid-Sep–Nov), a modest aquarium that entertains families on grey or wet days.

Just 6km west of Marina di Campo is the shingle-sand beach of Cavoli, well suited to families with its beach cafe, sun loungers and pedalos to rent, car park with a kids' playground and so on.

🍴 Sleeping & Eating

Montecristo   HOTEL €€
(☎0565 97 68 61; www.hotelmontecristo.it; Viale Nomelini; per person €40-140; P❄) Low-end rooms are a little spare; otherwise this is a pleasantly posh beachside hotel with flower-framed balconies and a bar and pool overlooking the sea. The large sunny rooms have Scandinavian-style light furnishings and king-size beds. There's a fitness centre, sauna and free bicycles.

TOP CHOICE Il Cantuccio   TRATTORIA €
(☎0565 97 67 75; www.ristoranteilcantuccio.eu; Largo Garibaldi 6; meals €25; ☺lunch & dinner)

Ignore the menu-touting waiters on the waterfront wanting to entice you in and head to this backstreet *trattoria* and *vineria* instead. In business since 1930, the place is unassuming and excellent value – hence the crowds of locals who come here for simple Tuscan classics, homemade pasta, wood-oven fired pizza and so on. Reservations recommended.

CAPOLIVERI & PORTO AZZURRO

From Marina di Campo it's a comparatively long drive along the south coast before climbing up a precipitous ridgeback in the southeast pocket of the island to Capoliveri (population 3840), another hilltop village flirting with too-enchanting-for-its-own-good designation. Its steep, narrow alleys and sandwiched houses are certainly pretty and the panorama of rooftop and sea beyond that fan out from the old stone terrace on its central square, Piazza Matteotti, is lovely indeed. But in August the tourist mob is particularly bad – avoid.

Backtrack down the ridge and head east to Porto Azzurro (population 3530), a pleasant seaside village overlooked by a fort (now a prison) built by Philip III of Spain in 1603. Its bijou maze of flower-bedecked pedestrian streets is laden with restaurant and cafe terraces, and there is a sweep of good beaches within bicycle shot. It is also a great place for easy wine tasting.

TOP-FIVE BEACH SPOTS

It pays to know your *spiaggia* (beaches), given that Elba's beaches on its 147km-long coast embrace everything in the way of shade and size of sand, pebble and rock. You'll find sandy strands on the south coast and in the Golfo della Biodola on the opposite side of Capo d'Enfola to Portoferraio. The quietest, prettiest beaches are tucked in bijou rocky coves and often involve a steep clamber down. Parking is invariably roadside and scant. Surf Info Elba (www.infoelba.com) for the complete lowdown.

Enfola

Just 6km west of Portoferraio, it's not so much the grey pebbles as the outdoor action that lures the crowds to this tiny fishing port in the shape of pedalos to rent, a beachside diving school, and a family-friendly 2.5km-long circular hiking trail around the green cape. The Parco Nazionale dell'Arcipelago Toscano (Tuscan Archipelago National Park; ☑0565 91 94 11; ⊙9am-1pm Mon & Fri, 2.30-4pm Tue & Thu) office also has a visitors centre here.

Procchio

This small bustling beach town, 10km west of Portoferraio, has one of Elba's longest stretches of golden sand and the island's best *gelato* and Sicilian *granita* at cafe-gelateria Scalo 70 (Via del Mare 10; cones €2-4); try the rice ice-cream or nut, fig and caramel. It's also a great spot to rent a bicycle and go for an island spin: Rent Procchio (☑335 7567764; www.rentprocchio.it; mountain bikes per day €10), with a stand on the main street, has the wheels and all the info on itineraries. West from Procchio, the road hugs cliffs above Spiaggia di Spartaia and Spiaggia della Paolina, beautiful little beaches requiring a steep clamber down.

Sansone & Sorgente

This twinset of cliff-ensnared, white-shingle and pebble beaches stands out for its turquoise, crystal-clear waters just made for snorkelling, and the naturally pretty camp site, Camping La Sorgente (☑0565 91 71 39; www.campinglasorgente.it; adult €14, child €9-12, tent €3, car €14, 4-person bungalows €60-150; ⊙reception 9am-9pm Apr–mid-Sep), that scales the terraced hillside from the shore of Sorgente. By car from Portoferraio, follow the SP27 to Enfola.

Morcone, Pareti & Innamorata

Find this trio of charming sandy-pebble coves framed by sweet-smelling pine and eucalyptus trees some 3km south of Capoliveri on the southeast part of the island. Rent a kayak and paddle out to sea on Innamorata, the wildest of the three; or fine dine and overnight on Pareti beach at Hotel Stella Maris (☑0565 96 84 25; www.albergostella maris.com; half-board per person in d €68-120; ℗❋), one of the island's few three-star hotels to be found on the sand.

Colle d'Orano & Fetovaia

The standout highlight of these two gorgeous swathes of golden sand on Elba's western coast is the dramatic drive – a real island highlight – between the two. The road follows the island's splendid southwest coastal road (SP25). Legend has it Napoleon frequented Colle d'Orano to sit and swoon over his native Corsica, which is visible across the water. A heavenly scented, maquis (herbal scrubland) covered promontory protects sandy Fetovaia, where nudists flop on nearby granite rocks known as Le Piscine.

✗ Eating & Drinking

TOP CHOICE Il Chiasso   TUSCAN, SEAFOOD €€
(☑0565 96 87 09, 335 332634; Via Cavour 32, Capoliveri; meals €40; ⊙dinner daily Easter-Oct) This address has been one of the hottest spots on the island for a dinner date since the 1970s. Tucked down a quiet little alley *(chiasso)* enlivened only by the odd line of washing hung out to dry, Il Chiasso has a classy set menu and excellent wine list. For a true taste of Capoliveri go for the octopus

soup (an old recipe of grandma's) or the fish soup *di Luciano* (€25) – cooked up by chef Luciano since time began and swimming with local catch. Advance reservations are recommended.

Summertime MODERN TUSCAN **€€**
(☑0565 93 51 80; Via Roma 56, Capoliveri; meals €30; ☺dinner Mon & Tue, lunch & dinner Wed-Sun) Yes, Ella Fitzgerald's dulcet tones can be heard in the background at this lovely address in Capoliveri village. The mixed platter of marinated and fried fish and veg is delicious, as is the homemade *schiaccia* (Elban cake with raisins and pine kernels) dipped in a glass of Aleatico Passito (Elban dessert wine). Get here sharp to grab a table outside on the street.

La Botte Gaia OSTERIA **€€**
(☑0565 9 56 07; www.labottegaia.com; Viale Europa 5-7, Porto Azzurro; meals €34-38; ☺dinner daily, closed Mon winter) Slow Food–featured and deservedly so, this is *the* revered dining address in Porto Azzurro – lots of homemade pasta, just-caught fish and island wines.

Fandango WINE BAR
(Via Cardenti 1, Capoliveri; ☺Tue-Sun) Steps lead down from the panoramic terrace at the far end of Piazza Matteotti to this pocket-sized *enoteca*. Sitting outside beneath its vine-clad pergola in the early evening is particularly atmospheric. Cocktails, live music and *piccolo cucina* (light snacks) add real after-dark flair.

I Sapori del Sole WINE BAR
(☑0565 92 00 81; Via Cavour 3-7, Porto Azzurro; ☺Mon-Sat) This bottle-packed wine bar and shop is a great place for tasting local Elba wines and olive oil, either on the move or as an *aperitivo* with a delicious oil-dripping bruschetta as companion.

RIO DELL'ELBA & AROUND
POP 1230

Time and energy permitting, a final bit of gorgeous driving can be done in the northeast corner of the island to this village, the heart of Elba's iron-mining operation. The village itself is slightly gloomy, but refreshingly tourist-free with what's left of tiny stone hermitage Eremo di Santa Caterina – great views – on its northern fringe.

Anyone interested in the island's industrial heritage should head 3.5km east to Rio Marina (population 2250), Rio dell'Elba's coastal sibling, where the story of iron mining is told in an engaging and interactive manner at the Parco Minerario dell'Isola d'Elba (☑0565 96 20 88; www.parcominelba.it; Via Magenta 26; adult/reduced €12/7.50; ☺Apr-Oct). The mineral park has a small museum (admission €2.50; ☺9.30am-12.30pm & 4.30-6.30pm daily May-Sep) and it organises some fantastic activities, including three-hour guided treks in Rio Marina's open-cast mine (adult/child €14/7), mineral-hunting expeditions (adult/child €5/2) and family workshops for budding geologists (adult/child €5/7.50). In season an electric train runs 1½-hour tours with commentary of the entire mining area

THE COUNT OF MONTECRISTO

This feel-good swashbuckling tale was born from author Alexandre Dumas' acquaintance with Jérome Bonaparte, Napoleon Bonaparte's brother, whom he accompanied on a trip to Elba. Dumas became aware of another island, deserted Montecristo, deeper in the Mediterranean, and determined to write a novel in remembrance of the trip. In the person of the swashbuckling Dantes, Dumas takes a dig at the corruption of the bourgeois world. The dashing officer is imprisoned for a crime he hasn't committed and vows to get even. He escapes and, after a tip-off, searches for treasure on the island of Montecristo where, after much adventure and jolly japes, our man wins all the prizes – getting rich, becoming the Count of Montecristo and exacting a full measure of revenge on those who framed him.

Of course, it's all a tall tale (and no one has ever found any treasure on Montecristo) but this particular story has made a lot of loot for a lot of people. At least 25 film and TV versions of the story have been made, with greater or lesser skill. Among the better ones are the oldies: Rowland Lee's 1935 film and the 1943 version by Robert Vernay were equally good celluloid yarns. In Italy, Andrea Giordana had women swooning at their TV sets in the 1966 series by Edmo Fenoglio. Richard Chamberlain had a go at the lead role in David Greene's 1975 *The Count of Montecristo*, as, more recently, did Gérard Depardieu in *Montecristo* (1997).

(adult/child €12/7.50). Before coming here, call ahead to check the day's activities and reserve a spot.

Gorgona & Capraia

Pinprick Gorgona is the greenest, northern-most of the Tuscan islands and can only be visited with a guide. Two towers built by the Pisans and Medicis of Florence keep watch over its plunging coastline and beautiful interior, part of which has been off-limits as a low-security prison since 1869.

By contrast the elliptical volcanic island of Capraia (population 403), just 31km from the French island of Corsica, is 8km long, 4km wide, peaks with Monte Castello (447m) and has three hotels, a campground and a handful of restaurants. A chequered history has seen Genoa, Sardinia, the Sara-cens from North Africa and Napoleon all have a bash at running it.

The easiest way to see both islands is as part of a boat trip from Livorno. May to Sep-tember, Atelier del Viaggio (📞0586 88 41 54; www.atelierdelviaggio.it; adult/child 4-10yr €68/38; ⊙Sat & Sun Apr & May, & Mon Jun-Sep) runs one-day trips to both islands. On Capraia, the tourist office (📞0586 90 51 38; www.proloco capraiaisola.it, www.isoladicapraia.it; Via Assunzione 42; ⊙9am-12.30pm & 4.30-7pm Fri-Wed Apr-Sep) can advise on walking (ask about the trail to Lake Stagnone), hiking and biking routes around the island, and diving off its shores.

Toremar (www.toremar.it, in Italian) operates car and passenger ferries from Livorno to Capraia (adult/car low season €10.50/26.90, high season €10.50/41.70; 2½ hours; one or two daily year-round); most days boat schedules allow a return trip in a day but triple-check before setting out.

Siena & Central Tuscany

Best Places to Eat

» Osteria di Passignano (p212)

» Da Nisio (p219)

» La Grotta (p234)

» Officina della Bistecca (p212)

» Enoteca I Terzi (p205)

Best Places to Stay

» La Bandita (p226)

» Podere San Lorenzo (p222)

» Campo Regio Relais (p203)

» Fattoria di Rignana (p209)

Why Go?

When people imagine classic Tuscan countryside, they usually conjure up images of central Tuscany. However, there's more to this popular region than gently rolling hills, sun-kissed vineyards and artistically planted avenues of cypress trees. Truth be told, the real gems here are the historic towns and cities, most of which are medieval and Renaissance time capsules magically transported to the modern day.

This privileged pocket of the country has maintained a high tourist profile ever since the Middle Ages, when Christian pilgrims followed the Via Francigena from Canterbury to Rome. Towns on the route catered to the needs of these pilgrims and local economies prospered as a result. Today, not a lot has changed, with tourism being the major industry and travellers being thick on the ground.

Come here for art, for architecture and for gastronomy. But most of all, come here for enchantment – we promise you won't be disappointed.

When to Go

This is a year-round destination, although the landscape south of Siena can get very hot in high summer – make sure your accommodation offers a pool and air-con. In the cities, locals tend to spend summer nights outside, making for atmospheric street scenes but meaning that you should book in advance to dine at an outdoor table. Summer is also when the festival season reaches its peak, with high-profile cultural festivals in Siena, San Gimignano, Volterra and Montalcino. Autumn/fall is when *La Vendemmia* (the grape harvest) is celebrated.

Itineraries

Val d'Elsa Two of the region's most compelling attractions are perched atop hills in this idyllic landscape. Spend your first day wandering the perfectly preserved medieval streets of San Gimignano, following an artistic itinerary that balances the gravitas of the old (Collegiata) with the exhilaration of the new (Galleria Continua). For lunch, enjoy a sandwich at Dal Bertelli, followed by a delectable gelato from Gelateria di Piazza. Overnight and dine at Podere San Lorenzo outside the walled city of Volterra, and devote the next day to exploring Volterran streets and ateliers where artisans have worked for millennia.

Chianti Base yourself at an *agriturismo* (farm stay) for a few nights and spend your days touring vineyards, visiting sculpture parks and sampling modern Tuscan cuisine. Cellar visits will be the highlight of your time here – prime your palate at Le Cantine di Greve in Chianti and then sign up for tours and wine tastings at Castello di Verrazzano, Badia a Passignano, Castello di Ama, Castello di Volpaia or Castello di Brolio.

South from Siena Start in Tuscany's Gothic heartland and then head south to explore the spectacular scenery of Le Crete, the Val di Chiana and the Val d'Orcia. Base yourself at a rural retreat and spend your days exploring the countryside around Montepulciano, Montalcino and Pienza, where the landscape is dotted with majestic medieval abbeys, picturesque fortified hill towns and sybaritic hot springs.

GETTING AROUND

Siena is the region's transport hub, with buses zooming up and down the RA3 *superstrada* (expressway) between it and Florence and also travelling to other major cities in the country. Buses travel between Siena and smaller towns throughout the area as well, although services can be infrequent and connections convoluted. There are few primary train routes, and the only truly useful service is between Siena and Grosseto. Most towns and cities have strictly enforced *Zone a Traffico Limitato* (Limited Traffic Zones; ZTLs) in their historic centres.

Where to Stay

Siena's wide array of B&Bs, *pensioni* and hotels caters to every budget, and most other towns have at least one good midrange option. If you are travelling by car, consider basing yourself at a rural villa or *agriturismo* and exploring the countryside and towns on day trips.

Best Wine Tastings

» **Castello di Ama** (p213) Taste-test Chianti Classico and admire a sculpture park.

» **Ristorante di Poggio Antico** (p226) Tour the high-tech cellars and then linger over award-winning Brunellos and Super Tuscans.

» **Badia a Passignano** (p208) Visit the historic cellars and vineyards of this Antinori-owned abbey.

Advance Planning

» Book terrace tickets for Siena's Palio at least a year in advance (p203).

» Book online if you wish to attend concerts organised by Siena's Accademia Musicale Chigiana (p202).

» Book ahead if you plan to attend San Gimignano Estate festival (p218).

» Check the website to time your visit to the Abbazia di Sant'Antimo to coincide with Gregorian chanting (p225).

Resources

» Terre di Siena: www.terresiena.it

» Lonely Planet: www.lonelyplanet.com/italy/tuscany, www.lonelyplanet.com/italy/tuscany/siena

Siena & Central Tuscany Highlights

1 Eat, drink and sleep in style when exploring the world-famous wine region of **Chianti** (p206)

2 Gorge on Gothic architecture and *panforte* (a rich cake of almonds, honey and candied fruit) in sublimely beautiful **Siena** (p194)

3 Meditate while listening to Gregorian chants at the Romanesque **Abbazia di Sant'Antimo** (p225)

4 Wander the magically preserved medieval streets of gorgeous **San Gimignano** (p215)

5 Savour Vino Nobile and locally raised Chianina beef in **Montepulciano** (p231)

6 Admire Etruscan artefacts and alabaster artworks in the artistic enclave of **Volterra** (p220)

7 Taste-test Tuscany's most famous wine in medieval **Montalcino** (p224)

8 Detour onto scenic back roads in the World Heritage–listed **Val d'Orcia** (p224)

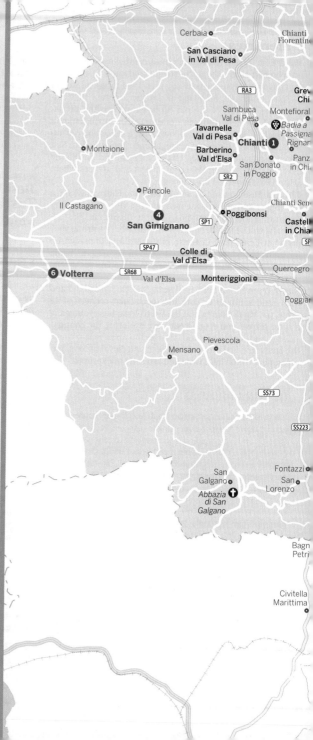

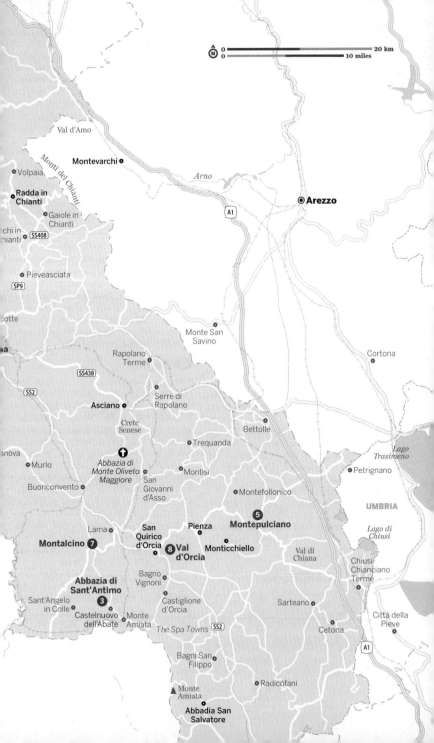

SIENA

POP 54,400

The rivalry between historic adversaries Siena and Florence continues to this day, and participation isn't limited to the locals – most travellers tend to develop a strong preference for one over the other. These allegiances often boil down to aesthetic preference: while Florence saw its greatest flourishing during the Renaissance, Siena's enduring artistic glories are largely Gothic.

History

Legend tells us that Siena was founded by the son of Remus, and the symbol of the wolf feeding the twins Romulus and Remus is as ubiquitous in Siena as it is in Rome. In reality the city was probably of Etruscan origin, although it didn't begin to grow into a proper town until the 1st century BC, when the Romans established a military colony here called Sena Julia.

In the 12th century, Siena's wealth, size and power grew along with its involvement in commerce and trade. Its rivalry with neighbouring Florence also grew proportionately, leading to numerous wars during the first half of the 13th century between Guelph Florence and Ghibelline Siena. In 1230 Florence besieged Siena and catapulted dung and donkeys over its walls. Siena's revenge came at the Battle of Montaperti in 1260, when it decisively defeated its rival, but its victory was short-lived. Only 10 years later, the Tuscan Ghibellines were defeated by Charles of Anjou and Siena was forced to ally with Florence, the chief town of the Tuscan Guelph League.

In the ensuing century, Siena was ruled by the Consiglio dei Nove (Council of Nine), a bourgeois group constantly bickering with the feudal nobles, and enjoyed its greatest prosperity. It was the Council that com-missioned many of the fine buildings in the Sienese-Gothic style that give the city its striking appearance, including lasting monuments such as the *duomo* (cathedral), Palazzo Comunale and Piazza del Campo.

The Sienese school of painting also had its origins at this time and reached its peak in the early 14th century, when artists such as Duccio di Buoninsegna and Ambrogio Lorenzetti were at work.

A plague outbreak in 1348 killed two-thirds of Siena's 100,000 inhabitants and led to a period of decline that culminated in the city being handed over to Florence's Cosimo I de' Medici, who barred the inhabitants from operating banks and thus severely curtailed its power.

This centuries-long economic downturn in the wake of the Medici takeover was a blessing in disguise, as lack of funds meant that its city centre was subject to very little redevelopment or new construction. In WWII, the French took Siena virtually unopposed, sparing it discernible damage. All of this has led to the historic centre's listing on Unesco's World Heritage list as the living embodiment of a medieval city.

◉ Sights

Piazza del Campo   PIAZZA

This sloping piazza, popularly known as Il Campo, has been Siena's civic and social centre since being staked out by the Consiglio dei Nove in the mid-12th century. It was built on the site of a former Roman marketplace, and its pie-piece paving design is divided into nine sectors to represent the number of members of the council. In 1346 water first bubbled forth from the Fonte Gaia (Happy Fountain) in the upper part of the square. These days, the fountain's panels are reproductions; the severely weathered originals, sculpted by Jacopo della Quercia in the early 15th century, are on display in the Complesso Museale Santa Maria della Scala.

At the lowest point of the square stands the spare, elegant Palazzo Comunale, conceived by the Consiglio dei Nove as a nerve centre for the republican government, uniting the offices and courts in one building and thus greatly reducing the symbolic and actual power of the feudal nobles.

Dating from 1297, the *palazzo* (palace) is one of the most graceful Gothic buildings in Italy, with an ingeniously designed concave facade that mirrors the opposing convex curve formed by the piazza. Also known as

ROAD DISTANCES (KM)

	Montepulciano	Siena	San Gimignano	Volterra
Siena	70			
San Gimignano	112	46		
Volterra	120	50	30	
Greve in Chianti	102	48	33	53

If you are planning to visit the major monuments, be sure to purchase one or more of the money-saving combined passes on offer:

» OPA SI Pass (*duomo*, Museo dell'Opera, Battistero di San Giovanni, Cripta and Oratorio di San Bernardino; €10, valid for three days)

» SIA Summer (Museo Civico, Complesso Museale Santa Maria della Scala, Museo dell'Opera, Battistero di San Giovanni, Oratorio di San Bernardino and Chiesa di San Agostino; €17, valid for seven days during period 15 March to 31 October)

» SIA Winter (Museo Civico, Complesso Museale Santa Maria della Scala, *duomo*, Museo dell'Opera and Battistero di San Giovanni; €14, valid for seven days during period 1 November to 14 March)

» Museo Civico and Torre del Mangia (€13)

» Musei Comunali (Museo Civico and Complesso Museale Santa Maria della Scala; €11, valid for two days)

The OPA SI Pass can be booked in advance at www.operaduomo.siena.it; all other passes are purchased directly at the museums.

SIENA SIGHTS

the Palazzo Pubblico, or town hall, it was purpose-built as the piazza's centrepiece, resulting in a wonderful amphitheatre effect. It now houses the Museo Civico.

Entry to the ground-floor central courtyard is free. From it soars the graceful **Torre del Mangia** (admission €8; ⊘10am-7pm Mar–mid-Oct, to 4pm mid-Oct–Feb), 102m high and with 500-odd steps. The views from the top are magnificent, but if you want to see them you should expect to wait in high season, as only 30 people are allowed up at any time.

The Campo is the undoubted heart of the city. Its magnificent pavement acts as a carpet on which students and tourists picnic and relax, and the cafes around the perimeter are the most popular *aperitivo* (predinner drinks) spots in town.

TOP CHOICE **Museo Civico** MUSEUM
(Piazza del Campo; adult/reduced €8/4.50; ⊘10am-7pm mid-Mar–Oct, to 6pm Nov–mid-Mar) The city's most impressive museum occupies rooms richly frescoed by artists of the Sienese school. These frescoes are unusual in that they were commissioned by the governing body of the city, rather than by the Church, and many depict secular subjects instead of the favoured religious themes of the time.

Upstairs, start in the **Sala del Risorgimento** with its impressive late-19th-century frescoes serialising key events in the campaign to unite Italy. Next is the **Sala di Balìa** (or Sala dei Priori). The 15 scenes depicted in

frescoes around the walls recount episodes in the life of Pope Alexander III (the Sienese Rolando Bandinelli), including his clashes with the Holy Roman Emperor Frederick Barbarossa. You then pass into the **Anticamera del Concistoro**, remarkable for the fresco (moved here in the 19th century) of *Saints Catherine of Alexandria, John and Augustine,* executed by Ambrogio Lorenzetti. The next hall, the **Sala del Concistoro**, is dominated by the allegorical ceiling frescoes of the Mannerist Domenico Beccafumi. Back in the Anticamera del Concistoro, you pass to your right into the **Vestibolo** (Vestibule), whose star attraction is a bronze wolf, the symbol of the city. Next door in the **Anticappella** are frescoes of scenes from Greco-Roman mythology and history, while the **Cappella** (Chapel) contains a fine *Holy Family and St Leonard* by Il Sodoma and intricately carved wooden choir stalls.

The best is saved for last, though. From the Cappella, you emerge into the **Sala del Mappamondo**, where you can admire the museum's masterpiece, Simone Martini's powerful and striking *Maestà* (Virgin Mary in Majesty). Completed in 1315, it features the Madonna beneath a canopy surrounded by saints and angels and is Martini's first known work. On the other side of the room is another work attributed to Martini, his oft-reproduced fresco (1328–30) of Guidoriccio da Fogliano, a captain of the Sienese army.

The next room, the **Sala della Pace**, is where the Council of Nine was based. It is decorated with Ambrogio Lorenzetti's fresco

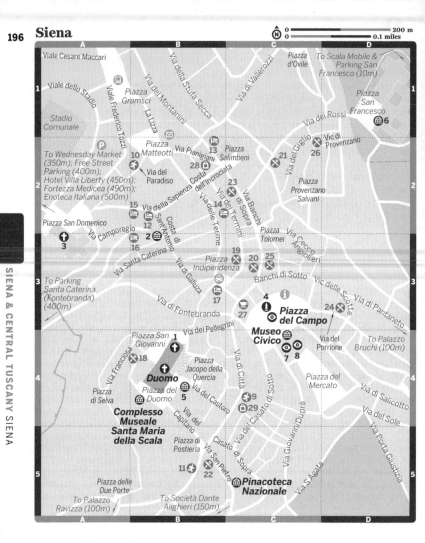

cycle known as the *Allegories of Good and Bad Government* (c 1338–40). The central allegory portrays scenes with personifications of Justice, Wisdom, Virtue and Peace, all unusually (at the time) depicted as women, rendered along with scenes of criminal punishment and rewards for righteousness. Set perpendicular from it are the frescoes *Allegory of Good Government* and *Allegory of Bad Government,* which feature intensely contrasting scenes set in the recognisable environs of Siena. The good depicts a sunlit, idyllic, serene city, with joyous citizens and a countryside filled with crops; the bad city is filled with vices, crime and disease. These frescoes are often described as the most important secular paintings of the Renaissance, and shouldn't be missed.

Finish by backtracking and climbing the stairs to the loggia, which looks southeast over Piazza del Mercato and the countryside.

Opera della Metropolitana di Siena

ECCLESIASTICAL COMPLEX

(www.operaduomo.siena.it; Piazza del Duomo) Siena's *duomo* is one of Italy's greatest Gothic churches, and is the focal point of this important group of ecclesiastical buildings. See

SIENA SIGHTS

the boxed text on p195 for details of the OPA SI Pass, which offers discounted admission to all of the attractions here.

Duomo

(admission €3, audioguide adult/child €5/3; ☉10.30am-7.30pm Mon-Sat, 1.30-5.30pm Sun Mar-May, 10.30am-8pm Mon-Sat, 1.30-6pm Sun Jun-Aug, 10.30am-5.30pm Mon-Sat, 1.30-5.30pm Sun Sep-Oct, 10.30am-6.30pm Mon-Sat, 1.30-5.30pm Sun Nov-Feb) Construction of the *duomo* started in 1215 and work continued well into the 14th century. The magnificent facade of white, green and red polychrome marble was designed by Giovanni Pisano (the statues of philosophers and prophets are copies; you'll find the originals in the Museo dell'Opera).

In 1339 the city's leaders planned to enlarge the cathedral and create one of Italy's biggest churches. Known as the Duomo Nuovo (New Cathedral), the remains of this project are on Piazza Jacopo della Quercia, on the eastern side of the cathedral. The daring plan, to build an immense new nave with the present church becoming the transept, was scotched by the plague of 1348.

The interior of the *duomo* is truly stunning. Walls and pillars continue the black-and-white-stripe theme of the exterior, while the vaults are painted blue with gold stars. The inlaid-marble floor, decorated with 56 panels by about 40 artists and executed over the course of 200 years (14th to 16th centuries), depicts historical and biblical subjects. The older rectangular panels, including *Wheel of Fortune* (1372) and *The She-Wolf of Siena with the Emblems of the Confederate Cities* (1373), are graffiti designs by unknown artists, both restored in 1864. Domenico di Niccoló dei Cori was the first known artist to work on the cathedral, contributing several panels between 1413 and 1423, followed by renowned painter Domenico di Bartolo, who contributed *Emperor Sigismund Enthroned* in 1434. In the 15th century, director Alberto Aringhieri and celebrated Sienese artist Domenico Beccafumi created the dramatic expansion of the floor scheme. These later panels were done in more advanced multicoloured marble, inlaid with hexagon and rhombus frames. Unfortunately, about half are obscured by unsightly, protective covering, and are revealed only from 21 August through to 27 October each year (admission is €6 during this period).

Medieval Masterpieces

The Middle Ages get a bad rap in the history books. Sure, this period may have been blighted by famines, plagues and wars, but it also saw an extraordinary flowering of art and architecture. Cities such as Siena, San Gimignano and Volterra are full of masterpieces from this time.

Museo Civico, Siena

1 This museum (p195) showcases a collection that is modest in size but monumental in quality. The highlights are Simone Martini's powerful *Maestà* (Virgin Mary in Majesty) and Ambrogio Lorenzetti's *Allegories of Good and Bad Government*.

Abbazia di Sant'Antimo

2 Benedictine monks have been performing Gregorian chants in this Romanesque abbey (p225) near Montalcino ever since the Middle Ages. Dating back to the time of Charlemagne, its austere beauty and idyllic setting make it an essential stop on every itinerary.

Piazza dei Priori, Volterra

3 Ringed by medieval palaces, Volterra's central square (p221) is presided over by the Torre del Porcellino (Piglet's Tower), named for the wild boar protruding from its upper section.

Duccio di Buoninsegna's Maestà, Siena

4 Originally displayed in Siena's *duomo* (cathedral) and now the prize exhibit in the Museo dell'Opera (p200), Duccio's altarpiece portrays the Virgin surrounded by angels, saints and prominent Sienese citizens of the period.

Collegiata, San Gimignano

5 Don't be fooled by its modest facade. Inside, the walls of this Romanesque cathedral (p215) are adorned with brightly coloured frescoes resembling a vast medieval comic strip.

Clockwise from top left
1. Martini's *Maestà* fresco 2. Abbazia di Sant'Antimo
3. Palazzo Pretorio on Volterra's central square

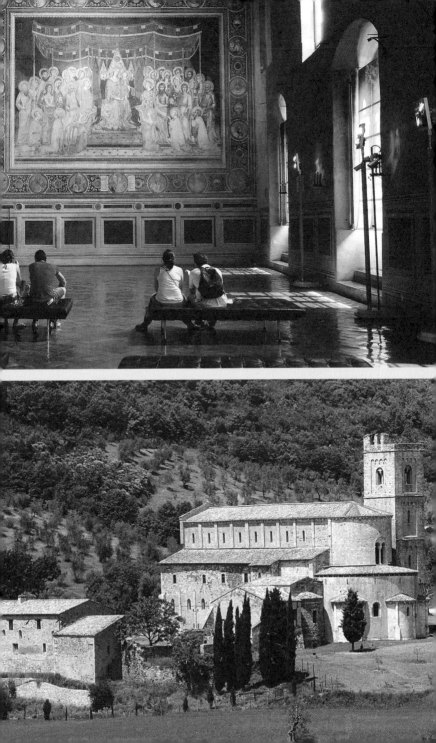

WORTH A TRIP

ABBAZIA DI SAN GALGANO

About 52km southwest of Siena via the SS73 are the evocative ruins of this 13th-century Cistercian abbey (admission free; ⊙8am-7.30pm), in its day one of the country's finest Gothic buildings.

On a hill overlooking the abbey is the tiny, round Romanesque Cappella di Monte Siepi (admission free), home to badly preserved frescoes by Ambrogio Lorenzetti depicting the life of local soldier and saint, San Galgano, who lived his last years here as a hermit. You'll need a couple of euro coins to illuminate the frescoes.

Other drawcards include the exquisitely crafted marble and porphyry pulpit carved by Nicola Pisano, assisted by Arnolfo di Cambio, who later designed the *duomo* in Florence. Intricately carved with vigorous, realistic crowd scenes, it's one of the masterpieces of Gothic sculpture.

Through a door from the north aisle is the enchanting Libreria Piccolomini, built to house the books of Enea Silvio Piccolomini, better known as Pius II. The walls of the small hall are decorated with vividly coloured narrative frescoes painted between 1502–07 by Bernardino Pinturicchio depicting events in the life of Piccolomini.

Museo dell'Opera

(admission €6; ⊙9.30am-7pm Mar-May & Sep-Oct, to 8pm Jun-Aug, 10am-7pm Nov-Feb) The collection here showcases artworks that formerly adorned the cathedral, including the 12 statues of prophets and philosophers by Giovanni Pisano that decorated the facade. Their creator designed them to be viewed from ground level, which is why they look so distorted as they crane uncomfortably forward.

The museum's highlight is Duccio di Buoninsegna's striking *Maestà* (1311), which was painted on both sides as a screen for the *duomo*'s high altar. The main painting portrays the Virgin surrounded by angels, saints and prominent Sienese citizens of the period; the rear panels (sadly incomplete) portray scenes from the Passion of Christ. Duccio also designed and painted the vibrant stained-glass window downstairs; it was originally in the *duomo*.

Battistero di San Giovanni

(Baptistry; Piazza San Giovanni; admission €3; ⊙9.30am-7pm Mar-May & Sep-Oct, to 8pm Jun-Aug) Behind the *duomo* and down a steep flight of steps is the Baptistry, which is richly decorated with frescoes. At its centre is a hexagonal marble font by Jacopo della Quercia decorated with bronze panels depicting the life of St John the Baptist by artists including Lorenzo Ghiberti *(Baptism of Christ* and *St John in Prison)* and Donatello *(The Head of John the Baptist Being Presented to Herod).*

Cripta

(Crypt; Piazza San Giovanni; admission incl audioguide €6; ⊙9.30am-7pm Mar-May & Sep-Oct, to 8pm Jun-Aug) Next to the Baptistry (and accessed through it) is this space below the cathedral's pulpit. It was rediscovered and restored in 1999 after having been filled to the roof with debris in the 1300s. The walls are completely covered with *pintura a secco* ('dry painting', better known as 'mural painting', as opposed to frescoes, which are painted on wet plaster, making them more durable) dating back to the 1200s. There's some 180 sq metres' worth, depicting several biblical stories, including the Passion of Jesus and the Crucifixion.

Complesso Museale
Santa Maria della Scala   CULTURAL CENTRE

(www.santamariadellascala.com; Piazza del Duomo 1; adult/reduced €6/3.50; ⊙10.30am-6.30pm) This former hospital, parts of which date to the 13th century, was built as a hospice for pilgrims travelling the Via Francigena but soon expanded its remit to shelter abandoned children and to care for the poor. Located directly opposite the *duomo,* it now functions as a cultural centre and houses three museums – the Archaeological Museum, Art Museum for Children and Center of Contemporary Art (SMS Contemporanea) – as well as a variety of historic halls, chapels and temporary exhibition spaces. Though the atmospheric Archaeological Museum housed in the basement tunnels is impressive, the complex's undoubted highlight is the upstairs Pellegrinaio (Pilgrim's Hall), with vivid 15th-century frescoes by Lorenzo Vecchietta, Priamo della Quercia and Domenico di Bartolo lauding the good works of the hospital and its patrons. The building's medieval *fienile* (hayloft) on level three houses Jacopo della Quercia's original *Fonte Gaia* sculptures.

Pinacoteca Nazionale   ART GALLERY

(Via San Pietro 29; adult/reduced €4/2; ⊙8.15am-7.15pm Tue-Sat, 9am-1pm Sun & Mon) Occupying the once grand but now sadly dishevelled 14th-century Palazzo Buonsignori, this labyrinthine gallery displays an incredible concentration of Gothic masterpieces from the Sienese school and also demonstrates the subsequent gulf cleaved between artistic life in Siena and Florence in the 15th century. While the Renaissance flourished 70km to the north, Siena's masters and their patrons remained firmly rooted in the Byzantine and Gothic precepts that had stood them in such good stead from the early 13th century. Stock religious images and episodes predominate,

typically pasted lavishly with gold and generally lacking any of the advances in painting (eg perspective, emotion or movement) that artists in Florence were exploring.

The highlights are all on the 2nd floor: Room 3 has Duccio's polyptych *Madonna with Child and Saints* (1305) and Simone Martini's *Madonna with Child* (c 1321); Room 5 has Martini's *The Blessed Agostino* altarpiece (1324); Room 7 houses Ambrogio Lorenzetti's luminous *Annunciation* (1343–44); Room 11 has Taddeo di Bartolo's *The Annunciation of the Virgin Mary* (1409); and Room 17 is home to three charming wooden sculptures by Jacopo della Quercia dating from the early 15th century.

ST CATHERINE OF SIENA

One of the two patron saints of Italy (with St Francis) and one of only three female Doctors of the Church (with St Teresa of Avilà and St Thérèse of Liseux), St Catherine was born in Siena in 1347, the 23rd child out of 25. Like a true prodigy, she had a religious fixation at a very early age. She is said to have entertained plans to impersonate a man so she could be a Dominican friar and occasionally raced out to the road to kiss the place where Dominicans had walked.

At the dubious age of seven, she consecrated her virginity to Christ, much to her family's despair. At 18 she assumed the life of a Dominican Tertiary (lay affiliate) and, as wayward teens are wont to do, chose initially to live as a recluse in the family's basement, focused on devotion and spiritual ecstasy. She was noted for her ability to fast for extended periods, living only on the Blessed Sacrament, which as nutritionists might attest, probably contributed to a delirium or two. Catherine described one such episode as a 'mystical marriage' with Jesus. Feeling a surge of humanity, she emerged from her cloistered path and began caring for the sick and poor at the Ospedale Santa Maria della Scala.

Another series of visions – this time set in Hell, Purgatory and Heaven – compelled Catherine to take her work to the next level and she began an ambitious and fearless letter-writing campaign to all variety of influential people, including lengthy correspondence with Pope Gregory XI. She beseeched royalty and religious leaders for everything from peace between Italy's republics to reform within the clergy. This go-getting, early form of activism was considered highly unusual for a woman at the time and her no-holds-barred style, sometimes scolding cardinals and queens like naughty children, was gutsy by any standard. And yet, rather than being persecuted for her insolence, she was admired, her powers of persuasion often winning the day where so many others had failed. She is said to have experienced the stigmata, but this event was suppressed as it was considered bad form at the time to associate the stigmata with anyone but St Francis.

Acting as an ambassador to Florence, Catherine went to Avignon and was able to convince Pope Gregory XI to bring the papacy back to Rome after a 73-year reign in France. A few years later she was invited to Rome by newly elected Pope Urban VI to campaign on his behalf during the pope/anti-pope struggle (the Great Western Schism), where she did her best to undo the effects that his temper and shortcomings were having on Rome. This heroic, utterly exhausting effort likely contributed to her untimely death in 1380 at the age of 33.

Catherine's abundant post-mortem accolades started relatively soon after her death, when Pope Pius II canonised her in 1461. More recently, Pope Paul VI bestowed Catherine with the title of Doctor of the Church in 1970 and Pope John Paul II made her one of Europe's patron saints in 1999. She is also one of the three patron saints of Siena (the others being Sts Ansanas and Ambrose).

For information about guided and self-guided walking tours of St Catherine's Siena, go to www.viaesiena.it.

Chiesa di San Domenico CHURCH
(Piazza San Domenico; ⊙9am-12.30pm & 3-7pm)
St Catherine was welcomed into the Dominican fold within this imposing church, and its **Cappella di Santa Caterina** is adorned with frescoes by Il Sodoma depicting events in her life. Catherine died in Rome, where most of her body is preserved, but her head was returned to Siena (it's in a 15th-century tabernacle above the altar in the *cappella*), as was her desiccated thumb (in a small window box to the right of the chapel). Next to the thumb is a nasty-looking chain that the saint flagellated herself with.

FREE **Casa Santuario di Santa Caterina** RELIGIOUS SIGHT
(Costa di Sant'Antonio 6; admission free; ⊙9am-6.30pm Mar-Nov, 10am-6pm Dec-Feb) If you want more of Santa Caterina – figuratively speaking – visit this pilgrimage sight where the saint, her parents and 24 siblings lived (locals like to joke that her mother must have been a saint, too). The rooms in the house were converted into small chapels in the 15th century and are decorated with paintings by Sienese artists, including Il Sodoma. The lower-level bedroom, frescoed in 1893 by Alessandro Franchi, includes her untouched, nearly bare cell.

Oratorio di San Bernardino ART GALLERY
(www.operaduomo.siena.it; Piazza San Francesco 9; admission €3; ⊙1-7pm mid-Mar–Oct) Nestled in the shadow of the huge Gothic church of San Francesco is this 15th-century oratory, which is dedicated to St Bernardino and decorated with Mannerist frescoes by Il Sodoma, Beccafumi and Pacchia. Upstairs, the small **Museo Diocesano di Arte Sacra** has some lovely paintings, including a *Madonna del Latte* (Nursing Madonna, c 1340) by Ambrogio Lorenzetti. Note that admission to the oratory is included in the OPA SI Pass.

🎓 Courses

Accademia Musicale Chigiana MUSIC
(☑0577 2 20 91; www.chigiana.it; Via di Città 89) Offers competitive-entry classical-music masterclasses and workshops every summer.

Fondazione Siena Jazz MUSIC
(☑0577 27 14 01; www.sienajazz.it; Fortezza Medicea 1) One of Europe's foremost institutions of its type, offering courses and workshops for experienced jazz musicians.

Scuola Leonardo da Vinci LANGUAGE
(☑0577 24 90 97; www.scuolaleonardo.com; Via del Paradiso 16) Italian-language school with supplementary cultural programs.

Società Dante Alighieri LANGUAGE
(☑0577 4 95 33; www.dantealighieri.com; Via Tommaso Pendola 37) Language and cultural courses southwest of the city centre.

Tuscan Wine School WINE TASTING
(☑333 7229716; www.tuscanwineschool.com; Via Stalloreggi 26) Two-hour wine-tasting classes introducing Italian and Tuscan wines (€40).

Università per Stranieri LANGUAGE
(University for Foreigners; ☑0577 24 03 02; www.unistrasi.it; Piazza Carlo Rosselli 27/28) Offers various courses in Italian language and culture. You'll find it near the train station.

WORTH A TRIP

ABBAZIA DI MONTE OLIVETO MAGGIORE

Still a retreat for Benedictine monks, the congregation of this medieval abbey (www.monteolivetomaggiore.it; admission free but library donation requested; ⊙9.15am-noon & 3.15-5pm Mon-Sat, to 6pm in summer, 9am-12.30pm Sun) 39km southeast of Siena was founded in 1313 by John Tolomei, although construction didn't begin on the monastery until 1393. Visitors come here for the wonderful fresco series in the Great Cloister, painted by Luca Signorelli and Il Sodoma, which illustrates events in the life of St Benedict, founder of the order. The entire cycle is a masterpiece, although the 36 frescoes by Sodoma are more impressive than the nine frescoes by Signorelli.

You can also visit the church, which features magnificent choir stalls of inlaid wood; the refectory, frescoed by Paolo Novelli; the magnificent library, built in 1518; the pharmacy; and the chapter house.

Downhill from the main building is the abbey's 14th-century Cantina Storica (Historic Wine Cellar; www.agricolamonteoliveto.com; ⊙10am-1pm & 2.30-6.30pm, to 6pm winter), where you can take a guided tour and enjoy a wine tasting.

Dating from the Middle Ages, this spectacular annual event includes a series of colourful pageants and a wild horse race on 2 July and 16 August. Ten of Siena's 17 *contrade* (town districts) compete for the coveted *palio* (silk banner). Each *contrada* has its own traditions, symbol and colours plus its own church and *palio* museum.

The race is staged in the Campo. From about 5pm, representatives from each *contrada* parade in historical costume, all bearing their individual banners. For scarcely one exhilarating minute, the 10 horses and their bareback riders tear three times around a temporarily constructed dirt racetrack with a speed and violence that makes spectators' hair stand on end.

The race is held at 7.45pm in July and 7pm in August. Join the crowds in the centre of the Campo at least four hours before the start if you want a place on the rails, but be aware that once there you won't be able to leave for toilet or drink breaks until the race has finished. Alternatively, the cafes in the Campo sell places on their terraces; these cost between €350 and €400 per ticket, and can be booked through the tourist office up to one year in advance.

Note that during the Palio, hotels raise their rates between 10% and 50% and enforce a minimum-stay requirement.

☞ Tours

Ninety-minute walking tours in English and Spanish leave from Piazza Gramsci at 1pm daily (€15 per person). From Easter through to October there are also extra two-hour tours in English and Italian (€20 including entry ticket to the *duomo*) departing from outside the tourist office in the Campo. Advance bookings aren't necessary. For details contact the tourist office.

The tourist office also takes bookings for a range of day tours operated by My Tour (✆0577 23 63 30; www.mytours.it). These include a package for the Palio; cooking classes; hot-air balloon rides; horse-riding; and trips to Chianti, Montalcino, San Gimignano and Montepulciano.

★ Festivals & Events

The Accademia Musicale Chigiana presents three highly regarded series of concerts featuring classical musicians from around the world: Micat in Vertice from April to May, Settimana Musicale Senese in July and Estate Musicale Chigiana between July and September. Venues include the Palazzo Comunale and Teatro dei Rinnovati in the Campo, Teatro dei Rozzi in Piazza Indipendenza, Palazzo Chigi Saraconi in Via di Città and the Abbazia di Sant'Antimo (see the boxed text, p225), near Montalcino.

The Associazione Musicale Quattro Quarti (www.quattroquarti.org) stages the Musica Senese – La Primavera Senese chamber music festival in April and May.

For more information about events, go to www.informacitta.net and download the Siena-specific PDF on the home page.

🛏 Sleeping

TOP CHOICE **Campo Regio Relais** BOUTIQUE HOTEL €€€
(✆0577 22 20 73; www.camporegio.com; Via della Sapienza 25; s €150-220, d €190-250, ste €250-450; ❄@🛜) Siena's most charming hotel has only six rooms, all of which are individually decorated and luxuriously equipped. Breakfast is served in the sumptuously decorated lounge or on the terrace, which has a sensational view of the *duomo* and Torre del Mangia.

Palazzo Ravizza HOTEL €€
(✆0577 28 04 62; www.palazzoravizza.com; Pian dei Mantellini 34; r €75-230, ste €150-320; P❄@🛜) Occupying a Renaissance-era *palazzo* located in a quiet but convenient corner of the city, this impressive hotel offers rooms with frescoed ceilings, huge beds, flat-screen TVs and small but well-equipped bathrooms. Suites are even more impressive, with views over the delightful rear garden. The three cheapest rooms are in the attic; though charming, they have small windows and even smaller bathrooms.

Hotel Alma Domus HOTEL €
(✆0577 4 41 77; www.hotelalmadomus.it; Via Camporegio 37; s €40-45, d €65-75; ❄@🛜) Owned by the Catholic diocese and still home to eight Dominican nuns who act as guardians at the Casa Santuario di Santa Caterina (located in

the same complex), this convent is now privately operated as a budget hotel. Most of the simple but spotlessly clean rooms have views over the narrow green Fontebranda valley across to the *duomo*. There's a 1am curfew.

Hotel Villa Liberty   HOTEL €€

(☏0577 4 49 66; www.villaliberty.it; Viale Vittorio Veneto 11; s €55-85, d €89-159; ❄️🛜) Located in a tree-lined boulevard opposite the Fortezza Medicea, this Liberty-style villa has been converted into a 17-room hotel and is one of the city's best midrange choices. Though the Campo is only a 15-minute walk away, the area is less touristy than the historic centre and there is free (but highly contested) parking right outside the hotel. Rooms are light and modern, with comfortable beds and small but perfectly adequate bathrooms.

Antica Residenza Cicogna   B&B €

(☏0577 28 56 13; www.anticaresidenzacicogna.it; Via dei Termini 67; s €70-75, d €85-100, ste €120-130; ❄️@🛜) Charming host Elisa supervised the recent restoration of this 13th-century building and will happily recount its history (it's been owned by her family for generations). The seven rooms are clean and well maintained, with comfortable beds, painted ceilings and tiled floors. There's also a tiny lounge where you can relax over complimentary Vin Santo and *cantucci* (hard, sweet almond biscuits). Reception has limited core hours (8am to 1pm), so arrange your arrival in advance.

Albergo Bernini   PENSIONE €

(☏0577 28 90 47; www.albergobernini.com; Via della Sapienza 15; s €78, d with shared bathroom €75, d €85, f with shared bathroom €115; 🛜) Pros: this is a welcoming, family-run hotel with clean and neat rooms and a gorgeous terrace sporting views across to the *duomo* and Chiesa di San Domenico. Cons: uncomfortable beds and the fact that only two rooms – the single and triple – have air-con. Breakfast costs €3 to €7.50, rates are negotiable in winter and payment is cash only.

Palazzo Bruchi   B&B €€

(☏0577 28 73 42; www.palazzobruchi.it; Via di Pantaneto 105; s €80-90, d €90-150; @🛜) This six-roomed B&B in a 17th-century *palazzo* close to the Campo is one of the few places in Siena where one wakes up to church bells and chirping birds rather than street noise (rooms overlook the Fontebranda valley). Host Camilla Masignani goes out of her way

to make guests feel at home. Reception closes at 4pm, so organise your arrival accordingly.

Hotel La Perla   HOTEL €

(☏0577 4 71 44; www.hotellaperlasiena.com; Piazza Indipendenza 25; s €40-60, d €60-85; ❄️@🛜) The bathrooms are tiny, some rooms are noisy and there is a steep staircase to contend with, but the central location of this friendly, cheap and well-run option certainly compensates. No breakfast.

Albergo Cannon d'Oro   HOTEL €

(☏0577 4 43 21; www.cannondoro.com; Via dei Montanini 28; s €48-85, d €60-105; ❄️🛜) Basic but perfectly acceptable rooms at keen prices are the draw here. Don't be deterred by the golden cannon (the very one that gave the place its name) trained upon you as you face the otherwise amicable reception desk. Only a few rooms have air-con and street noise can be a bit of a problem.

Villa Scacciapensieri   HOTEL €€€

(☏0577 4 14 41; www.villascacciapensieri.it; Via Scacciapensieri 10; s €75-140, d €110-305, ste €250-330; P❄️🛜🏊) Around 2.5km north of Siena, this 19th-century villa set in formal gardens has plenty of amenities, including a swimming pool, restaurant (dinner €38), tennis court and bicycles. If you are driving through the region, you can leave your car here and catch the bus into Florence for day trips (the bus stop is directly outside the property).

Camping Colleverde Siena   CAMPGROUND €

(☏0577 33 25 45; www.campingcolleverde.com; Strada di Scacciapensieri 47; camping 2 people, tent & car €33.70, tw mobile home €45-65; ☾Mar-early Jan; P🛜🏊) Three kilometres north of the historical centre (and 2km north of the train station), this popular place rents standard camp sites as well as mobile homes that sleep two to five people (some have full kitchens). There's an on-site restaurant/bar and mini-market. Buses 3 and 8 travel between the campground, the train station and the city centre. Wi-fi is €4 per day.

✗ Eating

Among many traditional Sienese dishes are *panzanella* (summer salad of soaked bread, basil, onion and tomatoes), *ribollita* (a rich vegetable, bean and bread soup), *pappardelle con la lepre* (ribbon pasta with hare) and *panforte* (a rich cake of almonds, honey and candied fruit). Keep an eye out for dishes featuring the region's signature *cinta senese* (indigenous Tuscan pig).

TOP CHOICE **Enoteca I Terzi** MODERN ITALIAN €€

(0577 4 43 29; www.enotecaiterzi.it; Via dei Termini 7; meals €39; 11am-1am Mon-Sat) Close to the Campo but off the well-beaten tourist trail, this classy modern *enoteca* (wine bar) is a favourite with bankers from the nearby headquarters of the Monte dei Paschi di Siena bank, who linger over their working lunches of light-as-air fried *baccalà* (cod), delicate handmade pasta, flavoursome risotto and succulent grilled meats. Servings aren't huge (a relief after the giant-sized plates that are often the norm in Tuscany) and there's an excellent choice of wine by the glass. Go.

Tree Cristi SEAFOOD €€

(0577 28 06 08; www.trecristi.com; Vicola di Provenzano 1-7; 4-course tasting menus €35-40, 6-course menus €60; closed Sun) Seafood restaurants are thin on the ground in this meat-obsessed region, so the long existence of Tre Cristi (it's been around since 1830) should be heartily celebrated. The menu here is as elegant as the decor, and added touches such as a complimentary glass of *prosecco* (dry sparkling wine) at the start of the meal add to the experience. Dishes are delicate and delicious, and the tasting menus offer excellent value.

Morbidi DELICATESSEN €

(Via Banchi di Sopra 75; 9am-8pm Mon-Sat) Local gastronomes shop here, as the range of cheese, cured meats and imported delicacies is the best in Siena. If you are self-catering you can join them, but make sure you also investigate the downstairs lunch buffet (from 12.30pm to 2.30pm), which offers fantastic value. For a mere €12, you can make your choice from platters of antipasti, salads, pastas and a dessert of the day; best of all is the fact that it's perfectly acceptable to return for second helpings! Bottled water is included in the price, wine and coffee cost extra.

Osteria Le Logge MODERN TUSCAN €€€

(0577 4 80 13; www.osterialelogge.it; Via del Porrione 33; meals €55; Mon-Sat) This place changes its menu of creative Tuscan cuisine almost daily. The best tables are in the downstairs dining room – once a pharmacy and still retaining its handsome display cabinets – or on the streetside terrace. The antipasti and *primi* (first courses) are con-sistently delicious, but mains can be disappointing. There's an excellent wine list.

Antica Osteria da Divo TRADITIONAL TUSCAN €€

(0577 28 60 54; www.osteriadadivo.it; Via Franciosa 25-29; meals €44) The background jazz at this long-standing favourite is as smooth as the walls are rough-hewn. At the lower, cellar level you're dining amid Etruscan tombs. The menu features traditional Tuscan fare given a modern accent, and is dominated by meat dishes.

Grom GELATERIA €

(www.grom.it; Via Banchi di Sopra 11-13; gelato €2.50-5; 11am-midnight Sun-Thu, to 1am Fri & Sat summer, 11am-11pm Sun-Thu, to midnight Fri & Sat winter) Delectable gelato with flavours that change with the season; many of the ingredients are organic or Slow Food–accredited. Also serves milkshakes.

Kopa Kabana GELATERIA €

(www.gelateriakopakabana.it; Via dei Rossi 52-55; gelato €1.70-2.30; 11am-midnight mid-Feb–mid-Nov) Come here for fresh gelato made by self-proclaimed ice-cream master Fabio (we're pleased to concur). There's a second location at Via San Pietro 20, close to the Pinacoteca Nazionale.

Pasticceria Nannini CAFE €

(Via Banchi di Sopra 24; coffee & biscuit at bar €2; 7.30am-11pm) Nannini serves the finest *cenci* (fried sweet pastry), *panforte* and *ricciarelli* (almond biscuits) in town, enjoyed with a cup of excellent coffee. Its refrigerator is cooled by water carried from 16km away by the same 13th-century tunnels that fuel many of the city's fountains, including the Fonte Gaia in Piazza del Campo.

Drinking

Caffè Fiorella CAFE

(www.torrefazionefiorella.it; Via di Città 13; 7am-8pm Mon-Sat) Squeeze into this tiny space behind the Campo to enjoy Siena's best coffee. In summer, the coffee granita with a dollop of cream is a wonderful indulgence.

Enoteca Italiana WINE BAR

(www.enoteca-italiana.it; Fortezza Medicea; noon-1am Mon-Sat Apr-Sep, to midnight Oct-Mar) The former munitions cellar and dungeon of this Medici fortress has been artfully transformed into a classy *enoteca* that carries over 1500 Italian labels. You can take a bottle with you, ship a case home or enjoy a glass or two in the attractive courtyard or atmospheric vaulted interior of the wine bar. There's usually food available, too.

🛍 Shopping

Wednesday market
MARKET

(⏱7.30am-1pm) Spreading around Fortezza Medicea and towards the Stadio Comunale, this is one of Tuscany's largest markets and is great for foodstuffs and cheap clothing.

Consorzio Agrario di Siena
FOOD

(Via Pianigiani 13; ⏱8am-7.30pm Mon-Sat) This farmer's co-op, operating since 1901, is a rich emporium of food and wine, much of which has been locally produced.

Pizzicheria de Miccoli
FOOD

(Via di Città 93-95; ⏱8am-8pm) Richly scented, de Miccoli has a stuffed boar's head over its entrance and windows festooned with sausages, stacks of cheese and sacks of *porcini* mushrooms. It also sells filled *panini* to go.

ℹ Information

Hospital (☎0577 58 51 11; Viale Bracci) Just north of Siena at Le Scotte.

Police station (☎0577 20 11 11; Via del Castoro 6)

Tourist office (☎0577 28 05 51; www.terre siena.it; Piazza del Campo 56; ⏱9am-7pm) Reserves accommodation, sells a map of Siena (€0.50), organises car and scooter hire, and sells train tickets.

ℹ Getting There & Away

Bus

Siena Mobilità (☎800 570530; www.siena mobilita.it), part of the **Tiemme** (☎0577 20 42 46; www.tiemmespa.it) network, runs services between Siena and other parts of Tuscany. It has a **ticket office** (⏱6.30am-7.30pm Mon-Fri, 7am-7.30pm Sat & Sun) underneath the main bus station in Piazza Gramsci; there's also a left-luggage office (per 24 hours €5.50).

A Siena Mobilità bus travels between Pisa airport and Siena (one-way/return €14/26, two hours), leaving Siena at 7.10am and Pisa at 1pm. Tickets should be purchased at least one day in advance from the bus station or online.

My Tour (☎0577 23 63 30; www.mytours. it) operates a shuttle service between Florence airport and Siena twice daily (one-way/return €30/50, two hours). Tickets can be booked through the tourist office.

Frequent 'Corse Rapide' (Express) buses race up to Florence (€7.10, 1¼ hours); they are a better option than the 'Corse Ordinarie' services, which stop in Poggibonsi and Colle di Val d'Elsa en route. Other regional destinations include San Gimignano (€5.50, one to 1½ hours, 10 daily either direct or changing in Poggibonsi), Montalcino (€3.65, 1½ hours, six daily), Poggibonsi (€3.95, 50 minutes, every 40 minutes), Montepulciano (€5.15, 1½ hours), Arezzo (€5.40, 1½ hours, eight daily) and Colle di Val d'Elsa (€2.70, 30 minutes, hourly), with connections for Volterra (€2.75). Note that all services run to dramatically reduced timetables on Sunday and holidays.

Sena (☎861 1991900; www.sena.it) buses run to/from Rome (€21, 3½ hours, eight daily), Milan (€35, 4¼ hours, four daily), Venice (€28, 5¼ hours, two daily) and Perugia (€12, 90 minutes, one daily). Its **ticket office** (⏱8.30am-7.45pm Mon-Sat) is also underneath the bus station in Piazza Gramsci.

Car & Motorcycle

For Florence, take the RA3 (Siena–Florence *superstrada*) or the more attractive SR222.

Train

Siena isn't on a major train line so buses are generally a better alternative; the exception is the direct service to Grosseto (€6.70, 90 minutes, seven daily). You'll need to change at Chiusi for Rome and at Empoli for Florence.

ℹ Getting Around

Bus

Siena Mobilità operates city bus services (€1 per 90 minutes). Buses 9 and 10 run between the train station and Piazza Gramsci.

Car & Motorcycle

There's a ZTL in the historical centre, although visitors can drop off luggage at their hotel, then get out (don't forget to have reception report your licence number or risk receiving a hefty fine).

There are large, conveniently located car parks at the Stadio Comunale and around the Fortezza Medicea, both just north of Piazza San Domenico. Some free street parking (look for white lines) is available in Viale Vittorio Veneto, on the southern edge of the Fortezza Medicea, but it is hotly contested. The paid car parks at San Francesco and Santa Caterina (aka Fontebranda) each have a *scala mobile* (escalator) to take you up into the centre.

All paid car parks charge €1.60 per hour. For more information on parking, go to www.siena parcheggi.com (in Italian).

CHIANTI

The ancient vineyards in this postcard-perfect part of Tuscany produce the grapes used in the ruby-red Chianti and Chianti Classico DOCGs, blends of red grapes with a minimum 75% (Chianti) or 80% (Chianti

Classico) Sangiovese component. Both are sold under the Gallo Nero (Black Cockerel/Rooster) trademark. They're not the only wines produced in this region, though: the Colli dell'Etruria Centrale, Pomino, Vin Santo del Chianti and Vin Santo del Chianti Classico DOCs are local drops, too. The biggest wine-producing estates have *cantine* (cellars) where you can taste and buy wine, but few vineyards – big or small – can be visited without an advance reservation; most only open their doors to tour groups.

Split between the provinces of Florence (Chianti Fiorentino) and Siena (Chianti Senese), Chianti is usually accessed via the SR222 (Via Chiantigiana) and is crisscrossed by a picturesque network of *strade provinciale* (provincial roads) and *strade secondaria* (secondary roads), some of which are unsealed. You'll pass immaculately maintained vineyards and olive groves, honey-coloured stone farmhouses, graceful Romanesque *pieve* (rural churches), handsome Renaissance villas and imposing castles built by Florentine and Sienese warlords during the Middle Ages.

Chianti Festival (www.chiantifestival.com), a program of arts events, is staged in July.

For information about the Consorzio Vino Chianti Classico (the high-profile consortium of local producers), go to www.chianti classico.com. For a handy guide to events in the region, go to www.classico-e.it.

Chianti Fiorentino

The northern half of this region is a popular day trip from Florence, with visitors arriving by bus, car and bicycle.

GREVE IN CHIANTI
POP 14,300

Located 26km south of Florence, Greve in Chianti is the main town in the Chianti Fiorentino. As well as being the hub of the local wine industry, it is home to the enthusiastic and entrepreneurial Falorni family, who operate the town's three main tourist attractions.

Greve's annual **wine fair** is held in the first or second week of September – make sure that you book accommodation well in advance if you plan to visit at this time.

Opened in 2010, the privately established and operated **Museo del Vino** (www. museovino.it; Piazza Nino Tirinnanzi 10; adult/reduced €5/4; ⊙11am-6pm Mon-Sat mid-Mar–mid-Oct) is a labour of love for brothers

❶ DRIVING IN CHIANTI

Chianti's roads can be frighteningly narrow and frustratingly difficult to navigate – to cut down on driving stress, be sure to purchase a copy of *Le strade del Gallo Nero* (€2), a useful map of the wine-producing zone that shows both major and secondary roads and also includes a comprehensive list of wine estates. It's available at the tourist offices in Greve in Chianti and Castellina in Chianti.

Lorenzo and Stefano Falorni, who have spent over 40 years documenting the history of the local wine industry and adding to their father's collection of artefacts and materials associated with it. The collection is as extensive as it is eclectic – including historic postcards featuring Chianti scenes, wine manuals and catalogues, wine-making machinery and implements, barriques (a type of wine barrel) and much more. The audioguide (included in the entry fee) provides a fascinating narrative, as does an interview-based audiovisual presentation.

Another Falorni family enterprise, **Le Cantine di Greve in Chianti** (www.lecantine. it; Piazza delle Cantine 2; ⊙10am-7pm) is a vast commercial *enoteca* that stocks more than 1200 varieties of wine. To indulge in some of the 140 different wines available for tasting here (including Super Tuscans, top DOCs and DOCGs, Vin Santo and grappa), buy a prepaid wine card costing €10 to €25 from the central bar, stick it into one of the many taps and out trickles your tipple of choice. Any unused credit will be refunded when you return the card. It's fabulous fun, though somewhat distressing for designated drivers. Fortunately, it's also possible to purchase bottles to drink back at the hotel or ship home. To find the *cantine,* look for the supermarket on the main road – it's down a staircase opposite the supermarket entrance.

Antica Macelleria Falorni (www.falorni. it; Piazza Matteotti 71; ⊙8am-1pm & 3.30-7.30pm Mon-Sat, 10am-1pm & 3.30-7pm Sun), an atmospheric *macellerìa* (butcher shop) in the main square, was established by the Falornis way back in 1729. Known for its *finocchiona briciolona* (pork salami made with fennel seeds and Chianti), it's the perfect pit stop if you're after picnic provisions.

ℹ️ Information

The **tourist office** (☎055 854 62 99; www.comune.greve-in-chianti.fi.it/ps/s/info-turismo; Piazza Matteotti 11; ⏱10am-1pm & 2-7pm Mon-Fri, & Sat May-Sep) is reasonably helpful, but is only open over the summer period.

ℹ️ Getting There & Around

BUS SITA buses travel between Greve in Chianti and Florence (€3.30, one hour, hourly).

CAR & MOTORCYCLE Greve is located on the Via Chiantigiana. There is free parking in the two-level, open-air car park on Piazza della Resistenza, on the opposite side of the main road to Piazza Matteotti.

AROUND GREVE IN CHIANTI

A narrow road leads from Greve in Chianti up to the medieval village of Montefioralle, the ancestral home of Amerigo Vespucci (1415–1512). An explorer, navigator and cartographer who made two early voyages to America following the route charted by Columbus, Vespucci wrote excitedly about the New World on his return to Europe, inspiring cartographer Martin Waldseemüller (creator of the 1507 *Universalis Cosmographia*) to name the new continent in his honour. It's an extremely steep walk or bike ride, but the panoramic view makes it worth the effort.

👁 Sights & Activities

Badia a Passignano   WINERY
This 11th-century abbey located 6km west of Montefioralle is owned by the Antinoris, one of Tuscany's oldest and most prestigious winemaking families, and is surrounded

OUTLET SHOPPING

Head to the Val d'Arno area in the northeast corner of Chianti to unleash your inner fashionista (and your credit cards). Bargains from the previous season's collections can be sourced at a number of outlets, the most popular of which are the Mall in Leccio Regello (see p117); Dolce & Gabbana (Via Pian dell'Isola 49, Località Santa Maria Maddalena; ⏱10am-7pm Mon-Sat, 3-7pm Sun), off the SR69 near Incisa Val d'Arno; and Prada (www.prada.com; Space Factory Outlets, Via Levanella Becorpi, Località Levanella; ⏱10.30am-7.30pm Mon-Fri & Sun, 9.30am-7.30pm Sat), off the SR69 on the southern edge of Montevarchi.

by vines and olive trees. At the time of research, the main building was undergoing a major restoration; its refectory (home to a 15th-century fresco of the *Last Supper* by Domenico and Davide Ghirlandaio) and cloisters will be open to the public when the restoration is complete.

There are a number of options if you are keen to take a guided wine tour (☎055 807 12 78; www.osteriadipassignano.com) of the vineyards and historic cellars. The 'Antinori and Badia a Passignano' tour (€150; Monday to Wednesday and Friday to Saturday at 11.15am) includes a tasting of four estate wines followed by a three-course lunch in the estate's restaurant; and the 'Antinori and the Osteria' tour (€200; Monday to Wednesday and Friday to Saturday at 5.45pm) includes a tasting of four estate wines plus a five-course dinner.

Other options include visits to the Tignanello vineyard (where the grapes for the Tignanello and Solaia Super Tuscans are grown) and to Montalcino, where the Antinori's acclaimed Pian delle Vigne Brunello is produced. Alternatively, you can enjoy a tour of the cellars and a paid tasting of four wines (€80; Monday to Saturday at 4pm). Bookings for all of these tours are essential. It's also possible to taste and purchase Antinori wines and olive oil at La Bottega (⏱10am-6.30pm Mon-Sat), the estate's wine shop. You don't need to make a reservation for this.

Castello di Verrazzano   WINERY
(☎055 85 42 43; www.verrazzano.com) The castle at this wine estate 3km north of Greve was once home to Giovanni da Verrazzano (1485–1528), who explored the North American coast and is commemorated in New York by the Verrazano Narrows bridge (the good captain lost a 'z' from his name somewhere in the mid-Atlantic). Today, the castle presides over a 220-hectare historic estate where Chianti Classico, Vin Santo, grappa, honey, olive oil and balsamic vinegar are produced.

There are four guided tours on offer, each of which incorporate a short visit to the historic wine cellar and gardens. The 'Classic Wine Tour' (1½ hours, €14, 10am and 3pm Monday to Friday) includes a tasting of wines; the 'Chianti Tradition Tour' (2½ hours, €28, 11am Monday to Saturday) includes a tasting of wine and gastronomic specialities; the 'Wine and Food Experience' (three hours, €48, noon Monday to Friday,

Exploring Chianti by bicycle is a highlight for many travellers. You can rent bicycles from **Ramuzzi** (☎055 85 30 37; www.ramuzzi.com; Via Italo Stecchi 23; touring bike/125cc scooter per day €20/55; ⏲9am-1pm & 3-7pm Mon-Fri, 9am-1pm Sat) in Greve in Chianti.

A number of companies offer guided cycling tours leaving from Florence:

Florence by Bike (☎055 48 89 92; www.florencebybike.it; Via San Zanobi 120r) Day tour of northern Chianti, including lunch and wine tasting (€74; March to October).

I Bike Florence (Map p66; ☎055 012 39 94; www.ibikeflorence.com; Via de' Lamberti 1) Two-day guided tour from Florence to Siena (€329; including one night's accommodation, two lunches and one dinner) every Monday and Thursday between April and October. A shuttle takes you from Florence to the starting point in Chianti.

I Bike Italy (Map p66; ☎055 012 39 94; www.ibikeflorence.com; Via de' Lamberti 1) Jointly runs the two-day tour with I Bike Florence, but also offers a day tour including lunch at a winery (€80; March to October). A shuttle takes you from Florence to the starting point in Chianti. Students receive a 10% discount.

I Bike Tuscany (☎335 8120769; www.ibiketuscany.com) Year-round one-day tours (€110 to €140) for riders of every skill level. The company transports you from your Florence hotel to Chianti by minibus, where you join the tour. Both hybrid and electric bikes are available, as is a support vehicle.

11am Saturday) includes a four-course lunch with estate wines; and the 'Executive Wine Tour' (€110, Tuesday to Friday) includes a private guide, lunch with estate wines and transport to/from Florence. Bookings are advisable.

🛏 Sleeping

Fattoria di Rignana   AGRITURISMO €€
(☎055 85 20 65; www.rignana.it; Rignana; s/d in fattoria €100/110, s/d in villa €120/140; P@☎) This old farmstead and noble villa 3.8km from Badia a Passignano has everything you'll need for the perfect Chianti experience – an historic setting, glorious views, a large swimming pool and walking access to a decent local *cantina*. Two accommodation options are on offer: elegant rooms in the 17th-century villa and more rustic rooms in the adjoining *fattoria* (farmhouse). Wi-fi access was being investigated when this book went to print.

Villa I Barronci   HOTEL €€
(☎055 82 05 98; www.villaibarronci.com; Via Sorripa 10, San Casciano in Val di Pesa; s €85-150, d €115-230; P✿@☎☎🐾) Located on the northwestern edge of Chianti between Florence and Pisa, this extremely comfortable modern country hotel offers exemplary service and amenities. You can relax in the bar and restaurant, rejuvenate in the spa, laze by the pool or head off for easy day trips to Volterra, San Gimignano and Siena.

🍃 Agriturismo   AGRITURISMO €
(☎339 5019849; www.agrifuturismo.com; Strada San Silvestro 11, Barberino Val d'Elsa; 2-/4-/6-person apt €70/120/140; ☎) Woods filled with oak, juniper, cypress and pine trees sit next to ancient terraces of olive trees on this farm estate 13km southwest of Greve in Chianti. All cultivation is pesticide-, herbicide- and fertilizer-free, and sustainable features such as solar panels, rain collection and recycling are utilised. The apartments are charming, with a strong and attractive design ethos. All have kitchens. No credit cards and minimum three-night stay.

Ostello del Chianti   HOSTEL €
(☎055 805 02 65; www.ostellodelchianti.it; Via Roma 137, Tavarnelle Val di Pesa; dm €16.50, d with shared bathroom €39, d €50; ⏲reception 8.30-11am & 4pm-midnight; hostel closed Nov–mid-Mar; P@) This is one of Italy's oldest hostels (it's been going strong since the 1950s). Staff members are extremely friendly, dorms max out at six beds and bike hire can be arranged for €10 per day. Breakfast costs €2. Florence is easily accessed by SITA bus (€3.30, one hour).

Villa Vignamaggio   AGRITURISMO €€
(☎055 854 66 53; www.vignamaggio.it; Via Petriolo 5, Greve in Chianti; r €150-450, apt €200-275; P✿@☎) Used as a location in Kenneth Branagh's film *Much Ado About Nothing*, this exquisite 15th-century manor house is

The Wine Roads

To indulge fully in the Tuscan idyll, hire a car or bicycle and follow a *strada del vino* (wine road). These trails have been set up by regional tourism authorities and local producers to showcase areas known for their wine, olive oil and *sapori* (good food).

Each *strada* has its own distinct emblem; look for road signs including something resembling a bunch of grapes and you'll probably be on the right track. All have their own map and itinerary, listing wine estates, *cantine* (cellars where wine can be tasted), *enoteche* (wine bars), olive-oil mills and producers of artisan food. There are more than 20 of these *strade* across Tuscany, although it must be said that some are marketed in a much more professional way than others.

Tourist offices usually carry maps and brochures about trails in their area, and information is available online at www.terreditoscana.regione.toscana.it/stradedelvino/. Other useful resources are www.strade-del-vino-italia.it, a listing of trails across the country, and the *Guida alle Strade del Vino, dell'Olio e dei Sapori di Toscana (Guide to the Wine Tours, Olive Oil and Good Food of Tuscany)*, a book of 22 enogastronomic itineraries covering the entire region. This can be accessed online at www.stradevinoditoscana.it/la_guida_online/.

BEST WINE ROADS

» **Strada del Vino Costa degli Etruschi** www.lastradadelvino.com, in Italian

» **Strada del Vino dei Colli di Candia e di Lunigiana** www.stradadelvinoms.it, in Italian

» **Strada del Vino delle Colline Pisane** www.stradadelvinocollinepisane.it, in Italian

» **Strada del Vino e dei Sapori Monteregio di Massa Marittima** www.stradavino.it

» **Strada del Vino Nobile di Montepulciano** www.stradavinonobile.it

Right

1. Vineyards in Chianti 2. Le Cantine di Greve in Chianti (p207)

Wine Tour of Chianti

A Four-Day Itinerary

Tuscany has more than its fair share of highlights, but few can match the glorious indulgence of a leisurely drive through Chianti. On offer is an intoxicating blend of scenery, acclaimed restaurants and ruby-red wine.

Florence
Chianti Fiorentino
CHIANTI
Castello di Verrazzano
Badia a Passignano
Greve in Chianti
Panzano in Chianti
Castello di Volpaia
Radda in Chianti
Castello di Ama
Chianti Senese
Castello di Brolio
Siena

Heading south from Florence along the R222 (Via Chiantigiana), stop to prime your palate with a wine tasting or lunch at the historic **Castello di Verrazzano** (p208).

Continue to the major town in the Chianti Fiorentino, **Greve in Chianti** (p207). Visit its Museo del Vino to learn about the history of Chianti's centuries-old wine industry and then test your newfound knowledge over a self-directed tasting in the nearby Cantine di Greve in Chianti.

» On the next day, head to the idyllically located wine estate of **Badia a Passignano** (p208) to enjoy a tour and tasting followed by lunch in the acclaimed Osteria di Passignano restaurant. In the late afternoon, watch the sun set over the vineyards at La Cantinetta di Passignano.

» On day three, meander along the narrow roads west of the Via Chiantigiana in the morning, lunch with Dario Cecchini (p212) in **Panzano in Chianti** (vegetarians steer clear!) and then spend the afternoon visiting the historic cellars at the **Castello di Volpaia** (p214) near Radda in Chianti.

» On the final day, head towards Siena. En route, take a tour at the ancient **Castello di Brolio** (p214) and investigate Chianti Classico and contemporary art at the **Castello di Ama** (p213).

Above
1. Chianti wine maturing in barrels **2.** Generations of winemakers at work

on a wine estate 5km south of Greve in Chianti. It offers B&B rooms and self-catering apartments to rent and sports an Italian garden, wellness centre, two swimming pools and a tennis court. From Greve in Chianti, follow the SR222 south for 2km, then turn left towards Lamole.

Eating & Drinking

TOP CHOICE **Osteria di Passignano** GASTRONOMIC €€€
(📞055 807 12 78; www.osteriadipassignano.com; Via di Passignano 33; meals €70, tasting menu €65; ⊙closed Sun) This elegant dining room on the Antinori Estate at Badia a Passignano is one of Tuscany's most impressive restaurants. The delectable food utilises local produce and is decidedly Tuscan in inspiration, but its execution is refined rather than rustic. The tasting menu with wine match (€110) is a total triumph.

La Locanda di Pietracupa GASTRONOMIC €€
(📞055 807 24 00; www.locandapietracupa.com; Via Madonna di Pietracupa 31, San Donato in Poggio; meals €40; ⊙closed Tue) The prices at this restaurant near the late-Renaissance sanctuary of the Madonna di Pietracupa are remarkably reasonable considering the quality of the modern Tuscan cuisine on offer. You can enjoy a long lunch on the pretty outdoor terrace, or book one of the four B&B rooms (single/double €70/80) in advance (parking is available) and settle in for an indulgent dinner in the elegant dining room. The wine list is as impressive as the food menu.

La Tenda Rossa GASTRONOMIC €€€
(📞055 82 61 32; www.latendarossa.it; Piazza del Monumento 9-14, Cerbaia; meals €90; ⊙closed Sun & lunch Mon) In the small town of Cerbaia near San Casciano in Val di Pesa, the 'Red Tent' serves award-winning modern Tuscan cuisine with more than a few twists – the results are often inspired but could be too fussy for some diners. The four-course 'Truffle Show' set menu (€85) is an indulgent showcase of the precious ingredient, which is sourced in the surrounding area.

La Cantinetta di Passignano TRADITIONAL ITALIAN €€
(📞055 807 19 75; www.lacantinettadipassignano.com; Via di Greve 1a, Badia a Passignano; meals €30; ⊙Thu-Tue) Lolling on a designer couch in the garden of this recently opened wine bar/restaurant is a perfect way to while away an hour or two in the late afternoon. The vineyard views are gorgeous, and the cheese and meat platters are a perfect accompaniment to the wines and designer beers on offer. On weekends, it's popular with groups of young Florentines (hence the Italian pop music on the sound system).

Il Giglio GELATERIA €
(Via del Giglio 13, San Donato in Poggio; gelato €1.50-4; ⊙3pm-midnight Mon-Fri, 11.30am-midnight Sat & Sun) The fortified medieval village of San Donato is on the Siena-Florence *superstrada* (RA3), close to Tavarnelle Val di Pesa and a short drive from Badia a Passignano. It has three claims to fame: a charming main street with a Renaissance *palazzo*; a beautiful 12th-century *pieve;* and this *gelateria,* which has a pretty rear courtyard where you can enjoy a coffee and delectable homemade gelato (try the fig and ricotta flavour).

L'Antica Scuderia TRADITIONAL ITALIAN €€
(📞055 807 16 23; www.ristorolanticascuderia.com; Via di Passignano 17, Badia a Passignano; meals €43, pizzas €6-10; ⊙Wed-Mon; 🖪) If you fancy the idea of lunching on a garden terrace over-

DON'T MISS

L'ANTICA MACELLERÌA CECCHINI

The small town of Panzano in Chianti southwest of Greve in Chianti is known throughout Italy for the *macelleria* (butcher shop) owned and run by extrovert butcher, Dario Cecchini (www.dariocecchini.com, Via XX Luglio 11; ⊙9am-2pm Mon-Thu & Sun, to 6pm Fri & Sat). This Tuscan celebrity has carved out a niche for himself as a poetry-spouting guardian of the *bistecca* (steak) and other Tuscan meaty treats, and he operates three eateries here as well as the *macelleria*: Officina della Bistecca (📞055 85 21 76; set menu €50; ⊙dinner 8pm Tue, Fri & Sat, lunch 1pm Sun), with a simple set menu built around the famous *bistecca;* Solociccia (📞055 85 27 27; set menu €30; ⊙dinner 7pm & 9pm Thu, Fri & Sat, lunch 1pm Sun), where guests share a communal table to sample meat dishes other than *bistecca;* and Dario + (burger with vegetables & potatoes €10, light menu €20; ⊙lunch Mon-Sat), his casual lunchtime-only eatery. Book ahead for the Officina and Solociccia.

SCULPTURE PARKS

To indulge in some art appreciation between wine tastings, take a scenic drive to these magnificent sculpture parks located near Gaiole in Chianti:

Castello di Ama (✆0577 74 60 31; http://arte.castellodiama.com; guided tours €10, with wine & oil tasting €35; ☺10am-4pm Tue-Sat Apr-Oct) The highly regarded Castello di Ama estate produces a delicious Chianti Classico and has developed a sculpture park showcasing 12 site-specific artworks by artists including Louise Bourgeois, Chen Zhen, Anish Kapoor, Kendell Geers and Daniel Buren. Guided tours of the cellar, villa and sculpture park are in English, French or Italian. You'll find the estate 11km southwest of Gaiole, near Lecchi in Chianti. Advance bookings are essential.

Parco Sculture del Chianti (Chianti Sculpture Park; ✆0577 35 71 51; www.chiantisculpture park.it; adult/child €7.50/5; ☺10am-sunset Apr-Oct, by appointment Nov-Mar; 🖐) This vast green wooded area studded with 26 site-specific contemporary artworks can be explored on a 1km walking trail. You'll find it in Pievasciata, 12km southwest of Gaiole off the SS408.

looking one of the Antinori vineyards, this casual eatery may well fit the bill. Lunch features antipasti, pastas and traditional grilled meats, while dinner sees plenty of pizza-oven action. It's also a good mid-afternoon coffee stop. Kids love the playground set, and adults love the fact that it's at the opposite end of the garden.

La Cantinetta di Rignana   TRADITIONAL ITALIAN €€
(✆055 85 26 01; www.lacantinettadirignana.it; Rignana; meals €35; ☺lunch & dinner Wed-Mon) Idyllically nestled in the old oil mill on the Rignana estate (p209), this eatery offers quintessential Tuscan views from its large terrace. The food is rustic and will please most palates. It's a 15-minute drive from Badia a Passignano, between Panzano in Chianti and Mercatale Val di Pesa. The approach is via a long dirt road.

Chianti Senese

Though it's now part of the province of Siena, this southern section of Chianti was once the stronghold of the *Lega del Chianti,* a military and administrative alliance within the city-state of Florence that comprised Castellina, Gaiole and Radda.

CASTELLINA IN CHIANTI
POP 2970

Established by the Etruscans and fortified by the Florentines in the 15th century as a defensive outpost against the Sienese, Castellina in Chianti is now a major centre of the wine industry, as the huge cylindrical silos brimming with Chianti Classico attest. To taste some of the local product, head to Antica Fattoria la Castellina (Via Ferruccio 26), the town's best-known wine shop.

From the southern car park, follow Via Ferruccio or the panoramic path under the town's eastern defensive walls to access the atmospheric Via delle Volte, an arched passageway that was originally used for ancient sacred rites and later enclosed with a roof and incorporated into the Florentine defensive structure.

Etruscan archaeological finds from the local area are on display at the Museo Archeologico del Chianti Sienese (www. museoarcheologicochianti.it; Piazza del Comune 18; adult/reduced €5/3; ☺11am-7pm daily Apr-Oct, 11am-5pm Sat & Sun Nov-Mar), located in the town's medieval *rocca* (fortress). Room 4 showcases artefacts found in the 7th-century-BC Etruscan tombs of Montecalvario (Ipogeo Etrusco di Monte Calvario; admission free; ☺24hr), which is located on the northern edge of town off the SR222.

ⓘ Information
The helpful **InCHIANTI tourist office** (✆0577 74 13 92; www.essenceoftuscany.it; Via Ferruccio 40; ☺9am-1pm Mon-Sat, 2-6pm Mon-Tue & Thu-Sat mid-Mar–Oct, closed Nov-mid–Mar) can book visits to wineries and cellars. It also provides maps, accommodation suggestions and other information.

ⓘ Getting There & Around
BUS Siena Mobilità buses travel between Castellina in Chianti and Siena (€2.55, 35 minutes, 10 daily).

CAR & MOTORCYCLE The most convenient car park is at the southern edge of town off Via IV Novembre (€1/5 per hour/day).

TRAIN It's possible to access Castellina in Chianti from Florence by train (€5.80, 90 minutes, hourly), but you'll need to change trains in Empoli.

🛏 Sleeping

TOP CHOICE Castello delle Serre
BOUTIQUE HOTEL €€€

(☑331 7339474; www.castellodelleserre.com; Piazza XX Settembre 1, Serre di Rapolano; r €175-250, ste €300-350; [P][✱][@][🐀][☒]) Though not officially in the Chianti Senese (it's in Le Crete), the prospect of spending the night in this fabulous medieval castle makes the 41km trip from Gaiole in Chianti well worth the effort. Meticulously restored by Italian-American restaurateur Salvatore Gangale, who is a magnificent host, it features huge rooms and a swish pool area. For a once-in-a-lifetime experience, book into the deluxe suite in the turret, which has a private terrace commanding suitably regal views.

La Locanda
HOTEL €€€

(☑0577 73 88 32; www.lalocanda.it; Montanino di Volpaia; r €220-310; [P][🐀][☒]) Overlooking the medieval village of Volpaia near Radda in Chianti, this country hotel offers seven charming rooms in the converted 16th-century farmhouse, as well as a lounge, library and dining room (dinner €35) in the former stables. The genial hosts are able to suggest plenty of activities around Chianti, including wine tastings at the nearby Castello di Volpaia estate.

Locanda La Capannuccia
RURAL INN €€

(☑0577 74 11 83; www.lacapannuccia.it; Borgo di Pietrafitta; s €80-90, d €96-130; ☺Mar-Nov; [P][🐀][☒]) Tucked down a valley at the end of a 1.5km dirt road, this is a true Tuscan getaway. A pretty country inn, it offers five simple but comfortable rooms and can provide dinner (€25 to €30) if you book in advance. To get here, head north along the SR222 from Castellina in Chianti and turn right to Pietrafitta.

🍴 Eating

TOP CHOICE Ristorante Albergaccio
GASTRONOMIC €€€

(☑0577 74 10 42; www.albergacciocast.com; Via Fiorentina 63, Castellina in Chianti; 4-course menus €58, 5-course menus €65; ☺lunch & dinner Mon-Sat, closed lunch Tue-Thu Oct–mid-Apr) One kilometre outside Castellina in Chianti on the road to San Donato in Poggio, this upmarket restaurant in a restored farmhouse showcases what it describes as 'the territory on the table', making full use of local, seasonal and organic produce. The menu is innovative, making it a favourite with local and in-

---

WORTH A TRIP

RADDA IN CHIANTI

Shields and escutcheons add a dash of drama to the facade of 16th-century Palazzo del Podestà on the main square in this important wine centre 11km east of Castellina in Chianti. The volunteer-staffed **Ufficio Pro Loco** (☑0577 73 84 94; www.chiantistorico.com; Piazza Castello 2; ☺10am-1pm & 3.15-7pm Mon-Sat, 10.30am-12.30pm Sun) can book accommodation and tours for this pocket of Chianti, and also supplies information about walks in the area. For picnic provisions or to try local wines, olive oil and home-cured meats, head to **Casa Porciatti** (www.casaporciatti.com; Piazza IV Novembre 1-3).

If wine-tasting, not walking, is on your agenda, head 6km north of town to the historic hilltop hamlet of Volpaia, where the **Castello di Volpaia** (☑0577 73 80 66; www.volpaia. it; Località Volpaia) estate has been producing wines, olive oils and vinegars for centuries. Book ahead to enjoy a 1½-hour guided tour of the castle and cellars followed by a tasting (€16), or to take a cooking class (€140). Alternatively, pop into the *enoteca* (wine bar), which is inside the main tower of the castle, to stock up on a few bottles.

Another wine estate worth investigating is **Castello di Brolio** (☑0577 73 02 80; www.ricasoli.it), owned by the Ricasoli family since the 12th century. Wander through its **formal gardens** (☺10am-6pm Apr-Oct), visit the small **museum** (☺10.30am-12.30pm & 2.30-5.30pm Tue-Sun Apr-Oct) or take a **guided tour** (☺10.30am Mon, Wed & Fri-Sun, 3pm daily, 5pm Mon & Fri Mar-Nov) of the castle, cellars and vineyards before adjourning to the estate's **osteria** (meals €38-50; ☺Fri-Wed Mar-Oct) for lunch or dinner. Bookings are essential for guided tours and to eat at the *osteria*.

ternational foodies. There's a thoughtful and well-priced wine list.

Osteria Le Panzanelle   OSTERIA €€
(🖉0577 73 35 11; www.lepanzanelle.it; Lucarelli; meals €25; ⊘closed Mon & part of Jan & Feb) A great lunch stop en route from Greve in Chianti to Siena, this roadside inn serves traditional Tuscan dishes in its pretty garden and downstairs bar/dining room. The menu changes monthly, reflecting what is in season. Find it 5km south of Panzano in Chianti on the SP2 to Radda in Chianti.

VAL D'ELSA

A convenient base for visiting the rest of Tuscany, this valley stretching from Chianti to the Maremma can be relied upon to tick many of the boxes on your Tuscan 'must-do' list, with plenty of opportunities to enjoy food, wine, museums and scenery. The valley's major towns are Colle di Val d'Elsa and Poggibonsi, but the major tourist drawcard is San Gimignano. Note that we have included nearby Volterra in this section despite the fact that it is officially located in the Val di Cecina, a province of Pisa.

San Gimignano

POP 7770

As you crest the hill coming from the east, the 15 towers of this walled hill town look like a medieval Manhattan. Originally an Etruscan village, the town was named after the bishop of Modena, San Gimignano, who is said to have saved the city from Attila the Hun. It became a *comune* (local government) in 1199 and was very prosperous due in part to its location on the Via Francigena – building a tower taller than that of one's neighbour (there were originally 72) became a popular way for the town's prominent families to flaunt their power and wealth. In 1348 plague wiped out much of the population and weakened the local economy, leading to the town's submission to Florence in 1353. Today, not even the plague would deter the swarms of summer day-trippers, who are lured by the town's palpable sense of history, intact medieval streetscapes and enchanting rural setting.

◉ Sights & Activities

Start in triangular Piazza della Cisterna, named after the 13th-century cistern at its

---

centre. In the Piazza del Duomo, the cathedral looks across to the late-13th-century **Palazzo del Podestà** and its tower, the **Torre della Rognosa**.

ᴛᴏᴘ ᴄʜᴏɪᴄᴇ〉Collegiata   DUOMO
(Piazza del Duomo; adult/child €3.50/1.50; ⊘10am-7.10pm Mon-Fri, to 5.10pm Sat, 12.30-7.10pm Sun Apr-Oct, 10am-4.40pm Mon-Sat, 12.30-4.40pm Sat & Sun Nov–mid-Jan & Feb-Mar, closed for religious celebrations 2nd half of Nov & Jan) San Gimignano's Romanesque cathedral, officially titled the Duomo Collegiata o Basilica di Santa Maria Assunta but commonly known as the Collegiata (referring to the college of priests who originally managed it), has a bare facade that belies the remarkably vivid frescoes inside.

Parts of the building date back to the second half of the 11th century, but the frescoes, which resemble a vast medieval comic strip, date from the 14th century. Entry is via the side stairs and through a loggia that was originally covered and functioned as the baptistry.

Facing the altar, along the left (north) wall, are scenes from Genesis and the Old Testament by Bartolo di Fredi, dating from around 1367. The top row runs from the creation of the world through to the forbidden fruit scene. This in turn leads to the next level and fresco, the expulsion of Adam and Eve from the Garden of Eden, which has sustained some war damage. Further scenes include Cain killing Abel, and the stories of Noah's ark and Joseph's coat. The last level continues with the tale of Moses leading the Jews out of Egypt, and the story of Job.

On the right (south) wall are scenes from the New Testament by the workshop of Simone Martini (probably led by Lippo Memmi, Martini's brother-in-law), which were completed in 1336. Again, the frescoes are spread over three levels, starting in the six lunettes at the top. Commencing with the Annunciation,

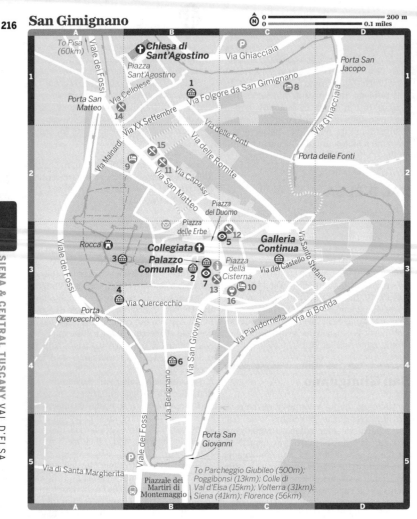

the panels proceed through episodes such as the Epiphany, the presentation of Christ in the temple and the massacre of the innocents on Herod's orders. The subsequent panels on the lower levels summarise the life and death of Christ, the Resurrection and so on. Again, some have sustained damage, but most are in good condition.

On the inside wall of the front facade, extending onto adjoining walls, is Taddeo di Bartolo's striking depiction of the Last Judgment – on the upper-left side is a fresco depicting *Paradiso* (Heaven) and on the upper-right *Inferno* (Hell). The fresco of San Sebastian next to the entrance is by Benozzo Gozzoli.

Off the south aisle, near the main altar, is the **Cappella di Santa Fina**, a Renaissance chapel adorned with naive and touching frescoes by Domenico Ghirlandaio depicting events in the life of one of the town's patron saints. These featured in Franco Zeffirelli's 1999 film *Tea with Mussolini*.

Palazzo Comunale   ART GALLERY
(Piazza del Duomo; adult/reduced €5/4; ☉9.30am-7pm Apr-Sep, 10am-5.30pm Oct-Mar) This 12th-century *palazzo* has always been the centre

San Gimignano

of local government; its Sala di Dante is where the great poet addressed the town's council in 1299, urging it to support the Guelph cause. You can't miss Lippo Memmi's early-14th-century *Maestà*, which portrays the enthroned Virgin and Child surrounded by angels, saints and local dignitaries – the kneeling noble in red-and-black stripes was the *podestà* (chief magistrate) of the time. Other frescoes in the room portray jousts, hunting scenes, castles and other medieval goings-on.

Above the Sala del Consiglio is the small but charming Pinacoteca, which features paintings from the Sienese and Florentine schools of the 12th to 15th centuries. Highlights of its collection are *Angel Annunciate* (1482) by Filippino Lippi, *Madonna and Child with Saints* (1466) by Benozzo Gozzoli and an altarpiece by Taddeo di Bartolo (1401) illustrating the life of St Gimignano.

In the Camera del Podestà, at the top of the stairs, is a recently restored cycle of frescoes by Memmo di Filippuccio illustrating a moral history – the rewards of marriage are shown in the scenes of the husband and wife naked in the bath and in the sack.

After visiting the Pinacoteca, be sure to climb the *palazzo's* Torre Grossa for a spectacular view of the town and surrounding countryside.

Chiesa di Sant'Agostino CHURCH
(Piazza Sant'Agostino; ☺7am-noon & 3-7pm mid-Apr–Oct, to 6pm Nov-Dec, 4-6pm Mon, 10am-noon & 3-6pm Tue-Sun Jan–mid-Apr) This late-13th-century church at the northern end of town is best known for Benozzo Gozzoli's charming fresco cycle illustrating the life of St Augustine. Gozzoli also painted the highly unusual fresco of San Sebastian on the north wall, which shows the fully clothed saint protecting the citizens of San Gimignano, helped by a bare-breasted Virgin Mary and semi-robed Jesus (it alluded to the saint's supposed intervention to protect citizens during the 1464 plague). On Sundays at 11am, an English-language mass is celebrated in the cloister.

FREE Museo del Vino MUSEUM, WINE TASTING
(Wine Museum; Parco della Rocca; ☺11.30am-6.30pm) San Gimignano's famous white wine, Vernaccia, has always had a loyal following – Dante in his *Divine Comedy* banished Pope Martin IV to purgatory because of it, Boccaccio fantasised about flowing streams of it, Pope Paul III reputedly bathed in it and the ever-demure St Catherine of Siena used it as medicine.

More a wine bar than a museum, this operation housed in an unmarked gallery next to the *rocca* has been set up to celebrate the delicate, golden-hued drop. It comprises a small exhibition on the history of the varietal (Italian language only) and an *enoteca* where you can enjoy a paid tasting (four/six wines €6/10) or purchase a glass (€3 to €5) to enjoy on the terrace, which has a panoramic view.

Museo Archeologico & Speziera di Santa Fina MUSEUM
(Via Folgore da San Gimignano 11; both museums adult/reduced €3.50/2.50; ☺11am-5.45pm mid-Mar–Dec) There are actually two museums and a gallery here. The Speziera section includes ceramic and glass storage vessels from the Speziera di Santa Fina, a reconstructed 16th-century pharmacy and herb garden. Many are beautifully painted and still contain curative concoctions. Follow

DON'T MISS

GALLERIA CONTINUA

It may seem strange that we're highlighting a showcase of contemporary art in this medieval time capsule of a town, but we do so for good reason. This **commercial art gallery** (www.galleriacontinua.com; Via del Castello 11; admission free; ☺10am-1pm & 2-7pm Tue-Sat) is one of the best in Europe, showing the work of 40 big-name artists, including Ai Weiwei, Daniel Buren, Carlos Garaicoa, Moataz Nasr, Kendell Geers, Liu Jianhua and Sophie Whettnall. There are also permanent exhibits by Anthony Gormley (*6 Times Ground*, 2009), Michelangelo Pistoletto (*Obellisco*, 2010) and the late Sol Lewitt (*Planes With Broken Bands of Colour*, 2007–2010) – don't miss the Pistoletto. Spread over three venues (an old cinema, a medieval tower and a medieval vaulted cellar), the gallery is one of San Gimignano's most compelling attractions.

your nose to the side room in Gallery 7, called 'the kitchen', which is filled with herbs and spices used for elixirs. Beyond here is a small **archaeological museum** divided into Etruscan/Roman and medieval sections with exhibits found locally.

Upstairs is the **Galleria d'Arte Moderna E Contemporanea**, a modern art gallery that in itself merits a visit. Permanent works include Renato Guttuso's impressive *Marina* (1970).

Museo d'Arte Sacra MUSEUM
(Piazza Pecori 1; adult/child €3/1.50; ☺10am-7.10pm Mon-Fri, to 5.10pm Sat, 12.30-7.10pm Sun Apr-Oct, 10am-4.40pm Mon-Sat, 12.30-4.40pm Sat & Sun Nov–mid-Jan & Feb-Mar, closed for religious celebrations 2nd half of Nov & Jan) Works of religious art from the Collegiata and other churches in the town are on display in this modest museum. Those who are interested in medieval religious objects will appreciate the items made from precious metals, including beautifully crafted chalices and thuribles (censers), as well as some exquisitely embroidered textiles.

San Gimignano del 1300 MUSEUM
(www.sangimignano1300.com; Via Berignano 23; adult/child €5/3; ☺9am-7pm; ⊕) San Gimignano's newest tourist attraction is particularly popular with young children. A handmade ceramic recreation of the medieval city, it shows houses, streets, towers and people as they would have looked in 1300. It's bound to inspire junior visitors to attempt bigger and better Lego projects on their return home.

☞ Tours

The tourist office has a range of tours. From mid-April to October it offers a **guided walking tour** (adult/child under 12yr €20/free,

incl admission to Palazzo Comunale) of the town on Saturday and Sunday at 11am. Advance bookings aren't necessary. Other activities include a **Vernaccia di San Gimignano Vineyard Visit** (€20; Tue & Thu Apr-Oct) that includes tastings of local foods and wines; and **nature walks** (€20) through the hills surrounding San Gimignano on Wednesday at 3pm and through Riserva Naturale di Castelvecchio, southwest of town, on Friday at 3pm. Advance bookings are essential for these.

★ Festivals & Events

San Gimignano Estate CULTURAL
(www.terresiena.it) Includes performances of opera in Piazza del Duomo, films in the *rocca*, concerts, theatre and dance. Held between June and September.

Ferie delle Messi CULTURAL
Held in June (usually the third weekend), this pageant evokes the town's medieval past through re-enacted battles, archery contests and plays.

Festival Barocco di San Gimignano MUSIC
A season of Baroque music concerts in September and early October.

⌂ Sleeping

Hotel L'Antico Pozzo BOUTIQUE HOTEL €€
(☎0577 94 20 14; www.anticopozzo.com; Via San Matteo 87; s €85-100, d €110-180; ☺closed 1st 2 weeks Nov & Jan; ❋@☎) The town's best hotel is named after the old, softly illuminated *pozzo* (well) just off the lobby. Each room in the 15th-century building features high ceilings, simple but elegant decor and good-sized bathrooms; the superior rooms are particularly attractive. There's a handsome breakfast room, but in summer most guests

choose to enjoy the first meal of the day in the charming rear courtyard.

Foresteria Monastero di
San Girolamo
HOSTEL €

(☏0577 94 05 73; www.monasterosangirolamo.it; Via Folgore da San Gimignano 26-32; dm €27) This is an excellent budget choice. Run by friendly nuns, it has basic but comfortable rooms with attached bathrooms, sleeping two to five people. Breakfast costs €3. Ring ahead as it is perpetually booked. If you don't have a reservation, arrive between 9am and 12.30pm or between 3.30pm and 5.45pm and ring the monastery bell (not the Foresteria one, which is never answered). Kitchen use is €3 per day; parking is €2 per day.

La Cisterna
HOTEL €€

(☏0577 94 03 28; www.hotelcisterna.it; Piazza della Cisterna 24; s €64-78, d €85-160; ✲@🛜) Although it is in sore need of a renovation, the Cisterna is worth considering due to its setting (a splendid 14th-century building on the piazza of the same name) and its rooftop breakfast room/restaurant, which has panoramic views. The cheaper rooms have cramped bathrooms and can be dark – opt for a superior or deluxe version if possible (Nos 58 and 82 have fabulous views). Internet costs €1 per day, but wi-fi is free.

✖ Eating & Drinking

San Gimignano is known for its *zafferano* (saffron). You can purchase meat, vegetables, fish and takeaway food at the **Thursday morning market** (Piazza delle Erbe).

TOP CHOICE Dal Bertelli
SANDWICH SHOP €

(Via Capassi 30; panino €3-5, glass of wine €1.50; ⊙1-7pm Mar-early Jan) The Bertelli family has lived in San Gimignano since 1779, and its current patriarch is fiercely proud of both his heritage and his sandwiches. Sig. Brunello Bertelli sources his salami, cheese, bread and wine from local artisan producers and sells his generously sized offerings from an atmospheric space as far away as possible from what he calls the town's 'tourist grand bazaar'. Fabulous.

TOP CHOICE Da Nisio
MODERN ITALIAN €€

(☏0577 94 10 29; www.danisio.com; Località Sovestro 32; meals €41; ⊙dinner Wed-Mon) The location's not the best (it's on the road to Poggibonsi, 1.5km before town, and is attached to the unattractive Le Colline hotel), but the food here is sensational. The chef/

owner grows all of the vegetables he uses in his imaginative dishes, and results are both light and full of flavour. The antipasti 'specialità' changes according to what is in season, all pasta and bread is homemade, and meats are cooked on a wood grill, imparting excellent flavour.

Gelateria di Piazza
GELATERIA €

(www.gelateriadipiazza.com; Piazza della Cisterna 4; gelato €1.80- 2.50; ⊙8.30am-11pm Mar–mid-Nov) Master gelato-maker Sergio Dondoli uses only the choicest ingredients to create his creamy and icy delights. Get into the local swing of things with a *Crema di Santa Fina* (saffron cream) gelato or a Vernaccia sorbet.

Perucà
TRADITIONAL ITALIAN €€

(☏0577 94 31 36; www.peruca.eu; Via Capassi 16; meals €34; ⊙Mar–mid-Jan) The lady owner here is as knowledgeable about regional food and wine as she is enthusiastic, and the food is excellent. Try the house speciality of *fagottini del contadino* (ravioli with *pecorino*, pears and saffron cream) with a glass of Fattoria San Donato's Vernaccia – it's a match made in heaven.

Dorandò
MODERN ITALIAN €€€

(☏0577 94 18 62; www.ristorantedorando.it; Vicolo dell'Oro 2; 5-course tasting menus €50; ⊙daily Easter-Oct, Tue-Sun Oct-Easter, closed Dec & Jan) The swankiest eatery in town, Dorandò has an old-fashioned decor but serves modern interpretations of traditional Tuscan dishes. It's where local families come to celebrate special occasions.

Il Pino
MODERN ITALIAN €€

(☏0577 94 04 15; www.ristoranteilpino.it; Via Cellolese 8-10; meals €44; ⊙lunch Sat-Wed, dinner Fri-Wed) A spruce, vaulted and airy space where a seasonal menu including excellent homemade pasta and bread is served. It's the only restaurant in town recommended by the highly regarded *Gambero Rosso* restaurant guide, so you're bound to be dining alongside local foodies.

DiVinorum
WINE BAR

(Piazza della Cisterna 30; ⊙11am-8pm Mar-Oct, to 4pm Nov-Dec) As cool as San Gimignano comes, this wine bar is housed in cavernous former stables and has a few outdoor tables with views over the historic town walls. There's a decent array of antipasti (cheese, meats, bruschettas, salads) on offer, and an excellent selection of wine by the glass.

ℹ Information

The extremely helpful **tourist office** (☎0577 94 00 08; www.sangimignano.com; Piazza del Duomo 1; ⊙9am-1pm & 3-7pm Mar-Oct, 9am-1pm & 2-6pm Nov-Feb) organises tours, supplies maps and can book accommodation. It also has information on the *Strada del Vino Vernaccia di San Gimignano* (Wine Road of the Vernaccia di San Gimignano).

ℹ Getting There & Away

BUS The bus station is beside Porta San Giovanni, the main entrance to town. Buy bus tickets at the tourist office. Buses run to/from Florence (€6.50, 1¼ hours, 14 daily) but almost always require a change at Poggibonsi. Buses also run to/from Siena (€5.50, one to 1½ hours, 10 daily Monday to Saturday). For Volterra you need to go to Colle di Val d'Elsa (€2.40, 35 minutes, four daily) and then buy a ticket for Volterra (€2.75, 50 minutes, four daily).

CAR & MOTORCYCLE From Florence and Siena, take the Siena–Florence *superstrada* (RA3), then the SR2 and finally the SP1 from Poggibonsi. From Volterra, take the SR68 east and follow the turn-off signs north to San Gimignano on the SP47.

Parking is expensive here. The cheapest option (per hour/24 hours €1.50/6) is at Parcheggio Giubileo (P1) on the southern edge of town; the most convenient is at Parcheggio Montemaggio (P2) next to Porta San Giovanni (per hour/24 hours €2/20).

TRAIN The closest train station is located at Poggibonsi (by bus €1.95, about 30 minutes, frequent).

Volterra

POP 11,100

Volterra's well-preserved medieval ramparts give the windswept town a proud, forbidding air that author Stephanie Meyer deemed ideal for the discriminating tastes of the planet's principal vampire coven in her wildly popular *Twilight* book series. Fortunately, the reality is considerably more welcoming, as a wander through the winding cobbled streets (refreshingly populated by locals rather than tourists) attests.

The Etruscan settlement of Velathri was an important trading centre and senior partner of the Dodecapolis. It is believed that as many as 25,000 people lived here in its Etruscan heyday. Partly because of the surrounding inhospitable terrain, the city was among the last to succumb to Rome – it was absorbed into the Roman confederation around 260 BC and renamed Volaterrae. The bulk of the old city was raised in the 12th and 13th centuries under a fiercely independent free *comune*. The city first entered Florence's orbit in 1361, but the people of Volterra fought hard against Medici rule – their rebellion was brought to a brutal end when Lorenzo Il Magnifico's soldiers sacked the city in 1472. There was another rebellion in 1530 – again brutally crushed by the Florentines – but Volterra would never again achieve self-government, moving from Florentine rule to that of the Grand Duchy of Tuscany before unification in 1860.

◎ Sights & Activities

Museo Etrusco Guarnacci MUSEUM
(Via Don Minzoni 15; adult/student €8/6; ⊙9am-7pm mid-Mar–Oct, 8.30am-1.45pm Nov–mid-Mar) One of Italy's most impressive collections of Etruscan artefacts is exhibited here. Much of the collection is displayed in the old-style didactic manner – badly labelled, mostly in Italian, and stuffy – though some exhibits on the upper levels have been artfully displayed in modern, stylish cases with subdued lighting. The multilingual audio guide (€3) is worth the investment for much-needed descriptions and to boost the overall pep factor.

All exhibits were unearthed locally. They include a vast collection of some 600 funerary urns carved mainly from alabaster and tufa and displayed according to subject and period. The best examples (those dating from later periods) are on the 2nd and 3rd floors; don't miss the *Urn of the Sposi*, a strikingly realistic terracotta rendering of an elderly couple.

Other exhibits to search out include a crested helmet excavated from the Tomba del Guernero at nearby Poggio alle Croci; and the *L'Ombra della Sera* (Shadow of the Evening), an elongated bronze nude figurine that bears a striking resemblance to the work of the Italian sculptor Alberto Giacometti.

Cattedrale di Santa Maria Assunta DUOMO
(Piazza San Giovanni; ⊙8am-12.30pm & 3-6pm) Built in the 12th and 13th centuries, the *duomo's* interior was remodelled in the 16th century and features a handsome coffered ceiling. The Chapel of Our Lady of Sorrows on the left as you enter from Piazza San Giovanni has two sculptures by Andrea della Robbia and a small fresco of the *Procession of the Magi* by Benozzo Gozzoli – be sure not to damage it by throwing a coin behind the glass, as some visitors do.

Volterra

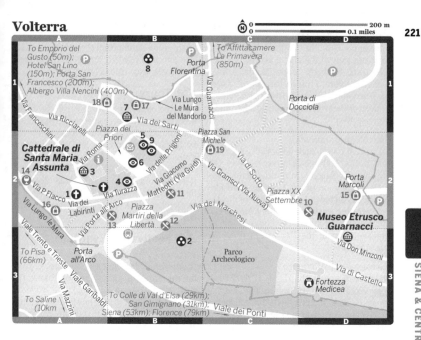

Volterra

◎ Top Sights

Cattedrale di Santa Maria Assunta	A2
Museo Etrusco Guarnacci	D3

◎ Sights

1 Baptistry	A2
Ecomuseo dell'Alabastro	(see 7)
2 Etruscan Acropolis	B3
3 Museo Diocesano d'Arte Sacra	A2
4 Palazzo dei Priori	B2
5 Palazzo Pretorio	B2
6 Piazza dei Priori	B2
7 Pinacoteca Comunale	B1
8 Roman Theatre	B1
9 Torre del Porcellino	B2

✪ Eating

10 La Carabaccia	D2
11 L'Incontro	B2
12 Ristorante-Enoteca Del Duca	B2
13 Web & Wine	B2

◎ Drinking

14 Caffè dei Fornelli	A2

⬢ Shopping

15 alab'Arte	D2
16 Alessandro Marzetti	A2
17 Fabula Etrusca	B1
18 Opus Artis	A1
19 Paolo Sabatini	C2

In front of the cathedral, a 13th-century **baptistry** features a small marble font (1502) by Andrea Sansovino. Nearby, the **Museo Diocesano d'Arte Sacra** (Via Roma 1; ☺9am-1pm & 3-6pm mid-Mar–Oct, 9am-1pm Nov–mid-Mar) merits a peek for its collection of illuminated manuscripts, ecclesiastical vestments, gold reliquaries and artworks by Andrea della Robbia, Taddeo di Bartolo and Rosso Fiorentino. Don't miss the exquisite marble tomb carving of Cavaliere Michele Pigi dei Bonaguidi in the first room.

Piazza dei Priori PIAZZA
The city's central square is ringed by austere medieval buildings, including the 13th-century **Palazzo dei Priori** (admission €1.50; ☺10.30am-5.30pm daily mid-Mar–Oct, 10am-5pm Sat & Sun Nov–mid-Mar), the oldest seat of local government in Tuscany. Highlights inside are a fresco on the staircase of the Crucifixion

by Piero Francesco Fiorentino, the magnificent cross-vaulted council hall and a small antechamber on the 1st floor that gives a bird's-eye view of the piazza below.

Palazzo Pretorio, opposite, dates back to the same era. From it thrusts the Torre del Porcellino (Piglet's Tower), so named because of the wild boar protruding from its upper section.

Pinacoteca Comunale ART GALLERY
(Via dei Sarti 1; adult/student €6/4.50; ⊙9am-7pm mid-Mar–Oct, 8.30am-1.45pm Nov–mid-Mar) Occupying the Palazzo Minucci Solaini, this modest collection of local, Sienese and Florentine art includes Taddeo di Bartolo's lovely *Madonna Enthroned with Child* (1411) and Rosso Fiorentino's strikingly modern representation of the *Deposition from the Cross* (1521).

Ecomuseo dell'Alabastro MUSEUM
(Via dei Sarti 1; adult/child/family €3.50/2.50/8; ⊙11am-5pm mid-Mar–Oct, 9am-1.30pm Sat & Sun Nov–mid-Mar) As befits a town that has hewn the precious rock from nearby quarries since Etruscan times, Volterra has an alabaster museum, which shares the same building as the Pinacoteca. On the ground floor are contemporary creations, including a finely chiselled mandolin and a bizarre fried egg, while on the two upper floors are choice examples from Etruscan times onwards as well as a re-created artisan's workshop.

Roman Theatre ARCHAEOLOGICAL SITE
(admission €3.50; ⊙10.30am-5.30pm mid-Mar–Oct, to 4pm Sat & Sun Nov–mid-Mar) On the city's northern edge is a Roman theatre, a well-preserved complex dating from the 1st century BC. Three arched niches, two stairways and 19 rows of seating are still easily identifiable. Behind the theatre is a Roman bathhouse dating from the 4th century AD. The site was used as landfill during medieval times; excavations began in 1951.

⏩ Tours

Volterra Walking Tour (☑0588 08 62 01; www.volterrawalkingtour.com) offers just that – a one-hour English-language tour of the city by foot costing only €5 per person (minimum four participants or €20 for tour to operate). Operated by licensed tour guides, it leaves from Piazza Martiri della Libertà at 6pm daily from April to July and September to October. Bookings aren't necessary and payment is cash only.

✨ Festivals & Events

Volterra AD 1398 CULTURAL
(www.volterra1398.it, in Italian; day pass €9) On the third and fourth Sundays of August, the citizens of Volterra roll back the calendar some 600 years, take to the streets in period costume and celebrate this event with gusto and all the fun of a medieval fair.

Volterragusto FOOD
(www.volterragusto.com) Between late October and early November, Volterragusto showcases local produce, including cheese, white truffles, olive oil and chocolate, with a market in the city centre. The same organisers stage a truffle festival in late March.

🛏 Sleeping

Podere San Lorenzo AGRITURISMO €
(☑0588 3 90 80; www.agriturismosanlorenzo.it; B&B d €90, 2-/3-/4-bed apt without breakfast €98/118/138; ❄🖙🐾) This model of slow tourism is located 3.4km outside Volterra off the road from Siena, Florence and San Gimignano. The two rooms and eight self-catering apartments are relatively basic, but the surrounds are bucolic and the alluring mountain spring–fed biological swimming pool comes complete with frogs and salamanders. Best of all are the gourmet dinners created by chef Marianna (per person €28), which are served in a 12th-century Franciscan chapel. Walking, biking, horse-riding and hands-on, seasonal olive-oil production (October to November) opportunities are available, as are cooking classes (per person €90). To find it, pass the sculpture of the red circle at the entrance to town and then turn right into the narrow lane after the car saleyard.

ⓘ COMBINED TICKETS

Two discount tickets are on offer. One gives admission to the Museo Etrusco Guarnacci, the Pinacoteca Comunale and the Museo Diocesano d'Arte Sacra (adult/student & child/family €10/6/20) and another gives entry to both the Roman Theatre and the acropolis at the Parco Archeologico (€3.50). Truth be told, the second ticket isn't really necessary as there is a great view over the theatre from Via Lungo Le Mura del Mandorlo and the acropolis is dilapidated and not really worth a visit.

A number of outfits offer walking tours in Tuscany. Recommended companies include the following:

Hedonistic Hiking (www.hedonistichiking.com.au) Runs an eight-day, seven-night guided tour that transfers participants from Pisa Airport, starts in Volterra, includes a walk from Volterra to San Gimignano and ends in Massa Marittima. The cost of €2235 includes accommodation, wine tastings and all meals.

Hidden Italy (www.hiddenitaly.com.au) This company has devised a six-day, five-night, self-guided walk from Montalcino to Montepulciano that is suitable for families. The cost of €1500 includes accommodation, breakfasts, dinners and baggage transfer between hotels.

Alternatively, devise your own Tuscan pilgrimage by following parts of the **Via Francigena**, a medieval pilgrimage route connecting Canterbury with Rome that goes past or through central Tuscan towns including San Gimignano, Monteriggioni, San Quirico d'Orcia and Radicófani. Globalmap has recently released *Via Francigena in Toscana*, an excellent hiking map (1:50,000) with detailed routes and information about accommodation for pilgrims. You'll find it for sale in tourist offices and bookshops throughout the region. You can also check www.francigenalibrari.beniculturali.it for route maps and GPS coordinates.

Chiosco delle Monache   HOSTEL €
(☑0588 8 66 13; www.ostellovolterra.it; Via delle Teatro 4; dm €16-18, B&B s €42-53, B&B d €53-69; ☺Apr-Sep; P🕾) Opened in 2009 after a major renovation, this excellent private hostel occupies a 13th-century monastery complete with a frescoed refectory where breakfast is served. It's outside town, near the hospital, but the historic centre is only a 30-minute (albeit steep) walk away and local buses from Piazza Martiri della Libertà stop right outside the entrance (€1). Airy rooms overlook the cloisters and have good beds and bathrooms; dorms sleep up to six. Reception is open 8am to noon and 5pm to 11pm, but often stays open for the full day in high summer. Wi-fi is €1 per hour; breakfast (for those in dorms) is €6.

Hotel San Lino   HOTEL €€
(☑0588 8 52 50; www.hotelsanlino.com; Via San Lino 26; s €60-90, d €90-105; ✳@🕾🏊) This former convent is the best sleeping option in the historic centre, but it's certainly not perfect. Pros include the swimming pool and reasonable rates. Cons come courtesy of small rooms with cramped bathrooms. Parking is €11 per day.

Affittacamere La Primavera   B&B €
(☑0588 8 72 95; www.affittacamere-laprimavera. com; Via Porta Diana 15; d €70; P🕾) Just outside the walls (near the Roman Theatre), this family-run place offers four pleasantly decorated rooms, a generous breakfast and free parking. An additional bed costs only €10.

Albergo Villa Nencini   HOTEL €
(☑0588 8 63 86; www.villanencini.it; Borgo Santo Stefano 55; s €67-73, d €88; P🏊) A somewhat shabby family-run hotel, Villa Nencini is a mere 200m beyond Porta San Francesco yet has a decidedly country feel. The pool is a major drawcard in summer.

✘ Eating & Drinking

TOP CHOICE La Carabaccia   TRADITIONAL ITALIAN €
(☑0588 8 62 39; Piazza XX Settembre 4-5; meals €20; ☺closed Mon) A trio of local women – Sara, Lala and Patrizia – have put their heart and soul into this fantastic trattoria, which is the city's best lunch option. Named after a humble Tuscan vegetable soup, it has a small menu that changes daily according to what local producers are offering and always has vegetarian options. Sit on the front terrace or head indoors to enjoy the Italian folk music played on the sound system.

L'Incontro   CAFE €
(Via G Matteotti 18; sandwiches €2.50-3.50; ☺6.30am-1am Thu-Tue) Come here for excellent coffee, delectable home-baked biscuits and great savoury snacks. The rear *salone* is a great spot to grab a quick antipasto plate or *panino* for lunch, and the long front bar is always crowded with locals enjoying a coffee or *aperitivo*.

Ristorante-Enoteca
Del Duca
TRADITIONAL ITALIAN €€

(☏0588 8 15 10; www.enoteca-delduca-ristorante.
it; Via di Castello 2; 5-course tasting menus €42;
☺Wed-Mon) Volterra's only fine-dining establishment serves traditional Tuscan dishes
in its vaulted dining areas and lovely rear
courtyard. It has an excellent wine list –
not surprising considering the owner has
his own vineyard (try his Giusto Alle Balze
merlot).

Web & Wine
VEGETARIAN €€

(☏0588 8 15 31; Via Porta all'Arco 11-19; meals €35;
☺9.30am-1am Fri-Wed; @) This place is hard
to characterise, being an internet point (€3
per hour), a stylish *enoteca* (with a good selection of tipples and food platters) and a
restaurant specialising in organic vegetarian food – all at the same time. The decor
features underlit Etruscan remains and the
sound system is ruled by cool jazz.

Caffè dei Fornelli
CAFE

(Piazza dei Fornelli; ☺9am-11pm Tue-Sat, to 6pm
Sun) The city's bohemian set congregates
here. Poetry readings and exhibitions are
regular occurrences, and the streetside terrace is the only place in town where you can
enjoy a coffee or glass of wine while enjoying
a view over the surrounding countryside.

🛍 Shopping

For information about artisans in Volterra,
see www.arteinbottegavolterra.it.

Emporio del Gusto
FOOD

(Via San Lino 2; ☺9.30am-1pm & 4.30-8pm Mon-
Fri) This food co-op is sponsored by the
comune and sells produce from around
the region. It stocks olive-oil products (including toiletries), fresh milk and yoghurt,
cheese, vegetables, locally grown saffron,
truffles, pasta, bread and wine.

Fabula Etrusca
JEWELLERY

(www.fabulaetrusca.it; Via Lungo Le Mura del Mandorlo 10; ☺10am-7pm Easter-Christmas) Distinctive pieces in 18-carat gold – many based on
Etruscan designs – are handmade in this
workshop on the city's northern walls.

Alabaster Workshops
ARTISANAL

Volterra is known as the city of alabaster,
and has a number of shops specialising in
hand-carved alabaster items; many of these
double as ateliers where the artisans work.
Among the best are Opus Artis (www.opu

sartis.com; Piazza Minucci 1); Paolo Sabatini
(www.paolosabatini.com; Via G Matteotti 56); and
the atelier of sculptor Alessandro Marzetti
(www.alessandromarzetti.it; Via dei Labirinti).
To watch alabaster being carved, head to
alab'Arte (Via Orti San Agostino 28).

ℹ Information

The efficient **tourist office** (☏0588 8 72 57;
www.volterratur.it; Piazza dei Priori 19-20;
☺10am-1pm & 2-6pm) provides free maps,
offers a free hotel-booking service, runs a guided
Twilight New Moon–themed walking tour and
rents out an audioguide tour (€5) of the town.

ℹ Getting There & Around

BUS The bus station is in Piazza Martiri della
Libertà. **CPT** (☏800 570530; www.cpt.pisa.
it) buses connect the town with Saline (€2, 20
minutes, frequent) and its train station.

You'll need to go to Colle di Val d'Elsa (€2.75,
50 minutes, four daily) to catch connecting bus
services to San Gimignano (€2.40, 35 minutes,
four daily) and Siena (€2.70, two hours). For
Florence, you'll need only one ticket (€7.85, two
hours, three to four daily), but you'll usually need
to change buses at Colle di Val d'Elsa.

CAR & MOTORCYCLE Volterra is accessed via
the SR68, which runs between Cecina on the
coast and Colle di Val d'Elsa, just off the RA3
(Siena–Florence *superstrada*).

A ZTL applies in the historic centre. The most
convenient car park is beneath Piazza Martiri
della Libertà (P1, per hour/day €1.50/11), but
there are other car parks around the circumference – P2, P3, P6 and P8 are free.

VAL D'ORCIA

This picturesque agricultural valley is a
Unesco World Heritage site, as is the town
of Pienza on its northeastern edge. Its distinctive landscape features flat chalk plains
out of which rise almost conical hills topped
with fortified settlements and with magnificent abbeys that were once important staging points on the Via Francigena.

Montalcino
POP 5280

Managing to hold out against Florence even
after Siena had fallen (hence its former title
of 'the Republic of Siena in Montalcino'),
this medieval hill town eventually gave up
on politics and channelled its energies into
winemaking. Today, it is known as the home

of one of the world's great wines, Brunello di Montalcino.

◉ Sights & Activities

The main activity in town is visiting *enoteche*. For non-alcoholic diversion, purchase a combined ticket (€6) for entry to the *fortezza* and the Museo Civico e Diocesano d'Arte Sacra.

Fortezza　　　　　　　　　　HISTORICAL BUILDING
(Piazzale Fortezza; courtyard free, ramparts adult/child €4/2; ⊘9am-8pm Apr-Oct, 10am-6pm Nov-Mar) An imposing 14th-century structure that was later expanded under the Medici dukes, Montalcino's fortress dominates the town's skyline. You can sample and buy local wines in the *enoteca* and also climb up to the fort's ramparts (though the view is almost as magnificent from the courtyard). Buy a ticket at the bar.

Museo Civico e Diocesano
d'Arte Sacra　　　　　　　　　　　MUSEUM
(Via Ricasoli 31; adult/child €4.50/3; ⊘10am-1pm & 2-5.40pm Tue-Sun) Occupying the former convent of the neighbouring Chiesa di Sant'Agostino, this collection of religious art from the town and surrounding region includes a triptych by Duccio and a *Madonna and Child* by Simone Martini. Other artists represented include the Lorenzetti brothers, Giovanni di Paolo and Sano di Pietro.

Museo del Brunello　　　　　　　　　MUSEUM
(www.museodelbrunello.it, in Italian; Fattoria dei Barbi, Podernovaccio; adult/child €4/2; ⊘10am-6pm Mon, Thu & Fri, 3-7pm Sat & Sun) Make your way south of town, off the road to the Abbazia di Sant'Antimo, to visit this new museum. The exhibits will be of interest to wine buffs, but most of the interpretative material is in Italian only.

✵ Festivals & Events

Benvenuto Brunello　　　　　　　　　WINE
The new vintage is celebrated at this weekend of tastings and award presentations in February. It's organised by the Consorzio del Vino Brunello di Montalcino (www.consorzio brunellodimontalcino.it).

Festa della Musica　　　　　　　　　MUSIC
(www.montalcinofestadellamusica.com) Held in mid-June.

International Chamber
Music Festival　　　　　　　　　　MUSIC
(www.musica-reale.com) Staged in July.

Jazz & Wine Festival　　　　　　　　MUSIC
(www.montalcinojazzandwine.com) Also in July.

DON'T MISS

ABBAZIA DI SANT'ANTIMO

This beautiful Romanesque church (www.antimo.it; Castelnuovo dell'Abate; admission free; ⊘10.30am-12.30pm & 3-6.30pm Mon-Sat, 9.15-10.45am & 3-6pm Sun) lies in an isolated valley just below the village of Castelnuovo dell'Abate, 10.5km from Montalcino. It's best visited in the morning, when the sun, streaming through the east windows, creates an almost surreal atmosphere. At night, too, it's impressive, lit up like a beacon.

Tradition tells us that Charlemagne founded the original monastery here in 781. The exterior, built in pale travertine stone, is simple but for the stone carvings, which include various fantastical animals. Inside, study the capitals of the columns lining the nave, especially the one representing Daniel in the lion's den (second on the right as you enter). Below it is a particularly intense polychrome 13th-century Madonna and Child and there's a haunting 12th-century Crucifixion above the main altar.

Monks perform Gregorian chants in the abbey during daily services – check times on the website.

Three to four buses daily (€1.35, 15 minutes, Monday to Saturday only) connect Montalcino with the village of Castelnuovo dell'Abate.

It's a two-hour walk from Montalcino to the abbey. The route starts next to the police station near the main roundabout in town; many visitors choose to walk there and return by bus – check the timetable with the tourist office.

The abbey has a guesthouse (foresterie@antimo.it) offering simple accommodation for pilgrims. Locanda Sant'Antimo (☑0577 83 56 15; www.locandasantantimo.it; Via Bassomondo 8) at Castelnuovo dell'Abate serves solid traditional cooking. A three-course, fixed menu with wine and coffee costs a mere €19.

🛏 Sleeping

Hotel Vecchia Oliviera
HOTEL €€

(📞0577 84 60 28; www.vecchiaoliviera.com; Via Landi 1; s €70-85, d €120-190; ⊘closed Dec–mid-Feb; 🅿❄🛜♨) Just beside the Porta Cerbaia, this former olive mill has been tastefully restored and converted into a stylish small hotel. Each of the 11 rooms is individually decorated; the superior ones come with view and jacuzzi. The garden terrace has stunning views, and the pool is in an attractive garden setting.

Hotel Il Giglio
HOTEL €€

(📞0577 84 81 67; www.gigliohotel.com; Via Soccorso Saloni 5; s €88, d €130-140, annex s/d €60/95, apt €100-140; 🅿🛜) The comfortable wrought-iron beds here are each gilded with a painted *giglio* (lily), and all doubles have panoramic views. Room 1 has a private terrace with a fantastic view, and the small single is very attractive.

Il Giardino
PENSIONE €

(📞0577 84 82 57; albergoilgiardino@virgilio.it; Piazza Cavour 4; s €45, d €55-60) The town's cheapest sleeping option is run by an elderly couple who don't speak languages other than Italian but go out of their way to welcome guests. Occupying a venerable building overlooking Piazza Cavour, its decor and furnishings date from the 1970s.

🍴 Eating & Drinking

For a quick and delicious snack, head to Pizzeria La Torre (pizza per slice €1; ⊘11am-9pm Tue-Sun) on Piazza del Popolo.

WORTH A TRIP

LA BANDITA

Sophisticated urban style melds with stupendous rural scenery at this rural retreat (📞333 4046704; www.la-bandita.com; r €235-375, apt €350-495; ⊘Mar-Dec; 🅿❄@🛜♨👟), set amid working sheep farms in one of the most stunning sections of the Val d'Orcia. Owned and operated by former NYC music executive John Voigtmann and his travel-writer wife (non–Lonely Planet, we hasten to add), it offers comfortable rooms, amenities galore and impressive levels of personalised service. Put simply, it's the type of place we all fantasise about retiring to, though few of us could afford to do so. Base yourself here to visit nearby Pienza, Montepulciano and Montalcino.

Osticcio
OSTERIA €€

(Via Matteotti 23; www.osticcio.it; antipasto plates €10, meals €36; ⊘11am-11pm Fri-Wed) A huge selection of Brunello and its more modest, but still very palatable, sibling Rosso di Montalcino joins dozens of bottles of wine from around the world at this excellent *enoteca/osteria*. After browsing the selection of wines downstairs, claim a table in the upstairs dining room for a glass of wine accompanied by a cheese and meat plate or a full meal. You can also enjoy a tasting session here (three Brunello €14.50, one Rosso and one Brunello €8).

Ristorante di Poggio Antico
MODERN ITALIAN €€€

(📞0577 84 92 00; www.poggioantico.com; meals €48, 6-/7-course tasting menus €50/70; ⊘lunch & dinner Tue-Sun Apr-Oct, lunch Tue-Sun Nov-Mar) It's obligatory to visit at least one vineyard when in this world-famous wine region, and combining an excellent meal with a tasting is the way to do this in style. Located 4.5km outside town on the road to Grosseto, Poggio Antico makes award-winning wines (try its Brunello or Madre IGT), conducts tours of the winery (free), offers paid tastings (€22 for five wines) and has one of the area's best restaurants.

Enoteca La Fortezza di Montalcino
WINE BAR

(www.enotecalafortezza.com; Piazzale Fortezza; tastings €12-26; ⊘9am-8pm) Set within the fort itself, this *enoteca* is the perfect place to try and buy one of countless varieties of Brunello. It carries a huge range.

Alle Logge di Piazza
CAFE

(Piazza del Popolo 1; ⊘7am-1am Thu-Tue; 🛜) This is one of Montalcino's primary social hubs, and it also serves the best coffee in town.

ⓘ Information

The **tourist office** (📞0577 84 93 31; www.prolocomontalcino.it, in Italian; Costa del Municipio 1; ⊘10am-1pm & 2-5.50pm Apr-Oct, closed Mon Nov-Mar) is just off the main square. It can supply information about vineyard visits and book accommodation.

ⓘ Getting There & Away

BUS Regular Siena Mobilità buses (€3.65, 1½ hours, six daily) run to/from Siena.

CAR & MOTORCYCLE From Siena, take the SR2 (Via Cassia) and exit onto the SP14 at Lama. There's free parking next to the *fortezza*.

In 2008, Montalcino drew the attention of the international wine world when a number of local producers were accused of secretly adulterating their vintages of Brunello di Montalcino with 'foreign' grapes such as merlot and cabernet sauvignon. The Disciplinare di Produzione dei Vini a Denominazione di Origine Controllata (Law Controlling Wine Appellations in Italy) decrees that Brunello must be 100% Sangiovese, so this breach was taken extremely seriously by the government, wine industry and international wine media.

As a result of the accusations, the USA blocked some imports of Brunello, hitting Montalcino's economy hard (approximately 25% of each vintage ends up in the States). Seventeen producers faced commercial fraud charges and possible jail sentences, and the local industry's reputation (not to mention that of its product) suffered as a consequence.

The scandal – known as Brunellopoli or Brunellogate – raised the question of whether winemakers should be able to vary the DOCG decree and add other grapes to broaden Brunello's marketing appeal, particularly for palates attuned to New World wines. Heated debates have occurred within the Consorzio del Vino Brunello, the peak consortium of local producers, about whether upholding tradition equates to halting progress.

At present, the vast majority of the consortium's 700-odd members believe that the 100% local Sangiovese rule should stand, arguing that it is the purest expression of terroir and the wine's strongest claim to quality and marketability. They also argue that allowing blending would simply be another step towards global wine homogenisation. Proponents of change argue that blending with other varieties makes economic sense and leads to the creation of better wines.

Only one thing is sure: the debate is unlikely to be resolved any time soon.

The Spa Towns

Medieval pilgrims walking the Via Francigena from Canterbury to Rome loved this part of central Tuscany, as it was the site of thermal springs. Having a long therapeutic soak is as popular today as it was back then, and there are two popular places where you can take to the waters: Bagno Vignoni and Bagni San Filippo.

⊙ Sights & Activities

Antiche Terme Bagno Vignoni   HOT SPRING
(☎0577 88 73 65; www.termebagnovignoni.it; Piazza del Moreto 12, Bagno Vignoni; bath €19, mud bath €28, massages €35-59; ☺8am-1pm Mon-Sat May-Oct) The tiny spa town of Bagno Vignoni dates back to Roman times. Hot sulphurous water (around 49°C) bubbles up into the picturesque pool in the centre of town, which was built by the Medicis and is surrounded by mellow stone buildings. You can't dunk yourself in the pool – which has at its centre the source of the thermal spring – but this adjoining thermal institute offers a thermal pool, mud therapy and various massages and health treatments. It's particularly popular with elderly Italians seeking relief from complaints such as discopathy, osteoporosis and periarthritis.

To try the waters over winter, when the *terme* (hot springs) are closed, go to the Hotel Posta Marcucci, which offers day passes (adult/child €15/10) to its thermal swimming pool.

Bagni San Filippo   HOT SPRING
Those who prefer free hot-water frolics could press on about 15km south of Bagno Vignoni along the SR2 to this tiny village, where there are thermal cascades in an open-air reserve. You'll find these just uphill from Hotel le Terme, the village's only hotel – follow a sign marked 'Fosso Bianco' down a lane for about 150m to limestone outcrops and you'll come to a set of warm tumbling cascades that get more spectacular the further downhill you walk. It's a pleasant if slightly whiffy spot for a picnic.

🛏 Sleeping & Eating

Le Case   AGRITURISMO €
(☎0577 88 89 83; www.agriturismolecase.com; Strada Provinciale 323 km 6, Castiglione d'Orcia; r €70; ☺mid-Mar–Dec; ◙🗢) Located just 5km south of Bagno Vignoni, close to the town of Castiglione d'Orcia, is this secluded and gloriously peaceful 18th-century stone farmhouse. Run by the charming Fabio and Valeria, it offers five tastefully decorated rooms

WORTH A TRIP

ABBAZIA DI SAN SALVATORE

At the southern edge of the Val d'Orcia, set amid chestnut trees covering the eastern slope of Monte Amiata, is Abbadia San Salvatore, an ugly mining town that grew rapidly in the late 19th and early 20th centuries. Its saving grace, the **Abbazia di San Salvatore** (abbaziasansalvatore@virgilio.it; Piazzale Michelangelo 8; entry to crypt €1; ⊙10am-12.30pm & 4-7pm), lies in the centre of town and was an important stage on the Via Francigena. Founded in 743 by the Lombard Erfo, the abbey eventually passed from the Benedictines into the hands of Cistercian monks, who still occupy it today. Little remains of the monastery, but the Romanesque church more than compensates. Built in the 11th century, it was reconstructed in the late 16th century. Don't miss the huge and extremely atmospheric Lombard crypt with its remarkable forest of stone columns.

The abbey can be hard to find. Claim a free car park in Via della Pace on the side of the Stadio Comunale (Sports Stadium), and then walk into the centre of town towards the crenulated stone tower. The entrance to the monastery is off Via Cavour, down a narrow street (Via Monastero) and through two stone arches.

and spectacular views. Two elderly farmers can be regularly spotted around the property, resolutely undertaking their daily chores. Fantastic value.

Hotel Posta Marcucci　　　SPA HOTEL €€
(☑0577 88 71 12; www.hotelpostamarcucci.it; s €100-120, d €176-220; P❄🐾🏊) Overnight at this old-fashioned hotel in the centre of town and you'll be in the company of elderly Italians taking advantage of the National Health Service–funded water therapies available at the Antiche Terme Bagno Vignoni. Meals are taken in the hotel's restaurant (buffet lunch €18, four-course dinner €28) and there's inevitably a queue to use the sauna, Turkish bath and tonic hydromassage in the in-house health centre. The hotel's major drawcard is its large swimming pool, which is fed by the thermal spring.

Osteria del Leone　　TRADITIONAL ITALIAN €€
(☑0577 88 73 00; Piazza del Moretto 28, Bagno Vignoni; meals €36; ⊙Tue-Sun) A pleasantly lit, rustic building sporting a heavy-beamed ceiling, this unassuming *osteria* is located a block back from the pool in Bagno Vignoni and serves solid Tuscan country fare.

Pienza

POP 2190

If the primary road to Montepulciano didn't pass right through town, Pienza might still be the sleepy hamlet it was before Enea Silvio Piccolomini (later Pius II) decided to rebuild it in magnificent Renaissance style. And, frankly, that could be a very good thing. Weekends here are horrendous, with tourists outnumbering locals by a ratio of around 50:1. Come mid-week if at all possible, but even then be prepared for a theme-park-style experience of overpriced shopping, underwhelming dining and only a few modest cultural attractions.

Unesco added Pienza's historic centre to its World Heritage list in 1996, citing the revolutionary vision of urban space realized in Piazza Pio II and the buildings around it.

◎ Sights

Piazza Pio II　　　　　　　　PIAZZA
Stand in this magnificent square and spin 360 degrees. You have just taken in Pienza's major monuments. Gems of the Renaissance constructed in a mere three years between 1459 and 1462, they are arranged according to the urban design of Bernardo Rossellino, who applied the principles of Renaissance town planning devised by his mentor, Leon Battista Alberti. The space available to Rossellino was limited, so to increase the sense of perspective and dignity of the great edifices that he had been commissioned to design, he set them off at angles to the cathedral around a magnificently paved piazza. It was a true masterstroke.

Palazzo Piccolomini
(www.palazzopiccolominipienza.it; 30min guided tours adult/reduced €7/5; ⊙10am-6.30pm Tue-Sun mid-Mar–mid-Oct, to 4.30pm mid-Oct–mid-Mar) To your right as you face the cathedral, this magnificent palace was the pope's residence and is considered Rossellino's masterpiece. Built on the site of former Piccolomini family houses, the building has a fine courtyard,

from which stairs lead up into the papal apartments. These are now filled with an assortment of period furnishings, minor art and the like. To the rear, a three-level loggia offers a spectacular panorama over the Val d'Orcia below. There are guided tours of the 1st floor every 30 minutes, but you can peek into the courtyard for free.

Duomo
(⊙8.30am-1pm & 2.15-6.30pm) The piazza's focal point, this cathedral was built on the site of the Romanesque Chiesa di Santa Maria, of which little remains. The Renaissance facade, in travertine stone, is of clear Albertian inspiration. The interior of the building, a strange mix of Gothic and Renaissance, contains a collection of five altarpieces painted by Sienese artists of the period, as well as a superb marble tabernacle by Rossellino containing a relic of St Andrew the Apostle, Pienza's patron saint. The papal bull of 1462 forbade any changes to the church, so revel in the thought that its appearance is virtually the same now as it was in the Middle Ages.

Museo Diocesano
(Corso Rossellino 30; adult/reduced €4.10/2.60; ⊙10am-1pm & 3-6pm Wed-Mon mid-Mar–Nov, 10am-1pm & 3-6pm Sat & Sun Dec–mid-Mar) To the left of the cathedral is Palazzo Vescovile, modified and enlarged in 1492 for Cardinal Borgia (later Pope Alexander VI), and now containing this museum. It displays an intriguing miscellany of artworks, illuminated manuscripts, tapestries and miniatures. Enter via Corso Rossellino.

Pieve di Corsignano   CHURCH
Be sure to take time to visit this Romanesque church at the entrance to town. It dates from the 10th century, when Pienza was called Corsignano, and boasts a strange circular bell tower with eight arched windows. Look closely to discern the carving of a two-headed siren over the main doorway and scenes of the Three Kings and Nativity on the side doorway on the right side of the church next to an abandoned farmhouse. Inside the church is the baptismal font where Pius II was christened. There are no fixed visiting times but it's usually open between Easter and November.

🛏 Sleeping

Hotel Lupaia   BOUTIQUE HOTEL €€€
(☑0577 66 80 28; www.lupaia.com; Località Lupaia 74; d €270-360; P❄🛜🏊) Occupying the buildings of a medieval *borgo* (small rural settlement) close to both Pienza and Montepulciano, this hotel has been uniquely and meticulously fitted out by the family matriarch, a 30-year veteran of fashion and interior design. Luxurious rooms are located in the old farm buildings and the main house contains the sitting/dining rooms (four-course set dinner €38). Stays here are largely occupied by enjoying sigh-inducing countryside views, lazing by the pool and admiring the dazzling creative use of medieval space.

Oliviera Camere   B&B €
(☑0578 74 82 74, 338 9520459; www.nautilus-mp.com/oliviera; Via Condotti 4b; s/d €35/48, apt €70) Squeezed into a side street and as close to dead-centre Pienza as the un-sainted can hope to get, this former olive-oil mill represents excellent value. Its three rooms are simple but fresh and attractive. There are also three slightly larger studio apartments with kitchenette.

🍴 Eating

TOP CHOICE **Osteria La Porta**   TRADITIONAL ITALIAN €€
(☑0578 75 51 63; Via del Piano 3; meals €40; ⊙Fri-Wed) A 15-minute drive southeast from Pienza will bring you to Monticchiello, a sleepy

---

PIUS II

Let's be honest: there have been a lot of popes over the centuries, and not all of them have possessed intellectual gifts, tact and moral rectitude (Rodrigo Borgia, aka Alexander VI, comes immediately to mind). But Pienza's favourite son, Pope Pius II (1405–64), possessed all of these qualities. Born Enea Silvio Piccolomini, the man was everywhere, evidenced by how many times we drop his name in this chapter alone. He was a tireless traveller, writer of erotic and comic stories, poet laureate, diplomat, bishop, exhaustive autobiographer (13 volumes!) and medieval urban-planning trendsetter. And most of that occurred before he got the top job. Noted above all for being the 'humanist pope', this towering intellectual figure is also remembered for his tireless diplomacy in the face of uncooperative leaders and insurmountable odds.

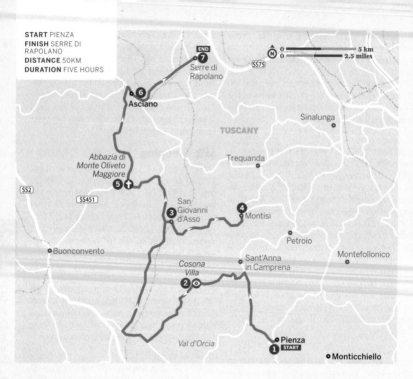

START PIENZA
FINISH SERRE DI RAPOLANO
DISTANCE 50KM
DURATION FIVE HOURS

Driving Tour
The Crete Senesi

❯ Le Crete (a Tuscan dialect word meaning clay) is an area of rolling hills scored by steep ravines offering a feast of classic Tuscan images – ridgelines topped by cypress trees, fields of wheat rippling in the breeze and silhouetted hills fading into the misty distance. This tour showcases some of its most spectacular scenery.

Leaving **1 Pienza**, follow the road signs to Siena and then turn right onto the SP71A heading towards San Giovanni d'Asso ('Trequanda Castelmúzio'). After a short drive, turn left onto the SP71 towards **2 Cosona Villa**; it's a dirt road but is perfectly drivable in a 2WD. Driving along the ridgeline, pass the historic villa at Cosona and then turn right towards Torrenieri. From here, follow road signs to **3 San Giovanni d'Asso**. As well as being home to a Museum of Truffles (www.museodeltartufo.it), this town is one of the 40 'Città del Tartufo' in Italy and hosts truffle festivals on the first weekend of March and the second and third weekends in November. For lunch, stop at **4 Da Roberto**

Taverna in Montisi (☎0577 84 51 59; www.tavernamontisi.com; Via Umberto I, 3; meals €28; ⊗closed Mon & mid-Jan–Feb). Owner/chef Roberto Crocenzi proudly tells diners that his kitchen has no freezer and microwave, and the fresh and flavoursome dishes he creates certainly back up this claim.

From San Giovanni d'Asso, take the SP60 and SS451 to **5 Abbazia di Monte Oliveto Maggiore**, an atmospheric religious retreat with a frescoed Great Cloister, internationally recognised library and historic wine cellar.

The 10km drive from Monte Oliveto Maggiore to the agricultural centre of **6 Asciano** is quite a thrill, both for drivers (a 1½ car-width, winding, heel-toe challenge) and for passengers (camera-ready countryside). If you have time, stop and wander around the town's medieval streets. Alternatively, continue on the SP26 and SP64 towards Rapolano Terme, concluding your tour at the fortified medieval hill town of **7 Serre di Rapolano**, where you can overnight in the magnificent **Castello delle Serre**.

medieval hilltop village. Positioned just inside the main gate, this highly regarded *osteria/enoteca/caffetteria* has a small terrace with panoramic views of Val d'Orcia and a reputation for food and service that behoves a reservation, even in low season. The €18 fixed menu at lunchtime offers great value, and *spuntini* (snacks) such as bruschettas, olives and cheese plates are served outside usual meal hours.

Osteria Sette di Vino   OSTERIA €

(☎0578 74 90 92; Piazza di Spagna 1; soups €6, bruschettas €3, cheese plates €6; ⏱Thu-Tue) Known for its *zuppa di pane e fagioli* (bread and white-bean soup) and *pecorino con lardo* (grilled *pecorino* cheese with *lardo* – cured strips of back fat), this simple place is run by the exuberant Luciano, who is immortalised as Bacchus in a copy of Caravaggio's famous painting hanging above the main counter. There are a few tables inside, and a few more on the piazza. Cash only; no coffee.

Trattoria Latte di Luna   TRATTORIA €€

(☎0578 74 86 06; Via San Carlo 6; meals €30; ⏱closed Tue & in Feb & Jul) On a kind of squarette where the street splits off from Corso Rossellino, this trattoria has a lovely terrace with plenty of shady umbrellas. Dishes are local and seasonal and there's a strong representation of local reds on the wine list.

🛍 Shopping

Bottega del Naturista   FOOD

(Corso Rossellino 16) Almost a monument in its own right, this pungent *bottega* (shop) stocks a truly mouth-watering array of local *pecorini* cheeses.

ℹ Information

Tourist office (☎0578 74 99 05; info.turismo@comune.pienza.si.it; Corso Rossellino 30; ⏱10am-1pm & 3-6pm Wed-Mon mid-Mar–Oct, 10am-1pm & 3-6pm Sat & Sun Nov–mid-Mar) Located inside the Museo Diocesano.

ℹ Getting There & Away

BUS Two Siena Mobilità buses run between Siena and Pienza (€4.15, 70 minutes) and nine travel to/from Montepulciano (€1.95). The bus terminal is just off Piazza Dante Alighieri. Buy tickets at the nearby bar.

CAR & MOTORCYCLE Finding a car park is extremely difficult on weekends as the public car park near the centre fills quickly. It costs €1.50 per hour. Be warned that local traffic officers are quick to fine cars that overstay their ticket.

VAL DI CHIANA

Straddling the provinces of Siena and Arezzo, this scenic valley is known for its food and wine. Dining in its major town, Montepulciano, is a highlight – particularly if you opt for the local Chianina beef washed down with a glass or two of the famous Vino Nobile.

Montepulciano

POP 14,500

This reclaimed narrow ridge of volcanic rock will push your quadriceps to their failure point. When this happens, self-medicate with a generous pour of the highly reputed Vino Nobile while drinking in the spectacular views over the Val di Chiana and Val d'Orcia.

SIENA & CENTRAL TUSCANY MONTEPULCIANO

WORTH A TRIP

THE TOMB OF THE INFERNAL CHARIOT

In 2003, archaeologists excavating an intact 4th-century-BC tomb in the necropolis of Pianacce, just outside Sarteano on the road to Cetona (signposted '*tombe etrusche delle Pianacce*'), discovered a unique fresco, its colours still as bright as the day they were applied. On the walls surrounding the alabaster sarcophagus, a demonic figure with wild flowing russet hair drives a chariot pulled by a pair of lions and two griffins. Fabulous monsters – a three-headed snake and a huge seahorse – rear up and two male figures (perhaps lovers or perhaps a father and son) have an affectionate moment.

The deceased chose his last resting place well, and the commanding views over the Val di Chiana make the tomb worth the short diversion on the strength of the panorama alone. Tours cost adult/child €7/5 and are only held on Saturday (9.30am and 6pm in summer, 11am in winter). Reserve through the Civic Archaeological Museum (☎0578 26 92 61; info.museo@comune.sarteano.si.it; Via Roma 24) in Sarteano.

A late-Etruscan fort was the first in a series of settlements here. During the Middle Ages, the town was a constant bone of contention between Florence and Siena. Florence eventually won the day in 1404 and the Marzocco, or lion of Florence, came to replace the she-wolf of Siena as the city's symbol. The new administration invited architects including Michelozzo and Sangallo il Vecchio to design new buildings and endow this Gothic stronghold with some Renaissance grace and style. That intriguing mix alone makes the steep climbs worthwhile.

Sights

Il Corso STREET

The main street, called in stages Via di Gracciano nel Corso, Via di Voltaia del Corso and Via dell'Opio nel Corso, climbs uphill from Porta al Prato, near the car park on Piazza Don Minzoni. At the upper end of Piazza Savonarola is the Colonna del Marzocca, erected in 1511 to confirm Montepulciano's allegiance to Florence. The splendid stone lion, squat as a pussycat atop this column is, in fact, a copy; the original is in the town's Museo Civico. The late-Renaissance Palazzo Avignonesi by Giacomo da Vignola is at No

Montepulciano

91. Several mansions line Via di Gracciano nel Corso, including the Palazzo di Bucelli at No 73, the lower courses of whose facade are recycled Etruscan and Latin inscriptions and reliefs. Sangallo il Vecchio designed Palazzo Cocconi at No 70. Continuing up Via di Gracciano nel Corso, you'll find Michelozzo's Chiesa di Sant'Agostino (Piazza Michelozzo; ◷9am-noon & 3-6pm), with its lunette above the entrance holding a terracotta Madonna and Child, John the Baptist and St Augustine. Opposite, the Torre di Pulcinella, a medieval tower house, is topped by the town clock and the hunched figure of Pulcinella (Punch of Punch and Judy fame), which strikes the hours. After passing historic Caffè Poliziano, the Corso eventually does a dog-leg at Via del Teatro, continuing uphill past Cantine Contucci (www.contucci.it; Via del Teatro 1; admission free, paid tastings; ◷8.30am-12.30pm & 2.30-6pm Mon-Fri, from 9.30am Sat & Sun), housed underneath the handsome *palazzo* of the same name. You can visit the historic cellars and taste local tipples here.

Piazza Grande   PIAZZA
This is the town's highest point and the location for the main crowd scene in *New Moon*, the second film in the *Twilight* series. The 14th-century Palazzo Comunale (access to panoramic terrace €2; ◷9am-6pm Mon-Sat) and the late-16th-century Duomo (◷9am-noon & 4-7pm), with its unfinished facade, are the piazza's major landmarks. Behind the high altar in the *duomo* is Taddeo di Bartolo's lovely *Assumption* triptych (1401).

Via Ricci   STREET
From Piazza Grande, Via Ricci runs downhill past Palazzo Ricci (www.palazzoricci.com; Via Ricci 9-11), now home to a German music academy. From the *palazzo*'s courtyard, stairs lead down to another historic wine cellar, Cantina del Redi (www.vecchiacantinadimontepulciano.com; admission free, paid tastings; ◷10.30am-1.30pm & 3-7.30pm mid-Mar–early Jan, Sat & Sun only early Jan–mid Mar). A bit further downhill is the Museo Civico (admission €5; ◷10am-1pm & 3-6pm Tue-Sun), home to an eclectic collection of artworks and artefacts. The street terminates in Piazza San Francesco, where you can admire a panoramic view of the Val di Chiana.

🍴 Courses & Tours

The office of the Strada del Vino Nobile di Montepulciano (www.stradavinonobile.it) organises a range of tours and courses, including cooking courses (€60 to €180), vineyard tours (€18 to €48), Slow Food tours (€100 to €155), wine-tasting lessons (€37) and walking tours in the vineyards culminating in a wine tasting (€45 to €60). You can make bookings at its information office in Piazza Grande.

🎭 Festivals & Events

A festival of classical music is held at Palazzo Ricci in June, and its lovely main salon hosts occasional concerts during the year; see www.palazzoricci.com for details.

🛏 Sleeping

TOP CHOICE **Locanda San Francesco**   B&B €€€
(☑349 6721302; www.locandasanfrancesco.it; Piazza San Francesco 5; r €195-215, ste €235; ◷closed mid-Jan–mid-Feb; ℗✳@🛜) Four handsome rooms (two with magnificent views) and an elegantly furnished lounge/breakfast room await at this luxury B&B. Host Cinzia Caporali runs both it and the E Lucevan Le Stelle wine bar with friendly efficiency.

Villa Cicolina
BOUTIQUE HOTEL €€€

(☎0578 75 86 20; www.villacicolina.it; Via Provinciale 11; s €150-210, d €185-270; P❄️🛜🏊) A five-minute drive from the town, this historic villa set in formal gardens has atmosphere and comfort in equal measure. There's a spectacular pool terrace and an excellent restaurant where dinner is served in the high season (six-course set menu €35).

Camere Bellavista
HOTEL €

(☎347 8232314; www.camerebellavista.it; Via Ricci 25; s €65-70, d €75; P🛜) Nearly all of the 10 high-ceilinged double rooms at this excellent budget hotel have fantastic views; room 6 also has a private terrace (€100). No-one lives here so phone ahead in order to be met and given a key (if you've omitted this stage, there's a phone in the lobby from where you can call). No breakfast.

🍴 Eating & Drinking

TOP CHOICE La Grotta
TRADITIONAL ITALIAN €€

(☎0578 75 74 79; www.lagrottamontepulciano.it; Via San Biagio 15; 6-course set menus €48; ⊘closed Wed) Facing the High Renaissance Tempio di San Biagio on the road to Chiusi, La Grotta has elegant dining rooms and a gorgeous courtyard garden that's perfect for summer dining. The food is simple but delicious, and service is exemplary. A hint: don't skip dessert.

Osteria Acquacheta
OSTERIA €

(☎0578 71 70 86; www.acquacheta.eu; Via del Teatro 22; meals €19; ⊘closed Tue) Hugely popular with locals and tourists alike, this bustling place specialises in *bistecca alla fiorentina* (chargrilled T-bone steak), which comes to the table in huge, lightly seared and exceptionally flavoursome slabs (don't even *think* of asking for it to be served otherwise). Lunch sittings are at 12.15pm and 2.15pm; dinner at 7.30pm and 9.15pm – book ahead.

Enoteca a Gambe di Gatto
TRADITIONAL ITALIAN €€

(☎0578 75 74 31; Via dell'Opio nel Corso 34; meals €34; ⊘closed Jan-Easter & Wed) Renowned throughout the region, exacting husband and wife team of Emanuel (front of house) and Laura (kitchen) travel the country each winter to acquire the best products from organic producers. The daily menu fluctuates wildly, depending on market offerings, and meals start with a complimentary tasting of wine and olive oil. Service stretches the Slow Food philosophy to its limits – don't come here if you're after a quick meal.

E Lucevan Le Stelle
WINE BAR

(www.locandasanfrancesco.it; Piazza San Francesco 5; ⊘11.30am-11pm Easter–mid-Nov; 🛜) Comfy couches, cool jazz (both on the sound system and live) and modern art on the walls are the hallmarks at this laid-back wine bar and bistro. Dishes (antipasto plates €4.50 to €8, *piadinas* €6, pastas €6.50 to €9) are simple but tasty and there's an outdoor terrace that's a perfect spot for an *aperitivo*.

Caffè Poliziano
CAFE

(Via di Voltaia nel Corso 27; 🛜) Established as a cafe in 1868, Poliziano has had a chequered past – at times functioning as a cafe-cabaret, mini-cinema and grocery store – but it was lovingly restored to its original form 20 years ago and has since regained its position as the town's favourite cafe. A sit-down coffee is expensive, but will be worth the outlay if you manage to score one of the tiny, precipitous balcony tables.

ℹ️ Information

Strada del Vino Nobile di Montepulciano Information Office (☎0578 71 74 84; www.stradavinonobile.it; Piazza Grande 7; ⊘10am-1pm & 3-6pm Mon-Fri) Books accommodation and arranges courses and tours.

Tourist office (☎0578 75 73 41; www.prolocomontepulciano.it; Piazza Don Minzoni; ⊘9.30am-12.30pm & 3-8pm Mon-Sat, 9.30am-12.30pm Sun) Reserves accommodation, offers internet access (€3.50 per hour), sells a map of the town (€0.50), rents bikes and scooters and sells bus and train tickets.

WORTH A TRIP

FATTORIA LE CAPEZZINE

Fifteen kilometres northeast of town, this **wine estate** (www.avignonesi.it; Valiano di Montepulciano; ⊘9am-6pm May-Oct, 9am-5pm Mon-Fri Nov-Apr) is part of the highly regarded Avignonesi company, which produces Vino Nobile di Montepulciano, Rosso di Montepulciano, Vin Santo, grappa and olive oil. Spread over 19 hectares, the estate is known for its 'Round Vineyard', which was designed to establish to what extent the quality of wine is influenced by density of planting and type of rootstock. Visit the *enoteca* to purchase wine and enjoy limited tastings.

ORVIETO *Joe Fullman*

This Umbrian city looms over the A1 *superstrada* (expressway) in truly spectacular fashion. Perched precariously on a craggy volcanic landform, its skyline is dominated by a huge cathedral (www.opsm.it; Piazza Duomo; admission €2, incl Cappella di San Brizio €3; ☺9.30am-77.30pm Apr-Oct, 9.30am-1pm & 2.30-5pm Nov-Mar), one of the great master-pieces of medieval architecture. Dating from 1290, this remarkable edifice was originally planned in the Romanesque style but, as work proceeded and architectural styles changed, Gothic features were incorporated into the structure and showcased on the magnificent facade. Inside, Luca Signorelli's fresco cycle *The Last Judgement* shimmers with life. Look for it to the right of the altar in the Cappella di San Brizio (☺closed during Mass). Signorelli began work on the series in 1499, and Michelangelo is said to have taken inspiration from it.

Orvieto is a mere one-hour drive from both Montepulciano and Arezzo, so can easily be visited in a day if you're staying in the Val di Chiana. If you wish to overnight, Hotel Maitani (☎0763 34 20 11; www.hotelmaitani.com; Via Lorenzo Maitani 5; s/d €77/126, breakfast €10; P�wi-fi) near the cathedral is a good choice. For meals, head to Trattoria dell'Orso (☎0763 34 16 42; Via della Misericordia 18; meals €32; ☺Wed-Sun), the city's oldest restaurant.

The tourist office (☎0763 34 17 72; info@iat.orvieto.tr.it; Piazza Duomo 24; ☺8.15am-1.50pm & 4-7pm Mon-Fri, 10am-1pm & 3-6pm Sat, Sun & holidays) can supply information on other sights as well as timetables for *regionale* train services to Florence and Rome.

For tips, recommendations and reviews, head to shop.lonelyplanet.com to purchase a downloadable PDF of the Umbria & Le Marche chapter from Lonely Planet's *Italy* guide.

ℹ Getting There & Around

BUS The bus station is next to Car Park No 5 (P5). Siena Mobilità runs four buses daily between Siena and Montepulciano (€5.15, 1½ hours) stopping at Pienza en route. To get here from Florence, you need to catch a Tiemme service to Bettolle (€7.90, 90 minutes, three daily) and connect with a Siena Mobilità bus (€1.95, 40 minutes, one daily).

Regular buses connect with Chiusi-Chianciano Terme (€2.55, 40 minutes), from where you can catch a train to Florence (€9.30, two hours, frequent) via Arezzo (€4.70, 50 minutes).

CAR & MOTORCYCLE Coming from Florence, take the Valdichiana exit off the A1 (direction Bettolle-Sinalunga) and then follow the signs; from Siena, take the Siena–Bettolle–Perugia autostrada.

A 24-hour ZTL applies in the historic centre between June and September; between October and May it applies from 7am to 5pm. Your hotel can usually supply a permit. The most convenient car park is at Piazza Don Minzoni (P1, €1.20 per hour), from where minibuses (€1) weave their way up the hill to Piazza Grande.

Southern Tuscany

Best Places to Eat

» Il Pellicano (p253)

» Antica Trattoria Aurora (p253)

» La Vecchia Hosteria (p244)

» La Tana del Brillo Parlante (p242)

» Rosso e Vino (p251)

Best Places to Stay

» Pieve di Caminino (p243)

» Montebelli Agriturismo & Country Hotel (p244)

» Tenuta del Fontino (p241)

» Podere Riparbella (p241)

» Le Camere del Ceccottino (p245)

Why Go?

If you love the great outdoors, southern Tuscany is for you. A landscape dotted with dramatically sited inland hill-towns, biologically diverse coastal plains and craggy mountain ranges stretching to the sea, it offers visitors activities of every description. Here, you can walk, horse-ride and bird-watch to your heart's content, spending your days in the fresh air and your nights relaxing in atmospheric *agriturismi* (farm stay accommodation).

Locals here are fiercely proud of the ancient customs of the Maremma, as the region is commonly called, and history resonates in every city, town and village. Inland, there's a wealth of Etruscan sites, including settlements, necropolises (burial sites) and the enigmatic sunken roads known as *vie cave*. There are also plenty of medieval and Renaissance towns scattered across the hills – exploration of these will inevitably culminate with lunch or dinner at a local eatery serving rustic Maremmese dishes that are perfectly complemented by the region's robust wines.

When to Go

The shoulder seasons (spring and autumn/fall) are the best times to visit. In summer, Romans descend upon the coast en masse, causing traffic to snarl, prices to skyrocket and hotels to overfill. Outdoor activities are best enjoyed outside summer also, as the heat can be oppressive and bushfires are an occasional threat. Birdwatching opportunities are plentiful in the two WWF reserves on the coast from September to April, and the spring season is welcomed with one of Tuscany's most evocative events, Pitigliano's Torciata di San Giuseppe.

Itineraries

Coastal Landscapes The southwest coast is home to three of Tuscany's most important nature reserves: the Parco Regionale della Maremma, the Riserva Naturale WWF Lago di Burano and the Riserva Naturale Laguna di Orbetello. Come here to walk, bicycle, canoe or horse-ride through the wild natural scenery, and consider signing up for a farm experience at Agienza Regionale Agricola di Alberese in the regional park, where the famous *butteri* (Maremmese cowboys) ride the range.

Etruscan Sites Though the Etruscans have left their mark on towns, cities and landscapes throughout this region, the southeast corner is a particularly rich repository of their heritage. Base yourself in picturesque Pitigliano and then explore the neighbouring settlements of Sorano and Sovana to see Etruscan necropolises and explore the mysterious *vie cave*. After a morning's exploration, head to the Etruscan town of Saturnia for a soak in its hot, sulphurous waters.

Rural Relaxation This part of Tuscany is home to some of the best *agriturismi* in the country. Turn your back on city life and sign up for a week in the country, visiting medieval towns such as Grosseto and Massa Marittima in the morning and exploring *strade del vino e dei sapori* (wine and speciality products routes) in the afternoon. At day's end, head back to relax by the pool or enjoy a late-afternoon *aperitivo* (pre-dinner drinks) on a vineyard-facing terrace before sampling flavourful local dishes over dinner.

GETTING AROUND

You'll need a car to explore this pocket of Tuscany thoroughly – try to veer off the S1 autostrada and explore secondary roads whenever possible. Train travel won't get you far – the *Frecciabianca* stops in Grosseto on its trip between Rome and Genoa and *regionale* (regional) trains servicing that route also stop in Capalbio (for Lago di Burano) and Orbatello-Monte Argentario, but the only other rail link is between Siena and Grosseto. Bus travel is even worse, with limited routes and infrequent services.

Where to Stay

Accommodation options in Grosseto and Massa Marittima leave a lot to be desired, so we highly recommend staying in an *agriturismo* instead – the area between Massa and Vetulonia is rich in alluring farm-stay options. There are also good budget *pensioni* in Pitigliano.

Best Walks

» Pitigliano to Sovana
Incorporating parts of *vie cave* (see the boxed text, p245).

» Le Biancane Park, Monterotondo Marittimo
Through a strange geothermal landscape (see the boxed text, p241).

» Parco Regionale della Maremma Along the beach and through a forest to reach the ruins of a 12th-century tower (p252).

Archaeological Sites

» Vetulonia (p243)

» Parco Archeologico della Città del Tufa (p249)

» Roselle (p251)

Resources

» Maremma Tourism: www. turismoinmaremma.it

» Parco degli Etruschi: www.parcodeglietruschi.it

Southern Tuscany Highlights

1 Become a Maremmese cowboy for the day in the **Parco Regionale della Maremma** (p252).

2 Admire a saucy fresco and one of Italy's most magnificent piazzas in **Massa Marittima** (p240).

3 Kick back and relax in some of Tuscany's best **agriturismi** (farm-stay accommodation).

4 Embark on a hike with a difference amid the strange geothermal landscape of **Monterotondo Marittimo** (see the boxed text, p241).

5 Observe exciting Etruscan excavation works at the archaeological site of **Vetulonia** (p243).

6 Visit an historic synagogue where the largest Jewish community in Italy once worshipped in the hilltop stronghold of **Pitigliano** (p244).

7 Walk in the footsteps of Etruscans while exploring the enigmatic landscape around **Sovana** (p248).

8 Follow tens of thousands of migrating birds to the unspoiled natural landscape of the **Riserva Naturale WWF Lago di Burano** (p254).

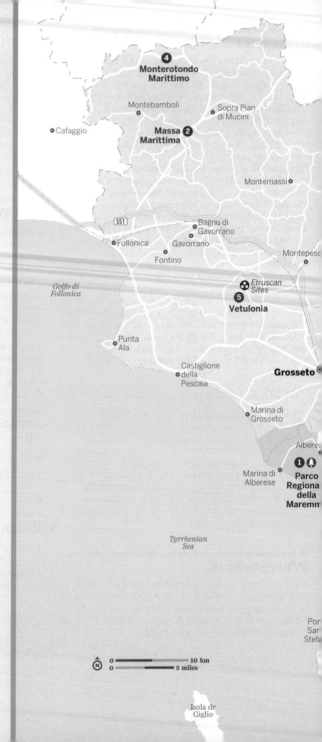

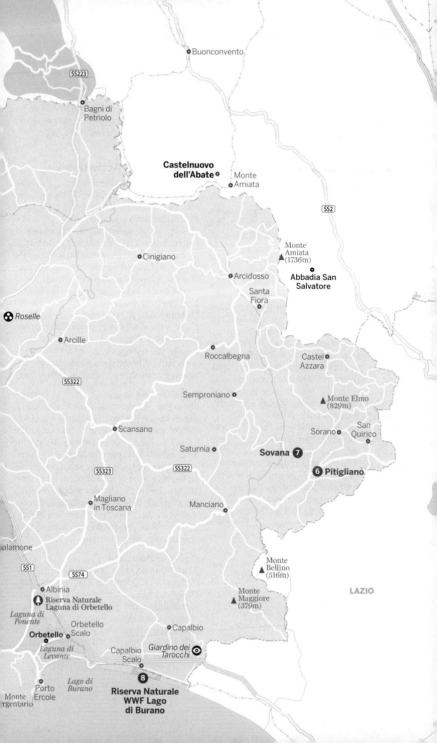

THE ALTA MAREMMA

The Alta (Upper) Maremma starts south of Livorno and continues down to Grosseto, incorporating Massa Marittima and the surrounding Colline Metallifere (metal-producing hills) that are now part of Unesco's European Geopark Network. It also covers inland territory including the hill towns south of the Crete Senesi and the mountainous terrain surrounding Monte Amiata.

Massa Marittima

POP 8820

This medieval hill town (commonly known as Massa) is located between Siena and the coast. Its lack of tourists is puzzling, as there's an eccentric yet endearing jumble of museums and the central piazza is one of the most magnificent in Tuscany.

Briefly under Pisan domination, Massa became an independent *comune* (city state) in 1225 but was swallowed up by Siena a century later. The plague in 1348 and the decline of its lucrative mining industry 50 years later reduced the town to the brink of extinction, a situation made even worse by the prevalence of malaria in surrounding marshlands. Fortunately, the draining of marshes in the 18th century and the re-establishment of mining shortly afterwards brought the town back to life.

The town is divided into three districts: the Città Vecchia (Old Town), Città Nuova (New Town) and Borgo (Borough). Access from the Città Vecchia to the Città Nuova is via the massive **Arco Senese** (Sienese Arch) linking defensive bastions in the old city walls to the **Torre del Candeliere** (Piazza Matteotti; adult/child €2.50/1.50; ⊙10am-1pm & 3-6pm Tue-Sun Apr-Oct, 11am-1pm & 2.30-4.30pm Tue-Sun Nov-Mar), a tower commanding stupendous views over the town.

ROAD DISTANCES (KM)

	Vetulonia	Massa Marittima	Grosseto	Pitigliano
Massa Marittima	38			
Grosseto	52	48		
Pitigliano	129	120	75	
Orbetello	91	90	43	60

MONEY SAVER

A **cumulative ticket** (☑0566 90 22 89; www.massamarittimamusei.it; adult/child 6-16 €15/10) gives access to all 12 of Massa's museums and monuments. A €6 ticket gives access to the Museo di Arte Sacra and Torre del Candeliere. All museums are closed on Mondays.

◉ Sights & Activities

Cattedrale di San Cerbone   DUOMO
(⊙8am-noon & 3-5pm) Massa's 13th-century *duomo* (cathedral) presides over photogenic Piazza Garibaldi (aka Piazza Duomo) and is cleverly set asymmetrical to the square to better show off its splendour. It is dedicated to St Cerbonius, the town's patron saint, who is always depicted surrounded with a flock of geese; carved panels on the facade depict scenes from his life. Inside, look behind the high alter for the *Arca di San Cerbone* (St Cerbone's Ark; 1324) carved by Goro di Gregorio. A wooden crucifix (early 14th century) by Giovanni Pisano sits on the altar itself. Beware the self-appointed custodian (an elderly lady), who firmly believes that the *duomo* is for worship rather than sightseeing.

Museo di Arte Sacra   MUSEUM
(Corso Diaz 36; adult/child €5/3; ⊙10am-1pm & 3-6pm Tue-Sun Apr-Sep, 11am-1pm & 3-5pm Tue-Sun Oct-Mar) This museum is housed in the former monastery of San Pietro all'Orto. Its main exhibit is a splendid *Maestà* (Majesty; c 1330) by Ambrogio Lorenzetti, originally on the high altar of the Chiesa di San Pietro all'Orto, but it also houses sculptures from the *duomo's* facade by Giovanni Pisano as well as a collection of primitive grey alabaster bas-reliefs. These were also from the *duomo* but originally date from an earlier era.

Museo Archeologico   MUSEUM
(Piazza Garibaldi 1; adult/child €3/2; ⊙10am-12.30pm & 3.30-7pm Tue-Sun Apr-Oct, 10am-12.30pm & 3-5pm Tue-Sun Nov-Mar) The 13th-century **Palazzo del Podestà** houses Massa's musty archaeological museum, whose only truly noteworthy exhibit is *La Stele del Vado all'Arancio,* a simple but compelling stone stela (funeral or commemorative marker) dating from the 3rd millennium BC.

Albero della Fecondità   FOUNTAIN
Downhill from Piazza Garibaldi, opposite the main car park, is a 13th-century build-

ing that was once used to store wheat. Under its loggia is the Fonte dell'Abbondanza (Fountain of Abundance), a now decommissioned public drinking fountain topped by an extraordinary fresco of the *Albero della Fecondità* (Fertility Tree). Look closely to see what type of fruit the tree bears!

Museo della Miniera   MUSEUM
(Via Corridoni; adult/child 6-16/child under 6 €5/3/free; ☉10am-5.30pm Tue-Sun Apr-Sep, to 4.30pm Oct-Mar) The city's long mining history is told at this museum, where the display includes a replica of a length of mine. Guided tours (in Italian, but with audioguide in English, French or German) last around 30 minutes.

✦ Festivals & Events

Massa's big event of the year is the **Balestro del Girifalco** (Contest of the Falcon's Heart), a crossbow competition held twice yearly on the first Sunday after 20 May and on a Sunday in either July or August (usually the second Sunday in August). Teams from the town's three *terzieri* (town districts) dress in medieval costume and compete for a golden arrow and large silk painted arrow.

🛏 Sleeping

Massa's clutch of hotels leave a lot to be desired, but there are fabulous villas and *ag-*riturismi* dotted around the surrounding area.

Tenuta del Fontino   AGRITURISMO €€
(☑0566 91 92 32; www.tenutafontino.it; Località Fontino; r per person €52-85, ste €158-340; ❋🅿🛜⛳) Surrounded by forests of cypress and pine trees, this attractive 19th-century villa and wine estate 20km southwest of Massa is an idyllic rural retreat. There's a great pool, a horse-riding centre and a glorious terrace where meals are served (dinner €18). Some of the rooms are simple; others have been recently refurbished and have mod-cons including air-con. Suites can sleep up to four people, and there are also two- and four-person apartments available for weekly rent (€530 to €1750).

🖊 Podere Riparbella   AGRITURISMO €€
(☑0566 91 55 57; www.riparbella.com; Località Sopra Pian di Mucini; s €82-94, d €156-176; ☉closed early Jan–mid-Apr; 🅿🛜) The Swiss owners of this 18-hectare estate 5km outside Massa have spent the last 20-odd years building an ecologically sustainable farm operation cultivating grapes and olives, and making jams. The 11 guest rooms are in a charming old building with communal lounge and terrace. A delicious four-course dinner utilises home-grown and local products and is included in the room price. No credit cards.

THE COLLINE METALLIFERE

Massa Marittima's handsome buildings and artistic treasures are the legacy of the town's location in the centre of Tuscany's Colline Metallifere (metal-producing hills). Mining occurred in these hills over three millennia, and has shaped the region's physical and cultural landscapes – a fact acknowledged by the recent addition of the Parco Nazionale Technologico Archeologico delle Colline Metallifere Grossetane (National Technological and Archaeological Park of the Colline Metallifere; www.parcocollinemetallifere.it) to the Unesco-auspiced European Geopark Network. The national park aims to preserve and promote the history of metallurgy and mining activities in the region.

The national park incorporates many sites, including '**Le Biancane**' (admission free; ☉information office 10.30am-12.30pm & 4-6pm daily Jun-Sep, 9.30am-12.30pm & 2-4pm daily Apr-May, 10.30am-12.30pm & 4-6pm Sat & Sun Oct) in Monterotondo Marittimo, a geothermal park 21km north of Massa where steam has been transformed into power by vapour turbines since 1916, supplying power to one million Tuscan households (and meeting 25% of Tuscany's overall energy demands). Visitors can take a two-hour walk through wooded terrain belching steam from under the earth's crust and sheltering amazing clumps of sulphur crystals.

Another site well worth a visit is the **Parco Minerario Naturalistico Gavorrano** (www.parcominerario.it; Località Ex Bagnetti, Gavorrano; adult/reduced €8/7; ☉10am-1pm Sat & Sun May–mid-Jun, 10am-1pm & 4-7pm Tue-Sun mid-Jun–Sep, 10am-1pm & 4-7pm Sun Oct, 10am-1pm & 3.30-5.30pm Sun Nov, 10am-5.30pm Sun Dec), a museum and education centre in a huge former pyrite mine that operated from 1898 to 1984 and was once the largest mine in Europe. A section of the mine's 180km of underground galleries can be visited in a fascinating guided tour incorporating social history commentary and interactive displays.

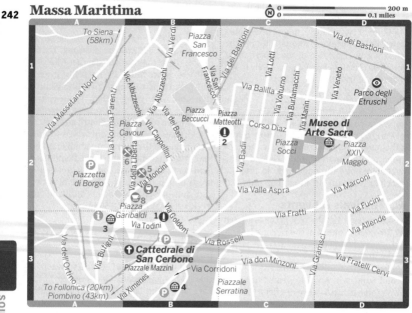

Massa Marittima

◎ Top Sights

Cattedrale di San Cerbone	B3
Museo di Arte Sacra	D2

◎ Sights

1	Albero della Fecondità	B3
2	Arco Senese	C2
3	Museo Archeologico	A3
4	Museo della Miniera	B3
	Palazzo del Podestà	(see 3)
	Torre del Candeliere	(see 2)

⊗ Eating

5	La Tana del Brillo Parlante	B2
6	L'Osteria da Tronca	B2

☺ Drinking

7	Il Bacchino	B2
8	Le Logge	B2

✖ Eating & Drinking

La Tana del Brillo Parlante
OSTERIA €€

(☎0566 90 12 74; Vicolo del Ciambellano 4; meals €32; ⊙closed Wed) Satisfying the Slow Food checklist to the letter, this self-described 'smallest *osteria* in Italy' seats a mere 10 people (in summer up to another four can

squeeze into tiny alley tables). If you intend to dine here in summer or on the weekend, reserve well in advance. Pork is the fixation, particularly the regional *cinghiale alla Maremmana* (Maremma wild boar).

L'Osteria da Tronca
TRADITIONAL ITALIAN €€

(☎0566 90 19 91; Vicolo Porte 5; meals €26; ⊙closed Wed & mid-Dec–Feb) Squeezed into a side street (it's behind Hotel Il Sole), this stone-walled restaurant specialises in the rustic dishes of the Maremma. Specialities include *acquacotta* (a hearty vegetable soup with bread and egg), *tortelli alla maremma* (pasta parcels filled with ricotta and a type of spinach) and *coniglio in porchetta* (roasted stuffed rabbit).

Il Bacchino
[TOP CHOICE] WINE BAR

(Via Moncini 8; ⊙daily Mar-Jan, Tue-Sun Feb) Owner Magdy Lamei may not be a local (in fact, he's from Cairo), but it would be hard to find anyone else as knowledgeable and passionate about local artisanal produce. Come here to stock up on wine, honey, jams, cheese and meats, and while you're here settle in for a tasting in the upstairs wine bar (€12 for three glasses of wine and a tasting plate).

Le Logge
CAFE

(Piazza Garibaldi 11; ⊙6am-9.30pm daily Jul & Aug, 6am-midnight Wed-Mon Sep-Jun) The tables of

Massa's best cafe spill out under the loggia of a handsome *palazzo* opposite the *duomo*, a 19th-century replica of the original Sienese marketplace building that occupied this spot. The town's undoubted social hub, it's equally enticing for a coffee or a drink.

❶ Information

Tourist office (☎0566 90 47 56; www.turismo inmaremma.it; Via Todini 5-7; ☉9.30am-1pm & 2-6.30pm Tue-Sun) Located down a side street beneath the Museo Archeologico.

❶ Getting There & Away

Bus
The bus station is at Piazza del Risorgimento, 800 m down the hill from Piazza Garibaldi. There is one bus daily to Grosseto (€3.30, one hour), two to Siena (€4.70, two hours) at 7.05am and 4.40pm, and around four to Volterra (changing at Monterotondo Marittimo). **Massa Veternensis** (Piazza Garibaldi 18) sells both bus and train tickets.

Train
The nearest train station is Massa-Follonica in Follonica, 22km southwest of Massa, served by a regular shuttle bus (€2.30, 25 minutes, 10 daily).

Vetulonia

This windswept hilltop village 23km northwest of Grosseto seems to rise out of nothing from the surrounding plains. Originally an important Etruscan settlement, it was colonised by the Romans in 224 BC.

◉ Sights & Activities

TOP **CHOICE** **Museo Civico Archeologico 'Isidoro Falchi'** MUSEUM
(adult/child €4.50/2.50; ☉10am-2pm & 4-8pm Tue-Sat Jun-Sep, to 4pm Oct-Feb, to 6pm Mar-May, open daily Jul & Aug) The town's main piazza boasts spectacular views over the surrounding countryside and is home to this small but extremely impressive museum, which houses a rich display of artefacts revealed by excavations at the Scavi di Città (Town Excavations; admission free; ☉10.10am-6.50pm Apr-Sep, 8.30am-4.50pm winter), located just below the village on the main road, and at two Etruscan tombs (admission free; ☉10.10am-6.50pm summer, 8.30am-4.50pm winter), situated a couple of kilometres further downhill and along a turn-off to the right.

⛏ Sleeping

TOP **CHOICE** **Pieve di Caminino** AGRITURISMO €€
(☎0564 56 97 37; www.caminino.com; Via Provinciale di Peruzzo, Roccatederighi; ste from €110, apt from €90; ❄ P ⌘ ⌗) It would be a hard task to find another sleeping option to match the historic atmosphere at this now-decommissioned 11th-century monastery 25km northeast of Vetulonia. Set on a 200-hectare estate planted with olive trees and vines, it offers charmingly decorated suites and apartments sleeping up to five persons. All have sitting rooms and basic kitchens, two have air-con.

SOUTHERN TUSCANY VETULONIA

LOCAL KNOWLEDGE

DR SIMONA RAFANELLI: DIRECTOR, MUSEUM & NECROPOLIS, VETULONIA

I think I have the perfect job! I am the director of the Museo Civico Archeologico 'Isidoro Falchi' in the town of Vetulonia and of the necropolis just outside the town. I am also in charge of the ongoing excavations at the Scavi di Città, which are very exciting at the moment.

What's exciting about these excavations?
Since 2009 we have been slowly excavating the foundations of a 2300-year-old Etruscan *domus* (house). In 2010 we uncovered dry-stone walls, a brick floor, a small terracotta altar, plenty of amphorae and a small fragment of wall fresco. We now know that it is the most intact villa from the Etruscan-Roman era in existence, and our work has led us to believe that there are other houses, shops and temples still to be discovered here.

What should visitors look forward to seeing at the Museo Civico Archeologico?
We have made a big effort to bring Etruscan history to life in our museum. Everybody seems to love the exhibit we organised especially for blind visitors, where they can actually pick up and feel Etruscan artefacts including vases and bowls. I guess it's not every day that people have a chance to hold a 3000-year-old artefact in their hands!

Montebelli Agriturismo &
Country Hotel   AGRITURISMO €€
(📞0566 88 71 00; www.montebelli.com; Località
Molinetto Caldana; s €62-190, d €180-240, ste
€180-270; ⊙closed Jan-end Mar; ✱🅿️🛜🏊🐎) A
country-club feel prevails on this sprawling
wine and olive-oil estate halfway between
Grosseto and Massa Marittima and 10km
north of Vetulonia. The facilities are sensational – tennis court, two swimming pools
(one indoor, one outdoor), horse-riding lessons, pony rides for children, a welcoming
restaurant (five-course dinner adult/child
€30/15), sleek health centre and walking
tracks through the vineyards. Rooms are
extremely comfortable, but air-con is only
available in the newly constructed country
house. Wi-fi €4 per hour.

✕ Eating

La Vecchia Hosteria   TRADITIONAL ITALIAN €€
(Viale Marconi 249, Bagno di Gavorrano; meals €28;
⊙Fri-Wed) The unassuming exterior of this
neighbourhood eatery on Bagno di Gavorrano's main street gives no clue as to the
excellence of the food on offer inside. The
handmade pasta is sensational (be sure to
order the *tortelli di ricotta* if it's on offer)
and the rustic mains pack a flavoursome
punch. You'll find the town 4.5km downhill
from the Parco Minerario Naturalistico Gavorrano and 14km north of Vetulonia.

ℹ️ Getting There & Away

To get to Vetulonia, exit the SS1 at Montepes-
cali/Braccagni (heading towards Braccagni)
and follow the SP152 and SP72 uphill to the
village.

PAESE DEL TUFA (LAND OF THE TUFA)

The picturesque towns of Pitigliano, Sovana
and Sorano form a triangle enclosing a dramatic landscape where local buildings have
been constructed from the volcanic porous
rock called tufa since Etruscan times.

Pitigliano

POP 3970

Check your mirrors before screeching to a
halt and indulging in an orgy of photography on the approach to this spectacularly
sited hilltop stronghold. Organically sprouting from a volcanic rocky outcrop towering

over the surrounding country, the town is
surrounded by gorges on three sides, con-
stituting a natural bastion completed to the
east by a manmade fort. Within the town,
twisting stairways disappear around corners, cobbled alleys bend tantalisingly out
of sight beneath graceful arches and quaint
stone houses are crammed next to each other in higgledy-piggledy fashion.

Originally built by the Etruscans, Pitigliano came under Roman rule and then in turn
became a fiefdom of the wealthy Aldobrandeschi and Orsini families; the Orsinis, who
were from Rome, enlarged the fortress, rein-
forced the defensive walls and built the imposing aqueduct. Their rule came to an end
in 1608 when the town was absorbed into the
grand duchy under Cosimo I de' Medici.

In 1944, 88 local residents were killed and
many buildings were damaged during Allied
bombings. A plaque near Piazza della Repubblica commemorates the victims.

◎ Sights & Activities

Palazzo Orsini   MUSEUM
(Piazza della Fortezza; adult/child €4/2.50;
⊙10am-1pm & 3-7pm Tue-Sun May–mid-Oct, 10am-
1pm & 3-8pm daily Aug, 10am-1pm & 3-5pm Tue-
Sun mid-Oct–mid-Jan & Apr) Interlinked Piazza
Petruccioli and Piazza Garibaldi provide a
majestic walkway towards this 13th-century
castle, which was enlarged by the Orsinis in
the 16th century, eventually became the residence of the local bishop and is now home
to a museum. Its rooms are filled with an
eclectic collection of artworks and ecclesias-
tic oddments from churches in the diocese,
including an unattributed and extremely
unusual painting of Jesus being circumcised
and a 14th-century wooden *Madonna and
Child* statue by Jacopo della Quercia.

Museo Civico Archeologico
della Civiltà Etrusca   MUSEUM
(Piazza della Fortezza; adult/child €2.50/1.50;
⊙10am-5pm Mon & Thu-Sun Apr–mid-Jun, 10am-

ℹ️ COMBINED TICKET

If you're keen to investigate the area's
Etruscan heritage, buy the combined
ticket (adult/child €5.50/2.50) giving
entry to the Museo Civico Archeologico
della Civiltà Etrusca and the Museo
Archeologico all'Aperto 'Alberto Manzi'
outside town.

There are at least 15 rock-sculpted passages spreading out in every direction from the valleys below Pitigliano. These *vie cave* (sunken roads) are enormous – up to 20m deep and 3m wide – and are believed to be sacred routes linking the necropolises and other sites associated with the Etruscan religious cult. A less popular, more mundane explanation is that these strange megalithic corridors were used to move livestock or as some kind of defence, allowing people to move from village to village unseen. Whatever the reason, every spring on the night of the equinox (19 March) there is a torch-lit procession down the Via Cava di San Giuseppe, which culminates in a huge bonfire in Pitigliano's Piazza Garibaldi. Known as the **Torciata di San Giuseppe**, the procession serves as a symbol of purification and renewal marking the end of winter.

The countryside around Pitigliano, Sovana and Sorano is also riddled with *vie cave*. Two particularly good examples, 500m west of Pitigliano on the road to Sovana, are Via Cava di Fratenuti, with its high vertical walls and Etruscan markings, and Via Cava di San Giuseppe, which passes the Fontana dell'Olmo, carved out of solid rock. From this fountain stares the sculpted head of Bacchus, the mythological god of fruitfulness, as the water flows from his mouth.

There's a fine walk from Pitigliano to Sovana (8km) that incorporates parts of the *vie cave*. For a description and map of the walk, go to www.trekking.it and download the pdf in the Maremma section. There's also an enjoyable 2km walk from the small stone bridge in the gorge below Sorano along the Via Cava San Rocco (2km) to the Necropoli di San Rocco, another Etruscan burial site.

The open-air **Museo Archeologico all'Aperto 'Alberto Manzi'** (adult/child €4/2; ☺10am-3pm Mon-Fri, to 6pm Sat & Sun), south of Pitigliano on the road to Saturnia, contains sections of *vie cave* and several necropolises.

5pm Wed-Mon 2nd half of Jun & Sep, 10am-7pm daily Jul & Aug, 10am-5pm Thu-Mon Oct) Accessed via a stone staircase opposite the entrance to Palazzo Orsini, this small but well-run museum has a rich display of finds from local Etruscan sites. Highlights include some huge intact *bucchero* (black earthenware pottery) urns dating from the 6th century BC and a collection of charming pinkish-cream clay oil containers in the form of small deer.

La Piccola Gerusalemme   MUSEUM
(Little Jerusalem; www.lapiccolagerusalemme.it; Vicolo Manin 30; adult/reduced €3/2; ☺10am-1.30pm & 2.30-6.30pm Sun-Fri Apr-Sep, 10am-12.30pm & 3-5.30pm Sun-Fri Oct-Mar) In the course of the 16th century, a Jewish community settled in Pitigliano, increasing notably when Pope Pius IV banned Jews from Rome in 1569. Under Medici rule, its members were moved into a tiny ghetto, where they remained until 1772. From then until well into the following century, the local community of 400 flourished, forming the largest Jewish community in Italy and leading to the town being dubbed 'Little Jerusalem'. By the time the Fascists introduced the race laws in 1938, most Jews had moved away; only 80 or so were left and precious few survived the war. Those that did survive were hidden from the Fascists by locals.

To visit the old Jewish ghetto, head down Via Zuccarelli and turn left at a sign indicating La Piccola Gerusalemme, a small museum of Jewish culture incorporating a tiny, richly adorned synagogue (established in 1598 and one of only five in Tuscany), ritual bath, kosher butcher, bakery, wine cellar and dyeing workshops.

★ Festivals and Events

Wines including the town's signature Bianco di Pitigliano, a dry and lively white varietal, are celebrated each year over the first weekend in September at **Settembre diVino – Festa delle Cantine** (Festival of the Wine Cellars; www.cantineneltufo.org).

⎑ Sleeping

Le Camere del Ceccottino   PENSIONE €
(☎0564 61 49 26; Via Roma 159; r €80-100; ❀ ⊛) Everything is brand-spanking new in this recently opened *pensione*. A new venture by the owners of the nearby Ceccottino restaurant, its excellent location near the *duomo*

1. Vie Cave, Pitigliano (p245)
The Via Cava San Rocca forms part of the Etruscan *vie cave* (sunken roads).

2. Monte Argentario (p253)
Scenic cove near Porto Ercole, which lies on the southern side of Monte Argentario.

3. Pitigliano (p244)
Pitigliano is set above a spectacular, rugged hilltop.

4. Massa Marittima (p240)
Buildings in the historic Old Town district at Massa Marittima.

and well-equipped rooms (satellite TV, tea-and-coffee-making facilities, comfortable beds) make it a great choice. Opt for the superior or prestige room if possible, as the standard versions are slightly cramped. No breakfast.

Il Tufo Rosa
PENSIONE €

(☑0564 61 70 19; www.iltuforosa.com; Piazza Petruccioli 97-101; s €40-42, d €65-75; ❄🏠) The lady owner of this old-fashioned *pensione* is very proud of her spick-n-span rooms, each of which is individually decorated and named after an Aldobrandeschi, Orsini or Medici countess. The rooms are located in an old bastion of the fortress on Piazza Petruccioli, conveniently near the town's main bus stop and opposite its best cafe. No breakfast, and air-con is only available in a few rooms.

Locanda Pantanello
RURAL INN €€

(☑0564 61 67 15; www.pantanello.it; Località Pantano; s €45-60, d €90-120; 🅿🐾) Six kilometres southeast of town, this country inn offers five simple rooms, a restaurant (dinner €45), horse-riding opportunities and a large swimming pool. No credit cards.

✖ Eating & Drinking

Il Tufo Allegro
TRADITIONAL ITALIAN €€

(☑0564 61 61 92; Vicolo della Costituzione 5; 3-course menus €22-24; ⊙closed Tue & Wed lunch) The aromas emanating from the kitchen door facing Via Zuccarelli should be enough to draw you down to the cavernous dining room, which is carved out of tufa foundations. The chef is known for his *menù Goym* (Gentiles menu), which features Jewish-influenced dishes such as *buglione d'agnello* (lamb soup with tomato and bread). You'll find it near Piccola Gerusalemme.

Hostaria del
Ceccottino
TRADITIONAL ITALIAN €€

(☑0564 61 42 73; Piazza San Gregorio VII 64; meals €36; ⊙Fri-Wed) Nestled in the shadow of the Baroque *duomo*, Ceccottino subscribes to both the Slow Food philosophy and the Km0 movement. It specialises in pasta, steaks and carpaccio. Tables on the piazza are hotly contested during summer.

La Cantina Incantata
WINE BAR

(Piazza Petruccioli 68; ⊙closed Wed afternoon) As well as being the best people-watching spot in town, this welcoming *cantina* is a perfect spot to enjoy a glass of wine and snack on local meats and cheeses.

ℹ Information

Staff in the **tourist office** (☑0564 61 71 11; www.comune.pitigliano.gr.it, in Italian; Piazza Garibaldi; ⊙9.30am-1pm & 4-7pm Tue-Sun Apr-Sep, 9.30am-1pm & 3-6pm Tue-Sun Oct-Mar) speak Italian only and were disinterested in assisting visitors when we last visited. If you're in need of advice or assistance, the staff at the Sovana or Sorano *fortezza* (fortress) offices are your best bets.

ℹ Getting There & Away

Bus

Rama Mobilità (☑199 848787; www.rama mobilita.it, in Italian) buses travel between Via Santa Chiara, just off Piazza Petruccioli, and Grosseto five times daily (€5.20, two hours). There's also one daily service to Siena (€7.90, three hours) and one or two services daily to Sorano (€1.20, 15 minutes) and Sovana (€1.20, 20 minutes). Buy tickets at Il Golosone next to the bus stop.

Car

There are plenty of free car parks around town; look for white lines. Alternatively, the car park near Piazza Petruccioli charges €0.50 per hour.

Sovana

The main attractions here are a very pretty main street and two austerely beautiful Romanesque churches; a museum of Roman times is planned to open in the future. Two significant archaeological sites are located just outside town, and Pitigliano is accessed via one of the most popular walks in Tuscany, some of which follows Etruscan *vie cave*.

◎ Sights

Duomo
DUOMO

(⊙daily summer, Sat & Sun rest of year) Built over a 200-year period starting in the 1100s, this Romanesque cathedral was commissioned by local boy-made-big Pope Gregory VII (Hildebrand of Sovana; c 1015–85). Its strangely positioned doorway is decorated with carvings of people, animals and plants, and its huge interior has a beauty that owes nothing to artworks and everything to the genius of its architect. A downstairs crypt houses relics of San Mamilianus, who preached in the district in the 6th century.

Santa Maria Maggiore
CHURCH

(⊙daily summer, Sat & Sun rest of year) Designed in a Romanesque-Gothic transitional style, this church is notable for the 16th-century frescoes in the apse and an unusual and quite lovely stone *ciborium* (vaulted canopy over the altar) dating from the 9th century.

✘ Eating

La Tavernetta   TRATTORIA
(Via del Pretorio 3; meals €22, pizzas €4-6; ⊘daily summer, Wed-Mon rest of year) Serving traditional Maremmana dishes all day and pizzas from its wood-fired oven at night, this casual eatery near the tourist office is a safe choice for a simple meal.

❶ Information

The extremely helpful **tourist office** (☏0564 61 40 74; ⊘10am-1pm & 3-7pm daily summer only) is in the Palazzo Pretorio on the main piazza.

❶ Getting There & Away

BUS Rama Mobilità buses travel to/from Pitigliano (€1.20, 15 minutes) and Sorano (€1.20, 15 minutes) once or twice daily.
CAR The car park at the entrance to town charges €0.50 per hour.

Around Sovana

Tuscany's most significant Etruscan tombs are found within the **Parco Archeologico della Città del Tufa** (Necropoli di Sovana; www.leviecave.it; admission €5; ⊘9am-7pm Tue-Sun late-Mar-Oct, 10am-5pm Fri-Sun Dec-Feb), 1.5km south of town. Interpretative panels in Italian and English impart interesting information about the site.

There are four tombs in total. The **Tomba dei Demoni Alati** (Tomb of the Winged Demons) was discovered in 2004 and features a headless recumbent figure in terracotta. The carving of a sea demon with huge wings

that was the original centrepiece of the tomb is now protected in a roofed enclosure nearby. The **Tomba Ildebranda**, named after Gregory VII, still preserves traces of its carved columns and stairs and is the park's headline exhibit. The **Tomba del Tifone** (Tomb of the Typhoon) is about 300m down a trail running alongside a rank of tomb facades cut from the rock face. Two arresting lengths of *via cave* (one known as 'Cavone' and the other 'Poggio Prisca') are nearby.

On the opposite side of the site is the **Tomba della Sirena** and another *via cava* ('San Sebastiano'), which was closed due to safety concerns at the time of research.

At the **Area Archeologica di Vitozza** (admission free; ⊘always open), due east of the village and signposted from the main square, you will find more than 200 rock caves peppering a high rock ridge. One of the largest troglodyte dwellings in Italy, the complex was first inhabited in prehistoric times. To explore the site, you'll need two hours and sturdy walking shoes.

Sorano

Sorano's setting isn't quite as dramatic as Pitigliano's, but it comes close. On a rocky outcrop, its weatherworn stone houses are built along a ridge overlooking the Lente gorge and river. Below the ridgeline are *cantine* (cellars) dug out of tufa, as well as a series of terraced gardens, many hidden from public view.

◎ Sights & Activities

If you're planning to visit both Sorano's *fortezza* and the Parco Archeologico della Città del Tufa outside Sorana, a combined ticket (€7) will save you money.

WORTH A TRIP

SATURNIA

The sulphurous thermal baths at **Terme di Saturnia** (www.termedisaturnia.it; day admission €44, after 3pm €39; ⊘9.30am-7.30pm Apr-Oct, to 5.30pm Nov-Mar; **P**) are 2.5km downhill from the village. You can happily do as the Romans did and spend a whole day dunking yourself in the hot pools and indulging in spa treatments at this luxury resort, or you can take the econo-bather option and avail yourself of the waters running parallel to the road for several hundred metres, starting just south of the Terme di Saturnia turn-off. Look for the telltale sign of other bathers' cars parked on the road, then forage down the dirt path until you find a suitable spot of gratis cascading water, with temperatures at a constant 37.5°C. Another alternative is to overnight in the **Hotel Saturno Fontepura** (☏0564 60 13 13; www.hotelsaturnofontepura.it; s €95-100, d €130-180; **P ✳ 🛜 ☎**), a spa resort with its own thermal pool. It's on the highway overlooking the *terme* (thermal baths).

Fortezza Orsini HISTORICAL BUILDING
(admission €4; ⊙guided tours 10.30am, 11.30am, 3.30pm, 4.30pm & 5.30pm) Standing sentinel over the town, this massive fortress was built in the 11th century and added to over the centuries. It has two bastions connected by sturdy walls and surrounded by a dry moat. You can visit a few of its frescoed rooms, but the highlight of any visit here would have to be a guided tour of the subterranean passages.

🛏 Sleeping

Hotel della Fortezza HOTEL €€
(☑0564 63 20 10; www.fortezzahotel.it; Piazza Cairoli 5; r €100-155; 🅿) Fancy the idea of sleeping in a medieval castle? If so, this comfortable hotel inside one of the fortress' bastions is just what you're looking for. Many of its 16 rooms have spectacular views, but the best is undoubtedly the massive Tower Room (€130 to €155).

🍴 Eating & Drinking

Hostaria Terrazza Aldobrandeschi MODERN ITALIAN €€
(☑0564 63 86 99; www.hostaria-aldobrandeschi. com, in Italian; Via del Borgo 44; 4-course set menu €35; ⊙Wed-Sun, closed Jan) With a terrace overlooking the Lente Valley and a menu featuring dishes constructed using organic, local and Slow Food–endorsed produce, this place earns its reputation as the area's best restaurant. Booking is advisable.

Cantina L'Ottava Rima WINE BAR
(www.cantinaottavarimait, in Italian; Via del Borgo 25; ⊙variable) Carved out of the tufa, this casual *cantina* is a great place to sample local wine and simple dishes (antipasto plates €12) that highlight quality Maremmese produce.

ℹ Information

The main **tourist office** (☑0564 63 30 99; ⊙10am-1pm & 3-6pm Thu-Tue) is at the *fortezza*; a second branch in the centre of town is nowhere near as helpful.

MOVING ON?

For tips, recommendations and reviews, head to shop.lonelyplanet com to purchase a downloadable PDF of the Rome & Lazio chapter from Lonely Planet's *Italy* guide.

ℹ Getting There & Away

BUS Rama Mobilità buses travel between Pitigliano, Sovana and Sorano once or twice daily (€1.20).
CAR The car park outside the Town Hall charges €0.50 per hour from 8am to 1pm and 3pm to 8pm daily. Parking at the *fortezza* is free.

THE BASSA MAREMMA

The Bassa (Lower) Maremma starts at Grosseto and travels along the coast, incorporating the peninsula of Monte Argentario, the Parco Regionale della Maremma and two biologically diverse WWF reserves.

Grosseto
POP 80,700

Poor Grosseto. Its uninviting name, unattractive surrounds and lack of headline sites lead to it being ignored by most tourists, relegated to a mere navigational marker for travellers taking the coastal highway down to Rome. However, it – like most Tuscan cities – has a distinct charm and is worth a short stop.

One of the last Siena-dominated towns to fall into Medici hands (in 1559), Grosseto's bastions, fortress and hexagonal-shaped walls were raised by the Florentines in order to protect what was then an important grain and salt depot for the grand duchy. These days the city is the provincial capital of the Maremma and its *centro storico* (historic centre) is one of the rare places in Tuscany where the oft-proclaimed 'no car zone' means almost that, making it a perfect place to wander during the day and experience the *passeggiata* (evening stroll) along Corso Carducci.

◉ Sights & Activities

Cattedrale di San Lorenzo DUOMO
(Piazza del Duomo; ⊙7.30am-noon & 3.30-7pm) Dating from the late 13th century, Grosseto's *duomo* has a distinctive Sienese air and a particularly beautiful rose window on the facade. Dedicated to St Lawrence, the city's patron saint, the building has been altered over time, with much of the facade renewed along neo-Romanesque lines during the 19th century. Inside, look for the baptismal font, which dates from 1470; the *Madonna delle Grazie* in the left transept, part of a

larger painting by Sienese artist Matteo di Giovanni; and the two 15th-century stained-glass windows depicting saints.

Next door, on Piazza Dante, the Palazzo della Provincia seems to be Sienese Gothic, which is exactly what its early 20th-century architects hoped you might think.

Museo Archeologico e d'Arte della Maremma
MUSEUM

(Piazza Baccarini 3; adult/child €5/2.50; ⊘10am-7pm Tue-Sat, 10am-1pm & 4-7pm Sun summer, 9am-5pm Tue-Sat, 10am-1pm & 4-7pm Sun winter) Grosseto's major tourist drawcard, this complex houses an archaeological museum on the ground floor and a museum of ecclesiastical art upstairs. On show are Etruscan and Roman artefacts unearthed from Roselle, Vetulonia and other Etruscan sites, as well as an impressive collection of paintings from the 13th to 17th centuries.

Museo di Storia Naturale della Maremma
MUSEUM

(www.museonaturalemaremma.it; Strada Corsini 5; adult/student/family €5/2/12; ⊘9am-1pm Wed-Fri, 9am-1pm & 4-8pm Sat, 4-8pm Sun) This newly opened museum of natural history faces Piazza Pacciardi, close to the Medici fortress. It showcases specimens including rocks and minerals, insects, birds, shells and fossils from the local area, the rest of Europe and some tropical areas.

Roselle
ARCHAEOLOGICAL SITE

(adult/student/child €4/2/free; ⊘8.30am-7pm May-Aug, to 6.30pm Mar, Apr-Sep & Oct, to 5.30pm Nov-Feb) Less than 7km northeast of Grosseto's centro storico, Roselle (Rusellae) was a middle-ranking Etruscan town populated as early as the 7th century BC. It came under Roman control in the 3rd century BC.

Although there are no great monuments left standing, the site retains its Roman defensive walls, an oddly elliptical amphitheatre, traces of houses, the forum and streets. You will also find remains of an abandoned medieval village. There are wonderful views down to the plains and out to the sea.

To get here, take Via Senese (SS223).

✖ Eating

Rosso e Vino
MODERN ITALIAN €€

(Piazza Pacciardi; meals €26; ⊘lunch & dinner Mon-Sat, wine bar 5pm-late) Owned by Fattoria Le Pupille, a highly regarded local winery, this sleek enoteca (wine bar) is Grosseto's style hub, and a great place to enjoy a meal

or aperitivo. The restaurant seating spills out onto Piazza Pacciardi, and the enoteca entrance is around the corner on Via Garibaldi. The excellent wine list is perfectly complemented by light tapas-style dishes.

Il Canto del Gallo
TRADITIONAL ITALIAN €€

(☏0564 41 45 89; Via Mazzini 29; meals €35; ⊘dinner Mon-Sat, lunch bookings only) If you're after a traditional Maremmese meal, head to the 'Cock Crow', which serves reliable food in an interior decorated with every possible variant upon the cockerel (rooster) theme, even down to the stoppers used on the grappa decanters.

⌨ Sleeping

There are very few decent accommodation options in Grosseto, so most visitors choose to stay in nearby agriturismi.

Grand Hotel Bastiani
HOTEL €€

(☏0564 2 00 47; www.hotelbastiani.com; Piazza Gioberti 64; s €78-110, d €115-180; ❀@☎) This old-fashioned hotel is located just inside the main gate into the centro storico, conveniently close to a public car park. Housed within a grand old building complete with a Gone with the Wind–type dance-down-me staircase, it offers comfortable rooms, efficient and friendly service, and a lavish buffet breakfast. Wi-fi €4 per hour.

⌂ Shopping

TOP CHOICE Dolci Tradizioni dalla Maremma Toscana
FOOD

(Via Garibaldi 60; ⊘daily) Specialising in local delicacies including lo sfratto, a traditional Jewish pastry made with honey and walnuts, this wonderful pasticceria (pastry shop) opposite the Medici fortress makes all of its products by hand and sells them in beautifully wrapped packages.

ⓘ Information

There is a **tourism information point** (☏0564 48 82 08; www.turismomaremma.it; Corso Carducci 1; ⊘9am-1pm & 4-7pm Mon-Thu, 9am-1pm & 5-8pm Fri & Sat) close to the duomo.

ⓘ Getting There & Away

Bus

Buses usually leave from the train station. There is only one direct bus daily to Massa Marittima (€3.30, one hour). Other destinations include Porto Santo Stefano (€3.80, one hour, three daily), Pitigliano (€5.20, two hours, five daily) and Siena (€6.60, 75 minutes, 13 daily).

Car

A Limited Traffic Zone (ZTL) applies in the *centro storico*. There's plenty of paid car parking surrounding the city walls; the most convenient is next to the city gate on Viale Zimenes, near Piazza Lamaremma (per hour €1).

Train

The main coastal train line runs between Rome (€25, 90 minutes) and Pisa (€20, 75 minutes), via Grosseto and Livorno (€20, one hour). The high-speed *Frecciabianca* runs between Rome and Genoa, stopping at Grosseto, Livorno (€20, one hour) and Pisa (€20, 75 minutes) en route. There are also nine direct *regionale* services to Siena daily (€6.70, 1½ hours), but you'll need to change trains at Pisa for Florence (€12.50, three hours).

Parco Regionale della Maremma

This spectacular regional park (www.parco -maremma.it; adult €6-15, reduced €4-12) incorporates the Uccellina mountain range, a 600-hectare pine forest, marshy plains and a 20km stretch of unspoiled coastline. The main visitor centre (☑0564 40 70 98; Via del Bersagliere 7-9; ◷8am-8.30pm mid-Jun–mid-Sep, 8.30am-5.30pm mid-Sep–mid Jun) is in Alberese, on the park's northern edge. A smaller visitor centre adjoins the Talamone Aquarium (☑0564 88 71 73; Via Nizza 24; ◷8.30am-noon & 5.30am-8pm mid-Jun–mid-Sep, 8.30am-5.30pm mid-Sep–mid Jun) at the park's southern extremity (the aquarium showcases the local lagoon environment and works to safeguard local turtles).

Park access is limited to 11 signed walking trails, varying in length from 2.5km to 13km; the most popular is A2 ('Le Torri'), a 5.8km walk to the beach. The entry fee (paid at the visitor centres) varies according to whether a park-operated bus transports you from the visitor centre to your chosen route. From 15 June to 15 September the park can only be visited on a guided tour due to possible bushfire threat. At the time of research these tours were being conducted in French on Tuesdays, German on Wednesdays and English on Fridays (all at 4pm), but it is wise to call ahead to check language and time.

As well as the walking trails, there is bicycle hire (per half-/full day €7/11) and a guided canoe trail (adult/reduced €16/10). A number of private operators offer horse and pony treks through the park – contact the Centro Turismo Equestre Il Gelsomino (☑347

ℹ️ **A TASTE OF SOUTHERN TUSCANY**

For itinerary ideas, check out the three online resources for *strade del vino e dei sapori* (wine and speciality products routes) in this part of Southern Tuscany: the Strada del Vino e dei Sapori Colli di Maremma (www. stradavinimaremma.it), the Strada del Vino e dei Sapori Monteregio di Massa Marittima (www.stradavino.it) and the Strada del Vino Montecucco e dei Sapori d'Amiata (www. stradadelvinomontecucco.it, in Italian). The first lists wine and food-related events in the Maremma and the other two provide a wealth of information about accommodation, restaurants, and food and wine producers in the areas around Massa Marittima and Monte Amiata.

7776476) or Tenuta Agricola dell'Uccellina Scuderia di Maremma (☑0564 59 71 04; www.tenutauccellina.it).

There are free tastings of local food and wine four times daily (mid-June to mid-September) in the upstairs *degustazion* (tasting) room at the Alberese visitor centre. Opposite the centre are a bar-cafe and I Briganti al Parco (antipasti €2.50-9, pasta & soup €8), a small and friendly *enoteca* with variable opening hours where you can grab a sandwich, *antipasto* plate or pasta accompanied by a glass of locally produced wine.

Parts of the regional park are farmed as they have been for centuries, mainly to graze the famous Maremma breed of cattle. The huge Agienza Regionale Agricola di Alberese (☑0564 40 71 80; www.alberese.com; Via della Spergolaia) farm operation produces beef, wine, olive oil and its own organic pasta and is a regional headquarters for the Slow Food organisation. It offers a Farm Experience (€25-40; ◷10am-1pm Thu summer), including an introduction to the work of the Maremma's famed *butteri* (traditional cowboys) and tastings of farm produce. Experienced horse riders can also sign up for a full day's work experience with a *buttero* (€50; daily from 7am to 7pm). The farm's fattoria (◷8.30am-12.30pm & 4.30-7.30pm Tue, Thu & Fri-Sun), located near the Alberese visitor centre, sells its own products and those of other Slow Food–accredited producers. It's a great place to stock up on supplies if you're self-catering (its Morellino di Scansano – a robust red wine – costs a mere €1.55 per litre, so bring a couple of bottles to fill!).

The *agienza* offers accommodation at the Fattoria Granducale (www.alberese.com/ita/villa; B&B d €180 per Sat & Sun, self-catering apt €255-310), a 15th-century villa once owned by Grand Duke Leopoldo II of Lorraine. It also rents out simple apartments (d/t/q €150/200/250) in the surrounding farm buildings.

Orbetello

POP 15,200

Set on a balance-beam isthmus running through the lagoon, Orbetello is a relatively laid-back seaside destination. Its modest main attraction is the cathedral (Piazza della Repubblica; ⊙9am-noon & 3-6pm), which has retained its 14th-century Gothic facade despite being remodelled in the Spanish style during the 16th century. Other reminders of the Spanish garrison that was stationed in the city for nearly 150 years include the viceroy's residence on Piazza Eroe dei Due Mondi, the fort and the city walls, parts of which are the original Etruscan fortification.

The best place for observing bird life on Orbetello Lagoon (where as many as 140 species have been identified) is at the Riserva Naturale Laguna di Orbetello (Località Ceriolo; www.wwf.it; 2hr guided tours adult/reduced

€8/6; ⊙guided visits 9.30am & 1.30pm Sat & Sun Sep-Apr) north of town, which is owned and operated by the Italian branch of the WWF.

Monte Argentario

POP 13,000

Once an island, this rugged promontory came to be linked to the mainland by an accumulation of sand that is now the isthmus of Orbetello. Further sandy bulwarks form the Tombolo della Giannella and Tombolo di Feniglia to the north and south. They enclose a lagoon that is now a protected nature reserve. Sadly, overdevelopment has spoiled the northern side of the promontory, particularly around the crowded harbour of Porto Santo Stefano, a favourite weekend getaway for Romans in the summer. Ambitious hotel and restaurant prices make it poor value in the high season, and parking is cutthroat; we suggest visiting on a day trip and then hightailing it inland for accommodation options.

If you're driving, follow signs for the narrow and sometimes dangerously overcrowded Via Panoramica, a circular route offering great coastal views over the water to the hazy whaleback of the Isola de Giglio.

There are several good beaches, mainly of the pebbly variety, just to the east and west of Porto Santo Stefano.

On the less-crowded southern side of the promontory is Porto Ercole, a smaller and more attractive harbour nestled between three Spanish forts. Here you can wander the hillside *centro storico* past the sandwiched Chiesa di Sant'Erasmo and up towards the largest of the fortresses. Down by the water, the beach is relatively clean but is cluttered with deck chairs and umbrellas.

✕ Eating & Drinking

Il Pellicano   GASTRONOMIC €€€

(☎0564 83 81 11; www.pellicanohotel.com; Località Lo Sbarcatello, Porto Ercole; set menu €125; ⊙dinner daily Apr-Oct) Proud possessor of two Michelin stars (one of only four such recipients in Tuscany), this classy restaurant at the five-star hotel of the same name specialises in seafood and has two outdoor terraces with spectacular views. There's also a less-expensive poolside grill and bar here.

Giulia   CAFE €

(Via del Molo 16/17, Porto Santo Stefano; ⊙6.30am-4am Tue-Sun, daily summer) Almost at the end of the *lungomare* (port promenade), Porto

WORTH A TRIP

GIARDINO DEI TAROCCHI

Twenty-two oversized Gaudí-influenced sculptures tumble down a hillside at this fantastic sculpture garden (www.nikidesaintphalle.com; Località Garavicchio-Capalbio; adult/reduced €10.50/6, free 1st Sat of month 9am-1pm Jan-Mar & Nov-Dec; ⊙2.30-7.30pm Apr–mid-Oct) created by Franco-American artist Niki de Saint Phalle (1930–2002). On a theme-park scale, the whimsical, mosaic-covered sculptures skilfully merge with surrounding nature, creating what the artist described as a 'garden of joy'. The colossal effort depicts the main players from the tarot card pack – the Moon, the Fool, Justice, the Falling Tower etc – and include one used by de Saint Phalle as a home during the garden's construction. Sculptor Jean Tinguely contributed moving sculptural elements to many of the figures and the visitor centre was designed by Swiss architect Mario Botta. Your interest in divination notwithstanding, these pleasing exhibits transcend aesthetic leanings and are particularly popular with young children. To get here, take the Pescia Fiorentina exit from the SS1.

Santo Sefano's best cafe is a great spot for a morning coffee, *panino* (sandwich) lunch or late-afternoon *aperitivo*.

ⓘ Information

Orbetello tourist office (☎0564 86 09 13; Piazza Giovanni Paolo II 2; ⊙9am-1pm & 4-8pm) Opposite the cathedral and has maps of the town and region.

Porto Santo Stefano tourist office (☎0564 81 42 08; www.lamaremma.info; Piazzale Sant'Andrea; ⊙9am-1pm & 4-8pm) Appallingly located at the eastern end of the port.

ⓘ Getting There & Away

BUS Frequent Rama Mobilità buses connect most towns on Monte Argentario with central Orbetello (€1.80, 20 minutes) and continue to the train station. They also run to Grosseto (€3.80, one hour, up to four daily).

CAR & MOTORCYCLE If driving, follow signs for Monte Argentario from the SS1, which connects Grosseto with Rome.

Riserva Naturale WWF Lago di Burano

This saltwater flat 10km east of Monte Argentario is home to a nature reserve (☎0564 89 88 29; www.wwf.it; Capalbio Scalo; free admission, 2hr guided tour adult/reduced

€8/6; ⊙visitor centre 8.30am-1pm & 2.30-8pm daily Sep-Apr, guided visits 10am & 2.30pm or 3pm Sun Sep-Apr) run by the WWF. Covering 410 hectares and stopping about 7km short of the regional frontier with Lazio, it is typical of the Maremma in its flora (600 species including spontaneous orchids) but is interesting above all for its migratory bird life. Tens of thousands of birds of 283 species winter here, including several kinds of duck, flamingos, hen harriers and even falcons. There's a tame kestrel that responds to the ranger's call and a butterfly garden next to the visitor centre.

There's a short, flat trail from the visitor centre to the lake as well as a wheelchair-friendly path with seven observation points, accessed only by guided tour.

Birdwatchers wanting to overnight here can stay in the basic accommodation (dm €25), which offers a few bedrooms, communal kitchen and small lounge.

The reserve is easily accessed by train from Grosseto. Alight at Capalbio (€4.20, 40 minutes, 11 daily) and walk 300m through the underground passage to the visitor centre. By car, take the Capalbio Scalo exit from the SS1, enter town, veer right when you reach the train station, drive until you reach an underpass on your left and then follow the signs to the reserve.

Eastern Tuscany

Best Places to Eat

» Da Mengrello (p274)

» Toscana Twist (p268)

» Ristorante Da Ventura (p266)

» Ristorante Fiorentino (p266)

» Il Goccino (p274)

Best Places to Stay

» Villa Fontelunga (p262)

» Borgo Corsignano (268)

» Il Borro (p262)

» Casa Chilenne (p273)

» Graziella Patio Hotel (p262)

Why Go?

There are two good reasons why so many local and international directors have chosen this part of Tuscany as a film location: its scenery offers oh-wow moments galore, and the excellent food, wine and accommodation on offer is the perfect bribe to ensure happy cooperation on a shoot. Up until now, visitor numbers have been largely limited to domestic tourists and these film crews, but we highly recommend that you buck this trend and devote a week or so to exploring here. The rewards are many and varied: spectacular mountain scenery and walks in the Casentino; magnificent art and architecture in the medieval cities of Arezzo, Sansepolcro and Cortona; and Tuscany's best *bistecca alla fiorentina* (chargrilled T-bone steak) in the Val di Chiana. Your travels will be often solitary but always rewarding – a particularly unusual and felicitous combination.

When to Go

Temperatures plummet and many hotels close in this corner of Tuscany over the winter months, so you are best off travelling at other times of the year. Summer is particularly alluring, as the cool Casentino forest offers shady walking tracks, and the historical centres of Arezzo and Cortona stage colourful medieval pageants. Autumn is the pilgrimage season at the important Franciscan sites of Assisi (in neighbouring Umbria) and the Santuario della Verna in the Casentino – book accommodation well in advance if you plan to visit on 4 October, the saint's feast day.

Best Museums

» **Museo Civico, Sansepolcro** (p264) Home to three magnificent paintings by Piero della Francesca.

» **Museo Diocesano, Cortona** (p271) Has a small but sensational collection of religious art.

» **Casa Museo di Ivan Bruschi, Arezzo** (p261) Showcases an antique dealer's eclectic personal collection.

Medieval Pageants

» Giostra del Saracino, Arezzo (p262)

» Palio della Ballestra, Sansepolcro (p264)

» Giostra dell'Archidado, Cortona (p273)

Resources

» Casentino: www.casentino.net

» Eventi & Turismo: www.eventiturismo.it, in Italian

» Provincia di Arezzo: www.turismo.provincia.arezzo.it

Itineraries

Lights, Camera, Action In recent years, three major films have been set in this region. Roberto Benigni filmed scenes of *La vita è bella* (Life is Beautiful) in Arezzo and Cortona, Anthony Minghella shot the most memorable scene of *The English Patient* in Arezzo's Cappella Bacci and Audrey Wells shot much of *Under the Tuscan Sun* in Cortona. Both cities well and truly live up to their cinematic selves.

The della Robbia Trail The famous family of sculptors took ceramics way beyond teacups in the 15th century, creating magnificent devotional sculptures for churches throughout the region. Start in the Casentino, where you can visit the Sacro Eremo di Camaldoli and Santuario della Verna, home to works by the most famous member of the family, Andrea. Next, move on to Sansepolcro, where you can admire another of Andrea's pieces in the Museo Civico by day and enjoy a meal at Ristorante Da Ventura or Ristorante Fiorentino at night – both restaurants also offer accommodation.

Val di Chiana Home to apple orchards, olive groves and lush pastures where porcelain-white Chianina cattle graze, this huge valley in the southern section of eastern Tuscany is worth exploring when travelling between Arezzo and Cortona, or from either town to central Tuscany. Base yourself at Villa Fontelunga or Il Borro to the west of Arezzo, and spend your days wandering the cobbled streets and lingering over lunch at towns such as Castiglion Fiorentino, Cortona, Foiano della Chiana and Lucignano.

Where to Stay

Most destinations in the region are an easy day trip apart, so we suggest basing yourself at a rural *agriturismo* or villa and exploring by car. If you are travelling by public transport, Arezzo and Cortona are the most convenient bases.

AREZZO

POP 99,500

Arezzo may not be a Tuscan centrefold, but those parts of its historic centre that survived merciless WWII bombings are as compelling as any destination in the region. A setting for two Oscar-winning films – Anthony Minghella's *The English Patient* and Roberto Benigni's *La vita è bella* (Life is Beautiful) – its photogenic historic centre is well worth a visit.

Once an important Etruscan trading post, Arezzo was later absorbed into the Roman Empire. A free republic as early as the 10th century, it supported the Ghibelline cause in the violent battles between pope and emperor and was eventually subjugated by Florence in 1384.

Today, the city is known for its churches, museums and shopping – Arentini (residents of Arezzo) flock to the huge antiques fair held in Piazza Grande on the first weekend of every month, and love nothing more than combining the *passeggiata* with a spot of upmarket retail therapy on Corso Italia.

The birthplace of two great Renaissance figures – the poet Petrarch and the painter, architect and art historian, Giorgio Vasari – it has a long and very proud reputation as an important cultural centre.

⊙ Sights & Activities

TOP CHOICE Cappella Bacci CHURCH

(www.pierodellafrancesca.it; Piazza San Francesco; adult/reduced €6/4; ⊙9am-6.30pm Mon-Fri, to 5.30pm Sat & 1-5.30pm Sun Apr-Oct, 9am-5.30pm Mon-Fri, to 5pm Sat & 1-5pm Sun Nov-Mar) Gracing the apse of the 14th-century **Chiesa di San Francesco** is one of the greatest works of Italian art, Piero della Francesca's fresco cycle of the *Legend of the True Cross*. Painted between 1452 and 1466, it relates in 10 episodes the story of the cross on which Christ was crucified. It was named in honour of the wealthy family that commissioned it.

The illustration of this medieval legend, as entertaining as it is inconceivable, begins in the top right-hand corner and follows the story of the tree that Seth plants on the grave of his father, Adam, and from which, eventually, the True Cross is made. A scene on the opposite wall shows the long-lost cross being rediscovered by Helena, mother of the emperor Constantine; behind her, the city of Jerusalem is represented by a medieval view of Arezzo. Other scenes show the

	Castiglion Fiorentino	Arezzo	Cortona	Sansepolcro
Arezzo	18			
Cortona	12	29		
Sansepolcro	40	38	52	
Poppi	51	33	60	71

victory of Heraclius over the Persian king Khosrau, who had been accused of stealing the cross; and Constantine sleeping in a tent on the eve of his battle with Maxentius – the following scene shows the emperor carrying the cross into the battle itself.

Two of the best-loved scenes depict the Queen of Sheba kneeling on a bridge over the Siloam River and meeting with King Solomon; she and her attendants are depicted wearing rich Renaissance-style gowns, and King Solomon's palace seems to be modelled on the designs of notable architect Leon Battista Alberti.

Rarely will you get a better sense of medieval frescoes as strip cartoon, telling a tale with vigour and sheer beauty. Likewise, art buffs will be struck by Piero's innovations with light, perspective and geometric perfection.

In Michael Ondaatje's novel of *The English Patient* (on which the film is based), Kip repays the kindness of a medieval scholar by showing him Piero's fresco of Maxentius' troops fleeing before the cross. In the film, Kip (Naveen Andrews) takes Hana (Juliette Binoche) into the chapel and hoists her aloft on ropes so that she can see the frescoes in the illuminated light of a flare – it's a lyrical and powerful scene.

Only 25 people are allowed into the chapel every half-hour (maximum 30-minute visit). At the time of research the ticket office was at Piazza San Francesco 4, to the right of the church's main entrance, but there was talk of this changing.

Pieve di Santa Maria CHURCH

(Corso Italia 7; ⊙8.30am-12.30pm & 3-7pm May-Sep, to noon & 3-6pm Oct-Apr) This 12th-century church (Arezzo's oldest) has a magnificent Romanesque arcaded facade adorned with dozens of carved columns, each uniquely decorated. Its 14th-century bell tower, with

Eastern Tuscany Highlights

1 Join the locals for a *passeggiata* (evening stroll) through the photogenic streets and squares of **Arezzo** (p257)

2 Admire the work of Renaissance painter Piero della Francesca in his birthplace of **Sansepolcro** (p263)

3 Explore a well-preserved medieval castle in the hilltop hamlet of **Poppi** (p268)

4 Visit two medieval monasteries in the secluded setting of the **Parco Nazionale delle Foreste Casentinesi, Monte Falterona e Campigna** (p269)

5 Enjoy the sensational views, food and hilltop villages of the **Val di Chiana** (p271)

6 Laze away a couple of days in the spectacularly sited hilltop town of **Cortona** (p271)

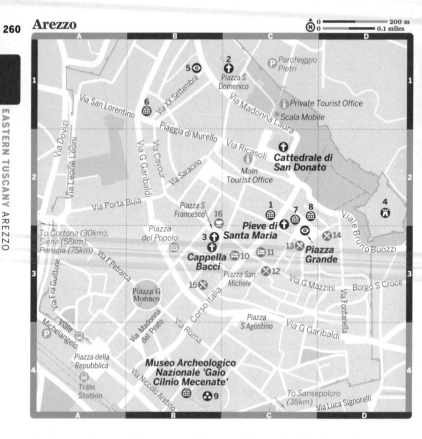

40 apertures, is something of an emblem for the city. Above the central doorway are 13th-century carved reliefs known as the *Cyclo dei Mesi,* which represent the months of the year. January's figure has two faces: one looks back on the previous year and the other looks forward.

Inside, the undoubted highlight is Pietro Lorenzetti's polyptych, *Madonna and Saints* (1320–24), located beneath the semi-dome of the apse. Below the altar is a 14th-century silver bust reliquary of the city's patron saint, San Donato. Other treasures on display include a 13th-century crucifix by Margherito di Arezzo, which hangs above the door to the sacristy.

Piazza Grande   PIAZZA

This lopsided and steeply sloping piazza is located behind the *pieve* and is overlooked at its upper end by the porticos of the **Palazzo delle Logge Vasariane,** completed in 1573. The church-like **Palazzo della Fra-**

ternità dei Laici in the northwest corner was started in 1375 in the Gothic style and finished after the onset of the Renaissance. In addition to being the venue for the Giostra del Saracino, the piazza is the venue for Arezzo's famous **antiques fair** (p262), which has been operating since 1968 and is one of the largest in Italy.

Cattedrale di San Donato   DUOMO

(Piazza Duomo; ⊙7am-12.30pm & 3-6.30pm) Though construction started in the 13th century, Arezzo's *duomo* (cathedral) wasn't completed until well into the 15th century. In the northeast corner, to the left of the bulky, intricately carved main altar, there's an exquisite fresco of *Mary Magdalene* (c 1460) by Piero della Francesca. This is dwarfed in size – but definitely not in beauty – by the multi-tiered marble reliefs of the adjoining tomb of Bishop Guido Tarlati, who died in 1327. The tomb features a frieze of priests and an acolyte chanting while holding a censer, a prayer book and candles.

Behind the southeast of the cathedral, across the peaceful gardens of the **Passeggio del Prato**, rears the **Fortezza Medicea** (admission free; ☉7am-8pm Apr-Oct, 7.30am-6pm Nov-Mar), completed in 1560 and offering grand views of the town and surrounding countryside.

Museo Archeologico Nazionale 'Gaio Cilnio Mecenate'　　　MUSEUM
(Via Margaritone 10; adult/reduced/child €4/2/ free; ☉8.30am-7.30pm) Overlooking the remains of a **Roman amphitheatre** (admission free; ☉8.30am-7pm Apr-Oct, to 6pm Nov-Mar) that once seated up to 10,000 spectators, this museum in a 14th-century convent has a sizeable collection of Etruscan and Roman artefacts, the highlights of which are the *Cratere di Euphronios,* a large 6th-century-BC Etruscan vase decorated with vivid scenes showing Hercules in battle, and an exquisite tiny portrait of a bearded man executed on glass in the 3rd century AD. You'll find the vase on the ground floor and the portrait upstairs.

Casa Museo di Ivan Bruschi　　　MUSEUM
(www.fondazionebruschi.it; Corso Italia 14; adult/reduced €5/3; ☉10am-6pm Tue-Sun late-Mar–Oct, 10am-1pm & 2-6pm Tue-Sun Nov–late-Mar) The 13th-century Palazzo del Capitano del Popolo opposite the *pieve* was restored in the 1960s by Ivan Bruschi, a wealthy antique dealer who was the instigator of Arezzo's antiques fair and whose family had owned the building since the start of the 20th century.

Since his death, it has opened its doors as a private house museum showcasing Bruschi's eclectic personal collection of furniture, art, coins, jewellery, costumes and ceramics dating from the prehistoric, Etruscan, Greek, Roman, medieval and Renaissance periods. Note that admission is discounted to €1 if you have a ticket for the Cappella Bacci.

Chiesa di San Domenico　　　CHURCH
(Piazza San Domenico 7; ☉8.30am-6pm) A short detour from the *duomo,* this church has an unusual, asymmetrical facade and an austere interior dominated by a haunting *Crucifixion* over the main altar, one of Cimabue's earliest works. Note, too, the well-preserved fresco of *Saint Philip and Saint Jacob and the Story of their Lives* by Spinello Aretino (1350–1410) on the inside of the facade. You'll need a €1 coin to illuminate the Cimabue.

Museo Statale d'Arte Medievale e Moderna　　　MUSEUM
(Via San Lorentino 8; adult/reduced/child €4/2/ free; ☉8.30am-7.30pm) A repository of art from churches in the Arezzo diocese, this time-worn museum is in urgent need of some tender loving care. If it wasn't for the

---

ⓘ MONEY SAVER

A combined ticket (€10) gives entry to the Cappella Bacci, Museo Archeologico Nazionale, Museo Statale d'Arte Medievale e Moderna and Museo di Casa di Vasari.

presence of Pietro Lorenzetti's *Madonna with Child and Saints Agnes and Catherine* (c 1310–15) and Parri di Spinello's *Madonna della Misericordia* (c 1437), we'd be tempted to advise giving it a miss.

Museo di Casa di Vasari MUSEUM
(Via XX Settembre 55; adult/reduced €2/free; ⊙8.30am-7.30pm Mon & Wed-Sat, to 1.30pm Sun)
Built and sumptuously decorated (in many cases, overwhelmingly so) by Vasari (1511–74) himself, this is where the Arezzo-born painter, architect and art historian lived and where the original manuscript of his *Lives of the Most Excellent Painters, Sculptors and Architects* (1550) – still in print under the title *The Lives of the Artists* – is kept.

☞ Tours

Two-hour guided English-language walking tours (☑0575 2 66 77; www.coloritoscani.com; adult/child under 12yr €10/free) are conducted every Thursday from 3pm between May and October. Bookings are essential.

✵ Festivals & Events

The Giostra del Saracino is the major event of the year, but the Fiera Antiquaria di Arezzo (Arezzo Antique Fair; www.arezzofiera antiquaria.org), held on the first Sunday and preceding Saturday of every month, is nearly as famous.

🛏 Sleeping

Arezzo has a dearth of decent sleeping options in the historical centre. When this book was being researched, the Cavaliere Palace Hotel on Via Madonna del Prato and the Hotel I Portici on Portici di Via Roma were undergoing major renovations. On reopening, they may be worth investigating.

Graziella Patio Hotel BOUTIQUE HOTEL €€
(☑0575 40 19 62; www.hotelpatio.it; Via Cavour 23; s €100-180, d €150-250, ste €250-320; ✳❄☎) Each of the 10 themed rooms in Arezzo's most characterful hotel is dedicated to one of Bruce Chatwin's travel books and decorated accordingly. Request 'Utz' – it's the nicest. Parking is €22 per day.

Palazzo dei Bostoli B&B €
(☑334 1490558; www.palazzobostoli.it, in Italian; 2nd fl, Via G Mazzini 1; s/d €60/80; ✳☎)
In a 13th-century *palazzo* close to Piazza Grande, this old-fashioned place offers five simple but comfortable rooms. The breakfast – a coffee and *cornetto* (croissant) – is served at Bar Stefano in nearby Corso Italia.

AROUND AREZZO

TOP CHOICE / **Villa Fontelunga** COUNTRY HOTEL €€
(☑0575 66 04 10; www.fontelunga.com; Via Cunicchio 5, Foiano della Chiana; r €179-265, ste €210-280; ⊙closed mid-Nov–late-Mar ☲✳❄☎☲)
Gorgeous is the only word to use when describing this 19th-century villa 30 minutes southwest of Arezzo. Restored, decorated and run by three charming friends (one an architect, one a landscape designer and one a former international banker), it perfectly balances traditional Tuscan elegance with jet-set pizazz. Two-night minimum stay.

Il Borro COUNTRY HOTEL €€€
(☑055 97 70 53; www.ilborro.com; Località Borro, San Giustino Valdarno; 3-day packages from €480 per person; ☲✳@❄☲) Incorporating a medieval village 20km northwest of Arezzo and well placed for forays into the Chianti region, this luxury resort on a wine estate is operated by the Ferragamo fashion empire. Choose between accommodation in a villa, converted farmhouse or apartment, and

---

GIOSTRA DEL SARACINO

Originating in the time of the Crusades, the Joust of the Saracino (www.giostradelsaracino. arezzo.it, in Italian) is one of those grand, noisy affairs involving extravagant fancy dress and neighbourhood rivalry. Like many such Tuscan folk spectacles, the tournament was revived in its present form in 1931 after long neglect. Held on the evening of the third Saturday in June and the afternoon of the first Sunday in September, the event begins with a procession of around 350 people in 14th-century dress accompanied by 31 horses. It's the highlight of the year for the city's four *quartieri* (quarters), each of which puts forward a team of 'knights'.

In the Piazza Grande, the knights try their hand jousting at a wooden effigy, known as the *buratto*. In one hand the *buratto* holds a shield, etched with various point-scores, which the knights aim for while trying to avoid being belted with the *mazzafrusto* – three heavy leather balls on ropes – which dangle from the *buratto's* other hand. The winning team takes home the coveted Golden Lance, bringing glory to its *quartiere*.

spend your days in the wellness spa, playing tennis, horse-riding, lazing by the pool or taking cooking classes. Accommodation packages include a spa treatment, one dinner, one lunch, a horseback ride, a wine tasting and a guided tour of Arezzo.

✗ Eating & Drinking

TOP CHOICE La Bottega di Gnicche SANDWICH SHOP € (www.bottegadignicche.com; Piazza Grande 4; panini €3-5; ☉11am-8pm Thu-Tue) There's a delectable array of artisan meats and cheeses to choose from when you order a *panini imbottiti* (roll filled with meat and cheese) at this wonderful *alimentari* (grocery store) on Arezzo's main piazza. Eat on the tiny front terrace, or perch on a stool inside.

La Torre di Gnicche TRADITIONAL ITALIAN €€ (☑0575 35 20 35; Piaggia San Martino 8; meals €28; ☉closed Wed & 2 weeks in Jan) Just off Piazza Grande, this is a fine restaurant specialising in traditional local dishes. Its soups are delicious – in summer try *pappa al pomodoro* (a thick bread and tomato soup), in winter *acquacotta* (a hearty vegetable soup with bread and egg) and *ribollita* (a 'reboiled' bean, vegetable and bread soup with black cabbage). Afterwards, choose from the ample range of local *pecorino* (cheese made from sheep's milk) and cured meats accompanied by a choice red from the extensive wine list.

La Tua Piadina SANDWICH SHOP € (Via de' Cenci 18; piadine €3.50) Hidden away down a side street, this justifiably popular takeaway place serves a range of hot, tasty *piadine,* Emilia-Romagna's version of the wrap. A busy mix of neighbourhood folk, students and visitors vie for the limited seating out on the street.

Antica Osteria Agania TRADITIONAL ITALIAN € (☑0575 29 53 81; www.agania.com; Via G Mazzini 10; meals €25; ☉Tue-Sun) There are no surprises on the menu here, just simple food offered at good prices. Kick off with an *antipasto misto della casa* (mixed house antipasto plate) and then take your pick from the robust pastas, soups and mains on offer.

Caffè dei Costanti CAFE (www.caffedeicostanti.it, in Italian; Piazza San Francesco 19-20; ☉8.30am-10pm Wed-Sun, to midnight summer) Arezzo's oldest and most atmospheric cafe is located directly opposite the Chiesa di San Francesco, so it's a perfect coffee stop before or after a visit to the Cappella Bacci. The coffee is excellent, as are the home-baked pastries.

MOVING ON?

For tips, recommendations and reviews, head to shop.lonelyplanet.com to purchase downloadable PDFs of the Umbria & Le Marche and Rome & Lazio chapters from Lonely Planet's *Italy* guide.

ⓘ Information

Centro di Accoglienza Turistica Benvenuti ad Arezzo (☑0575 40 19 45; www.turismo.provincia.arezzo.it; Palazzo Comunale, Via Ricasoli; ☉10am-7pm) The region's main tourist office is located opposite the *duomo.*

Na Vetrina per Arezzo e Le Sue Vallate (☑0575 182 27 70; ☉9.30am-7pm) A private tourist office located on the *scala mobile* leading up to Piazza del Duomo.

Nuovo Ospedale San Donato (☑0575 25 50 01; Via A de Gasperi) Hospital located outside the city walls.

Police station (☑0575 31 81; Via Fra Guittone 3)

ⓘ Getting There & Away

BUS Siena Mobilità (www.sienamobilita.it) buses go to Siena (€5.40, 1½ hours, eight daily), **Baschetti** (www.baschetti.it) buses go to Sansepolcro (€3.50, one hour, frequent on weekdays, fewer services on weekends) and **Tiemme** (www.lfi.it) services Cortona (€3.10, one hour, frequent). Buses depart from Piazza della Repubblica.

CAR & MOTORCYCLE To drive here from Florence, take the A1; the SS73 heads west to Siena. There is free car parking at Via Pietri, from where a *scala mobile* takes you up to Piazza del Duomo. Parking at the train station costs €1.50 per hour.

TRAIN Arezzo is on the Florence–Rome train line, and there are frequent services to Florence (€5.80, 1½ hours) and Rome (€23, 2½ hours). Trains also call by Cortona (€2.40, 20 minutes, hourly).

SANSEPOLCRO

POP 16,400

The term 'hidden gem' is bandied about with gay abandon in travel brochures and books, but this is one place that truly deserves the description. Dating from AD 1000, Sansepolcro reached its current size in the 15th century and was walled in the 16th century. Today, its historic centre remains blessedly untouched by development or tourism – something that certainly can't be said of many other Tuscan cities.

⊙ Sights

The streets of the historic centre are littered with *palazzi* and churches – look out for the Chiesa di Sant'Antonio Abate (cnr Via San Antonio & Via del Campaccio; ⊘8.30am-12.30pm & 3-7pm summer, 8.30am-12.30pm & 3.30-6pm winter), which houses a processional banner painted by Luca Signorelli; the deconsecrated Chiesa di San Lorenzo (cnr Via di San Croce & Via Lucca Pacioli), where you'll find the Rosso Fiorentino masterpiece *Deposition of Christ* dating from 1528 (ring the bell at 2 Via di San Croce for entrance); and the Chiesa di Santa Maria delle Grazie (Piazza Beato Ranieri; ⊘8.30am-12.30pm & 3-7pm summer, 8.30am-12.30pm & 3.30-6pm winter), home to Raffaellino del Colle's *Madonna delle Grazie* (1555), a painting of a pregnant Madonna that may slightly predate Piero's *Parto* in Monterchi.

TOP CHOICE Museo Civico   MUSEUM
(www.museocivicosansepolcro.it, in Italian; Via Niccolò Aggiunti 65; adult/reduced/child €6/4.50/3; ⊘9.30am-1.30pm & 2.30-7pm mid-Jun–mid-Sep, 9.30am-1pm & 2.30-6pm mid-Sep–mid-Jun) The town's flagship museum is home to a small but top-notch collection of artworks, the highlights of which are three Piero della Francesca masterpieces: *Resurrection* (c 1460), the *Madonna della Misericordia* polyptych (c 1455–60) and *Saint Julian* (1455–58). Piero's authorship of a fourth work, *Saint Louis of Toulouse* (1460), is disputed by modern art historians – see what you think.

The museum also holds paintings by Raffaellino del Colle, Matteo di Giovanni and Santi di Tito; di Tito's *Rest during the Flight into Egypt* portrays the Holy Family in a tender and humanistic light and is particularly charming. Also look out for Andrea della Robbia's gorgeous tondo (circular sculpture) known as the *Virgin and Child with Manetti Coat of Arms* (1503).

Downstairs, there's a small archaeological collection, ecclesiastical objects and a splendid collection of intricate locks and keys.

Cattedrale di San Giovanni Evangelista   DUOMO
(Via Giacomo Matteotti 4; ⊘8.30am-12.30pm & 3-7pm mid-Jun–mid-Sep, 8.30am-12.30pm & 3-6pm mid-Sep–mid-Jun) Sansepolcro's 14th-century *duomo* contains an *Ascension* by Perugino and the striking *Volto Santo* (Sacred Face), a wooden crucifix with a wide-eyed Christ that dates back to the 10th century AD, perhaps even earlier. The polyptych behind the altar is by Niccolò di Segna and is thought to have influenced Piero's *Resurrection*.

🎟 Festivals & Events

On the second Sunday of September, Sansepolcro hosts the Palio della Ballestra, a crossbow tournament between local archers and rivals from nearby town of Gubbio. Contestants and the crowd dress in medieval costumes, and a great time is had by all.

🛏 Sleeping

Locanda del Giglio   B&B €
(✆0575 74 20 33; www.ristorantefiorentino.it; Via Luca Pacioli 60; s/d €60/85; ✳✿) These four

---

THE PREGNANT MADONNA

If you are travelling along the SS73 between Sansepolcro and Arezzo, be sure to take a small detour to the unassuming village of Monterchi, home to Piero della Francesca's much-loved fresco fragment of the Madonna del Parto (Pregnant Madonna; Via della Reglia 1, Monterchi; adult/reduced/child €3.50/€2/free; ⊘9am-1pm & 2-7pm Tue-Fri, 9am-7pm Sat-Sun Apr-Oct, 9am-1pm & 2-5pm Tue-Sun Nov-Mar). Painted c 1460, it once graced the walls of the church of Santa Maria a Momentana (since demolished), but was moved to a nearby chapel in 1785 and then, recently, to an architecturally undistinguished concrete school building on the main road, where it is the sole exhibit.

In the fresco, a heavily pregnant Madonna wears a simple blue gown and is standing in a tent, flanked by two angels who hold back the tent's curtains as a charming framing device. Piero painted it in a mere seven days, and it possesses a pleasing simplicity and grace.

Note: in a nice touch, the museum gives free entry to pregnant women!

Piero della Francesca

Though many details about his life are hazy, it is believed that this great Renaissance painter was born around 1420 in Sansepolcro and died in 1492. Trained as a painter from the age of 15, his distinctive use of perspective, mastery of light and skilful synthesis of form and colour set him apart from his artistic contemporaries, and the serene grace of his figures remains unsurpassed to this day. In his book *The Lives of the Artists,* Piero's fellow townsman Giorgio Vasari called him the 'best geometrician of his time' and lamented the fact that so few of his works were preserved for posterity, leading to him being 'robbed of the honour that [was] due to his labours'.

Piero's most famous works are the *Legend of the True Cross* in Arezzo's Cappella Bacci and his *Resurrection* in Sansepolcro's Museo Civico, but he is most fondly remembered for his luminous *Madonna del Parto* (Pregnant Madonna) on display in Monterchi, a village located in the Tiber Valley between Sansepolcro and Arezzo.

Devotees can follow a trail of Piero's paintings through the region of Arezzo. Check http://turismo.provincia.arezzo.it for details or pick up the *Piero della Francesca: In and Around Arezzo* brochure from museums and tourist offices throughout the region.

VIEWING THE PAINTINGS

» **Cappella Bacci, Arezzo** (p257) *Legend of the True Cross*

» **Cattedrale di San Donato, Arezzo** (p260) *Mary Magdalene*

» **Uffizi Gallery, Florence** (p61) *Federico da Montefeltro and Battista Sforza, the Duke and Duchess of Urbino*

» **Monterchi** (see the boxed text, p264) *Madonna del Parto*

» **Museo Civico, Sansepolcro** (p264) *Resurrection,* the *Madonna della Misericordia* polyptych and *Saint Julian*

Left
1. *Legend of the True Cross* (detail) **2.** *The Duke and Duchess of Urbino* (detail)

rooms on the floor above Ristorante Fiorentino have been given a stylish modern fit out by Alessia Uccellini, whose family has operated the restaurant for over half a century. Rooms feature clever lighting, small but attractive bathrooms and – alas – uncomfortable futon-style beds.

✗ Eating & Drinking

TOP CHOICE **Ristorante Da Ventura** TRADITIONAL ITALIAN €
(☏0575 74 25 60; www.albergodaventura.it; Via Niccolò Aggiunti 30; meals €23; ⊘closed Mon & dinner Sun) Beware the trollies at this fabulous local eatery; heavily laden with the huge joints of roasted meat that the place is famous for (roast pork, beef stewed in Chianti Classico and roasted veal shank), they zoom around the dining room pushed by waiters high on piling diners' plates high. Vegetarians have no need to fear, though – the *uova con tartufo marzolino fresco* (omelette topped with shaved black truffles) is a total triumph, as are the generous plates of homemade pasta served with truffles or fresh *porcini* mushrooms. There's a simple B&B (s/d €45/65 or half-board per person €50) upstairs.

Ristorante Fiorentino TRADITIONAL ITALIAN €€
(☏0575 74 20 33; www.ristorantefiorentino.it; Via Luca Pacioli 60; meals €37; ⊘closed Wed & 1 week in Nov, Jul & Feb) No wonder locals come here to celebrate birthdays and big dates – the dining room is stuffed with antique furniture, chandeliers and objets d'art, and the genial host Alessio makes everyone feel like special guests. The food is traditional with an occasional modern twist, and there's an excellent wine list.

Enoteca Guidi WINE BAR
(Via Luca Pacioli 44; ⊘lunch & dinner Mon, Tue, Thu & Fri, dinner Sat & Sun) You'll receive a friendly welcome from owner Severio when you enter this tiny wine bar. Enjoy a local artisan beer (Severio recommends 'La Tipografica') or a glass of *vino* (everything from local drops to fashionable Super Tuscans). If you so choose, you can then move to the rear dining room, where simple meals (€28) are served. There's also an attached B&B (☏0575 74 19 07; www.locandaguidi.com; s €40-45, d €75-90; ❄).

❶ Information

The helpful **tourist office** (☏0575 74 05 36; infosansepolcro@apt.arezzo.it; Via Giacomo

---

TERRE DI AREZZO

The Arezzo region boasts one DOCG and five DOC wines: Chianti Colli Arentini DOCG, Vinsanto del Chianti Colli Arentini DOC, Vinsanto del Chianti Colli Arentini Occhio di Pernice DOC, Valdichiana DOC, Cortona DOC and Pietraviva DOC. To investigate these fully, you can follow the **Strada del Vino Terre di Arezzo** (www.stradadelvino. arezzo.it, Italian) or take full advantage of their regular appearances on the wine menus of restaurants across the region.

Matteotti 8; ⊘9am-1pm & 3.30-7pm) is opposite the *duomo*.

❶ Getting There & Away

BUS Baschetti (www.baschetti.it) buses link Sansepolcro with Arezzo (€3.50, one hour, frequent on weekdays, fewer on weekends). **Sulga** (www.sulga.it) operates one daily service to Rome (€18.50, 3½ hours), leaving at 7am. All buses leave from the bus station off Via G Marconi, near the Porta Fiorentina; purchase tickets at the Bar Autostazione.

CAR & MOTORCYCLE A Zona a Traffico Limitato (ZTL; Limited Traffic Zone) applies within the city walls; you'll find free parking just outside.

THE CASENTINO

The northeastern corner of Tuscany is home to spectacular mountain scenery, historic monasteries and little-visited hamlets where the traditional customs and cuisine are proudly maintained.

Castello di Romena

Approaching from Florence, you'll be on the SR70 (Passo della Consuma), which winds its way through heavily forested scenery to the pretty town of Poppi. En route, consider stopping at the ruins of this 11th-century castle (adult/child €3/1.50; ⊘10am-1.30pm & 2.30-5pm Thu-Sun mid-Mar–Jun & Sep, 10am-1.30pm & 2.30-6pm daily Jul & Aug), a stronghold of the Guidi counts who ruled the Casentino until being supplanted by the Florentine Republic in 1440. After walking through the central courtyard, investigating the towers and admiring the view of the surrounding

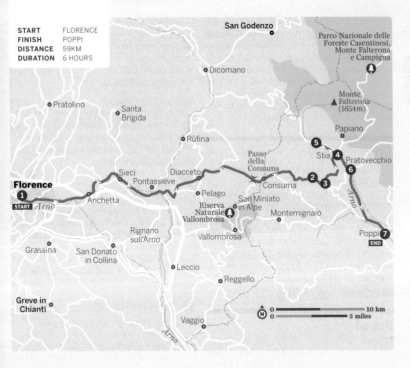

START	FLORENCE
FINISH	POPPI
DISTANCE	59KM
DURATION	6 HOURS

Driving Tour
The Casentino

❯ For a foray into this little-visited corner of Tuscany, head southeast from ❶ **Florence** and follow the Arno river along the SR69 (Via Aretina) through Pontassieve and over the Passo della Consuma (SR70), a scenic mountain pass over this Tuscan section of the Apennine Mountains. The road will eventually bring you to the turn-off to the ❷ **Castello di Romena**, on the left-hand-side. After admiring the cypress-edged courtyard and panoramic view at this 11th-century castle that Dante once visited, visit the Romanesque ❸ **Pieve di Romena** down the hill and then follow the road signs to the towns of Stia and Pratovecchio. The Arno meets its first tributary, the Staggia, at ❹ **Stia** and the town was for many years the centre of the local wool industry. It's now home to a wool museum whose gift shop sells examples of the Casentino's brightly coloured and 'nubby' woollen blankets and clothing.

From Stia, it's a short drive northwest to the ❺ **Chiesa Santa Maria delle Grazie**, a gorgeous Renaissance church – see if you can find a local who will let you inside to admire a fresco by Ghirlandaio and two very pretty ceramic lunettes by Benedetto Buglioni. Backtracking to Stia, proceed south to nearby ❻ **Pratovecchio**, where you should stop for a late-ish lunch at the unfortunately monikered – but nonetheless fabulous – Toscana Twist. From here, continue on to the regional centre of ❼ **Poppi**, where you can visit the magnificent Castello dei Conti Guidi and wander the picturesque streets of the upper town before heading to your accommodation for the night.

countryside, make your way down the hill behind the castle to the exquisite Pieve di Romena, a Romanesque church with interior capitals featuring primitive carvings of human and animal figures. A walking track leads around the castle's fortified walls and down the hill, or you can drive from the castle car park. To gain entry, try knocking on the door of the adjoining building.

Stia

Close to the Castello di Romena, this attractive town sits on the banks of the Staggia river, a tributary of the Arno. For centuries, it was the centre of the Casentino's famous wool industry, and its historic wool mill, which operated until 1985, has recently been restored and opened as the Lanificio di Stia (www.museo dellalana.it, in Italian; Via Sartori 2; adult/reduced €3/2; ◌4-7pm Sat, 10am-1pm & 4-7pm Sun Jun-Sep, 3-6pm Sat, 10am-1pm & 3-6pm Sun Oct-May), a museum dedicated to 'the art of woolmaking'.

Poppi

POP 6380

Perched high above the Arno plain, Poppi Alta (the historic upper section of the town) is crowned by the gaunt, commanding presence of the Castello dei Conti Guidi (www. buonconte.com, in Italian; Piazza Repubblica 1; adult/child €5/4; ◌10am-6.30pm daily May-Sep, 10am-12.30pm & 2.30-5.30pm Tue-Sun Oct-Apr), built in the late 13th century by Count Simone da Battifolle, head of the Guidi family.

Inside, there's a fairy-tale courtyard, handsome staircase, library full of medieval manuscripts and chapel with frescoes by Taddeo Gaddi. The scene of *Herod's Feast* shows Salome apparently clicking her fingers as she dances, accompanied by a lute player, while John the Baptist's headless corpse lies slumped in the corner.

The kiosk in the piazza outside the castle is the social hub of the town during the summer months; at other times locals tend to socialise in Ponte a Poppi (the lower town).

🛏 Sleeping

TOP
CHOICE ⧸ Borgo Corsignano   COUNTRY HOTEL €€
(☑0575 50 02 94; www.borgocorsignano.it; Località Corsignano; d €80-120; P @) Occupying a *borgo* (medieval village) that was once home to Camaldoli monks, this gorgeous country hotel is the best accommodation option in the

Casentino. A mere five-minute drive from Poppi, it offers self-contained apartments and a wealth of facilities, including two swimming pools, a sybaritic wellness centre, tennis court, *cantinetta* (small wine cellar) and sculpture-filled gardens.

Albergo San Lorenzo   B&B €
(☑0575 52 01 76; www.poppi-sanlorenzo.com; Piazza Bordoni 2-5; d €84; ◌mid-Mar–mid-Nov; @) This 10-room hotel in Poppi Alta abuts the external wall of the castle and has a laid-back, vaguely arty feel.

🍴 Eating

L'Antica Cantina   TRADITIONAL ITALIAN €€
(☑0575 52 98 44; www.anticacantina.com; Via Lapucci 2; set menus €28-30; ◌closed Mon, Tue lunch & all Jan) An old-fashioned vaulted dining space located on a side street off Via Cesare Battisti, 'The Old Cantina' is Poppi's best eatery. It offers set three-course menus and genial service.

❶ Information

The **tourist office** (☑0575 52 05 11; www. casentino.net; Via Roma 203, Ponte a Poppi; ◌9am-1pm & 3-6pm Mon-Thu, 9am-1pm Fri) is at the eastern edge of town near the turn-off to Camaldoli.

❶ Getting There & Away

BUS SITA (www.sitabus.it) buses travel between Poppi and Florence (€4.60, two hours, four daily), however local services within the Casentino are pretty well non-existent.

CAR & MOTORCYCLE From Florence, take the SR67 and SR69 (Via Aretina) and veer onto the SR70 (Passo della Consuma). To Arezzo, take the SR70 and SS71.

WORTH A TRIP

TOSCANA TWIST

There's only one compelling reason to visit the small town of Pratovecchio on the road between Poppi and Stia, and that's to eat at this fantastic osteria (☑320 2342762; Via della Libertà 3; meals €25; ◌lunch daily, aperitivi & dinner Sat & Sun). Chef Patrizia Vignati uses the best local produce to create her light and flavoursome interpretations of Tuscan classics, and she certainly does Pratovecchio proud. You'll find it in an ugly building on the main road.

TRAIN Trasporto Ferroviario Toscano (TFT;
www.trasportoferroviariotoscano.it) trains link
Poppi with Arezzo (€2.90, one hour, 16 daily).

Parco Nazionale delle Foreste Casentinesi, Monte Falterona e Campigna

One of only three national parks in Tuscany, this protected nature reserve (www.parco forestecasentinesi.it, www.parks.it/parco.nazionale. for.casentinesi) straddles the Tuscany–Emilia-Romagna border, taking in some of the most scenic stretches of the Apennines and protecting the largest and best preserved forest and woodlands in the country.

One of the highest peaks, Monte Falterona (1654m), marks the source of the Arno. Apart from the human population, which includes the inhabitants of two historic monasteries, the park is also home to a rich assortment of wildlife plus nearly 100 bird species. Nine self-guided walking trails have been created within the park; the most popular is the 4.5km uphill hike to the Acquacheta waterfall.

The major settlement in the park is Badia Prataglia, a small village in the Alpe di Serra, near the border with Emilia-Romagna. Its visitors centre (☎0575 55 94 77; www.ba diaprataglia.com, in Italian; Via Nazionale 14; ☺9am-12.30pm Sat & Sun Apr & Jun, 9am-12.30pm Thu-Sun May, 9am-12.30pm & 3.30-6pm daily Jul, to 7pm daily Aug, 9am-12.30pm & 3.30-6pm Sat & Sun Sep, 9am-12.30pm Sat & Sun Oct-Dec) carries a wealth of information about the park and also hires mountain bikes (per half/full day €6/10).

◉ Sights

**Monasterio & Sacro
Eremo di Camaldoli**   MONASTERY
(www.camaldoli.it; ☺monastery 9am-1pm & 2.30-7pm, hermitage 9am-noon & 3-5pm) Hidden in the thick forest of the national park are the Benedictine monastery and hermitage of Camaldoli, founded between 1024 and 1025 by St Romuald and now home to a community of approximately 20 monks.

From Poppi, take Via Camaldoli (SR67) and follow it up through the forest. Eventually, you will come to a fork in the road – the hermitage is uphill to the right and the monastery is downhill to the left.

At the monastery you can visit its church, which houses three paintings by Vasari: *Deposition from the Cross; Virgin with Child, St John the Baptist and St Giro-lamo;* and a *Nativity.* Down a set of stairs off the main road are the somewhat forbidding cloisters and the austere Cappella dello Spirito Santo, a stone space where a photographic exhibition about daily life in the monastery is displayed. For a souvenir of your visit, pop into the 16th-century pharmacy (☺9am-12.30pm & 2.30-6pm), which is accessed from the side of the main building. It sells soap, perfumes and other items made by members of the monastic community.

At the hermitage there is a small church housing a Bronzino altarpiece of the *Crucifixion and Four Saints,* but the highlight is the Cappella di San Antonio Abate, to the left as you enter the church building. Inside is an exquisite altarpiece by Andrea della Robbia.

Santuario della Verna   MONASTERY
(www.santuariolaverna.org, in Italian; Via del Santuario 45; ☺8am-7pm) This Franciscan monastic complex is dramatically positioned on a windswept mountainside. It's where St Francis of Assisi is said to have received the stigmata and is thus a major pilgrimage destination.

At the sanctuary, the Basilica houses some remarkably fine glazed ceramics by Andrea della Robbia – a *Madonna and Child Enthroned Between Saints* to your right as you enter the church, an *Adoration* to the right of the altar, a charming *Annunciation* to the left and a huge *Ascension* in the chapel to the left of the presbytery.

Beside the Basilica entrance is the Cappella della Pietà. From it, the Corridoio delle Stimmate, decorated with modern frescoes recounting the saint's life, leads to the Cappella delle Stimmate, built in 1263 on the spot where the saint supposedly received the stigmata. It is decorated with a magnificent *Crucifixion* by Andrea della Robbia and a smaller *Madonna and Child* tondo by Andrea's uncle, Luca.

By car, follow signs just outside the hamlet of Chiusi della Verna for the sanctuary or take the mildly taxing but agreeable 30-minute uphill hike from the visitor centre (☎0575 53 20 98; cv.chiusiverna@par coforestecasentinesi.it; Parco Martiri della Libertà 21; ☺9am-noon & 3.30-6pm Jul & Aug, 10.30am-4.30pm Feast of the Stigmata in Sep, 2-6.30pm 4 Oct). The sanctuary is located 23km east of the Casentino's major town, Bibbiena, and is accessed via the SP208. There is a foresteria (guesthouse; per person €55), refectory (set lunch €18) and bar/cafe on site.

Magnificent Monasteries

Consider yourself warned: after visiting these medieval monasteries, many visitors find themselves entertaining serious thoughts about leaving their fast-paced urban existences to embrace the contemplative life.

Assisi

1 Every year, more than five million pilgrims make their way to this medieval hill town in Umbria where St Francis was born. Incredibly, the streets have changed little since St Francis and his friend St Clare lived here (p273).

Abbazia di Monte Oliveto Maggiore

2 The Benedictine monks living in this medieval abbey southeast of Siena (p202) tend the ancient vineyard and olive grove, study in one of Italy's most important medieval libraries and walk through a cloister frescoed by Luca Signorelli and Il Sodoma.

Monasterio & Sacro Eremo di Camaldoli

3 Deep in the forest of the Casentino, amid a landscape that has changed little for centuries, lie this Benedictine monastery and hermitage (p269). Treasures include paintings by Vasari and Bronzino, as well as one of Andrea della Robbia's greatest terracotta sculptures.

Santuario della Verna

4 St Francis of Assisi is said to have received the stigmata at this spectacularly located monastery on the southeastern edge of the Casentino (p269). Pilgrims flock here to worship in the Cappella delle Stimmate and to admire the della Robbia artworks in the church.

Eremo Le Celle

5 A babbling stream, old stone bridge and terraces of olive trees contribute to the fairy-tale feel of this picturesque Franciscan hermitage just outside Cortona (p272).

Right
1. Basilica di San Francisco in Assisi 2. Fresco in Abbazia di Monte Oliveto Maggiore

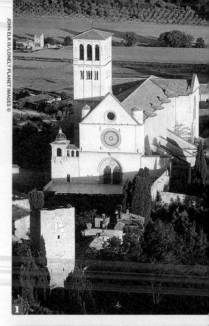

JOHN ELK III/LONELY PLANET IMAGES ©

ROBIN CHAPMAN/LONELY PLANET IMAGES ©

VAL DI CHIANA

South of Arezzo stretches the Val di Chiana, a wide green valley punctuated by gently rolling hills crowned with medieval villages. This prized agricultural land is rich in orchards and olive groves, but is primarily known as the home of Tuscany's famed Chianina cows, one of the oldest breeds of cattle in the world and the essential ingredient in Tuscany's signature dish, *bistecca alla fiorentina*.

Castiglion Fiorentino

POP 13,500

If you're driving from Arezzo to Cortona, be sure to stop en route at this picturesque walled town to visit its impressively restored Cassero (www.icec-cf.it, in Italian; Via del Tribunale). Inside this huge medieval fortress are the Pinacoteca Comunale (adult/reduced/child €3/2/0.50; ⊙10am-12.30pm & 4-6.30pm Tue-Sat, 4-7pm Sun Apr-Oct, 10am-12.30pm & 3.30-6pm Tue-Sun Nov-Mar), with a small collection including Taddeo Gaddi's delightful *Virgin and Child;* the Museo Archeologico Sezione Antica e Medievale (adult/reduced/child €3/2/0.50; ⊙10am-12.30pm & 4-6.30pm Tue-Sat, 4-7pm Sun Apr-Oct, 10am-12.30pm & 3.30-6pm Tue-Sun Nov-Mar), which incorporates the remains of an Etruscan temple dating from the end of the 6th century BC and an Etruscan house from the end of the 4th century BC; and the Torre del Cassero (admission €1.50; ⊙10am-1pm & 4-7pm Sun May-Sep), a medieval tower commanding panoramic views over the valley. A combined adult/reduced/child ticket costs €5/3/1.

A ZTL applies in the streets immediately surrounding the Cassero, but a public car park is close by at Porta Fiorentina (€1 per hour). Also here is a tourist information booth (☑0575 65 82 78; proloco.castiglioni@tin.it; ⊙9.30-11.30am Mon, 9.30-11.30am & 4-6pm Tue-Sat).

Cortona

POP 23,100

Rooms with a view are the rule rather than the exception in this spectacularly sited hilltop town. In the late 14th century Fra' Angelico lived and worked here, and fellow artists Luca Signorelli and Pietro da Cortona were both born within the walls – all three are represented in the Museo Diocesano's small

but sensational collection. More recently, large chunks of *Under the Tuscan Sun,* the soap-in-the-sun film of the book by Frances Mayes, were shot here.

⊙ Sights

Museo dell'Accademia Etrusca   MUSEUM
(MAEC; www.cortonamaec.org; Piazza Signorelli 9; adult/child 6-12yr €8/4; ⊙10am-7pm daily Apr-Oct, to 5pm Tue-Sun Nov-Mar) Brooding over lopsided Piazza della Repubblica is the Palazzo Comunale, built in the 13th century. To the north is attractive Piazza Signorelli and, on its north side, the 13th-century Palazzo Casali, whose rather plain facade was added in the 17th century. Inside is the fascinating Museo dell'Accademia Etrusca, which displays substantial local Etruscan and Roman finds, Renaissance globes, 18th-century decorative arts and contemporary paintings. The well-presented Etruscan collection is the highlight, particularly those objects excavated from the tombs at Sodo, just outside town. Book in advance for a guided tour (☑0575 63 72 35; archeoparco@libero.it; per group €120) of the museum and two of the tombs.

Museo Diocesano   MUSEUM
(Piazza del Duomo 1; adult/child €5/3, audioguide €3; ⊙10am-7pm Tue-Sun Apr-Oct, to 5pm Tue-Sun Nov-Mar) Little is left of the original Romanesque character of Cortona's *duomo,* which is situated northwest of Piazza Signorelli and has been rebuilt several times in a less-than-felicitous fashion. Fortunately, its artworks have been saved and are on display in this museum, which occupies the former church of the Gesù on the opposite side of the piazza.

Room 1 features a remarkable Roman sarcophagus decorated with a frenzied battle scene between Dionysus and the Amazons, but the museum's real treasures are in Room 3. These include a moving *Crucifixion* (1320) by Pietro Lorenzetti and two beautiful works by Fra' Angelico: *Annunciation* (1436) and *Madonna with Child and Saints* (1436–37).

ⓘ MONEY SAVER

A combined ticket (adult/child €10/6) gives entry to the Museo dell'Accademia Etrusca and the Museo Diocesano.

Cortona

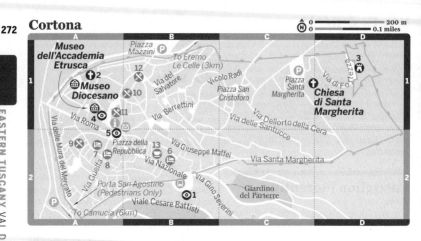

Cortona

◉ Top Sights

◉ Sights

🛏 Sleeping

✕ Eating

◉ Drinking

Chiesa di Santa Margherita CHURCH
(Piazza Santa Margherita; ⊙8am-noon & 3-7pm Apr-Oct, 9am-noon & 3-6pm Nov-Mar) For the most effective cardiovascular workout in Tuscany, hike up to this largely 19th-century church through the sleepy warren of steep cobbled lanes in the eastern part of town. Inside, the remains of St Margaret, the patron saint of Cortona, are on display in a 14th-century, glass-sided tomb above the main altar.

St Margaret's story is the archetypical sinner-to-saint tale. After spending her early life as a mistress and a mother to an illegitimate son, she was transformed after arriving in Cortona. After a few false-starts with local dreamboats, Margaret formed her own congregation, opened a hospital, received ecstasy-charged messages from heaven, prophesised the date of her death and surrounded herself with the poor, ill, pious and penitent. She was canonised in 1728.

Fortezza Medicea LANDMARK
(adult/child €3/1.50; ⊙10am-1.30pm & 2.30-6pm May, Jun & Sep, to 7pm Jul & Aug) There's a stupendous view over the Val di Chiana to Lake Trasimeno in Umbria from the remains of this Medici fortress, which stands atop the highest point in town. For the less fit, a **belvedere** at the eastern end of Via Nazionale, down in the centre of town, also has a panoramic view.

Eremo Le Celle MONASTERY
(www.lecelle.it; Strada dei Cappuccini 1) Adopting the contemplative religious life becomes everyone's fantasy after a visit to this Franciscan hermitage set amid dense woodland 3km north of Cortona. The group of rustic buildings sits next to a picturesque stream complete with an 18th-century stone bridge, and the wonderfully tranquil atmosphere is disturbed only by the bells calling the resident friars to vespers and mass in the cave-like **Chiesa Cella di San Francesco**.

⌒ Tours

English-language **walking tours** (🖉0575 2 66 77; www.coloritoscani.com; adult/child under 12yr €10/free) are conducted every Monday from 11am to 1pm between May and October. The ticket includes entrance to Museo dell'Accademia Etrusca. Bookings essential.

✹ Festivals & Events

Giostra dell'Archidado   CULTURAL
A full week of medieval merriment in May or June (the date varies to coincide with Ascension Day) culminates in a crossbow competition.

Festival of Sacred Music   MUSIC
(www.cortonacristiana.it) Held in early July each year.

Tuscan Sun Festival   CULTURAL
(www.tuscansunfestival.com) Music and art festival held in late July–early August each year.

🛏 Sleeping

TOP CHOICE Casa Chilenne   B&B €
(🖉0575 60 33 20; www.casachilenne.com; Via Nazionale 65; s €80-85, d €88-110; ❋@❄🖐) Run by American-born Jeanette and her Cortonese husband Luciano, this wonderfully welcoming B&B has it all – great hosts, a central location, comfortable rooms, a lavish breakfast spread and keen prices. Each of the five rooms has a satellite TV, but there's also a communal lounge with TV, small terrace and cooking corner.

Hotel San Michele   HOTEL €€
(🖉0575 60 43 48; www.hotelsanmichele.net; Via Guelfa 15; d €99-250; ⊘closed Jan–mid-Mar; ❋@❄) This is Cortona's finest hotel. Primarily Renaissance, but with elements dating from the 12th century and modifications over subsequent centuries, it's like a little history of Cortona in stone. Rooms are airy and comfortable, if a little faded. Prices vary wildly due to special offers and festivals. Parking is €20 per night and there is wi-fi only in the foyer.

Dolce Maria   B&B €
(🖉0575 63 03 97; www.cortonastorica.com; Via Ghini 12; s €70-80, d €90-100; ❋❄) A 15th-century *palazzo* tucked into a warren of streets near Piazza Signorelli, this slightly musty but highly atmospheric B&B is operated by a friendly husband and wife team who also operate the downstairs restaurant. The six

---

WORTH A TRIP

ASSISI

Thanks to St Francis, who was born here in 1182, this medieval hilltop town in the neighbouring region of Umbria is a major destination for millions of pilgrims. Its major drawcard is the **Basilica di San Francesco** (Piazza di San Francesco), which comprises two churches filled with magnificent Renaissance art. The **upper church** (⊘8.30am-6.45pm Easter-Nov, to 5.45pm Dec-Easter) was built between 1230 and 1253 in the Italian Gothic style and features superb frescoes by Giotto and works by Cimabue and Pietro Cavallini. Downstairs, in the dimly lit **lower church** (⊘6am-6.45pm Easter-Nov, to 5.45pm Dec-Easter), there's a series of colourful frescoes by Simone Martini, Cimabue and Pietro Lorenzetti.

To book English-language guided tours of the basilica, contact its **information office** (🖉0758 19 00 84; www.sanfrancescoassisi.org; Piazza San Francesco; ⊘9am-noon & 2-5.30pm Mon-Sat) or fill out the form on the website. The **tourist office** (🖉0758 13 86 80; www.assisi.regioneumbria.eu; ⊘8am-2pm & 3-6pm Mon-Sat, 10am-1pm Sun) on Piazza del Comune can supply general information about the town.

Assisi is a popular overnight destination, so you'll need to book ahead during peak times: Easter, August, September and the Feast of St Francis (4 October). For a comfortable and well located sleeping option, try **Hotel Alexander** (🖉0758 1 61 90; www.hotelalexanderassisi.it; Piazza Chiesa Nuova 6; s €60-80, d €78-140; ❋❄). To eat, head to **Trattoria Da Erminio** (🖉0758 1 25 06; www.trattoriadaerminio.it; Via Montecavallo 19; 4-course set menu €16; ⊘closed Thu, Feb & 1st half of Jul) for traditional Umbrian dishes, or to trendy **MagnaVino** (🖉0758 1 68 14; Corso Giuseppe Mazzini 12; meals €25; ⊘noon-4pm & 6pm-2am) for modern Tuscan creations; the latter is also a great place for an *aperitivo*.

Sulga buses connect Assisi with Florence (€12.50, 2½ hours, twice weekly). A Zona a Traffico Limitato (ZTL; Limited Traffic Zone) applies in the historic centre, but there are plenty of paid car parks (€1.15/10 per hour/day) just outside the walls.

GREAT LUNCH STOPS

To sample the most flavoursome Chianina beef in the valley that gave this Tuscan speciality its name, head to **Da Mengrello** (☑0575 64 05 81; www.ristorantemengrello.it; Viale della Resistenza 20; meals €30; ☺Wed-Mon) in the small agricultural town of Foiano della Chiana. A cavernous vaulted space set in a converted stable, it serves truly sensational *bistecca alla fiorentina* and *tagliata* (sliced beef sirloin).

Another excellent restaurant in this area is **Il Goccino** (☑0575 83 67 07; www.ilgoccino. it; Via Giorgio Matteotti 90; meals €35; ☺daily), in the pretty hilltop village of Lucignano. Its €25 four-course 'Tuscan menu' is extremely good value and its rear terrace commands panoramic views over the valley.

rooms are large, with antique furnishings and small but modern bathrooms; the pick is 'Torretta', which has a private rooftop terrace accessed via a narrow stone staircase.

✖ Eating & Drinking

La Bucaccia   TRADITIONAL ITALIAN €€
(☑0575 60 60 39; www.labucaccia.it; Via Ghibellina 17; meals €35) Set in a medieval stable that was incorporated into a Renaissance *palazzo*, this is an atmospheric and enjoyable dinner venue, but is a bit dark at lunchtime. The set menu (€29) of four courses, one glass of wine and water offers extremely good value.

Trattoria Dardano   TRATTORIA €
(☑0575 60 19 44; www.trattoriadardano.com; Via Dardano 24; meals €20; ☺Thu-Tue) Dardano is one of those no-nonsense yet still unexpectedly wonderful trattorias that feature prominently in every Tuscany travel memoir, doing amazing things with ostensibly simple dishes. You'll be elbow-to-elbow with locals and giddy, idealistic visitors who are seriously considering buying and fixing up a nearby farmhouse on the strength of their delicious and inexpensive meal.

Osteria del Teatro   TRADITIONAL ITALIAN €€
(☑0575 63 05 56; www.osteria-del-teatro.it; Via Maffei 2; meals €39; ☺Thu-Tue) The walls are clad with photos of actors who have dined here after performing in the nearby theatre, and service is suitably theatrical – waiters wield what could well be the biggest pepper grinder in the world, and blocks of locally produced chocolate are attacked with a butcher's knife for a sweet finale. The menu relies heavily on seasonal local produce.

Taverna Pane e Vino   WINE BAR
(www.pane-vino.it; Piazza Signorelli 27; ☺closed Mon & lunch Jan-Easter) Serving over 900 wines, this casual place is a perfect spot for

a light lunch (bruschetta €3.50, meat and cheese platters €6 to €10, pasta €7.50 to €10), afternoon drink or rustic dinner. Claim a table in the front courtyard or vaulted interior, settle back over a glass or two of wine and relax with the local bon vivants.

Tuscher Caffè   CAFE
(www.caffetuschercortona.com; Via Nazionale 43; ☺closed Mon) Coffee is the main drawcard of this modern cafe on the main *passeggiata* route, although many visitors end up staying for a light meal (served all day), glass of wine or professionally shaken cocktail.

ⓘ Information

The **tourist office** (☑0575 63 72 23; infocortona@apt.arezzo.it; Palazzo Comunale; ☺9am-1pm & 3-6pm Mon-Sat, 9am-1pm Sun May-Sep, 9am-1pm & 3-6pm Mon-Fri, 9am-1pm Sat Oct-Apr) stocks maps and brochures and can book hotels.

ⓘ Getting There & Away

BUS From Piazza Garibaldi, Tiemme buses connect the town with Arezzo (€3.10, one hour, frequent) via Castiglion Fiorentino (€2.10).

CAR & MOTORCYCLE The city is on the north-south SS71 that runs to Arezzo. It's also close to the Siena–Bettolle–Perugia autostrada, which connects to the A1. There are free car parks around the circumference of the city walls; the most convenient is at Porta San Agostino. A ZTL applies inside the walls.

TRAIN The nearest train station is located about 6km away at Camucia, and can be accessed via a local bus (€1.20, 15 minutes, hourly). Destinations include Arezzo (€2.40, 20 minutes, hourly), Florence (€7.30, 1½ hours, hourly), Rome (€10.25, 2½ hours, eight daily) and Perugia (€3.85, 50 minutes, six daily).

Note that Camucia station has no ticket office, only machines. If you need assistance purchasing or booking tickets, you'll need to go to the station at Terontola, south of Camucia, instead.

Understand Florence & Tuscany

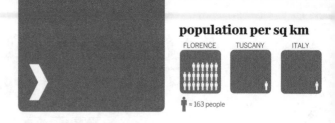

Florence & Tuscany Today

Famously Red

Tuscany has been a stronghold of the Italian left ever since rapid industrialisation post-WWII. And regional elections in 2010 proved no exception. Much-loved incumbent Regione Toscane president Claudio Martini (p289) chose not to stand for a third term, only for fellow centre-left candidate Enrico Rossi (b 1958) to storm into office with an easy landslide victory over the centre-right. What made the red Tuscan politician's victory so poignant was the fact that other like-minded, traditionally left regions (such as neighbouring Lazio) fell to Berlusconi's governing centre-right coalition (p289). But famously red Tuscany stood firm.

» Population: 3.73 million (2010)

» Area: 22,994 sq km

» GDP: €106 billion (6.7% of national GDP)

» Annual inflation: 1.9%

» Unemployment rate: 6.3%

Tuscany 2.0

Tuscans rapidly warmed to their region's new president, who tweets at @ rossipresidente and uses Facebook to chat with them, answer questions and communicate key developments in Tuscany – such as the region-wide switch to digital TV in November 2011; Pisa being hailed as one of Italy's most wi-fi–connected cities; and the opening of the first leg of the controversial, Rome-bound toll motorway that will run from just south of Livorno to Civitavecchia, 206km further south, when complete in 2016.

Green for Go

In a region known for its traditional agriculture, soft rolling green hills and century-old cypress alleys (visited by 47 million tourists in 2010), it is natural that ecofriendly travel should be of increasing importance. In notoriously traffic-clogged Florence, the city's smart young mayor, Matteo Renzi (another big 2.0 guy who cleverly combines all the social media tools with old-fashioned visits to local schools and so on), is considering a London-style scheme limiting the number of cars entering downtown

Tuscan Icons

» The Vespa scooter
» Gucci
» Chianti wine
» Michelangelo's *David*
» Renaissance art

Dos & Don'ts

» Flip-flops and singlets are reserved for the beach.

» When visiting someone's home, take *dolcetti* (sweet cakes or biscuits) for your host.

» Splitting the bill is uncouth. The person who invites pays, but close friends often go Dutch.

Out & About

» Strangers and acquaintances – men or women – shake hands.

» Friends exchange a peck of a kiss on each cheek.

» Italians are chic. Make an effort with your presentation and never remove your shoes in public.

belief systems
(% of population)

85

Roman Catholic

15

Jewish,
Protestant &
Muslim

if Tuscany were 100 people

91 would be Italian
2 would be Albanian
2 would be Romanian
5 would be Other

Florence. The obvious moment to introduce it would be 2016, when Florence's state-of-the-art tramlines will be completed – the first opened in 2010 to the joy of its 40,000 daily passengers and the 3000 motorists who now travel each day to work, in a much greener fashion, by tram.

Countryside by Design

Tuscany is not all about old stone farmsteads romantically lost in cinematic rushes of green hills, vineyards and sun-gold wheat fields. Thoroughly contemporary *cantine* (cellars) designed by some of the world's top architects are cropping up in the Tuscan countryside – or rather beneath it – like mushrooms after the rain. Examples include Renzo Piano's brilliant-red Rocca di Frassinello in the Maremma, and the striking Petra wineries near Suvereto by world-class Swiss architect Mario Botta.

Innovation is the New Idyll

Such grand architectural designs are as much about raising the technological bar in the wine cellar as aesthetic beauty. Innovation is the new idyll and Tuscan wines are more creative, more fashionable and better than ever before. In 2010 Italian wine exports (€3.93 billion) exceeded domestic consumption (€3.85 billion) for the first time.

More international wine producers are turning to Tuscan soil to blend Super Tuscans and other modern wines. In 2011 it was American-owned Castello Banfi (actually in the Tuscan biz for over three decades) who scooped the prestigious Vinitaly wine prize, quietly underscoring the demise of winemaking as the exclusive domain of old, blue-blooded, Tuscan winemaking families. These days, in this ancient land first cultivated by the Etruscans, Tuscany's oldest craft is open to anyone with wine-wizardry nous.

Unesco World Heritage Sites

» Historic centre of Florence

» Piazza dei Miracoli, Pisa

» Historic centre of Siena

» Val d'Orcia

» Historic centre of San Gimignano

» Historic centre of Pienza

Top Wines

» Brunello di Montalcino
» Vino Nobile di Montepulciano
» Chianti
» Vernaccia di San Gimignano
» Super Tuscan Sassicaia

Cafe Etiquette

» Sitting down at a table in a cafe to have a coffee is three times more expensive than drinking it standing at the bar.

Church Matters

» Never intrude on a mass or service.

» Be it to worship or sightsee, cover your shoulders when entering a church – and no short skirts.

History

Tuscan history is an opera that quietly opens with the wine-loving Etruscans around the 9th century BC, staccatos with feisty clashes between medieval city states, and crescendos with Florence's powerful Medici dynasty and the birth of the Renaissance. To this day, it is the Renaissance with its extraordinary art and architecture (p306) that defines the region's largest city and inspires an overwhelming sense of pride and gratitude in its beauty-ensnared, art-loving inhabitants. It remains Tuscany's greatest moment, and the region has not been at the cusp of such momentous change since.

Florence enjoyed a brief stint as capital of Giuseppe Garibaldi's fledgling kingdom of Italy from 1865 until 1870 when Rome fell and the whole of Italy was unified. Italy's post-war economic miracle brought an influx of wealth to Tuscany, but also unregulated real estate developments to its legendary green rolling hills. Political violence marred the late 20th century, Florence's mayor being killed in 1986 and a bomb blowing up part of the Uffizi and its infamous Vasarian Corridor in 1993.

New-millennium Tuscany with its Super Tuscan wines, world-class fashion designers and beautiful countryside is once again an enviable part of the world. Agriculture and travel are defining features of the region, 'go slow' being the spindle around which that traditional Tuscan cart turns just as it did three millennia ago.

> Learn to speak Etruscan at Etruscology Online: www.etruskisch.de/pgs/vc.htm. Favourite words: *netshvis* (a fortune teller who reads animal entrails) and *thuta* (which can mean either 'chaste' or 'only married once').

The Etruscans

No one knows exactly why the ancient Etruscans headed to Tuscany in the 9th century BC, but Etruscan artefacts give clues as to why they stayed: dinner. The wild boar roaming the Tuscan hills was a favourite item on the Etruscan menu, and boar hunts are a recurring theme on Etruscan ceramics, tomb paintings and even bronze hand mirrors. In case the odd boar bristle tickled the throat or a truffle shaving headed

TIMELINE	9th century BC	265 BC	59 BC
	Etruscans bring highly civilised wine, women and song to the hills of Tuscany – never has life been so good. Unfortunately they fail to invite the Romans and war ensues.	Etruria falls to Rome, but remains unruly and conspires with Hannibal against Rome during the Punic Wars.	After emerging victorious from a corrupt election campaign for the position of Roman consul, Julius Caesar establishes a soldier-retiree resort called Florentia.

down the windpipe while eating, Etruscans washed down their meals with plenty of wine, thereby introducing viticulture to Italy.

Tomb paintings show Etruscan women keeping pace with men in banquets so decadent they scandalised even the orgy-happy Romans. Many middle-class and aristocratic women had the means to do what they wished, including indulging in music and romance, participating in politics and overseeing a vast underclass of servants. Roman military histories boast of conquests of Etruscan women along with Etruscan territory starting in the 3rd century BC (probably exaggerated). According to recent genetic tests, Etruscans did not mingle much with their captors – their genetic material is distinct from modern Italians, who are the descendants of ancient Romans.

Etruscans didn't take kindly to Roman authority, nor were they keen on being enslaved to establish Roman plantations. They secretly allied with Hannibal to bring about the ignominious defeat of the Romans – one of the deadliest battles in all of Roman history – at Lago Trasimeno in neighbouring Umbria: 16,000 Roman soldiers were lost in approximately three hours.

After that Rome took a more hands-off approach with the Etruscans, granting them citizenship in 88 BC to manage their own affairs in the new province of Tuscia (Tuscany) and in return securing safe passage along the major inland Roman trade route via the Via Flaminia. Little did the Romans realise when they paved the road that they were also paving the way for their own replacements in the 5th to 8th centuries AD: first came German emperor Theodoric, then Byzantine emperor Justinian, then the Lombards and finally Charlemagne in 800.

Medieval Scandal

Political power constantly changed hands in medieval Tuscany. Nevertheless, two notorious women wielded power effectively against a shifting backdrop of kings and popes. The daughter of a Roman senator and a notorious prostitute-turned-senatrix, Marozia already had one illegitimate son by her lover Pope Sergius III and was pregnant again when she married the Lombard duke of Spoleto, Alberic I, in 909 AD. He was hardly scrupulous himself: he'd achieved his position by murdering the previous duke, and he soon had Sergius III deposed. When Alberic was in turn killed, Marozia married Guy of Tuscany and conspired with him to smother Pope John X and install (in lethally rapid succession) Pope Leo VI and Stephen VIII.

After Guy's death, she wooed his half-brother Hugh of Arles, the new king of Italy. No matter that he already had a wife: his previous marriage was soon annulled. But at the wedding ceremony, Marozia's son, Alberic II, who had been named Pope John XI, had the happy couple arrested.

Best Etruscan Ruins

» Vie Cave, Pitigliano

» Parco Archeologico di Baratti e Populonia, Golfi di Baratti

» Necropoli, Sovana

AD 476	570–774	773–74	800
German king Odovacar snatches Rome out from under Romulus Augustulus, and becomes the first of many foreign kings of Italy.	The Lombards rule Italy as far south as Florence, and manage to turn the tiny duchy of Spoleto into a booming trade empire.	Charlemagne crosses the Alps into Italy, fighting the Lombards and having his ownership of Tuscany, Emilia, Venice and Corsica confirmed by Pope Hadrian I.	Pope Leo III crowns Charlemagne Holy Roman Emperor on Christmas Day.

Marozia spent the rest of her life in prison, but her legacy lived on: no fewer than five popes were her direct descendants.

Countess Matilda of Tuscany (1046–1115) was another power woman. Rumour has it that she was more than just an ally to Pope Gregory VII, and there's no doubt she was a formidable strategist on and off the battlefield. To consolidate her family's Tuscan holdings, she married her own stepbrother, Godfrey the Hunchback. She soon arranged for him to be sent off to Germany, annulling the marriage and finding herself a powerful prince 26 years her junior to marry.

When Matilda's ally Pope Gregory VII excommunicated Holy Roman Emperor Henry IV in 1077 for threatening to replace him with an anti-pope, the emperor showed up outside her castle barefoot and kneeling in the snow to beg the pope's forgiveness. Gregory, who was Matilda's guest, kept him waiting for three days before rescinding the excommunication. Henry retaliated for what he saw as Matilda's complicity in his humiliation by conspiring with Matilda's neighbours to seize her property, and even turned her trophy husband against her – but Matilda soon dislodged Henry's power base in the north with the support of his own son, Conrad. Disgraced by his own family and humbled on the battlefield by a woman, Henry died in 1106.

FLAGELLATING MONKS & NUNS

The first known case of religious self-flagellation dates from the mid-13th century in Perugia in neighbouring Umbria, when a strange, spontaneous parade of believers began whipping themselves while singing.

By 1260 roving bands of Flagellants appeared in major Tuscan cities, stripped to the waist, hooded and ecstatically whipping themselves while singing *laudi* (songs about the passion of Christ). They made quite an impression in Florence and Siena where adherents formed *scuole di battuti* (schools of beatings) to build *case di Dio* (houses of God) that served as charity centres, hospices and host to mass flagellation sessions.

The Church remained neutral on the issue until the fledgling Flagellants claimed their activities could grant temporary relief from sin. This posed direct competition for the Church's practice of confession, not to mention its steady business in indulgences, pardons and tithes. The Flagellant movement was banned in 1262, only to regain momentum a century later during the plague and recur periodically until the 15th century, when the Inquisition subjected Flagellants to the ultimate mortification of the flesh: burning at the stake.

Self-flagellation processions continued to be held in Tuscany under the Church's guidance into the late 19th century.

1080	1082	1136	1167
Henry IV deposes Pope Gregory VII for the second time, installing Clement III in his place and marching against Gregory's supporter Matilda of Tuscany, confiscating her territory.	Florence picks a fight with Siena over ownership of the Chianti region, starting a bitter rivalry that will last the next 400 years.	Scrappy, seafaring Pisa adds Amalfi to its list of conquests, which included Jerusalem, Valencia, Tripoli and Mallorca, and colonies in Constantinople and Cairo, among others.	Siena's *comune* (town council) establishes a written constitution, declaring that elected terms should be short and money should be pretty; it's soon amended to guarantee Sienese public boxing matches.

A New Law & Order

By the 13th century Tuscans wanted change. Farmers who had painstakingly reclaimed their fields wanted to get their produce to market alive; merchants needed peaceful piazzas in which to conduct their business; and the populace at large began to entertain hopes of actually living past the age of 40.

In a bid to reorganise their communities in a more orderly and civilised fashion, *comuni* (town councils) were established in Florence, Siena and other towns. In this new power-sharing arrangement, representatives were drawn from influential families, guilds and the merchant classes. Building projects were undertaken to give citizens a new sense of shared purpose and civic identity. Hospitals and public charities helped serve the needy, and new public squares, marketplaces and town halls became crucial meeting places for civic society.

Law and order was kept by a *podestà*, an independent judiciary often brought in from outside the city for limited terms of office to prevent corruption. Each *comune* (city state) developed its own style of government: Siena's was the most imaginative. To curb bloody turf battles among its *contrade* (neighbourhoods), Siena channelled its fighting spirit into organised boxing matches, bullfights and Il Palio, an annual horse race. Anyone who broke the peace was fined and the city's coffers soon swelled with monies collected in the city's *osterie* (casual tavern or eatery presided over by a host) for cursing.

After Florence won yet another battle against Siena by cutting off the town's water supply, Siena's *comune* was faced with a funding choice: build an underground aqueduct to fend off Florence or build a cathedral to establish Siena as creative capital of the medieval world. The council voted unanimously for the latter. Work began in 1215 and continued for more than three centuries.

Dante's Circle of Hell

'Midway on our life's journey, I found myself in dark woods, the right road lost...' So begins the ominous year 1300 in Dante Alighieri's *Inferno*, where our hero Dante (1265–1321) escapes from one circle of hell only to tumble into the next – gloomy but uncannily accurate. In the 14th century, Dante and his fellow Tuscans endured a hellish succession of famine, economic collapses, plague, war and tyranny.

When medieval mystics predicted the year 1300 would bring doom, they were off by barely 50 years. Approximately two-thirds of the population were decimated in cities across Tuscany in the bubonic plague outbreak of 1348, and since the carriers of the plague (fleas and rats) weren't correctly identified or eradicated, the Black Death repeatedly

---

Best Roman Relics

» Area Archeologica, Fiesole

» Roselle, near Grosseto

» Roman theatre, Volterra

» Vetulonia

Medieval Tuscany was criminal: leaders of powerful families were stabbed by rivals while attending Mass; peasants were ambushed by brigands; and bystanders were maimed in neighbourhood disputes that all too easily escalated to murderous brawls. Petty crimes were punished with steep fines, corporal punishment and public flogging or mutilation.

1314–21

Dante Alighieri writes his *Divina Commedia*, told in the first person, using Tuscan dialect instead of the usual formal Latin, and peppered with political satire, pathos, adventure and light humour.

» Statue of Dante, Florence

DALLAS STRIBLEY / LONELY PLANET IMAGES ©

1348–50

Black Death ravages Tuscany, wiping out approximately two-thirds of the population in dense urban areas, and it doesn't stop there: further outbreaks are recorded until 1500.

1375–1406

Colluccio Salutati serves as chancellor of Florence, promoting a secular civic identity to trump old feudal tendencies; it's a bold, new model of citizenship for Europe that occasionally even works.

From Siena's dark days emerged its magnificent *duomo* and an expressive, eerily glowing style of painting known as the Sienese School, aka precocious precursor to the Renaissance.

ravaged the area for decades afterwards. Blame for the disease was placed on the usual suspects – lepers, immigrants, Romany people, heretics, Jewish communities, women of loose morals. Entire hospital and monastery populations were wiped out, leaving treatment to opportunists promising miracle cures. Flagellation, liquor, sugar and spices were prescribed, as was abstinence from bathing, fruit and olive oil – all to no avail. Florentine author and 1348 plague eyewitness Giovanni Boccaccio (1313–75) writes of quarantined families left to starve, sick children abandoned by parents and family members dumped still breathing in mass graves.

But amid the ample evidence of human failings there were also more reassuring signs of humanity. Meals were shared, and orphans cared for by strangers. Doctors and devout clergy who cared for the sick were the most obvious heroes of the day; though they lacked the medical knowledge to save plague victims, they knowingly risked their own lives just to provide a dignified death for their patients. At age 19, St Catherine of Siena overruled her family's understandable objections and dedicated her life to serving the plague-ridden. She wrote long, eloquent letters to the pope and powerful families in the region, imploring them to reconsider their warring ways and allow the troubled region peace.

Relive 14th-century Florence: visiting Dante's Florentine home comes with the chapel where he met his muse and a traditional tripe shop. For Dante with a pop-culture twist, read Sandow Birk and Marcus Sanders' *The Divine Comedy,* which sets *Inferno* in Los Angeles' traffic, *Purgatorio* in foggy San Francisco and *Paradiso* in New York.

Painful though those days must have been to record, writers such as Boccaccio, Dante and Marchione di Coppo Stefani (c 1336–85) wrote frank assessments of their time, believing their critiques might one day serve the greater good. More than any painterly tricks of perspective or shading, it's this rounded view of humanity that brought truth to Renaissance art.

Renaissance Belligerence & Beauty

The Renaissance was a time of great art and great tyrants, between which there was an uneasy relationship. The careful balance of power of the *comuni* became a casualty of the plague in the 14th century; political control was mostly left to those who survived and were either strong enough or unscrupulous enough to claim it. In *comuni* such as Florence and Siena, powerful families assumed control of the *signoria,* the city council ostensibly run by guild representatives and merchants.

Cities, commercial entities and individual families took sides with either the Rome-backed Guelphs or the imperial Ghibellines, loyalists of the Holy Roman Empire. Since each of these factions was eager to put itself on the map, this competition might have meant a bonanza for artists and architects – but shifting fortunes in the battlefield meant funds for pet art projects could disappear just as quickly as they appeared.

Tuscany began to resemble a chess game, with feudal castles appearing only to be overtaken, powerful bishops aligning with nobles before

1378	1469–92	1478–80	1494
The Florentine *signoria* (city council) ignores a petition from the city's *ciompi* (wool carders), who want guild representation: cue the Revolt of Ciompi, an ultimately unsuccessful democratic uprising.	Lorenzo de' Medici unofficially rules Florence, despite the 1478 Pazzi Conspiracy, an attempted overthrow that left his brother Giuliano torn to shreds in the *duomo*.	A confusing set of overlapping wars break out among the papacy, Siena, Florence, Venice, Milan and Naples, as individual families broker secret pacts and the dwindling Tuscan population pays the price.	The Medici are expelled by Charles VIII of France, and Savonarola declares a theocratic republic with his Consiglia di Cinquecento.

being toppled and minor players backed by key commercial interests occasionally rising to power. Nowhere was the chess game harder to follow than in the Ghibelline *comune* of Pistoia: first it was conquered by the Florentine Guelphs, then it split into White and Black Guelph splinter groups, then it was captured by Lucca (which was at that time Ghibelline backed) before being reclaimed by the Florentines.

The Medicis

The Medici family were not exempt from the usual failings of Renaissance tyrants, but early on in his rise to power Cosimo the Elder (1389–1464) revealed a surprisingly enlightened self-interest and an exceptional eye for art. Although he held no elected office, he served as ambassador for the Church, and through his behind-the-scenes diplomatic skills managed to finagle a rare 25-year stretch of relative peace for Florence. When a conspiracy led by competing banking interests exiled him from the city in 1433, some of Cosimo's favourite artists split town with him, including Donatello and Fra' Angelico.

But they weren't gone long: Cosimo's banking interests were too important to Florence, and he returned triumphant after just a year to crush his rivals, exert even greater behind-the-scenes control and sponsor masterpieces such as Brunelleschi's legendary dome for Florence's *duomo* (cathedral).

But sponsorship from even the most enlightened and powerful patrons had its downside: their whims could make or break artists and they attracted powerful enemies. Lorenzo de' Medici (Lorenzo Il Magnifico; 1449–92) was a legendary supporter of the arts and humanities, providing crucial early recognition and support for Leonardo da Vinci, Sandro Botticelli and Michelangelo Buonarroti, among others.

But after Lorenzo escaped an assassination attempt by a conspiracy among the rival Florentine Pazzi family, the king of Naples and the pope, the artists he supported had to look elsewhere for sponsorship until Lorenzo could regain his position. Religious reformer Savonarola took an even darker view of Lorenzo and the classically influenced art he promoted, viewing it as a sinful indulgence in a time of great suffering. When Savonarola ousted the Medici in 1494, he decided that their decadent art had to go, too, and works by Botticelli, Michelangelo and others went up in flames in the massive 'Bonfire of the Vanities' on Florence's Piazza della Signoria.

The Original Machiavelli

Few names have such resonance as Niccolò Machiavelli (1469–1527), the Florentine scholar and political thinker who said 'the times are more powerful than our brains'. He was born into a poor offshoot of one of Florence's leading families and his essential premise – 'the end justifies

The Medici have nothing to hide – at least, not anymore. Dig your own dirt on Florence's dynamic dynasty in the archives at www.medici.org.

Most unelected Renaissance rulers weren't great tyrants but rather petty ones, obsessed with accumulating personal power and wealth, and their lasting contributions to civic life were costly wars of conquest and internal strife.

1498	1527–30	1571	1633
To test Savonarola's beliefs, rival Franciscans invite him to a trial by fire. He sends a representative to be burned instead, but is eventually tortured, hung and burned as heretic.	Florentines run the Medici out of town. The Republic of Florence holds out for three years, until the emperor's and pope's combined cannon power reinstalls the Medici.	Painters are no longer obliged to belong to guilds, so individual artistic expression means you don't have to pay your dues first.	Galileo Galilei is condemned for heresy in Rome. True to his observations of a pendulum in motion, the Inquisition's extreme measures yielded an opposite reaction: Enlightenment.

Il Principe (The Prince) is Machiavelli's allegory of absolute power – but was it a cautionary tale against the Medici who'd had him tortured for suspected treason, or an instructional manual to get back in the Medici's good graces? Five centuries later, the debate continues.

the means' – is one that continues to live with disturbing terrorism five centuries on.

Impoverished as Machiavelli's family was, his father – a small-time lawyer continually in debt – had a well-stocked library, which the young Machiavelli devoured. When he was 29 Machiavelli landed a post in the city's second chancery marking the start of his colourful career as a Florentine public servant. By 1500 he was in France on his first diplomatic mission in the service of the Republic. Indeed, so impressed was he by the martial success of Cesare Borgia and the centralised state of France that Machiavelli concluded Florence, too, needed a standing army.

Florence, like so many other towns and cities on the Italian peninsula, had always employed mercenaries to fight its wars. The problem was that mercenaries had few reasons to fight and die for anyone. They took their pay and often did their best to avoid mortal combat. Machiavelli convinced the Republic of the advantages of a conscripted militia, which he formed in 1506. Three years later it was bloodied in battle against the rebellious city of Pisa, whose fall was mainly attributed to the troops led by the wily statesman.

The return to power of the Medici family in 1512 was a blow for Machiavelli, who was promptly removed from office. Suspected of plotting against the Medici, he was even thrown into Florence's infamous Le Stinche (the earliest known jail in Tuscany, dating from 1297 and among the first in Europe) in 1513 and tortured with six rounds of interrogation on the prison's notorious rack. Yet he maintained his innocence and, once freed, retired a poor man to his small property outside Florence.

Tuscany's Renaissance legacy was almost lost by the 1966 Great Flood of Florence that left thousands homeless and three million manuscripts and thousands of artworks under mud, stone and sewage. Those heroes who helped dig the treasures from the mud are honoured as gli angeli del fango (angels of mud).

But it was during these years, far from political power, that Machiavelli did his greatest writing. Il Principe (The Prince) is his classic treatise on the nature of power and its administration, a work reflecting the confusing and corrupt times in which he lived and his desire for strong and just rule in Florence and beyond.

Machiavelli never got back into the mainstream of public life. He was commissioned to write an official history of Florence, the Istorie Fiorentine, and towards the end of his life he was appointed to a defence commission to improve the city walls. In 1526 he joined the papal army in its futile fight against imperial forces.

By the time the latter had sacked Rome in 1527, Florence had again rid itself of Medici rule. Machiavelli hoped that he would be restored to a position of dignity, but by now he was suspected almost as much by the Medici opponents as he had been years before by the Medici. He died frustrated and, as in his youth, impoverished.

1656	1716	1737	1760s
Oh no, not again: the plague kills at least 300,000 people across central and southern Italy.	The growing region of Italy's oldest known wine is clearly defined: Chianti Classico has received favourable reviews since the 14th century.	Maria Theresa ends the Medici's dynastic rule by installing her husband as grand duke of Tuscany. She remains the brains of the operation, reforming Tuscany from behind the scenes.	Florence, along with Venice, Milan and Turin, becomes an essential stop for British aristocrats on the Grand Tour, a trend that continues until the 1840s.

Galileo

One of the most notable faculty members at the revitalised University of Pisa was a professor of mathematics named Galileo Galilei (1564–1642). To put it in mathematical terms, Galileo was a logical paradox: a Catholic who fathered three illegitimate children; a man of science with a poetic streak, who lectured on the dimensions of hell according to Dante's *Inferno;* and an inventor of telescopes whose head was quite literally in the clouds, yet who kept in close contact with many friends who were the leading intellectuals of their day.

Galileo's meticulous observations of the physical universe attracted the attention of the Church, which by the 16th century had a difficult relationship with the stars. Pope Paul III kept several astrologers on hand, and no major papal initiative or construction project could be undertaken without first searching the sky with an astrolabe for auspicious signs. Yet theologian (and sometime astrologer) Tommaso Campanella was found guilty of heresy for dissenting views that emphasised observation. Research into the universe's guiding physical principles was entrusted by Paul III to his consulting theologians, who determined from close examination of the scriptures that the sun must revolve around the earth.

Equipped with telescopes that he'd adjusted and improved, Galileo came to a different conclusion. His observations supported Nicolaus Copernicus' theory that the planets revolved around the sun, and a cautious body of Vatican Inquisitors initially allowed him to publish his findings as long as he also presented a case for the alternate view. But when Galileo's research turned out to be dangerously convincing, the Vatican reversed its position and tried him for heresy. By then Galileo was quite ill, and his weakened state and widespread support may have spared him

He needed that one for the Inquisitors: see Galileo's preserved middle finger (and other body parts) in Florence's superb and wholly interactive Museo Galileo, just around the corner from the Uffizi. Online, explore Galileo's life, times, religious context and scientific advances in The Galileo Project (http://galileo.rice.edu).

A BLOW TO INTELLECTUAL THOUGHT

Savonarola's theocratic rule over Florence (1494–98) might well have only lasted four years, until his denunciation of decadence got him excommunicated and executed by Pope Alexander VI, who didn't appreciate Savonarola critiquing his extravagant spending, illegitimate children and pursuit of personal vendettas.

But Savonarola's short reign had an impact on Tuscany for centuries to come: it made the Church see a need to exert more direct control over the independent-minded region, and to guard against humanist philosophies that might contradict the Church's divine authority, hence the Inquisition: heretical ideas were made punishable by death, leading to an understandably chilling effect on intellectual inquiry. Celebrated universities in Pisa and Siena were subject to close scrutiny, and the University of Pisa was effectively closed for about 50 years until Cosimo I de' Medici (1519–74) reinaugurated it in 1543.

1765–90	1796–1801	1805–14
Enlightenment leader Leopold I continues his mother's reforms. Moved by Cesare Beccaria's case for criminal justice reform, he makes Tuscany the first sovereign state to outlaw the death penalty.	Italy becomes a battleground between Napoleon, the Habsburgs and their Russian allies, and Tuscans witness much of their cultural patrimony divvied up as spoils of war.	Napoleon establishes himself as king of Italy, with the military assistance of Italian soldiers he'd conscripted; when his conscripts desert, Napoleon loses Tuscany to Grand Duke Ferdinando III in 1814.

MANFRED HOFER / LONELY PLANET IMAGES ©

» Napoleon's home on Elba

the usual heresy sentence of execution. Under official threat of torture, Galileo stated in writing that he may have overstated the case for the Copernican view of the universe, and was allowed to carry out his prison sentence under house arrest. Pope Urban VIII alternately indulged his further studies and denied him access to doctors, but Galileo kept on pursuing scientific research even after he began losing his sight. Meanwhile, Tommaso Campanella was taken out of prison and brought to Rome, where he became Urban VIII's personal astrologer in 1629.

Gold Gilt: Going for Baroque

With his astrologers on hand, the pope might have seen Italy's foreign domination coming. Far from cementing the Church's authority, the Inquisition created a power vacuum on the ground while papal authorities were otherwise occupied with lofty theological matters. While local Italian nobles and successful capitalists vied among themselves for influence as usual, the Austrian Holy Roman Empress Maria Theresa took charge of the situation in 1737, and set up her husband Francis as the grand duke of Tuscany.

The mother of 16 children (including the now-notorious Marie Antoinette) and self-taught military strategist soon put local potentates in check, and pushed through reforms that curbed witch burning, outlawed torture, established mandatory education and allowed Italian peasants to keep a modest share of their crops. She also brought the Habsburgs' signature flashy style to Tuscany, and kicked off a frenzy of redecoration that included flamboyant frescoes packed with cherubs, ornate architectural details that were surely a nightmare to dust, and gilding whenever and wherever possible. Perhaps fearing that her family's priceless art collection might factor into Maria Theresa's redecorating plans, Medici heiress Anna Maria Luisa de' Medici willed everything to the city of Florence upon her death in 1743, on the condition that it all must remain in the city.

Naturally the glint of gold captured the attention of Napoleon Bonaparte, who took over swathes of Tuscany in 1799. So appreciative was Napoleon of the area's cultural heritage, in fact, that he decided to take as much as possible home with him. What he couldn't take he gave as gifts to various relatives – never mind that all those Tuscan villas and church altarpieces weren't technically his to give. When Habsburg Ferdinando III took over the title of grand duke of Tuscany in 1814, Napoleon's sister Elisa Bonaparte and various other relations refused to budge from the luxe Lucchesi villas they had usurped, and concessions had to be made to accommodate them all.

Still more upmarket expats arrived in Tuscany and Umbria with the inauguration of Italy's cross-country train lines in 1840. Soon no

1861	1871	1915	1921
Two decades of insurrections culminate in a new Italian government, with a parliament and a king. Florence becomes Italy's capital in 1865, despite extensive poverty and periodic bread riots.	After French troops are withdrawn from Rome, the forces of the Kingdom of Italy defeat the Papal States to take power in Rome; the capital moves there from Florence.	Italy enters WWI fighting a familiar foe: the Austro-Hungarian Empire. War casualties, stranded POWs, heating-oil shortages and food rationing make for a hard-won victory by 1918.	Mussolini forms the Fascist Party, and Tuscan supporters fall in line by 1922. The 1924 elections are 'overseen' by Fascist paramilitary groups, and the Fascists win a parliamentary majority.

finishing-school education would be complete without a Grand Tour of Italy, and the landmarks and museums of Tuscany were required reading. Trainloads of debutantes, dour chaperones and career bachelors arrived, setting the stage for EM Forster novels, Tuscan timeshare investors and George Clooney wannabes.

Red & Black: A Chequered Past

While an upper-crust expat community was exporting Romantic notions about Italy, the country was facing some harsh realities. Commercial agriculture provided tidy sums to absentee royal Austrian landlords while reducing peasants to poverty and creating stiff competition for small family farms. In rural areas, three-quarters of the family income was spent on a meagre diet of mostly grains. The promise of work in the burgeoning industrial sector lured many to cities, where long working hours and dangerous working conditions simply led to another dead end, and 70% of family income was still spent on food. Upward mobility was rare, since university admissions were strictly limited, and the Habsburgs were cautious about allowing locals into their imperial army or bureaucratic positions. Increasingly, the most reliable means for Tuscans to support their families was emigration to the Americas.

America was named after Amerigo Vespucci, a Florentine navigator who, from 1497 to 1504, made several voyages of discovery in what would one day be known as South America.

Austrian rule provided a common enemy that, for once, united Italians across provinces and classes. The Risorgimento (reunification period) was not so much a reorganisation of some previously unified Italian states (which hadn't existed since Roman times) as a revival of city-state ideals of an independent citizenry. The secret societies that had flourished right under the noses of the French as a local check on colonial control soon formed a network of support for nationalist sentiment. During 1848 and 1849 revolution broke out, and a radical government was temporarily installed in Florence.

Nervous that the Austrians would invade, conservative Florentine leaders invited Habsburg Leopold II to return as archduke of Tuscany. But when rural unrest in Tuscany made Austria's return to power difficult, Austrian retaliation and brutal repression galvanised nationalist sentiment in the region. Although the country was united under one flag in 1861, this early split between radicals and conservatives would define the region's political landscape in the years ahead.

Unification didn't end unemployment or unrest; only 2% of Italy's population gained the right to vote in 1861 – the same 2% that controlled most of the country's wealth. Strikes were held across the country to protest working conditions, and their brutal suppression gave rise to a new Socialist Party in 1881. The new Italian government's money-making scheme to establish itself as a colonial power in Ethiopia and Eritrea proved a costly failure: 17,000 Italian soldiers were lost near Adowa in

1940–43	1943–45	1946	1959–63
The Fascist Italian Empire joins Germany in declaring war on Great Britain and France. Italy surrenders in 1943; Mussolini refuses to comply and war continues.	The Italian Resistance joins the Allies against Mussolini and the Nazis; Tuscany is liberated. When civil warfare ends in 1945, a coalition government is formed.	Umberto II is exiled after a referendum to make Italy a republic is successful; 71.6% of Tuscans vote for a republic.	Italy's economy revives via industrialisation, entrepreneurship and US Marshall Plan investments designed to stop it from joining the Soviet Bloc.

1896, in what was the worst defeat of any European colonial power in Africa. When grain prices were raised in 1898, many impoverished Italians could no longer afford to buy food, and riots broke out. Rural workers unionised, and when a strike was called in 1902, 200,000 rural labourers came out en masse.

Finally Italian politicians began to take the hint and initiated some reforms. Child labour was banned, working hours were set and the right to vote was extended to all men over the age of 30 by 1912 (women would have to wait for their turn at the polls until 1945). But as soon as the government promised the Socialists to fund an old-age pension scheme, it reneged, and opted to invade Tunisia instead.

Italy then got more war than it had budgeted for in 1914, when WWI broke out. A young but prominent Socialist firebrand named Benito Mussolini (1883–1945) led the call for Italy to intervene in support of the Allies, though most Socialists were opposed to such an action. As a result, Mussolini was expelled from the Socialist Party and went on to join the Italian army and serve in the war. After being injured and discharged from the army, he formed the Italian Combat Squad in 1919, the forerunner of the National Fascist Party.

Inter-War Blues

Though Italy had been on the winning side in WWI, few Italians were in the mood to celebrate. In addition to war casualties, 600,000 Italians served time as POWs (prisoners of war), and another 100,000 died primarily due to the Italian government's failure to send food, clothing and medical supplies to its own soldiers. Wartime decrees that extended working hours and outlawed strikes had made factory conditions so deplorable that women led mass strikes even under threat of prison. Bread shortages spread nationwide, along with bread riots. Mussolini had found support for his call to order in the Tuscan countryside, and by 1922 his black-shirted squads could be seen parading through Florence, echoing his call for the ousting of the national government and the purging of socialists and communists from all local positions of power. In 1922 the Fascists marched on Rome and staged a coup d'etat, installing Mussolini as prime minister.

But no amount of purging prevented the country from plunging into recession in the 1930s after Mussolini demanded (and obtained) a revaluation of the Italian lira. While the free fall of wages won Mussolini allies among industrialists, it created further desperation among his power base. New military conquests in Libya and Ethiopia initially provided a feeble boost to the failing economy, but when the enormous bill came due in the late 1930s, Mussolini hastily agreed to an economic and military alliance with Germany. Contrary to the bold claims of Mus-

On Screen

» *Life is Beautiful* (Roberto Benigni, 1997) This uplifting Holocaust film became a modern-day classic overnight; it's partly set in Arezzo.

» *Tea with Mussolini* (Franco Zeffirelli, 1999) Florence and San Gimignano are the backdrop for this great director's semi-autobiographical film, set in 1930s and 1940s Tuscany.

1966

The Arno bursts its banks, submerging Florence in metres of mud and water. Some 5000 people are left homeless and thousands of art works and manuscripts destroyed.

1969

Strikes and university-student uprisings demand social change and promote sweeping reforms, not just in working conditions but also housing, social services, pensions and civil rights.

1970s–'80s

The Anni di Piombo (Years of Lead) terrorise the country with extremist violence and reprisals; police kill anarchist Franco Serantini in Pisa, and Red Brigades kill Florence's mayor in 1986.

» Arno river, Florence

Unbelievable as it may sound, this trio became heroes of the Italian Resistance during WWII. Giorgio Nissim was a Jewish accountant in Pisa who belonged to a secret Tuscan Resistance group that helped Jewish Italians escape from fascist Italy. The network was discovered by the Fascists, and everyone involved was sent to concentration camps, except for Giorgio, who remained undetected.

It seemed nowhere was safe for Jewish refugees – until Franciscan friar Rufino Niccacci helped organise the Assisi Underground, which hid hundreds of Jewish refugees from all over Italy in convents and monasteries across Umbria in 1943 and 1944. In Assisi, nuns who'd never met Jewish people before learned to cook kosher meals for their guests, and locals risked their lives to provide shelter to total strangers.

The next problem was getting forged travel documents to the refugees, and quick. Enter Gino Bartali, world-famous Tuscan cyclist, Tour de France winner and three-time champion of the Giro d'Italia. After his death in 2003, documents revealed that during his 'training rides' during the war years, Bartali had carried Resistance intelligence and falsified documents that were used to transport Jewish refugees to safe locations. Suspected of involvement, Bartali was once interrogated at the dreaded Villa Triste in Florence, where political prisoners were held and tortured – but he revealed nothing. Until his death he refused to discuss his efforts to save Jewish refugees, even with his children, saying, 'One does these things, and then that's that.'

solini's propaganda machine, Italy was ill-prepared for the war it entered in 1940.

Post-WWII: The Tuscan Left

A new Italian government surrendered to the Allies in 1943, but Mussolini refused to concede defeat, and dragged Italy through two more years of civil war, Allied campaigns and German occupation. Tuscany emerged from these black years redder than ever, and Tuscany in particular became a staunch Socialist power base.

Immediately after the war, three coalition governments succeeded one another. Italy became a republic in 1946 and the newly formed right-wing Democrazia Cristiana (DC; Christian Democrats), led by Alcide de Gasperi, who remained prime minister until 1953, won the first elections under the new constitution in 1948.

Until the 1980s the Partito Comunista Italiano (PCI; Italian Communist Party), despite being systematically kept out of government, played a crucial role in Italy's social and political development. The very popularity of the party – actually founded in the Tuscan port town of Livorno in 1921 – prompted the so-called *anni di piombo* (years of lead) in the 1970s, dominated by terrorism and social unrest. In 1978 the Brigate

A powerful Resistance movement emerged in Tuscany during WWII, but not soon enough to prevent hundreds of thousands of Italian casualties, plus a still-unknown number of Italians shipped off to 23 Italian concentration camps (including one near Arezzo) and death camps in Germany.

1993	1995	2001	2005
A car bomb at the Uffizi kills six and causes US$10 million damage to artworks. The mafia is suspected, but never indicted. The same year 200,000 people protest mafia violence.	Maurizio Gucci, heir to the Florence-born Gucci fashion empire, is gunned down outside his Milan offices. Three years later, his estranged wife Patrizia Reggiani is jailed for ordering his murder.	Silvio Berlusconi's right-wing Casa delle Libertà (Liberties House) coalition wins an absolute majority in national polls. The following five years are marked by economic stagnation.	Regional elections in Tuscany see centre-left president Claudio Martini win a second term in office, with a landslide victory, reconfirming Tuscany as Italy's true bastion of the left.

Tuscany's regional government is headed by the president, elected every five years. In turn he is aided by 10 ministers and a legislative regional council comprising 65 members, also elected by proportional representation for the same five-year term. Keep tabs on regional government and council at www.regione. toscana.it and www.consiglio. regione.toscana.it respectively.

Rosse (Red Brigades, a group of young left-wing militants responsible for several bomb blasts and assassinations) claimed their most important victim – former DC prime minister Aldo Moro. His kidnap and (54 days later) murder (the subject of the 2004 film *Buongiorno Notte*) shook the country.

Despite the disquiet, the 1970s enjoyed positive change: divorce and abortion became legal, and legislation was passed allowing women to keep their own names after marriage. Significantly, regional governments with limited powers were formed in 15 of the country's 20 regions, including Tuscany.

And, in a predictable Tuscan centre-left fashion, from its creation in 1970 until 1983, Tuscany's regional government was headed up by Italy's dominant leftist party, the Partito Socialista Italiano (PSI; Italian Socialist Party).

With the disbanding of the Socialist party following the Tangentopoli ('kickback city') scandal, which broke in Milan in 1992, the door was left open in Tuscany's political arena for the Partito Democratico della Sinistra (Democratic Party of the Left; PDS) – an equally socialist political party created in 1991 to replace the disbanded PCI – to dominate the decade: on a national level, the PDS was part of Romano Prodi's winning centre-left coalition that defeated Berlusconi in 1996 (only for Berlusconi to sweep back into power with an unassailable majority at the head of a right-wing coalition known as Popolo della Libertà; PdL).

Regional elections in April 2005 saw incumbent Tuscan president Claudio Martini of the left-wing Democratici di Sinistra (DS; Democrats of the Left), in power since 2000, win a second term in office with a landslide victory over Berlusconi's centre-right PdL candidate, gaining 57.4% of votes. Utterly unique and innovative for an Italian politician, Tunis-born Claudio Martini (b 1951), who moved to Italy aged 10, worked tirelessly to revamp the healthcare system in Tuscany during his time in office. He rid the region of a serious health service deficit and strived to forge closer ties with the rest of Europe and Tuscans abroad. He chose not to stand for a third term in the 2010 regional elections (see p276).

2007	2008	2009	2011
Almost a decade after the project was announced, the first crane is spotted above Florence's Uffizi gallery. The multimillion-euro renovation project will double the gallery size. Completion date unknown.	Silvio Berlusconi and his right-wing allies triumph in the national elections. Tuscany's traditional support of leftist candidates and parties is diluted, with support for the Rainbow Left coalition falling dramatically.	Italy's Constitutional Court overturns a law giving Berlusconi immunity from prosecution while in office, opening the possibility that he could stand trial in several court cases. He refuses to resign.	Berlusconi stands trial in Milan in April on charges of abuse of power and paying for sex with an under-aged Moroccan prostitute called Karima El Mahroug (aka 'Ruby Heart Stealer').

The Tuscan Way of Life

It's a lifestyle that's the envy of so many. Romanticised the world over, Tuscany has impassioned more writers, more designers, more filmmakers and musicians than any other region. Yet just what is it that makes the birthplace of Gucci, Cavalli and the Vespa scooter so inspiring, so iconic, so exquisitely *dolce*?

Rural Roots

Deeply attached to their patch of land, people in this predominantly rural neck of the woods with only a sugar dusting of small towns are not simply Italian or Tuscan. Harking back to centuries of coexistence as rival political entities with their own style of architecture, school of painting, bell tower and so on, it is the *paese* (home town) or, in the case of Siena, the *contrada* (neighbourhood) in which one is born that reigns supreme. For most, such *campanilismo* (literally, loyalty to one's bell tower) is all-consuming.

Passionate, proud, reserved, hard-working, family-oriented, fond of food and wine, thrifty, extremely self-conscious and proud of their appearance are characteristics attributed to Tuscans across the board.

Brash, no, but in Florence Florentines like to make it known where they stand in society. From oversized doorknobs to sculpted stonework, overt statements of wealth and power are everywhere in this class-driven city, whose dialect – penned for the world to read by literary greats Dante, Boccaccio and Petrarch in the 14th century – is deemed the purest form of Italian.

La Dolce Vita

Life is *dolce* (sweet) for this privileged pocket of Italy, one of the country's wealthiest enclaves where the family reigns supreme, and tradition and quality reign over quantity. From the great names in viticulture to the flower-producing industry of Pescia and the small-scale farms of rural Tuscany, it is family-run businesses handed between generations that form the backbone of this proud, strong region.

In Florence – the only city with a faint hint of the cosmopolitan – daily life is the fastest paced. Florentines rise early, drop their kids at school by 8am then flit from espresso to the office by 9am. Lunch is a lengthy affair for these food- and wine-mad people, as is the early-evening *aperitivo,* enjoyed in a bar with friends to whet the appetite for dinner. For younger Florentines, who bear the biggest brunt of Florence's ever-rising rent and salaries that scarcely rise, it is quite common to treat the lavish *aperitivo* spread like dinner – enter *apericena.* Smokers meanwhile, fast dwindling, puff on pavements outside.

There is no better time of day or week than late Sunday afternoon to witness the *passeggiata* (early evening stroll), a wonderful tradition that

Best Passeggiata Strips

» Via de' Tornabuoni & Ponte Vecchio, Florence

» Via Banchi di Sopra, Siena

» 'The Corso' (aka Corso Italia), Arezzo

» Corso Carducci, Grosetto

With their gargantuan artistic heritage and tradition of master craftsmanship, it is not surprising that Florentines are known for their natural style, attention to detail, quest for perfection, appreciation of beauty, pride in their dialect and deep respect for the past.

sees Tuscans in towns don a suitable outfit and walk – to get a gelato, chat, meet friends, mooch, contemplate the sunset and, quite simply, relish the close of the day at an exceedingly relaxed pace.

Theatre, concerts, art exhibitions (the free opening on Thursday evenings at Florence's Palazzo Strozzi is always packed) and *il calcio* (football) entertain after hours. Tuscany's top professional football club, ACF Fiorentina, has a fanatical fan base (check the memorabilia in Florence's Trattoria Mario).

Weekends see many flee their city apartments for less urban climes, where the din of *motorini* (scooters) whizzing through the night lessens and there's more space and light: green countryside is a mere 15-minute getaway from lucky old Florence, unlike many urban centres where industrial sprawl really sprawls.

No title better delves into the essence of Tuscan lifestyle than *The Wisdom of Tuscany: Simplicity, Security and the Good Life – Making the Tuscan Lifestyle Your Own* by Ferenc Màté.

Casa Dolce Casa

By their very nature, family-orientated Tuscans travel little (many spend a lifetime living in the town of their birth) and place great importance on *casa dolce casa* (home sweet home) – the rate of home ownership in Tuscany is among Europe's highest.

Rural lifestyle is slavishly driven by close-knit, ancient communities in small towns and villages, where local matters and gossip are more important than national or world affairs. Everyone knows everyone to the point of being clannish, making assimilation for outsiders hard – if not impossible. Farming is the self-sufficient way of life, albeit one that is becoming increasingly difficult – hence the mushrooming of *agriturismi* (farm-stay accommodation), as farmers stoically utilise every resource they have to make ends meet.

'Better a death in the family than a Pisan at the door' says an old Florentine proverb with reference to the historic rivalry between Tuscan towns.

At one time the domain of Tuscany's substantial well-off British population (there's good reason why playwright John Mortimer dubbed Chianti 'Chiantishire' in his 1989 TV adaptation *Summer Lease*), the region's bounty of stylish stone villas and farmhouses with terracotta floors, wood-burning fireplaces and terraces with views are now increasingly passing back into the hands of Tuscans eagerly rediscovering their countryside.

Urban or rural, children typically remain at home until they reach their 30s, often only fleeing the nest to wed. In line with national trends, Tuscan families are small – one or two kids, with around 20% of families childless and 26% of households being single. Despite increasing numbers of women working, chauvinistic attitudes remain well entrenched in more rural areas.

La Festa

Delve into the mindset of a Tuscan and a holy trinity of popular folklore, agricultural tradition and religious rite of passage dances before your eyes – which pretty much translates as *la festa* (party!). No cultural agenda is more jam-packed with ancient festivity than theirs: patron

---

VIRTUAL TUSCAN LIFESTYLE

» **Florence Night & Day** (http://lovingflorence.blogspot.com) Compelling diary of a 30-something Florentine gal.

» **One Hundred Years Later in Florence** (http://bellabiker.blogspot.com) Post 9/11 and overnight disappearance of the neighbourhood in which she lived, a New York executive follows her Italian ancestors to Florence and becomes a bike-tour leader.

» **Notes from the Boot** (http://notesfromtheboot.blogspot.com) Intelligent, often amusing insights and musings on local culture.

Coffee is not just a drink but a way of life for Tuscans, whose typical day is regimentally punctuated with caffeine, the type of coffee depending wholly on time of day and occasion.

The number one cardinal rule: cappuccino (espresso topped with hot, frothy milk), caffè latte (milkier version with less froth) and latte macchiato (warmed milk 'stained' with a spot of coffee) are only ever drunk at breakfast or in the early morning. If you're truly Tuscan, though, the chances are you'll probably grab a speed espresso (short, sharp shot of strong, black coffee) or *caffè doppio* (double espresso) standing up at the bar – substantially cheaper than sitting down at a table – at your favourite cafe on the way to work.

Lunch and dinner only end one way, with *un caffè* (literally 'a coffee', meaning an espresso and nothing else), although come dusk it is quite acceptable to perhaps finish with *un caffè corretto* (espresso with a dash of grappa or other spirit).

saints alone provide weeks of celebration given that every village, town, profession, trade and social group has a saint they call their own and venerate religiously.

La festa climaxes, not once but twice, with Siena's soul-stirring Il Palio, a hot-blooded horse race conceived in the 12th century to honour the Virgin Mary and revamped six centuries on to celebrate the miracles of the Madonna of Provenzano (2 July) and Assumption (16 August). Deeply embroiled in its religious roots is a fierce *contrada* rivalry, not to mention a fervent penchant for dressing up and a widespread respect of tradition that sees horses blessed before the race, jockeys riding saddleless and the silk banner for the winner of August's race ritually designed by local Sienese artists and July's by non-Sienese. Legend says that a Sienese bride marrying in far-off lands took with her earth from her *contrada* to put beneath the legs of her marital bed to ensure her offspring would be conceived on home soil.

Although it's by no means the social force it once was, Catholicism (the religion of 85% of the region) and its rituals nevertheless play a key role in daily lives: first Communions, church weddings and religious feast days are an integral part of Tuscan society.

Bella Figura

A sense of style is vital to Tuscans, who take great pride in their dress and appearance to ensure their *bella figura* (good public face). Dressing impeccably comes naturally to most and for most Florentines, chic is a byword. Indeed, it was in that naturally beautiful city that the Italian fashion industry was born and bred.

Guccio Gucci and Salvatore Ferragamo got the haute-couture ball rolling in the 1920s with boutiques in Florence. And in 1951 a well-heeled Florentine nobleman called Giovanni Battista Giorgini held a fashion soirée in his Florence home to spawn Italy's first prêt-à-porter fashion shows. The catwalk quickly shifted to Florence's Palazzo Pitti, where Europe's most prestigious fashion shows dazzled until 1971 (when the women's shows moved to Milan). The menswear shows stayed put, though, and top designers still leg it to Florence twice a year to unveil their menswear collections at the Pitti Immagine Uomo fashion shows and their creations for *bambini* (kids) at Pitti Bimbo.

Tuscany continues to inspire fashion and the fashionable. Take American actor and dandy John Malkovich, who chose the Tuscan town of Prato to create his designer fashion label Technobohemian (www.technobohemian.it).

Just what is behind the average Florentine's front door? Take a peek with Andrew Losowsky's *The Doorbells of Florence* (http://losowsky.com/doorbells/), a collection of photographs of doorbells in Florence accompanied by a fictional story about the fun and antics behind them. Published first on Flickr, the award-winning title pioneered the term 'flicktion'.

The Tuscan Table

Be it by sinking your teeth into a beefy blue *bistecca alla fiorentina* (chargrilled T-bone steak), wine tasting in Chianti, savouring Livorno fish stew or devouring white truffles unearthed around San Miniato near Pisa, travelling Tuscany is a magnificent banquet of gastronomic and viticultural experiences.

For tips on when to go and what to eat, see the Eat & Drink Like a Local chapter (p35). For guidance on what you can expect to spend eating out, see p328.

A Country Kitchen

It was over an open wood fire in *la cucina contadina* (the farmer's kitchen) that Tuscan cuisine was cooked up. Its basic premise: don't waste a crumb.

During the 13th and 14th centuries, when Florence prospered and the wealthy started using silver cutlery instead of their fingers, simplicity remained the hallmark of dishes cooked up at the lavish banquets held by feuding families as a show of wealth. And while the Medici passion for flaunting the finer things in life during the Renaissance gave Tuscan cuisine a fanciful kick, with spectacular sculptures of sugar starring alongside spit-roasted suckling pig on the banquet table, ordinary Tuscans continued to rely on the age-old *cucina povera* (poor dishes) to keep hunger at bay.

Contemporary Tuscan cuisine remains faithful to these humble rural roots, relying on fresh local produce and eschewing fussy execution.

Virtual Kitchen

» Panini Girl (http://paninigirl. wordpress.com)

» Lucullian Delights (http://lucullian. blogspot.com)

» Faith Willinger (www.faithwilling er.com)

» Elizabeth Minchilli (www. elizabethminchilli. com)

A Bloody Affair: Meat & Game

The icon of Tuscan cuisine is Florence's *bistecca alla fiorentina,* a chargrilled T-bone steak rubbed with olive oil, seared on the chargrill, garnished with salt and pepper and only served one way – *al sangue* (brilliantly blue and bloody). A born-and-bred rebel, this feisty cut of meat of magnificent proportion (weighed before it's cooked and priced on menus by *l'etto* or 100g) was actually outlawed by the EU from 2001 to 2006 for fear of mad-cow disease.

Tuscan markets conjure up an orgy of animal parts many wouldn't dream of eating. In the past, prime beef cuts were the domain of the wealthy and offal was the staple peasant fare: tripe was simmered in the pot for hours with onions, carrots and herbs to make *lampredotto* or with tomatoes and herbs to make *trippa alla fiorentina* – two Florentine classics still going strong.

Fortunately *pasto,* a gruesome mix of *picchiante* (cow's lungs) and chopped potatoes, is not even a gastronomic curiosity these days – unlike *cibrèo* (chicken's kidney, liver, heart and cockscomb stew) and *colle ripieno* (stuffed chicken's neck), two dishes that can still be sampled at Florence's Trattoria Cibrèo in Santa Croce. Another fabulous golden oldie (cooked by the Etruscans, no less, as many a fresco illustrates) still going strong is *pollo al mattone* – boned chicken splattered beneath a brick, rubbed with herbs and baked beneath the brick. The end result is handsomely crispy.

Cinghiale (wild boar), hunted in autumn, is turned into *salsicce di cinghiale* (wild-boar sausages) or simmered with tomatoes, pepper and herbs to create a rich stew.

In Tuscany the family pig invariably ends up on the plate as a salty slice of *soprassata* (head, skin and tongue boiled, chopped and spiced with garlic, rosemary and other herbs and spices), *finocchiona* (fennel-spiced sausage), prosciutto, nearly black *mallegato* (spiked with nutmeg, cinnamon, raisins and pine kernels from San Miniato) or mortadella (a smooth-textured pork sausage speckled with cubes of white fat). *Lardo di colonnata* (thin slices of local pork fat aged in a mix of herbs and oils for at least six months) is among the Tuscan food products highlighted by Slow Food's Ark of Taste.

Best Creative Tuscan

» Il Santo Bevitore, Florence

» Filippo, Pietrasanta

» Antica Trattoria Aurora, Magliano in Toscana

» Ristorante Albergaccio, Castellina in Chianti

» La Locanda di Pietracupa, San Donato in Poggio

Best on Friday: Fish

Livorno leads the region in seafood, fishy *cacciucco* (one 'c' for each type of fish thrown into it) being its signature dish. Deriving its name from the Turkish *kukut,* meaning 'small fry', *cacciucco* is a stew of five fish simmered with tomatoes and red peppers, served atop stale bread. *Triglie alla livornese* is red or white mullet cooked in tomatoes, and *baccalà alla livornese,* also with tomatoes, features cod traditionally salted aboard the ships en route to the old Medici port. *Baccalà* (salted cod), not to be confused with *stoccofisso* (unsalted air-dried stockfish) is a Tuscan trattoria mainstay, served on Fridays as tradition and old-style Catholicism demands.

Poor Man's Meat: Pulses, Grains & Vegetables

Poor man's meat was precisely what pulses were to Tuscans centuries ago. Jam-packed with protein, cheap and available year-round (eaten fresh in summer, dried in winter), pulses go into traditional dishes such as *minestra di fagioli* (bean soup), *pasta e ceci* (chickpea pasta), *minestra di pane* (bread and bean soup) and *ribollita* (a 'reboiled' bean,

THE ARK OF TASTE

A project born and headquartered in Florence, the Ark of Taste is an international catalogue of endangered food products drawn up by the Slow Food Foundation for Biodiversity in partnership with the region of Tuscany. It aims to protect and promote traditional, indigenous edibles threatened with extinction by industrialisation, globalisation, hygiene laws, environmental dangers and so on.

In Tuscany 30-odd products risk disappearing, including Chianina beef, *lardo di colonnata*, Certaldo onions, Casola chestnut bread, Cetica red potatoes, Garfagnana potato bread and *farro* (spelt), Carmignano dried figs, *cinta senese* (the indigenous Tuscan pig), Londa Regina peaches, Pistoian Mountain *pecorino* cheese, Orbetello *bottarga* (salted mullet roe), Zeri lamb and *zolfino* beans. Among the many cured meats that make the list: San Miniato *mallegato*, Prato mortadella (smooth-textured pork sausage made dull-pink with drops of alkermes liqueur and speckled white with cubes of fat), Sienese *buristo* (a type of pork salami made in the province of Siena), Valdarno *tarese* (a 50cm-to-80cm-long pancetta spiced with red garlic, orange peel and covered in pepper), Florentine *bardiccio* (fresh fennel-flavoured sausage encased in a natural skin of pig intestine and eaten immediately) and *biroldo* (spiced blood sausage made in Garfagnana from pig's head and blood).

Dining on or sampling any of these items in Tuscany guarantees an authentic and delicious tasting experience. For the complete list see www.fondazioneslowfood.it.

ORGANIC FOOD

Cibo biologico (organic food) is increasingly popular in farm-rich Tuscany, where several stand-out dining choices (such as Podere del Grillo near San Miniato or La Cerreta near Sassetta) are created solely from organic farm produce. Italian organic super-market NaturaSi (www.naturasi. it) has shops in Siena, Lucca and Florence.

vegetable and bread soup with black cabbage, left to sit for a day before being served).

Amid the dozens of different bean varieties, *cannellini* and dappled *borlotti* are the most common; both are delicious drizzled with olive oil to accompany meat. The round yellow *zolfino* from Pratomagno and silky smooth *sorano* bean from Pescia are prized. Of huge local pride to farmers in Garfagnana is *farro della garfagnana* (spelt), an ancient grain grown in Europe as early as 2500 BC.

Tuscany's lush vegetable garden sees medieval vegetables grow alongside typical tomatoes and zucchini. Wild fennel, black celery (braised as a side dish), sweet red onions (delicious oven-baked), artichokes and zucchini flowers (stuffed and oven-baked), black cabbage, broad beans, chicory, chard, thistle-like cardoons and green tomatoes are among the more unusual ones to look out for.

Prized as one of the most expensive spices, saffron is all the rage again, particularly around San Gimignano where it was enthusiastically traded in medieval times. Fiery red and as fine as dust by the time it reaches the kitchen, saffron in its rawest state is, in fact, the dried flower stigma of the saffron crocus.

Where's the Salt: Bread

One bite and the difference is striking: Tuscan *pane* (bread) is unsalted, creating a disconcertingly bland taste many a bread lover might never learn to love.

Yet it is this centuries-old staple, deliberately unsalted to ensure it lasted for a good week and to complement the region's salty cured meats, that forms the backbone of Tuscany's most famous dishes: *pappa al pomodoro* (a thick bread and tomato soup, eaten hot or cold), *panzanella* (a tomato and basil salad mixed with a mush of bread soaked in cold water) and *ribollita*. None sound or look particularly appetising, but their depth of flavour is extraordinary.

Thick-crusted *pane toscana* (also known as *pane casalingo*) is the basis of two antipasti delights, traditionally served on festive occasions but a staple on every menu: *crostini* (lightly toasted slices of bread topped with liver pâté) and *fettunta* or Tuscan bruschetta (also called *crogiantina*; toast fingers doused in garlic, salt and olive oil).

A Dowry Skill: Cheese

So important was cheesemaking in the past, it was deemed a dowry skill. Still highly respected, the sheep's-milk *pecorino* crafted in Pienza ranks among Italy's greatest *pecorini*: taste it young and mild in the company of fava beans, fresh pear or chestnuts and honey; or try it more mature and tangier, spiked with *toscanello* (black peppercorns) or as *pecorino di tartufo* (infused with black-truffle shavings). *Pecorino* massaged with olive oil during the ageing process turns red and is called *rossellino*.

OLIVE OIL

Olive oil heads Tuscany's culinary trinity (bread and wine are the other two) and epitomises the earthy simplicity of Tuscan cuisine: dipping chunks of bread into pools of this liquid gold or biting into a slice of oil-doused *fettunta* (bruschetta) are sweet pleasures in life here.

The Etruscans were the first to cultivate olive trees and press the fruit to make oil, a process later refined by the Romans. As with wine, strict rules govern when and how olives are harvested (October through to 31 December), the varieties used, and so on.

The best Tuscan oils wear a Chianti Classico DOP or Terre di Siena DOP label and an IGP certificate of quality issued by the region's Consortium of Tuscan Olive Oil.

In 1986 McDonald's was about to open a restaurant at the famed Spanish Steps in Rome. Carlo Petrini, a wine writer, was so appalled at this prospect that he started a movement that has since grown to include more than 100,000 members in 132 countries. Called Slow Food (www.fondazioneslowfood.com), about half of its members are based in Italy, but branches are opening around the world at a rapid pace as people follow the Italian lead, seeking to preserve local food traditions and encouraging interest in the food they eat, where it comes from, how it tastes and how our food choices affect the rest of the world.

From the Slow Food Movement grew the Slow City Movement (www.cittaslow. blogspot.com). Its members are concerned that globalisation is wiping out differences in traditions and culture and replacing them with a watered-down homogeneity.

To become a Slow City (Città Lenta), towns have to pass a rigid set of standards, including having a visible and distinct culture. The towns must follow principles such as relying heavily on autochthonous (from within) resources instead of mass-produced food and culture; cutting down on air and noise pollution; and increasingly relying on sustainable development, such as organic farming and public transport. The following are Tuscan Slow Cities: Anghiari, Barga, Castelnuovo Berardenga, Civitella in Val di Chiana, Greve in Chianti, Massa Marittima, Pratovecchio, San Miniato, San Vincenzo and Suvereto.

THE TUSCAN TABLE A COUNTRY KITCHEN

Festive Frolics: Sweets, Chocolate & Ice

Be it the simple honey, almond and sugar-cane sweets traditionally served at the start of 14th-century banquets in Florence, or the sugar sculptures made to impress at the flamboyant 16th- and 17th-century feasts of the power-greedy Medici, *dolci* (sweets) have always been reserved for festive occasions. In more humble circles street vendors sold *bomboloni* (doughnuts) and *pandiramerino* (rosemary-bread buns), while Carnivale in Florence was marked by *stiacchiata* (Florentine flat bread made from eggs, flour, sugar and lard, then dusted with icing sugar).

As early as the 13th century, servants at the Abbazia di Montecelso near Siena paid tax to the nuns in the form of *panpepato* (a pepper and honey flat bread), although legend tells a different tale: following a siege in Siena, the good-hearted Sister Berta baked a revitalising flat cake of honey, dried fruit, almonds and pepper to pep up the city's weakened inhabitants. Subsequently sweetened with spices, sprinkled with icing sugar and feasted on once a year at Christmas, Siena's *panforte* (literally 'strong bread') – a flat, hard cake with nuts and candied fruit – is eaten year-round today. An old wife's tale says it stops couples quarrelling.

Unsurprisingly, it was at the Florentine court of Catherine de' Medici that Italy's most famous product, gelato (ice cream), first appeared thanks to court maestro Bernardo Buontalenti (1536–1608), who engineered a way of freezing sweetened milk and egg yolks together; the ice house he designed still stands in the Giardino di Boboli in Florence. For centuries, ice cream and sherbets – a mix of shaved ice and fruit juice served between courses at Renaissance banquets to aid digestion – only appeared on wealthy tables.

Tuscan *biscotti* (biscuits) – once served with candied fruits and sugared almonds at the start of and between courses at Renaissance banquets – are dry, crisp and often double-baked. *Cantucci* are hard, sweet biscuits studded with almonds. *Brighidini di lamporecchio* are small, round aniseed-flavoured wafers; *ricciarelli* are almond biscuits, sometimes with candied orange; and *lardpinocchiati* are studded with pine kernels. In Lucca, locals are proud of their *buccellato* (a sweet bread loaf

Pasta is as much Tuscan as it is Italian, and no Tuscan banquet would be quite right without a *primo* (first course) of homemade *maccheroni* (wide, flat ribbon pasta), *pappardelle* (wider flat ribbon pasta) or Sienese *pici* (a thick, hand-rolled version of spaghetti) served with a duck, hare, rabbit or boar sauce.

with sultanas and aniseed seeds), a treat given by godparents to their godchild on their first Holy Communion and eaten with alacrity at all other times.

Buone Feste

Be it the start of a harvest, a wedding, a birth or a religious holiday, traditional celebrations are intrinsically woven into Tuscan culinary culture. These are by no means as raucous as festivals of the past, when an animal was sacrificed, but most remain meaty affairs. As integral to the festive calendar as these madcap days of overindulgence are the days of eating *magro* (lean) – fasting days, usually preceding every feast day and in place for 40 days during Lent.

Tuscans have baked simple breads and cakes such as ring-shaped *berlingozzo* (Tuscan sweet bread) and *schiacciata alla fiorentina* (a flattish, spongey bread-cum-cake best made with old-fashioned lard) for centuries during Carnevale, the period of merrymaking leading up to Ash Wednesday. Fritters are another sweet Carnevale treat: *cenci* are plain twists (literally 'rags') of fried, sweet dough sprinkled with icing sugar; *castagnole* look like puffed-up cushions; and *fritelle di mele* are slices of apple battered, deep fried and eaten warm with plenty of sugar.

Pasqua (Easter) is big. On Easter Sunday, families take baskets of hard-boiled white eggs covered in a white-cloth napkin to church to be blessed, and return home to a luncheon feast of roast lamb gently spiced with garlic and rosemary, pre-empted by the blessed eggs.

September's grape harvest sees grapes stuck on top of *schiacciata* to make *schiacciata con l'uva* (grape cake), and autumn's chestnut harvest brings a flurry of chestnut festivals and *castagnaccio* (chestnut cake baked with chestnut flower, studded with raisins, topped with a rosemary sprig and delicious served with a slice of ricotta) to the Tuscan table.

Come Natale (Christmas), a *bollito misto* (boiled meat) with all the trimmings is the traditional festive dish in many families: various meaty animal parts, trotters et al, are thrown into the cooking pot and simmered for hours with a vegetable and herb stock. The meat is later served with mustard, salsa verde and other sauces. A whole pig, notably the recently revived ancient white-and-black *cinta senese* indigenous breed, roasted on a spit is the other option.

Food festivals – a great excuse to dine well, drink and sometimes dance 'til dawn – cover the region's rich cultural calendar; see Month by Month (p24) for more details.

Best Farm Meals

» Pradaccio di Sopra, near Castelnuovo di Garfagnana

» Podere San Lorenzo, near Volterra

» Montebelli Agriturismo & Country Hotel, near Vetulonia

LABELS OF QUALITY

Quality and origin of Tuscan wine is flagged with a trio of official classifications:

» **DOC** (Denominazione d'Origine Controllata; Protected Designation of Origin) Must be produced within a specified region using defined methods to meet a certain quality; the rules spell out production area, grape varietals and viticultural/bottling techniques.

» **DOCG** (Denominazione d'Origine Controllata e Garantita; Protected Designation of Origin and Quality) The most prestigious stamp of quality, DOCG wines are particularly good ones, produced in subterritories of DOC areas. Of Italy's 44 DOCGs, eight are Tuscan – Brunello di Montalcino, Carmignano, Chianti, Chianti Classico, Morellino di Scansano, Vernaccia di San Gimignano, Vino Nobile di Montepulciano and Elba Aleatico Passito.

» **IGT** (Indicazione Geografica Tipica; Protected Geographical Indication) High-quality wines that don't meet DOC or DOCG definitions but are high quality nevertheless. Super Tuscans fall into this category.

In addition to Tuscany's bevy of wine roads, six tasty Strade del Vino & dell'Olio meander past olive groves, vines and farms plump with local produce. For routes in Chianti, see p210.

» **Strada del Vino e dei Sapori Colli di Maremma** (www.stradavinimaremma. it) This route southeast of Grossetto highlights Morellino di Scansano DOC and DOCG; Ansonica Costa dell'Argentario, Bianco di Pitigliano, Capalbio, Parrina and Sovana DOCs; extra-virgin olive oil Toscano IGP (Indicazione Geografica Protetta; Protected Geographical Indication); and the Maremma breed of cattle.

» **Strada del Vino e dell'Olio Lucca Montecarlo e Versilia** (www.stradavinoeo liolucca.it) Travels between Seravezza in the Apuane Alps to Lucca and then east to Montecarlo and Pescia, passing dramatic scenery and ornate villas on the way. Features Lucca's famous DOP olive oil and the Colline Lucchesi and Montecarlo di Lucca DOCs.

» **Strada del Vino Montecucco e dei Sapori d'Amiata** (www.stradadelvinomon tecucco.it) Follow the trail south of Montalcino, home to Montecucco DOC and Seggiano DOP extra-virgin olive oil.

On the Wine Trail

There's far more to this vine-rich region than cheap, raffia-wrapped bottled Chianti – *that* was the 1970s, darling! Something of a viticultural powerhouse, Tuscany excites oenophiles with its myriad of full-bodied, highly respected reds. Wine tasting is an endless pleasure and the region is peppered with *enoteche* (wine bars) and *cantine* (wine cellars) designed especially for tasting and buying.

Many are planted on Tuscany's *strade del vino* (wine roads), signposted itineraries that lead motorists and cyclists along wonderfully scenic back roads into the heart of Tuscan wine country. See p210 for more details and images.

Brunello di Montalcino

Brunello is up there at the top with Italy's most prized: count up to €10 for a glass, €30 to €100 for an average bottle and €5000 for a 1940s collectible. The product of Sangiovese grapes grown south of Siena, it must spend at least two years ageing in oak. It is intense and complex with an ethereal fragrance, and is best paired with game, wild boar and roasts. Brunello grape rejects go into Rossi di Montalcino, Brunello's substantially cheaper but wholly drinkable kid sister.

Vino Nobile di Montepulciano

Prugnolo Gentile grapes (a clone of Sangiovese) form the backbone of the distinguished Vino Nobile di Montepulciano (2006 was an exceptional year). Its intense but delicate nose and dry, vaguely tannic taste make it the perfect companion to red meat and mature cheese.

Chianti

This cheery, full and dry fellow is known the world over as being easy to drink, suited to any dish and wholly affordable. More famous than it was good in the 1970s, contemporary Chianti gets the thumbs up from wine critics today. Produced in seven subzones from Sangiovese and a mix of other grape varieties, Chianti Classico – the traditional heart of this longstanding wine-growing area – is the best known, with a DOCG (Denominazione d'Origine Controllata e Garantita; Protected Designation of Origin and Quality) guarantee of quality and a Gallo Nero (Black Cockerel) emblem that once symbolised the medieval Chianti League.

Tuscan white amounts to one label loved by Renaissance popes and artists alike: the aromatic Vernaccia di San Gimignano, best drunk as an aperitif on a terrace in or around San Gimignano.

THE TUSCAN TABLE ON THE WINE TRAIL

Young, fun Chianti Colli Senesi from the Siena hills is the largest sub-zone; Chianti delle Colline Pisane is light and soft in style; and Chianti Rùfina comes from the hills east of Florence.

Super Tuscans

One result of Chianti's 'cheap wine for the masses' reputation in the 1970s was the realisation by some Tuscans – including the Antinoris, Tuscany's most famous wine-producing family – that wines with a rich, complex, internationally acceptable taste following the New World tradition of blending mixes could be sold for a lot more than local wines. Thus, innovative, exciting wines were developed and cleverly marketed to appeal to buyers both in New York and in Florence. And when an English-speaking scribe dubbed the end product 'Super Tuscans', the name stuck. Sassacaia, Solaia, Bolgheri, Tignanello and Luce are all superhot Super Tuscans.

Celebrity Wine

With the birth of Super Tuscans so was born a gaggle of celebrity-backed wines: Sting owns a vast wine-producing estate near Figline Valdarno in Chianti, where he produces a Chianti Colli Aretini known as Il Serrestori (after the silk-weaving family who once owned his pad), sold under his own private label, limited and signed.

Sinatra Family Estates (yes, as in Frank) meanwhile owns a small 3-hectare vineyard (http://sinatrafamilyestates.com) in the Fiesole hills near Florence where grapes are grown to make Le Noce (literally 'the Voice'), a limited-edition Super Tuscan blend of Colorino and Sangiovese grapes.

Other celebrity wines to look out for are the Super Tuscan reds produced by the son of Florentine designer Roberto Cavalli at the Tenuta degli Dei (www.deglidei.it) outside Panzano in Chianti (top-of-the-range bottles are packaged in a typical Cavalli, flashy leopard-skin box); and those produced southeast of Pisa on the family estate of opera singer Andrea Bocelli, sold at Cantina Bocelli in La Sterza.

If celebrity design is more your cup of tea, taste wine at the subterranean, design-driven Rocca di Frassinello (www.roccadifrassinello.it) winery near Grossetto by Renzo Piano; or the equally breathtaking Petra (www.petrawine.it) winery by Swiss architect Mario Botta in the Etruscan hills near Suvereto.

Best Wine Bars

» Le Volpi e l'uva, Florence

» Enoteca Marcucci, Pietrasanta

» Enoteca I Terzi, Siena

» Osticcio, Montalcino

» Rosso e Vino, Grosseto

Tuscany on Page & Screen

Tuscany in Print

In the late Middle Ages, a cheeky chap named Dante Alighieri decided that he would shake up the literary establishment by writing in Italian rather than Latin. In so doing, he laid the foundations for the development of a rich literary culture that continues to nurture both local and foreign writers to this day.

In 2010, the US video-game developer Electronic Arts released its version of Dante's *Inferno* for Xbox and PlayStation consols.

Local Voices

Prior to the 13th century, all Italian literature was written in Latin. But all that changed with the arrival of Florentine-born Dante Alighieri (c 1265–1321) on the literary scene. One of the founders of the *Dolce Stil Novo* (Sweet New Style) literary movement, whose members wrote lyric poetry in the Tuscan vernacular, Dante went on to use the local language when writing the epic poem that was to become the first, and greatest, literary work published in the Italian language: *La grande commedia*

THE REAL ADVENTURES OF PINOCCHIO

A timeless tale of a wooden puppet that turns into a boy, *Le avventure di Pinocchio* (The Adventures of Pinocchio) is among the most widely read and internationally popular pieces of literature ever to emerge from Italy.

In the early 1880s, Carlo Collodi (1826–90), a Florentine journalist, wrote a series for *Il Giornale dei Bambini,* the first Italian newspaper for children. Entitled *Storia di un burattino* (Story of a Puppet) and subsequently renamed, it would have made Collodi (real name Lorenzini) a multimillionaire had he lived to exploit the film and translation rights.

The character of Pinocchio is a frustrating mix of the likeable and the odious. At his worst he's a wilful, obnoxious, deceitful little monster who deserves just about everything he gets. Humble and blubbering when things go wrong, he has the oh-so-human tendency to resume his wayward behaviour when he thinks he's in the clear.

The story, weaving between fantasy and reality, is a mine of references, some more veiled than others, to the society of late-19th-century Italy – a troubled country with enormous socio-economic problems compounded by the general apathy of those in power. Pinocchio waits the length of the story to become a real boy. But, while his persona may provoke laughter, his encounters with poverty, petty crime, skewed justice and just plain bad luck constitute a painful education in the machinations of the 'real' world.

Disney made a much-loved animated film of the story in 1940. It won two Academy Awards – one for Best Original Score and one for Best Original Song ('When You Wish Upon a Star'). A number of Italian adaptations have also been made, including one directed by Roberto Benigni in 2002.

(The Great Comedy), published around 1317 and later renamed *La divina commedia* (The Divine Comedy) by his fellow poet Boccaccio. Divided into three parts – *Inferno, Purgatorio* and *Paradiso* – the *Divine Comedy* delivered an allegorical vision of the afterlife that made an immediate and profound impression on readers and, through its wide-reaching popularity, established the Tuscan dialect as the new standardised form of written Italian.

Another early adaptor to the new language of literature was Giovanni Boccaccio (1303–75), who hailed from Certaldo. His masterpiece, *Decameron*, was written in the years following the plague of 1348. A collection of 100 allegorical tales recounted by 10 characters, it delivered a vast panorama of personalities, events and symbolism to contemporary readers and was nearly as popular and influential as the *Divine Comedy*.

The remaining member of the influential triumvirate that laid down the course for the development of a rich literature in Italian was Petrarch (Francesco Petrarca; 1304–74), born in Arezzo to Florentine parents. Although most of his writings were in Latin, he wrote his most popular works, the poems, in Italian. *Il canzoniere* (Songbook; c 1327–68) is the distilled result of his finest poetry. Although the core subject is his unrequited love for a woman named Laura, the breadth of human grief and joy is treated with a lyrical quality hitherto unmatched. His influence spread far and across time: the Petrarchan sonnet form, rhyme scheme and even subject matter was adopted by English Metaphysical poets of 17th-century England such as John Donne.

Another outstanding writer of this period was Niccolò Machiavelli (1469–1527), known above all for his work on power and politics, *Il Principe* (The Prince; 1532).

19th Century Onwards

After its stellar start during the Renaissance, Tuscany took a literary break between the 17th and 18th centuries. It wasn't until the 19th century that the scene started to regain some momentum.

Giosue Carducci (1835–1907) was one of the key figures of 19th-century Tuscan literature. Born in the Maremma, he spent the second half of his life in Bologna. The best of his poetry, written in the 1870s, ranged in tone from pensive evocation of death (such as in *Pianto antico*) or memories of youthful passion *(Idillio Maremmano)* to an historic nostalgia harking back to the glories of ancient Rome.

Florence's Aldo Palazzeschi (1885–1974) was in the vanguard of the Futurist movement during the pre-WWI years. In 1911 he published

---

Decameron on Screen

» *Decameron Nights* (Hugo Fregonese; 1953)

» *Decameron* (Pier Paolo Pasolini; 1971)

» *Virgin Territory* (David Leland; 2007)

Food forms the subject of many Tuscan memoirs. Two good examples are *A Culinary Traveller in Tuscany: Exploring & Eating Off The Beaten Track* (Beth Elon; 2006) and *The Tuscan Year: Life and Food in an Italian Valley* (Elizabeth Romer; 1985).

TUSCAN MEMOIRS

After visiting Tuscany, many people dream of moving there permanently. The following writers did just that, some establishing wildly successful literary franchises in the process.

» **Dario Castagno** (*Too Much Tuscan Sun; A Day in Tuscany; Too Much Tuscan Wine; 2004–2009*)

» **Mark Gordon Smith** (*Tuscan Echoes; Tuscan Light: Memories of Italy; 2003–2007*)

» **Ferenc Máté** (*The Hills of Tuscany; A Vineyard in Tuscany: A Wine-Lover's Dream; The Wisdom of Tuscany; 1999–2009*)

» **Frances Mayes** (*Under the Tuscan Sun: At Home in Italy; Bella Tuscany; In Tuscany; Every Day in Tuscany; 1996–2010*)

» **Don McPherson** (*Ah! Tuscany: The Enlightenment of an Expatriate; 2006*)

» **Eric Newby** (*A Small Place in Italy; 1994*)

Tuscany features as the setting for some great crime fiction written by local and international authors. If you're a fan of the genre, you may like to read the following before or during your visit.

» **Michael Dibdin** His popular Aurelio Zen novels include *And Then You Die* (2002), set on the Tuscan coast.

» **Michele Giuttari** A former high-ranking Florentine policeman, Giuttari has set two of his Michel Ferrara novels here: *A Florentine Death* (2007) and *A Death in Tuscany* (2008). A new title, *The Black Rose of Florence,* is due in 2012.

» **Thomas Harris** Florence is the setting for *Hannibal,* Harris' 1999 sequel to *The Silence of the Lambs.*

» **John Spencer Hill** The late Canadian writer set two historical crime titles here: *The Last Castrato* (1995) in Florence and *Ghirlandaio's Daughter* (1996) in Lucca.

» **Christobel Kent** Florentine-based private detective Sandro Cellini features in *A Florentine Revenge* (2006), *A Time of Mourning* (aka *The Drowning River;* 2009) and *A Fine and Private Place* (aka *Murder in Tuscany;* 2010). A fourth title, *The Dead Season,* is due for publication in 2012.

» **Giulio Leoni** *The Third Heaven Conspiracy* (aka *The Mosaic Crimes;* 2004) is a historical crime fiction title in which Dante solves the murder of a mosaicist in a ruined church just outside Florence.

» **Magdalen Nabb** The prolific British crime writer wrote 14 novels featuring Florentine policeman Marshal Guarnaccia.

» **Iain Pears** The Jonathan Argyll/Flavia di Stefano series includes *The Raphael Affair* (1991), set in Siena; *Giotto's Hand* (1994), set in Florence; and *The Immaculate Deception* (2000), set in various Tuscan locations.

» **Marco Vichi** Italian crime fiction writer whose latest title, *Death in August* (2011), is set in Florence in 1962.

arguably his best work, *Il codice di Perelà* (Perelà's Code), an at times bitter allegory that in part becomes a farcical imitation of the life of Christ.

By the 1920s and '30s Florence was bubbling with activity as a series of literary magazines flourished in spite of the Fascist regime. Publications such as *Solaria,* which lasted from 1926 to 1934, its successor *Letteratura* (which began circulating in 1937) and *Il frontespizio* (1929–40) gave writers from across Italy a platform from which to launch and discuss their work. One of its founding authors, Alessandro Bonsanti (1904–84), wrote essays and literary criticism. Guglielmo Petroni (1911–93), from Lucca, was another contributor to *Letteratura.* Although a poet of some note, he's chiefly recognised for his novel *Il mondo è una prigione* (The World is a Prison; 1948), a vivid account of a political prison and the Italian Resistance. Mario Tobino (1910–91), from Viareggio, used his experience as director of a mental asylum to great effect in *Le libere donne di Magliano* (The Free Women of Magliano; 1953).

Florentine Vasco Pratolini (1913–91) set four highly regarded Neorealist novels in his birthplace: *Le ragazze di San Frediano* (1949), *Cronaca familiare* (1947), *Cronache di poveri amanti* (1947) and *Metello* (1955).

Tuscan-born Dacia Maraini (b 1936), for many years the partner of author Alberto Moravia, is one of Italy's most lauded contemporary writers, with novels, plays and poetry to her credit. Her best-known works include *Buio* (1999), which won the Premio Strega, Italy's most prestigious literary award, and *La lunga vita di Marianna Ucrìa* (published in English as The Silent Duchess; 1990).

Americans Abroad

» *Italian Hours* (Henry James; 1909)

» *The Stones of Florence* (Mary McCarthy; 1956)

» *The City of Florence* (RWB Lewis; 1995)

Through Foreign Eyes

The trend of setting English-language novels in Tuscany kicked off during the era of the Grand Tour, when wealthy young men from Britain and Northern Europe travelled around Europe to view the cultural legacies of classical antiquity and the Renaissance, completing their liberal educations and being introduced to polite society in the process. The Grand Tour's heyday was from the mid-17th century to the mid-19th century.

With the advent of rail travel in the 1840s, the prospect of a cultural odyssey opened to the middle classes. Wealthy travellers from Britain, America and Australasia flocked to Italy, some of whom wrote about their experiences. Notable among these were Henry James, who set parts of *The Portrait of a Lady* (1881) and *Roderick Hudson* (1875) here; George Eliot, whose *Romola* (1862) was set in 15th-century Florence; and EM Forster, who set *A Room with a View* (1908) in Florence and *Where Angels Fear to Tread* (1905) in San Gimignano (fictionalised as Monteriano).

Things slowed down in the early 20th century, with only a few major novelists choosing to set their work here. These included Somerset Maugham (*Up at the Villa;* 1941) and Aldous Huxley (*Time Must Have a Stop;* 1944).

In recent decades, a number of highly regarded novels have been set in Tuscany. Perhaps the best known of these are by English writer Linda Proud, whose Botticelli trilogy – *A Tabernacle for the Sun, Pallas and the Centaur* and *The Rebirth of Venus* – is set in Renaissance Florence during the Pazzi Conspiracy, the Medici exile and the rise of Savonarola. The historical detail in all three is exemplary, and each is a cracking good read. A prequel, *A Gift for the Magus,* is due to be published in 2011.

Other writers who have used Renaissance Florence as a setting include Sarah Dunant (*The Birth of Venus;* 2003), Salman Rushdie (*The Enchantress of Florence;* 2008), Michaela-Marie Roessner-Hermann (*The Stars Dispose,* 1997; *The Stars Dispel,* 1999) and Jack Dann (*The Memory Cathedral;* 1995). Of these, Dann wins the prize for constructing the most bizarre plot, setting his novel in a version of the Renaissance in which Leonardo da Vinci actually constructs a number of his inventions (eg the flying machine) and uses them during a battle in the Middle East while in the service of a Syrian general.

Also set here are *Innocence* (1986) by Booker Prize–winning novelist Penelope Fitzgerald, which is set in Florence during the 1950s; *The Sixteen Pleasures* (1994) by Robert Hellenga, set in the same city after the devastating flood of 1966; and *The English Patient* (1992) by Michael Ondaatje, partly set in a villa outside Florence.

Britons Abroad

» *Pictures from Italy* (Charles Dickens; 1846)

» *Along the Road* (Aldous Huxley; 1925)

» *Etruscan Places* (DH Lawrence; 1932)

Tuscany on Film

Cinema heavyweight Franco Zeffirelli was born in Florence in 1923 and has set many of his films in the region. His career has taken him from radio and theatre to opera (both stage productions and film versions) and his films include *Romeo and Juliet* (1968), *Brother Sun, Sister Moon* (1972), *Hamlet* (1990) and the semiautobiographical *Tea with Mussolini* (1999).

Actor, comedian and director Roberto Benigni was born near Castiglion Fiorentino in 1952. He picked up four Oscars and created a genre all of his own – Holocaust comedy – with the extraordinarily powerful *La vita é bella* (Life is Beautiful; 1998), a film that he directed, co-wrote and starred in. Often compared with Charlie Chaplin and Buster Keaton, he has directed nine films (two set in Tuscany) and acted in many more, including three directed by American independent film-maker Jim Jarmusch.

Four films based on Neorealist novels by Vasco Pratolini were shot in Florence: *Le ragazze di San Frediano* (The Girls of San Frediano; Valerio

Don't Miss

» *Life is Beautiful*

» *A Room with a View*

» *The Night of the Shooting Stars*

Don't Bother

» *Under the Tuscan Sun*

» *Letters to Juliet*

» *Obsession*

INTERNATIONAL FILM PRODUCTIONS SET IN TUSCANY

» **The English Patient** (Anthony Minghella; 1996) Known for its lyrically beautiful scene set in Arezzo's Cappella Bacci.

» **Hannibal** (Ridley Scott; 2001) Parts of the sequel to *The Silence of the Lambs* were shot in Florence.

» **Letters to Juliet** (Gary Winick; 2010) Could equally have been titled 'Under the Tuscan Schmaltz'. What was Vanessa Redgrave thinking?!

» **Miracle at St. Anna** (Spike Lee; 2008) Based on James McBride's novel about four black American soldiers who get trapped in a Tuscan village near Lucca during WWII.

» **Much Ado about Nothing** (Kenneth Branagh; 1993) Branagh, Emma Thompson and Keanu Reeves star in this adaptation of Shakespeare's comedy; shot in Chianti.

» **New Moon** (Chris Weitz; 2009) Parts of the second film in the Twilight trilogy were shot in Montepulciano's main piazza, despite the fact that in the book the action occurs in Volterra.

» **Obsession** (Brian De Palma; 1976) Clearly influenced by Hitchcock's *Vertigo*, this lacklustre effort is only redeemed by some lovely shots of Florence.

» **The Portrait of a Lady** (Jane Campion; 1996) Features a couple of scenes shot in Florence.

» **Quantum of Solace** (Marc Forster; 2008) The 22nd Bond film featured great action sequences shot in Carrara and Siena.

» **Romola** (Henry King; 1924) The silent film version of George Eliot's novel starred Lillian Gish and was filmed in Florence.

» **A Room with a View** (James Ivory; 1985) Hugely popular period drama set in Florence; there was also a 2007 UK ITV adaptation by Andrew Davies.

» **September Affair** (William Dieterle; 1950) Joseph Cotten and Joan Fontaine fall in love in Florence; features Kurt Weill's famous 'September Song'.

» **Stealing Beauty** (Bernardo Bertolucci; 1996) In her first film role, Liv Tyler grapples with her grief and burgeoning sexuality in the lush Tuscan countryside.

» **Under the Tuscan Sun** (Audrey Wells; 2003) A lightweight film version of the wildly popular memoir set in Cortona.

» **Up at the Villa** (Philip Haas; 2000) Sean Penn and Kristin Scott Thomas star in an adaptation of Somerset Maugham's novel.

» **Where Angels Fear to Tread** (Charles Sturridge; 1991) A fine cast including Helen Mirren, Judy Davis and Helena Bonham Carter stars in this period film shot in San Gimignano.

Zurlini; 1954), *Cronache di poveri amanti* (Chronicle of Poor Lovers; Carlo Lizzani; 1954), *Cronaca familiare* (Family Diary; Valerio Zurlini; 1962) and *Metello* (Mauro Bolognini; 1970).

Award-winning film-makers Paolo and Vittorio Taviani were born in San Miniato and have set parts of three of their films in Tuscany: *La notte di San Lorenzo* (aka The Night of the Shooting Stars; 1982), *Le affinità elettive* (Elective Affinities; 1996) and *Good Morning Babylon* (1987).

Art & Architecture

In many respects, the history of Tuscan art is also the history of Western art. Browse through any text on the subject and you'll quickly develop an understanding of how influential the Italian Renaissance, which kicked off and reached its greatest flowering in Florence, has been over the past 500 years. Indeed, it's no exaggeration to say that architecture, painting and sculpture rely on its technical innovations and take inspiration from its major works to this very day.

Tuscany itself is one huge art gallery, full of museums, *palazzi* (palaces) and churches housing a treasure trove of art that is unmatched anywhere in the world. There's no way you'll be able to see everything, but a few days in Florence, Siena and Pisa should give you a great introduction – as well as an excellent excuse to return and see more.

The Etruscans

Etruscan necropoli (tombs) are found throughout Tuscany. Excavation of these often yields cinerary urns (used for body ashes) made from terracotta and alabaster, earthenware pottery (particularly the glossy black ceramic known as *bucchero*) and bronze votive offerings.

Roughly 2800 years before we all started dreaming of a hilltop getaway in Tuscany, the Etruscans had a similar idea. Dotting the countryside are towns that they founded to keep a watchful eye on the crops below – as well as on the neighbours across the valley.

From the 8th to the 3rd century BC, Etruscans held their own against friends, Romans and countrymen, worshipped their own gods and goddesses, and farmed lowlands using sophisticated drainage systems of their own invention. How well the Etruscans lived between sieges and war is unclear, but they sure knew how to throw a funeral: a wealth of jewellery, ceramics and other creature comforts for the afterlife have been found in Etruscan stone tombs throughout southern, central and eastern Tuscany.

Despite the tantalising clues they left behind, no one seems to know who the Etruscans were or where they came from. Recent studies of their genetic material suggest they have more in common with Anatolia than with modern Italians, and early Roman historians suggested a connection with Asia Minor. You'll be able to come up with your own theories at the impressive array of Etruscan museums this region has to offer.

Of course, the Romans knew a good thing when they plundered it. After conquering swaths of Etruscan territory in Tuscany in the 3rd century BC, they incorporated the Etruscans' highly refined, geometric style into their own art and architecture. But even after another 800 years of trying, Rome never entirely succeeded in establishing its authority throughout Etruscan territory. This would become a recurring theme, with local municipal authorities battling with papal emissaries from Rome for control over the region right through to the 15th century AD.

Enter Christianity

Roman centurions may have failed to make much of an impression on Etruscan territory, but Christianity began to take hold when a young man from the region named Benedict abandoned his studies and a promising career in Rome to adopt the contemplative life around AD 500. After three years living as a hermit in a cave near Subiaco, south of Rome, the monks of a nearby abbey begged him to become their abbot. He agreed, but the monks soon found community life under his direction way too strict and tried to poison him – twice. They were unsuccessful, and Benedict went on to achieve a number of miracles, personally establish 12 monasteries and inspire the founding of many more. His story is visually narrated in great detail in the stunning fresco series (1497–1505) by Il Sodoma and Luca Signorelli in the Great Cloister at Abbazia di Monte Oliveto Maggiore near Siena.

One early Benedictine monastery, San Pietro in Valle, was built in neighbouring Umbria by order of the Longobard duke of Spoleto, Faroaldo II. It kick-started a craze for the blend of Lombard and Roman styles known as Romanesque, and many local ecclesiastical structures were built in this style. The basic template was simple: a stark nave stripped of extra columns ending in a domed apse, surrounded by chapels usually donated by wealthy patrons. Gone were the colonnaded Roman facades seen on earlier buildings; the new look was more spare and austere, befitting a place where hermits might feel at home and nobles may feel inspired to surrender worldly possessions.

In the 11th century, the Romanesque style acquired a distinctly Tuscan twist in Pisa, when the coloured marble banding and veneering of the city's *duomo* (cathedral) set a new gold standard for architectural decoration. This new style (sometimes described as Pisan) was then applied to a swathe of churches throughout the region, including the Basilica di San Miniato al Monte in Florence and the Chiesa di San Michele in Foro and Cattedrale di San Martino in Lucca.

Siena was not about to be outdone in the architectural stakes by its rivals, Florence and Pisa, and so in 1196 its city council approved a no-expenses-spared program to build a new *duomo*. They certainly got their money's worth, ending up with a spectacular Gothic facade by Giovanni Pisano, a pulpit by Nicola Pisano and a rose window designed by Duccio di Buoninsegna.

While Tuscany's churches were becoming increasingly more spectacular, nothing prepared pilgrims for what they would find inside the upper and lower churches of the Basilica di San Francesco in Assisi, Umbria. Not long after St Francis' death in 1226, an all-star team of Tuscan artists was hired to decorate these churches in his honour, kicking off a craze for frescoes that wouldn't abate for centuries. Cimabue, Giotto, Pietro Lorenzetti and Simone Martini captured the life and gentle spirit of St Francis while his memory was still fresh in the minds of the faithful. For medieval pilgrims unaccustomed to multiplexes and special effects, entering a space that had been covered from floor to ceiling with stories told in living colour must have been a dazzling, overwhelming experience. Painter, art historian and Renaissance man Giorgio Vasari praised Cimabue for setting the standard for realistic modelling and perspective with his lower church frescoes, which you can still make out despite the extensive damage caused over the years by earthquakes – not to mention art thieves who plundered fresco fragments after the devastating 1997 quake.

But the most startling achievement in the Basilica di San Francesco is Giotto's fresco cycle, which shows Francis not just rolling up but tearing off his sleeves to provide aid to lepers and the needy, as onlookers and

ART & ARCHITECTURE

Top Etruscan Museums

» Museo Etrusco Guarnacci, Volterra

» Museo dell'Accademia Etrusca, Cortona

» Museo Civico Archeologico 'Isidoro Falchi', Vetulonia

» Museo Archeologico Nazionale 'Gaio Cilnio Mecenate', Arezzo

Romanesque Churches

» Duomo di San Cristoforo, Barga

» Collegiata, San Gimignano

» Abbazia di Sant'Antimo, outside Montalcino

» Pieve di Corsignano, Pienza

» Duomo, Sovana

» Pieve di Santa Maria, Arezzo

Tuscan Artists

Plenty of big names jostle for precedence in the pantheon of Tuscan artists, so narrowing any list down to a 'Top Five' is a near impossible task. Here's our best attempt.

Michelangelo Buonarroti (1475–1564)

1 The quintessential Renaissance man. A painter, sculptor and architect with more masterpieces to his credit than any other artist either before or after. In Florence, view his *David* in the Galleria dell'Accademia (p83) and his *Tondo Doni* (Holy Family) in the Uffizi (p68).

Sandro Botticelli (c 1444–1510)

2 His Renaissance beauties charmed commissions out of the Medicis and continue to exert their siren call on the millions who visit the Uffizi Gallery (p65) each year. Don't miss his *Primavera* and *Birth of Venus*.

Giotto di Bondone (c 1266–1337)

3 Giotto kick-started the Renaissance with action-packed frescoes in which each character pinpoints emotions with facial expressions and poses that need no translation. Make the pilgrimage to Assisi to see his *Life of St Francis* fresco cycle (p273).

Fra' Angelico (c 1395–1455)

4 Few artists are saints – they're far more likely to be sinners. One of the exceptions was Beato Angelico, who was canonised in 1982. His best-loved work is the *Annunciation* in the convent of the Museo di San Marco (p83).

Duccio di Buoninsegna (c 1255–1318)

5 Head honcho of the Sienese school; known for his riveting Madonnas with level gazes and pale-green skin against glowing gold backgrounds. His masterwork is the *Maestà* in the Museo dell'Opera in Siena (p200).

Clockwise from top left

1. Michelangelo's *David* 2. Botticelli's *Primavera* (Spring)
3. *St Francis Expelling the Demons from Arezzo*, by Giotto

JON DAVISON/LONELY PLANET IMAGES ©

SUPERSTOCK/ALAMY ©

family members gasp and look away in shock. These images had an emotional, immediate impact on viewers, creating a much more theatrical setting for church services. Chants and solos added to the liturgy provided a surround-sound component to the fresco cycles, and the drama reached fever pitch with passion plays and other theatrical elements. The basilica drew hundreds of thousands of pilgrims each year when its decoration was in progress and even more when it was completed; today, annual attendance figures top five million.

The Middle Ages: the Rise of the Comune

While communities sprang up around hermits and holy men in the hinterlands, cities began taking on a life of their own from the 13th and 14th centuries. Roman road networks had been serving as handy trade routes starting in the 11th century, and farming estates and villas began to spring up outside major trading centres as a new middle class of merchants, farmers and skilled craftspeople emerged. Taxes and donations sponsored the building of hospitals such as the Ospedale Santa Maria della Scala in Siena. Streets were paved, town walls erected and sewage systems built to accommodate an increasingly sophisticated urban population not keen on sprawl or squalor.

Once townsfolk came into a bit of money, they weren't necessarily keen to part with it, and didn't always agree how their tax dollars should be spent. Town councils *(comuni)* were formed to represent the various interests of merchants, guilds and competing noble families, and the first order of business on the agenda in major medieval cities such as Siena, Florence and Volterra was the construction of an impressive town hall to reflect the importance and authority of the *comune*. Surprisingly, these democratic monuments don't look as though they were designed by committee – the greatest example, Siena's Palazzo Comunale, has become a global icon of civic pride with its pointed Sienese arches, a splendid

Best Art Galleries

MASTERPIECES IN MARBLE

Tuscan artists and architects have always loved working in marble, and many of the seminal works of the medieval and Renaissance periods were constructed using this material. Michelangelo wasn't the first local artist to become fixated by the stuff – white marble has been sourced from the huge marble quarries in Carrara since Roman times, and green and red marble are also widely used. Marble masterpieces include the following:

» **Baptistry, Florence** The facade features green and white marble banding; inside, there's a marble tomb sculpted by Donatello.

» **Duomo, Pisa** Green and cream banding on the exterior attracts attention, but the true masterpiece here is Giovanni Pisano's marble pulpit.

» **Baptistry, Pisa** Nicola Pisano's 13th-century hexagonal pulpit is covered with deep reliefs of Old and New Testament characters who seem to be almost twisting free of the structure.

» **Duomo, Siena** The tricolour facade of white, green and red marble was designed by Giovanni Pisano. Inside, there's a riot of black and white marble stripes, an inlaid marble floor and a marble and porphyry pulpit carved by Nicola Pisano.

» **Chiesa di Santa Maria della Spina, Pisa** A gloriously Gothic confection featuring an ornately spired exterior encrusted with marble tabernacles and statues.

» **David, Galleria dell'Accademia, Florence** With his famous sculpture of the nude warrior, Michelangelo showed what miracles could be wrought with a block of stone. Unfortunately, his plans to clad the exterior of the Basilica di San Lorenzo with Carrara marble never eventuated and the facade remains unfinished to this day.

marble loggia contributed by Sienese Black Death survivors, and the tall Torre del Mangia clock tower that serves as the compass needle orienting the entire city.

In addition to being savvy political lobbyists and fans of grand architectural projects that kept their constituents gainfully employed, medieval *comuni* were masters of propaganda, and perfectly understood the influence that art and architecture could wield. A perfect case in point is Ambrogio Lorenzetti's *Allegories of Good and Bad Government* fresco series in Siena's Museo Civico, which is better and bigger than any political billboard could ever be. In the *Allegory of Good Government,* Lorenzetti's grey-bearded figure of Legitimate Authority is flanked by an entourage who'd put White House interns to shame: Peace, Fortitude, Prudence, Magnanimity, Temperance and Justice. Above them flit Faith, Hope and Charity, and to the left Concord sits confidently on her throne while the reins of justice are held taut overhead.

Next to this fresco is another depicting the effects of good government: townsfolk make their way through town in an orderly fashion, pausing to do business, greet one another, join hands and dance a merry jig. But things couldn't be more different in the *Allegory of Bad Government,* where horned and fanged Tyrannia rules over a scene of chaos surrounded by winged vices and Justice lies unconscious, her scales shattered. Like the best campaign speeches, this cautionary tale was brilliantly rendered, but not always heeded.

As well as endowing churches, building palaces and funding frescoes, the wealthy merchant families of the Renaissance commissioned plenty of portraits. Cosimo I de' Medici's favourite portrait painter was Agnolo di Cosimo (1503–72), called Bronzino because of his dark complexion. Look for his Medici portraits in the Uffizi, Florence.

On the World Stage

When they weren't busy politicking, late-medieval farmers, craftspeople and merchants did quite well for themselves. Elegant, locally made ceramics, tiles and marbles were showcased in churches across Tuscany and became all the rage throughout Europe and the Mediterranean when pilgrims returned home to England and France with examples after following the Via Francigena pilgrimage route from Canterbury to Rome. Artisans were kept busy applying their skills to civic works projects and churches, which had to be expanded and updated to keep up with the growing numbers and rising expectations of pilgrims in the area.

With outside interest came outside influence, and local styles adapted to international markets. Florence became famous for lustrous, tin-glazed *maiolica* (majolica ware) tiles and plates painted with vibrant metallic pigments that were inspired by the Islamic ceramics of Majorca (Spain). The prolific della Robbia family started to create richly glazed ceramic reliefs that are now enshrined at the Museo del Bargello in Florence and in churches and museums across the region.

Modest Romanesque cathedrals were given an International Gothic makeover befitting their appeal to pilgrims of all nations, but the Italian take on the French style was more colourful than the grey-stone spires and flying buttresses of Paris. The local version often featured a simple layout and striped stone naves fronted by multilayer birthday-cake facades, which might be frosted with pink paint, glittering mosaics and rows of arches capped with sculptures. The most famous example of this confectionary approach is the *duomo* in Siena.

The evolution from solid Romanesque to airy Gothic to a yin and yang balance of the two can be witnessed in buildings throughout the region. The Gothic trend started while the upper church of the Basilica di San Francesco in Assisi was under construction, and the resulting blend of a relatively austere Romanesque exterior with high Gothic drama indoors set a new ecclesiastical architecture standard that was quickly exported into Tuscany and on to the rest of Europe.

Gothic Churches

» Duomo, Siena

» Abbazia di San Galgano, south of Siena

» Chiesa di Santa Maria della Spina, Pisa

Dark Times

By the 14th century, the smiling Sienese townsfolk of Ambrogio Loren-zetti's *Allegory of Good Government* must have seemed like the figment of a fertile imagination. After a major famine in 1329 followed by a bank collapse, Siena's *comune* went into debt to maintain roads, continue work on the *duomo*, help the needy and jump-start the local economy. But just when it seemed set for a comeback, the plague devastated the city in 1348. Three-quarters of Siena's population – including artists Pietro and Ambrogio Lorenzetti – died, and virtually all economic and artistic activity ground to a halt. The *comune* rallied with tough fines on lawbreakers, new business taxes and rules against wearing black mourning attire (too depressing), and within five years Siena had bounced back. Alas, another plague hit in 1374, killing 80,000 Sienese, and was swiftly followed by a famine. It was too much – the city never entirely recovered.

Florence was also hit by the plague in 1348, and despite fervent public prayer rituals, 96,000 Florentines died in just seven months. Those who survived experienced a crisis of faith, making Florence fertile territory for humanist ideals – not to mention macabre superstition, attempts to raise the dead, and a fascination with corpses that the likes of Leonardo da Vinci would call science and others morbid curiosity.

At plague's end, a building boom ensued when upstart merchants such as Cosimo I de' Medici (Cosimo the Elder) and Filippo Strozzi competed to put their stamp on a city that needed to be reimagined after the horrors it had undergone.

The Renaissance

It wasn't only merchants who were jockeying for power at this time. To put an end to the competing claims of the Tuscan Ghibelline faction that was allied with the Holy Roman Empire, the Rome-backed Guelph faction had marked its territory with impressive new landmarks, predominantly in Florence. Giotto – often described as the founding artist of the

GIOTTO DI BONDONE

The 14th-century Tuscan poet Giovanni Boccaccio wrote in his *Decameron* that his fellow Tuscan Giotto di Bondone (c 1266–1337) was 'a genius so sublime that there was nothing produced by nature...that he could not depict to the life'.

Boccaccio wasn't the only prominent critic of the time to consider Giotto extraordinary – Giorgio Vasari was also a huge fan, arguing that Giotto initiated the 'rebirth' (*rinascità* or *renaissance*) in art. Giotto's most famous works are all in the medium of the fresco, and his supreme achievement is the cycle gracing the walls of the Cappella degli Scrovegni in Padua, near Venice. In his paintings, he abandoned popular conventions such as the three-quarter view of head and body and presented his figures from behind, from the side or turning around, just as the story demanded. Giotto had no need for lashings of gold paint and elaborate ornamentation to impress the viewer with the significance of the subject. Instead, he enabled the viewer to feel the dramatic tension of a scene through a naturalistic rendition of figures and a radical composition that created the illusion of depth.

Giotto's important works in Tuscany include an altarpiece portraying the Madonna and Child among angels and saints in Florence's Uffizi Gallery, a painted wooden crucifix in the Basilica di Santa Maria Novella and frescoes in the Basilica di Santa Croce. His magnificent *Life of St Francis* fresco cycle graces the walls of the upper church of the Basilica di San Francesco in Assisi, Umbria.

Many Renaissance painters included self-portraits in their major works. Giotto didn't, possibly due to the fact that friends such as Boccaccio described him as the ugliest man in Florence. With friends like those...

RENAISSANCE FRESCOES

They may look like ordinary bible stories now, but in their heyday, Renaissance frescoes provided running social commentary as well as religious inspiration. In them, human adversity looked divine, and vice versa.

Fantastic examples are found throughout Tuscany, but to see the very best head to the following churches and museums:

» **Collegiata, San Gimignano** There are hardly any undecorated surfaces in this cathedral, with every wall sporting huge, comic-strip-like frescoes by Bartolo di Fredi, Lippo Memmi, Domenico Ghirlandaio and Benozzo Gozzoli. The highlight is Taddeo di Bartolo's gleefully grotesque *Final Judgment* (1396).

» **Libreria Piccolomini, Duomo, Siena** Umbrian artist Bernardino Pinturicchio extols the glory of Siena in 10 vibrant fresco panels (c 1502–1507) celebrating Enea Silvio Piccolomini, aka the humanist Pope Pius II. St Catherine of Siena makes a cameo appearance.

» **Museo di San Marco, Florence** Fra' Angelico's frescoes portray religious figures in all-too-human moments of uncertainty, reflecting the humanist spirit of the Renaissance. The highlight is his *Annunciation* (c 1440).

» **Museo Civico, Siena** Magnificent is the only word to use when describing Ambrogio Lorenzetti's *Allegories of Good and Bad Government* (1338–40) and Simone Martini's *Maestà* (Virgin Mary in Majesty; 1315).

» **Cappella Brancacci, Florence** Masaccio's *The Expulsion of Adam and Eve from Paradise* and *The Tribute Money* (c 1427) showcase architectural perspective and sly political satire.

» **Cappella Bacci, Chiesa di San Francesco, Arezzo** Piero della Francesca's *Legend of the True Cross* (c 1452–66) displays a veritable encyclopaedia of Renaissance painting tricks (directional lighting, steep perspective etc).

» **Chiesa di Sant'Agostino, San Gimignano** Benozzo Gozzoli's bizarre fresco of San Sebastian (c 1464) shows the fully clothed saint protecting the citizens of San Gimignano, helped by a bare-breasted Virgin Mary and semi-robed Jesus. Wins the prize for the weirdest religious iconography.

» **Cappella dei Magi, Palazzo Medici-Riccardi, Florence** More Gozzoli, but this time there's nothing strange about his subject matter, which has members of the Medici family making a guest appearance in the *Procession of the Magi to Bethlehem* (c 1459–63).

Renaissance – had been commissioned to design the city's iconic 85m-tall square *campanile* (bell tower) and one-up the 57m-tall tower under construction in Ghibelline Pisa that was already looking a bit off kilter. And this was only one of many such projects.

'Mess with Florence, and you take on Rome' was the not-so-subtle hint delivered by Florentine architects, who made frequent reference to the glories of the ancient power and its classical architecture when designing the new churches, *palazzi* and public buildings that started sprouting across the city. This new Florentine style became known as Renaissance or 'rebirth', and really started to hit its swing after architect Filippo Brunelleschi won a competition to design the dome of Florence's *duomo*. Brunelleschi was heavily influenced by the achievements of the classical masters, but he was able to do something that they hadn't been able to do themselves – discover and record the mathematical rules by which objects appear to diminish as they recede from us. In so doing, he gave local artists and architects a whole new visual perspective and a means to glorious artistic ends.

To decorate the new buildings, artists enjoyed a bonanza of commissions to paint heroic battle scenes, fresco private chapels and carve busts

Florence is home to many works by the great painter, sculptor and architect, Michelangelo Buonarroti. To see them, head to the Uffizi, Museo dell'Opera di Santa Maria del Fiore, Palazzo Vecchio, Cappelle Medicee, Galleria dell'Accademia and Museo del Bargello.

1. Colours of Libreria Piccolomini (p200)
The interior of the Libreria Piccolomini in Siena's *duomo*.

2. Masaccio's Masterpieces (p89)
Fresco by Masaccio in Florence's Cappella Brancacchi.

3. Homage to St Francis of Assisi (p273)
The Basilica di San Francesco in Assisi is filled with Renaissance art.

4. Museo di San Marco (p83)
Frescoes in the cloister of Florence's Museo di San Marco.

Masaccio's *Trinity*, a wall painting in the Basilica di Santa Maria Novella in Florence, is often described as one of the founding works of Renaissance painting and the inspiration for Leonardo da Vinci's *Last Supper* fresco.

of the latest power players – works that sometimes outlived their patrons' clout. A good example is the Peruzzi family, whose members had risen to prominence in 14th-century Florence as bankers with interests reaching from London to the Middle East, and who set the trend for art patronage by commissioning Giotto to fresco the family's memorial chapel in Santa Croce, completed in 1320. When Peruzzi client King Edward III of England defaulted on loans the family went bankrupt – but as patrons of Giotto's precocious experiments in perspective and Renaissance illusionism, their legacy set the tone for the artistic flowering of Florence.

One Florentine family to follow the Peruzzis' lead was the prominent Brancacci, who commissioned Masolino da Panicale and his precocious assistant Masaccio to decorate a chapel in the Basilica di Santa Maria del Carmine in Florence. After Masaccio's premature death aged only 27, the frescoes were completed by Filippino Lippi. In these dramatic frescoes, framed in astonishingly convincing architectural sets, select scenes from the life of St Peter allude to pressing Florentine concerns of the day: the new income tax, unfair imprisonment and hoarded wealth. Masaccio's image of the expulsion of Adam and Eve from the Garden of Eden proved especially prophetic: the Brancacci were allied with the Strozzi family, and were similarly exiled by the Medici before they could see the work completed.

But the patrons with the greatest impact on the course of art history were, of course, the Medici. Patriarch Cosimo the Elder was exiled in 1433 by a consortium of Florentine families who considered him a triple threat: powerful banker, ambassador of the Church, and consummate politician with the savvy to sway emperors and popes. But the flight of capital from Florence after his departure created such a fiscal panic that the exile was hastily rescinded and within a year the Medici were well and truly back in town. To announce his return in grand style, Cosimo

FILIPPO BRUNELLESCHI

Many Renaissance men left their mark on Florence, but few did so with as much grace and glory as Filippo Brunelleschi (1377–1446). An architect, mathematician, engineer and sculptor, Brunelleschi trained as a master goldsmith and showed early promise as a sculptor – he was an entrant in the 1401 competition to design the doors of the Baptistry in Florence (won by fellow goldsmith Lorenzo Ghiberti) and shortly after travelled to Rome with Donatello, another goldsmith by training, to study that city's ancient architecture and art. When he returned to Florence in 1419 he took up an architectural commission from the silk merchant's guild to design a hospital for foundlings on Piazza della Santissima Annunziata in San Marco. Known as the Ospedale degli Innocenti (Hospital of the Innocents), his classically proportioned and detailed building featured a distinctive nine-arched loggia and was a radical departure from the High Gothic style that many of his artistic contemporaries were still embracing. Its design was sober, secular and sophisticated, epitomising the new humanist age.

In 1419, after completing his work on the foundling hospital, Brunelleschi moved on to a commission that was to occupy him for the next 42 years – the dome of Florence's *duomo*. His mathematical brain and talent for devising innovative engineering solutions enabled him to do what many Florentines had thought impossible: deliver the largest dome to be built in Italy since antiquity.

Brunelleschi's other works in Florence include the Basilica di San Lorenzo, the Basilica di Santa Spirito and the Cappella de' Pazzi in the Basilica di Santa Croce. Vasari said of him: 'The world having for so long been without artists of lofty soul or inspired talent, heaven ordained that it should receive from the hand of Filippo the greatest, the tallest, and the finest edifice of ancient and modern times, demonstrating that Tuscan genius, although moribund, was not yet dead.' He is buried in the *duomo*, under the dome that was his finest achievement.

GIORGIO VASARI'S 'LIVES OF THE ARTISTS'

Painter, architect and writer Giorgio Vasari (1511–74) was one of those figures rightfully described as a 'Renaissance man'. Born in Arezzo, he trained as a painter in Florence, working with artists such as Andrea del Sarto and Michelangelo (he idolised the latter). As a painter, he is best remembered for his floor-to-ceiling frescoes in the Salone dei Cinquecento in Florence's Palazzo Vecchio. As an architect, his most accomplished work was the elegant loggia of the Uffizi Gallery (he also designed the enclosed, elevated corridor that connected the Palazzo Vecchio with the Uffizi and Palazzo Pitti and was dubbed the 'Corridoio Vasariano' in his honour). But posterity remembers him predominantly for his work as an art historian. His *Lives of the Most Excellent Painters, Sculptors and Architects, from Cimabue to Our Time,* an encyclopaedia of artistic biographies published in 1550 and dedicated to Cosimo I de' Medici, is still in print (as *The Lives of the Artists*) and is full of wonderful anecdotes and gossip about his artistic contemporaries in 16th-century Florence.

Memorable passages include his recollection of visiting Donatello's studio one day only to find the great sculptor staring at his extremely life-like statue of the *Prophet Habakkuk* and imploring it to talk (we can only assume that Donatello had been working too hard). Vasari also writes about a young Giotto painting a fly on the surface of a work by Cimabue that the older master then tried to brush away. The book makes wonderful predeparture reading for anyone planning to visit Florence and its museums.

funded the 1437 rebuilding of the Convento di San Marco (now Museo di San Marco) by Michelozzo, and commissioned Fra' Angelico to fresco the monks' quarters with scenes from the life of Christ. Another artist pleased to see Cosimo return was Donatello, who had completed his lithe bronze statue of *David* (now in the city's Museo del Bargello) with his patronage.

Through such commissions, early Renaissance innovations in perspective, closely observed realism and chiaroscuro (the play of light and dark) began to catch on throughout the region. In Sansepolcro, a painter named Piero della Francesca earned a reputation for figures who were glowing with otherworldly light, and who were caught in personal predicaments that people could relate to: Roman soldiers snoozing on the job, crowds left goggle-eyed by miracles, bystanders distressed to witness cruel persecution. His fresco series *Legend of the True Cross,* commissioned by the Bacci family for a chapel in Arezzo's Chiesa di San Francesco, was one of the supreme artistic achievements of the time.

The High Renaissance

The decades leading up to and starting the Cinquecento (1500s) are often seen as a kind of university faculty meeting, with genteel, silver-haired sages engaged in a collegial exchange of ideas. A bar brawl might be closer to the metaphorical truth, with artists, scientists, politicians and clergy mixing it up and everyone emerging bruised. The debate was never as simple as Church versus state, science versus art or seeing versus believing; in those days, politicians could be clergy, scientists could be artists, and artists could be clergy. Nor was debate strictly academic: any statement, however artistic, could mark a person as a menace, a has-been, a heretic or a dead man.

There were many artistic superstars during this period, and most were locals who ended up honing their skills in Florence and then moving elsewhere in Italy. Their careers were well documented by Giorgio Vasari in his gossipy *Lives of the Artists*.

Inspired by Masaccio, tutored by Fra' Filippo Lippi and backed by Lorenzo de' Medici, Sandro Botticelli was a rising Florentine art star

ART & ARCHITECTURE

FRA' FILIPPO LIPPI: THE RENEGADE MONK

Filippo Lippi (1406–69), one of the greatest Tuscan painters of his era, entered the Carmelite order as a monk aged only 14. Vasari writes in his *Lives of the Artists* that 'Instead of studying, he spent all of his time scrawling pictures on his own books and those of others.' It's perhaps not surprising, then, that Lippi eventually left the order. In fact, he abducted a novice who was sitting for the figure of the Madonna in a fresco he was painting for the *duomo* in Prato, renounced his vows and married her. Their son Filippino (1457–1504) followed in his father's artistic footsteps, but history doesn't relate whether he shared his dad's peccadilloes.

who was sent to Rome to paint a fresco celebrating papal authority in the Sistine Chapel. The golden boy who'd painted the *Birth of Venus* for Lorenzo de' Medici's private villa in 1485 (now in Florence's Uffizi) could do no wrong until he was accused of sodomy in 1501. The charges didn't stick but the rumours did, and Botticelli's work was critiqued as too decadently sensual for religious subjects. When religious reformer Savonarola ousted the Medici and began to purge Florence of decadent excess in the face of surely imminent Armageddon, Botticelli paintings went up in flames in the massive Bonfire of the Vanities. Botticelli repudiated mythology and turned his attention to Madonnas, some of whom bear a marked family resemblance to his Venus.

Michelangelo was another of Lorenzo de' Medici's protégées, and his classically inspired work was uniformly admired until the Medici were ousted by Savonarola in 1494. By some accounts, Savonarola tossed rare early paintings by Michelangelo onto his bonfires (ouch). Without his Medici protectors, Michelangelo seemed unsure of his next move: he briefly hid in the basement of San Lorenzo and then roamed around Italy. In Rome he carved a Bacchus for Cardinal Raffaele Riario that the patron deemed unsuitable – which only seemed to spur Michelangelo to make a bigger and still more sensuous statue of *David* in 1501. It's now exhibited in Florence's Galleria dell'Accademia.

Leonardo, who hailed from Vinci southwest of Florence, had so many talents that it is hard to isolate only a few for comment. In his painting, he took what some critics have described as the decisive step in the history of Western art – namely, abandoning the balance that had previously been maintained between colour and line and choosing to modulate his contours using shading. This technique is called sfumato and it is perfectly displayed in his *Mona Lisa* (now in the Louvre in Paris). Few of his works live in her birthplace; the exceptions are his *Adoration of the Magi* and *Annunciation*, both in the Uffizi.

In 1542, the Inquisition arrived in Italy, marking a definitive end to the Renaissance exploration of humanity in all its glorious imperfections. Tuscan art and architecture would never again lead the world by example.

A Stop on the Grand Tour

In the centuries that followed the sack of Rome by Charles V in 1527, artistic production in Tuscany came to be defined by passing trends, imperial excess and periodic pillaging. The region soon had the dubious luck of being the holiday destination of choice for despots, generals and imperial relations, with Lucca in particular beginning to look distinctly French. As a consolation prize for separating from her husband, Elisa Bonaparte had been dubbed Duchess of Tuscany by her brother Napoleon Bonaparte, and soon established the trend for Italian vacation villas with her Villa Reale outside that town.

Artistic genius, like madness and profligacy, often runs through families. Italian artistic dynasties include the della Robbias (Luca, Marco, Andrea, Giovanni and Girolamo), Lorenzettis (Ambrogio and Pietro) and Pisanos (Andrea, Nicola and Giovanni).

DYNASTIES

A 'Grand Tour' of Italy became an obligatory display of culture and class status by the 18th century, and Tuscany was a key stop on the itinerary. German and English artists enraptured with Michelangelo, Perugino and other early High Renaissance painters took the inspiration home. Conversely, Italian artists picked up on artistic trends making a splash in northern Europe without having to leave home. Impressionism, plein-air painting and romanticism became trendy among Italian artists, as witnessed in the collection at Florence's Galleria d'Arte Moderna in the Palazzo Pitti, which is dominated by late-19th-century works by artists of the Tuscan Macchiaioli school (the local equivalent of Impressionism). These include Telemaco Signorini (1835–1901) and Giovanni Fattori (1825–1908).

In architecture, the most fascinating case of artistic import-export is Italian art nouveau, often referred to as Liberty after the London store that put William Morris' Italian-inspired visual ideals into commercial action.

The 20th Century

After centuries under the thumbs of popes and sundry imperial powers, Tuscany had acquired a certain forced cosmopolitanism, and local artists could identify with Rome, Paris or other big cities in addition to their own *contrada* (neighbourhood). The two biggest stars in the early decades of this century were Livorno-born painter and sculptor Amedeo Modigliani (1884–1920), who lived most of his adult life in Paris, and Greek-born painter Giorgio de Chirico (1888–1978), who studied in Florence and painted the first of his 'Metaphysical Town Square' series there.

Other than Modigliani and di Chirico, no Tuscan painters of note were represented within the major artistic movements of the century: *Futurismo* (Futurism), *Pittura Metafisica* (Metaphysical Painting), *Spazialismo* (Spatialism) and *Arte Povera* (conceptual art using materials of little worth). Architecture didn't have many local stars either, with the only exception being Giovanni Michelucci (1891–1990), whose buildings include Santa Maria Novella Railway Station in Florence (1932–34) and the Chiesa di San Giovanni Battista on the Autostrada del Sole (1964).

In the 1980s, there was a return to painting and sculpture in a traditional (primarily figurative) sense. Dubbed 'Transavanguardia', this movement broke with the prevailing international focus on conceptual art and was thought by some critics to signal the death of avant-garde. Tuscan artists who were part of this movement include Sandro Chia (b 1946).

Contemporary Art

A heritage of rich artistic traditions spanning three millennia means job security for legions of Tuscan art conservation specialists and art historians, but can have a stultifying effect on artists attempting to create something wholly new. Fortunately, even though Tuscany isn't known for its contemporary art scene, there's more going on than the dreadful daubs being created by sidewalk artists outside major museums and tourist attractions would seem to indicate.

One of the most notable visual artists working here is Massimo Bartolini (b 1962), who radically alters the local landscape with just a few deceptively simple (and quintessentially Tuscan) adjustments of light and perspective that fundamentally change our experience: a bedroom where all the furniture appears to be sinking into the floor, Venice style, or a gallery where the viewer wears special shoes that subtly change the lighting in the gallery with each step. Bartolini has also changed the local flora of the tiny Tuscan town of Cecina, near Livorno, where he lives

The term 'Macchiaioli' (the name given to a 19th-century group of Tuscan plein-air artists) was coined by a journalist in 1862. It mockingly implied that the artists' finished works were no more than sketches, and was drawn from the phrase 'darsi alla macchia' (to hide in bushes or scrubland).

Tuscany has a wealth of sculpture gardens showcasing site-specific contemporary works in gorgeous surrounds. These include the Fattoria di Celle outside Pistoia, Il Giardino dei Tarocchi in southern Tuscany and the Parco Sculture del Chianti and Castello di Ama in Chianti.

Architecture as Artform

Painters and sculptors tend to be awarded the credit for ushering in the Renaissance, but in reality it was their architectural colleagues who first sought to emulate the ancients in forging a strong and easily accessible visual language to celebrate humanity's achievements.

Palazzo Comunale, Siena

1 A triumph of spatial geometry and secular architecture, this graceful Gothic building (p194) has an ingeniously designed concave facade that mirrors the opposing convex curve formed by the famous Piazza del Campo.

Ospedale degli Innocenti, Florence

2 Everyone knows Brunelleschi's dome (most of us suffer from *duomo*-sickness after leaving Florence), but architecture buffs also admire his foundling hospital in San Marco (p84).

Basilica di San Miniato al Monte, Florence

3 Another lesser-known Florentine gem, this basilica (p94) overlooking the Florentine skyline has a Tuscan-Romanesque multicoloured marble facade that is one of the most beautiful in all of Italy.

Duomo, Pisa

4 Adding a distinctly Tuscan twist to Romanesque architecture, the striking bands of green and cream marble on the exterior of this cathedral (p129) prototyped the popular Pisan style and added a jaunty note to the city's famous Field of Miracles.

Piazza Pio II, Pienza

5 This harmonious vision of urban space (p228) is so unique and impressive that it was added to the World Heritage list in 1996.

Clockwise from top left
1. Aerial view of Piazza del Campo 2. Portico of Ospedale degli Innocenti 3. Basilica di San Miniato al Monte

and works, attracting colourful flocks of contemporary art collectors and curators.

The bijou town of Pietrasanta in the hinterland of the Versilian coast in northwestern Tuscany has a vibrant arts community and is home to the much-lauded Colombian-born sculptor Fernando Botero (b 1932).

Also notable is San Gimignano's Galleria Continua, a world-class commercial gallery whose stable of artists includes Tuscans Giovanni Ozzola (b 1982) and Luca Pancrazzi (b 1961).

Art & Architecture Glossary

Annunciation	the appearance of the Angel Gabriel to Mary to tell her that she will bear the Son of God
apse	a vaulted semicircular or polygonal recess, especially at the end of a choir in a church
architrave	1. the part of the entablature that holds columns in place; 2. a band of mouldings or other ornamentation atop or around openings or panels
atrium	forecourt
badia	abbey
baldacchino	canopy, usually over a high altar in a basilica
basilica	an early or medieval Christian church with a ground plan similar to or derived from the Roman basilica
bas-relief	sculpture in low relief
battistero	a church building in which baptism was/is administered
Byzantine	art and architecture of the Byzantine Empire; predated the Romanesque, Gothic and Renaissance movements
campanile	bell tower
cappella	chapel
cartoon	a full-size preparatory drawing for a painting or fresco
cella	sanctuary of a temple
cenacolo	scene of the Last Supper (often in the refectory of a convent or monastery)
chiaroscuro	literally 'light-dark'; artistic distribution of light and dark areas in a painting
chiostro	cloister; a rectangular open space surrounded by a covered walkway
clerestory	upper part of the nave wall of a church featuring windows
coffer	ornamental sunken panel in a ceiling
colonnade	a series of columns set at regular intervals, and usually supporting an entablature, a roof or a series of arches
cornice	1. a horizontal moulded projection that crowns or finishes a wall or building; 2. the uppermost division of an entablature, resting on the frieze; 3. the moulding(s) between the walls and ceiling of a room
cortile	courtyard
cruciform	cross-shaped
crypt	underground chamber or vault used as a burial place
cupola	a rounded vault or dome
diptych	painting or carving with two panels; usually small and portable and often used as an altarpiece
duomo	cathedral
entablature	sits on top of a row of columns on a classical facade; includes an architrave, the decorative frieze atop that and the triangular pediment to cap it off
exedra	semicircular recess

ex-voto	tablet or small painting expressing gratitude to a saint
font	receptacle, usually made of stone, that holds the water used in baptisms
fontana	fountain
fresco	painting executed on wet plaster
frieze	the part of an entablature between the architrave and the cornice, commonly ornamented with sculpture
Gothic	style of art and architecture in the late medieval period; popular from the 12th century
grisaille	technique of monochrome painting in shades of grey
loggia	covered area on the side of a building; porch; lodge
lunette	semicircular space in a vault or ceiling or above a door or window; often decorated with a fresco or painting
Madonna della Misericordia	literally 'Madonna of Mercy'; in art, an iconic formula showing a group of people seeking protection under the outspread cloak of the Madonna
Maestà	literally 'Majesty'; in art, an iconic formula of the enthroned Madonna with Christ Child, often surrounded by angels and saints
mausoleo	mausoleum; stately and magnificent tomb
narthex	vestibule along the facade of an early Christian church
nave	the main body, or middle part (lengthwise), of a church, flanked by aisles and extending typically from the entrance to the apse
necropolis	ancient cemetery or burial site
oculus	round window
palazzo	palace
pediment	a low triangular gable crowned with a projecting cornice, especially over a portico or porch at the end of a gable-roofed building
piano nobile	main floor of a palace
Pietà	literally 'pity' or 'compassion'; sculpture, drawing or painting of the dead Christ being held by the Madonna
pietra forte	fine sandstone used as a building material
pietra serena	greenish-grey 'serene stone'
pieve	parish church, usually in a rural setting
pinacoteca	art gallery
podium	a low continuous structure serving as a base or terrace wall
polyptych	painting or carving consisting of more than three panels; usually used as an altarpiece
porphyry	dark blue-, purple- or red-coloured rock
portico	a structure consisting of a roof supported by columns or piers forming the entrance to a church or other building
predella	small painting or panel attached below a large altarpiece
presbytery	eastern part of a church chancel, beyond the choir
pulpit	a platform or raised structure in a church from which a priest delivers a sermon
quadriporto	four-sided porch
quatrefoil	four-lobed design
relief	an apparent projection of parts in a sculpture or frieze giving the appearance of the third dimension
Renaissance	cultural movement that started in Florence; c 14th to 17th centuries
Romanesque	architecture of the early Western Christian empire c 6th to 12th centuries

rose window	circular window divided into sections by stone mullions and tracery; usually found in Gothic churches
rustification	stone with a chiselled, rough-hewn look
sacristy	room in a church where the sacred vessels, vestments etc are kept
sanctuaio	sanctuary; the part of a church above the altar
sfumato	hazy blending of colours and blurring of outlines; used in painting
sgraffito	a surface covered with plaster, then scratched away to create a 3D trompe l'œil effect of carved stone or brick
sinopia	working sketch for a fresco
spolia	creative reuse of ancient monuments in new structures
stele	upright stone with carved inscription or image
stemma	coat of arms
stigmata	marks appearing on a saint's body in the same places as the wounds of Christ
stucco	plasterwork
tabernacle	in Christianity, a locked box in which the communion wafers and wine are stored
tempera	powdered pigment bound together with a mixture of egg and water; used in painting
tesoro	treasury
tesserae	small cubes of marble, stone or glass used in mosaic work
tondo	circular painting or relief
torre	tower
transept	the transverse portion(s) of a cruciform church
travertine	limestone used in paving and building
triptych	painting or carving over three panels, hinged so that the outer panels fold over the middle one; often used as an altarpiece
tufa	soft volcanic rock
vault	arched structure forming a ceiling or roof
vestibule	passage, hall or antechamber between the outer door and interior parts of a building

Survival Guide

Directory A–Z

Accommodation

Tuscany is blessed with accommodation styles and options to suit every taste and budget. In cities and large towns there are plenty of family-run *pensioni* (guest houses) and B&Bs; in rural areas *agriturismi* (farm-stay accommodation) reigns supreme. Boutique and luxury options are also relatively common. We use the following pricing system throughout the book. Unless otherwise stated, prices quoted are for a double room with private bathroom and breakfast.

» **€** up to €100
» **€€** €100 to €200
» **€€€** €200-plus

For more information on accommodation in the region, see p31.

Business Hours

In this book, opening times for individual businesses are only included when they deviate from the following standard hours.

Banks 8.30am to 1.30pm and 3.30pm to 4.30pm Monday to Friday

Main post offices 8am to 7pm Monday to Friday, 8.30am to noon Saturday
Branch post offices 8am to 2pm Monday to Friday, 8.30am to noon Saturday
Restaurants 12.30pm to 2.30pm and 7.30pm to 10pm or midnight
Cafes 7.30am to 8pm
Bars & pubs 10am to 1am
Nightclubs 10pm to late

Shops 9am to 1pm and 3.30pm to 7.30pm (or 4pm to 8pm) Monday to Saturday
Pharmacies 9am to 12.30pm and 3.30pm to 7pm Monday to Friday, 9am to 12.30pm Saturday and Sunday

Customs Regulations

Visitors coming into Italy from non-EU countries can import the following items duty free:
» 1L spirits (or 4L wine)
» 200 cigarettes
» up to a total of €430 for other goods, including perfume and eau de toilette

Anything over these limits must be declared on arrival and the appropriate duty paid. On leaving the EU, non-EU citizens can reclaim any Value Added Tax (VAT) on expensive purchases (see p329).

Discount Cards

Free admission to many galleries and cultural sites is available to youths under 18 and seniors over 65 years

Climate

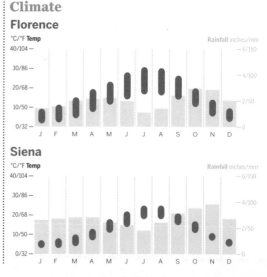

Florence

Siena

old. In addition, visitors aged between 18 and 25 often qualify for a 50% discount. In many cases, these discounts only apply to EU citizens. In our reviews, we have indicated this by using the description 'reduced' when citing admission charges.

When in Florence, consider purchasing a **Firenze Card** (www.firenzecard.it; €50), which is valid for 72 hours and covers admission to 33 museums, villas and gardens in Florence as well as unlimited use of public transport.

You can also often save money by purchasing a *biglietto cumulativo*, a ticket that allows admission to a number of associated sights for less than the combined cost of separate admission fees. We have included information about these in Practical Tip boxes throughout the book.

Youth, Student & Teacher Cards

If you're aged under 30, the European Youth Card (*Carta Giovani*; www.europeanyouthcard.org, www.cartagiovani.it; €11) offers thousands of discounts on Italian hotels, museums, restaurants, shops and clubs and is available for purchase online. Student, teacher or youth travel cards (www.isic.org;) can save you money on flights to Italy and are available worldwide from student unions, hostelling organisations and youth travel agencies such as **STA Travel** (www.statravel.com). They cost US$22, UK£9 or €10 and options include the International Student Identity Card (for full-time students), International Teacher Identity Card (for full-time teachers) and the International Youth Travel Card (for travellers under 26 years).

Note that many places in Italy give discounts according to age rather than student status. An ISIC may not always be accepted without proof of age (eg passport).

230V/50Hz

230V/50Hz

Embassies & Consulates

For foreign embassies and consulates in Italy that are not listed here, look under 'Ambasciate' or 'Consolati' in the telephone directory. In addition to the following, some countries run honorary consulates in other cities.

Australia Rome (☑06 85 27 21; www.italy.embassy.gov.au; Via Antonio Bosio 5); Milan (☑02 7767 4217; www.austrade.it; Via Borgogna 2)

Austria Rome (☑06 844 01 41; www.austria.it; Via Pergolesi 3); Milan (☑02 78 37 43; mailand-gk@bmeia.gv.at; Piazza del Liberty 8/4)

Canada (☑06 85 44 41; www.canadainternational.gc.ca/italy-italie; Via Zara 30, Rome)

France (www.ambafrance-it.org) Rome (☑06 68 60 11; Piazza Farnese 67); Milan (☑02 655 91 41; Via della Moscova 12); Naples (☑081 598 07 11; Via Francesco Crispi 86); Turin (☑011 573 23 11; Via Roma 366)

Germany Rome (☑06 49 21 31; www.rom.diplo.de; Via San Martino della Battaglia 4); Milan (☑02 623 11 01; www.mailand.diplo.de; Via Solferino 40); Naples (☑081 248 85 11; www.neapel.diplo.de; Via Francesco Crispi 69)

Ireland (☑06 697 91 21; www.ambasciata-irlanda.it; Piazza Campitelli 3, Rome)

Japan Rome (☑06 48 79 91; www.it.emb-japan.go.jp; Via Quintino Sella 60); Milan (☑02 624 11 41; www.milano.it.emb-japan.go.jp; Via Cesare Mangili 2/4)

Netherlands (www.olanda.it) Rome (☑06 3228 6001; Via Michele Mercati 8); Milan (☑02 485 58 41; Via Gaetano Donizetti 20)

New Zealand (www.nzembassy.com) Rome (☑06 853 75 01; Via Clitunno 44); Milan (☑02 7217 0001; Via Terraggio 17)

Slovenia Rome (☑06 8091 4310; vri@gov.si; Via Leonardo Pisano 10); Trieste (☑040 30 78 55; kts@gov.si; Via S Giorgio 1)

Switzerland Rome (☑06 80 95 71; www.eda.admin.ch/roma; Via Barnarba Oriani 61); Milan (☑02 777 91 61; www.eda.admin.ch/milano; Via Palestro 2)

UK (http://ukinitaly.fco.gov.uk) Rome (☑06 4220 0001; Via XX Settembre 80a); Florence (☑055 28 41 33;

BOOK YOUR STAY ONLINE

For more accommodation reviews by Lonely Planet authors, check out hotels.lonelyplanet.com/Italy. You'll find independent reviews, as well as recommendations on the best places to stay. Best of all, you can book online.

Lungarno Corsini 2); Milan (☏02 72 30 01; Via San Paolo 7); Naples (☏081 423 89 11; Via dei Mille 40)

USA Rome (☏06 4 67 41; http://italy.usembassy.gov; Via Vittorio Veneto 121); Florence (☏055 26 69 51; http://florence.usconsulate.gov; Lungarno Vespucci 38); Milan (☏02 29 03 51; http://milan.usconsulate.gov; Via Principe Amedeo 2/10); Naples (☏081 583 81 11; http://naples.usconsulate.gov; Piazza della Repubblica)

Food & Drink

In this book, we include approximate meal prices in our restaurant reviews. These are based on a *primo* (first course), *secondo* (main course/entrée), *dolce* (dessert) and *bicchiere di vino della casa* (glass of house wine). The pricing system is as follows:

» **€** up to €25
» **€€** €25 to €45
» **€€€** €45-plus

For information about Tuscany's food, wine and all-important eating culture, see p35 and p294.

Gay & Lesbian Travellers

Homosexuality is legal in Italy and well accepted in the major cities. On the Tuscan coast, Torre del Lago has a lively gay scene, best expressed by **Friendly Versilia** (www.friendlyversilia.it), a summer campaign that encourages gays and lesbians to revel in Torre del Lago's

fun-in-the-sun frolics from late April to September.

Resources include the following:

Arcigay & Arcilesbica (www.arcigay.it) Bologna-based national organisation for gays and lesbians.

Azione Gay e Lesbica Firenze (☏055 22 02 50; www.azionegayelesbica.it, in Italian; Via Pisana 32r) Active Florence-based organisation for gays and lesbians.

GayFriendlyItaly.com (www.gayfriendlyitaly.com) English-language site produced by Gay.it, featuring information on everything from hotels to homophobia issues and the law.

Gay.it (www.gay.it, in Italian) Website listing gay bars and hotels across the country.

Pride (www.prideonline.it) National monthly magazine of art, music, politics and gay culture.

Health

Recommended Vaccinations

No jabs are required to travel to Italy. However, the World Health Organization (WHO) recommends that all travellers should be covered for diphtheria, tetanus, the measles, mumps, rubella and polio, as well as hepatitis B.

Health Insurance

If you're an EU citizen (or from Switzerland, Norway or Iceland), a European Health Insurance Card (EHIC) covers you for most medical care in public hospitals free of charge, but not for emergency repatriation home or non-emergencies. The card is

available from health centres and (in the UK) from post offices. Citizens from other countries should find out if there is a reciprocal arrangement for free medical care between their country and Italy (Australia, for instance, has such an agreement; carry your Medicare card).

If you do need health insurance, make sure you get a policy that covers you for the worst possible scenario, such as an accident requiring an emergency flight home. Find out in advance if your insurance plan will make payments directly to providers or reimburse you later for overseas health expenditures.

Availability of Health Care

Pharmacists can give you valuable advice and sell over-the-counter medication for minor illnesses. They can also advise you when more specialised help is required and point you in the right direction.

Pharmacies generally keep the same hours as other shops, closing at night and on Sundays. However, a handful remain open on a rotation basis *(farmacie di turno)* for emergency purposes. These are listed online at www.miniportale.it (click on Farmacie di Turno and then the region you want). You can also check the door of any pharmacy that is closed for business – it will display a list of the nearest emergency pharmacies.

If you need an ambulance, call ☏118. For emergency treatment, head straight to the *pronto soccorso* (casualty) section of a public hospital, where you can also get emergency dental treatment.

Insurance

A travel-insurance policy to cover theft, loss and medical problems is a good idea. Some policies specifically exclude dangerous activities, which can include scuba diving, motorcycling and even hiking – read the fine print. For information on car insurance, see p336. For information on health insurance, see p328.

Worldwide travel insurance is available at www.lonelyplanet.com/bookings/insurance.do. You can buy, extend and claim online any time – even if you're already on the road.

Internet Access

Throughout this guide we use the @ icon to indicate venues that offer an internet terminal (an actual computer) for guests' use, and the 🛜 icon to designate places with a wi-fi network. If charges apply for either, we mention this in the review.

Internet access has improved markedly in the past couple of years, with most locals now having home connections and a large percentage of hotels, B&Bs, hostels and *agriturismi* now offering free wi-fi. As a result, internet cafes are thin on the ground; when you do find one, it will charge around €3 per hour).

Certain provisions of Italy's anti-terrorism law, which required all internet users to present a photo ID and allowed the government to monitor internet usage, were rescinded in January 2011, but internet cafes and some hotels will still sometimes request identification before allowing you to use their facilities.

Legal Matters

The average tourist will only have a brush with the law if robbed by a bag-snatcher or pickpocket, or if their car is towed away. See p335 for information about traffic laws.

Maps

We have recommended useful cycling, walking and city maps in regional chapters throughout the book. You can choose from a number of sheet maps covering the region: Michelin's *Toscana* (1:200,000), Euro Cart's *Toscana* (1: 300,000), Marco Polo's *Toscana/Tuscany* (1:200,000), DeAgostini's *Carta Stradale/Road Map*

Toscana (1:200,000), Touring Editore's *Toscana* (1:200,000) and the AA's *Tuscany* (1:200,000). All are regularly updated.

Money

The euro is Italy's currency. Notes come in denominations of €500, €200, €100, €50, €20, €10 and €5. Coins are in denominations of €2 and €1, and 50, 20, 10, five, two and one cents.

For the latest exchange rates, check out www.xe.com.

ATMs

Bancomats (ATM machines) are widely available throughout Tuscany and are the best way to obtain local currency.

Credit Cards

International credit and debit cards can be used at any *bancomat* displaying the appropriate sign. Cards are also good for payment in most hotels, restaurants, shops, supermarkets and tollbooths.

If your card is lost, stolen or swallowed by an ATM, you can telephone toll free to have an immediate stop put on its use:

Amex (☑06 7290 0347 or your national call number)
Diners Club (☑800 864064)
MasterCard (☑800 870866)
Visa (☑800 819014)

Moneychangers

You can change money in banks, at the post office or in a *cambio* (exchange office). Post offices and banks tend to offer the best rates; exchange offices keep longer hours, but watch for high commissions and inferior rates.

Taxes & Refunds

A Value Added Tax (VAT) of around 20%, known as IVA (Imposta di Valore Aggiunto), is slapped onto just about everything in Italy. If you are a non-EU resident and spend

---

ITALY'S POLICE FORCES

There are six national police forces in Italy, as well as a number of local police forces. The main forces are shown in the table below.

ORGANISATION	JURISDICTION	UNIFORM
polizia di stato (civil national police)	thefts, visa extensions and permits; based at the local *questura* (police station)	powder blue trousers with a fuchsia stripe and a navy blue jacket
arma dei carabinieri (military police)	general crime, public order and drug enforcement (often overlapping with the *polizia statale*)	black uniforms with a red stripe
polizia municipale (aka *vigili urbani*; municipal police)	parking tickets, towed cars, public order, petty crime	varies according to province

PRACTICALITIES

» Italy uses the metric system for weights and measures.

» Smoking is banned in all closed public spaces.

» The major daily newspapers are *Corriere della Sera* (www.corriere.it), which publishes in both Italian and English, and the Florentine edition of *La Repubblica* (www.firenze.repubblica.it), which is only in Italian.

» For news, views and classifieds in English, pick up a copy of the free bimonthly newspaper *The Florentine* (www.theflorentine.net), distributed at select hotels, cafes, bookshops and bars in Florence. Another useful resource is the glossy *Toscana & Chianti News* (www.toscanaechiantinews.com), published monthly and available at tourist offices.

more than €155 (€154.94 to be precise!) on a purchase, you can claim a refund when you leave. The refund only applies to purchases from affiliated retail outlets that display a 'tax free for tourists' (or similar) sign. You have to complete a form at the point of sale, then have it stamped by EU customs as you leave the zone (if you are visiting one or more EU countries after visiting Italy, you'll need to submit the form at your final port of exit). For information, visit **Tax Refund for Tourists** (www.taxrefund.it) or pick up a pamphlet on the scheme from participating stores.

Post

Le Poste (www.poste.it, in Italian), Italy's postal system, is reasonably reliable but if you are sending a package you might want to use DHL or FedEx, which are safer. For post office opening hours, see p326.

Francobolli (stamps) are available at post offices and authorised *tabacchi* (tobacconists; look for the official sign: a big 'T', often white on black). Since letters often need to be weighed, what you get at the tobacconist for international airmail will occasionally be an approximation of the proper rate.

Tobacconists keep regular shop hours (p326).

Public Holidays

Most Italians take their annual holiday in August, with the busiest period occurring around August 15, known locally as *Ferragosto*. This means that many businesses and shops close for at least a part of that month. *Settimana Santa* (Easter Week) is another busy holiday period for Italians.

Individual towns have public holidays to celebrate the feasts of their patron saints. National public holidays include the following:

New Year's Day (Capodanno or Anno Nuovo) 1 January

Epiphany (Epifania or Befana) 6 January

Easter Sunday (Domenica di Pasqua) March/April

Easter Monday (Pasquetta or Lunedì dell'Angelo) March/April

Liberation Day (Giorno della Liberazione) On 25 April – marks the Allied Victory in Italy, and the end of the German presence and Mussolini, in 1945.

Labour Day (Festa del Lavoro) 1 May

Republic Day (Festa della Repubblica) 2 June

Feast of the Assumption (Assunzione or Ferragosto) 15 August

All Saints' Day (Ognissanti) 1 November

Feast of the Immaculate Conception (Immaculata Concezione) 8 December

Christmas Day (Natale) 25 December

Boxing Day (Festa di Santo Stefano) 26 December

Telephone

Domestic Calls

Italian telephone area codes all begin with 0 and consist of up to four digits. The area code is followed by a number of anything from four to eight digits. The area code is an integral part of the telephone number and must always be dialled, even when calling from next door. Mobile-phone numbers begin with a three-digit prefix such as 330. Toll-free (free-phone) numbers are known as *numeri verdi* and usually start with 800. Nongeographical numbers start with 840, 841, 848, 892, 899, 163, 166 or 199. Some six-digit national rate numbers are also in use (such as those for Alitalia, rail and postal information).

As elsewhere in Europe, Italians choose from a host of providers of phone plans and rates, making it difficult to make generalisations about costs.

International Calls

The cheapest options for calling internationally are free or low-cost computer programs such as Skype, cut-rate call centres or international calling cards, which are sold at news-stands and tobacconists. Cut-price call centres can be found in all of the main cities, and rates can be considerably lower than from Telecom payphones for international calls. You simply place your call from a private booth inside the centre and pay for it when you've finished. Direct international calls can also easily be made from public telephones with a phonecard. Dial ☑00 to get out of Italy, then the relevant country and area codes, followed by the telephone number.

To call Italy from abroad, call the international access number (☑011 in the USA, ☑00 from most other countries), Italy's country code (☑39) and then the area code of the location you want, including the leading 0.

Mobile Phones

Italy uses GSM 900/1800, which is compatible with the rest of Europe and Australia but not with North American GSM 1900 or the totally different Japanese system (though some GSM 1900/900 phones do work here). If you have a GSM phone, check with your service provider about using it in Italy and beware of calls being routed internationally (very expensive for a 'local' call).

Italy has one of the highest levels of mobile-phone penetration in Europe, and you can get a temporary or prepaid account from several companies if you already own a GSM, dual- or tri-band mobile phone. Always check with your mobile-service provider in your home country to ascertain whether your handset allows use of another SIM card. If yours does, it can cost as little as €10 to activate a local prepaid SIM card (sometimes with €10 worth of calls on the card). You'll need to register with a mobile-phone shop, bring your passport and wait for approximately 24 hours for your account to be activated. After that, buy *ricarica* (prepaid minutes) from your selected mobile company at shops and tobacconists everywhere.

TIM (Telecom Italia Mobile; www.tim.it), **Vodafone** (www.vodafone.it) and **Wind** (www.wind.it) have the densest networks of outlets across the country.

Payphones & Phonecards

You'll find Telecom Italia payphones on the streets, in train stations and in Telecom offices. Most payphones accept only *carte/schede telefoniche* (phonecards), although some also accept credit cards. Telecom offers a wide range of prepaid cards for both domestic and international use; for a full list, see www.telecomitalia.it/telefono/carte-telefoniche. You can buy phonecards (most commonly €3, €5 or €10) at post offices, tobacconists and news-stands. You must break off the top left-hand corner of the card before you can use it. All phonecards have an expiry date, printed on the face of the card.

Time

Italy operates on a 24-hour clock. It is one hour ahead of GMT/UTC. Daylight-saving time starts on the last Sunday in March, when clocks are put forward one hour. Clocks are put back an hour on the last Sunday in October. This is especially valuable to know in Italy, as 'summer' and 'winter' hours at museums and other sights are usually based on daylight-saving time.

Tourist Information

Practically every village and town has a tourist office of sorts (listed under the relevant towns and cities throughout this book). These operate under a variety of names but are often known as 'Pro Loco'.

Note that when this book went to print, Tuscany's *Azienda di Promozione Turistica* (Agency for the Promotion of Tourism; APT) network was in the process of being disbanded, and tourist office locations and opening hours were likely to change. In the future, responsibility for tourism information will be devolved to the provinces rather than being run by the regional government.

Travellers with Disabilities

Italy is not an easy country for disabled travellers and getting around can be a problem for wheelchair users. Even a short journey in a city or town can become a major expedition if cobblestone streets have to be negotiated. Although many buildings have lifts, they are not always wide enough for wheelchairs. Not an awful lot has been done to make life for the hearing impaired and/or blind any easier either.

Italy's national rail company, **Trenitalia** (www.trenitalia.com) offers a helpline for disabled passengers at ☑199 303060 (7am to 9pm daily).

Some organisations that may help:

Accessible Italy (www.accessibleitaly.com) A San Marino–based company that specialises in holiday services for the disabled, ranging from tours to the hiring of adapted transport to romantic Italian weddings. This is the best first port of call.

Consorzio Cooperative Integrate (www.coinsociale.it) This Rome-based organisation provides information on the capital and is happy to share its contacts throughout Italy. Its 'Turismo per Tutti' program seeks to improve infrastructure and access for tourists with disabilities.

Tourism for All (www.tourismforall.org.uk) This UK-based group has information on hotels with access for guests with disabilities, where to hire equipment and tour operators dealing with travellers with disabilities.

Visas

Italy is one of 25 member countries of the Schengen Convention, under which EU countries (except Bulgaria, Cyprus, Ireland, Romania and the UK) plus Iceland, Norway and Switzerland have abolished permanent checks at common borders.

Legal residents of one Schengen country do not require a visa for another. Residents of 28 non-EU countries, including Australia, Brazil, Canada, Israel, Japan, New Zealand and the USA, do not require visas for tourist visits of up to 90 days.

All non-EU and non-Schengen nationals entering Italy for more than 90 days, or for any reason other than tourism (such as study or work) may need a specific visa. For details, visit www.esteri.it/visti/home_eng.asp or contact an Italian consulate.

You should also have your passport stamped on entry as, without a stamp, you could encounter problems if trying to obtain a residence permit (permesso di soggiorno). If you enter the EU via another member state, get your passport stamped there.

EU citizens do not require any permits to live or work in Italy but, after three months' residence, are supposed to register themselves at the municipal registry office where they live and offer proof of work or sufficient funds to support themselves. Non-EU foreign citizens with five years' continuous legal residence may apply for permanent residence.

Permesso di Soggiorno

Non-EU citizens planning to stay at the same address for more than one week are supposed to report to the police station to receive a permesso di soggiorno (a permit to remain in the country). Tourists staying in hotels are not required to do this.

A permesso di soggiorno only really becomes a necessity if you plan to study, work (legally) or live in Italy. Obtaining one is never a pleasant experience; it often involves long queues and the frustration of arriving at the counter only to find you don't have the necessary documents.

The exact requirements, such as specific documents and marche da bollo (official stamps), can change. In general, you will need a valid passport (if possible containing a stamp with your date of entry into Italy), a special visa issued in your own country if you are planning to study (for non-EU citizens), four passport photos and proof of your ability to support yourself financially. You can apply at the ufficio stranieri (foreigners' bureau) of the police station closest to where you're staying.

EU citizens do not require a permesso di soggiorno.

Study Visas

Non-EU citizens who want to study at a university or language school in Italy must have a study visa. These can be obtained from your nearest Italian embassy or consulate. You will normally require confirmation of your enrolment, proof of payment of fees and adequate funds to support yourself. The visa covers only the period of the enrolment. This type of visa is renewable within Italy but, again, only with confirmation of ongoing enrolment and proof that you are able to support yourself (bank statements are preferred).

Women Travellers

As with most places in the world, women travelling alone need to take certain precautions and be prepared for more than their fair share of unwanted attention (wolf whistles, sleazy looks etc). Foreign women particularly attract male attention in tourist towns like Florence and Siena; usually the best way to deal with local Lotharios is to ignore them. If that doesn't work, politely tell your interlocutors you're waiting for your marito (husband) or fidanzato (boyfriend) and, if necessary, walk away.

Watch out for men with wandering hands on crowded buses. Either keep your back to the wall or make a loud fuss if someone starts fondling your behind. A loud 'Che schifo!' (How disgusting!) will usually do the trick. If a more serious incident occurs, report it to the police, who are then required to press charges.

Transport

GETTING THERE & AWAY

Entering the Country

EU and Swiss citizens can travel to Italy with their national identity card alone. All other nationalities must have a valid passport and may be required to fill out a landing card (at airports).

By law you are supposed to have your passport or ID card with you at all times. You'll need one of these documents for police registration every time you check into a hotel.

In theory, there are no passport checks at land crossings from neighbouring countries, but random customs controls do occasionally still take place between Italy and Switzerland.

Air

High season for air travel to Italy is May to September. Shoulder season often runs from mid-September to the end of October and in April. Low season is generally November to March, but tickets around Christmas and Easter often increase in price or sell out in advance. Flights, tours and rail tickets can be booked at lonelyplanet.com/bookings.

Airlines

International airlines flying into the region include the following:

Aegean Airlines (www. aegeanair.com)

Aer Lingus (www.aerlingus. com)

Air Berlin (www.airberlin. com)

Air France (www.airfrance. com)

Air Malta (www.airmalta.com)

Albanian Airlines (www. albanianair.com)

Austrian (www.aua.com)

British Airways (www. ba.com)

Brussels Airlines (www. brusselsairlines.com)

Carpatair (www.carpatair. com)

Czech Airlines (www. czechairlines.com)

Delta (www.delta.com)

easyJet (www.easyjet.com)

Finnair (www.finnair.com)

Germanwings (www.german wings.com)

Iberia (www.iberia.com)

Iceland Express (www. icelandexpress.com)

Jet2 (www.jet2.com)

Jet4you (www.jet4you.com)

KLM (www.klm.com)

Lufthansa (www.lufthansa. com)

Luxair (www.luxair.lu)

Meridiana (www.meridiana.it)

Norwegian (www.norwegian. com)

Royal Air Maroc (www. royalairmaroc.com)

Ryanair (www.ryanair.com)

SAS (www.flysas.com)

Swiss (www.swiss.com)

TAP (www.flytap.com)

Thomsonfly (www.thomson fly.com)

Transavia (www.transavia. com)

CLIMATE CHANGE & TRAVEL

Every form of transport that relies on carbon-based fuel generates CO_2, the main cause of human-induced climate change. Modern travel is dependent on aeroplanes, which might use less fuel per kilometre per person than most cars but travel much greater distances. The altitude at which aircraft emit gases (including CO_2) and particles also contributes to their climate change impact. Many websites offer 'carbon calculators' that allow people to estimate the carbon emissions generated by their journey and, for those who wish to do so, to offset the impact of the greenhouse gases emitted with contributions to portfolios of climate-friendly initiatives throughout the world. Lonely Planet offsets the carbon footprint of all staff and author travel.

AIRPORTS SERVICING TUSCANY

AIRPORT	ALTERNATIVE NAMES	LOCATION	WEBSITE
Pisa International Airport (PSA)	Aeroporto Galileo Galilei	Pisa	www.pisa-airport.com
Florence airport (FLR)	Amerigo Vespucci; Peretola	Florence	www.aeroporto.firenze.it
Umbria International Airport (PEG)	S Egidio	Perugia, Umbria	www.airport.umbria.it
Bologna Airport (BLQ)	Aeroporto G Marconi	Bologna, Emilia-Romagna	www.bologna-airport.it

Turkish Airlines (www.thy.com)

Vueling (www.vueling.com)

Wizzair (http://wizzair.com)

Domestic airlines flying into the region include the following:

Air Italy (www.airitaly.it)

Air One (www.flyairone.it)

AirDolomiti (www.airdolomiti.it)

Alitalia (www.alitalia.it)

Belleair (wwwbelleair.it)

Blue Air (www.blueairweb.com)

Neos (www.neosair.it)

Prima (www.primair.it)

Skybridge AirOps (www.skybridgeairops.com)

WindJet (http://w4.vola windjet.it)

Land

Border Crossings

Entering Italy is relatively simple. If you are arriving from a neighbouring EU country, you do not require a passport check.

Bus

Buses are the cheapest overland option to Italy, but services are less frequent, less comfortable and significantly slower than the train. **Eurolines** (www.eurolines.com) is a consortium of coach companies with offices throughout

Europe. The company offers a low-season bus pass (www.eurolines-pass.com) valid for 15/30 days that costs €205/310 (€175/240 for under-26s and senior citizens over 60). This pass allows unlimited travel between 40 European cities, including Florence and Siena. Fares increase to €345/455 (€290/375) in midsummer.

Car & Motorcycle

Every vehicle travelling across the border should display a valid national licence plate and an accompanying registration card.

Train

Milan is the major rail hub in northern Italy, so if you are arriving from a European destination you will usually arrive there and change

trains to get to Florence. From France, you can also change at Turin to catch a connecting service to Pisa, or book onto the Artesia Euronight service that travels from Paris Bercy to Rome, stopping at Florence en route. Euronight services from Vienna Meidling and Munich HbF also stop at Florence en route to Rome.

For timetables, consult the comprehensive European Rail Timetable (UK£13.99), updated monthly, available from **Thomas Cook Publishing** (www.thomascookpublishing.com).

Sea

Ferries connect Italy with its islands and countries all over the Mediterranean. However, the only options for reaching

EXPRESS TRAINS FROM CONTINENTAL EUROPE

FROM	TO	FREQUENCY	DURATION (HR)	COST (€)
Paris	Milan	3 daily	7	98
Paris	Florence	nightly	12¼	130
Geneva	Milan	4 daily	4	72
Zurich	Milan	7 daily	3¾	65
Munich	Florence	nightly	9¼	94
Vienna	Florence	nightly	11	89

Tuscany directly by sea are the ferry crossings to Livorno from Sardinia, Corsica and Sicily. See p172 for more details.

For a comprehensive guide to all ferry services into and out of Italy, check out **Traghettionline** (www. traghettionline.com, in Italian). The website lists every route and includes links to ferry companies, where you can buy tickets or search for deals.

GETTING AROUND

To/From the Airport

Buses and trains connect Pisa International Airport with Pisa and Florence, and there is also one bus per day between Pisa airport and Siena. Buses link Florence airport with central Florence, and there is also a private shuttle service from the airport to Siena. If you fly into Bologna airport, you'll need to take a shuttle bus to Bologna Centrale station, from where you can take a train to Florence. From Umbria International Airport you'll need to take a shuttle bus to Perugia and then a bus or train to Tuscany.

Bicycle

Cycling is a national pastime in Italy. Bikes are prohibited on the autostrada (expressway), but there are few other special road rules.

Bikes can be taken on any train that carries the bicycle logo. The cheapest way to do this is to buy a separate bicycle ticket (€3.50 for regionale services, €5 for intercity services and €12 for Eurostar and Euronight services), which are available even at the self-service kiosks. You can use this ticket for 24 hours, making

a day trip quite economical. Bicycles that are dismantled and stored in a bag can be taken for free, even on night trains, and all ferries allow free bicycle passage.

See p46 for more information about cycling around the region.

Boat

Regular ferries connect Piombino on the mainland with Portoferraio on Elba. From Livorno, ferries run to the island of Capraia via Gorgona. See p172 and p183 for more details.

Bus

Although trains are the most convenient and economical way to travel between major towns, a bus is often the best link between small towns and villages. For a few intercity routes, such as the one between Florence and Siena, the bus is your best bet.

Dozens of different companies – loosely affiliated under the **Tiemme** (www. lfi.it) network – service the region. Most reduce or even drop services on holidays and weekends, especially

Sundays; in this book we have cited frequency of services on weekdays. Local tourist offices often carry bus timetables.

You can purchase tickets at most *tabacchi* (tobacconists) and news-stands, or from ticket booths and dispensing machines at bus stations; they must be validated in the machine on board. Tickets are also usually available on board for a slightly higher cost. In larger cities, ticket companies often have offices at the bus terminal and some larger cities offer good-value daily tourist tickets.

Turn up on time; in defiance of deep-seated Italian tradition, buses are almost always punctual.

Car & Motorcycle

Automobile Associations

The **Automobile Club d'Italia** (ACI; www.aci.it) is a driver's best resource in Italy. For 24-hour roadside emergency service, dial ☏803116 from a landline or ☏800 116800 from a mobile phone. Foreigners do not have to join but instead pay a per-incident fee.

BUS COMPANIES IN TUSCANY

REGIONAL BUS COMPANY	WEBSITE (MOST IN ITALIAN ONLY)	SERVICES
ATL	www.atl.livorno.it	Livorno
Baschetti	www.baschetti.it	Sansepolcro
CAT	www.catspa.it	Lunigiana
CPT	www.cpt.pisa.it	Pisa
Rama Mobilità	www.ramamobilita.it	Southern Tuscany
Siena Mobilità	www.sienamobilita.it	Siena & around
SITA	www.sitabus.it	Florence & Chianti
CPT	www.cpt.pisa.it	Pisa
Vaibus	www.vaibus.it	Lucca, Garfagnana & Versilia

CAR

To rent a car you must be at least 25 years old and have a credit card. Car-rental agencies expect you to bring the car back with a full tank of petrol and will charge astronomically if you don't. You should also make sure that the office where you are returning your car will be open when you arrive – we receive many complaints from travellers who have been hit with late fines because offices were closed when they tried to return their hire vehicles.

Make sure you understand what is included in the price (unlimited kilometres, tax, insurance, collision damage waiver and so on). Also consider vehicle size carefully. High fuel prices, extremely narrow streets and tight parking conditions mean that smaller is always better.

Following are among the most competitive multinational and Italian car-hire agencies:

Avis (☑199 100133; www.avis.com)

Budget (☑800 4723325; www.budget.com)

Europcar (☑199 307030; www.europcar.com)

Hertz (☑199 112211; www.hertz.com)

Italy by Car (☑091 6393120; www.italybycar.it) Partners with Thrifty.

Maggiore (☑199 151120; www.maggiore.it) Partners with Alamo and National.

SPEED LIMITS

» Urban areas: 50km/h

» Secondary roads: 90km/h

» Main roads: cars 110km/h; caravans 80km/h

» Autostradas: cars 130km/h; caravans 100km/h

MOTORCYCLE

Agencies throughout Tuscany rent everything from small Vespas to larger touring bikes. Prices start around €20/140 per day/week for a 50cc scooter, or upwards of €80/400 per day/week for a 650cc motorcycle.

Most agencies will not rent motorcycles to people aged under 18. Many require a sizeable deposit, and you could be responsible for reimbursing part of the cost of the bike if it is stolen.

You don't need a licence to ride a scooter under 50cc. The speed limit is 40km/h, you must be 14 or over and you can't carry passengers. To ride a motorcycle or scooter between 50cc and 125cc, you must be aged 16 or over and have a licence (a car licence will do). For motorcycles over 125cc you will need a motorcycle licence.

On a motorcycle, you can ride freely in the heart of cities that have *Zona a Traffico Limitato* (ZTLs; Limited Traffic Zones), including Florence.

Driving Licence

All EU member states' driving licences are fully recognised throughout Europe. Drivers with a non-EU licence are supposed to obtain an International Driving Permit (IDP) to accompany their national licence, though copious anecdotal testimonies indicate that this rule is rarely enforced.

Fuel & Spare Parts

Italy's petrol prices are among the highest in Europe and vary from one service station (*benzinaio, stazione di servizio*) to another. When this book was researched, lead-free gasoline (*senza piombo;* 95 octane) averaged €1.47 per litre, with diesel (*gasolio*) averaging €1.57 per litre.

Spare parts are available at many garages or via the 24-hour ACI motorist assistance number (☑803116).

Insurance

Always carry proof of vehicle ownership and evidence of third-party insurance. If driving an EU-registered vehicle, your home country insurance is sufficient. Ask your insurer for a European Accident Statement (EAS) form, which can simplify matters in the event of an accident.

Limited Traffic Zones (ZTLs)

Many Tuscan towns and cities have a *Zona a Traffico Limitato* (ZTL; Limited Traffic Zone) in their historic centre. This means that only local vehicles with parking permits can enter – all other vehicles must stay outside the ZTL or be hit with a hefty fine. Being in a hire car will not exempt you from this rule – we receive regular reports from travellers who have unknowingly breached a ZTL and have ended up with a hefty charge (fine plus administrative fee) on their credit card. ZTLs in specific towns and cities are noted in destination chapters.

Parking

Parking spaces outlined in blue are designated for paid parking (look for a nearby ticket machine and display the ticket on your dashboard). White or yellow outlines almost always indicate that residential permits are needed. Traffic police generally turn a blind eye to motorcycles or scooters parked on footpaths.

Road Network

Tuscany has an excellent road network, including autostradas and major highways. Most of these are untolled, with the main exceptions being the A11 and A12 (FI-PI-LI) autostrada connecting Florence, Pisa and Livorno and the A1 autostrada linking Milan and Rome via Florence and Arezzo. For information about driving times and toll charges on these, check www.autostrade.it/en/.

PASSING

You might call it passing or overtaking, but Italians call it a national pastime. On first glance, it seems as if the overtaker will soon be introduced to an undertaker, but there are actually a few rules in place.

The major hard-and-fast rule: stay in the right lane unless you're passing or going Italian-driver-on-three-espressos fast!

Italians joke that they don't use their rear-view mirrors when driving. This means that you don't have to either. When a driver is on your tail at 160km/h and you're in the right-hand lane, it's not your responsibility to pull over or slow down. If they want to pass, they will have to wait until it is safe (or not seriously dangerous) to do so.

When you overtake, make sure you have your left-turn signal on. Wait until the solid yellow middle line turns into dots or dashes. Don't even think about passing on a curve. Oh, yes, and make sure there isn't a car coming from the opposite direction.

There are several minor road categories, listed below in descending order of importance.

Strade statali (state highways) Represented on maps by 'S' or 'SS'. Vary from toll-free, four-lane highways to two-lane main roads. The latter can be extremely slow, especially in mountainous regions.

Strade regionali (regional highways connecting small villages) Coded SR or R.

Strade provinciali (provincial highways) Coded SP or P.

Strade locali Often not even paved or mapped.

Road Rules

Cars drive on the right and overtake on the left. Unless otherwise indicated, you must always give way to cars entering an intersection from a road on your right.

Seatbelt use (front and rear) is required by law; violators are subject to an on-the-spot fine. Children under 12 must travel in the back seat, and those under four must use child seats.

In the event of a breakdown, a warning triangle is compulsory, as is use of an approved yellow or orange safety vest if you leave your vehicle. Recommended accessories include a first-aid kit, spare-bulb kit and fire extinguisher.

Italy's blood-alcohol limit is 0.05%, and random breath tests take place. If you're involved in an accident and under the influence, the penalties can be severe.

Speeding fines follow EU standards and are proportionate with the number of kilometres that you are caught driving over the speed limit, reaching up to €2000 with possible suspension of your driving licence.

On all two-wheeled transport, helmets are required. The speed limit for mopeds is 40km/h. Headlights are compulsory day and night for all vehicles on the autostradas, and advisable for motorcycles even on smaller roads.

Local Transport

Taxi

You can usually find taxi ranks at train and bus stations, or you can telephone for taxis. It's best to go to a designated taxi stand, as it's illegal for taxis to stop in the street if hailed. If you phone a taxi, bear in mind that the meter starts running from the moment of your call rather than when it picks you up.

Tram

Florence has a new tram network, but it services residential areas rather than tourist hotspots.

Train

The train network throughout Tuscany is limited. Local *regionale* trains are slow and stop at nearly all stations, while faster trains such as the Intercity (IC), Alta Velocità (AV; High Speed) or Eurostar (ES) call at major towns and cities.

Trenitalia (☑800 892021, Italian speaking; www.trenitalia.com) is the partially privatised state train system, which runs most of the services in Italy. We indicate the few other private Italian train lines within relevant destination sections of this book.

Reservations are not really necessary unless you are travelling on a Eurostar or AV train (when they are mandatory). Tickets can be purchased from the ticket office or automatic ticket machines when you get to the station.

Almost all train journeys require you to validate your ticket *before* boarding – just punch it in the yellow *convalida* machines installed at the entrance to all train platforms. On many buses, you'll need to validate your ticket on the bus itself. Getting caught freeloading or with a ticket that hasn't been validated risks a fine of up to €50. It's paid on the spot to an inspector who will be kind enough to escort you to an ATM if you don't have the cash on you. Don't even think about trying the '*Ma sono turista!*' line; it won't wash.

Train Routes

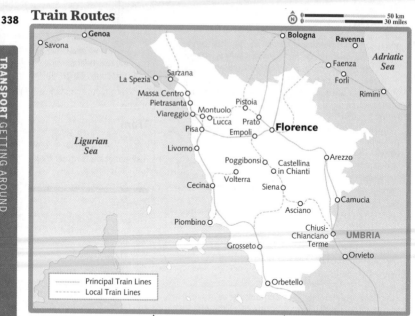

0 ____ 50 km
0 ____ 30 miles

Principal Train Lines
Local Train Lines

Classes & Costs

Train timetables at stations generally display *arrivi* (arrivals) on a white background and *partenze* (departures) on a yellow one.

There are 1st and 2nd classes on most Italian trains; a 1st-class ticket costs just less than double the price of a 2nd-class one. There are special deals for families and group travel. If you are simply travelling to a town a stop or two up the line, check the difference between the *regionale* and IC/ES ticket prices, as *regionale* tickets are always considerably cheaper – you might arrive 10 minutes earlier on an IC or ES service, but you'll also pay €5 or more for the privilege. Check up-to-date prices of routes on www.trenitalia.com.

Left Luggage

Most train stations have either a guarded left-luggage office or self-service lockers. The guarded offices are usually open 24 hours or 6am to midnight and charge around €3 per 12 hours for each piece of luggage. In Florence, it's €4 for the first five hours and then €0.60 per hour from six to 12 hours.

Train Passes

Trenitalia offers various discount passes, including the Carta Verde for youth and Carta d'Argento for seniors, but these are mainly useful for residents or long-term visitors, as they only pay for themselves with regular use over an extended period. If you are only travelling within Tuscany, it makes no sense to buy one.

Language

WANT MORE?

For in-depth language information and handy phrases, check out Lonely Planet's *Italian Phrasebook*. You'll find it at **shop. lonelyplanet.com**, or you can buy Lonely Planet's iPhone phrasebooks at the Apple App Store.

Modern standard Italian began to develop in the 13th and 14th centuries, predominantly through the works of Dante, Petrarch and Boccaccio – all Tuscans – who wrote chiefly in the Florentine dialect. The language drew on its Latin heritage and many dialects to develop into the standard Italian of today. Although many dialects are spoken in every-day conversation in Italy, standard Italian is understood throughout the country. Despite the Florentine roots of standard Italian – and the fact that standard Italian is widely used in Florence and Tuscany – anyone who has learned some Italian will notice the peculiari-ty of the local accent. In Florence, as in other parts of Tuscany, you are bound to hear the hard 'c' pronounced as a heavy 'h'. For example, *Voglio una cannuccia per la Coca Cola* (I want a straw for my Coca Cola) sounds more like *Voglio una hannuccia per la Hoha Hola*.

Italian pronunciation is relatively easy as the sounds used in spoken Italian can all be found in English. If you read our coloured pronunciation guides as if they were English, you'll be understood. The stressed syllables are indicated with italics. Note that ai is pronounced as in 'aisle', ay as in 'say', ow as in 'how', dz as the 'ds' in 'lids', and that r is a strong and rolled sound. Keep in mind that Italian consonants can have a stronger, emphatic pronunciation – if the consonant is written as a double letter, it should be pronounced a little stronger, eg *sonno son·*no (sleep) versus *sono so·*no (I am).

BASICS

Italian has two words for 'you' – use the polite form *Lei* lay if you're talking to strang-ers, officials or people older than you. With people familiar to you or younger than you, you can use the informal form *tu* too.

In Italian, all nouns and adjectives are either masculine or feminine, and so are the articles *il/la* eel/la (the) and *un/una* oon/oo·na (a) that go with the nouns.

In this chapter the polite/informal and masculine/feminine options are included where necessary, separated with a slash and indicated with 'pol/inf' and 'm/f'.

Hello.	*Buongiorno.*	bwon·*jor*·no
Goodbye.	*Arrivederci.*	a·ree·ve·*der*·chee
Yes./No.	*Sì./No.*	see/no
Excuse me.	*Mi scusi.* (pol)	mee *skoo*·zee
	Scusami. (inf)	*skoo*·za·mee
Sorry.	*Mi dispiace.*	mee dees·*pya*·che
Please.	*Per favore.*	per fa·*vo*·re
Thank you.	*Grazie.*	*gra*·tsye
You're welcome.	*Prego.*	*pre*·go

How are you?
Come sta/stai? (pol/inf) *ko*·me sta/stai

Fine. And you?
Bene. E Lei/tu? (pol/inf) *be*·ne e lay/too

What's your name?
Come si chiama? *ko*·me see *kya*·ma

My name is ...
Mi chiamo ... mee *kya*·mo ...

Do you speak English?
Parla/Parli inglese? (pol/inf) *par*·la/*par*·lee een·*gle*·ze

I don't understand.
Non capisco. non ka·*pee*·sko

ACCOMMODATION

Do you have a ... room?	Avete una camera ...?	a·ve·te oo·na ka·me·ra ...
double	doppia con letto matri-moniale	do·pya kon le·to ma·tree-mo·nya·le
single	singola	seen·go·la

How much is it per ...?	Quanto costa per ...?	kwan·to kos·ta per ...
night	una notte	oo·na no·te
person	persona	per·so·na

Is breakfast included?
La colazione è compresa? — la ko·la·tsyo·ne e kom·pre·sa

air-con	aria condizionata	a·rya kon-dee-tsyo·na·ta
bathroom	bagno	ba·nyo
campsite	campeggio	kam·pe·jo
guesthouse	pensione	pen·syo·ne
hotel	albergo	al·ber·go
youth hostel	ostello della gioventù	os·te·lo de·la jo·ven·too
window	finestra	fee·nes·tra

DIRECTIONS

Where's ...?
Dov'è ...? — do·ve ...

What's the address?
Qual'è l'indirizzo? — kwa·le leen·dee·ree·tso

Could you please write it down?
Può scriverlo, per favore? — pwo skree·ver·lo per fa·vo·re

Can you show me (on the map)?
Può mostrarmi (sulla pianta)? — pwo mos·trar·mee (soo·la pyan·ta)

at the corner	all'angolo	a·lan·go·lo
at the traffic lights	al semaforo	al se·ma·fo·ro
behind	dietro	dye·tro
far	lontano	lon·ta·no
in front of	davanti a	da·van·tee a
left	a sinistra	a see·nee·stra
near	vicino	vee·chee·no
next to	accanto a	a·kan·to a
opposite	di fronte a	dee fron·te a
right	a destra	a de·stra
straight ahead	sempre diritto	sem·pre dee·ree·to

To get by in Italian, mix and match these simple patterns with words of your choice:

When's (the next flight)?
A che ora è (il prossimo volo)? — a ke o·ra e (eel pro·see·mo vo·lo)

Where's (the station)?
Dov'è (la stazione)? — do·ve (la sta·tsyo·ne)

I'm looking for (a hotel).
Sto cercando (un albergo). — sto cher·kan·do (oon al·ber·go)

Do you have (a map)?
Ha (una pianta)? — a (oo·na pyan·ta)

Is there (a toilet)?
C'è (un gabinetto)? — che (oon ga·bee·ne·to)

I'd like (a coffee).
Vorrei (un caffè). — vo·ray (oon ka·fe)

I'd like to (hire a car).
Vorrei (noleggiare una macchina). — vo·ray (no·le·ja·re oo·na ma·kee·na)

Can I (enter)?
Posso (entrare)? — po·so (en·tra·re)

Could you please (help me)?
Può (aiutarmi), per favore? — pwo (a·yoo·tar·mee) per fa·vo·re

EATING & DRINKING

What would you recommend?
Cosa mi consiglia? — ko·za mee kon·see·lya

What's in that dish?
Quali ingredienti ci sono in questo piatto? — kwa·li een·gre·dyen·tee chee so·no een kwe·sto pya·to

That was delicious!
Era squisito! — e·ra skwee·zee·to

Cheers!
Salute! — sa·loo·te

Please bring the bill.
Mi porta il conto, per favore? — mee por·ta eel kon·to per fa·vo·re

I'd like to reserve a table for ...	Vorrei prenotare un tavolo per ...	vo·ray pre·no·ta·re oon ta·vo·lo per ...
(two) people	(due) persone	(doo·e) per·so·ne
(eight) o'clock	le (otto)	le (o·to)

I don't eat ...	Non mangio ...	non man·jo ...
eggs	uova	wo·va
fish	pesce	pe·she
nuts	noci	no·chee
(red) meat	carne (rossa)	kar·ne (ro·sa)

Key Words

bar	locale	lo·ka·le
bottle	bottiglia	bo·tee·lya
breakfast	prima colazione	pree·ma ko·la·tsyo·ne
cafe	bar	bar
cold	freddo	fre·do
dinner	cena	che·na
drink list	lista delle bevande	lee·sta de·le be·van·de
fork	forchetta	for·ke·ta
glass	bicchiere	bee·kye·re
grocery store	alimentari	a·lee·men·ta·ree
hot	caldo	kal·do
knife	coltello	kol·te·lo
lunch	pranzo	pran·dzo
market	mercato	mer·ka·to
menu	menù	me·noo
plate	piatto	pya·to
restaurant	ristorante	ree·sto·ran·te
spicy	piccante	pee·kan·te
spoon	cucchiaio	koo·kya·yo
vegetarian (food)	vegetariano	ve·je·ta·rya·no
with	con	kon
without	senza	sen·tsa

Meat & Fish

beef	manzo	man·dzo
chicken	pollo	po·lo
(dried) cod	baccalà	ba·ka·la
crab	granchio	gran·kyo
duck	anatra	a·na·tra
fish	pesce	pe·she
(cured) ham	prosciutto	pro·shoo·to

herring	aringa	a·reen·ga
lamb	agnello	a·nye·lo
lobster	aragosta	a·ra·gos·ta
meat	carne	kar·ne
mussels	cozze	ko·tse
octopus	polpi	pol·pee
oysters	ostriche	o·stree·ke
pork	maiale	ma·ya·le
prawn	gambero	gam·be·ro
rabbit	coniglio	ko·nee·lyo
salmon	salmone	sal·mo·ne
sausage	salsiccia	sal·see·cha
scallops	capasante	ka·pa·san·te
seafood	frutti di mare	froo·tee dee ma·re
shrimp	gambero	gam·be·ro
squid	calamari	ka·la·ma·ree
thinly sliced raw meat	carpaccio	kar·pa·cho
tripe	trippa	tree·pa
trout	trota	tro·ta
tuna	tonno	to·no
turkey	tacchino	ta·kee·no
veal	vitello	vee·te·lo

Vegetables

artichokes	carciofi	kar·cho·fee
asparagus	asparagi	as·pa·ra·jee
aubergine/ eggplant	melanzane	me·lan·dza·ne
beans	fagioli	fa·jo·lee
black cabbage	cavolo nero	ka·vo·lo ne·ro
cabbage	cavolo	ka·vo·lo
capsicum	peperone	pe·pe·ro·ne
carrot	carota	ka·ro·ta
cauliflower	cavolfiore	ka·vol·fyo·re
cucumber	cetriolo	che·tree·o·lo
fennel	finocchio	fee·no·kyo
lentils	lenticchie	len·tee·kye
lettuce	lattuga	la·too·ga
mushroom	funghi	foon·gee
nuts	noci	no·chee
olive	oliva	o·lee·va
onions	cipolle	chee·po·le
peas	piselli	pee·ze·lee
potatoes	patate	pa·ta·te
rocket	rucola	roo·ko·la
salad	insalata	een·sa·la·ta

spinach	spinaci	spee·na·chee
tomatoes	pomodori	po·mo·do·ree
vegetables	verdura	ver·doo·ra

Fruit & Gelato Flavours

apple	mela	me·la
cherry	ciliegia	chee·lee·e·ja
chocolate	cioccolata	cho·ko·la·ta
chocolate and hazelnuts	bacio	ba·cho
forest fruits (wild berries)	frutta di bosco	froo·ta dee bos·ko
fruit	frutta	froo·ta
grapes	uva	oo·va
hazelnut	nocciola	no·cho·la
lemon	limone	lee·mo·ne
melon	melone	me·lo·ne
orange	arancia	a·ran·cha
peach	pesca	pe·ska
pear	pere	pe·re
pineapple	ananas	a·na·nas
plum	prugna	proo·nya
strawberry	fragola	fra·go·la
trifle (lit: 'English soup')	zuppa inglese	tsoo·pa een·gle·ze
vanilla	vaniglia	va·nee·ya
wild/sour cherry	amarena	a·ma·re·na

Other

bread	pane	pa·ne
butter	burro	boo·ro
cheese	formaggio	for·ma·jo
cream	panna	pa·na
cone	cono	ko·no
cup	coppa	ko·pa
eggs	uova	wo·va
honey	miele	mye·le
ice	ghiaccio	gya·cho

Question Words

How?	Come?	ko·me
What?	Che cosa?	ke ko·za
When?	Quando?	kwan·do
Where?	Dove?	do·ve
Who?	Chi?	kee
Why?	Perché?	per·ke

jam	marmellata	mar·me·la·ta
noodles	pasta	pas·ta
oil	olio	o·lyo
pepper	pepe	pe·pe
rice	riso	ree·zo
salt	sale	sa·le
soup	minestra	mee·nes·tra
soy sauce	salsa di soia	sal·sa dee so·ya
sugar	zucchero	tsoo·ke·ro
truffle	tartufo	tar·too·fo
vinegar	aceto	a·che·to

Drinks

beer	birra	bee·ra
coffee	caffè	ka·fe
(orange) juice	succo (d'arancia)	soo·ko (da·ran·cha)
milk	latte	la·te
red wine	vino rosso	vee·no ro·so
soft drink	bibita	bee·bee·ta
tea	tè	te
(mineral) water	acqua (minerale)	a·kwa (mee·ne·ra·le)
white wine	vino bianco	vee·no byan·ko

For additional food and drink terms, check out the Eat & Drink Like a Local chapter (p35).

EMERGENCIES

Help!
Aiuto!   a·yoo·to

Leave me alone!
Lasciami in pace!   la·sha·mee een pa·che

I'm lost.
Mi sono perso/a. (m/f)   mee so·no per·so/a

There's been an accident.
C'è stato un   che sta·to oon
incidente.   een·chee·den·te

Call the police!
Chiami la polizia!   kya·mee la po·lee·tsee·a

Call a doctor!
Chiami un medico!   kya·mee oon me·dee·ko

Where are the toilets?
Dove sono i   do·ve so·no ee
gabinetti?   ga·bee·ne·tee

I'm sick.
Mi sento male.   mee sen·to ma·le

It hurts here.
Mi fa male qui.   mee fa ma·le kwee

I'm allergic to ...
Sono allergico/a a ... (m/f)   so·no a·ler·jee·ko/a a ...

SHOPPING & SERVICES

I'd like to buy ...
Vorrei comprare ...   vo·*ray* kom·*pra*·re ...

I'm just looking.
Sto solo guardando.   sto *so*·lo gwar·*dan*·do

Can I look at it?
Posso dare un'occhiata?   po·so *da*·re oo·no·*kya*·ta

How much is this?
Quanto costa questo?   kwan·to kos·ta *kwe*·sto

It's too expensive.
È troppo caro/a. (m/f)   e *tro*·po *ka*·ro/a

Can you lower the price?
Può farmi lo sconto?   pwo *far*·mee lo *skon*·to

There's a mistake in the bill.
C'è un errore nel conto. che oo·ne·*ro*·re nel *kon*·to

ATM	*Bancomat*	ban·ko·mat
post office	*ufficio postale*	oo·*fee*·cho pos·*ta*·le
tourist office	*ufficio del turismo*	oo·*fee*·cho del too·*reez*·mo

TIME & DATES

What time is it?	*Che ora è?*	ke o·ra e
It's one o'clock.	*È l'una.*	e *loo*·na
It's (two) o'clock.	*Sono le (due).*	*so*·no le (*doo*·e)
Half past (one).	*(L'una) e mezza.*	(*loo*·na) e *me*·dza
in the morning	*di mattina*	dee ma·*tee*·na
in the afternoon	*di pomeriggio*	dee po·me·*ree*·jo
in the evening	*di sera*	dee *se*·ra
yesterday	*ieri*	*ye*·ree
today	*oggi*	o·*jee*
tomorrow	*domani*	do·*ma*·nee
Monday	*lunedì*	loo·ne·*dee*
Tuesday	*martedì*	mar·te·*dee*
Wednesday	*mercoledì*	mer·ko·le·*dee*
Thursday	*giovedì*	jo·ve·*dee*
Friday	*venerdì*	ve·ner·*dee*
Saturday	*sabato*	*sa*·ba·to
Sunday	*domenica*	do·*me*·nee·ka
January	*gennaio*	je·*na*·yo
February	*febbraio*	fe·*bra*·yo
March	*marzo*	*mar*·tso
April	*aprile*	a·*pree*·le
May	*maggio*	*ma*·jo

June	*giugno*	*joo*·nyo
July	*luglio*	*loo*·lyo
August	*agosto*	a·*gos*·to
September	*settembre*	se·*tem*·bre
October	*ottobre*	o·*to*·bre
November	*novembre*	no·*vem*·bre
December	*dicembre*	dee·*chem*·bre

NUMBERS

1	*uno*	oo·no
2	*due*	*doo*·e
3	*tre*	tre
4	*quattro*	*kwa*·tro
5	*cinque*	*cheen*·kwe
6	*sei*	say
7	*sette*	*se*·te
8	*otto*	o·to
9	*nove*	*no*·ve
10	*dieci*	*dye*·chee
20	*venti*	*ven*·tee
30	*trenta*	*tren*·ta
40	*quaranta*	kwa·*ran*·ta
50	*cinquanta*	cheen·*kwan*·ta
60	*sessanta*	se·*san*·ta
70	*settanta*	se·*tan*·ta
80	*ottanta*	o·*tan*·ta
90	*novanta*	no·*van*·ta
100	*cento*	*chen*·to
1000	*mille*	*mee*·lel

TRANSPORT

Public Transport

At what time does the ... leave/arrive?	*A che ora parte/ arriva ...?*	a ke o·ra *par*·te/ a·*ree*·va ...
boat	*la nave*	la *na*·ve
bus	*l'autobus*	*low*·to·boos
ferry	*il traghetto*	eel tra·*ge*·to
metro	*la metropolitana*	la me·tro·po·lee·*ta*·na
plane	*l'aereo*	la·e·*re*·o
train	*il treno*	eel *tre*·no
... ticket	*un biglietto ...*	oon bee·*lye*·to
one-way	*di sola andata*	dee *so*·la an·*da*·ta
return	*di andata e ritorno*	dee an·*da*·ta e ree·*tor*·no

bus stop	fermata dell'autobus	fer·ma·ta del ow·to·boos
platform	binario	bee·na·ryo
ticket office	biglietteria	bee·lye·te·ree·a
timetable	orario	o·ra·ryo
train station	stazione ferroviaria	sta·tsyo·ne fe·ro·vyar·ya

Does it stop at ...?
Si ferma a ...?   see fer·ma a ...

Please tell me when we get to ...
Mi dica per favore   mee dee·ka per fa·vo·re
quando arriviamo a ...   kwan·do a·ree·vya·mo a ...

I want to get off here.
Voglio scendere qui.   vo·lyo shen·de·re kwee

Driving & Cycling

I'd like	Vorrei	vo·ray
to hire	noleggiare	no·le·ja·re
a/an ...	un/una ... (m/f)	oon/oo·na ...
4WD	fuoristrada (m)	fwo·ree·stra·da
bicycle	bicicletta (f)	bee·chee·kle·ta
car	macchina (f)	ma·kee·na
motorbike	moto (f)	mo·to

bicycle pump	pompa della bicicletta	pom·pa de·la bee·chee·kle·ta
child seat	seggiolino	se·jo·lee·no
helmet	casco	kas·ko
mechanic	meccanico	me·ka·nee·ko
petrol/gas	benzina	ben·dzee·na
puncture	gomma bucata	go·ma boo·ka·ta
service station	stazione di servizio	sta·tsyo·ne dee ser·vee·tsyo

Is this the road to ...?
Questa strada porta a ...?   kwe·sta stra·da por·ta a ...

(How long) Can I park here?
(Per quanto tempo)   (per kwan·to tem·po)
Posso parcheggiare qui?   po·so par·ke·ja·re kwee

The car/motorbike has broken down (at ...).
La macchina/moto si è   la ma·kee·na/mo·to see e
guastata (a ...).   gwas·ta·ta (a ...)

I have a flat tyre.
Ho una gomma bucata.   o oo·na go·ma boo·ka·ta

I've run out of petrol.
Ho esaurito la   o e·zow·ree·to la
benzina.   ben·dzee·na

I've lost my car keys.
Ho perso le chiavi della   o per·so le kya·vee de·la
macchina.   ma·kee·na

GLOSSARY

For art and architecture terms, see p322.

abbazia – abbey

aeroporto – airport

affittacamere – rooms for rent in private houses

agriturismo – farm-stay accommodation

albergo – hotel

alimentari – grocery shop

alto – high

ambulanza – ambulance

anfiteatro – amphitheatre

autostazione – bus station/ terminal

autostrada – motorway, highway

basilica – Christian church with a rectangular hall, aisles and an apse at the end

battistero – baptistry

biblioteca – library

biglietto – ticket

biglietto cumulativo – combined ticket that allows entrance to a number of associated sights

borgo – ancient town or village; farm hamlet

cabinovia – two-seater cable car

caffetiera – cafeteria

calcio – football

camera doppia – room with twin beds

camera matrimoniale – room with a double bed

camera singola – single room

campanile – bell tower

campeggio – camping

campo – field

cantinetta – small cellar where wine is served

cappella – chapel

carabinieri – military police

Carnevale – carnival period between Epiphany and Lent

casa – house, home

castello – castle

cattedrale – cathedral

cava – quarry

centro – city centre

centro storico – literally, 'historical centre'; old town

chiesa – church

colle – hill

colonna – column

comune – equivalent to a municipality; town or city council; historically, a commune (self-governing town or city)

contrada – town district

convalida – ticket-stamping machine

coperto – cover charge

corso – main street, avenue

deposito bagagli – left luggage

dolce – sweet; also dessert course
duomo – cathedral

enoteca – wine bar (see also *fiaschetteria*)

fattoria – farmhouse
ferrovia – train station
festa – festival
fiaschetteria – small tavern serving wine and snacks (see also *enoteca*)
fontana – fountain
forno – bakery
foro – forum

gelateria – ice-cream shop
golfo – gulf
grotta – cave

isola – island

lago – lake
largo – small square
libreria – bookshop
locanda – inn, small hotel
loggia – covered area on the side of a building; porch
lungomare – seafront road, promenade

macchia – scrub, bush
macellerìa – butcher shop
mare – sea
mercato – market

monte – mountain, mount
motorino – scooter
municipio – town hall
museo – museum

nave – ship
necropoli – ancient cemetery, burial site

osteria – casual tavern or eatery presided over by a host

palazzo – palace; a large building of any type, including an apartment block
parcheggio – car park
parco – park
passeggiata – traditional evening stroll
pasticceria – shop selling cakes and pastries
pensione – small hotel
permesso di soggiorno – residence permit
piazza – square
piazzale – large open square
pinacoteca – art gallery
ponte – bridge
porta – door, city gate
portico – walkway, often on the outside of buildings
porto – port

questura – police station

rifugio – mountain hut
rocca – fort

sagra – festival (usually with a culinary theme)
sala – room in a museum or a gallery
santuario – sanctuary
scalinata – flight of stairs
scavi – excavations
spiaggia – beach
stazione – station
stazione di servizio – service/petrol station
stazione marittima – ferry terminal
strada – street, road
superstrada – expressway; highway with divided lanes

tabaccheria/tabaccaio – tobacconist's shop/tobacconist
teatro – theatre
tempio – temple
terme – thermal bath
torre – tower
trattoria – simple restaurant

ufficio stranieri – foreigners' bureau
uffizi – offices

via – street, road
vicoli – alley, alleyway

ZTL – *(Zona a Traffico Limitato)* Limited Traffic Zone

behind the scenes

SEND US YOUR FEEDBACK

We love to hear from travellers – your comments keep us on our toes and help make our books better. Our well-travelled team reads every word on what you loved or loathed about this book. Although we cannot reply individually to postal submissions, we always guarantee that your feedback goes straight to the appropriate authors, in time for the next edition. Each person who sends us information is thanked in the next edition – and the most useful submissions are rewarded with a free book.

Visit **lonelyplanet.com/contact** to submit your updates and suggestions or to ask for help. Our award-winning website also features inspirational travel stories, news and discussions.

Note: We may edit, reproduce and incorporate your comments in Lonely Planet products such as guidebooks, websites and digital products, so let us know if you don't want your comments reproduced or your name acknowledged. For a copy of our privacy policy visit lonelyplanet.com/privacy.

OUR READERS

Many thanks to the travellers who used the last edition and wrote to us with helpful hints, useful advice and interesting anecdotes: Dan Bertauche, Zver Domonkos, Kenny and Alexia Hilton, Chris Kidwell, Dietmar Krumpl, Gary McDade, Ramona, Micky Schoenmaker, James Sinclair, Gillian Wilkinson

AUTHOR THANKS

Virginia Maxwell

Greatest thanks to my travelling companions on this job: Peter and Max Handsaker, Ryan Ver Berkmoes and Giancarlo and Margie Paolucci. Thanks also to Ilaria Crescioli, Roberta Romoli, Chiara Olmastroni, Sara Caprarotta, Roberta Vichi, Chiara Ponzuoli, Luigina Benci, Cecilia Rosa and Caterina Bencistà Falorni. A *mille grazie* goes to fellow authors Nicola Williams and Joe Fullman and also to commissioning editor Joe Bindloss. Finally, thanks to Freya Middleton, Filippo Giabboni and Robert Landon for the great dinner in Florence!

Nicola Williams

Heartfelt thanks to everyone who helped me delve into the Tuscan heart: in Florence, Doreen and daughter Francesca Privitera

(Hotel Scoti), fashion stylist Jennifer Tattanelli, father Georgio and assistant Olga (Casini Firenze), Alessio (Hotel Cestelli), Vasarian Corridor guide Michele Colloca (Florencetown), Ilaria Crescioli (Toscana Promozione), Roberta Romoli (APT) and guide extraordinaire Freya Middleton. Elsewhere, Guido Manfredi (Barbialla Nuova), Fabrizio Quochi (Pisa), Francesca Geppetti (Livorno), Kristin Walton (Lucca), @allafiorentina, @emikodavies, @Morgannelefay13. And, of course, my ever-fabulous travel companions Matthias, Niko, Mischa and Kaya Lüfkens.

ACKNOWLEDGMENTS

Climate map data adapted from Peel MC, Finlayson BL & McMahon TA (2007) 'Updated World Map of the Köppen-Geiger Climate Classification', *Hydrology and Earth System Sciences*, 11, 163344.

Illustrations pp62-3 by Javier Zarracina.

Cover photograph: The *duomo*, Florence, Oliver Strewe/Lonely Planet Images.

Many of the images in this guide are available for licensing from Lonely Planet Images: www.lonelyplanetimages.com.

THIS BOOK

This 7th edition of Lonely Planet's *Florence & Tuscany* guidebook was researched and written by Virginia Maxwell and Nicola Williams. Edition 6 was updated by Virginia Maxwell, Alex Leviton and Leif Pettersen, and edition 5 by Nicola Williams, Alison Bing, Alex Leviton, Leif Pettersen and Miles Roddis. This guidebook was commissioned in Lonely Planet's London office, and produced by the following:

Commissioning Editors Joe Bindloss, Catherine Craddock

Coordinating Editor Carolyn Boicos

Coordinating Cartographer Valentina Kremenchutskaya

Coordinating Layout Designer Carlos Solarte

Senior Editor Susan Paterson

Managing Editor Brigitte Ellemor

Managing Cartographer Amanda Sierp

Managing Layout Designer Chris Girdler

Assisting Editors Alice Barker, Kristin Odijk, Helen Yeates

Assisting Cartographers Enes Basic, Valeska Cañas, Karusha Ganga, Eve Kelly

Cover Research Naomi Parker

Internal Image Research Aude Vauconsant

Language Content Annelies Mertens

Thanks to Sasha Baskett, Yvonne Bischofberger, Nicholas Colicchia, Brendan Dempsey, Ryan Evans, Joshua Geoghegan, Evan Jones, Anna Metcalfe, Trent Paton, Jessica Rose, Wibowo Rusli, Kerrianne Southway, Sophie Splatt, Gerard Walker, Kate Whitfield

how to use this book

These symbols will help you find the listings you want:

◉ Sights	☞ Tours	🍷 Drinking
🏖 Beaches	🎊 Festivals & Events	☆ Entertainment
🏃 Activities	🛏 Sleeping	🔒 Shopping
🍴 Courses	🍴 Eating	❶ Information/Transport

These symbols give you the vital information for each listing:

📞 Telephone Numbers	🤝 Wi-Fi Access	🚌 Bus
🕙 Opening Hours	🏊 Swimming Pool	⛴ Ferry
Ⓟ Parking	🥦 Vegetarian Selection	Ⓜ Metro
⊝ Nonsmoking	📖 English-Language Menu	Ⓢ Subway
✳ Air-Conditioning	👶 Family-Friendly	⊖ London Tube
@ Internet Access	🐾 Pet-Friendly	🚋 Tram
		🚆 Train

Reviews are organised by author preference.

Look out for these icons:

TOP CHOICE	Our author's recommendation
FREE	No payment required
🌿	A green or sustainable option

Our authors have nominated these places as demonstrating a strong commitment to sustainability – for example by supporting local communities and producers, operating in an environmentally friendly way, or supporting conservation projects.

Map Legend

Sights
- ◉ Beach
- ▲ Buddhist
- 🏰 Castle
- ✛ Christian
- ⬡ Hindu
- ☪ Islamic
- ✡ Jewish
- ❶ Monument
- 🏛 Museum/Gallery
- ❸ Ruin
- 🍇 Winery/Vineyard
- 🐘 Zoo
- ◉ Other Sight

Activities, Courses & Tours
- 🤿 Diving/Snorkelling
- 🛶 Canoeing/Kayaking
- ⛷ Skiing
- 🏄 Surfing
- 🏊 Swimming/Pool
- 🚶 Walking
- 🏄 Windsurfing
- ✛ Other Activity/Course/Tour

Sleeping
- 🛏 Sleeping
- ⛺ Camping

Eating
- 🍴 Eating

Drinking
- ☕ Drinking
- ☕ Cafe

Entertainment
- 🎭 Entertainment

Shopping
- 🛍 Shopping

Information
- ✉ Post Office
- ❶ Tourist Information

Transport
- ✈ Airport
- ⊗ Border Crossing
- 🚌 Bus
- 🚠 Cable Car/Funicular
- 🚲 Cycling
- ⛴ Ferry
- Ⓜ Metro
- 🚝 Monorail
- Ⓟ Parking
- Ⓢ S-Bahn
- 🚕 Taxi
- 🚆 Train/Railway
- 🚋 Tram
- ⊖ Tube Station
- Ⓤ U-Bahn
- • Other Transport

Routes
- Tollway
- Freeway
- Primary
- Secondary
- Tertiary
- Lane
- Unsealed Road
- Plaza/Mall
- Steps
-)=(Tunnel
- Pedestrian Overpass
- Walking Tour
- Walking Tour Detour
- Path

Boundaries
- International
- State/Province
- Disputed
- Regional/Suburb
- Marine Park
- Cliff
- Wall

Population
- ✪ Capital (National)
- ◉ Capital (State/Province)
- ● City/Large Town
- ◦ Town/Village

Geographic
- 🏠 Hut/Shelter
- 🗼 Lighthouse
- 👁 Lookout
- ▲ Mountain/Volcano
- ✿ Oasis
- ❶ Park
-)(Pass
- 🏕 Picnic Area
- ♨ Waterfall

Hydrography
- River/Creek
- Intermittent River
- Swamp/Mangrove
- Reef
- Canal
- Water
- Dry/Salt/Intermittent Lake
- Glacier

Areas
- Beach/Desert
- Cemetery (Christian)
- Cemetery (Other)
- Park/Forest
- Sportsground
- Sight (Building)
- Top Sight (Building)

689

OUR STORY

A beat-up old car, a few dollars in the pocket and a sense of adventure. In 1972 that's all Tony and Maureen Wheeler needed for the trip of a lifetime – across Europe and Asia overland to Australia. It took several months, and at the end – broke but inspired – they sat at their kitchen table writing and stapling together their first travel guide, *Across Asia on the Cheap*. Within a week they'd sold 1500 copies. Lonely Planet was born.

Today, Lonely Planet has offices in Melbourne, London and Oakland, with more than 600 staff and writers. We share Tony's belief that 'a great guidebook should do three things: inform, educate and amuse'.

OUR WRITERS

Virginia Maxwell

Coordinating Author, Siena & Central Tuscany, Southern Tuscany, Eastern Tuscany Based in Australia, Virginia spends part of every year in Italy indulging her passions for history, art, architecture, food and wine. As well as having been the coordinating author of the previous edition of this guide, she works on Lonely Planet's *Sicily* guidebook and covers other parts of the country for the *Western Europe* book. Though reticent to choose a favourite Tuscan destination (arguing that they're all wonderful), she usually nominates Florence if pressed.

Read more about Virginia at:
lonelyplanet.com/members/virginiamaxwell

Nicola Williams

Florence, Northwestern Tuscany, Central Coast & Elba Nicola is a British writer, editorial consultant, newbie video journalist and mother-of-three. For over a decade she has lived on the shores of Lake Geneva in France, an easy getaway through the Mont Blanc Tunnel to Italy, where she's spent years eating her way around and revelling in its extraordinary art and landscape. When she's not working she skis the Alps, dines fine, hunts truffles... This time around she travelled camera-in-hand to catch the region on film. Nicola has worked on numerous titles for Lonely Planet, including *Florence & Tuscany, Milan, Turin & Genoa* and *Piedmont*. She blogs at tripalong.word press.com and tweets @Tripalong.

Read more about Nicola at:
lonelyplanet.com/members/nicolawilliams

Published by Lonely Planet Publications Pty Ltd
ABN 36 005 607 983
7th edition – Jan 2012
ISBN 978 1 74179 853 1
© Lonely Planet 2012   Photographs © as indicated 2012
10 9 8 7 6 5 4 3 2 1
Printed in China

Although the authors and Lonely Planet have taken all reasonable care in preparing this book, we make no warranty about the accuracy or completeness of its content and, to the maximum extent permitted, disclaim all liability arising from its use.